# Macmillan/McGraw-Hill READING

**Mc Graw Hill** **Macmillan McGraw-Hill**

New York          Farmington

**Contributors**

The Princeton Review, Time Magazine, Accelerated Reader

The Princeton Review is not
affiliated with Princeton
University or ETS.

**RFB&D** 🎧
learning through listening

Students with print disabilities may be eligible to obtain an accessible audio version of the
pupil edition of this textbook. Please call Recording for the Blind & Dyslexic at 1-800-221-4792
for complete information.

*Macmillan/McGraw-Hill*

*A Division of The McGraw·Hill Companies*

Published by Macmillan/McGraw-Hill, a division of The McGraw-Hill Companies, Inc., Two Penn Plaza, NY, NY 10121

Printed in the United States of America

2 3 4 5 6 7 8 9  006/043  05 04 03 02

# Macmillan/McGraw-Hill READING

## Authors

James Flood

Jan E. Hasbrouck

James V. Hoffman

Diane Lapp

Donna Lubcker

Angela Shelf Medearis

Scott Paris

Steven Stahl

Josefina Villamil Tinajero

Karen D. Wood

**Macmillan McGraw-Hill**

New York          Farmington

Computer Center

Working with Words Station

Writing Station

Reading and Listening Station

Welcome!

Word Box

# Managing the

# Classroom

**Social Studies Station**

**Teacher Directed Small Group Instruction**

## Sample Management Plan

| Group 1 | Group 2 | Group 3 | Group 4 |
|---|---|---|---|
| **With Teacher** | Reading or Writing Workstation | Working with Words Station | Cross-Curricular or Computer Station |
| Reading or Writing Workstation | **With Teacher** | Cross-Curricular or Computer Station | Working with Words Station |
| Working with Words Station | Cross-Curricular or Computer Station | **With Teacher** | Reading or Writing Workstation |
| Cross-Curricular or Computer Station | Working with Words Station | Reading or Writing Workstation | **With Teacher** |

# Creating

# WORKSTATIONS

**Establishing independent workstations and other independent activities is the key to helping you manage the classroom as you meet with small groups.**

## Reading

Set up a classroom library for independent reading. Add Leveled Books as read during small-group instruction. Add other titles, also grouped by reading level. See the Theme Bibliography on pages T78–T79 for suggestions. Include titles based on discussions of students' fiction and nonfiction preferences.

- Self-Selected Reading
- Paired Reading
- Student Anthology selection from the Listening Library

## Writing

Focus the unit's writing projects on Expository Writing. Weekly writing assignments are found at the end of each selection. The unit writing process project, Expository Writing, can also be the focus of the Writing Station. Equip the Writing Station with the following materials:

- Samples of published Expository Writing
- Expository Writing samples, available in the **Teacher's Writing Resource Handbook**, pages 24–25

## Computer

Students can access the Internet to complete the Research and Inquiry activities suggested throughout the unit. Look for Internet connections in the following Research and Inquiry projects:

- Find Out More project at the end of each selection
- Cooperative Theme Project: Investigating Important Issues
- Cross-Curricular Activities
- Bringing Groups Together project

## Working with Words

heritage    thrive    navigate

**Selection Vocabulary**

Each student writes each selection vocabulary word on a card and then writes random letters before and after it. Then partners trade cards, circle the words, and give a synonym or antonym.

**High-Frequency Words**

Have students use these high-frequency words: *nothing, idea, special, island, back, call.* Ask them to write each word twice on a note card, each time omitting two or three different letters. They then trade cards with partners, fill in the missing letters, and use the word in a sentence.

## Cross-Curricular
# STATIONS

Set up a Cross-Curricular station to help extend selection concepts and ideas. Suggestions for Cross-Curricular activities can be found in the Teacher's Edition.

### Science

- Skunks, 392
- Heating Systems, 398
- Sir Francis Bacon, 418
- Erosion, 440
- Satellites, 476

### Social Studies

- Map Skills, 390, 416
- Tsunami, 454
- Track the Storm, 470

### Math

- Measurement, 394
- Probability, 424
- Geometry, 448
- Time and Distance, 480

### Art

- Still Lifes, 450
- Storms, 472

# Additional Independent Activities

The following independent activities offer a means to practice and reinforce concepts and skills taught in the unit.

### PUPIL EDITION: READER RESPONSE

**Story Questions** to monitor the student's comprehension of the selection. The questions are leveled progressing from literal to critical thinking.

**Story Activities** related to each selection. Four activities are provided: one writing activity, two cross-curricular activities, and a research and inquiry activity in the Find Out More project. Students are encouraged to use the Internet for research.

### LEVELED PRACTICE

Each week, Reteach, Practice, and Extend pages are offered to address the individual needs of students as they learn and review skills.

# McGraw-Hill Reading

**MULTI-AGE Classroom**

Using the same global themes at each grade level facilitates the use of materials in multi-age classrooms.

| GRADE LEVEL | Experience<br>Experiences can tell us about ourselves and our world. | Connections<br>Making connections develops new understandings. |
| --- | --- | --- |
| Kindergarten | **My World**<br>We learn a lot from all the things we see and do at home and in school. | **All Kinds of Friends**<br>When we work and play together, we learn more about ourselves. |
| Subtheme 1 | At Home | Working Together |
| Subtheme 2 | School Days | Playing Together |
| 1 | **Day by Day**<br>Each day brings new experiences. | **Together Is Better**<br>We like to share ideas and experiences with others. |
| 2 | **What's New?**<br>With each day, we learn something new. | **Just Between Us**<br>Family and friends help us see the world in new ways. |
| 3 | **Great Adventures**<br>Life is made up of big and small experiences. | **Nature Links**<br>Nature can give us new ideas. |
| 4 | **Reflections**<br>Stories let us share the experiences of others. | **Something in Common**<br>Sharing ideas can lead to meaningful cooperation. |
| 5 | **Time of My Life**<br>We sometimes find memorable experiences in unexpected places. | **Building Bridges**<br>Knowing what we have in common helps us appreciate our differences. |
| 6 | **Pathways**<br>Reflecting on life's experiences can lead to new understandings. | **A Common Thread**<br>A look beneath the surface may uncover hidden connections. |

# Themes: Kindergarten – Grade 6

**Six Units IN EVERY GRADE**

| Expression | Inquiry | Problem-Solving | Making Decisions |
|---|---|---|---|
| There are many styles and forms for expressing ourselves. | By exploring and asking questions, we make discoveries. | Analyzing information can help us solve problems. | Using what we know helps us evaluate situations. |
| **Time to Shine**<br>We can use our ideas and our imagination to do many wonderful things. | **I Wonder**<br>We can make discoveries about the wonders of nature in our own backyard. | **Let's Work It Out**<br>Working as part of a team can help me find a way to solve problems. | **Choices**<br>We can make many good choices and decisions every day |
| Great Ideas | In My Backyard | Try and Try Again | Good Choices |
| Let's Pretend | Wonders of Nature | Teamwork | Let's Decide |
| **Stories to Tell**<br>Each one of us has a different story to tell. | **Let's Find Out!**<br>Looking for answers is an adventure. | **Think About It!**<br>It takes time to solve problems. | **Many Paths**<br>Each decision opens the door to a new path. |
| **Express Yourself**<br>We share our ideas in many ways. | **Look Around**<br>There are surprises all around us. | **Figure It Out**<br>We can solve problems by working together. | **Starting Now**<br>Unexpected events can lead to new decisions. |
| **Be Creative!**<br>We can all express ourselves in creative, wonderful ways. | **Tell Me More**<br>Looking and listening closely will help us find out the facts. | **Think It Through**<br>Solutions come in many shapes and sizes. | **Turning Points**<br>We make new judgments based on our experiences. |
| **Our Voices**<br>We can each use our talents to communicate ideas. | **Just Curious**<br>We can find answers in surprising places. | **Make a Plan**<br>Often we have to think carefully about a problem in order to solve it. | **Sorting It Out**<br>We make decisions that can lead to new ideas and discoveries. |
| **Imagine That**<br>The way we express our thoughts and feelings can take different forms. | **Investigate!**<br>We never know where the search for answers might lead us. | **Bright Ideas**<br>Some problems require unusual approaches. | **Crossroads**<br>Decisions cause changes that can enrich our lives. |
| **With Flying Colors**<br>Creative people help us see the world from different perspectives. | **Seek and Discover**<br>To make new discoveries, we must observe and explore. | **Brainstorms**<br>We can meet any challenge with determination and ingenuity. | **All Things Considered**<br>Encountering new places and people can help us make decisions. |

# Investigate!

*We never know where the search for answers might lead us.*

## CARLOS AND THE SKUNK ...... 386A

Written by **Jan Romero Stevens**
illustrated by **Jeanne Arnold**

**REALISTIC FICTION**

| SKILLS | | | |
|---|---|---|---|
| **Comprehension** | **Vocabulary** | **Study Skill** | **Phonics** |
| • **Introduce** Judgments, Decisions | • **Introduce** Suffixes | • Graphic Aids: Diagram | • **Review** /ô/ and /ôr/ |
| • **Review** Judgments, Decisions | | | |
| • **Introduce** Draw Conclusions | | | |

## HOW TO THINK LIKE A SCIENTIST ..................... 408A

written by **Stephen P. Kramer**
illustrated by **Kim Behm**

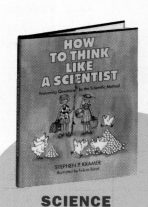

**SCIENCE NONFICTION**

| SKILLS | | | |
|---|---|---|---|
| **Comprehension** | **Vocabulary** | **Study Skill** | **Phonics** |
| • **Introduce** Important Information | • **Introduce** Root Words | • Graphic Aids: Outline | • **Review** /är/ and /âr/ |
| • **Review** Important Information | | | |
| • **Review** Draw Conclusions | | | |

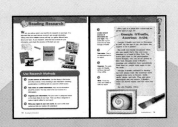

**INFORMATIONAL TEXT**

| | **WEEK 1** Carlos and the Skunk | **WEEK 2** How to Think Like a Scientist |
|---|---|---|
|  **Leveled Books** | **Easy:** *Kelley in Charge* <br> **Independent:** *The Lesson* <br> **Challenge:** *The Red Book* | **Easy:** *On Track* <br> **Independent:** *The Ladder of Truth: Forensic Detectives at Work* <br> **Challenge:** *The Speckled Monster* |
| ☑ **Tested Skills** | ☑ **Comprehension** <br> Judgments and Decisions, 387A–387B, 407E–407F <br> Draw Conclusions, 407G–407H <br> ☑ **Vocabulary** <br> Suffixes, 407I–407J <br> ☑ **Study Skills** <br> Graphic Aids, 406 | ☑ **Comprehension** <br> Important and Unimportant Information, 409A–409B, 431E– 431F <br> Draw Conclusions, 431G–431H <br> ☑ **Vocabulary** <br> Root Words, 431I–431J <br> ☑ **Study Skills** <br> Graphic Aids, 430 |
| **Minilessons** | **Phonics and Decoding: /ô/ and /ôr/,** 395 <br> **Genre:** Realistic Fiction, 389 <br> **Problem and Solution,** 391 <br> **Main Idea,** 399 | **Phonics and Decoding: /är/ and /âr/,** 413 <br> **Genre:** Informational Story, 411 <br> **Summarize,** 415 <br> **Suffixes,** 421 <br> **Root Words,** 423 <br> **Problem and Solution,** 425 |
| **Language Arts** | ✎ **Writing:** Expository Writing, 407K <br> **Grammar:** Adjectives, 407M <br> **Spelling:** Words with /ô/ and /ôr/, 407O | ✎ **Writing:** Expository Writing, 431K <br> **Grammar:** Articles, 431M <br> **Spelling:** Words with /är/ and /âr/, 431O |

**Activities**

| **Curriculum Connections** | **Read Aloud:** "The Lobster and the Crab," 386E <br><br> **Stories in Art:** *The Human Condition, II,* 386 <br><br> **Social Studies:** Map Skills, 390 <br><br> **Science:** Skunks, 392 <br><br> **Math:** Measurement, 394 <br><br> **Science:** Heating Systems, 398 <br><br> **Science:** Tomatoes, 405 | **Read Aloud:** "Archimedes and the King's Gold Crown," 408E <br><br> **Stories in Art:** *Basil Rathbone as Sherlock Holmes,* 408 <br><br> **Social Studies:** Map Skills, 416 <br><br> **Science:** Sir Francis Bacon, 418 <br><br> **Math:** Probability, 424 <br><br> **Math:** Identifying Unimportant Information, 429 |
| 🖐 **CULTURAL PERSPECTIVES** | Cooking, 400 | Superstitions, 412 |

| **WEEK 3** An Island Scrapbook | **WEEK 4** The Big Storm | **WEEK 5** Catching Up with Lewis and Clark | **WEEK 6** Review, Writing, Reading Information, Assessment |
|---|---|---|---|
| **Easy:** *Tourist Trap Island* **Independent:** *The Galapagos Islands* **Challenge:** *All About Islands* | **Easy:** *Tornado!* **Independent:** *Animals Sense the Weather* **Challenge:** *The Great Galveston Hurricane* | *Self-Selected Reading of Leveled Books* | *Self-Selected Reading* |

| | | | |
|---|---|---|---|
| ☑ **Comprehension** Fact and Nonfact, 433A–433B, 463E–463F Important and Unimportant Information, 463G–463H ☑ **Vocabulary** Suffixes, 463I–431J ☑ **Study Skills** Graphic Aids, 462 | ☑ **Comprehension** Judgments and Decisions, 465A–465B, 491E–491F Draw Conclusions, 491G–491H ☑ **Vocabulary** Root Words, 491I–491J ☑ **Study Skills** Graphic Aids, 490 | ☑ **Comprehension** Fact and Nonfact, 493A–493B Important and Unimportant Information, 501E–501F ☑ **Vocabulary** Root Words, 501G–501H Suffixes 501I–501J ☑ **Study Skills** Graphic Aids, 500 | ☑ **Assess Skills** Judgments and Decisions Draw Conclusions Fact and Nonfact Important and Unimportant Information Root Words Suffixes Graphic Aids ☑ **Assess Grammar and Spelling** Review Adjectives, 503I Review Spelling Patterns, 503J ☑ **Unit Progress Assessment** ☑ **Standardized Test Preparation** |

| | | | |
|---|---|---|---|
| **Phonics and Decoding:** /îr/ and /ûr/, 441 **Genre:** Narrative Nonfiction, 435 **Root Words,** 443; **Suffixes,** 445 **Main Idea,** 447 **Sequence of Events,** 451 **Make Inferences,** 453 **Figurative Language,** 455 | **Phonics and Decoding:** /îr/ and /ûr/, 479 **Genre:** Narrative Nonfiction, 467 **Cause and Effect,** 473 **Draw Conclusions,** 475 **Compound Words,** 477 **Sequence of Events,** 481 **Summarize,** 483 | **Genre: Social Studies Article,** 495 | **Reading Research** 503A |

| | | | |
|---|---|---|---|
| ✎ **Writing:** Expository Writing, 463K **Grammar:** Adjectives That Compare, 463M **Spelling:** Words with /îr/ and /ûr/, 463O | ✎ **Writing:** Expository Writing, 491K **Grammar:** Comparing with *More* and *Most*, 491M **Spelling:** Compound Words, 491O | ✎ **Writing:** Expository Writing, 501K **Grammar:** Comparing with *Good* and *Bad*, 501M **Spelling:** Words from Social Studies, 501O | ✎ **Unit Writing Process:** Expository Writing, 503C–503H |

| | | | |
|---|---|---|---|
| **Read Aloud:** "Souvenir," 432E **Stories in Art:** *Marble Inlay Tabletop of the Seabed,* 432 **Science:** Erosion, 440 **Math:** Geometry, 448 **Art:** Still Lifes, 450 **Social Studies:** Tsunami, 454 **Art:** Environment Mobiles, 461 **Natural Remedies,** 444 | **Read Aloud:** "Snowmaker Torments the People," 464E **Stories in Art:** *Satellite Image of Hurricane Andrew,* 464 **Social Studies:** Track the Storm, 470 **Music:** Storms, 472 **Science:** Satellites, 476 **Math:** Time and Distance, 480 **Science:** Hurricanes, 489 **Predicting the Weather,** 482 | **Read Aloud:** "Western Wagons," 492E **Stories in Art:** *Ships of the Long Range Pioneer Fleet,* 492 **Math:** *How Long Would It Take?,* 499 |  **GROUP** **Cooperative Theme Project Research and Inquiry:** Investigating Important Issues, 503 |

# Unit Resources

## LITERATURE

### LEVELED BOOKS

 **Easy:**
- *Kelley in Charge*
- *On Track*
- *Tourist Trap Island*
- *Tornado!*

 **Independent**
- *The Lesson*
- *The Ladder of Truth: Forensic Detectives at Work*
- *The Galapagos Islands*
- *Animals Sense the Weather*

 **Challenge:**
- *The Red Book*
- *The Speckled Monster*
- *All About Islands*
- *The Great Galveston Hurricane*

 **LISTENING LIBRARY**
Recordings of the student book selections and poetry. Available on **audiocassette** or **compact disc.**

*Macmillan/McGraw-Hill*

 **Intervention**
Easy Leveled Books
Skills Intervention Guide
Phonics Intervention Guide

## SKILLS

### LEVELED PRACTICE

**Practice Book:** Student practice for comprehension, vocabulary, and study skills plus practice for instructional vocabulary and story comprehension. Take-Home Story included for each lesson.

**Reteach:** Reteaching opportunities for students who need more help with assessed skills.

**Extend:** Extension activities for vocabulary, comprehension, story, and study skills.

 **TEACHING CHARTS** Instructional charts for modeling vocabulary and tested skills. Also available as **transparencies.**

### WORD BUILDING MANIPULATIVE CARDS
Cards with words and structural elements for word building and practicing vocabulary.

### LANGUAGE SUPPORT BOOK
**ESL** Parallel lessons and practice for students needing language support.

### PHONICS AND PHONEMIC AWARENESS PRACTICE BOOK
Additional practice focusing on vowel sounds, phonograms, blends, digraphs, and key phonetic elements.

### FLUENCY ASSESSMENT
Evaluation and practice for building reading fluency.

## LANGUAGE ARTS

### GRAMMAR PRACTICE BOOK
Provides practice for grammar and mechanics lessons.

### SPELLING PRACTICE BOOK
Provides practice with the word list and spelling patterns. Includes home involvement activities.

### DAILY LANGUAGE ACTIVITIES
Provide practice and reinforcement of grammar, mechanics, and usage skills. Available as **blackline masters** and **transparencies.**

### WRITING PROCESS TRANSPARENCIES
Model each stage of the writing process.

### HANDWRITING HANDBOOKS
Available for instruction and practice.

*McGraw-Hill School*
**TECHNOLOGY**

**interNET CONNECTION** Extend lesson activities through Research & inquiry ideas. Visit **www.mhschool.com/reading**

 **Vocabulary Puzzle-Maker** Provides practice with instructional vocabulary.

 **MindJogger Videos** Review grammar and writing skills.

 **Handwriting CD-ROM** Provides practice activities.

# Resources for Meeting Individual Needs

| | EASY | ON-LEVEL | CHALLENGE | LANGUAGE SUPPORT |
|---|---|---|---|---|

## UNIT 4

**Carlos and the Skunk**

| EASY | ON-LEVEL | CHALLENGE | LANGUAGE SUPPORT |
|---|---|---|---|
| **Leveled Book:** *Kelley in Charge* Reteach, 112–118 **Alternate Teaching Strategies,** T60–T66 **Writing:** Cartoons, 407L **Intervention** | **Leveled Book:** *The Lesson* Practice, 112–118 **Alternate Teaching Strategies,** T60–T66 **Writing:** A Personal Account, 407L | **Leveled Book:** *The Red Book* Extend, 112–118 **Writing:** Another Adventure, 407L **Science:** Tomatoes, 405 | **Teaching Strategies,** 388A, 388C, 389, 397, 399, 407E, 407L Language Support, 121–128 **Alternate Teaching Strategies,** T60–T66 **Writing:** Write a TV News Story, 407K–407L |

**How to Think Like a Scientist**

| EASY | ON-LEVEL | CHALLENGE | LANGUAGE SUPPORT |
|---|---|---|---|
| **Leveled Book:** *On Track* Reteach, 119–125 **Alternate Teaching Strategies,** T60–T66 **Writing:** Comic Strip, 431L **Intervention** | **Leveled Book:** *The Ladder of Truth: Forensic Detectives at Work* Practice, 119–125 **Alternate Teaching Strategies,** T60–T66 **Writing:** News Report, 431L | **Leveled Book:** *The Speckled Monster* Extend, 119–125 **Writing:** Summary, 431L **Math:** Identifying Unimportant Information, 429 | **Teaching Strategies,** 410A, 410C, 411, 419, 420, 425, 431L Language Support, 129–136 **Alternate Teaching Strategies,** T60–T66 **Writing:** Write a Scientific Report, 431K–431L |

**An Island Scrapbook**

| EASY | ON-LEVEL | CHALLENGE | LANGUAGE SUPPORT |
|---|---|---|---|
| **Leveled Book:** *Tourist Trap Island* Reteach, 126–132 **Alternate Teaching Strategies,** T60–T66 **Writing:** A Favorite Animal, 463L **Intervention** | **Leveled Book:** *The Galapagos Islands* Practice, 126–132 **Alternate Teaching Strategies,** T60–T66 **Writing:** Another Home, 463L | **Leveled Book:** *All About Islands* Extend, 126–132 **Writing:** Report, 463L **Art:** Environmental Mobiles, 461 | **Teaching Strategies,** 434A, 434C, 435, 436, 439, 447, 449, 463L Language Support, 137–144 **Alternate Teaching Strategies,** T60–T66 **Writing:** Write an Observation Report, 463K–463L |

**The Big Storm**

| EASY | ON-LEVEL | CHALLENGE | LANGUAGE SUPPORT |
|---|---|---|---|
| **Leveled Book:** *Tornado!* Reteach, 133–139 **Alternate Teaching Strategies,** T60–T66 **Writing:** Summary, 491L **Intervention** | **Leveled Book:** *Animals Sense the Weather* Practice, 133–139 **Alternate Teaching Strategies,** T60–T66 **Writing:** Warnings, 491L | **Leveled Book:** *The Great Galveston Hurricane* Extend, 133–139 **Writing:** Weather Report, 491L **Science:** Hurricanes, 489 | **Teaching Strategies,** 466A, 466C, 467, 469, 471, 473, 484, 491E, 491L Language Support, 145–152 **Alternate Teaching Strategies,** T60–T66 **Writing:** Write a Report, 491K–491L |

**Time for Kids: Catching Up with Lewis and Clark**

| EASY | ON-LEVEL | CHALLENGE | LANGUAGE SUPPORT |
|---|---|---|---|
| Review Reteach, 140–146 **Alternate Teaching Strategies,** T60–T66 **Writing:** Book Jacket, 501L **Intervention** | Review Practice, 140–146 **Alternate Teaching Strategies,** T60–T66 **Writing:** Travel Brochure, 501L | Review Extend, 140–146 **Writing:** A Press Release, 501L **Math:** How Long Would It Take?, 499 | **Teaching Strategies,** 494A, 494C, 495, 501L Language Support, 153–160 **Alternate Teaching Strategies,** T60–T66 **Writing:** Write a Magazine Article, 501K–501L |

## INFORMAL

### Informal Assessment

- Comprehension, 387B, 402, 403, 407F, 407H; 409B, 426, 427, 431F, 431H; 433B, 458, 459, 463F, 463H; 465B, 486, 487, 491F, 491H; 493B, 497, 501F
- Vocabulary, 407J, 431J, 463J, 491J, 501H, 501J

### Performance Assessment

- Scoring Rubrics, 407L, 431L, 463L, 491L, 501L, 503H
- Research and Inquiry, 384J, 503
- Writing Process, 407K, 431K, 463K, 491K, 501K
- Listening, Speaking, Viewing Representing Activities, 386E, 386, 388A, 388–405, 407D, 407L; 408E, 408, 410A, 410–429, 431D, 431L; 432E, 432, 434A, 434–461, 463D, 463L; 464E, 464, 466A, 466–489, 491D, 491L; 492E, 492, 494A, 494–499, 501D, 501L
- Portfolio, 407L, 431L, 463L, 493L, 501L
- Writing, 407K–L, 431K–L, 463K–L, 491K–L, 501K–L, 503C–H
- Cross-Curricular Activities, 390, 392, 394, 398, 405, 416, 418, 424, 429, 440, 448, 450, 454, 461, 470, 472, 476, 480, 489, 499
- Fluency, 402, 426, 458, 486, 496

### Leveled Practice
#### Practice, Reteach, Extend

- **Comprehension**
  Judgments and Decisions, 112, 116, 133, 137
  Draw Conclusions, 117, 124, 138
  Important and Unimportant Information, 119, 123, 131, 144
  Fact and Nonfact, 126, 130, 140
- **Vocabulary Strategies**
  Suffixes, 118, 132, 146
  Root Words, 125, 139, 145
- **Study Skills**
  Graphic Aids, 115, 122, 129, 136, 143

## FORMAL

### Selection Assessments

- **Skills and Vocabulary Words**
  *Carlos and the Skunk, 31–32*
  *How to Think Like a Scientist, 33–34*
  *An Island Scrapbook, 35–36*
  *The Big Storm, 37–38*
  *Catching Up with Lewis and Clark, 39–40*

### Unit 4 Test

- **Comprehension**
  Judgments and Decisions
  Draw Conclusions
  Important and Unimportant Information
  Fact and Nonfact
- **Vocabulary Strategies**
  Suffixes
  Root Words
- **Study Skills**
  Graphic Aids

### Grammar and Spelling Assessment

- **Grammar**
  Adjectives, 101, 107, 113, 119, 125, 127–128
- **Spelling**
  Unit 4 Assessment, 127–128

### Fluency Assessment

- Fluency Passages, 34–37

### Diagnostic/Placement Evaluation

- Informal Reading Inventory
- Running Record
- Placement Tests

### Test Preparation

- Test Power in Teacher's Edition, 407, 431, 463, 491, 501
- Additional standardized test preparation materials available

 **Reading Test Generator**

- Assessment Software

# Assessment Checklist

**Student** ............................ **Grade** .........

**Teacher** ....................................................

| | Carlos and the Skunk | How to Think Like a Scientist | An Island Scrapbook | The Big Storm | Catching Up with Lewis and Clark | Assessment Summary |
|---|---|---|---|---|---|---|
| **LISTENING/SPEAKING** | | | | | | |
| Participates in oral language experiences | | | | | | |
| Listens and speaks to gain knowledge of culture | | | | | | |
| Speaks appropriately to audiences for different purposes | | | | | | |
| Communicates clearly | | | | | | |
| **READING** | | | | | | |
| Uses a variety of word identification strategies, including: | | | | | | |
| • Suffixes | | | | | | |
| • Root Words | | | | | | |
| Reads with fluency and understanding | | | | | | |
| Reads widely for different purposes in varied sources | | | | | | |
| Develops an extensive vocabulary | | | | | | |
| Uses a variety of strategies to comprehend selections: | | | | | | |
| • Judgments and Decisions | | | | | | |
| • Draw Conclusions | | | | | | |
| • Important and Unimportant Information | | | | | | |
| • Fact and Nonfact | | | | | | |
| Responds to various texts | | | | | | |
| Analyzes the characteristics of various types of texts | | | | | | |
| Conducts research using various sources, including: | | | | | | |
| • Graphic Aids | | | | | | |
| Reads to increase knowledge | | | | | | |
| **WRITING** | | | | | | |
| Writes for a variety of audiences and purposes | | | | | | |
| Composes original texts using the conventions of written language such as capitalization and penmanship | | | | | | |
| Spells proficiently | | | | | | |
| Composes texts applying knowledge of grammar and usage | | | | | | |
| Uses writing processes | | | | | | |
| Evaluates own writing and writing of others | | | | | | |

+ Observed      − Not Observed

**384H**

# Introduce the Theme

# Investigate!

*We never know where the search for answers might lead us.*

**DISCUSS THE THEME** Write the theme statement on the board and read it aloud with students. Explain that there are many sources we can use to obtain information. Ask:

- What are some of the standard resources you use to search for answers to questions?

- How might songs, books, or movies be good resources?

- How can other ways of investigating, such as observing, asking questions, looking for connections, and experimenting be helpful in finding answers?

**PREVIEW UNIT SELECTIONS**
Have students preview the unit by reading the selection titles and looking at the illustrations. Ask:

- How might the stories, poems, and the *Time for Kids* magazine article relate to the theme?

- Which of these selections seems to be fiction and which nonfiction?

As students read the selections in this unit, encourage them to discuss their similarities and differences and how each develops the unit theme Investigate!

## THEME CONNECTIONS

Each of the five selections relates to the unit theme Investigate! as well as to the global theme Inquiry. These thematic links will help students to make connections across texts.

*Carlos and the Skunk* Carlos learns an unpleasant lesson when he tries to impress his friend Gloria.

*How to Think Like a Scientist* Four examples highlight the value of the scientific method in everyday life.

*An Island Scrapbook* The author and her daughter investigate everyday life and beauty on a barrier island.

*The Big Storm* People are still talking about the storm that blew across the United States in 1982.

*Catching Up with Lewis and Clark* Historians are trying to trace the steps of explorers Lewis and Clark.

# Research and Inquiry

**GROUP**

**Theme Project: Investigating Important Issues** Have students work in teams to brainstorm scientific or historical issues. Have them choose one issue as the basis for a project searching for answers to unanswered questions.

**Make a Resource Chart** Have teams list what they already know about their issue. Next ask students to brainstorm questions they would need to answer in order to prepare their presentation. Have students create a three-column chart, listing their questions in the first column.

In the second column have them list resources that will help them answer their questions. After they finish their research, they can write the answers in the third column. Remind students to take notes about important details and to identify their sources properly.

**Create a Presentation** When their research is complete, students will present the results of their investigation. Encourage them to be creative. They may create a documentary, an in-depth report, or a poster presentation. Suggest that they use audio and visual aids in their presentations.

| QUESTIONS | RESOURCES | ANSWERS |
|---|---|---|
| • Why were there so many avalanches this year? <br> • What causes avalanches? <br> • Where have they occurred? <br> • Can they be prevented? | • Newspapers <br> • Encyclopedias <br> • Search on the Internet <br> • Government agencies <br> • Interviews with experts | |

See **Wrap Up the Theme**, page 503.

## Research Strategies

Share these tips with students about how to use multiple sources of information.

- Skim a text to get an overview of its contents. Look at titles, section headings, captions, and graphics such as maps and photographs.

- Scan a text to find a particular fact or piece of information. Scan titles, headings, captions, text in

dark or italic (slanted) type, and graphics to help locate the specific information you are seeking.

- Take good notes. Include your sources of information.

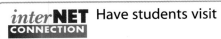
**interNET CONNECTION** Have students visit

**www.mhschool.com/reading**

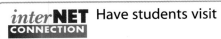

**384J**

# Poetry

## Read the Poem

**READ ALOUD** Read "First Flight" aloud to students. Afterward, ask:

- What investigation is the poem about?

- What is the mood of the poem— suspenseful, sad, humorous?

**Listening Library** The poem is available on **audiocassette** and on **compact disc.**

**DRAMATIC READING** Have volunteers take turns reading the poem as they think Wilbur might have said the lines. Tell each reader to use gestures and intonation to enhance reading.

## Learn About Poetry

**IRONY** Explain:

- **Irony** is the use of words to express the unexpected in an otherwise predictable situation; for example, saying "What perfect weather!" when the rain spoils your picnic.

Ask students to discuss what is ironic about Wilbur's words.

**DIALOGUE** Review:

- **Dialogue** is a conversation between two or more people.

- In this poem, we read only one character's words.

Discuss what Wilbur says to his brother. Ask students what they think Orville might have replied.

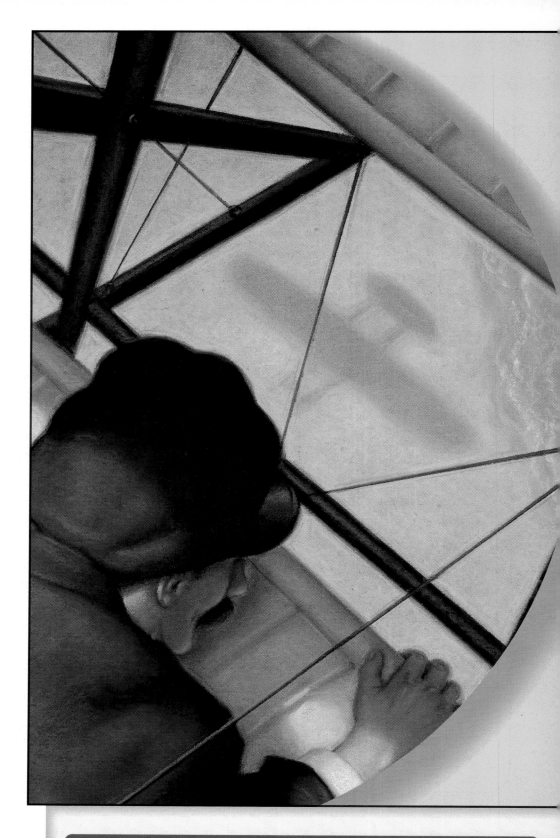

### MEET THE POET

**ABOUT FRANK RICHARDS**
Frank Richards (Charles Harold St. John Hamilton) was born in 1876. A prolific fiction author, he wrote not only school stories, but also adventure, travel, and crime tales. He is said to have written well over 5,000 full-length stories (of 25,000 words or more).

# Investigate!

**FIRST FLIGHT**

Said Wilbur Wright, "Oh, this is grand,
But, Orville, you must understand.
   We've discovered all right
   The secret of flight—
The question is, how do we land?"

*by Frank Richards*

385

# Poetry

**LITERARY DEVICES: Rhyme and Rhythm** Read the poem aloud, emphasizing the stressed syllables. Have a volunteer read the poem again, while students clap along. Point out that this poem is a limerick, a funny poem with a set rhythm and rhyme pattern.

Have students note that the first, second, and last lines have four beats, while the third and fourth lines have only two beats. Ask whether the rhyme scheme is related to the meter. Then discuss how the bouncy meter adds to the humorous tone of the poem.

## Oral Response

**SMALL-GROUP DISCUSSIONS** Have 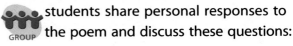 students share personal responses to the poem and discuss these questions:

* Where do you think this speech takes place?
* What kind of person do you think Wilbur is?
* What do you know about Wilbur and Orville's early flights? Do you think they ever had problems landing?
* How do you feel about flying?
* What possible human predicaments might be symbolized by the situation described in the poem?

## WRITE A POEM

**Write a Poem** Ask students if they have ever gotten into a situation and not known how to get out of it. Do they know anyone else to whom this has happened? Invite students to write a poem describing such an experience. They may choose to write about the predicament in a humorous way, using a limerick, or they may wish to look at the problem more seriously, using another form of poetry.

**Have a Poetry Reading** Plan with students a time to gather for a poetry reading. Have students either read their poems or recite them from memory.

**385**

## Concept
- **Learning a Lesson**

## Comprehension
- **Judgments and Decisions**

## Vocabulary
- **nestled**
- **peculiar**
- **stunned**
- **tortillas**
- **unbearable**
- **unpleasant**

# Reaching All Learners

### Anthology

# Carlos and the Skunk

**Selection Summary** In this amusing story set in the Southwest, a young boy named Carlos has an encounter with a skunk and learns that you can't believe everything you hear.

**Stories in Art** focuses on the **comprehension** skill

**Reading Strategy** applies the **comprehension** skill

**Listening Library**

**INSTRUCTIONAL** pages 388–403

**About the Author** The series of "Carlos" books, from which this story came, grew out of Jan Romero Stevens's experiences of rearing two sons in the Southwest. In fact, Stevens reads drafts of her works to her sons. They are my "best and most helpful critics," she says.

**About the Illustrator** Jeanne Arnold, who has illustrated the entire "Carlos" series, enjoys working with Jan Romero Stevens. Their mutual respect for the Southwest is an important part of their collaboration.

# Same Concept, Skills and Vocabulary!

## Leveled Books

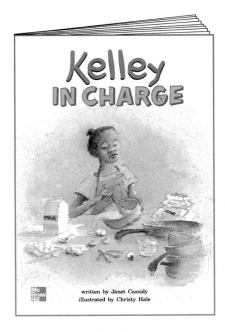

**EASY**
**Lesson on pages 407A and 407D**

**INDEPENDENT**
**Lesson on pages 407B and 407D**

🏠 *Take-Home version available*

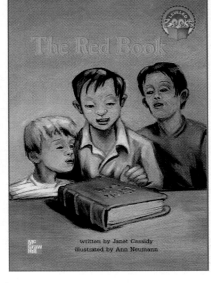

**CHALLENGE**
**Lesson on pages 407C and 407D**

## Leveled Practice

### EASY
**Reteach,** 112–118 Blackline masters with reteaching opportunities for each assessed skill

### INDEPENDENT/ON-LEVEL
**Practice,** 112–118 Workbook with Take-Home stories and practice opportunities for each assessed skill and story comprehension

### CHALLENGE
**Extend,** 112–118 Blackline masters that offer challenge activities for each assessed skill

**Quizzes Prepared by**  Accelerated Reader®

# WORKSTATION Activities

**Social Studies** . . . **Map Skills,** *390*

**Science** . . . . . . . . . . . **Skunks,** *392*
**Heating Systems,** *398*
**Tomatoes,** *405*

**Math** . . . . . . . . . . . . . . **Measurement,** *394*

**Language Arts** . . **Read Aloud,** *386E*

**Cultural Perspectives** . . . . . **Cooking,** *400*

**Writing** . . . . . . . . . . . **TV News Story,** *404*

**Research and Inquiry** . . . . . **Find Out More,** *405*

 **Internet Activities** . . . . . . . . **www.mhschool.com/reading**

# Suggested Lesson Planner

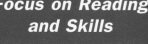

## READING AND LANGUAGE ARTS

 **DAY 1** *Focus on Reading and Skills*

 **DAY 2** *Read the Literature*

### Comprehension
### Vocabulary
### Phonics/Decoding
### Study Skills
### Listening, Speaking, Viewing, Representing

**DAY 1**

 **Read** **Read Aloud: Fable,** 386E
"The Lobster and the Crab"

**Develop Visual Literacy,** 386

 **Introduce Judgments and Decisions,** 387A–387B
 **Teaching Chart 91**
 **Reteach, Practice, Extend,** 112

 **Read** **Reading Strategy:** Make Judgments and Decisions, 387
"The Pest"

**Intervention Program**

**DAY 2**

**Build Background,** 388A
 Develop Oral Language

**Vocabulary,** 388B–388C

| | | |
|---|---|---|
| *nestled* | *stunned* | *unbearable* |
| *peculiar* | *tortillas* | *unpleasant* |

 **Teaching Chart 92**
 Word Building Manipulative Cards
 **Reteach, Practice, Extend,** 113

 **Read** **Read the Selection,** 388–403
  **Judgments and Decisions**

**Genre: Realistic Fiction,** 389

**Cultural Perspectives,** 400

**Intervention Program**

### Curriculum Connections

**Link** Fine Arts, 386

**Link** Language Arts, 388A

### Writing

 **Writing Prompt:** Describe how you might be able to show someone that you are brave or smart. Be sure to include what might happen if your plans do not turn out as you hope.

**Writing Prompt:** Shoes are expensive. Write what Carlos's parents might have said as they discussed whether or not to get him new ones.

 **Journal Writing,** 403
 Quick-Write

### Grammar

**Introduce the Concept: Adjectives,** 407M
 Daily Language Activity
 1. His mother chopped a _____ tomato. (red)
 2. The sweet _____ corn tasted good. (yellow)
 3. The skunk was black and _____. (white)

**Grammar Practice Book,** 97

**Teach the Concept: Adjectives,** 407M
 Daily Language Activity
 1. They ran through _____ cornfield. (this)
 2. Carlos ran to _____ river. (that)
 3. His mother liked _____ shoes. (those)

**Grammar Practice Book,** 98

### Spelling

**Pretest: Words with /ô/ and /ôr/,** 407O
 **Spelling Practice Book,** 97–98

**Explore the Pattern: Words with /ô/ and /ôr/,** 407O
 **Spelling Practice Book,** 99

**Meeting Individual Needs**

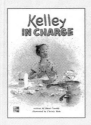
*Kelley IN CHARGE*

*The Lesson*

 = **Skill Assessed in Unit Test**

 **Intervention Program Available**

**Read EVERY DAY**

## DAY 3 — Read the Literature

**Rereading for Fluency,** 402

**Story Questions and Activities,** 404–405
Reteach, Practice, Extend, 114

**Study Skill,** 406
☑ **Read a Diagram**
**Teaching Chart 93**
Reteach, Practice, Extend, 115

**Test Power,** 407

**Read the Leveled Books,** 407A–407D
Guided Reading
/ô/ and /ôr/
☑ **Judgments and Decisions**
☑ **Instructional Vocabulary**

ⓘ **Intervention Program**

 **Activity** Social Studies, 390

 **Writing Prompt:** Write a summary of Carlos's adventure with the skunk from Gloria's point of view.

**Writing Process: Expository Writing,** 407K
Prewrite, Draft

**Review and Practice: Adjectives,** 407N
Daily Language Activity
1. It was a _____ day. (sunny)
2. At first the church was very_____. (quiet)
3. Carlos was sitting near_____ air vent. (this)

**Grammar Practice Book,** 99

**Practice and Extend: Words with /ô/ and /ôr/,** 407P
**Spelling Practice Book,** 100

## DAY 4 — Build Skills

 **Read the Leveled Books and Self-Selected Books**

☑ **Review Judgments and Decisions,** 407E–407F
**Teaching Chart 94**
Reteach, Practice, Extend, 116
Language Support, 126

☑ **Introduce Draw Conclusions,** 407G–407H
**Teaching Chart 95**
Reteach, Practice, Extend, 117
Language Support, 127

**Minilessons,** 391, 395, 399

ⓘ **Intervention Program**

 **Activity** Science, 392, 398

 **Writing Prompt:** Pretend you are Carlos. Write a letter to a friend explaining what you have just learned about skunks and their spray.

**Writing Process: Expository Writing,** 407K
Revise
**Meeting Individual Needs for Writing,** 407L

**Review and Practice: Adjectives,** 407N
Daily Language Activity
1. The _____ children were best friends. (two)
2. Carlos's shoes had a _____ odor. (terrible)
3. He tried to catch _____ skunk. (that)

**Grammar Practice Book,** 100

**Proofread and Write: Words with /ô/ and /ôr/,** 407P
**Spelling Practice Book,** 101

## DAY 5 — Build Skills

 **Read Self-Selected Books**

☑ **Introduce Suffixes,** 407I–407J
**Teaching Chart 96**
Reteach, Practice, Extend, 118
Language Support, 128

**Listening, Speaking, Viewing, Representing,** 407L

**Minilessons,** 391, 399

**Phonics Review,** /ô/ and /ôr/, 395

**Phonics/Phonemic Awareness Practice Book,** 67–68

ⓘ **Intervention Program**

 **Activity** Math, 394

 **Writing Prompt:** Write instructions for how to get rid of the odor if you get sprayed by a skunk.

**Writing Process: Expository Writing,** 407K
Edit/Proofread, Publish

**Assess and Reteach: Adjectives,** 407N
Daily Language Activity
1. His father bought him_____ shoes. (new)
2. Carlos was very _____ . (pleased)
3. He learned _____ important lesson. (this)

**Grammar Practice Book,** 101–102

**Assess and Reteach: Words with /ô/ and /ôr/,** 407P
**Spelling Practice Book,** 102

**Language Arts**

# Read Aloud

## The Lobster and the Crab
### a fable by Arnold Lobel

On a stormy day, the Crab went strolling along the beach. He was surprised to see the Lobster preparing to set sail in his boat.

"Lobster," said the Crab, "it is foolhardy to venture out on a day like this."

"Perhaps so," said the Lobster, "but I love a squall at sea!"

"I will come with you," said the Crab. "I will not let you face such danger alone."

The Lobster and the Crab began their voyage. Soon they found themselves far from shore. Their boat was tossed and buffeted by the turbulent waters.

"Crab!" shouted the Lobster above the roar of the wind. "For me, the splashing of the salt spray is thrilling! The crashing of every wave takes my breath away!"

"Lobster, I think we are sinking!" cried the Crab.

**Continued on page T2**

## Oral Comprehension

**LISTENING AND SPEAKING** Read the fable aloud. Ask students to think about the judgments and decisions that each character makes. Afterward, ask:

- What decision did the Lobster and the Crab make?
- During their trip, how did their judgments differ?

Then reread the fable. Explain that in a fable, characters are often animals with human traits. Ask: In what way do the characters' reactions to the events reflect human attitudes?

**GENRE STUDY: FABLE** Discuss some of the literary devices and techniques used in "The Lobster and the Crab."

- Point out that, in a fable, the characters are usually stereotypes. Ask: How would you describe the character of the Lobster? of the Crab?

- Most fables focus on one incident. Going to sea in a leaky boat would be dangerous for humans. Ask: Why was this situation only a "small risk" for the Lobster and the Crab?

- Explain that all fables end with a moral. Ask: What is the moral of this fable?

**Activity** Invite students to dramatize the fable with puppets. Remind students to use props and to assign someone to be the narrator. After the performance, discuss the value of taking small risks versus larger risks.

▶ **Kinesthetic/Linguistic/Interpersonal**

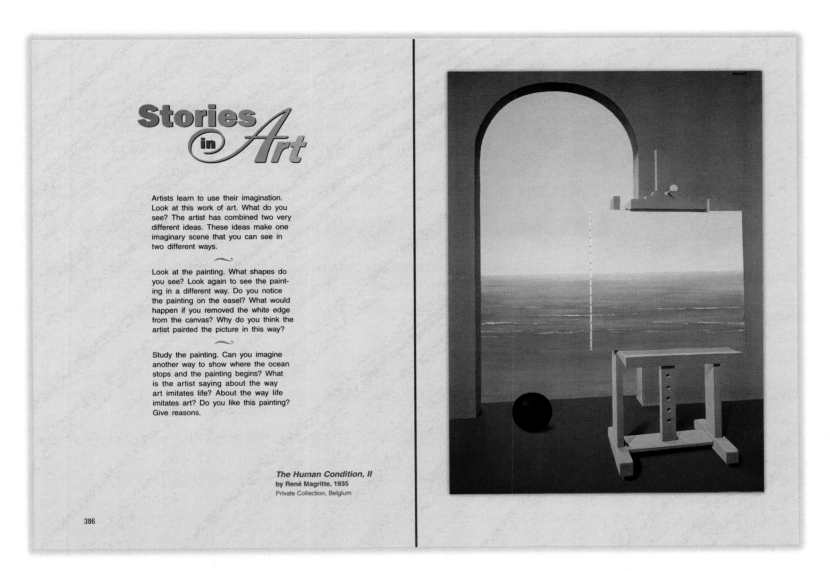

Stories in Art

Artists learn to use their imagination. Look at this work of art. What do you see? The artist has combined two very different ideas. These ideas make one imaginary scene that you can see in two different ways.

Look at the painting. What shapes do you see? Look again to see the painting in a different way. Do you notice the painting on the easel? What would happen if you removed the white edge from the canvas? Why do you think the artist painted the picture in this way?

Study the painting. Can you imagine another way to show where the ocean stops and the painting begins? What is the artist saying about the way art imitates life? About the way life imitates art? Do you like this painting? Give reasons.

*The Human Condition, II*
by René Magritte, 1935
Private Collection, Belgium

386

## Objective: Identify Judgments and Decisions

**VIEWING** In his surrealist painting, René Magritte has played with space so that the foreground and background become linked in a dreamlike way. Invite students to describe the painting in their own words. Ask them where the painting in the foreground stops and the ocean in the background begins. Lead students to see that the painting makes a statement about how art and life imitate each other.

Read the page with students, encouraging individual interpretations of the painting.

Encourage students to make judgments about the painting. For example:

- The painting tricks the eye. Where does the ocean stop and the painting on the easel begin?
- The ball helps signal where the room ends and the beach begins.

**REPRESENTING** Invite students to create dreamlike drawings that dispute reality. Then have them judge or assess their own work. Help them come up with an assessment checklist before they begin their evaluations.

**OBJECTIVES**

Students will make judgments and decisions based on a story.

### Skills Finder

**Judgments and Decisions**

| Introduce | 387A-B |
|---|---|
| Review | 407E-F, 465A-B, 491E-F, 617A-B, 647E-F, 699A-B |
| Test | Unit 4, Unit 6 |

### TEACHING TIP

**CLUES** Explain to the students that often there are clues that explain why a judgment or decision is made. Clues may describe an event or setting or even a character. Challenge them to look for descriptive information that may help them understand a decision or judgment. Tell the students to pay careful attention to the details of the text so they can understand why judgments or decisions were made.

# Introduce Judgments and Decisions

**PREPARE**

**Discuss a Familiar Example**

Discuss this example: Baby animals are often cute. When you are out exploring nature, you may judge it safe and fun to approach one. You may be sorry, though, if you decide to feed a baby bear. As a result of your decision, an angry mother bear might attack you. Knowing this fact may change the way you think, or make a judgment, about approaching wild baby animals.

**TEACH**

**Define Judgments and Decisions**

Explain: Judgments are the opinions we reach about something after carefully thinking it over. Decisions are what we choose to do based on those judgments.

### Gloria, Carlos, and the Skunk

Carlos and Gloria were playing hide and seek one afternoon. Suddenly, Carlos saw a skunk darting through the corn plants. Gloria saw the skunk, too, and immediately stepped back.

"Leave it alone, Carlos," she said. "If we frighten the skunk, it will spray us."

But Carlos wouldn't listen to her. "It's easy. All you have to do is sneak up behind the skunk and grab it by its tail," he said.

"I don't think the skunk will like that, and then you'll be in big trouble," Gloria said.

"It's the best way to catch a skunk," Carlos said stubbornly. "Just watch me."

Teaching Chart 91

**Read the Passage and Model the Skill**

Display **Teaching Chart 91.** Have students pay attention to clues about judgments and decisions as the story is read.

**MODEL** Carlos and Gloria judge the skunk in different ways. Gloria believes they should stay away from the animal, while Carlos thinks he can catch it by grabbing its tail. It seems clear Carlos has made a decision to catch the skunk his way.

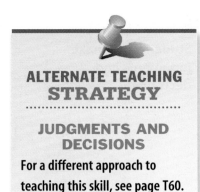

## PRACTICE

**Create a Judgments and Decisions Chart**

GROUP

Have students circle Carlos's and Gloria's judgments about the skunk and underline phrases that explain why they each made that judgment. Have groups discuss their judgments about the skunk. Then have them make a Judgments and Decisions chart like the one below.

| JUDGMENTS | DECISIONS |
|---|---|
| Gloria thinks that if Carlos frightens the skunk, it will spray him. | Gloria stays away from the skunk. |
| Carlos thinks it's safe to catch the skunk by grabbing it by the tail. | Carlos decides to try and catch the skunk. |

## ASSESS/CLOSE

**Make Judgments and Decisions**

Have students suppose that the children see a fox, not a skunk.
Ask: What decision might Carlos and Gloria each make?

---

**ALTERNATE TEACHING STRATEGY**

**JUDGMENTS AND DECISIONS**

For a different approach to teaching this skill, see page T60.

**Intervention ➤ Skills Intervention Guide,** for direct instruction and extra practice with judgments and decisions

---

# Meeting Individual Needs for Comprehension

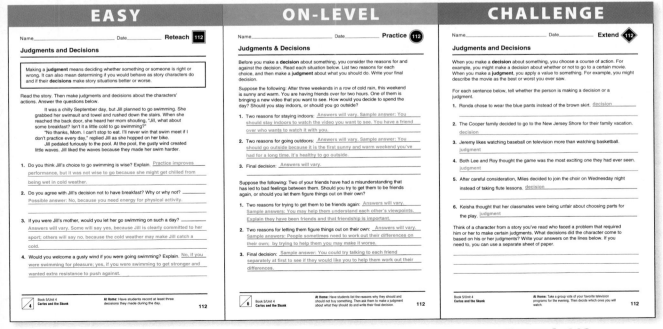

Reteach, 112          Practice, 112          Extend, 112

**TESTED OBJECTIVES**

Students will make judgments and decisions.

## Apply Judgments and Decisions

**READING STRATEGY**

### Make Judgments and Decisions

Develop a strategy for making judgments and decisions.

1. **Think about the actions** of the main character.

2. **Decide on the reasons** for those actions.

3. **Think about what** you would do in a similar situation. How would you feel?

4. **Compare what you** would do with what Tom did.

5. **Make a judgment** based on evidence from the selection and your own beliefs and opinions.

387

# The Pest

Tom's younger brother Brian followed him everywhere. He begged to go with Tom to the park and to the community pool. Brian played with Tom's favorite toys and even read his favorite books. Brian was a pest!

One afternoon, Tom's best friend Mike came over for a game of checkers. Tom and Mike had been playing checkers for years. As they began to set up the game on the edge of Tom's bed, Brian came wandering into the room.

"May I play?" Brian asked.

"You don't know how to play checkers. Besides, you're much too young," said Tom.

"Please! Just let me watch. I bet if I watch long enough, I'll learn how to play," said Brian.

"Fine. You can watch, but just for a few minutes," said Tom.

Brian sat so quietly that Tom and Mike played for almost two hours before they realized he was still in the bedroom.

Just after dinner, Brian pleaded with his brother to play a game of checkers. Tom finally agreed and thought to himself, "This will be an easy win."

Tom and Brian played three games of checkers, and to Tom's surprise, Brian won all three games. Brian was a great player! "Maybe I'll even ask him to go to the park with me next week," Tom thought.

**READING STRATEGY**

---

**PREVIEW** Have students preview "The Pest" by reading the title and first paragraph. Ask:

- What does the title suggest about the subject of the story? (The story will be about someone or something that is a pest.)

- Who are the main characters? (Tom and his younger brother Brian)

**SET PURPOSES** Explain that students will apply what they have learned about making judgments and decisions as they read "The Pest."

**APPLY THE STRATEGY** Discuss this strategy for making judgments and decisions.

- How had Tom been acting toward Brian?

- Why do you think Tom acted the way he did toward Brian?

- What would you do in a similar situation?

- Compare what you would do with what Tom did.

- What is your judgment about Tom's actions?

**Activity** Have students reread the passage and side notes. Then have them create a Judgments and Decisions chart for the passage.

# Build Background

## Concept: Learning a Lesson

**Anthology and Leveled Books**

## Evaluate Prior Knowledge

**CONCEPT: LEARNING A LESSON** The main characters in this story and the Leveled Books all make mistakes and learn an important lesson. Have students think about a lesson they have learned, either through a mistake or from a person who was older and wiser.

**IDENTIFY A CHAIN OF EVENTS** Have students reflect on the chain of events that caused them to learn a lesson. Ask them to identify the events by completing a Cause and Effect chain. ▶ **Logical/Visual**

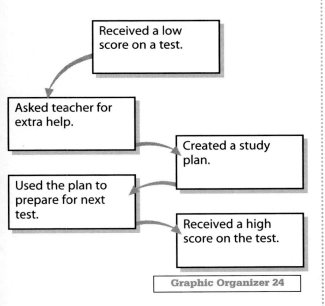

Received a low score on a test.

Asked teacher for extra help.

Created a study plan.

Used the plan to prepare for next test.

Received a high score on the test.

**Graphic Organizer 24**

**WRITE A THANK-YOU NOTE** Have
  students write thank-you notes to individuals who have taught them life lessons. Encourage students to include descriptions of how the learning experiences enriched their lives.

## Develop Oral Language

**DISCUSS LIFE LESSONS** Have students **ESL** reflect on times when they were considered to be older or wiser than others. Ask them to describe how it feels to be viewed this way. Invite volunteers to describe experiences in which they helped other people learn life lessons. Choose two of the stories and briefly outline on the board the chain of events that took place in them. Then ask other students to use the notes to describe the life lesson experiences outlined on the board.

### TEACHING TIP

**MANAGEMENT** You may want to show students a sample thank-you note before beginning the writing activity. Stress that while the tone of such correspondence is friendly, the message should clearly identify the lesson the writer has learned.

**LANGUAGE SUPPORT**

See Language Support Book, pages 121–124, for teaching suggestions for Build Background.

**OBJECTIVES**

Students will use context clues to determine the meanings of vocabulary words.

tortillas
peculiar
unpleasant
unbearable
stunned
nestled

**Definitions**

**tortillas** (p. 390) round, flat bread made from cornmeal

**peculiar** (p. 399) odd; unusual

**unpleasant** (p. 396) not pleasing; disagreeable

**unbearable** (p. 394) difficult to put up with

**stunned** (p. 394) shocked and confused

**nestled** (p. 390) settled down snugly and comfortably

### Story Words

These words from the selection may be unfamiliar. Before students read, have them check the meanings and pronunciations of the words in the Glossary beginning on page 760 or in a dictionary.

- chiles, p. 390
- fertile, p. 390
- adobe, p. 390
- arroyo, p. 394

# Vocabulary

## Teach Vocabulary in Context

**Identify Vocabulary Words**

Display **Teaching Chart 92** and read it with students. Have students circle each vocabulary word and underline other words that are clues to its meaning.

**Under the Sink**

1. Ron went into the kitchen to get some tortillas, the flat breads he enjoys most. 2. He noticed a peculiar smell but couldn't figure out where the odd scent was coming from. 3. He covered his nose because he found the scent unpleasant. 4. Ron discovered the bad odor was unbearable in one part of the kitchen. 5. Opening a cabinet beneath the sink, he was stunned by the surprising discovery he made. 6. A sack of rotting potatoes was nestled snugly in the corner of the cabinet.

**Teaching Chart 92**

**Discuss Meanings**

Ask questions like these to help clarify word meanings:

- What would you eat with tortillas?
- What is the most peculiar thing you have ever seen?
- Would you like to spend time with an unpleasant person?
- What task would you find unbearable?
- Have you ever been stunned by the size or beauty of an animal at the zoo?
- How do you feel when you are nestled in your bed?

## Practice

**Demonstrate Word Meaning**

PARTNERS

Have partners choose vocabulary cards from a pile and demonstrate each word meaning with pantomime, drawings, or verbal clues.

▶ **Kinesthetic/Linguistic**

 peculiar  stunned  nestled

Word Building Manipulative Cards

**Write a Poem**

WRITING

Have partners use vocabulary words to write a poem. Tell them to use as many vocabulary words as they can in their poems. Have students refer to their Glossary as needed.

▶ **Linguistic**

## Assess Vocabulary

**Use Words in Context**

GROUP

Have students work in small groups to create a five-panel cartoon strip about a funny situation. Tell students to use all of the vocabulary words in speech balloons as part of the comic strip. Make a bulletin board display of the cartoon strips so that all students can enjoy each group's finished work.

**SPELLING/VOCABULARY CONNECTIONS**

See Spelling Challenge Words, pages 4070–407P.

**LANGUAGE SUPPORT**

See the **Language Support Book**, pages 121–124, for teaching suggestions for Vocabulary.

**Vocabulary PuzzleMaker**

Provides vocabulary activities

# Meeting Individual Needs for Vocabulary

| EASY | ON-LEVEL | ON-LEVEL | CHALLENGE |
| --- | --- | --- | --- |

**EASY**

Name_____ Date_____ Reteach 113

**Vocabulary**

Complete each sentence using the correct vocabulary word.

| unbearable | peculiar | unpleasant | stunned | tortillas | nestled |

1. When she dines in a Mexican restaurant, Kate usually orders _tortillas_ wrapped around cheese with sour cream.

2. The house was _nestled_ between a stone ledge and a hill covered with apple trees.

3. After cleaning the barn and working in the fields, Lucas thought his clothing smelled _unbearable_.

4. When Dawn was accidentally hit hard by the ball, she was so _stunned_ that it took her some time to realize what had happened.

5. Samir felt sick. His homework had mistakes, and he forgot his lunch. All in all, it was turning out to be a very _unpleasant_ day.

6. Jaime never went anywhere without his guitar. He played constantly. So everyone thought it was _peculiar_ when he stopped playing.

☐ 6

**Story Comprehension**

Reteach 114

Read each sentence about "Carlos and the Skunk." Write T if the sentence is true and F it is false.

1. Carlos didn't want to touch the skunk. _F_
2. Carlos avoided Gloria for a while. _T_
3. The church service ended earlier than usual. _T_
4. Carlos didn't know where the terrible smell was coming from. _F_
5. Carlos asked his father for a new pair of shoes. _F_

At Home: Have students tell what clues helped them realize why Carlos was avoiding Gloria.
113–114    Carlos and the Skunk 5

**Reteach, 113**

---

**ON-LEVEL**

Name_____ Date_____ Practice 113

**Vocabulary**

Write a vocabulary word from the list that means almost the same thing as the underlined words in the sentences.

| nestled | peculiar | stunned | tortillas | unbearable | unpleasant |

1. The cold water was _unbearable_. The temperature was intolerable.

2. The star of the film was very _unpleasant_. She had a disagreeable personality.

3. We were all shocked to hear he had won the prize. It _stunned_ us.

4. I like _tortillas_. They remind me of thin pancakes.

5. After a long day of hiking, we lay comfortably _nestled_ in our tent. That night we snuggled in our sleeping bags to stay warm.

6. The story is a little odd. Some people think what happened is _peculiar_.

At Home: Have students use the vocabulary words in sentences
113    Carlos and the Skunk 6

**Practice, 113**

---

**ON-LEVEL**

### Very Good Cooking

"I could go for some good food," Maria thought to herself. "I could go for some tortillas. I could make them myself. How hard could it be?"

Usually, Maria thought cooking was unpleasant, but this time she was actually enjoying herself. Maria poured corn flour and water into a bowl just like she had seen her grandmother do. "That's peculiar," said Maria. "There must be more ingredients in the recipe." But Maria didn't have the recipe. So she decided to create her own. She found a box of raisins nestled in a drawer. She added those. Then she added some molasses and a little sugar.

Maria was finishing cooking her tortillas when her grandmother came into the kitchen. Maria proudly told her the recipe she had invented. Her grandmother was stunned. "Well, normally, you need only flour and water, but yours does sound interesting. I'm sure it won't be unbearable," said her grandmother. "I'm sure we'll enjoy eating them." They did enjoy eating them. They were very good!

1. What did Maria decide to cook? _tortillas_

2. What did Maria think was peculiar? _There were only two ingredients she could remember._

3. What was nestled in the drawer? _a box of raisins_

4. How did Maria's grandmother react to her recipe? _She was stunned._

5. Why do you think Maria's grandmother said the tortillas would not be unbearable? _She didn't want to hurt Maria's feelings; also the tortillas had sweet ingredients so they probably would taste fine._

Book 5/Unit 4
Carlos and the Skunk    At Home: Have students write a story about a time they cooked.    113a

**Practice, 113a
Take-Home Story**

---

**CHALLENGE**

Name_____ Date_____ Extend 113

**Vocabulary**

| nestled | peculiar | stunned |
| tortillas | unbearable | unpleasant |

Suppose that Carlos writes about the things that happen to him each day in a journal. Write a journal entry for the day that Carlos encountered the skunk. Use as many of the vocabulary words in the box as you can.

Answers will vary but should be written in correct context and with correct parts of speech.

Extend 114

**Story Comprehension**

The main character of "Carlos and the Skunk" is a boy named Carlos. His best friend is a girl named Gloria, but the story doesn't give many details about her. What inferences can you make about what Gloria is like? Reread the parts of the story where Gloria is mentioned. Write a description of Gloria.

Answers will vary. Students may say that Gloria is wiser about the ways of skunks than Carlos. She laughs when she tells him not to believe everything he has heard, so she probably also laughs when the skunk sprays Carlos. But she must also be sympathetic to Carlos, since they are still good friends at the end of the story.

At Home: Talk about animals you see around your home or the home of a friend or relative. What do they do when they meet up with a person? Has anyone in your family ever encountered a skunk?
113–114    Carlos and the Skunk

**Extend, 113**

**388C**

# Comprehension

## Prereading Strategies

**PREVIEW AND PREDICT** Have students read the title and preview the selection, noting pictures that tell about the setting and characters.

- Where might this story take place?
- What clues about the main character do the title and picture give?
- What will the story most likely be about?
- Why do you think this story might be realistic fiction? (The people and characters look real.) *Genre*

Have students record their predictions about the setting and the main character.

| PREDICTIONS | WHAT HAPPENED |
|---|---|
| The story takes place in a rural area. | |
| The main character is a boy named Carlos who likes skunks. | |

**SET PURPOSES** What do students want to find out by reading the story? For example:

- Who is the girl in the field?
- Why are the children following a skunk?

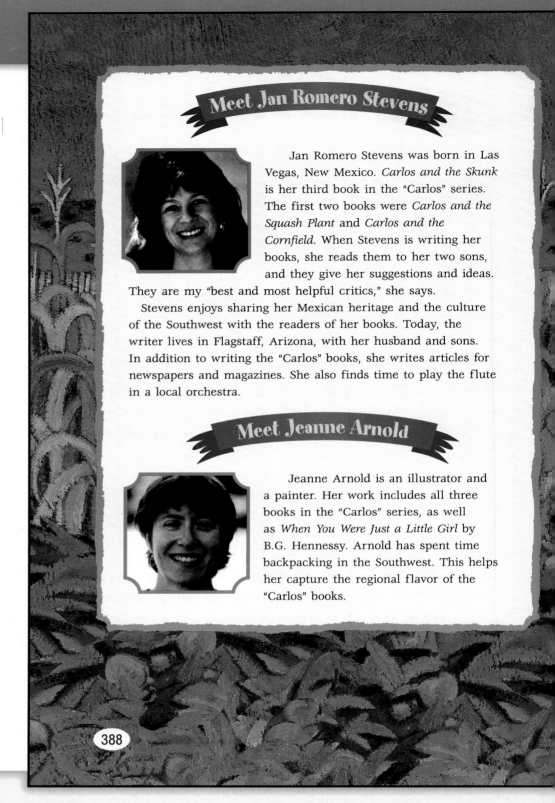

### Meet Jan Romero Stevens

Jan Romero Stevens was born in Las Vegas, New Mexico. *Carlos and the Skunk* is her third book in the "Carlos" series. The first two books were *Carlos and the Squash Plant* and *Carlos and the Cornfield*. When Stevens is writing her books, she reads them to her two sons, and they give her suggestions and ideas. They are my "best and most helpful critics," she says.

Stevens enjoys sharing her Mexican heritage and the culture of the Southwest with the readers of her books. Today, the writer lives in Flagstaff, Arizona, with her husband and sons. In addition to writing the "Carlos" books, she writes articles for newspapers and magazines. She also finds time to play the flute in a local orchestra.

### Meet Jeanne Arnold

Jeanne Arnold is an illustrator and a painter. Her work includes all three books in the "Carlos" series, as well as *When You Were Just a Little Girl* by B.G. Hennessy. Arnold has spent time backpacking in the Southwest. This helps her capture the regional flavor of the "Carlos" books.

388

# Meeting Individual Needs · Grouping Suggestions for Strategic Reading

| EASY | ON-LEVEL | CHALLENGE |
|---|---|---|
| **Read Together** Read the story together or invite students to use the **Listening Library.** Have students use the Judgments and Decisions chart to record important information about the characters and setting. Comprehension and Intervention prompts offer additional help with decoding, vocabulary, and comprehension. | **Guided Instruction** Choose from the Comprehension questions as you read the story with students. Have them use the Judgments and Decisions chart to record meaningful information during reading. | **Read Independently** Have students set up Judgments and Decisions charts as shown on page 389. After reading independently, they can use their charts to summarize the story. Remind students that making inferences about the characters and setting will help them understand the story. |

# Carlos and the Skunk

Written by Jan Romero Stevens  Illustrated by Jeanne Arnold

## ☑ Apply Judgments and Decisions

**STRATEGIC READING** Paying attention to what characters say, feel, and do will help you understand how and why they make their judgments and decisions. Before we begin to read this selection, let's make a Judgments and Decisions chart so that we can keep track of judgments and decisions the characters make.

| JUDGMENTS | DECISIONS |
|-----------|-----------|
|           |           |
|           |           |

 What clues in the illustration do you see about the characters in this story? (The boy and girl both appear to be about ten or eleven years old. They probably live on a farm or in a village, since they are standing in a field with tall corn plants. They see a skunk in the field.) *Character*

## LANGUAGE SUPPORT

A blackline master of the Judgments and Decisions chart is available in the **Language Support Book.**

### Genre

## Realistic Fiction

Explain that realistic fiction:

- features events, characters, and settings that could be found in the real world.
- includes well-developed characters.
- may have a setting that affects the plot.

**Activity** After students read *Carlos and the Skunk*, have them describe Carlos, including what he is like at the beginning of the story and how he has changed by the end. Then discuss how the setting affects what happens to Carlos. Ask how the story might be different if Carlos lived in a city.

**389**

# Comprehension

**②** **JUDGMENTS AND DECISIONS** In your judgment, what makes Carlos and Gloria such good friends?

*MODEL* The story says that when Carlos and Gloria were little, they used to play together. I know I love spending time with friends I've known for such a long time. We know each other so well. Probably a big reason they are close friends is because they have spent time together for as long as they can remember.

**③** How can you tell that Carlos's feelings for Gloria have changed? (He shows off for her and is concerned about his appearance. He is starting to think of her as his girlfriend.) *Character*

**C**arlos could not remember how long he and Gloria had been best friends.

When they were little, Gloria's mother would prop them up on old catalogs at the kitchen table while she strung red chiles together or rolled the dough for tortillas. If they were at Carlos's house, his mother would let them play in the garden

**②** while she sorted through the shiny green chiles, ripe red tomatoes, and sweet corn.

It seemed as if Carlos and Gloria were always together, but as they grew older, Carlos's feelings toward his friend started to

**③** change. He began gazing at himself in the mirror, combing his hair this way and that to see which looked better. He started showing off for Gloria, wanting her to notice how brave and smart he was becoming.

Carlos and Gloria lived in the fertile Española Valley nestled in the mountains of northern New Mexico. Their thick-walled adobe homes, with high tin roofs and matching

**④** gardens, were within walking distance from one another.

390

---

## Cross Curricular: Social Studies

**MAP SKILLS** Display a United States map. Have students:

- locate the state and area in which they live.
- locate New Mexico.
- name the states that border New

Mexico and a river that runs through New Mexico.

- identify a fraction that represents the size of New Mexico compared to the size of their home state.

▶ **Mathematical/Spatial**

SOUTHWESTERN UNITED STATES

391

# Comprehension

**④** When do you think the story takes place? (present) What clues did you use to decide? (Pictures show present time.) Do you think they live in a big town or small one? Explain. (probably a small town, because the area looks very rural) *Setting*

**p/i** **MULTIPLE-MEANING WORDS** Find the word *change* in the third paragraph. What does the word mean here? Can you think of another meaning for *change*? *Semantic Cues*

**REVIEW/MAINTAIN**

## Problem and Solution

Tell students that the main character of a story often faces some type of problem. During the course of the story, the character performs various actions to solve this problem.

- Ask students to identify the problem Carlos faces as described on page 390. (He wants Gloria to notice how brave and smart he has become.)

- Have them describe the actions Carlos has taken so far to solve his problem. (He tries to improve his grooming and he shows off for her.)

**Activity** Have students scan the story's illustrations. Then have them use information gleaned from their observations to predict two other actions Carlos will take to solve his problem.

**p/i** **PREVENTION/INTERVENTION**

**MULTIPLE-MEANING WORDS**
Review: Many words have more than one meaning; a reader must use context clues to determine the meaning the author intended. Use the word *change* as an example. Ask:

- What meaning of this word did the author intend here? (to become different)

- What clues did you use to determine this meaning? (The next sentences describe ways that Carlos's actions became different.)

- Does the word have the same meaning in the sentence *Carlos's pocket was full of change*? (no)

- What does *change* mean in that sentence? (coins) *Semantic Cues*

**391**

# Comprehension

**⑤ JUDGMENTS AND DECISIONS**
Carlos and Gloria see a skunk. What would you do if you saw a skunk? (avoid it) Why? (because it shoots a liquid that makes a terrible smell) What does Gloria decide to do? What judgment lies behind her decision?

*MODEL* Gloria thinks she will make the skunk angry if she goes near it. This judgment helps her to decide to stay away from it.

Let's add this information to the chart.

| JUDGMENTS | DECISIONS |
|---|---|
| Gloria knows the skunk may become angry. | Gloria decides to stay away from the skunk. |

392

## Cross Curricular: Science

**SKUNKS** When frightened or in danger, a skunk sprays a foul-smelling liquid at its enemy. Have students research this unique defense mechanism of skunks as well as other facts about the animal.

Challenge students to find out the name of the liquid, how it is released from a skunk's body, and warning signs that a skunk is about to spray an enemy.

Have groups create a 2-minute public service announcement advising the public about this unique ability of skunks.

▶ **Interpersonal/Linguistic**

After school each day, Gloria and Carlos did their chores—weeding the garden, feeding the chickens, and doing their homework. After dinner, they were allowed to play.

One fall evening, when they were running through the cornfield playing hide and seek, they caught a glimpse of a striped skunk slinking through the shadows of the garden. The children had seen the skunk many times before. It had only two toes on its right front paw, and they had nicknamed it Dos Dedos (Two Toes). **⑤**

Gloria feared the chance of arousing the skunk's anger and kept far away from it. But one afternoon, Carlos, wanting to impress Gloria, moved closer and closer until he could clearly see the narrow, single white stripe running from its head onto its tail.

"Carlos, you'd better be careful," whispered Gloria as Carlos inched along on his stomach toward the skunk.

"Gloria, don't worry. I know just how to catch a skunk," Carlos boasted. "You know what I heard? If you pick a skunk up by its tail, it can't spray you."

Gloria covered her mouth and giggled.

"Oh, Carlos," she said. *"No puedes creer todo lo que te dicen—* **⑥** you can't believe everything you hear."

"But it's true," Carlos insisted to his doubting friend, and he became more determined than ever to prove himself right. He went to sleep that night still pondering over how to catch **⑦** the skunk.

# Comprehension

**⑥** What do Gloria's actions tell you about her? (She is careful and smart and has good common sense.) ***Draw Conclusions***

**⑦** Why do you think Carlos is so determined to prove to Gloria that he is right about catching the skunk? (He wants to impress her.) ***Make Inferences***

---

### TEACHING TIP

**BILINGUAL TEXT** Direct students' attention to the second-to-last paragraph on page 393. Point out that the second sentence gives the saying in both Spanish and English. If possible, have a Spanish-speaking student read it aloud. Explain that, like many Spanish-speaking people in this country, Carlos and Gloria are comfortable speaking both languages and sometimes switch back and forth between the two when talking with other bilingual people. Point out this way of speaking is common in the region and culture in which the story is set.

---

# Comprehension

**8** **JUDGMENTS AND DECISIONS**
Read the fourth paragraph. What judgment and decision does Carlos make?

*MODEL* When Carlos sees the skunk, he thinks that it would be a good time to catch it. He decides to sneak up behind it and then grab its tail, believing that the skunk won't spray him.

Let's add this information to the chart.

| JUDGMENTS | DECISIONS |
|-----------|-----------|
| Gloria knows the skunk may become angry. | Gloria decides to stay away from the skunk. |
| Carlos thinks it's a good idea to catch the skunk. | Carlos picks up the skunk by the tail. |

**9** What do you learn about Carlos from the way he acts here? (He is so eager to impress Gloria that he doesn't consider the consequences of his actions.)
*Draw Conclusions*

The next day, Carlos had planned to take Gloria fishing so he awoke early and got dressed. His mother prepared warm flour tortillas, fried eggs, and fresh salsa for breakfast. Salsa was a family tradition in Carlos's home. Made from tomatoes and green chiles grown in the garden, the salsa was spicy and tasty. Carlos spooned it on just about everything—from breakfast to dinner.

After breakfast, Carlos rushed outside to get his fishing pole and a can for worms. Rounding the corner of his house, he saw Gloria waiting for him by the gate. As they began walking down the road together, they saw Dos Dedos in the garden.

*Qué suerte!* (What luck!) thought Carlos. "I will catch Dos Dedos this time!"

**8** Carlos gave no thought to what he might do with the skunk if he did catch it, but instead began creeping up behind it. He got closer and closer until he was inches away. For just a moment, Carlos hesitated, then winked at Gloria before he reached out and grabbed the tail. In an instant, the skunk's tail

**9** arched, and Carlos was sprayed from head to toe.

With a gasp, Carlos fell backward onto the ground. He was so stunned he hardly realized what had happened. He had never smelled such a strong odor. His eyes itched. He coughed and snorted and blew his nose. He did his best not to cry in

**10** front of Gloria.

Quite unconcerned, Dos Dedos disappeared down the side of an arroyo. And Carlos ran off to the river—leaving both Gloria and his fishing pole far behind.

Carlos chose a secluded spot and pulled off all his clothes as fast as he could. The smell of them was unbearable. He jumped into the stream and washed out his clothing, laying it out on a branch to dry in the sun. By afternoon his shirt and pants were dry, but the strong odor still lingered, especially on

**11** his shoes. He dressed and walked the long way home, climbing up and down the sides of the arroyos and stopping to gather piñon nuts. When he finally reached his house, he carefully took off his shoes and left them by the back door.

394

---

## Activity

## Cross Curricular: Math

**MEASUREMENT** Point out the recipe on page 402. Explain: Most recipes identify the number of people the given ingredients will serve. At times, a cook will reduce the ingredient amounts by half to serve half as many people. Other times, a cook needs to double the ingredient amounts to make twice as much of the recipe.

Have students apply their knowledge of multiplication and division of fractions to prepare an ingredient list for a half batch of salsa and a double batch of salsa.

▶ **Mathematical**

395

# Comprehension

**10** Why did Carlos try not to cry in front of Gloria? (He didn't want to appear weak in front of her because he wants to impress her.) *Make Inferences*

**11** Why does Carlos leave his shoes by the back door? (He doesn't want to bring them into the house because they still have a strong odor.) *Make Inferences*

**p/i** **DECODING/CONTEXT CLUES** Look at the first sentence of the last paragraph on page 394. How do you say the word spelled *s-e-c-l-u-d-e-d*? Can you tell what the word means? *Semantic Cues*

## Minilesson

### REVIEW/MAINTAIN

### /ô/ and /ôr/

Review the sounds /ô/ and /ôr/.

- Ask students to find two words on page 394 with the /ô/ sound spelled *a* as in *all*. *(salsa, walking)*

- Ask students to find one word on page 394 with the /ô/ sound spelled *aw* as in *law*. *(saw)*

- Ask students to find three words on page 394 with the sound /ôr/ as in *bored*. *(Gloria, tortillas, for)* *Graphophonic Cues*

**Activity** Have small groups brainstorm other words with these sounds. Then have them write silly sentences using three examples of words with /ô/ and /ôr/ in each.

 **Phonics Intervention Guide**

---

**p/i** **PREVENTION/INTERVENTION**

**DECODING/CONTEXT CLUES** Write *secluded* on the chalkboard.

- Ask a volunteer to name another word ending with *-cluded*. (included) Help students see that the last two syllables of both words are pronounced the same.

- Write *secret, select,* and *second* on the board. Discuss the different sounds the letters *se-* stand for in

these words. Explain that *secluded* begins with /si/, like *select*.

- Ask students how they could figure out the meaning of *secluded*. (Read the rest of the paragraph. Look at the illustration.)

Have partners discuss different meanings that would make sense for the word in the sentence. Have them use a dictionary to check their ideas. *Semantic Cues*

**395**

# Comprehension

**(12) JUDGMENTS AND DECISIONS**
How does Carlos think that tomato juice will help him? What does he decide to do as a result? (He believes tomato juice will help get rid of the smell of skunk. He picks all the ripe tomatoes, squeezes them in the bathtub, and washes with the tomato juice.)

Let's add Carlos's judgment and decision to the chart.

| JUDGMENTS | DECISIONS |
|---|---|
| Gloria knows the skunk may become angry. | Gloria decides to stay away from the skunk. |
| Carlos thinks it's a good idea to catch the skunk. | Carlos picks up the skunk by the tail. |
| Carlos believes tomato juice will get rid of the smell of the skunk. | He takes a bath in tomato juice. |

## Fluency

**READ DIALOGUE** Have students point out the punctuation marks in the dialogue on page 396. Have students read the dialogue aloud as partners with one student taking the role of Carlos and the other acting as Mamá. Remind them to pause briefly at commas, and that question marks indicate an interrogative rising tone. Encourage student partners to read the dialogue with expression.

**396** *Carlos and the Skunk*

---

When his mother came into the kitchen, she noticed a strange smell, but before she could question Carlos, he slipped out the door and into the garden.

Carlos had heard that tomato juice helped to get rid of the smell of skunk, so he picked every ripe tomato he could find and sneaked into the bathroom. He squeezed the tomatoes into the bathtub and all over his hair, scrubbing himself as hard as he could with a washrag.

**(12)** Beginning to think he smelled better, he crawled into bed and fell asleep quickly after his very unpleasant day.

The next morning was Sunday, and Mamá was up early, patting and shaping the dough for tortillas.

Dressed in his best shirt and pants, Carlos sat down at the table.

"Carlos, you look very nice for church this morning," said Mamá as she untied her flowered apron. "Where are your shoes?"

**(13)** "They're outside, Mamá. I will get them when we leave," said Carlos, feeling uneasy.

396

# Comprehension

**13** Why does Carlos feel uneasy? Would someone like to play Carlos and tell us what he might be thinking? *Role-Play*

---

### TEACHING TIP

**COMPOUND WORDS** Direct students' attention to the compound word *bathtub* on page 396. Ask a volunteer to explain what a compound word is. (a word made up of two smaller words whose meaning is a combination of the meanings of the words it contains) **Challenge students to find another compound word on this page.** (washrag)

---

## LANGUAGE SUPPORT

**ESL** Help students understand the expression *crawled into bed*. First, ask a volunteer to pantomime how a baby crawls across a floor. Explain that the term means "moving on all fours." Then have students reread the sentence on page 394 containing the word *crawled*. Ask students if they think Carlos moved from the bathroom to his bed on all fours. (no) Develop the idea that this phrase means "to move slowly and with great effort." Reinforce student understanding by reading the following sentences to students, having them respond with one finger if the word *crawled* in context refers to "moving on all fours" or two fingers if the term means "moving with great effort": *The traffic crawled along the highway.* (2) *The small puppy crawled toward his owner.* (1)

# Comprehension

**(14)** What words describe the mood as Carlos and his family enter the church? (formal, still, quiet) How does the mood change? (People begin to move about uncomfortably. People begin to leave the church.) What causes this change? (the foul odor of Carlos's shoes) *Setting*

## SELF-MONITORING STRATEGY

**ASK FOR HELP** Explain: Sometimes a story can include information about a topic that the reader is unfamiliar with. By asking for help to clear up confusing aspects of the story, the reader increases the likelihood of fully comprehending the selection. Have students recall some times when they needed to ask for help to understand what they were reading or describe some types of books that they might need some help to understand.

398

## Activity

## Cross Curricular: Science

**HEATING SYSTEMS** Most buildings are heated by a central heating system. In this system, air or water is warmed in a central location and then circulated throughout the building.

**RESEARCH AND INQUIRY** Have students determine how their homes are heated. Have them create a visual display, such as a chart or diagram that illustrates their home heating system.

▶ **Logical/Spatial**

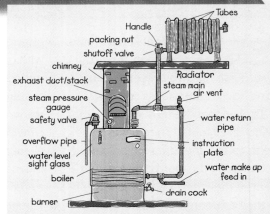

Carlos's family walked to the church near their home. When they arrived, they squeezed into a bench near the back. Carlos was pleased that he was able to sit next to Gloria.

But a most peculiar thing happened in church that day.

As the choir began a hymn, some of the singers began to make strange faces and cover their noses with handkerchiefs. The priest, as he walked to the altar, sneezed loudly and cleared his throat.

The people in the first few rows of the congregation turned to each other with puzzled looks. The women began vigorously fanning their faces with their church programs. The children started squirming and pinched their noses. Little by little the strange behavior began working its way toward the back of the church.

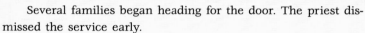

Carlos couldn't figure out what was going on until he looked down at his feet. He was sitting next to an air vent for the church's heating system. The smell from his shoes, which he had forgotten to clean after being sprayed by Dos Dedos, was spreading through the heating ducts to the entire church.

"Papá I think we better go home," whispered Carlos, hoping no one would realize he was the source of the terrible smell.

Several families began heading for the door. The priest dismissed the service early.

Embarrassed, Carlos pushed his way out of the church. He heard Gloria calling to him, but he bolted through the door, and ran all the way home. He untied his shoes, pulled them off, and left them on the back doorstep. Then he hurried to his room and shut the door.

399

# Comprehension

**(15) JUDGMENTS AND DECISIONS**
**What does Carlos think is causing the problem in church?** (The smell from his shoes is being spread by the church's heating system.) **What does he try to do?** (persuade his father that they should go home)

Let's add this information to our chart.

| JUDGMENTS | DECISIONS |
|---|---|
| Gloria knows the skunk may become angry. | Gloria decides to stay away from the skunk. |
| Carlos thinks it's a good idea to catch the skunk. | Carlos picks up the skunk by the tail. |
| Carlos believes tomato juice will get rid of the smell of the skunk. | He takes a bath in tomato juice. |
| Carlos realizes that his shoes are causing the church to smell. | He suggests to his father that they leave church early. |

## Minilesson
### REVIEW/MAINTAIN
### Main Idea

Remind students that the main idea refers to what a passage is about. Pieces of information that support this main idea are called supporting details.

- Ask students to identify the main idea of page 399. (Carlos's shoes are giving off a foul odor that is being carried throughout the church by the heating system.)

- Have students identify details that support this main idea. (People are holding their noses, sneezing, and making strange faces; people leave the church.)

**Activity** Have students work in groups to brainstorm a list of ways—no matter how fantastic—Carlos might eliminate the odor without leaving the church. Have the groups act out their best solutions.

# Comprehension

**16** According to Papá, why does Carlos need a new pair of shoes? (His old shoes are getting small.) **Why do you think Papá glanced at Mamá as he volunteered to buy Carlos new shoes? Is size the real problem with Carlos's old shoes?** (no) **What can you infer is the true reason?** (The old shoes have a terrible odor.) **Why do you think Papá doesn't come right out and say that Carlos's shoes smell bad?** (He doesn't want to embarrass Carlos.) *Make Inferences*

Troubled over how he might rid himself of the strong-smelling shoes, Carlos stayed in his bedroom until his mother called him for dinner. While they were eating, his parents noticed he was unusually quiet but said nothing to him.

Finally, when dinner was over, Papá turned to Carlos.

**16** "Carlos, I've noticed your shoes are looking a little small," said Papá, with a glance toward Mamá. "Isn't it time for a new pair?"

Carlos nodded, breathing a sigh of relief.

"Oh, *sí, sí,* Papá," he stammered. "My feet are getting too big for those shoes now."

The next day, Carlos and Papá drove to town. After trying on several pairs of shoes, Carlos chose a pair of heeled cowboy boots that made him appear much taller.

A few weeks passed and Carlos forgot about his encounter with the skunk. One evening, after a big dinner of pinto beans, rice, tortillas, and his favorite salsa, he decided to visit Gloria. He put on his new boots and took a good look at his hair in the mirror. As he was getting ready to leave, his father called him outside.

"I need your help," said Papá, and he pointed beneath the bushes alongside the house.

Carlos could just make out the shape of a small, black-and-white animal with three little ones that had made their home under the leaves.

"*Dios mío!*" ("Oh my goodness!") said Carlos. "What will we do?"

"It's no problem, Carlos," said Papá. "You know what I hear? You can catch a skunk if you pick it up by its tail. You go first."

**17** Carlos's nose and eyes began to water just with the thought of it.

"Oh, Papá, *no puedes creer todo lo que te dicen*—you know you can't believe everything you hear," Carlos said, and he drew **18** himself up a little taller, smoothed back his hair, and headed for Gloria's house.

400

# CULTURAL PERSPECTIVES

**COOKING** Explain: Thousands of years ago, the native peoples of Mexico discovered a way to grow corn. Since that time, corn has been a major ingredient in Mexican cooking. Kernels of corn are soaked in limewater, boiled, and then ground into cornmeal.

**RESEARCH AND INQUIRY** Have groups look for recipes for Mexican foods using corn. ▶ **Interpersonal**

*inter*NET **CONNECTION** Students can find more information about Mexican cooking by visiting **www.mhschool.com/reading**

401

# Comprehension

**17** Who wants to role-play Carlos for us? Carlos, you have just had a glimpse of Dos Dedos. Immediately, you recall being sprayed by this animal. Show us how you feel at the sight of the skunk. *Role-Play*

**18** **JUDGMENTS AND DECISIONS** Why do you think Papá tells Carlos that he can catch the skunk by picking it up by its tail? (He knows that's what Carlos tried to do.) How does Carlos's answer show that he has changed? (His answer shows that he understands it was foolish to pick up the skunk and that you can't believe everything you hear.)

**P/i** **MULTIPLE-MEANING WORDS** Read the last sentence on page 400. Focus on the word *drew*. This word has more than one meaning. What do you think it means in this sentence? *Semantic/Syntactic Cues*

---

**P/i PREVENTION/INTERVENTION**

**MULTIPLE-MEANING WORDS**
Explain that the word *drew* is used here in a manner that may be unfamiliar. Guide students in realizing that the word means "to move in a given direction." Invite a volunteer to show how Carlos "drew himself up a little taller." Lead students to note that this word is a verb or action word. Challenge them to use a different meaning of this term in a sentence. (For example, *Carlos drew a picture of the skunk.*) *Semantic/Syntactic Cues*

**401**

# Comprehension

**(19) JUDGMENTS AND DECISIONS**
What will Carlos probably do when he sees the skunk in the future? (avoid it) Let's complete our charts.

| JUDGMENTS | DECISIONS |
|---|---|
| Gloria knows the skunk may become angry. | Gloria decides to stay away from the skunk. |
| Carlos thinks it's a good idea to catch the skunk. | Carlos picks up the skunk by the tail. |
| Carlos believes tomato juice will get rid of the smell of the skunk. | He takes a bath in tomato juice. |
| Carlos realizes that his shoes are causing the church to smell. | He suggests to his father that they leave church early. |
| He understands that it was foolish to pick up the skunk. | He'll try to avoid the skunk from now on. |

**RETELL THE STORY** Ask volunteers to retell the story. Students may refer to their charts. Then have partners write one or two sentences that summarize the story. *Summarize*

## STUDENT SELF-ASSESSMENT

- How did using the strategy of analyzing judgments and decisions help me understand the story?

### TRANSFERRING THE STRATEGY

- When might I try using this strategy again? In what other reading could the chart help me?

---

**(19)**

### FRESH TOMATO SALSA

3 tomatoes, diced

1/4 white or yellow onion, diced

2–3 scallions with green tops, chopped

1 medium clove garlic, minced

2 teaspoons vinegar

1 teaspoon vegetable or olive oil

3–4 sprigs of cilantro, chopped

1 roasted green chile or 2 serrano chiles, diced
(or 2 tablespoons canned green chile)

1 teaspoon salt

1/4 teaspoon pepper

Mix all ingredients in a food processor, leaving salsa chunky, or stir by hand. Chill. Spoon over anything—eggs, beans, tacos—or use as a dip for tortilla chips.

## REREADING FOR *Fluency*

**GROUP** Have students choose a section to reread by themselves. Encourage them to read a part that they found difficult to understand during their first read.

**READING RATE** When you evaluate rate, have the student read aloud from the story for one minute. Place a stick-on note after the last word read. Count words read. To evaluate

students' performance, see the Running Record in the **Fluency Assessment** book.

 **Intervention** For leveled fluency lessons, passages, and norms charts, see **Skills Intervention Guide,** Part 4, Fluency.

---

# Comprehension

## Return to Predictions and Purposes

Review with students their story predictions and reasons for reading the story. Were their predictions correct? Did they find out what they wanted to know?

| PREDICTIONS | WHAT HAPPENED |
|---|---|
| The story takes place in a rural area. | The story takes place in the Española Valley of northern New Mexico at the present time. |
| The main character is a boy named Carlos who likes skunks. | Carlos is determined to catch a skunk and ends up being sprayed by it. |

### INFORMAL ASSESSMENT

#### JUDGMENTS AND DECISIONS

**HOW TO ASSESS**

• Can students make judgments and decisions about how they would act in Carlos's situation, based on details in the story?

Students should realize that everyone, including story characters, makes judgments and decisions based on experience, knowledge, and feelings. Point out that their own judgments about Carlos's actions should be based on logic and be supported by story details and/or personal experience.

**FOLLOW UP** If students have difficulty analyzing judgments and decisions, choose an example from some experience your class has shared and model the skill.

## LITERARY RESPONSE

**QUICK-WRITE** Invite students to record their thoughts about the selection. These questions may help them get started:

• How would you describe Carlos?

• Why does Carlos want to impress Gloria?

**ORAL RESPONSE** Have students share their journal writings and discuss the parts of the book they enjoyed the most. Which illustrations did they find most interesting?

# Story Questions

Have students discuss or write answers to the questions on page 404.

**Answers:**

1. The story takes place in the Española Valley, in northern New Mexico. *Literal/Setting*

2. Carlos wants to impress Gloria; he wants to show her how brave and smart he is by catching the skunk. *Inferential/Judgments and Decisions*

3. Carlos is the most important character in the story. The story is about what happens to him. *Inferential/Character*

4. The story teaches that you can't believe everything you hear and that it isn't wise to do something just to impress another person. *Critical/Summarize*

5. Answers will vary. *Critical/Reading Across Texts*

**Write a TV News Story** For a full writing process lesson, see pages 407K–407L.

## Story Questions & Activities

1 Where does the story take place?

2 Why does Carlos pick up the skunk?

3 Who is the main character in this story? How do you know?

4 What lesson does this story teach?

5 Does Carlos remind you of any other character you have read about or anyone you know in real life? Why or why not?

### Write a TV News Story

Imagine you are a television news reporter. You have about 90 seconds on camera to describe what happened when Carlos went to church on Sunday. Make sure you cover all the facts: Who was involved? What happened? When and where did the incident take place? If you can, videotape your report and play it for your classmates.

## Meeting Individual Needs

### EASY

Name_____ Date_____ Reteach **113**

**Vocabulary**

Complete each sentence using the correct vocabulary word.

| unbearable | peculiar | unpleasant | stunned | tortillas | nestled |

1. When she dines in a Mexican restaurant, Kate usually orders _____tortillas_____ wrapped around cheese with sour cream.

2. The house was _____nestled_____ between a stone ledge and a hill covered with apple trees.

3. After cleaning the barn and working in the fields, Lucas thought his clothing smelled _____unbearable_____

4. When Dawn was accidentally hit hard by the ball, she was so _____stunned_____ that it took her some time to realize what had happened.

5. Samir felt sick. His homework had mistakes, and he forgot his lunch. All in all, it was turning out to be a very _____unpleasant_____ day.

6. Jaime never went anywhere without his guitar. He played constantly. So everyone thought it was _____peculiar_____ when he stopped playing.

**Story Comprehension** Reteach **114**

Read each sentence about "Carlos and the Skunk." Write T if the sentence is true and F if it is false.

1. Carlos didn't want to touch the skunk. ____F____
2. Carlos avoided Gloria for a while. ____T____
3. The church service ended earlier than usual. ____T____
4. Carlos didn't know where the terrible smell was coming from. ____F____
5. Carlos asked his father for a new pair of shoes. ____F____

At Home: Have students tell what clues helped them realize why Carlos was avoiding Gloria.
113–114 Carlos and the Skunk 5

**Reteach, 114**

### ON-LEVEL

Name_____ Date_____ Practice **114**

**Story Comprehension**

Answer the questions about "Carlos and the Skunk."

1. Who is Gloria? Is she a main character? Why is she important to the story? _____ Gloria is Carlos's best friend. She is a main character and is important to the story because she is the one Carlos wants to impress.

2. What happens to Carlos's feelings for Gloria as they grow older? _His feelings_ about Gloria change. He likes her more as a girlfriend and not just as a childhood friend. He wants to impress her so that she likes him.

3. Who is Dos Dedos (Two Toes)? Why is Dos Dedos important to the story? _____ Dos Dedos is the skunk that Carlos tries to catch. Dos Dedos sets up the plot by spraying Carlos and ruining his shoes.

4. What does Carlos think will happen if he picks up the skunk by its tail? _____ He thinks he will not be sprayed if he catches the skunk by its tail.

5. How does Carlos try to get rid of the skunk smell? _He first runs to the river to_ wash the skunk's stinky odor off his body and his clothes. Then he takes a bath, using the juice of fresh tomatoes, to get rid of the smell.

6. How does the fact that Carlos forgets to clean his shoes affect the plot? _He has to_ wear them to church, and they still smell.

7. What happens at church that embarrasses Carlos? _The odor from his shoes_ fills the church with such a bad smell that people have to leave.

8. How do you know Carlos's father knows about the skunk and Carlos's smelly shoes? Explain. _Carlos's father offers to buy him new shoes. Then he makes a_ remark about catching a skunk by the tail.

At Home: Have students write about another way Carlos might have impressed Gloria.
114 Carlos and the Skunk Book 5/Unit 4 **6**

**Practice, 114**

### CHALLENGE

Name_____ Date_____ Extend **113**

**Vocabulary**

| nestled | peculiar | stunned |
| tortillas | unbearable | unpleasant |

Suppose that Carlos writes about the things that happen to him each day in a journal. Write a journal entry for the day that Carlos encountered the skunk. Use as many of the vocabulary words in the box as you can.

Answers will vary but should be written in correct context and with correct parts of speech.

Extend **114**

**Story Comprehension**

The main character of "Carlos and the Skunk" is a boy named Carlos. His best friend is a girl named Gloria, but the story doesn't give many details about her. What inferences can you make about what Gloria is like? Reread the parts of the story where Gloria is mentioned. Write a description of Gloria.

Answers will vary. Students may say that Gloria is wiser about the ways of skunks than Carlos. She laughs when she tells him not to believe everything he has heard, so she probably also laughs when the skunk sprays Carlos. But she must also be sympathetic to Carlos, since they are still good friends at the end of the story.

At Home: Talk about animals you see around your home or the home of a friend or relative. What do they do when they meet up with a person? Has anyone in your family ever encountered a skunk?
113–114 Carlos and the Skunk Book 5/Unit 4

**Extend, 114**

## Find a Recipe

Carlos loves fresh tomato salsa. He puts it on almost everything. Do you have a favorite Mexican food? Find a recipe for a Mexican or a Southwestern treat, such as tortillas or *chile con carne*, and write it down. Share the recipe with your friends. You might want to try the recipe and tell how it tasted!

## Make a Poster

What kind of skunk does Carlos catch in the story? Choose one kind of skunk—striped, hog-nosed, or spotted. Create a "skunk" poster. Draw a picture of your skunk, and tell where it lives. Include at least three other facts, such as what a skunk's spray—musk—is used for.

## Find Out More

This story takes place in the Southwest, in New Mexico. What do you know about this area? What people lived there 1,000 years ago? Start by checking in your social studies textbook or an encyclopedia. Find out about the Anasazi. Who were these early American people? How and where did they build their unusual houses? What were their villages like? Share what you learn with your classmates.

405

# Story Activities

### Find a Recipe

**Materials:** Mexican cookbook, empty binder, hole punch

**GROUP** Have students work in groups to create a recipe book of Mexican dishes. Each group can prepare a section of the book, such as appetizers, breads, main dishes, and desserts.

### Make a Poster

**Materials:** poster board, markers or crayons, colored pencils, encyclopedia or wildlife books

**ONE** Encourage students to add a map to their poster, showing where their skunk lives. They might develop a key to the map and show where other kinds of skunks live as well.

### Find Out More

**RESEARCH AND INQUIRY** Have students **GROUP** brainstorm questions they would like answered about the Southwest, New Mexico, and the Anasazi. Groups can use videos of the Southwest, skim encyclopedias and other books, the Internet, and magazines to locate specific information.

**inter**NET **CONNECTION** For more information on the Southwest and the Anasazi, students can visit *www.mhschool.com/reading*

### FORMAL ASSESSMENT

After page 405, see the Selection Assessment.

**SCIENCE: TOMATOES** Tomatoes play an important role in the story. Have students research some interesting facts about tomatoes, such as whether they are fruits or vegetables; which states produce the most tomatoes; the uses of tomatoes; or the history of the tomato. Ask students to prepare a short report about one aspect of tomatoes and include charts, photographs, or diagrams if appropriate.

**What To Look For** A short report on one interesting aspect of tomatoes, which includes appropriate visuals

CHALLENGE

# Study Skills

## GRAPHIC AIDS

**OBJECTIVES**  Students will

• understand the parts of a diagram

• learn how to read a diagram.

**PREPARE**  Read the passage with students. Display **Teaching Chart 93.**

**TEACH**  Review the labels for the parts of the garden. Have volunteers determine and explain each family member's responsibilities.

**PRACTICE**  Have students answer questions 1–5. Review the answers with them.

**1.** six **2.** Dos Dedos **3.** corn **4.** lettuce and zucchini **5.** so that they have everything they need near the garden

**ASSESS/CLOSE**  Have students plan their own garden. Ask what they would plant and whom they would get to help. Then have them make a simple diagram.

# Study Skills

## Read a Diagram

Carlos and Gloria's families both keep gardens. Before planting a garden, you may want to make a plan. A **diagram** is a plan in the form of a picture.

**Use the diagram to answer these questions.**

1 How many different types of fruits and vegetables are in the garden?

2 What should you look out for near the tomatoes?

3 Which plant gets the largest part of the garden?

4 Which plants are Mamá's responsibility?

5 Why do you think they want to build a tool shed?

# Meeting Individual Needs

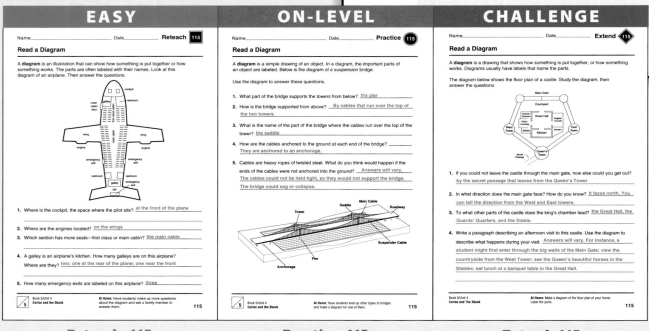

Reteach, 115                    Practice, 115                    Extend, 115

# TEST POWER

**Test Tip**
Always remember to look for the best answer to the question.

**DIRECTIONS**

Read the sample story. Then read each question about the story.

**SAMPLE**

## Jackie's Dilemma

Jackie's parakeet, Tatters, wouldn't calm down. Jackie knew that Tatters could be <u>clamorous</u>, but today the tiny bird was making an unbearable amount of noise. Everyone who came near the bird became extremely annoyed.

"What's disturbing your bird?" growled Jackie's father.

Jackie's mother covered her ears and said, "Jackie, will you please ask your feathered friend to keep it down?"

Jackie didn't know what to do. Tatters had been loud on a few occasions before, but it had only been when his water dish had been empty.

"That's it!" Jackie exclaimed. She slipped a tiny dish of water inside the cage. "Last time he was this noisy, he just needed some water," she said.

Sure enough, the little parakeet became silent as he hopped over to the water dish.

1  How did Jackie realize that Tatters was thirsty?

   **A**  She saw his water dish was empty.

   **(B)**  She remembered that Tatters had done this before.

   **C**  She could tell that he had a sore throat.

   **D**  She realized that she, too, was thirsty for some water.

2  When something is <u>clamorous</u>, it is very —

   **F**  foolish

   **G**  hungry

   **H**  ugly

   **(J)**  loud

## Read the Page

Tell students to note the underlined word as they read the passage.

## Discuss the Questions

**Question 1:** This question requires students to understand what helps Jackie realize that Tatters needs water. Remind students they should *not* rely on their memories; they should *always* refer back to the passage.

**Question 2:** This question asks students to define a word in context. Ask, "What are the clues that can help you answer this question?" After the underlined word, the sentence says that Tatters "was making an unbearable amount of noise." Have students read each answer choice. Remind students that there will always be clues in the passage about what the underlined word means.

# Leveled Books

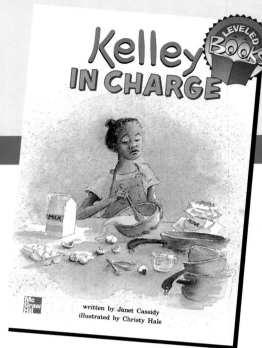

Kelley IN CHARGE

written by Janet Cassidy
illustrated by Christy Hale

## EASY

### Kelley in Charge

/ô/ and /ôr/

☑ **Judgments and Decisions**

☑ **Instructional Vocabulary:**
*nestled, peculiar, stunned,
tortillas, unbearable, unpleasant*

## Guided Reading

**PREVIEW AND PREDICT** Discuss the
chapter headings. Have students predict
what the story is about. List their ideas on
the board.

**SET PURPOSES** Ask students to discuss
what Kelley might be in charge of. List their
three top predictions on the board.

**READ THE BOOK** Have students read
the story independently as you observe
their reading behaviors. After they have
read the story, use the questions below to
reinforce reading strategies.

**Pages 4–5:** How would you describe
Kelley? (She is unhappy about her father's
cooking; she misses her mom's cooking.)
*Character*

**Page 5:** Reread the sentence with the
word *peculiar*. What does *peculiar* mean?
(strange, odd, unusual) *Vocabulary*

**Pages 12–14:** What are four words that
describe the kitchen? (Answers will vary,
but should convey the sense of a very
disorderly kitchen.) *Setting*

**Page 13:** What word on this page has the
/ô/ sound? (awful) What words have the
/ôr/ sound? (poured, tortillas) *Phonics*

**Pages 13–14:** What is Kelley's judgment
when she sees the pancakes? (They don't
look right.) What does she decide to do?
(make them into a kind of breakfast tortilla)
*Judgments and Decisions*

**RETURN TO PREDICTIONS AND
PURPOSES** Review students' predictions
about the story. Encourage them to discuss
whether or not their predictions were accurate and why.

**LITERARY RESPONSE** Discuss these
questions:

- How are Tess and Kelley alike? How are
they different?

- Which girl would you pick for a friend?
Why?

Also see the story questions and activity in
*Kelley in Charge.*

### Answers to Story Questions

1. They had complained about
having boring meals.
2. She knew that her parents were
losing patience.
3. She probably learned that
planning and cooking a meal is
not as easy as she thought.
4. It is about a girl who has to
prepare breakfast for her family.
It is almost a disaster, but it turns
out okay in the end.
5. Answers will vary.

The *Story Questions* and *Activity*
below appear in the *Easy Book.*

### Story Questions and Activity

1. Why did Kelley and her sister have to fix
breakfast on Saturday?
2. Why did Tess give Kelley a warning kick
under the table?
3. Do you think Kelley learned anything from
this experience?
4. What is the story mostly about?
5. Compare this story to *Carlos and the
Skunk.* How are the two stories similar?
How are they different?

### Record a Recipe

Look in a cookbook and find a recipe for
pancakes made from scratch. (Not from a
mix.) Then compare the recipe with the
way Kelley made the pancakes. Were any
ingredients different? Write out Kelley's
recipe, including the ingredients and
directions for making pancakes the way
she made them. Write her recipe the way it
would appear in a cookbook.

*from Kelley in Charge*

# Leveled Books

## INDEPENDENT

### The Lesson

☑ **Judgments and Decisions**

☑ **Instructional Vocabulary:**
*nestled, peculiar, stunned, tortillas, unbearable, unpleasant*

## Guided Reading

**PREVIEW AND PREDICT** Discuss the illustrations in the beginning of the book through page 6. Have students predict what the story is about. Have them record their predictions in their journals.

**SET PURPOSES** Have students list questions they have about the characters in these illustrations, and tell what they think they know about the characters, based on the illustrations.

**READ THE BOOK** Use the following questions to guide students' reading or after they have read the book independently.

**Page 4:** Compare The Stanton School to your school. How is it similar to or different from your school? (Answers will vary but should show understanding of what Tall Pines is like.) *Setting*

**Pages 6–7:** What decision does Meg need to make? (She needs to decide whether to tell the truth about not being able to ride.) What does she decide? (She decides to say she can ride.) What leads Meg to make this decision? (She wants to impress the other girls.) *Judgments and Decisions*

**Page 15:** Reread the sentence with the word *stunned*. What does *stunned* mean? (confused, dazed, bewildered) What context clues helped you figure out the meaning? (wind knocked out of) *Vocabulary*

**RETURN TO PREDICTIONS AND PURPOSES** Review students' predictions and their guesses about the characters in the story. Which predictions were accurate? On what basis did they make their original guesses about the characters? What confirmed or changed these judgments?

**LITERARY RESPONSE** Discuss these questions:

- What was your favorite part of the book?
- What would be another good name for this story?

Also see the story questions and activity in *The Lesson*.

### Answers to Story Questions

1. Her parents had to fly to England because her other grandmother was sick.
2. She felt shy and embarrassed, like she didn't fit in.
3. She didn't like the way they were making fun of her.
4. It is about a girl who pretends she can ride to impress some other girls, and gets into an embarrassing situation.
5. Answers will vary.

The *Story Questions* and *Activity* below appear in the *Independent Book*.

### Story Questions and Activity

1. Why was Meg staying with her grandmother?
2. How did Meg feel when she had to introduce herself to the class?
3. Why did Meg let Saundra and Beth think she knew how to ride?
4. What is this story mostly about?
5. In what ways is this story similar to *Carlos and the Skunk*? In what ways is it different?

### Was My Face Red!

Write a journal entry in which you tell about a time when something embarrassing happened to you. Try to make others understand the way you felt.

*from The Lesson*

# Leveled Books

## CHALLENGE

### The Red Book

☑ **Judgments and Decisions**

☑ **Instructional Vocabulary:**
*nestled, peculiar, stunned, tortillas, unbearable, unpleasant*

written by Janet Cassidy
illustrated by Ann Neumann

## Guided Reading

**PREVIEW AND PREDICT** Discuss the illustrations through page 6. Have students predict what the story is about. List their ideas.

**SET PURPOSES** Have students list questions they would like to have answered by reading the book. Review the questions and ask students which three questions they think the book is most likely to answer. Star these questions.

**READ THE BOOK** Use the following questions to reinforce reading strategies after students have read the story.

**Page 3:** In what way does Mr. Libro look peculiar? (Answers will vary.) *Vocabulary*

**Page 5:** Describe Sam's personality. (Answers will vary, but should indicate that he is a younger sibling.) *Character and Setting*

**Page 7–9:** What judgment does Joe have to make? (He has to judge whether Sammy is really in the book or not.) **Why is this hard?** (It looks like he is, but that seems to be impossible.) **What does Joe decide to do?**

(He decides to try to get into the book to rescue Sammy.) *Judgments and Decisions*

**Page 16:** Based on their adventure, do you think the boys will go back and examine the other books in the carton? (Answers will vary) *Make Inferences*

**RETURN TO PREDICTIONS AND PURPOSES** Review students' predictions and questions. Discuss which questions were or were not answered.

**LITERARY RESPONSE** Discuss these questions:

• If you were Joe and Matt, would you go back the next day? Why or why not?

• Can you name any other books that have a theme of traveling to a mysterious place through magic?

Also see the story questions and activity in *The Red Book*.

---

### Answers to Story Questions

1. He told them not to touch a certain carton of books.
2. The first part meant they should take the stairs on the left; the second part meant that they should open the back of the book. Blood to blood means brother to brother.
3. Answers will vary, but may include: He opened the book and somehow followed the cat in.
4. It is about a boy who learns a lesson from not looking after his younger brother, who gets trapped inside a book.
5. Answers will vary.

**The *Story Questions and Activity* below appear in the *Challenge Book*.**

**Story Questions and Activity**

1. What did Mr. Libro caution the boys against?
2. What did each part of the old woman's words mean?
3. How do you think Sammy got into the picture?
4. What is this story mostly about?
5. If Joe met Carlos from *Carlos and the Skunk* what do you think the two boys could teach each other?

**Predict Through Drawing**

What do you think might be in the rest of the red book? Write a page that you think may also be in the book. Be sure to include an illustration.

**from *The Red Book***

# Bringing Groups Together

## Anthology and Leveled Books

 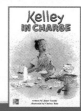  

## Connecting Texts

**UNIT THEME** Write the story titles on a chart. Discuss how the unit theme "Time of My Life" applies to each of the stories. Then chart the action taken by the main character in each story. What was the consequence of the action?

Three of the four stories are about everyday events. How do the authors make these stories about ordinary people interesting? Do any of the characters' experiences remind students of experiences they have had? Do they think students in other parts of the world may have had similar experiences, too?

| Story | Main Character | Action Taken | Consequence |
|---|---|---|---|
| • Carlos and the Skunk | Carlos | Carlos tries to impress his friend by catching a skunk. | The skunk sprays Carlos and his shoes are ruined. |
| • Kelley in Charge | Kelley | Kelley criticizes her father's cooking. | Kelley's parents suggest she cook breakfast. She learns that cooking isn't easy. |
| • The Lesson | Meg | Meg lies to impress her peers. | She embarrasses herself as a result of her lie. |
| • The Red Book | Joe | Joe neglects his younger brother, Sam. | Sam becomes trapped inside a book and Joe goes in to rescue him. |

## Viewing/Representing

**GROUP PRESENTATIONS** Divide students into small groups and have each group identify an "everyday adventure" that happened to someone in the group. The adventure can be either humorous or dramatic. Have them present the adventure by creating a short skit showing what happened or by creating a comic book that illustrates the adventure.

**AUDIENCE RESPONSE** Have students tell what they found interesting about the skits or comic book. Allow time for questions after each presentation.

## Research and Inquiry

**MORE ON ADVENTURE** Have students choose another person who overcame great challenges in his or her life. Students can work in small groups to:

- find information about their subject
- write stories about their subject
- gather photos of their subject and/or draw illustrations for their stories
- present their findings to the class.

**inter NET CONNECTION** Have students visit **www.mhschool.com/reading** to find out more about overcoming difficulties.

## OBJECTIVES

Students will

- make judgments and decisions.
- evaluate choices.

### Skills Finder

**Judgments and Decisions**

| Introduce | 387A-B |
|---|---|
| Review | 407E-F, 465A-B, 491E-F, 617A-B, 647E-F, 699A-B |
| Test | Unit 4, Unit 6 |

### LANGUAGE SUPPORT

**ESL** Students may need an explanation of the difference between a value and a choice.

*value*—a principle or quality considered desirable

*choice*—a decision about a course of action

## SELF-SELECTED Reading

*Students may choose from the following titles.*

### ANTHOLOGY
- Carlos and the Skunk

### LEVELED BOOKS
- The Red Book
- The Lesson
- Kelley in Charge

Bibliography, pages T78–T79

# Review Judgments and Decisions

### PREPARE

**Discuss Judgments and Decisions**

Review: Making a judgment involves applying values to determine what you should do. Making a decision involves choosing a course of action. Sometimes values are in conflict. Ask: Can you think of a time when two things you valued were in conflict?

### TEACH

**Read the Story and Model the Skill**

Read "The Choice" with students. Have students think about the values that are in conflict in this selection.

---

### The Choice

Gina looked at her math book and sighed. The test was tomorrow. That meant two hours of study and review before bedtime. But her favorite movie was on TV in fifteen minutes. "Well, I'll just have to study quickly," she thought, "or during the commercials."

The next morning, Gina struggled through the math test. She hadn't studied carefully enough. She knew she wouldn't get a good grade.

"Guess I made the wrong choice last night," Gina thought. "But I really enjoyed the movie."

Teaching Chart 94

---

Discuss with students the values that affected Gina's judgment and the choice she made.

**MODEL** Gina seems to value being entertained more than getting a good grade because she chooses to watch the movie rather than to study well for the test.

## PRACTICE

**Evaluate Choices**

GROUP

Have students underline the phrases in "The Choice" that show Gina's judgment and decision. Have students role-play Gina discussing her choice with two friends or her parents. Have each character evaluate Gina's decision. Suggest they express different points of view.

▶ **Logical**

## ASSESS/CLOSE

**Make Judgments and Decisions**

PARTNERS

Have partners work together to rewrite "The Choice" to show a different judgment and decision. They can create a new situation and characters if they wish. Have them discuss their work with the class.

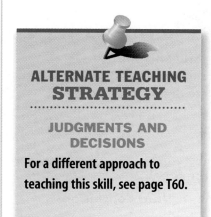

**ALTERNATE TEACHING**
## STRATEGY

.........................

**JUDGMENTS AND DECISIONS**

**For a different approach to teaching this skill, see page T60.**

---

**i** **Intervention** ▶ **Skills**

**Intervention Guide,** for direct instruction and extra practice with judgments and decisions

---

# Meeting Individual Needs for Comprehension

| EASY | ON-LEVEL | CHALLENGE | LANGUAGE SUPPORT |
|---|---|---|---|

**Reteach, 116**  **Practice, 116**  **Extend, 116**  **Language Support, 126**

**OBJECTIVES**

Students will use
information from text
to draw conclusions.

## Skills Finder

**Draw Conclusions**

| | |
|---|---|
| Introduce | 407G-H |
| Review | 431G-H, 491G-H, 647G-H, 673G-H, 717G-H |
| Test | Unit 4, Unit 6 |
| Maintain | 687 |

### TEACHING TIP

**UNSTATED MAIN
IDEAS** Tell students that
sometimes authors do not state
the main idea of a story. In this
case they will have to draw
their own conclusions based on
the details in the text.

# Introduce Draw Conclusions

**PREPARE**

Discuss Drawing
Conclusions

Introduce: Drawing conclusions requires logical reasoning—putting
together two or more ideas or pieces of information to reach a
conclusion.

**TEACH**

Read the Story
and Model
the Skill

Display **Teaching Chart 95.**

Read "Just a Dream?" with the students. Ask them to watch for clues that
will help them draw conclusions about what is happening in the story.

### Just a Dream?

I was in the park, and I saw a <u>strange skunk walking</u> on the sidewalk. It wore a pointed hat, and a red dog nipped at its tail. Then the
skunk smiled at me and <u>mumbled something I couldn't hear.</u>
Suddenly, I was <u>inside a box with transparent sides.</u> I could see
the park, the sidewalk, and a dog. I reached out to touch the dog, but
<u>the box moved with me keeping me from it.</u> Then I heard the strange
skunk laugh. But I couldn't see it. Instead, the bright sunlight blinded
me. <u>I blinked and found myself in my room, on my bed.</u>

**Teaching Chart 95**

Discuss clues in the story that help readers conclude whether or not it is
a dream.

**MODEL** I think the narrator was dreaming. The story is about fantastic
things, such as a talking skunk and a moving transparent box. Also,
being on a bed and blinking are clues that the narrator was asleep
and just woke up.

## PRACTICE

**Identify Information Used to Draw Conclusions**

GROUP

Invite volunteers to underline clues in "Just a Dream?" that point to the conclusion that the narrator was dreaming. Then have small groups each write three sentences that show how they reach the conclusion.

▶ **Logical/Interpersonal**

## ASSESS/CLOSE

**Draw Conclusions**

PARTNERS

Have students write a paragraph about a common event, such as wearing a coat, eating, or passing a test. Have them include information that will help readers to draw a conclusion about the event. Then ask partners to exchange paragraphs, draw conclusions, and identify the clues that support the conclusions.

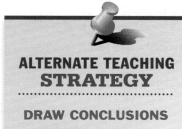

**ALTERNATE TEACHING STRATEGY**

**DRAW CONCLUSIONS**

For a different approach to teaching this skill, see page T62.

**Intervention** ▶ **Skills**

**Intervention Guide,** for direct instruction and extra practice with drawing conclusions

# Meeting Individual Needs for Comprehension

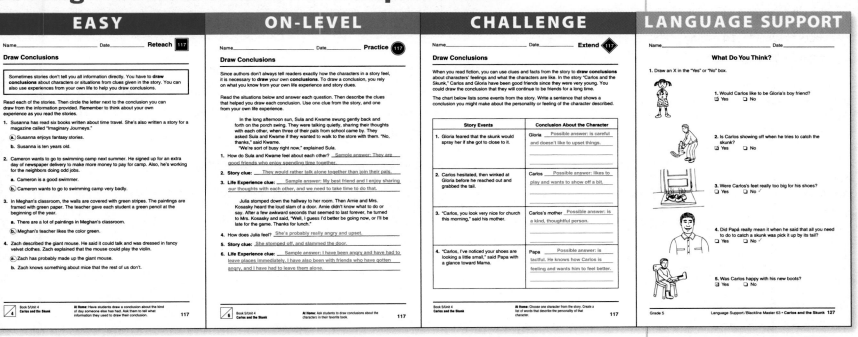

Reteach, 117          Practice, 117          Extend, 117          Language Support, 127

**407H**

**OBJECTIVES**

Students will learn how the suffixes *-able* and *-less* change word meaning.

| Skills Finder | |
|---|---|
| **Suffixes** | |
| Introduce | 407I-J |
| Review | 463I-J, 501I-J |
| Test | Unit 4 |
| Maintain | 547, 573, 587, 635 |

**TEACHING TIP**

**DECODING** Share with students a few tips on how to decode the meaning of an unfamiliar word.

- See if the word has familiar parts, such as a familiar base word and suffix.

- Put the meanings of the familiar parts of the word together to figure out the meaning of the whole word.

- Check to see if that meaning makes sense in the context.

# Introduce Suffixes

**PREPARE**

**Discuss Meaning of *-able* and *-less***

Explain: A suffix is a word part added to the end of a base word. Suffixes have their own meanings. The suffix *-able* means "capable or worthy of being." The suffix *-less* means "without." When a suffix is added to a word, the meaning of the word changes.

**TEACH**

**Read the Passage and Model the Skill**

Have students read the passage on **Teaching Chart 96.**

**Running Partners**

Gloria and Carlos were in training for a race. Carlos was not comfort<u>able</u>. He was hot and tired. Mud from the track had splattered his <u>spotless</u> new running shoes.

Gloria's speed was remark<u>able</u>. Carlos was <u>breathless</u> just trying to keep up. "I don't know how you do it," he gasped, almost <u>speechless</u> from running so fast. "It's unbeliev<u>able</u>."

"No, it's not," Gloria said. "I've been practicing every day for a month. You just started today."

**Teaching Chart 96**

**MODEL** The word *breathless* in the second paragraph ends in *-less*. The base word is *breath*. If *-less* means "without," then *breathless* means "without breath." Let me read that sentence again and see if that meaning makes sense.

Have students define *speechless* in the second paragraph, using the meaning of the suffix *-less*. (without speech) Ask them whether that meaning makes sense in the sentence.

## PRACTICE

**Identify Words with -able and -less**

GROUP

Have volunteers underline the words in "Running Partners" that end in the suffixes *-able* and *-less*, and then circle each suffix. Point out that some words, such as *unbelievable,* drop the final *e* before adding the suffix. Have students discuss the meanings of the words.

▶ **Linguistic/Interpersonal**

## ASSESS/CLOSE

**Form Words with -able and -less and Use Them in a Paragraph**

PARTNERS

Have students write each of the words below. Have them add either *-able* or *-less* to each word. Then ask them to work with a partner to write a paragraph containing these words.

| thought | mind | home |
|---------|------|------|
| break | work | laugh |

---

## ALTERNATE TEACHING STRATEGY
·······················
### SUFFIXES

For a different approach to teaching this skill, see page T63.

**i** **Intervention** ▶ **Skills Intervention Guide,** for direct instruction and extra practice with suffixes

---

# Meeting Individual Needs for Vocabulary

| EASY | ON-LEVEL | CHALLENGE | LANGUAGE SUPPORT |
|------|----------|-----------|------------------|

**EASY**

Name_____ Date_____ Reteach 118

**Suffixes**

**Suffixes** are word parts added to the ends of base words to change their meanings or their parts of speech. The suffix *-less* means "without." The suffix *-able* means "able to be" or "to cause to be."

Circle the suffix *-less* or *-able* in each word. Think about the meanings of the base word and the suffix. Then write a meaning for the whole word.

1. endless — *without end; going on forever*
2. careless — *without care; not careful*
3. meaningless — *without meaning*
4. comfortable — *able to be with comfort*
5. worthless — *without worth; not important*
6. reachable — *able to be reached*

Now write a word from above to complete each sentence.

7. The sparkling stones were really glass, so the necklace that looked so valuable was actually *worthless*.
8. She went camping and was not *reachable* by phone.
9. The ship had very *comfortable* cabins.
10. In June, summer vacation seemed like an *endless* adventure, but the children soon became bored and missed going to school.
11. Malik apologized for teasing his sister, but the apology was not sincere so it felt *meaningless*.
12. Leaving her new bike out in the rain was a *careless* act.

At Home: Ask students to add *-less* to weight, joy and harm and to use the new words in sentences.
118 — Book 5/Unit 4 — **Carlos and the Skunk** 12

**ON-LEVEL**

Name_____ Date_____ Practice 118

**Suffixes**

A **suffix** is a word part that can be added to the end of a word to change the word's meaning. Knowing what a suffix means can help you define the word. The suffix *-less* means "not having" or "without." The suffix *-able* means "able to be" or "cause to be."

| Word | + | Suffix = | New Word | Meaning |
|------|---|----------|----------|---------|
| hope | + | less = | hopeless | without hope |
| bear | + | able = | bearable | tolerable |

Write the suffix of each word. Write the word's meaning. Then use the word in a sentence of your own.

1. breathless **Suffix:** *less* **Meaning:** *without breath*
   **Sentence:** *Sample answer: The race left me breathless.*
2. likable **Suffix:** *able* **Meaning:** *pleasing*
   **Sentence:** *Sample answer: Sonya was a likable person.*
3. powerful **Suffix:** *ful* **Meaning:** *full of power, very strong*
   **Sentence:** *Sample answer: Paul Bunyan was a very powerful character.*
4. laughable **Suffix:** *able* **Meaning:** *causing laughter or scorn*
   **Sentence:** *Sample answer: His attempt to paint the door was laughable.*
5. homeless **Suffix:** *less* **Meaning:** *not having a home*
   **Sentence:** *Sample answer: How do you help the homeless?*
6. thoughtful **Suffix:** *ful* **Meaning:** *full of thought, considerate*
   **Sentence:** *Sample answer: Jorge is very thoughtful towards his grandfather.*
7. youthful **Suffix:** *ful* **Meaning:** *having the qualities of youth*
   **Sentence:** *Sample answer: That eighty-year-old woman looks very youthful.*
8. agreeable **Suffix:** *able* **Meaning:** *pleasant*
   **Sentence:** *Sample answer: His answer seemed agreeable.*

At Home: Ask students to name two other words that end with *-ful* and two other words that end with *-less.* Have them write each word's meaning, and then use each word in a sentence.
118 — Book 5/Unit 4 — **Carlos and the Skunk** 8

**CHALLENGE**

Name_____ Date_____ Extend 118

**Suffixes**

A **suffix** is a word part added to the end of a word. A suffix can change the meaning of a word. For example, *adapt* means "to adjust." When the suffix *-able* is added, the new word, *adaptable,* means "capable to adjust." The suffix *-less* means "without." *Shoeless* means "without shoes."

Use the suffix *-able* or *-less* to change the meaning of each word below. Then write sentences using the words you created.

1. like *able* *Sentences will vary.*
2. move *able* *Sentences will vary.*
3. fear *less* *Sentences will vary.*
4. tire *less* *Sentences will vary.*
5. bear *able* *Sentences will vary.*
6. care *less* *Sentences will vary.*

At Home: The suffix *-ton* is added to the names of many towns. Look on a map to find towns that end in *-ton* in your state.
118 — Book 5/Unit 4 — **Carlos and the Skunk**

**LANGUAGE SUPPORT**

Name_____ Date_____

**Helpful Endings**

1. Read the sentences. 2. Look at the word endings in the box below. 3. Write the correct ending on the line.

| -less = without | -able = capable of being |
|-----------------|--------------------------|

1. She ran fast. She was soon breath*less*
2. They had fun. Their day was enjoy*able*
3. He spilled some juice. He was care*less*
4. The shot did not hurt. It was bear*able*

128 **Carlos and the Skunk** • Language Support/Blackline Master 64 — Grade 5

---

Reteach, 118       Practice, 118       Extend, 118       Language Support, 128

# Expository Writing

## GRAMMAR/SPELLING
### CONNECTIONS

See the 5-Day Grammar and Usage Plan on adjectives, pages 407M–407N.

See the 5-Day Spelling Plan on words with /ô/ and /ôr/, pages 4070–407P.

## TEACHING TIP

**Technology** Point out to students that many word-processing programs provide a thesaurus. Help students use this feature to replace repeated or general words with more varied and specific choices.

**Handwriting** Remind students to take time to write neatly. All letters should slant evenly and they should be evenly spaced, leaving slightly wider spaces between words. For specific instruction on handwriting, see pages T68-T73.

**Handwriting CD-ROM**

## Prewrite

**WRITE A TV NEWS STORY** Present the following assignment: Imagine you are a television news reporter. You have about 90 seconds on camera to describe what happened when Carlos went to church on Sunday. Make sure you cover all the facts: Who was involved? What happened? When and where did the incident take place?

**USE A CLUSTER MAP** Ask students to gather details for the report on a cluster map. Tell them to write "Carlos in Church" in the center circle, and to label smaller circles *Who? What? When? Where? How?* and *Why?* Then have students record the answers on the spokes connecting each small circle to the center circle.

**Strategy: Choose a Beginning** Explain that a news report should have a strong beginning, or lead. The lead tells who, what, when, and where. Have students circle items in their cluster maps that would make up the lead.

## Draft

**ANSWER THE QUESTIONS** Explain that a news report answers all the questions in their cluster maps. Next, point out that this report is a human interest story because it tells what happened to ordinary people. Such a story often includes details about the people. Tell partners to review their clusters and talk about how they would complete these sentences.

- I will begin by . . .
- To report the news, I will include . . .
- Since this a human interest story, I will ...

Then have students write their first draft, using the cluster map for help.

## Revise

**EVALUATE THE 5 Ws AND HOW** Ask students to assess their drafts for improvement.

- What can I do to the beginning of the report to make someone stop and listen?
- Does my report tell who, what, when, why, where, and how? What might I add?
- Can I read my report in 90 seconds? If not, what do I need to take out or condense?

Have students reread their reports, this time aloud, and create a second draft. Conference with students on ways to improve the lead and tighten the writing.

## Edit/Proofread

**CHECK FOR ERRORS AND DETAILS** Students should reread their reports for spelling, grammar and punctuation—and revise accordingly.

## Publish

**SHARE THE REPORTS** Ask volunteers to read their news reports to the class.

### Strange Outbreak on Sunday

Carlos, a boy from this town, caused a commotion in church on Sunday. Shortly after the choir began singing, a strange odor spread throughout the building. People sneezed, made faces, and covered their noses. No one knew what had caused the terrible smell. The priest ended the service early.

Carlos later admitted that he was responsible. While playing in a cornfield, he had spotted a skunk. Carlos says he had heard you could safely catch a skunk by picking it up by the tail. However, when he tried, the skunk sprayed him with a terrible odor! Carlos was able to wash the smell out of his clothes but forgot about his shoes. On Sunday he sat near an air vent in church. This caused the odor to spread and made the whole church smell like skunk!

"It was horrible," said Carlos. "I guess you shouldn't believe everything you hear—especially about skunks!"

## Presentation Ideas

**MAKE AN ILLUSTRATION**  Point out that many news reports have visuals. Suggest that students make a supporting illustration of the people holding their noses in church.

▶ **Viewing/Representing**

**RECORD**  Invite students to video or tape record their news reports.

▶ **Speaking/Listening**

Consider students' creative efforts, possibly adding a plus (+) for originality, wit, and imagination.

| Scoring Rubric | | | |
|---|---|---|---|
| **Excellent** | **Good** | **Fair** | **Unsatisfactory** |
| **4:** The writer | **3:** The writer | **2:** The writer | **1:** The writer |
| • has a strong opening that tells who, what, when, where, why, and how. | • provides an accurate opening that tells who, what, when, where, why, and how. | • may not state all the 5Ws. | • may not grasp the writing task. |
| • includes imaginative details on the 5Ws. | • includes the 5Ws with essential details. | • may lose control of the main topic after the introduction. | • may not address the 5Ws, or may list disconnected ideas and details. |
| • provides vivid information about people in the event. | • may or may not include elaboration on people in the event. | • may or may not present detailed elaboration on people and events. | • may have trouble with basic writing conventions and skills. |

**Incomplete 0:** The writer leaves the page blank or fails to respond to the writing task. The student does not address the topic or simply paraphrases the prompt. The response is illegible or incoherent.

For a 6-point or an 8-point scale, see pages T107–T108.

## Meeting Individual Needs for Writing

| EASY | ON-LEVEL | CHALLENGE |
|---|---|---|
| **Cartoons**  Have students draw a comic strip that shows important scenes from *Carlos and the Skunk.* Each frame should include a few sentences of dialogue that help to tell the story. Students can use the cartoons to help them summarize the story. | **A Personal Account**  Ask students to write a diary entry from the point of view of either Gloria or Carlos. The entry should briefly describe the events in the story from the character's point of view. Encourage students to use descriptive language as well as supporting details. | **Another Adventure**  Ask students to write another adventure starring Carlos and Gloria. They can use other characters from the story or create new ones. Encourage them to use incidents from their own lives or the lives of their friends as jumping-off points. |

### Listening and Speaking

**LISTENING STRATEGIES**

As TV news reports are presented, have students:

• listen alertly.

• reflect on how engaging the report is.

**SPEAKING STRATEGIES**

Encourage students to:

• vary volume and tone of voice for emphasis.

• use appropriate facial and hand gestures to make the report lively.

• use body language and posture suitable to the material.

**LANGUAGE SUPPORT**

 Before having classmates act out the church scene, ask each character to tell who he or she is. Act out the skit. After each event, ask: What happened?

Then have students review their drafts to be sure they have included all the important events.

 Invite students to include their news stories in their portfolios.

# 5 Day Grammar and Usage Plan

**ESL** To demonstrate how adjectives can come before and after a noun, write these sentences on the board: *This is my red tie. My tie is red.* Point out that we never say, *This is my tie red.*

## DAILY LANGUAGE ACTIVITIES

Write each day's Activities on the board or use **Transparency 16.** Have students correct the sentences orally.

### Day 1
1. His mother chopped a _____ tomato.
2. The sweet _____ corn tasted good.
3. The skunk was black and _____.

### Day 2
1. They ran through _____ cornfield.
2. Carlos ran to _____ river.
3. His mother liked _____ shoes.

### Day 3
1. It was a _____ day.
2. At first the church was very _____.
3. Carlos was sitting near _____ air vent.

### Day 4
1. The _____ children were best friends.
2. Carlos's shoes had a _____ odor.
3. He tried to catch _____ skunk.

### Day 5
1. His father bought him _____ shoes.
2. Carlos was very _____.
3. He learned _____ important lesson.

---

Daily Language Transparency 16
**Suggested Answers on Transparency**

---

## DAY 1 — Introduce the Concept

**Oral Warm-Up** Ask students to describe an object in the room. Identify the adjectives that students use in their descriptions.

**Introduce Adjectives** Some words describe nouns. Present the following:

### Adjectives

- An **adjective** is a word that describes a noun and tells *what kind* or *how many*.
- An adjective can come after the noun it describes. The noun and the adjective are connected by a linking verb.

Present the Daily Language Activity and have students complete the sentences orally. Then ask students to write more sentences using number and color adjectives.

 **WRITING** Assign the daily Writing Prompt on page 386C.

---

Name_____ Date_____ LEARN **Grammar 97**

**Adjectives**

- An **adjective** is a word that describes a noun and tells *what kind* or *how many*.
- An adjective can come after the noun it describes. The noun and the adjective are connected by a linking verb.

Complete each of the following sentences with one of the adjectives from the box.

| doubting | strange | unbearable | shiny | foolish |
| uneasy | one | best | adobe | striped |

1. Carlos and Gloria played in the garden where _____**shiny**_____ chiles grew.
2. The children lived in thick-walled _____**adobe**_____ homes.
3. In just _____**one**_____ year, Carlos had grown several inches.
4. Dos Dedos had a _____**striped**_____ tail.
5. Gloria thought that Carlos was _____**foolish**_____.
6. The _____**doubting**_____ girl told him not to believe everything he heard.
7. The smell of Carlos's clothes was _____**unbearable**_____.
8. Carlos wore his _____**best**_____ shirt and pants to church.
9. He felt _____**uneasy**_____ when Mama asked him where his shoes were.
10. People in the church made _____**strange**_____ faces and held their noses.

Grade 5/Unit 4
*Carlos and the Skunk*

Extension: Have students write eight sentences about an embarrassing incident they have experienced. Ask them to include at least six adjectives and to circle each one.

97

**GRAMMAR PRACTICE BOOK, PAGE 97**

---

## DAY 2 — Teach the Concept

**Review Adjectives** Have students list as many adjectives as they can think of to describe their hair. (blond, brown, long, short, straight, curly, thick, smooth, fluffy, frizzy, spiky, wavy, shiny)

**Introduce Demonstrative Adjectives** Present and discuss:

### Adjectives

- A **demonstrative adjective** tells *which one*.
- Use *this* and *that* with singular nouns. Use *these* and *those* with plural nouns.
- *This* and *these* refer to nouns that are nearby; *that* and *those* refer to nouns that are farther away.

Present the Daily Language Activity. Have students complete the sentences orally. Then ask students to write sentences using *this* and *that*, *these* and *those*.

 **WRITING** Assign the daily Writing Prompt on page 386C.

---

Name_____ Date_____ LEARN AND PRACTICE **Grammar 98**

**Demonstrative Adjectives**

- A **demonstrative adjective** tells *which one*.
- Use *this* and *that* with singular nouns. Use *these* and *those* with plural nouns.
- *This* and *these* refer to nouns that are nearby; *that* and *those* refer to nouns that are farther away.

Read each sentence. Rewrite it using the correct form of the demonstrative adjective.

1. Carlos thought, "I wonder if this tomatoes are ripe."
   Carlos thought, "I wonder if these tomatoes are ripe."
2. "What is those?" Gloria yelled suddenly and pointed to a skunk.
   "What is that?" Gloria yelled suddenly and pointed to a skunk.
3. Carlos said, "These is the biggest skunk I ever saw."
   Carlos said, "This is the biggest skunk I ever saw."
4. He said, "I will catch these animal."
   He said, "I will catch this animal."
5. "Those is a bad idea," said Gloria.
   "That is a bad idea," said Gloria.
6. She watched the skunk spray Carlos and said, "These is a boy in trouble."
   She watched the skunk spray Carlos and said, "This is a boy in trouble."
7. Carlos said, "This shoes smell really bad."
   Carlos said, "These shoes smell really bad."
8. His friend said, "That pants are ruined, too."
   His friend said, "Those pants are ruined, too."
9. Mama ordered, "Get rid of these striped creature!"
   Mama ordered, "Get rid of that striped creature!"
10. Carlos nodded, "These is a smelly pest."
    Carlos nodded, "This is a smelly pest."

98

Grade 5/Unit 4
*Carlos and the Skunk*

**GRAMMAR PRACTICE BOOK, PAGE 98**

---

# Adjectives

## DAY 3 — Review and Practice

**Learn from the Literature** Review adjectives. Read aloud the following description from page 394 of the food that Carlos's mother made.

> His mother prepared warm flour tortillas, fried eggs, and fresh salsa for breakfast. The spicy salsa was made from tomatoes and green chilies grown in their garden.

Help students identify the adjectives that describe the food.

**Identify Adjectives** Present the Daily Language Activity and have students complete the sentences orally.

Ask students to read the last paragraph on page 390 of *Carlos and the Skunk* and write the adjectives used to describe the homes where Carlos and Gloria lived. Have students write a sentence about their homes using *this, that, these,* or *those.*

 Assign the daily Writing Prompt on page 386D.

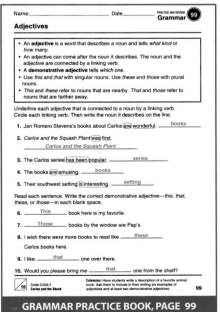

**GRAMMAR PRACTICE BOOK, PAGE 99**

## DAY 4 — Review and Practice

**Review Adjectives** Have students list adjectives from the Daily Language Activities for Days 1 through 3. Then present the Daily Language Activity for Day 4. Have students complete the sentences orally.

**Mechanics and Usage** Review the rules for proper adjectives. Display and discuss:

### Proper Adjectives

- A proper adjective is formed from a proper noun.
- A proper adjective begins with a capital letter.

 Assign the daily Writing Prompt on page 386D.

**GRAMMAR PRACTICE BOOK, PAGE 100**

## DAY 5 — Assess and Reteach

**Assess** Use the Daily Language Activity and page 101 of the **Grammar Practice Book** for assessment.

**Reteach** Display photos from magazines and play audio recordings from nature, such as water, wind, or animal sounds. Ask students to write sentences using adjectives that describe what they see and hear.

Have students add adjectives from their sentences to a classroom word wall.

Use page 102 of the **Grammar Practice Book** for additional reteaching.

 Assign the daily Writing Prompt on page 386D.

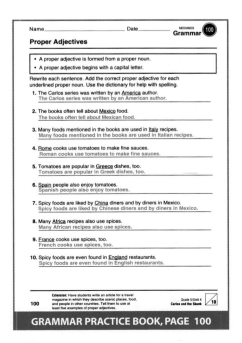

**GRAMMAR PRACTICE BOOK, PAGE 101**

**GRAMMAR PRACTICE BOOK, PAGE 102**

# 5 Day Spelling Plan

**ESL** Write *for* on the board and ask students to repeat the /ôr/ sound. Then ask them to think of other words with that sound that are spelled differently. Repeat with the /ô/ sound in the word *lawn*.

## DICTATION SENTENCES

### Spelling Words

1. The car rolled <u>forward</u>.
2. We kept the sailboat on <u>course</u>.
3. The <u>audience</u> enjoyed the show.
4. The sailor went <u>aboard</u> ship.
5. He thought the book might <u>bore</u> you.
6. The deer and <u>fawn</u> slept.
7. <u>Install</u> a phone in my bedroom.
8. I am <u>longing</u> to go for a swim.
9. The police are <u>performing</u> their jobs.
10. An <u>astronaut</u> travels in space.
11. I want to <u>soar</u> like a bird.
12. Cleaning is a <u>chore</u>.
13. She will <u>withdraw</u> some money.
14. Try to keep the <u>wallpaper</u> clean.
15. She drinks too much <u>coffee</u>.
16. Draw a <u>border</u> around the picture.
17. Did you find the <u>source</u> of the article?
18. Baseball fans <u>applaud</u> a home run.
19. The <u>coarse</u> fabric is not comfortable.
20. The weather <u>forecast</u> calls for snow.

### Challenge Words

21. The baby was <u>nestled</u> in the blanket.
22. I had a <u>peculiar</u> dream.
23. The bad news <u>stunned</u> us.
24. The heat was <u>unbearable</u>.
25. Loud noises are <u>unpleasant</u>.

---

## DAY 1 — Pretest

**Assess Prior Knowledge** Use the Dictation Sentences at the left and **Spelling Practice Book** page 97 for the pretest. Allow students to correct their own papers. Students who require a modified list may be tested on the first ten words.

| Spelling Words | | Challenge Words |
|---|---|---|
| 1. forward | 11. soar | 21. **nestled** |
| 2. course | 12. **chore** | 22. **peculiar** |
| 3. audience | 13. withdraw | 23. **stunned** |
| 4. aboard | 14. wallpaper | 24. **unbearable** |
| 5. bore | 15. coffee | 25. **unpleasant** |
| 6. fawn | 16. border | |
| 7. install | 17. **source** | |
| 8. longing | 18. applaud | |
| 9. performing | 19. coarse | |
| 10. astronaut | 20. forecast | |

*Note: Words in **dark type** are from the story.*

**Word Study** On page 98 of the **Spelling Practice Book** are word study steps and an at-home activity.

**SPELLING PRACTICE BOOK, PAGE 97**
**WORD STUDY STEPS AND ACTIVITY, PAGE 98**

---

## DAY 2 — Explore the Pattern

**Sort and Spell Words** Say *fawn*. Ask students what vowel sound they hear. (/ô/) Have students read the Spelling Words aloud and sort them as below.

| Words with /ô/ spelled | | | |
|---|---|---|---|
| *au* | *aw* | *a* | *o* |
| audience | fawn | install | longing |
| astronaut | withdraw | wallpaper | coffee |
| applaud | | | |

| /ôr/ spelled | | | |
|---|---|---|---|
| *or* | *our* | *oar* | *ore* |
| forward | course | aboard | bore |
| performing | source | soar | chore |
| border | | coarse | forecast |

**Word Wall** Have students create a word wall based on the word sort and add more words from their reading.

**SPELLING PRACTICE BOOK, PAGE 99**

---

# Words with /ô/ and /ôr/

**Practice and Extend**

**Word Meaning: Synonyms** Review that a *synonym* is a word that means about the same as another word. Ask students to think of synonyms for as many of the Spelling Words as they can (Examples: applaud/clap, soar/fly). Write sentences using the words.

If students need extra practice, have partners give each other a midweek test.

**Glossary** Review that some words in the Glossary have synonyms listed. Have partners:

- write each Challenge Word and look it up in the Glossary.

- find the Challenge Word that has a synonym.

- use the Challenge Word and its synonym in a sentence.

**Proofread and Write**

**Proofread Sentences** Write these sentences on the chalkboard, including the misspelled words. Ask students to proofread, circling incorrect spellings and writing the correct spellings. There are two spelling errors in each sentence.

> The awdience will aplaude at the end of the show. (audience, applaud)
>
> It is a chor to get everybody aborde the plane. (chore, aboard)

Have students create additional sentences with errors for partners to correct.

 Have students use as many spelling words as possible in the daily Writing Prompt on page 386D. Remind students to proofread their writing for errors in spelling, grammar, and punctuation.

**Assess and Reteach**

**Assess Students' Knowledge** Use page 102 of the **Spelling Practice Book** or the Dictation Sentences on page 407O for the posttest.

**Personal Word List** If students have  trouble with any words in the lesson, have them add to their personal list of troublesome words in their journals. Have students underline the spelling patterns for /ô/ or /ôr/ in each word.

Students should refer to their word lists during later writing activities.

---

**SPELLING PRACTICE BOOK, PAGE 100**

Name_____ Date_____ PRACTICE AND EXTEND **Spelling 100**

Words with /ô/ and /ôr/

| forward | bore | performing | withdraw | source |
| course | fawn | astronaut | wallpaper | applaud |
| audience | install | soar | coffee | coarse |
| aboard | longing | chore | border | forecast |

**We Go Together**
Write the spelling word that matches each clue below.

1. clap — applaud
2. put in — install
3. predict — forecast
4. listeners — audience
5. task — chore
6. draw back — withdraw
7. fly high — soar
8. rough — coarse
9. edge or rim — border
10. make a hole — bore
11. deer — fawn
12. acting — performing
13. craving — longing
14. onward — forward

Write a sentence using each of the spelling words below.

15. aboard
16. course
17. astronaut
18. wallpaper
19. coffee
20. source

**Challenge Extension:** Have students write fill-in sentences for each Challenge Word. Then have each student exchange his/her sentences with a partner and try to fill them in correctly.

100                                                          Grade 5/Unit 4
Carlos and the Skunk 20

---

**SPELLING PRACTICE BOOK, PAGE 101**

Name_____ Date_____ PROOFREAD AND WRITE **Spelling 101**

Words with /ô/ and /ôr/

**Proofreading Activity**
Find the six spelling errors in the diary entry below. Circle each incorrectly spelled word. Write the words correctly on the lines below.

Gloria and I had a great time at the pet show. We saw a preforming dog named Pepe. Pepe walked forward on his hind legs. Then he climbed abored a toy rocket. You should have seen that rocket sore! The audiense loved Pepe. His dancing made everyone aplaud.

1. performing    3. aboard    5. audience
2. forward       4. soar      6. applaud

**Writing Activity**
Imagine having Pepe for a pet. Write a paragraph about what you and Pepe might do together. Use four words from the spelling list.

10  Grade 5/Unit 4
Carlos and the Skunk                                          101

---

**SPELLING PRACTICE BOOK, PAGE 102**

Name_____ Date_____ POSTTEST **Spelling 102**

Words with /ô/ and /ôr/

Look at the words in each set below. One word in each set is spelled correctly. Use a pencil to fill in the circle next to the correct word. Before you begin, look at the sample sets of words. Sample A has been done for you. Do Sample B by yourself. When you are sure you know what to do, you may go on with the rest of the page.

| Sample A: | Sample B: |
|---|---|
| (A) exploar | (A) craul |
| (B) exploir | (B) crual |
| (C) explor | ● crawl |
| ● explore | (D) crall |

1. (A) fourcast  (B) foarecast  (C) forcast  ● forecast
2. (E) applawd  (F) applayd  ● applaud  (H) applod
3. ● coarse  (B) corse  (C) corrse  (D) corese
4. (E) caffee  ● coffee  (G) cauffee  (H) cawffee
5. ● source  (B) sorce  (C) soarce  (D) sorece

6. (E) bourder  (F) bauder  (G) border  (H) boreder
7. (A) waullpaper  ● wallpaper  (C) wawllpaper  (D) wollpaper
8. (E) withdrauw  (F) withdrow  (G) withdra  ● withdraw
9. (A) chaore  ● chore  (C) choure  (D) chor
10. (E) sor  (F) sawr  ● soar  (H) saor

11. (A) astronawt  (B) astronat  ● astronaut  (H) astronot
12. (E) longeng  (F) lawnging  (G) launging  ● longing
13. (A) faun  ● fawn  (C) fon  (D) fawne
14. (E) instaull  (F) instawll  ● install  (H) instoll
15. (A) performance  (B) perfoamance  (C) performence  ● performance

16. ● bore  (F) bor  (G) boure  (H) boare
17. (A) abord  ● aboard  (C) abourd  (D) abored
18. (E) awdience  (F) adience  ● audience  (H) oudience
19. ● course  (B) corse  (C) corrse  (D) corese
20. (E) founward  (F) foarward  (G) foreward  ● forward

102                                                          Grade 5/Unit 4
Carlos and the Skunk 20

**407P**

**Reaching All Learners**

### Concept
- **Scientific Discoveries**

### Comprehension
- **Important and Unimportant Information**

### Vocabulary
- **assignments**
- **automatically**
- **carelessly**
- **normally**
- **observations**
- **swerved**

## Anthology

# How to Think Like a Scientist

**Selection Summary** This selection offers several short stories designed to illuminate various principles of research and inquiry used by scientists.

**Stories in Art** focuses on the **comprehension** skill

**Reading Strategy** applies the **comprehension** skill

**Listening Library**

**INSTRUCTIONAL** pages 410–431

**About the Author**  Writing a book about the scientific method was a logical next step for writer Stephen P. Kramer. A biology student in college, Kramer taught science for several years on a Navajo reservation. His books draw on his training as a biologist and his experience as a science teacher.

## Leveled Books

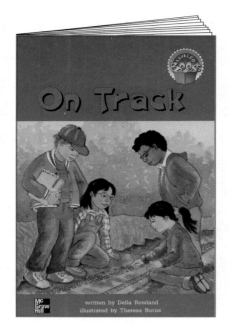

**EASY**
Lesson on pages 431A and 431D

**INDEPENDENT**
Lesson on pages 431B and 431D

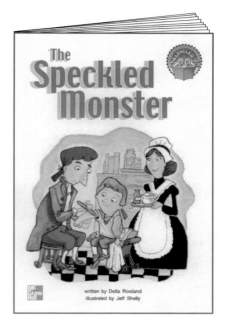

**CHALLENGE**
Lesson on pages 431C and 431D

## Leveled Practice

### EASY

**Reteach,** 119–125 Blackline masters with reteaching opportunities for each assessed skill

### INDEPENDENT/ON-LEVEL

**Practice,** 119–125 Workbook with Take-Home stories and practice opportunities for each assessed skill and story comprehension

### CHALLENGE

**Extend,** 119–125 Blackline masters that offer challenge activities for each assessed skill

**Quizzes Prepared by** Accelerated Reader

## WORKSTATION Activities

| | |
|---|---|
| **Social Studies** | Map Skills, *416* |
| **Science** | Sir Francis Bacon, *418* |
| **Math** | Probability, *424* |
| | Identifying Unimportant Information, *429* |
| **Language Arts** | Read Aloud, *408E* |
| **Cultural Perspectives** | Superstitions, *412* |
| **Writing** | Scientific Report, *428* |
| **Research and Inquiry** | Find Out More, *429* |
|  **Internet Activities** | www.mhschool.com/reading |

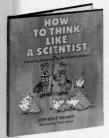

HOW TO THINK LIKE A SCIENTIST

# Suggested Lesson Planner

| READING AND LANGUAGE ARTS | DAY 1 — Focus on Reading and Skills | DAY 2 — Read the Literature |
|---|---|---|
| ● **Comprehension**<br>● **Vocabulary**<br>● **Phonics/Decoding**<br>● **Study Skills**<br>● **Listening, Speaking, Viewing, Representing** | **Read** **Read Aloud: Legend,** 408E<br>"Archimedes and the King's Gold Crown"<br><br>**Develop Visual Literacy,** 408<br><br>☑ **Introduce Important and Unimportant Information,** 409A–409B<br>**Teaching Chart 97**<br>**Reteach, Practice, Extend,** 119<br><br>**Read** **Reading Strategy:** Important and Unimportant Information, 409<br>"Woolly Mammoth Found in Siberia"<br><br>ⓘ Intervention Program | **Build Background,** 410A<br>Develop Oral Language<br><br>**Vocabulary,** 410B–410C<br><br>*assignments carelessly observations*<br>*automatically normally swerved*<br><br>**Teaching Chart 98**<br>Word Building Manipulative Cards<br>**Reteach, Practice, Extend,** 120<br>**Read** **Read the Selection,** 410–427<br>☑ **Important and Unimportant Information**<br>☑ **Draw Conclusions**<br><br>**Genre: Informational Story,** 411<br><br>**Cultural Perspectives,** 412<br><br>ⓘ Intervention Program |
| ● **Curriculum Connections** | **Link** Works of Art, 408 | **Link** Science, 410A |
| ● **Writing** | **Writing Prompt:** Choose an animal you know well. Write a pet manual for it. | **Writing Prompt:** In one of the stories, a boy chooses to see a movie instead of doing his homework. Think about your favorite movie. Write a review of it.<br><br>**Journal Writing,** 427<br>Quick-Write |
| ● **Grammar** | **Introduce the Concept: Articles,** 431M<br>Daily Language Activity<br>1. Pete ran over snake. a<br>2. It wasn't inner tube. an<br>3. Could it be rain snake? a<br><br>**Grammar Practice Book,** 103 | **Teach the Concept: Articles,** 431M<br>Daily Language Activity<br>1. Ask yourself question. a<br>2. Someone went into Murphys' house. the<br>3. You didn't see men. the<br><br>**Grammar Practice Book,** 104 |
| ● **Spelling** | **Pretest: Words with /är/ and /âr/,** 431O<br>**Spelling Practice Book,** 103–104 | **Explore the Pattern: Words with /är/ and /âr/,** 431O<br>**Spelling Practice Book,** 105 |

**Meeting Individual Needs**

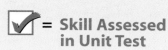

✓ = **Skill Assessed in Unit Test**

ⓘ **Intervention Program Available**

**Read EVERY DAY**

---

## DAY 3 — Read the Literature

**Rereading for Fluency,** 426

**Story Questions and Activities,** 428–429
   Reteach, Practice, Extend, 121

**Study Skill,** 430
   ✓ **Use an Outline**
   **Teaching Chart 99**
   Reteach, Practice, Extend, 122

**Test Power,** 431

**Read the Leveled Books,** 431A–431D
   Guided Reading
   /är/ and /âr/
   ✓ **Important and Unimportant Information**
   ✓ **Instructional Vocabulary**

ⓘ Intervention Program

---

**Activity** Social Studies, 416

✎ **Writing Prompt:** Write a description of what Ralphie saw happening at the Murphys' house.

**Writing Process: Expository Writing,** 431K
   Prewrite/Draft

**Review and Practice: Articles,** 431N
   Daily Language Activity
   1. Mr. Murphy called on telephone. the
   2. You saw truck parked in front of the house. a
   3. Who were burglars? the

   **Grammar Practice Book,** 105

**Practice and Extend: Words with /är/ and /âr/,** 431P
   **Spelling Practice Book,** 106

---

## DAY 4 — Build Skills

**Read the Leveled Books and Self-Selected Books**

✓ **Review Important and Unimportant Information,** 431E–431F
   **Teaching Chart 100**
   Reteach, Practice, Extend, 123
   Language Support, 134

✓ **Review Draw Conclusions,** 431G–431H
   **Teaching Chart 101**
   Reteach, Practice, Extend, 124
   Language Support, 135

**Minilessons,** 413, 415, 421, 423, 425

ⓘ Intervention Program

---

**Activity** Science, 418

✎ **Writing Prompt:** Write a dialogue between Ralphie and his sister after they discover that someone really was stealing something from the Murphys' home.

**Writing Process: Expository Writing,** 431K
   Revise
**Meeting Individual Needs for Writing,** 431L

**Review and Practice: Articles,** 431N
   Daily Language Activity
   1. Be careful how you answer question. the
   2. Someone from zoo came to the class. the
   3. Fish live in aquarium at the zoo. an

   **Grammar Practice Book,** 106

**Proofread and Write: Words with /är/ and /âr/,** 431P
   **Spelling Practice Book,** 107

---

## DAY 5 — Build Skills

**Read Self-Selected Books**

✓ **Introduce Root Words,** 431I–431J
   **Teaching Chart 102**
   Reteach, Practice, Extend, 125
   Language Support, 136

**Listening, Speaking, Viewing, Representing,** 431L

**Minilessons,** 415, 421, 423, 425

**Phonics Review,** /âr/ and /är/ , 413

**Phonics/Phonemic Awareness Practice Book,** 47–50

ⓘ Intervention Program

---

**Activity** Math, 424

✎ **Writing Prompt:** Write a paragraph telling what you think Pete and Jim will do to figure out whether or not hanging a dead snake in a tree would bring rain.

**Writing Process: Expository Writing,** 431K
   Edit/Proofread, Publish

**Assess and Reteach: Articles,** 431N
   Daily Language Activity
   1. He went to basketball game on Friday night. a
   2. She might forget about assignment. the
   3. He didn't know answer. the

   **Grammar Practice Book,** 107–108

**Assess and Reteach: Words with /är/ and /âr/,** 431P
   **Spelling Practice Book,** 108

---

# Read Aloud

## Archimedes and the King's Gold Crown
### a legendary story by Linda W. Girard

King Hiero, who lived in Syracuse on the island of Sicily, had a new crown of solid gold. The king had given his goldsmith pure gold and ordered him to hammer and mold it into just the crown the king wanted.

At last the crown was finished, and the king wore it all day. It was rather large, but the king was happy, for kings love to wear golden crowns that sway a bit as they walk.

Not until King Hiero was ready to go to sleep did he reach up to remove the crown. Hmm, he said to himself. This solid gold crown isn't as heavy as I thought it would be. It looks like solid gold. It shines. It's the right size. But it seems a bit light. He bounced it in his hands.

A black thought crept into the king's mind. Maybe his royal goldsmith had cheated him by melting the gold and mixing it with silver. Silver is much lighter than gold, and it's also cheaper than gold. Every king knows that. Had the goldsmith kept some of that gold for himself, and

**Continued on pages T2–T3**

## Oral Comprehension

**LISTENING AND SPEAKING**  As you read the legend aloud, ask students to think about the problem and its solution. Afterward, ask:

- What problem did Archimedes have to solve?

Have students think about important and unimportant information. Ask: Which facts were important to Archimedes as he tried to find the solution to his problem? Which facts were not as important?

**GENRE STUDY: LEGEND**  Discuss some of the literary devices and techniques used in "Archimedes and the King's Gold Crown."

- A legend often tells about a person who actually lived.

Ask: What do you learn about Archimedes? Does he seem like a real person? Why or why not?

- Legends often tell about someone who solves a difficult problem. Ask: Was it easy for Archimedes to solve the problem? Do you think this legend could be true?

**Activity**  Have students duplicate Archimedes' solution to the problem. Provide various weighted materials, scales, and bowls of water. Ask students to find two objects that weigh the same, immerse them in water, and carefully measure the amount of water displaced. Ask students to explain what the experiment tells them about the objects. ▶Logical/Mathematical

**Stories in Art**

This photograph shows a scene from a movie about the great English detective Sherlock Holmes. Think about the job of a detective. How do detectives sift through clues to solve mysteries?

Look at the photograph. Notice what Holmes is doing. Why is he looking through a magnifying glass? How is a magnifying glass like a scientist's microscope? How is a detective like a scientist? Explain.

Imagine that you are Sherlock Holmes. Besides a magnifying glass, what methods could you use to discover information? How would you separate the unimportant clues from the important ones? How would this help you solve a mystery?

*Basil Rathbone as Sherlock Holmes, c. 1940*

408

## Objective: Identify Important and Unimportant Information

**VIEWING** The character Sherlock Holmes was created by Sir Arthur Conan Doyle, whose background as a doctor enabled him to make his great detective think like a scientist as he searched for clues in solving mysteries. Invite students to describe what is happening in this black-and-white still photograph from a Sherlock Holmes film. Ask how the lack of color affects the mood of the scene while eliminating superfluous or unimportant information.

Read the page with students, encouraging individual interpretations of the photograph.

Have students examine the photograph and explain which information is important for the viewer to note. For example:

- The magnifying glass helps Holmes find clues.
- Holmes is focusing on a particular spot, suggesting he may have found an important clue.

**REPRESENTING** Have students hum music matching the mood of the photograph. Invite them to increase the tension and suspense of the music, imagining Holmes getting closer to the important clues.

## OBJECTIVES

Students will distinguish between important and unimportant information.

| Skills Finder | |
|---|---|
| **Important and Unimportant Information** | |
| Introduce | 409A-B |
| Review | 431E-F, 463G-H, 501E-F |
| Test | Unit 4 |

---

**TEACHING TIP**

**MAIN IDEA** Explain to students that the skill of distinguishing between important and unimportant information is much like the skill of summarizing. In applying both, readers must first determine the main idea.

---

# Introduce Important and Unimportant Information

**PREPARE**

**Discuss Important and Unimportant Information**

Explain to students that some information in stories is more important than other information. To determine what is important, readers must first identify the main idea and then choose the information that supports or develops this idea.

**TEACH**

**Read the Passage and Model the Skill**

Display **Teaching Chart 97.** Have students note important and unimportant information as the story is read.

### Can You Guess?

(Tomas was very curious.) He asked, "Why do birds sing? How high can a grasshopper hop? Where does the sun go at night?" (He asked questions) all day long. He asked his mom. He asked his dad. He asked his teachers. He asked his next-door neighbor, the mailman, and his best friend. Mostly they replied, "I don't know." Tomas's (biggest question was, "How can I find the answers?") Tomas's mom and dad are planning a surprise for his birthday gift. (It will answer many of his questions.) What do you think it is?

*Teaching Chart 97*

**MODEL** I wonder what Tomas is going to get for his birthday. I know it's important to remember that Tomas is curious and asks a lot of questions. I don't think it's important to remember each question, but it is important to remember that he didn't get many answers.

**Identify the Important Information**

Have students determine the main idea of the paragraph. (It's a riddle asking us to guess what Tomas will get for his birthday. Possible gifts: a set of encyclopedias, a library card, an encyclopedia disc for his computer) Ask students to circle the important information in the paragraph that will help them guess the gift.

## PRACTICE

**Chart Important and Unimportant Information**

GROUP

Have students use a chart to record the important and unimportant information from "Can You Guess?" ▶ **Interpersonal/Spatial**

| IMPORTANT | UNIMPORTANT |
|-----------|-------------|
| Tomas is curious. | Why do birds sing? |
| He asks questions. | He asked the mailman. |
| His gift will answer questions. | His gift will be a surprise. |

## ASSESS/CLOSE

**Use Important and Unimportant Information**

PARTNERS

Have partners think of an object or animal and write clues for a guessing game. Encourage them to provide accurate and precise information. Ask them to prepare two clues with unimportant but related information and three clues with important information. Have sets of partners exchange clues and guess the item. Then have them use a chart to list the important and unimportant information.

**ALTERNATE TEACHING STRATEGY**
........................................

**IMPORTANT AND UNIMPORTANT INFORMATION**

*For a different approach to teaching this skill, see page T64.*

**i** **Intervention** ▶ **Skills Intervention Guide,** for direct instruction and extra practice with important and unimportant information

# Meeting Individual Needs for Comprehension

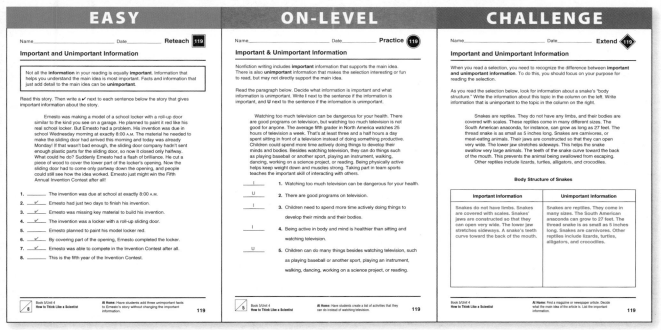

Reteach, 119          Practice, 119          Extend, 119

**409B**

**OBJECTIVES**

Students will understand how to identify important and unimportant information.

# Apply Important and Unimportant Information

**READING STRATEGY**

## Important and Unimportant Information

Develop a strategy to identify important and unimportant information.

**1** **Find the main idea.** What is the main point of the article?

**2** **Identify details** that are needed to understand the main idea. This is the important information.

**3** **Decide which details** are unimportant. They add interest to the story but aren't necessary for you to understand it.

**4** **Review the important information** and restate it in your own words.

## Woolly Mammoth Found

**READING STRATEGY**

Mammoths were huge, elephant-like creatures that once roamed most of the Earth's continents. About 10,000 years ago, these creatures died out.

In October of 1999, on the frozen tundra of central Siberia, an amazing event took place. An expedition led by French explorer Bernard Buigues dug out from the permafrost (a layer of soil and water that is permanently frozen) the carcass of a 20,000-year-old woolly mammoth. It was so well preserved that it still had some of its hair, skin, muscle, and other tissue.

The chunk of permafrost containing the mammoth was lifted by helicopter and flown 150 miles to an ice cave. Scientists there began defrosting the huge beast with hair dryers, one small section at a time, over a period of months. They called it the "Jarkov Mammoth" for the Siberian family who first discovered it.

Dutch scientist Dick Mol has been working on mammoths for more than 25 years. He is supervising the analysis of the mammoth. "This is a dream for me—to find the parts and touch them," said Mol. "It's very exciting."

Mol believes that this creature can help scientists learn why mammoths became extinct. Were they killed off by disease? The frozen mammoth may give scientists real answers to this question and to many others.

409

**PREVIEW** Have students preview "Woolly Mammoth Found," by reading the title and first paragraph. Ask:

• What is the subject of the story? (finding a woolly mammoth)

• Are there still living woolly mammoths? (no)

**SET PURPOSES** Explain that students will apply what they have learned about distinguishing important and unimportant information as they read "Woolly Mammoth Found."

**APPLY THE STRATEGY** Discuss this strategy for distinguishing between important and unimportant information.

• What is the main idea of the article?

• List three details that support the main idea.

• List two details that do not support the main idea.

• Tell the main idea and important details in your own words.

**Activity** Have students reread the passage and side notes. Then have them create an Important and Unimportant Information chart for the passage.

# Build Background

**Science**

## Concept: Scientific Discoveries

## Evaluate Prior Knowledge

**CONCEPT: SCIENTIFIC DISCOVERIES**
In this story, students will learn about the scientific method and specifically about observation, a key step in this process. Have students think about and share instances in which they came to a conclusion based on their observations.

**USE YOUR SENSES** Show students an object, such as a watch. Challenge them to observe the watch using at least three different senses. Have students record their observations in a Sense Star. ▶ **Logical/Visual**

### Graphic Organizer 35

**WRITE A THANK-YOU NOTE** Over

**PARTNERS**   **WRITING**

the years, scientists have made many discoveries using the scientific method of research and inquiry. Have students work in pairs to identify a scientific discovery of great importance in their lives. Then have each pair write a thank-you note to the scientist responsible for the discovery.

## Develop Oral Language

**DISCUSS SIMILARITIES** Guide students

**ESL** in recognizing that scientists often look for similarities among objects. Display a piece of chalk, a crayon, and a pencil. Ask students to name a trait the items share. (All leave a mark on a surface.) Then ask them to look back at the objects that leave a mark and describe how they are different from each other.

### TEACHING TIP

**MANAGEMENT** Some students may need assistance in identifying great scientific discoveries. It might help to brainstorm a list of notable discoveries before assigning the writing task, including the polio vaccine (Jonas Salk), the laws of motion (Isaac Newton), and the cell (Robert Hooke).

### LANGUAGE SUPPORT

See the **Language Support Book**, pages 129–132, for teaching suggestions for Build Background.

**OBJECTIVES**

Students will use context clues to determine the meanings of vocabulary words.

normally
assignments
automatically
observations
carelessly
swerved

# Vocabulary

## Teach Vocabulary in Context

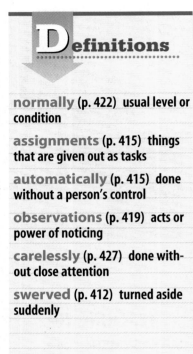

**Definitions**

**normally** (p. 422)  usual level or condition

**assignments** (p. 415)  things that are given out as tasks

**automatically** (p. 415)  done without a person's control

**observations** (p. 419)  acts or power of noticing

**carelessly** (p. 427)  done without close attention

**swerved** (p. 412)  turned aside suddenly

**Identifying Vocabulary Words**  Display **Teaching Chart 98** and read the passage with students. Have volunteers circle each vocabulary word and underline other words that are clues to its meaning.

### Changing Habits

1. Dom displays good study habits normally, but lately he's not his underline{usual} self. 2. In the past, he often completed assignments the day the underline{work was given}. 3. He studied in the library every day, automatically, underline{not waiting until the day of a test}. 4. But recent observations of Dom's work habits underline{show} that he's slipping. 5. His teacher watched him throw a science report together carelessly, underline{without making the slightest effort}. 6. Dom's teacher has decided to ask him why his work habits have swerved underline{downward}.

Teaching Chart 98

**Story Words**

These words from the selection may be unfamiliar. Before students read, have them check the meanings and pronunciations of the words in the Glossary beginning on page 760 or in a dictionary.

• avalanche, p. 416
• incorrectly, p. 419
• iguana, p. 421
• mongoose, p. 421
• skeptical, p. 427

**Discuss Meanings**  Ask questions like these to help clarify word meanings:

• How do you spend your free time normally?
• What were your favorite class assignments this year?
• What task can you do automatically, without thinking?
• Where would you go to make observations of the night sky?
• What might happen if you carry a pail of water carelessly?
• If a car swerved toward the sidewalk, where might it end up?

## Practice

**Act It Out**

GROUP

Have students work in groups of six. They should each choose a vocabulary card and write a sentence using it. Then have them take turns pantomiming clues to their sentences, challenging other students to guess the sentence. ▶ **Kinesthetic/Interpersonal**

 carelessly

 observations

swerved

> **Word Building Manipulative Cards**

**Write a Sketch**

WRITING

Have students write a sketch in which the vocabulary words appear as dialogue. Invite them to perform their sketch for the class.
▶ **Kinesthetic**

### SPELLING/VOCABULARY CONNECTIONS
See Spelling Challenge Words, pages 4310–431P.

### LANGUAGE SUPPORT
See the **Language Support Book,** pages 129-132, for teaching suggestions for Vocabulary.

**Vocabulary PuzzleMaker**

Provides vocabulary activities

## Assess Vocabulary

**Use Words in Context**

PARTNERS

Challenge students to write a paragraph about a recent event using as many of the vocabulary words as possible. Students should then exchange papers with a partner and check that the words are used correctly.

# Meeting Individual Needs for Vocabulary

| EASY | ON-LEVEL | ON-LEVEL | CHALLENGE |
|---|---|---|---|
| Reteach, 120 | Practice, 120 | Practice, 120a Take-Home Story | Extend, 120 |

# Comprehension

## Prereading Strategies

**PREVIEW AND PREDICT** Have the students read the title and preview the selection, noting how the pictures give clues to what the selection will be about.

- What is the topic of this selection?
- What will the story most likely be about?
- Do you think it will be a fiction or nonfiction story? Why? (Since science deals with facts, it will be a nonfiction story.) **Genre**

Have students prepare a Predictions chart telling what they think they will learn by reading the story.

| PREDICTIONS | WHAT HAPPENED |
|---|---|
| I will learn how scientists think. | |
| I will learn about the scientific method. | |

**SET PURPOSES** What questions do students want the story to answer?

- How do scientists think?
- How do scientists find answers to questions?

HOW to THiNK

ANSWERING QUESTIONS BY

410

## Meeting Individual Needs • Grouping Suggestions for Strategic Reading

| EASY | ON-LEVEL | CHALLENGE |
|---|---|---|
| **Read Together** Read the story together or have students use the **Listening Library.** Students may use the Important and Unimportant Information chart to record information. Comprehension and Intervention prompts offer help with decoding, vocabulary, and comprehension. | **Guided Instruction** Choose from the Comprehension questions as you read the story with students or after they have played the **Listening Library.** Have them use the Important and Unimportant Information chart to record information. | **Read Independently** Have students read independently. Set up an Important and Unimportant Information chart with students, as on page 411, and have them fill it in as they read. After reading, they can use their charts to discuss what they learned about the scientific method. |

# LiKe a SciENtiST

## THE SCIENTIFIC METHOD

by Stephen P. Kramer
illustrated by Kim Behm

411

# Comprehension

☑ **Apply Important and Unimportant Information**

☑ **Apply Draw Conclusions**

**STRATEGIC READING** As you read, try to determine which information is important and which is unimportant. This strategy can help you better understand the story's main idea.

Before we begin let's develop an Important and Unimportant Information chart to record information as we read.

| IMPORTANT | UNIMPORTANT |
| --- | --- |
|  |  |

**1 IMPORTANT AND UNIMPORTANT INFORMATION** The title and subtitle of the story give us an important piece of information. What is it? (The story will explain the scientific method of inquiry.)

## Genre

### Informational Story

Explain that an informational story:

- tells a story about events that actually happened or could happen.
- gives information in an easy-to-understand way.
- features realistic characters and settings.

**Activity** After students read *How to Think Like a Scientist,* have them describe in a few sentences the key plot events of one section of the story. Then discuss what they learned about the scientific method from that section.

# Comprehension

**② IMPORTANT AND UNIMPORTANT INFORMATION** Are some facts on this page more important than others? Which facts? Why?

*MODEL* I meet two boys on this page. They're riding bicycles. It's dark. Pete thinks he ran over a snake. Jim thinks it was an old inner tube. I think the time of day is important, because Pete can't be certain he ran over a snake. It's probably not as important to remember what Jim said, because the action of the story centers around the snake. As I continue to read, I'll find out if I'm right.

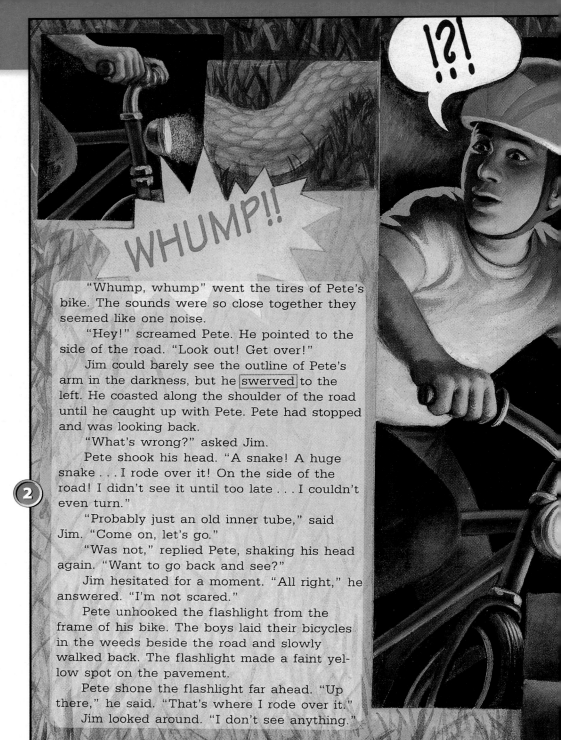

WHUMP!!

"Whump, whump" went the tires of Pete's bike. The sounds were so close together they seemed like one noise.

"Hey!" screamed Pete. He pointed to the side of the road. "Look out! Get over!"

Jim could barely see the outline of Pete's arm in the darkness, but he swerved to the left. He coasted along the shoulder of the road until he caught up with Pete. Pete had stopped and was looking back.

"What's wrong?" asked Jim.

Pete shook his head. "A snake! A huge snake . . . I rode over it! On the side of the road! I didn't see it until too late . . . I couldn't even turn."

"Probably just an old inner tube," said Jim. "Come on, let's go."

"Was not," replied Pete, shaking his head again. "Want to go back and see?"

Jim hesitated for a moment. "All right," he answered. "I'm not scared."

Pete unhooked the flashlight from the frame of his bike. The boys laid their bicycles in the weeds beside the road and slowly walked back. The flashlight made a faint yellow spot on the pavement.

Pete shone the flashlight far ahead. "Up there," he said. "That's where I rode over it."

Jim looked around. "I don't see anything."

412

---

# CULTURAL PERSPECTIVES

**SUPERSTITIONS** A superstition is a belief that a certain action or event can affect an unrelated event. In Japan people give live plants rather than cut flowers to a sick person because a live plant represents hope of recovery.

• Ask students to share a superstition they know.

**RESEARCH AND INQUIRY** Have students work with a partner to research superstitions in other cultures. Direct them to write their findings on poster paper for displaying. ▶ **Linguistic**

If you spill salt, throw a pinch of it over your left shoulder to avoid bad luck.

Pete shone the flashlight at the edge of the road. For a moment everything was still. Then, suddenly, the back half of a very large gopher snake disappeared into the roadside weeds.

Jim took a slow step backward. "You rode over that?"

Pete nodded. "I told you it wasn't an inner tube." He shone the flashlight directly on the spot where the snake had disappeared. "Think it's hurt?"

Jim shrugged. "It seems to be crawling all right."

"Maybe we should come back and look around tomorrow."

"OK," Jim agreed. "Let's wait until there's a little more light."

The boys turned and walked back to their bicycles. Pete kept the beam of light on the road.

"You know," said Jim, "my grandpa would call that a rain snake."

**413**

# Comprehension

**3** **DRAW CONCLUSIONS** Why do Pete and Jim draw the conclusion that the snake is okay? List at least two reasons.

*MODEL* The snake had moved away from the spot where Jim hit it. That told the boys it might be okay. The boys also saw the snake's tail move as it crawled into the brush, and Jim said it seemed to be crawling okay. Based on those two pieces of evidence, the boys concluded the snake was okay.

## TEACHING TIP

**MAKE IT PERSONAL** Ask students to personalize the situation described here. Have they ever been in a similar situation? For example, have they ever heard a noise at night and tried to figure out what it was?

## Minilesson

### REVIEW/MAINTAIN
### /âr/ and /är/

Review with students that the sound /âr/ as in *care* and *pair* can have several different spellings including *are*, *air*, and *ar*. Distinguish this sound from the sound /är/ as in *far*.

- Point out the word *darkness* on page 412. Ask if it has the /är/ or /âr/ sound.
- Ask students to locate two words on page 412 with the /âr/ sound. (barely, scared) *Graphophonic Cues*

**Activity** Have students make a chart with a column for each spelling pattern of /âr/ and record additional story words in the correct columns. (silverware, stare, care, aquariums, fairly, carelessly)

 Phonics Intervention Guide

**413**

# Comprehension

④ At first Jim didn't think a snake could bring rain. But he had second thoughts. Why? Who would like to role-play Jim and answer the question? *Role-Play*

**READ WITH INTONATION** Pages 412 to 414 provide an opportunity for students to read with dramatic intonation. Punctuation and vivid verbs indicate tone of voice.

You may wish to model fluent reading of the passage by

• infusing your voice with excitement as indicated by exclamation marks and the verb *screamed*

• slowing down and pausing at the ellipses as well as at the verb *hesitated.*

**PARTNERS** Have students select a section and practice reading it aloud to each other. Then ask volunteers to present their reading to the class.

"What?" asked Pete.

"A rain snake. He'd say you could make it rain for sure with a snake like that."

"How?"

"Well," said Jim, "my grandpa grew up way back in the hills. When he was a boy, the farmers would sometimes use a dead snake to make it rain. They'd find a large tree with a strong low branch and throw the snake over the branch. A big snake like that would bring rain for sure."

Pete leaned over and picked up his bike. "You believe that?"

④ "Naw," answered Jim quickly. Then he scratched his head and looked back down the road. "But, well, I never tried it. I don't know. My grandpa says they did it a lot. Maybe it'd work for some people, sometimes. . . ."

414

W̲hat do you think? Can throwing a dead snake over a tree branch bring rain? **⑤**

Every day you answer questions—dozens or even hundreds of them. What should I wear today? What assignments do I need for school? Can I eat an extra piece of toast and still get to the bus on time? What should I do tonight?

Some questions you answer correctly. Others you don't. Some questions are important. You spend lots of time thinking about them. Other questions aren't important. You guess at the answer or just choose an answer automatically.

415

# Comprehension

**⑤** Up to this point, I thought we were reading a story. How does this sentence differ from the ones before it? (It addresses the reader.) Why do you think the author does this? Do any of these questions apply to you? Does the author's use of "you" draw you deeper into the reading? *Author's Purpose, Point of View*

## Minilesson

### REVIEW/MAINTAIN

### Summarize

Review with students that a good summary is short, includes only important information, and tells the story events in order.

• Have volunteers help you summarize the episode on pages 412–414. Record information on the chalkboard.

**Activity** Direct pairs of students to choose a story within the selection to summarize. Possible stories appear on pages 416–418, 421–423, and 424–426.

**415**

# Comprehension

**6** **IMPORTANT AND UNIMPORTANT INFORMATION** Reread the first two paragraphs on page 416. What does the author say the rest of the story will be about? (ways people answer questions) Knowing that will help us distinguish important and unimportant information as we read the rest of the selection.

---

### TEACHING TIP

**OBSERVATIONS** As students read the story, ask them to identify the observations made by both characters. For example, Ralphie observed a man carrying something out of the neighbors' house and made the observation that he was a thief. His sister observed a television repair truck parked in the street and made the observation that the man was just taking the television in for repair. Ask students how scientists might use observations in their work (for example: observing the effects of sun and water on the growth of plants).

---

# How Do You Answer Questions?

You think about many things when you try to answer a question. You try to remember things you know that might help you. You look for new information about the question. Sometimes you try to guess how someone else would answer the question. Other times you might pick an answer because of what you would *like* the answer to be.

Sometimes these things help you find a correct answer. Other times they lead you to a wrong answer.

Here are three stories. Each story has a question. Each story tells about something that could happen to you, and each story will show a different way of answering a question.

**6**

## INFORMATION

You're sitting on your bed one afternoon reading a book about a mountain climber. Things are getting very exciting (an avalanche has just started) when your little brother Ralphie walks into the room. He strolls past your bed and looks out the window.

"Hey," he says, "someone's in Mr. Murphy's backyard."

Your teeth start to grind. You've lost your place but you try not to show it. A long time ago you learned that sometimes the best way to get along with Ralphie is to ignore him.

"Hey," says Ralphie, "they're going into the Murphys' house."

You frown and roll over, wondering when Ralphie is going to go away.

"Hey," says Ralphie, "they're coming out of the Murphys' house. They're carrying something that's all covered up. They're stealing something from the Murphys!"

You sit up straight. The Murphys? Someone is stealing something from the Murphys?

AVALANCHE!

416

---

Activity

## Cross Curricular: Social Studies

**MAP SKILLS** Maps are typically drawn from an aerial perspective. They help us understand the relationships among various locations.

• Ask students to identify where the television repair van was parked in relation to the Murphys' house.

**Activity** Have students draw a map of the neighborhood in the story and label each location mentioned. Then have them indicate the possible movements of the "bad men" using arrows drawn on the map.

▶ Intrapersonal/Spatial

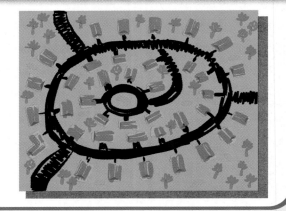

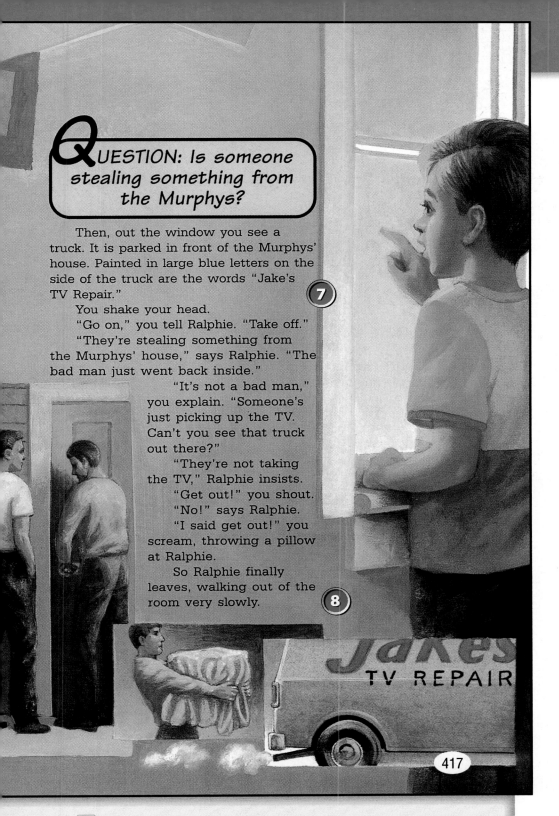

**QUESTION: Is someone stealing something from the Murphys?**

Then, out the window you see a truck. It is parked in front of the Murphys' house. Painted in large blue letters on the side of the truck are the words "Jake's TV Repair."

You shake your head.

"Go on," you tell Ralphie. "Take off."

"They're stealing something from the Murphys' house," says Ralphie. "The bad man just went back inside."

"It's not a bad man," you explain. "Someone's just picking up the TV. Can't you see that truck out there?"

"They're not taking the TV," Ralphie insists.

"Get out!" you shout.

"No!" says Ralphie.

"I said get out!" you scream, throwing a pillow at Ralphie.

So Ralphie finally leaves, walking out of the room very slowly.

**⑦**

**⑧**

*417*

Jakes
**TV REPAIR**

# Comprehension

**⑦ DRAW CONCLUSIONS** Do you have enough information to answer the question on this page? (No, there has been only one observation so far.) **Read on to find an answer.**

**⑧ DRAW CONCLUSIONS** What do you think is happening next door? (A television is being picked up for repair.) What information helped you reach this conclusion? (The sign on the truck says television repair and the man is carrying something about the size and shape of a portable television.)

**CONTEXT CLUES** Reread the first paragraph on page 416 under the heading *Information*. Do you know what the word *avalanche* means? *Semantic Cues*

 **PREVENTION/INTERVENTION**

**CONTEXT CLUES** Help students identify and use context clues for the word *avalanche*. For example, point out the words *mountain climber* in the previous sentence.

Explain that an avalanche is the swift, sudden fall of a mass of snow, rocks, or ice down a mountainside. Demonstrate by placing a few pebbles on a tilted book. Hold them in place with your hand, ask a student to call out a warning, "Avalanche!" and release the pebbles. Ask students how they could simulate a snow avalanche. Ask what might happen to a tree in the path of an avalanche. *Semantic Cues*

**417**

# Comprehension

**9** **IMPORTANT AND UNIMPORTANT INFORMATION** Which pieces of information in this story are important? Why? (Ralphie is a pesky little brother. The television repair truck was parked in the street—not in the Murphys' driveway. A man carried something out of the Murphys' house. The television repairman was at the Johnsons' house.) **Which pieces of information are unimportant? Why?** (Ralphie's sister was reading about an avalanche. The letters in the sign on the truck were painted blue.)

**10** Ralphie nodded "yes" to father's question because he had seen something. What do you think he saw that his sister didn't? What made him so certain that a robbery was taking place? (Maybe he saw the "bad men" put the covered box in another vehicle, not the television repair truck.) *Make Inferences*

RRRING!

**9** That night at dinner the telephone rings. Your father answers it. When he returns to the table, he says, "The Murphys just got home. While they were gone this afternoon, someone broke into their house and stole some money. The burglars also took some silverware and Mr. Murphy's violin.

"Most of our neighbors were gone this afternoon. The Johnsons didn't see anything because they were watching a repairman fix their TV all afternoon. Did any of you see anything?"

**10** Ralphie sits up straight and begins nodding.

418

## Cross Curricular: Science

**SIR FRANCIS BACON** Sixteenth-century philosopher Sir Francis Bacon was one of the first to insist that scientific investigation should begin with facts, not ideas.

**RESEARCH AND INQUIRY** Ask students to research with a partner the scientific discoveries of Bacon and prepare an oral report on their findings.
▶ **Interpersonal/Linguistic**

*inter* **NET** **CONNECTION** Students can learn more about Sir Francis Bacon by visiting **www.mhschool.com/reading**

What happened? The question was: Is someone stealing something from the Murphys? You and Ralphie both made observations. Ralphie's observations told him the answer was yes. Your observations told you the answer was no. Why did you and Ralphie end up with different answers to the same question?

You answered the question incorrectly because of the way you used an observation. You saw a TV repair truck through the front window. Your observation was a good one. You noticed what kind of truck was on your street and where it was parked. The problem was how you used your observation. You thought the truck was giving you information about who was in the Murphys' house. Actually, Ralphie was giving you better information.

Information must be used carefully. Having information does not always mean you will answer a question correctly. If the information is not true or is not used in the right way, it can lead to a wrong answer.

419

# Comprehension

**11 DRAW CONCLUSIONS** How did the girl's attitude about her brother help lead her to the wrong conclusion? (She thought of him as a pest and didn't value his information enough to investigate further.) Does the trust you put in information ever depend on from whom it is coming? Do you think it should? What does the story say about this? (Information must be thought about carefully or it can lead to a wrong answer.)

**12 IMPORTANT AND UNIMPORTANT INFORMATION** Why did the girl's observation lead her to the wrong answer?

*MODEL* The girl was correct when she said she saw a TV repair truck parked on the street. However, since she didn't observe the men loading a television into the truck, she didn't have enough information to say that the men were working for the Murphys. Her observation was incomplete.

Let's add what we know about making observations to our Important and Unimportant Information chart. We'll put information to focus on in the Important column and information to ignore in the Unimportant column.

| IMPORTANT | UNIMPORTANT |
|---|---|
| Scientists make careful, complete observations. | Ignore observations unrelated to the scientific investigation. |

# Comprehension

**13** What can we predict about this section after reading the heading? What do you think "What Other People Say" will have to do with answering questions? (Sample answer: The girl who's raising her hand thinks she knows the answer to the question. However, she may change her mind after the man talks some more.) *Make Predictions*

---

**TEACHING TIP**

**ROLE–PLAY** Ask the students to imagine themselves in the classroom in the story. Challenge them to visualize the details. How would they feel if they were there? Invite volunteers to role-play the scene.

**LANGUAGE SUPPORT**

**ESL** The words *mongoose* and *iguana* may be unfamiliar to students. Ask students to identify two familiar animals in the illustration. (fish, snake) Explain that a *mongoose* is a small, furry animal.

Have them point to the mongoose in the illustration. Explain that an *iguana* is a lizard. Have students point to the iguana in the illustration. To verify understanding, ask students to describe the animals.

It's Wednesday morning, just before lunch. Your teacher arranged for someone from the zoo to come and show your class some animals. You have seen an iguana, a mongoose, and a large snake. Now the zookeeper reaches into a wooden box and pulls out a fishbowl. He sets the bowl on a low table at the front of the room. Three small gray fish swim back and forth.

"Who knows the name of these fish?" asks the zookeeper.

Everyone is quiet. You stare at the fish for a moment. Of course you know what they are. They're guppies! They look just like the fish in your sister's aquarium. You've spent hours watching guppies.

Quickly, you raise your hand, but you're sitting in the last row and the zookeeper doesn't see you.

You wave your hand back and forth. The girl next to you ducks.

"These are gastromorphs," says the zookeeper. "They live in slow, muddy streams in Africa. They are very danger-ous. They will eat almost anything that moves."

Quickly, you pull your hand down and look around. "Whew," you think. "That could have been embarrass-ing." Then you lean forward and squint **(14)** at those fish again.

"We always keep a strong screen over this fishbowl when we visit schools. If anyone were to stick a hand in the water, well, these little fish would immediately attack and begin taking bites out of it."

421

# Comprehension

**(14)** **IMPORTANT AND UNIMPORTANT INFORMATION** What information causes the girl to raise her hand? (She observes that the fish look like the guppies in her sister's fishbowl.) What information causes her to lower her hand? (The zookeeper says the fish are gastromorphs.) What mistake did she make? (She depended too much on someone else's information.) Let's add this information to our chart.

| IMPORTANT | UNIMPORTANT |
|---|---|
| Scientists make careful, complete observations. | Ignore observations unrelated to the scientific investigation. |
| Trust your observations. Verify information from others. | Ignore who's provid-ing the information, because even experts can be wrong. |

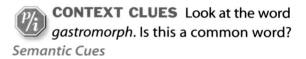 **CONTEXT CLUES** Look at the word *gastromorph*. Is this a common word? *Semantic Cues*

## Minilesson

### REVIEW/MAINTAIN

#### Suffixes

Remind students that many adverbs are formed by adding the suffix *-ly* to an adjec-tive. Also, remind them that adverbs tell when, where, or how something is done.

- Have the students find the first *-ly* word on page 421. (quickly)
- Have students identify the adjective used to form the adverb. (quick)

**Activity** Have students list other *-ly* adverbs in the selection and write the adjec-tival root next to each.

 **PREVENTION/INTERVENTION**

**CONTEXT CLUES** Explain that the scientific term *gastromorphs* is an example of specialized vocabulary. When writing for a general audience, authors often define specialized words or give strong clues to the meaning. Help students identify the clues for *gastromorphs* later in the paragraph and in the art.

Have students reread the text about *gastromorphs*—flesh-eating fish indigenous to Africa. Explain: *Gastromorph* is the scientific name of a type of fish. Most animals have both scientific and common names. For example, the scientific name of the desert iguana is *Dipsosaurus dorsairs*. *Semantic Cues*

**421**

# Comprehension ⑮

**⑮ DRAW CONCLUSIONS** Given what you know so far, how would you answer the question? List two pieces of evidence to support your answer. (Sample answer: The fish are gastromorphs. The zookeeper says they are gastromorphs. The zookeeper is an expert and should know. Since the girl is in the back of the room, maybe she can't see the fish well enough to be certain that they are guppies. Maybe they just look like guppies.)

**CONTEXT CLUES** Reread the second sentence in the last paragraph on this page. What is an *aquarium*? Can you guess what it is by rereading the sentence? *Semantic Cues*

---

## SELF-MONITORING STRATEGY

**REREAD** Rereading a part of the story can help a reader understand what happens in the story.

**MODEL** When I first read this part of the story, I wasn't certain how the zookeeper made the mistake of netting guppies instead of gastromorphs. In rereading the section, I realized the mistake occurred when the zookeeper looked away from what he was doing to return the snake to the bag. He must have moved the net from over the gastromorphs' aquarium to over the guppies' aquarium.

---

**QUESTION: What kind of fish is in the bowl?**

This time the question seems easy. The fish look a lot like guppies. They swim like guppies. They're even the size and color of guppies. But would you stick your hand in the bowl? Of course not! The zookeeper just told you they are gastromorphs. Zookeepers know their animals, right? So the fish must be gastromorphs. Maybe.

Here's what really happened. The zookeeper who was supposed to visit your class got sick. The zoo sent over the person who [normally] takes care of birds. The zookeeper who came to your class knew a lot about birds, but not much about fish.

His first stop that morning was at the mammal house to pick up the mongoose. Then he went to the reptile house to get the iguana and the snake. He took all three animals with him into the fish house.

It was dark in the fish house. All the fish were arranged alphabetically in separate aquariums. The guppies were in the aquarium next to the gastromorphs. The zookeeper picked up a net, walked over to the gastromorphs, and leaned over the aquarium to dip some out. Just then the snake began to crawl out of its bag, so the zookeeper reached down to push it back in. When he stood up straight again he had three fish in his net. He dumped them into the fishbowl and hurried to your school. What he didn't know was that he had accidentally dipped the net into the wrong tank. He had netted three guppies instead of three gastromorphs.

422

---

**p/i PREVENTION/INTERVENTION**

**CONTEXT CLUES** Explain that students can find clues to the meaning of *aquarium* by looking at the rest of the sentence. Explain that an aquarium is a tank, bowl, or similar water-filled container in which fish and other water animals are kept. Have students look at the rest of the paragraph for two more words that have similar meanings. (tank, fishbowl) *Semantic Cues*

MORPHS?

You really were right! The fish were guppies, but you changed your mind because of what the zookeeper said.

Sometimes other people are wrong. Usually zookeepers know much more about animals than you do, but maybe not every time. If you answer questions by depending too much on other people's answers, you probably will make mistakes. **16**

423

# Comprehension

**16** The answer to the question was wrong. What kind of fish is in the bowl? The girl could have provided the correct answer, but she assumed the zookeeper was correct. How is this the opposite of what happened in the last episode, the one about the robbery? (The sister's response was wrong because she didn't depend enough on someone else's information.) What have you learned about depending on someone else's information? (Both the source and the content of the information needs to be checked.) *Make Inferences*

## Minilesson

### REVIEW/MAINTAIN

### Root Words

Remind students that knowing the meaning of Latin and Greek roots of words can help figure out meanings.

- Have students analyze a word they know: *zookeeper*. Explain that *zoo* comes from the Greek word *zoio* meaning animal.

- Ask students to list other words with this root, such as *zoology* and *zoologist* and write their definitions.

**Activity** Ask students to analyze the word *reptile* by determining its root word (from the Latin word *repere* which means *to creep*). If necessary, model finding and using etymologies in a dictionary.

**423**

# Comprehension

**17** What does the boy think he should do? Why? (Stay home and do his math assignment. That way he'll get a better grade on his report card.) *Make Inferences*

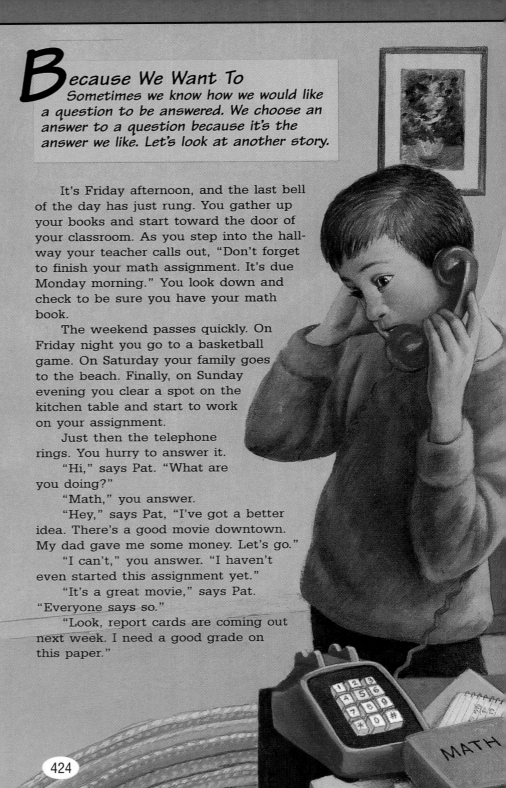

**B**ecause We Want To
Sometimes we know how we would like a question to be answered. We choose an answer to a question because it's the answer we like. Let's look at another story.

It's Friday afternoon, and the last bell of the day has just rung. You gather up your books and start toward the door of your classroom. As you step into the hallway your teacher calls out, "Don't forget to finish your math assignment. It's due Monday morning." You look down and check to be sure you have your math book.

The weekend passes quickly. On Friday night you go to a basketball game. On Saturday your family goes to the beach. Finally, on Sunday evening you clear a spot on the kitchen table and start to work on your assignment.

Just then the telephone rings. You hurry to answer it.

"Hi," says Pat. "What are you doing?"

"Math," you answer.

"Hey," says Pat, "I've got a better idea. There's a good movie downtown. My dad gave me some money. Let's go."

"I can't," you answer. "I haven't even started this assignment yet."

"It's a great movie," says Pat. "Everyone says so."

**17** "Look, report cards are coming out next week. I need a good grade on this paper."

424

# Cross Curricular: Math

**PROBABILITY** Probability deals with the likelihood of observing one of several possible outcomes that can occur in an event.

**RESEARCH AND INQUIRY** Have students design simple probability tests, by rolling a number cube, flipping a coin, or shaking colored marbles in a box. Ask students to predict the probability of certain outcomes and then create a chart to record the results of their trials.

▶ **Logical/Mathematical**

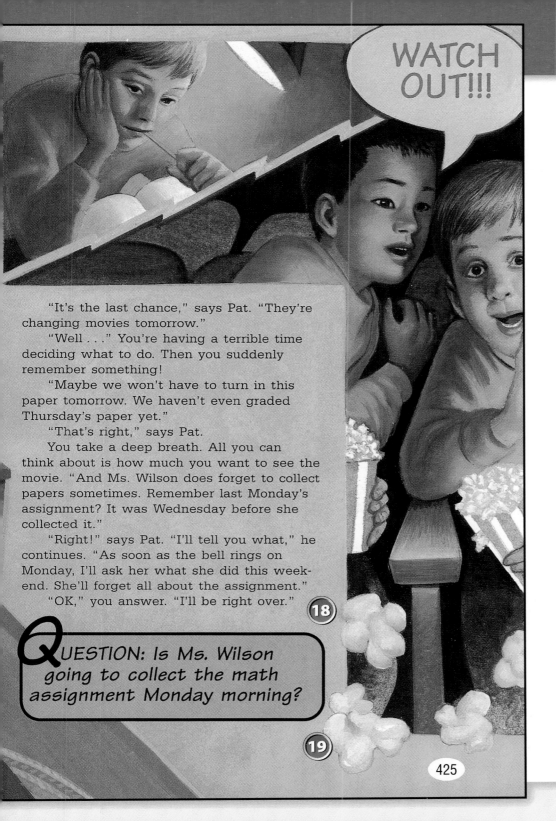

"It's the last chance," says Pat. "They're changing movies tomorrow."

"Well . . ." You're having a terrible time deciding what to do. Then you suddenly remember something!

"Maybe we won't have to turn in this paper tomorrow. We haven't even graded Thursday's paper yet."

"That's right," says Pat.

You take a deep breath. All you can think about is how much you want to see the movie. "And Ms. Wilson does forget to collect papers sometimes. Remember last Monday's assignment? It was Wednesday before she collected it."

"Right!" says Pat. "I'll tell you what," he continues. "As soon as the bell rings on Monday, I'll ask her what she did this weekend. She'll forget all about the assignment."

"OK," you answer. "I'll be right over." 18

QUESTION: Is Ms. Wilson going to collect the math assignment Monday morning?

19

425

# Comprehension

18 **DRAW CONCLUSIONS** Why does the boy decide to go to the movies? Give two or more reasons for your answer. (Sample answer: He really wants to go. He thinks his teacher won't collect the homework on Monday, so he'll have time to complete the assignment.)

19 **DRAW CONCLUSIONS** What evidence in the story might help you answer the question on this page? Is there enough evidence for you to draw a conclusion? (Sample answer: No, there's only one piece of evidence: Ms. Wilson did not collect homework last Monday. A conclusion should be based on two or more pieces of evidence.)

**425**

# Comprehension

**(20)** **IMPORTANT AND UNIMPORTANT INFORMATION** How did the character in the story arrive at the wrong answer? (He chose an answer he wished would be true instead of basing his answer on fact.) Let's add this information to our chart.

| IMPORTANT | UNIMPORTANT |
|---|---|
| Scientists make careful, complete observations. | Ignore observations unrelated to the scientific investigation. |
| Trust your own observations. Verify information from others. | Ignore who's providing the information. Even experts can be wrong. |
| Base conclusions on provable, reliable observations and information. | Ignore information that only fits in with the answer you want. |

**RETELL THE STORY** Ask volunteers to tell the main ideas of the story. Have them focus on the important information they learned regarding the scientific process. They may refer to their Important and Unimportant Information charts. *Summarize*

## STUDENT SELF-ASSESSMENT

- How did the strategy of sifting out the important from the unimportant information help me understand the main idea of the story?

- How did the Important and Unimportant Information chart help me?

**TRANSFERRING THE STRATEGY**

- When might I try using this strategy again? In what other reading could the chart help me?

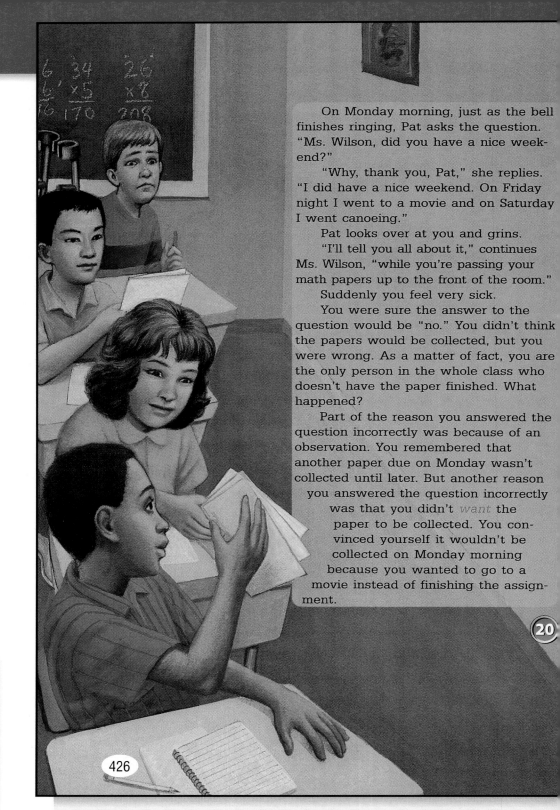

On Monday morning, just as the bell finishes ringing, Pat asks the question. "Ms. Wilson, did you have a nice weekend?"

"Why, thank you, Pat," she replies. "I did have a nice weekend. On Friday night I went to a movie and on Saturday I went canoeing."

Pat looks over at you and grins.

"I'll tell you all about it," continues Ms. Wilson, "while you're passing your math papers up to the front of the room."

Suddenly you feel very sick.

You were sure the answer to the question would be "no." You didn't think the papers would be collected, but you were wrong. As a matter of fact, you are the only person in the whole class who doesn't have the paper finished. What happened?

Part of the reason you answered the question incorrectly was because of an observation. You remembered that another paper due on Monday wasn't collected until later. But another reason you answered the question incorrectly was that you didn't *want* the paper to be collected. You convinced yourself it wouldn't be collected on Monday morning because you wanted to go to a movie instead of finishing the assignment.

**(20)**

426

## REREADING FOR *Fluency*

**(ONE)** Have students choose a section to practice reading aloud. Encourage them to read a part that they found difficult to understand during the first reading.

**READING RATE** When you evaluate rate, have the student read aloud from the story for one minute. Place a stick-on note after the last word read. Count words read. To evaluate

students' performance, see the Running Record in the **Fluency Assessment** book.

**(i) Intervention** ▶ For leveled fluency lessons, passages, and norms charts, see **Skills Intervention Guide**, Part 4, Fluency.

Sometimes we really want the answer to a question to turn out in a certain way. Such a question can be difficult to answer correctly or fairly. Often it is easier to find an answer we like than an answer that is correct.

Carelessly used information, what others think, what we want to happen—none of these are very reliable ways of answering questions. Too many times they lead to wrong answers. Is there a better way? How can you find out whether throwing a dead snake over a tree branch really will bring rain?

There is a better way to find answers. Scientists use a series of steps called the scientific method to find accurate and reliable answers to their questions.

Good scientists are skeptical, but they keep an open mind. They know that experiments sometimes show that the correct answer to a question is not always the one you think it will be!

# MEET STEPHEN P. KRAMER

Science has always fascinated Stephen P. Kramer. In college, he studied biology, the science of living things. After graduation, he taught science for four years on a Navajo reservation. Today, Kramer lives in Vancouver, Washington, where he writes and helps care for his two sons. His books combine his training as a biologist and his experience as a teacher. His first book, **Getting Oxygen: What Do You Do If You're Cell Twenty-Two?**, explains how the body gets and uses oxygen. **How to Think Like a Scientist** describes the scientific method, the step-by-step process that scientists use to learn about our world.

427

## LITERARY RESPONSE

**QUICK-WRITE** Invite students to record their thoughts about the selection. These questions may help them:

- What did you learn from reading the story?

- How can thinking like a scientist help you?

**ORAL RESPONSE** Have students share their journal entries or discuss the episode they liked best.

# Comprehension

## Return to Predictions and Purposes

Review with students their story predictions and purposes for reading the selection. Were their predictions accurate? Did they find out what they wanted to know?

| PREDICTIONS | WHAT HAPPENED |
|---|---|
| I will learn how scientists think. | Scientists do not let anything influence the answer to a question except facts. |
| I will learn about the scientific method. | The scientific method involves asking a question and looking for ways to answer it. |

## INFORMAL ASSESSMENT

### IMPORTANT AND UNIMPORTANT INFORMATION

#### HOW TO ASSESS

- Have students review the important information in the story about how to answer questions.

- Ask them why it is sometimes faulty either to rely on or to disregard information supplied by someone else.

Students should recognize that scientists make careful observations, verify all information, and accept only proven answers.

**FOLLOW UP** If students are having difficulty determining important and unimportant information, model how you would choose the important information to order your favorite ice cream cone and what information you wouldn't include.

# Story Questions

Have the students discuss or write answers to the questions on page 428.

**Answers:**

1. Ralphie was right. Bad men were in the Murphys' house. *Literal/Details*

2. The zookeeper called the fish gastromorphs, and the girl concluded her answer must be wrong. *Inferential/Draw Conclusions*

3. A wrong answer can result from misinterpreted information. *Inferential/Form Generalizations*

4. Scientists observe carefully, check all information, and accept only proven answers. *Critical/Summarize*

5. Similarities: Ask questions, gather information, draw conclusions. Differences: Conduct experiments, trust instincts. *Critical/Reading Across Texts*

**WRITE A SCIENTIFIC REPORT** For a full writing process lesson related to this suggestion, see pages 431K–431L.

# Story Questions & Activities

1. Did Ralphie or his sister have the correct answer to the question, "Is someone stealing something from the Murphys"? Explain.

2. Why didn't the girl in the zookeeper story give the answer "guppies" when she knew she was right?

3. Why do scientists need to use information correctly when answering a question?

4. What is the main idea of this selection?

5. Imagine that a famous scientist had a chance to meet the detective in the picture on page 408. Do you think they would see similarities in their jobs? What would the differences be?

## Write a Scientific Report

How does your cat let you know when it wants to come inside? How does a person eat an ice-cream cone? Choose an action to observe closely. Write a scientific report that presents clear and accurate facts. State the purpose of your report in the introduction. Supply the facts in the body of your report. End by summarizing your findings. Tell why they are important.

## Meeting Individual Needs

| EASY | ON-LEVEL | CHALLENGE |
|---|---|---|
| Reteach, 121 | Practice, 121 | Extend, 121 |

# Draw a Scene

In the theft story, Ralphie saw people robbing the Murphys' house, while his sister saw a TV repairman simply taking the Murphys' TV set to the fix-it shop. Draw a scene like the one Ralphie and his sister witnessed. Include details that could be interpreted differently by two different people. Ask your partner to observe the scene. Under your drawing, write what you and your partner observed from looking at the same picture.

# Create Two Comic Strips

Create two comic strips that both start with the same beginning but have two different endings. Show how one scene or situation can have a different ending depending on who is telling the story. Show what is happening in each picture with clear drawings and thought or speech balloons.

# Find Out More

In the story you learned that many discoveries are made by answering questions in the right way. Choose a scientist, such as Albert Einstein or Marie Curie. What was the scientist's major discovery? How did the scientist become interested in his or her research project? Start by checking an encyclopedia, a book about science, a video, or a true story about the scientist. Take notes. Use your notes to prepare an oral report.

E=MC²

429

# Story Activities

## Draw a Scene

**Materials:** paper, markers, or crayons

**PARTNERS** When students complete their scenes, have them cover the explanations they provided and show the drawings to partners. Encourage them to listen to their partners' interpretation of the drawing before revealing the explanations. Ask them to discuss differences in interpretation.

## Create Two Comic Strips

**Materials:** paper, markers, or crayons

**PARTNERS** Brainstorm types of events to use as a topic for a comic strip. Help students see that who or what the characters are determines how they act. For example, what might happen if a monkey were sent to buy bananas for dinner? What might happen if a dog tried to fly?

## Find Out More

**RESEARCH AND INQUIRY** Have students make a list of scientists and choose one to research, working in small groups. Suggest they report their findings to the class by role-playing an interview.

**GROUP**

inter**NET** **CONNECTION** For more information on famous scientists, students can visit **www.mhschool.com/reading**

FORMAL **A**SSESSMENT

After page 429, see the Selection Assessment.

MATH: IDENTIFYING UNIMPORTANT INFORMATION Ask students to identify the information that is unimportant (not needed) to solve the problem below. Then have them write three similar math problems and have partners identify the unimportant information in each.

• A train leaves New York at 8:00 A.M. It arrives in Boston at 12:15 P.M. The train averages 60 mph. How long does it take to travel from New York to Boston?

**What To Look For** Original math problems that include unnecessary information written by one student and identified by another.

CHALLENGE

# Study Skills

## GRAPHIC AIDS

**OBJECTIVES**  Students will learn how to use an outline.

**PREPARE**  Read the passage with students. Display **Teaching Chart 99.**

**TEACH**  Explain that the information in an outline is organized under two or more main topics. Have students note that an outline is concise and easy to read.

**PRACTICE**  Have students answer questions 1–5. Review the answers with them. **1.** Edison's Early Life, Menlo Park, The Light Bulb **2.** before **3.** Edison's Early Life **4.** III., A. **5.** Yes, an outline would show the most important facts in an easy to read format.

**ASSESS/CLOSE**  Have students outline a passage in their books. Also have them discuss why making an outline might help them with their own writing.

# Study SKILLS

## Use an Outline

An **outline** is a summary that shows how the information in a report, chapter, or story is or will be organized. When you have to write a report, making an outline first can help you group facts and ideas.

This outline is for a report about the inventor Thomas Edison. Roman numerals indicate the main topics. Capital letters indicate facts or details that support or explain the main topics.

I. Edison's Early Life
  A.  Born in Ohio, 1847; spent childhood in Michigan
  B.  Worked as newspaper boy on railroad; lost hearing in accident
  C.  Became a telegraph operator

II. Menlo Park
  A.  Sold first invention; used money to open research lab in Menlo Park, NJ
  B.  Improved Alexander Graham Bell's telephone design
  C.  Invented phonograph, many other things

III. The Light Bulb
  A.  1879: Made first practical light bulb
  B.  1880: Set up factory to manufacture light bulbs
  C.  1882: Built power plant that provided electricity to New York City

**Use the outline to answer these questions.**

**1**  What are the three main topics of the report?

**2**  Did Edison open the lab in Menlo Park before or after he invented the light bulb?

**3**  Where would you put information about Edison's school years?

**4**  Where would you add details about the design of the light bulb?

**5**  If you wanted to remember the key points of a magazine article, would making an outline be helpful? Explain.

## Meeting Individual Needs

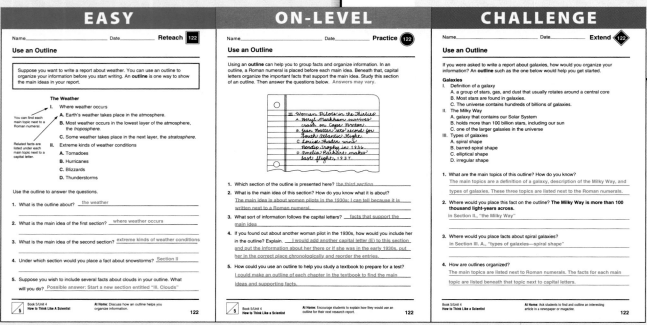

Reteach, 122          Practice, 122          Extend, 122

# TEST POWER

**DIRECTIONS**

**Read the sample story. Then read each question about the story.**

**SAMPLE**

## Erica's Drawings

Erica wasn't a very good speller or a great mathematician. But she loved to draw. Whenever her teacher gave her the chance, Erica turned to the back of her notebook and drew a picture.

The other students in her class liked Erica's pictures so much that they often passed their notebooks to her. They, too, wanted to have wonderful pictures in the backs of their notebooks.

One day, Erica's teacher collected everyone's notebooks. "I see that there are a lot of drawings in all of your notebooks. Where did they come from?" the teacher asked.

Nobody said a word.

"I'm asking because I'd like to hang some of these beautiful pictures on the walls," the teacher continued.

The class cheered. Soon Erica's drawings covered the walls of the classroom.

1   Information in the passage shows that Erica is very —

   **A**  playful

   **(B)**  talented

   **C**  organized

   **D**  gloomy

2   In the future, Erica will probably NOT —

   **F**  draw at lunchtime

   **G**  study her spelling words

   **(H)**  refuse to share her drawings

   **J**  hang her drawings on the wall

431

## Test Power

THE PRINCETON REVIEW

### Read the Page

Remind students to choose the *best* answer to each question.

### Discuss the Questions

**Question 1:**  This question requires students to make a conclusion about Erica. Remind students to look for clues or facts from the passage that support their answers. Information in the passage tells the reader that Erica's teacher and Erica's classmates liked Erica's pictures; it can be assumed that Erica is talented.

**Question 2:**  This question requires students to determine, based on the information in the passage, what Erica will *probably not do* in the future. Ask, "What clue is given about what Erica will probably *not* do in the future?" In the passage, Erica shares her pictures with her classmates and with her teacher.

# Leveled Books

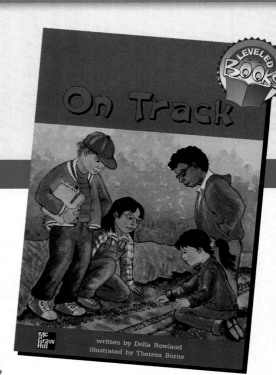

**EASY**

## On Track

/är/ and /âr/

☑ **Important and Unimportant Information**

☑ **Instructional Vocabulary** *assignments, automatically, carelessly, normally, observations, swerved*

## Guided Reading

**PREVIEW AND PREDICT** Have students preview the illustrations through page 7. Ask them to predict what the story is going to be about.

**SET PURPOSES** Have students write questions they would like to have answered by the story.

**READ THE BOOK** Use the questions below to help students apply reading strategies as they read.

**Pages 2 and 3:** Ask students to look on pages 2 and 3 for words with the /är/ sound as in car. (Marshall, handlebar, marks, started) *Phonics*

**Pages 6 and 7:** Ask students to look for words on pages 6 and 7 with the /âr/ sound as in pair. (grandparents, compared, carelessly) Ask them to compare the spellings of the words—pair, grandparents, compared, and carelessly—to determine three spellings of the /âr/ sound. (air, ar, are) *Phonics*

**Page 10:** Ask students to identify the important information in the first two paragraphs on page 10. (Franklin's initials were on a boy's bike. The boy's parents had purchased the bike at the Mountain Bike Shop.) Ask them to identify an example of unimportant information. (The team won. The kids ate hot dogs.) *Important and Unimportant Information*

**RETURN TO PREDICTIONS AND PURPOSES** Have students review their predictions. Which were accurate? Which questions were answered? Not answered?

**LITERARY RESPONSE** Discuss these questions with students:

- Did you guess the solution to the mystery before Franklin figured it out?

- Did the chapter organization of this book help you keep track of the action?

Also see the story questions and activity in *On Track*.

---

**Intervention** ➤ **Skills**

**Intervention Guide,** for direct instruction and extra practice in vocabulary and comprehension

### Answers to Story Questions

1. He could sell stolen bike parts there.
2. If his bicycle was stolen and brought to the shed there would be only one set of his tire tracks.
3. He figured out how extra weight on a bicycle can affect the look of the tire treads.
4. Marshall and the other kids solved the thefts by observing drawings of the tire tracks and comparing them to those made by the thieves.
5. Answers will vary.

The *Story Questions* and *Activity* below appear in the *Easy Book.*

### Story Questions and Activity

1. Why do you think Gary wanted to work in a bicycle shop?
2. How did the kids decide Phil was in on the robberies by looking at his bike tracks at the shed?
3. What important information did Marshall find that led him to solving the mystery?
4. What is the main idea of the story?
5. Explain how the four friends in this story used some of the scientific methods described in *How to Think Like a Scientist.*

### Your Own Special ID Mark

The marks Franklin made on his bike helped him identify his bike. On a sheet of paper, design a personal ID mark or logo that you might use to label your bike or another special possession. Explain how you came up with the ID mark and what you would plan to use it for.

*from On Track*

# Leveled Books

## INDEPENDENT

### The Ladder of Truth

☑ **Important and Unimportant Information**

☑ **Instructional Vocabulary:** *assignments, automatically, carelessly, normally, observations, swerved*

## Guided Reading

**PREVIEW AND PREDICT** Ask students to preview the illustrations and to predict what the story will be about.

**SET PURPOSES** Students should decide what they want to learn before they begin to read.

**READ THE BOOK** Have students read the story independently. Then use the questions below to emphasize reading strategies.

**Pages 2, 3, and 4:** List the information that was important and unimportant in solving the mystery. (Uncle Jim's comparison of a cat and skunk was important information —as was noticing the cat's paw prints were deeper than the others. The name of the cat and the fact that she was under a raspberry bush were unimportant.) *Important and Unimportant Information*

**Page 6:** How did Faulds know that the first burglary suspect was innocent? (His hand prints did not match the prints left on the wall.) *Draw Conclusions*

**Pages 12 and 13:** How did Koehler reach the conclusion that Hauptmann was the kidnapper? (The ladder provided the clues leading Koehler to suspect Hauptmann.) *Draw Conclusions*

**Page 16:** What does *swerved* mean? (turned from a straight course) What are some synonyms for this word? (turned, veered) *Instructional Vocabulary*

**RETURN TO PREDICTIONS AND PURPOSES** Review students' predictions and reasons for reading. Which predictions were accurate? Did they find answers to their questions?

**LITERARY RESPONSE** Discuss these questions with students:

- Which of the four mysteries—the missing cat, the mistaken thief, the kidnapping, or the traffic accident—did you think was the most interesting? Why?

- How do you think forensic science has changed crime investigation?

Also see the story questions and activity in *The Ladder of Truth.*

### Answers to Story Questions

1. Her first four tracks were deeper than the rest.
2. If he could find where the second piece came from, he might find a connection between it and the first piece of wood he traced. That connection might lead him to the kidnapper.
3. The dimensions are needed to reconstruct the room accurately in the animation.
4. Forensic scientists use scientific methods to uncover the truth and solve crimes.
5. Answers will vary.

The *Story Questions* and *Activity* below appear in the *Independent Book.*

### Story Questions and Activity

1. How did Uncle Jim know Fluffy had jumped down from something into the snow?
2. Why do you think Koehler began tracing the second piece of wood from the ladder?
3. Why would a computer animator need the dimensions of a room to make a 3-D animation?
4. What is the main idea of the book?
5. Compare the forensic methods described in this story with the scientific methods described in *How to Think Like a Scientist.* What similarities can you find?

### Your Unique Prints

Use an inkpad and some white paper to make your own fingerprints. Carefully compare them to your classmates' fingerprints, using a magnifying glass. What makes each person's print unique?

*from The Ladder of Truth*

# Leveled Books

*The Speckled Monster*

written by Della Rowland
illustrated by Jeff Shelly

## CHALLENGE

### The Speckled Monster

☑ **Important and Unimportant Information**

☑ **Instructional Vocabulary:** *assignments, automatically, carelessly, normally, observation, swerved*

## Guided Reading

**PREVIEW AND PREDICT** Ask students to look at the illustrations through page 9 and predict what will happen in the story.

**SET PURPOSES** Students should note what they want to learn before reading the story. Have them write down a few questions they would like to have answered by the story.

**READ THE BOOK** After students have read the book independently, return to the text to apply strategies.

**Page 3:** List the important and unimportant information in the first paragraph on page 3. (The important information is the discovery of the smallpox vaccine. The information about the downfall of three civilizations and the mummy is unimportant information.) *Important and Unimportant Information*

**Page 5:** Find the word *normally* in the first paragraph. What are some synonyms for this word? (usually, ordinarily, generally) *Instructional Vocabulary*

**Pages 10-13:** What were the steps Jenner followed in proving his theory? (First, he proved that people who had either cowpox

or horsepox would not contract smallpox. Then he proved that if someone was injected with cowpox from a cow and developed an infection that person would be immune to smallpox. Then he proved that the cowpox injection did not have to come from a cow.) *Steps in a Process*

**RETURN TO PREDICTIONS AND PURPOSES** Review students' predictions and reasons for reading. Which predictions were accurate? Which were not? Did they find answers to their questions?

**LITERARY RESPONSE** Discuss these questions with students:

- How do you feel about Jenner's decision to experiment with his vaccine by injecting a young boy?

- Do you know of other viruses that some people believe you can have only once?

Also see the story questions and activity in *The Speckled Monster*.

---

### Answers to Story Questions

1. They thought if they could catch a mild case of smallpox, they would get well and then be immune from it.
2. He knew how to do controlled experiments.
3. Yes, because he realized that cowpox was stronger at different times.
4. Jenner proved his vaccine theory by using scientific methods, recording his observations, and doing step by step experiments.
5. Answers will vary.

The *Story Questions and Activity* below appear in the *Challenge Book*.

### Story Questions and Activity

1. Why were people trying to catch smallpox if it was so severe?
2. How did Jenner come up with an effective vaccine when others had failed?
3. Was it important for Jenner to know that just one milkmaid got smallpox after she had had cowpox? Why?
4. What is the main idea of the book?
5. Which of the scientific methods discussed in *How to Think Like a Scientist* would have been most useful to Edward Jenner? Explain why.

### What Do You Think?

Do you agree with the WHO's decision to save one stock of the virus for future research? Or do you think that even the last smallpox sample should have been destroyed? Write a paragraph arguing your point.

*from the Speckled Monster*

# Bringing Groups Together

## Anthology and Leveled Books

## Connecting Texts

**IMPORTANT AND UNIMPORTANT INFORMATION** Draw a chart like the one shown here on the chalkboard. Ask students to list important and unimportant information from each of the stories. Remind them that important information is information that would be included in a summary of the story and unimportant information would not be included.

| | How to Think Like a Scientist | On Track | The Ladder of Truth | The Speckled Monster |
|---|---|---|---|---|
| **Important Information** | • Make careful, complete observations. Gather your own information. | • Franklin scratched his initials on the bike. Yung Sun's cat and kittens have six toes. | • Uncle Jim is a forensic scientist. Skunks' claws are larger than cats'. | • Jenner discovered a vaccine for smallpox. It was the first vaccine ever. |
| **Unimportant Information** | • Observations not related to activity. Inaccurate information. | • Yung Sun belongs to a baseball team. The kids played a video game. | • The cat's name is Fluffy. The cat hid under a raspberry bush. | • Egyptian mummies show evidence of smallpox. |

## Viewing/Representing

**GROUP PRESENTATIONS** Divide the class into groups, one for each of the books read in the lesson. (For *How to Think Like a Scientist* combine students of different reading levels.) Have each group summarize their assigned book or a segment of the book in the case of *The Ladder of Truth*. Ask them to prepare a story-board to use in presenting the summary to the class.

**AUDIENCE RESPONSE** Ask students to pay careful attention to each group's presentation. Ask them if any important information was not presented on the storyboards. Allow time for questions after each presentation.

## Research and Inquiry

**MORE ABOUT THE SCIENTIFIC PROCESS** Each of the books has shown ways that asking thoughtful questions and making careful observations can help solve mysteries. Ask students to research the steps in the scientific process and find other situations in which the scientific method has been applied. Have students

- make a chart showing the steps in the scientific process

- add examples to the chart exemplifying how someone has followed the steps to find a solution

- combine the best of each chart to produce a wall chart for the classroom detailing the scientific process.

 Have students log on to **www.mhschool.com/reading** to find out more about the scientific process.

**OBJECTIVES**

Students will:

- distinguish between important and unimportant information.
- tell why facts are important or unimportant.

### Skills Finder

**Important and Unimportant Information**

| Introduce | 409A-B |
|---|---|
| Review | 431E-F, 463G-H, 501E-F |
| Test | Unit 4 |

## TEACHING TIP

**MISSING INFORMA-TION** Before reading "Science Fair" direct students to think about what important information might be missing from the report.

## SELF-SELECTED Reading

*Students may choose from the following titles.*

#### ANTHOLOGY

- How to Think Like a Scientist

#### LEVELED BOOKS

- On Track
- The Ladder of Truth
- The Speckled Monster

Bibliography, pages T78–T79

# Review Important and Unimportant Information

### PREPARE

**Review Important and Unimportant Information**

Review: Important information contributes to the writer's main theme or purpose. Unimportant information might add interesting details, but does not build on the main idea and can distract or confuse readers.

### TEACH

**Read "Science Fair" and Model the Skill**

Read the story "Science Fair" with students. Ask them to listen for important and unimportant information.

---

**Science Fair**

Your little sister asks you for help with her science project. "I've written my report," she says, "but I don't know if it has the right information." Her report reads:

"On Monday, I put different amounts of sugar and water in three glasses. I hung a piece of string in each glass. I put the glasses in a sunny spot on a shelf next to my bedroom window. ~~The ground outside was covered with snow. The pond was frozen solid.~~ The next day, I saw that the crystals had formed on the string in Glass #2 and #3. By Friday, there were lots of crystals in Glass #3 and none at all in Glass #1. I think more sugar helps crystals form. The End."

Teaching Chart 100

---

Ask a volunteer to identify the important and unimportant information in the story.

**MODEL** After reading the story I had a question: How much sugar and water were put into each glass? Without this information, the experiment is meaningless. The information about the frozen pond is off the subject. The information about the snow on the ground may also be unimportant.

Have students draw a line through the unimportant information and have them circle important information.

## PRACTICE

**Distinguish Between Important and Unimportant Information**

ONE

Create an Important and Unimportant Informational chart on the board. You may wish to set the chart up and have students copy and complete it themselves.

| IMPORTANT FACTS | UNIMPORTANT FACTS |
|---|---|
| how much sugar and water in each glass | snow on the ground |
| which glass had most, fewer, fewest crystals? | the pond is frozen |

## ASSESS/CLOSE

**Tell Why Facts Are Important or Unimportant**

GROUP

Go through the chart with the class, discussing why each fact is important or unimportant. Student assessments may differ; therefore, stress the importance of justifying their assessments.

**ALTERNATE TEACHING STRATEGY**

**IMPORTANT AND UNIMPORTANT INFORMATION**

**For a different approach to teaching this skill, see page T64.**

**i Intervention ▶ Skills Intervention Guide,** for direct instruction and extra practice with important and unimportant information

# Meeting Individual Needs for Comprehension

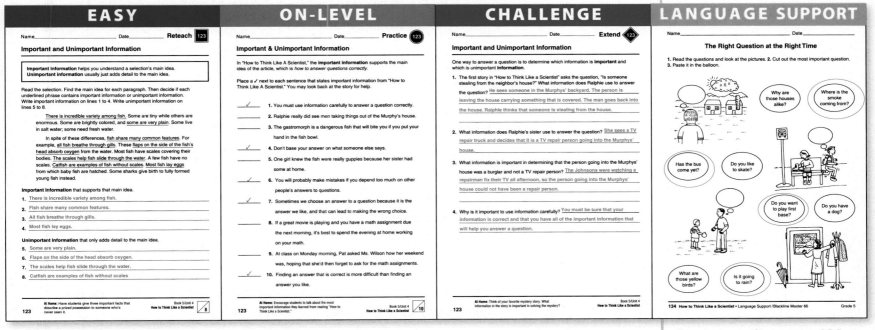

**Reteach, 123**          **Practice, 123**          **Extend, 123**          **Language Support, 134**

**431F**

**OBJECTIVES**

**Students will:**

- identify relevant information.
- use information to draw conclusion.

### Skills Finder

**Draw Conclusions**

| | |
|---|---|
| Introduce | 407G-H |
| Review | 431G-H, 491G-H, 647G-H, 673G-H, 717G-H |
| Test | Unit 4, Unit 6 |
| Maintain | 687 |

### TEACHING TIP

**MANAGEMENT** Before beginning to read "Sarah and Nick," tell students to take out blank paper and drawing materials.

# Review Draw Conclusions

**PREPARE**

**Discuss Drawing Conclusions**

Review: Drawing conclusions requires logical reasoning—putting together two or more ideas or pieces of information to reach a conclusion.

**TEACH**

**Read "Sarah and Nick" and Model the Skill**

Read the story "Sarah and Nick" with students. Ask students to think about what Nick looks like.

---

**Sarah and Nick**

Nick really wanted to go sledding with Sarah. He liked to jump and run and dig in the snow. And he loved to be with Sarah.

Nick watched Sarah as she put on her coat and hat and mittens. Nick's big, brown eyes begged silently. "Please take me along!"

Sarah thought about it. She couldn't take Nick on the sled. Maybe her friends would watch him as she rode downhill.

But Nick always whines when she leaves him with someone. Yet Nick needs fun and exercise, too.

Teaching Chart 101

---

Ask students to draw a picture of Nick, but keep their pictures private.

**MODEL** At first, I thought Nick might be Sarah's little brother. The story says he has big, brown eyes and that he likes to jump and run. However, as I continued to read and learned that he "begged silently" and that he couldn't go on the sled, I began to change my mind. Then when I read that he "whines" when left behind, I realized that Nick was Sarah's pet dog.

Reread the story. Have students underline information that supports their conclusions about Nick.

**Identify Relevant Information**

GROUP

Have small groups of students share their pictures. Then have them list all the facts they know about Nick. Ask: Do you have enough information to draw a conclusion about Nick? If not, what additional information would be helpful?

### ASSESS/CLOSE

**Use Information to Draw Conclusions**

GROUP

Give students three additional facts about Nick: He has brown hair. He is one year old. He weighs 45 pounds. Ask: Does this information change your conclusion about Nick? (Sample answer: No. Nick is a dog. The additional information confirms my conclusion.)

**ALTERNATE TEACHING STRATEGY**

**DRAW CONCLUSIONS**

For a different approach to teaching this skill, see page T62.

**i Intervention** **Skills Intervention Guide**, for direct instruction and extra practice with drawing conclusions

---

# Meeting Individual Needs for Comprehension

## EASY

Name_____ Date_____ Reteach 124

**Draw Conclusions**

**Drawing conclusions** means making decisions based on information. The information can come from clues in your reading or from your own experience.

Read each story. Then circle YES or NO after each sentence to tell whether or not it contains a conclusion that can be drawn from the story. Give at least one clue for each Yes answer. Remember to use clues from your own experience.

Tomás couldn't reach the light switch. He began to cry. Stomping his feet, he tugged furiously on his mother's pant leg until she noticed him. Smiling, his mother scooped Tomás up in her arms. She saw him point at the light switch, so she quickly turned it on.

1. Tomás is a very young child. (Yes) No

Clues: Possible answers: He can't reach light; he cries in frustration; he reaches only to his mother's pant leg; she can carry him.

2. Tomás's mother is impatient with him. Yes (No)

Clues: (None.)

Sweat poured down Shasta's back as she ran across the pavement rippling with heat. It was only 6:00 A.M. Shasta paused briefly. She always took a short break during her workout to help herself regain her strength. Still, she had to get going. She had another 10 miles to run that morning.

3. The story is set in a very cold place. Yes (No)

Clues: (None.)

4. Shasta is a serious long-distance runner. (Yes) No

Clues: Possible answers: She was out jogging at 6:00 A.M.; she had a workout plan based on experience; she had 10 more miles to run.

Book 5/Unit 4
**How to Think Like a Scientist**
At Home: Have students tell what other reasonable conclusions they can draw from the stories.
124

## ON-LEVEL

Name_____ Date_____ Practice 124

**Draw Conclusions**

Since authors don't always tell readers exactly how the characters in a story feel, you must sometimes draw your own conclusions. To **draw a conclusion**, you rely on what you know from personal life experience and story clues.

Read the situation below, and answer each question. Then describe the clues that helped you draw each conclusion.

Andrea and Mario had been working in their grandfather's garden all afternoon. Mario squinted into the sun. It was time for a rest. He slumped down in the shade and wiped his sweaty brow. Then he reached for the water bottle for a cool, refreshing drink. Andrea stopped weeding and joined him under the pear tree. He passed her the cold water bottle from their picnic basket. Andrea quickly gulped down what was left of it. As usual, Mario hadn't left much for her. Andrea went to back to work, while Mario rested.

1. From what you just read, how do you think Andrea and Mario are related? _____
They are either brother and sister or cousins.

2. Story clue: They are working in their grandfather's garden; they know each other's habits.

3. What is the weather like? It is hot and sunny.

4. Story clue: Mario squinted into the sun; he slumped down in the shade to rest; his brow was sweaty.

5. What kind of worker is Andrea? She is a hard worker; she rests for only a short time.

6. Story clue: Andrea goes right back to work; she doesn't rest very long.

Book 5/Unit 4
**How to Think Like a Scientist**
At Home: Encourage students to draw conclusions about some stories that they have read.
124

## CHALLENGE

Name_____ Date_____ Extend 124

**Draw Conclusions**

The characters in all three stories answer questions by **drawing conclusions**. Choose one story in "How to Think Like a Scientist." Use the drawing conclusions chart to show how the character arrived at his or her conclusion. Make sure you fill in the important information.

**What is the Question?**

Possible Answers: Is someone stealing from the Murphys? What kind of fish is in the bowl? Is Ms. Wilson going to collect the math assignment on Monday?

**Examples of Important Information** Answers will vary.

| Someone goes into the Murphys' house and carries out a covered item. | You know what guppies look like. | Ms. Wilson has collected papers late before. |

**Conclusion**

Answers will vary.
The Murphys are being robbed.
The fish in the bowl are guppies.
Ms. Wilson won't collect papers on Monday.

Was the conclusion correct? Explain. Answers will vary.
Yes. _____
Yes. _____
No. _____

Book 5/Unit 4
**How to Think Like a Scientist**
At Home: The newspaper is missing from your front porch. The neighbor's dog was seen chewing on something. Does the neighbor's dog have your paper? What conclusions do you make?
124

## LANGUAGE SUPPORT

Name_____ Date_____

**What Makes You Think So?**

1. Read the questions and study the pictures. 2. Write the answer to each question.

Answers will vary.

Mike's game starts at 2:00. Will Mike go to the movie before the game? no

What makes you think so?
Because movies last more than half an hour.

Is it summer? no

What makes you think so?
Because they are wearing winter clothes.

Maria sits next to Amy. Are Maria and Amy friends? yes

What makes you think so?
Because they are sharing one tub of popcorn.

Grade 5     Language Support/Blackline Master 67 • How to Think Like a Scientist    135

---

**Reteach, 124**          **Practice, 124**          **Extend, 124**          Language Support, 135

# Introduce Root Words

## OBJECTIVES

Students will:

- learn to recognize a root word.
- learn to use root words to determine the meanings of words.

### Skills Finder

**Root Words**

| Introduce | 431I–J |
| Review | 491I–J, 501G–H |
| Test | Unit 4 |

**TEACHING TIP**

**WORD MEANING** To figure out the meaning of a word,

- look at the word parts you know.
- look at the part you don't know and ask yourself, "What other words do I know that have this same part?"
- use what you know to figure out meaning.
- check your hunch. Read to see if the meaning makes sense.
- if possible, check the word in a dictionary or glossary. For technical words, try checking a textbook or handbook related to the subject.

**PREPARE**

**Discuss the Meaning of Root Words**

Explain: Root words are word parts that form the basis for other words. Most modern English words have their roots in ancient Greek and Latin languages. Knowing the Greek and Latin roots of words can help students understand difficult words they read.

**TEACH**

**Read the Passage and Model the Skill**

Have students read the passage on **Teaching Chart 102.**

---

### The Art of Scientific Thinking

The scientific method is a step-by-step approach to scientific investigation. It is designed to help scientists find accurate answers to problems.

Mr. Murphy used the scientific method when he telephoned his neighbors to ask if anyone had seen the burglars. He was questioning, as scientists question.

The zookeeper identified the fish as gastromorphs. Yet the girl thought they looked like the guppies in her aquarium. Had the girl acted as a scientist, she would have told the zookeeper.

Teaching Chart 102

---

Help students identify root words.

**MODEL** In the second sentence I can see that the word *telephoned* has the root word *phon. Phon* comes from the Greek language and means "sound." *Tele* also comes from Greek and means "far." So when we use a telephone, the sound comes from far away.

Discuss with students other words that have the root *tele* (telegraph, television) and *phon* (phonograph, symphony).

**Using Root Words to Determine Meaning**

Have students locate the word *aquarium* in the passage. If no one knows the meaning of the root *aqua*, tell students that it means "water." Have students explain how this helps to determine the word's meaning. Have them use a dictionary to verify the meaning.

▶ **Linguistic**

**Creating Word Trees with Root Words**

Have students create a word tree using one of the roots they have studied. They could draw a graphic that looks like a tree, with the root word at the bottom, and its derivative words making up the branches. Students may find a dictionary helpful in completing this exercise.

▶ **Spatial**

**ALTERNATE TEACHING STRATEGY**

**ROOT WORDS**

**For a different approach to teaching this skill, see page T65.**

**Intervention** **Skills Intervention Guide,** for direct instruction and extra practice with root words

# Meeting Individual Needs for Vocabulary

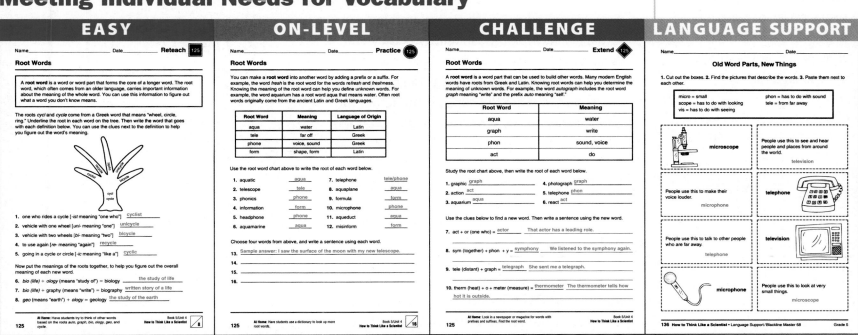

Reteach, 125     Practice, 125     Extend, 125     Language Support, 136

**431J**

# Expository Writing

## GRAMMAR/SPELLING
### CONNECTIONS

See the 5-Day Grammar and Usage Plan on articles, pages 431M–431N.

See the 5-Day Spelling Plan on words with /är/ and /âr/, pages 431O–431P.

## TEACHING TIP

**Technology** Some students may know word-processing tips or shortcuts that are worth sharing with the class. Invite them to explain and demonstrate what they know.

**Supporting Details** Have students review their drafts to make sure they have provided specific details to support their observations and the conclusions they reached, based upon these observations.

**Handwriting CD-ROM**

## Prewrite

**WRITE A SCIENTIFIC REPORT** Present this writing assignment: How does your cat let you know when it wants to come inside? How does a person eat an ice-cream cone? Choose an action to observe closely. Write a report that presents clear and accurate facts. State the purpose of your report in the introduction. Supply detailed facts in the body. End with a conclusion that summarizes your findings and tells why they are important.

**COLLECT FACTS IN A JOURNAL** Ask partners to brainstorm ideas about what to observe. Next, let students select their topics and determine how and where they will collect facts. Give students several days to collect and record data in their journals.

**Strategy: Organize Facts in a Chart** Have students use a three-column chart to create a story board with the following headings: Purpose (Introduction), Supporting Details and Facts (Body), Conclusion (Summary). Explain that the purpose tells why they are observing particular actions. Point out that the facts they collect will form the body of the report and are the supporting details for the conclusion. The conclusion tells what the observed details prove.

| Purpose | Supporting Details and Facts | Conclusion |
|---|---|---|
|  |  |  |

## Draft

**USE THE CHART** Ask students to review the facts listed on their charts. Tell them to check that their observations are in step order. If not, students should number them.

## Revise

**TAKE TIME OUT** Give students time to set aside their work before revising it. Then ask them to assess their drafts for improvement.

- How can I make the purpose in the introduction clearer?
- What important facts should I expand on?
- What should I cut?
- Does my conclusion summarize my findings?
- Do I show why my findings are important?

**PARTNERS** Have partners trade reports to get another point of view and then create second drafts.

## Edit/Proofread

**CHECK FOR ERRORS AND DETAILS** Students should reread their reports for spelling, grammar, accuracy, and punctuation. Have them revise once more to improve the clarity and organization of their facts.

## Publish

**SHARE REPORTS** Ask volunteers to read their reports aloud in small groups.

### A Scientific Report

I wanted to know how cold water has to be to become ice cubes.

1. I filled an ice cube tray with cold water and put it in the freezer. The water was 66°F and the freezer was 24°F.

2. After one hour, the water was just starting to freeze over. The water temperature was 40°F.

3. After two hours, the water was almost frozen over at 36°F.

4. After three hours, ice cubes were starting to form at 34°F.

5. After four hours, there were ice cubes.

Water must be less than 34°F to make ice cubes. When we buy a picnic cooler, we will want one that keeps things under 34°F.

## Presentation Ideas

**SKETCH** Have students make a sketch to accompany their reports. It should show the materials they used and any special way they were organized. ▶ **Viewing/Representing**

**INTERVIEW** Ask partners to take turns role-playing a scientist and a news reporter. Have reporters interview the scientists about their discoveries. ▶ **Speaking/Listening**

Consider students' creative efforts, possibly adding a plus (+) for originality, wit, and imagination.

### Scoring Rubric

| Excellent | Good | Fair | Unsatisfactory |
|---|---|---|---|
| **4:** The writer | **3:** The writer | **2:** The writer | **1:** The writer |
| • vividly states the reason for the observations in the Purpose | • states the purpose for the observations in the introduction | • may not state a clear purpose | • may not focus on the topic |
| • fluently states the observations that he or she has made | • states the behavior that he or she observed | • provides few observant details | • may give details that are not related to the purpose |
| • accurately describes the findings | • sums up the findings | • gives a vague summary of the findings | • does not summarize the findings. |
| • shows why the findings are important. | • attempts to show why the findings are important. | • is vague, or does not tell why the findings are important. | |

**Incomplete 0:** The writer leaves the page blank or fails to respond to the writing task. The writer does not address the topic or simply paraphrases the prompt. The response is illegible or incoherent.

For a 6-point or an 8-point scale, see pages T107–T108.

## Meeting Individual Needs for Writing

### EASY

**Comic Strip** Have students create a comic strip for one of the episodes in *How to Think Like a Scientist*. Have them use Graphic Organizer 30 for the cartoon frames. Tell students to use speech balloons for the dialogue. You may want to remind students how to convert dialogue in quotation marks into speech balloons.

### ON-LEVEL

**News Report** Have students reread page 418, paying attention to what father says about the robbery at the Murphy's. Then ask students to write a newspaper report about the robbery. Remind them to answer who, what, where, when, why, and how in the report.

### CHALLENGE

**Summary** Ask students to select a situation in the selection and relate it to a personal experience. For example, maybe you or a friend misinterpreted something that was said because it suited your interests. Have students describe how the expected and actual outcomes differed.

## Viewing and Speaking

**VIEWING STRATEGIES**
Encourage students to:

• tell the main ideas of the sketches that illustrate the reports.

• explain how the details in the sketches support those main ideas.

**SPEAKING STRATEGIES**
As students role-play, have them:

• ask questions to clarify what their partners say.

• make comments that reflect an understanding of the topic.

### LANGUAGE SUPPORT

**ESL** Select an observation for which students can make a tally and/or graph on which to record results. For example, put a bird feeder in one tree and none in another tree of the same kind. Have students tally how often birds visit one tree rather than the other.

 Invite students to include their reports in their portfolios.

# 5 Day Grammar and Usage Plan

**ESL** All languages have their own rules for using articles with nouns. Ask students to describe some of the differences in article usage between English and their first language.

## DAILY LANGUAGE ACTIVITIES

Write each day's Activities on the board or use **Transparency 17.** Have students correct the sentences orally.

### Day 1
1. Pete ran over snake.
2. It wasn't inner tube.
3. Could it be rain snake?

### Day 2
1. Ask yourself question.
2. Someone went into Murphys' house.
3. You didn't see men.

### Day 3
1. Mr. Murphy called on telephone.
2. You saw truck parked in front of the house.
3. Who were burglars?

### Day 4
1. Be careful how you answer question.
2. Someone from zoo came to the class.
3. Fish live in aquarium at the zoo.

### Day 5
1. He went to basketball game on Friday night.
2. She might forget about assignment.
3. He didn't know answer.

---

**Daily Language Transparency 17**

**Suggested Answers on Transparency**

---

## DAY 1 — Introduce the Concept

**Oral Warm-Up** Tell students that some adjectives appear before nouns. Ask students if they know any other words used only before nouns.

**Introduce Articles** Articles appear before nouns. Present the following:

### Articles

- The words *a, an,* and *the* are special adjectives called **articles.**
- Use *a* and *an* with singular nouns.
- Use *a* if the next word starts with a consonant sound.
- Use *an* if the next word starts with a vowel sound.

Present the Daily Language Activity and have students correct orally. Then ask students to write sentences using *a* and *an*.

 **WRITING** Assign the daily Writing Prompt on page 408C.

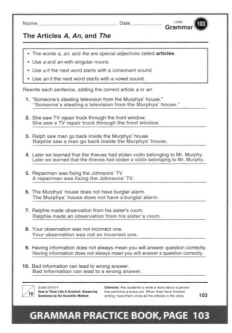

**GRAMMAR PRACTICE BOOK, PAGE 103**

---

## DAY 2 — Teach the Concept

**Review Articles** Ask students which is correct: *an answer* or *a answer, an question* or *a question.*

**Introduce the Article *the*** The article *the* is used with both singular and plural nouns. Present and discuss:

### Articles

- Use *the* with singular nouns that name a particular person, place, or thing.
- Use *the* before all plural nouns.

Present the Daily Language Activity. Have students correct the sentences orally. Then ask students to write sentences using *the* with a singular noun and with a plural noun.

 **WRITING** Assign the daily Writing Prompt on page 408C.

**GRAMMAR PRACTICE BOOK, PAGE 104**

# Articles

**Learn from the Literature** Review articles. Read aloud this sentence from page 412 of *How To Think Like a Scientist*.

> **The flashlight made a faint yellow spot on the pavement.**

Have students identify the nouns and their articles in the sentence. Ask students what article they would use if *flashlight* were plural.

**Identify the Rule** Present the Daily Language Activity and have students correct the sentences orally.

Ask students to read page 422 of *How To Think Like a Scientist* and write the articles and nouns that they find. Then have students write the rules for using articles at the top of a 5-column chart. Ask students to write the articles and nouns under the appropriate rule.

 Assign the daily Writing Prompt on page 408D.

**Review Articles** Write the articles and their nouns from the Daily Language Activities for Days 1 through 3 on the board. Have students list the articles and nouns under the appropriate rule on their charts from Day 3. Then present the Daily Language Activity for Day 4. Have students correct these sentences orally.

**Mechanics and Usage** Before students begin the daily Writing Prompt on page 408D, review the rules of quotations. Display and discuss:

### Quotations

- Use quotation marks to set off a direct quotation from the rest of the sentence.
- Use a comma before the quotation when the speaker's name comes first.
- Use a comma, a question mark, or an exclamation point to end the quotation when the speaker's name comes last.

 Assign the daily Writing Prompt on page 408D.

**Assess** Use the Daily Language Activity and page 107 of the **Grammar Practice Book** for assessment.

**Reteach** Write the following incomplete sentence on the chalkboard: *You see …* Display different pictures of singular and plural nouns and ask students to supply the article and the noun that completes the sentence for each picture. Have students write their sentences and then share them with a partner.

Have students transfer their charts from Days 3 and 4 to a classroom word wall and add any new nouns with their articles under the rules.

Use page 108 of the **Grammar Practice Book** for additional reteaching.

 Assign the daily Writing Prompt on page 408D.

---

# 5 Day Spelling Plan

The letter *r* has a strong influence on adjacent vowel sounds providing a variety of pronunciations. Pronounce each word and point out the spelling patterns of /är/ and /âr/.

## DICTATION SENTENCES

### Spelling Words

1. Do you like to play cards?
2. My mom will carve the meat.
3. I barely got there on time.
4. That stairway goes to the cellar.
5. His remark made us laugh.
6. I vary what I do because I like change.
7. We found a rare coin in the yard.
8. The workers are aboard the airline.
9. The cut left a scar.
10. Dolphins are scarce near the coast.
11. Draw the points on the chart.
12. He drew a circle and a square.
13. The repairman brought his tools.
14. She aimed at the target.
15. The fish are in an aquarium.
16. The barge carries freight.
17. Beware of the lions.
18. The foxes slept in their lair.
19. The artistic girl drew that picture.
20. Regard the storm with care.

### Challenge Words

21. Have you started the assignments?
22. I tie my shoes automatically.
23. Normally I walk home every day.
24. We make observations in science.
25. The car swerved around the cat.

---

## DAY 1 — Pretest

**Assess Prior Knowledge** Use the Dictation Sentences at the left and **Spelling Practice Book** page 103 for the pretest. Allow students to correct their own papers. Students who require a modified list may be tested on the first ten words.

| Spelling Words | | Challenge Words |
|---|---|---|
| 1. **cards** | 11. chart | 21. **assignments** |
| 2. carve | 12. square | 22. **automatically** |
| 3. **barely** | 13. **repairman** | 23. **normally** |
| 4. stairway | 14. target | 24. **observations** |
| 5. remark | 15. **aquarium** | 25. **swerved** |
| 6. vary | 16. barge | |
| 7. rare | 17. beware | |
| 8. airline | 18. lair | |
| 9. scar | 19. artistic | |
| 10. scarce | 20. regard | |

*Note: Words in **dark type** are from the story.*

**Word Study** On page 104 of the **Spelling Practice Book** are word study steps and an at-home activity.

---

## DAY 2 — Explore the Pattern

**Sort and Spell Words** Say *scar* and *scarce*. Ask students what vowel sound they hear in each word. (/är/, /âr/) Have students read the Spelling Words aloud and sort them as below.

### Words with
**/är/ spelled *ar***

| | | |
|---|---|---|
| cards | scar | barge |
| carve | chart | artistic |
| remark | target | regard |

**/âr/ spelled**

| *are* | *air* | *ar* |
|---|---|---|
| barely | stairway | vary |
| rare | airline | scarce |
| square | repairman | aquarium |
| beware | lair | |

**Word Wall** Have students create a word wall based on the word sort and add more words from their reading.

---

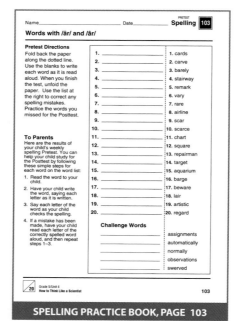

**SPELLING PRACTICE BOOK, PAGE 103**

**WORD STUDY STEPS AND ACTIVITY, PAGE 104**

**SPELLING PRACTICE BOOK, PAGE 105**

# Words with /är/ and /âr/

**Word Meaning: Analogies** Guide students in completing these analogies using the Spelling Words.

- road: truck, river:_____ (barge)

- dog: kennel, fish:_____ (aquarium)

- three: triangle, four:____ (square)

If students need extra practice, have partners give each other a midweek test.

**Glossary** Point out that each entry word in the Glossary has an illustrative sentence, which helps define the word. Have partners:

- write each Challenge Word and look it up in the Glossary.

- read each illustrative sentence.

- write an original illustrative sentence.

**Proofread Sentences** Write these sentences on the chalkboard, including the misspelled words. Ask students to proofread, circling incorrect spellings and writing the correct spellings. There are two spelling errors in each sentence.

> Bewair of the loose steps on the stareway. (beware, stairway)
>
> We saw rair fish at the aquairium. (aquarium, rare)

Have students create additional sentences with errors for partners to correct.

**WRITING** Have students use as many Spelling Words as possible in the daily Writing Prompt on page 408D. Remind students to proofread their writing for errors in spelling, grammar, and punctuation.

**Assess Students' Knowledge** Use page 108 of the **Spelling Practice Book** or the Dictation Sentences on page 431O for the posttest.

**Personal Word List** If students have trouble with any words in the **JOURNAL** lesson, have them add to their personal list of troublesome words in their journals. Have students underline the spelling patterns of /är/ or /âr/ in each word.

Students should refer to their word lists during later writing activities.

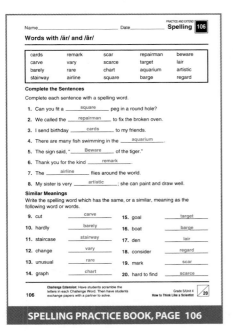

SPELLING PRACTICE BOOK, PAGE 106

SPELLING PRACTICE BOOK, PAGE 107

SPELLING PRACTICE BOOK, PAGE 108

**Concept**
- **Living on an Island**

**Comprehension**
- **Fact and Nonfact**

**Vocabulary**
- **barrier**
- **emerge**
- **fireball**
- **naturalist**
- **parallel**
- **teeming**

## Anthology

# An Island Scrapbook

**Selection Summary**  A mother and daughter make fascinating discoveries as they explore a barrier island from dawn to dusk, taking their sketch pads with them.

**Stories in Art** focuses on the **comprehension** skill

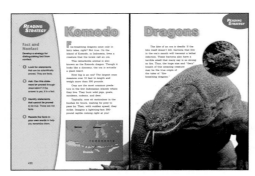

**Reading Strategy** applies the **comprehension** skill

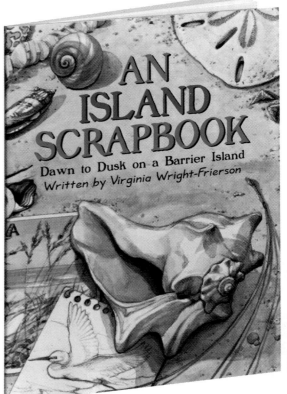

Listening Library

**INSTRUCTIONAL** pages 434–459

**About the Author and Illustrator**  Since she was a young

girl, Virginia Wright-Frierson has been drawing pictures. She often wrote stories to accompany her sketches. Today, Wright-Frierson is a professional writer and illustrator of books. Her daughter Amy appears to be following in her mother's footsteps. Amy enjoys drawing pictures, too, some of which appear in *An Island Scrapbook*. Wright-Frierson has dedicated the book to Amy, saying "[Amy] added so beautifully to this book and shared the discovery of this special island with me."

# Same Concept, Skills and Vocabulary!

## Leveled Books

**EASY**
Lesson on pages 463A and 463D

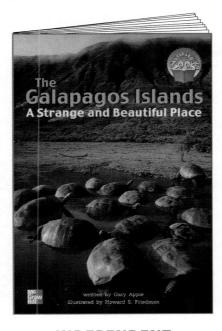

**INDEPENDENT**
Lesson on pages 463B and 463D

📙 *Take-Home version available*

**CHALLENGE**
Lesson on pages 463C and 463D

## Leveled Practice

**EASY**
**Reteach, 126–132** Blackline masters with reteaching opportunities for each assessed skill

**INDEPENDENT/ON-LEVEL**
**Practice, 126–132** Workbook with Take-Home stories and practice opportunities for each assessed skill and story comprehension

**CHALLENGE**
**Extend, 126–132** Blackline masters that offer challenge activities for each assessed skill

**Quizzes Prepared by** Accelerated Reader®

## WORKSTATION Activities

Social Studies ... **Tsunami,** *454*

Science ............ **Erosion,** *440*

Math ............... **Geometry,** *448*

Art ................. **Still Lifes,** *450*
                      **Environment Mobiles,** *461*

Language Arts .. **Read Aloud,** *432E*

Cultural
Perspectives ..... **Natural Remedies,** *444*

Writing ............ **Observation Report,** *460*

Research
and Inquiry ...... **Find Out More,** *461*

 Internet
Activities ........ **www.mhschool.com/reading**

**432B**

# Suggested
# Lesson Planner

An Island Scrapbook

## READING AND LANGUAGE ARTS

- Comprehension
- Vocabulary
- Phonics/Decoding
- Study Skills
- Listening, Speaking, Viewing, Representing

### DAY 1 — Focus on Reading and Skills

 **Read Aloud: Poetry,** 432E
"Souvenir"

**Develop Visual Literacy,** 432

☑ Review Fact and Nonfact, 433A–433B
**Teaching Chart 103**
Reteach, Practice, Extend, 126

 **Reading Strategy:** Fact and Nonfact, 433
"Komodo Dragons"

 **Intervention Program**

### DAY 2 — Read the Literature

**Build Background,** 434A
Develop Oral Language

**Vocabulary,** 434B–434D

| | | |
|---|---|---|
| barrier | fireball | parallel |
| emerge | naturalist | teeming |

**Teaching Chart 104**
Word Building Manipulative Cards
Reteach, Practice, Extend, 127

 **Read the Selection,** 434–459
☑ Fact and Nonfact
☑ Draw Conclusions

**Genre: Narrative Nonfiction,** 435

**Cultural Perspectives,** 444

 **Intervention Program**

---

## Curriculum Connections

**Link** Works of Art, 432

**Link** Social Studies, 434A

---

## Writing

 **Writing Prompt:** Choose one of the insects pictured on page 443, such as the honey bee or the cricket. Write a brief encyclopedia entry for it.

 **Writing Prompt:** Think of a time when you hunted for things such as shells. Explain how you found them.

 **Journal Writing,** 459
Quick-Write

---

## Grammar

**Introduce the Concept: Adjectives That Compare,** 463M
Daily Language Activity
1. This summer was warmest than last summer. warmer
2. We found the smoother sea glass of all. smoothest
3. That dock is oldest than our house. older

**Grammar Practice Book,** 109

**Teach the Concept: Adjectives That Compare,** 463M
Daily Language Activity
1. One crab is bravest than the others. braver
2. This crab has one claw biggest than the other. bigger
3. Crabs prefer the murkyer water. murkier

**Grammar Practice Book,** 110

---

## Spelling

**Pretest: Words with /îr/ and /ûr/,** 463O
**Spelling Practice Book,** 109–110

**Explore the Pattern: Words with /îr/ and /ûr/,** 463O
**Spelling Practice Book,** 111

---

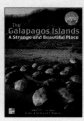

 = **Skill Assessed in Unit Test**

 **Intervention Program Available**

Read EVERY DAY

---

## DAY 3 — Read the Literature

**Rereading for Fluency,** 458

**Story Questions and Activities,** 460–461

**Study Skill,** 462
☑ **Read an Observation Chart**
**Teaching Chart 105**
**Reteach, Practice, Extend,** 129

**Test Power,** 463

 **Read the Leveled Books,** 463A–463D
Guided Reading
/îr/ and /ûr/
☑ **Fact and Nonfact**
☑ **Instructional Vocabulary**

 Intervention Program

---

## DAY 4 — Build Skills

 **Read the Leveled Books and Self-Selected Books**

☑ **Review Fact and Nonfact,** 463E–463F
**Teaching Chart 106**
**Reteach, Practice, Extend,** 130
**Language Support,** 142

☑ **Review Important and Unimportant Information,** 463G–463H
**Teaching Chart 107**
**Reteach, Practice, Extend,** 131
**Language Support,** 143

**Minilessons,** 411, 443, 445, 447, 451, 453, 455

**Writer's Craft,** 438

 Intervention Program

---

## DAY 5 — Build Skills

 **Read Self-Selected Books**

☑ **Review Suffixes,** 463I–463J
**Teaching Chart 108**
**Reteach, Practice, Extend,** 132
**Language Support,** 144

**Listening, Speaking, Viewing, Representing,** 463L

**Minilessons,** 443, 445, 447, 451, 453, 455

**Phonics Review** /îr/ and /ûr/, 441

**Phonics/Phonemic Awareness Practice Book,** 47–50

 Intervention Program

---

**Activity** Science, 440

**Activity** Math, 448; Art, 450

**Activity** Social Studies, 454

---

 **Writing Prompt:** Look at the shell collection on page 448. Write a paragraph comparing two of the shells.

**Writing Process: Expository Writing,** 463K
Prewrite, Draft

**Writing Prompt:** Pretend you are on the barrier island. Write a letter to a friend telling about the different animals you see. Include a description of the prettiest animal.

**Writing Process: Expository Writing,** 463K
Revise
**Meeting Individual Needs for Writing,** 463L

**Writing Prompt:** Study the list of things on page 454 that wreck the beach. Write a paragraph explaining which you think causes the most harm.

**Writing Process: Expository Writing,** 463K
Edit/Proofread, Publish

---

**Review and Practice: Adjectives That Compare,** 463N
Daily Language Activity
1. Raccoons are the larger animals on the beach. largest
2. The beach is rockyest than I remember. rockier
3. We took a longest walk today than yesterday. longer

**Grammar Practice Book,** 111

**Review and Practice: Adjectives That Compare,** 463N
Daily Language Activity
1. We saw the prettyer view of all from the dunes. prettiest
2. I found the rounder sand dollar today. roundest
3. Amy's paintings are largest than mine. larger

**Grammar Practice Book,** 112

**Assess and Reteach: Adjectives That Compare,** 463N
Daily Language Activity
1. Those are the thinner fish I have ever seen. thinnest
2. The sand on the beach is cleanest than on the road. cleaner
3. These shells are shinyest than those. shinier

**Grammar Practice Book,** 113–114

---

**Practice and Extend: Words with /îr/ and /ûr/,** 463P
Spelling Practice Book, 112

**Proofread and Write: Words with /îr/ and /ûr/,** 463P
Spelling Practice Book, 113

**Assess and Reteach: Words with /îr/ and /ûr/,** 463P
Spelling Practice Book, 114

# Read Aloud

## Souvenir
### a poem by Eve Merriam

I bring back a shell so I can always
    hear
the music of the ocean when I
    hold it to my ear:

then I feel again the grains of sand
trickle sun-warm through my hand

the sea gulls dip and swoop and cry
as they dive for fish then climb the
    sky

the sailboats race with wings
    spread wide
as the wind spins them round and
    they glide ride glide

my lips taste a crust of salty foam
and sandpipers skitter and crabs
    scuttle home

where I build a castle of Yesterday
that the high tide washes away away

while I keep the shell so I can
    always hear
the music of the ocean when I
    hold it to my ear.

## Oral Comprehension

**LISTENING AND SPEAKING**  Read the poem aloud. Ask students to listen for factual information and for information that is not factual. Afterward, ask:

- What facts about the seashore did you hear?

- What did you hear that was not a fact?

Then reread the poem. Point out that the poet calls the poem "Souvenir." Ask: In what way is the seashell a souvenir?

**GENRE STUDY: POETRY** Discuss some of the literary devices and techniques used in "Souvenir."

- Point out the use of alliteration (*wings* and *wide*) and assonance (*dive, climb, sky*). Have students identify

other examples in the poem.

- Explain that the sound heard in a seashell is actually air movement. The poet calls that sound "the music of the ocean." Ask: How does this metaphor fit the poem?

- Point out that the images in the poem appeal to different senses. Ask students to find images and identify the sense associated with each.

**Activity**  Give students copies of the poem. Ask one student to read the poem as the other mimes the actions. Invite students to switch roles and repeat. Consider videotaping students' performances.

▶ **Kinesthetic/Interpersonal**

# Develop Visual Literacy

**Works of Art**

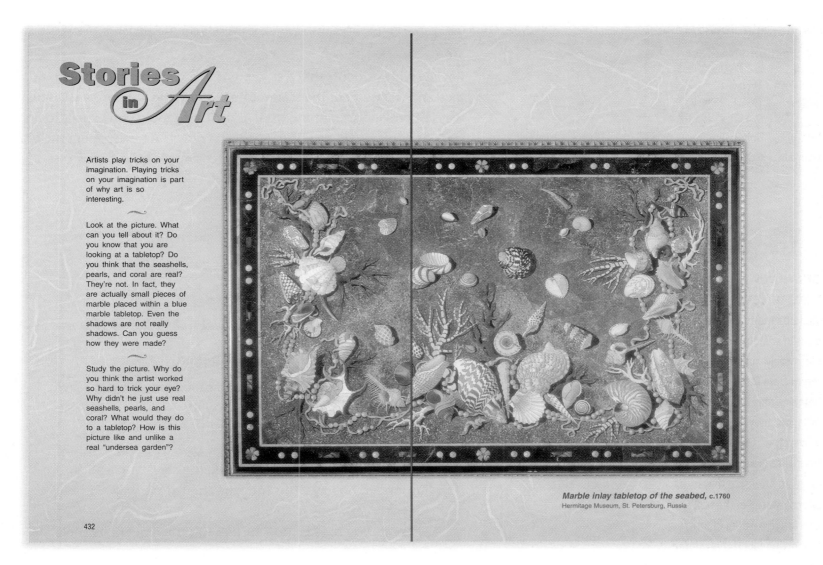

**Stories in Art**

Artists play tricks on your imagination. Playing tricks on your imagination is part of why art is so interesting.

Look at the picture. What can you tell about it? Do you know that you are looking at a tabletop? Do you think that the seashells, pearls, and coral are real? They're not. In fact, they are actually small pieces of marble placed within a blue marble tabletop. Even the shadows are not really shadows. Can you guess how they were made?

Study the picture. Why do you think the artist worked so hard to trick your eye? Why didn't he just use real seashells, pearls, and coral? What would they do to a tabletop? How is this picture like and unlike a real "undersea garden"?

*Marble inlay tabletop of the seabed,* c.1760
Hermitage Museum, St. Petersburg, Russia

432

## Objective: Distinguish Between Fact and Nonfact

**VIEWING** The artist who created this piece tricks the viewer's eye using light. Ask students to describe the artwork. Discuss how the artist made the tabletop look three-dimensional. Then challenge students to figure out where the light is coming from. Looking at the shadows will help students discover the answer.

Read the page with students, encouraging individual interpretations of the picture.

Encourage students to analyze the picture, differentiating between reality (fact) and illusion (nonfact). For example:

- The elements in the picture, such as shells and shadows, look real, but they have been created using pieces of colored marble.

- The shadows make the tabletop appear three-dimensional, but it's a flat surface.

**REPRESENTING** Have students create a mobile of an "undersea garden" that uses real and unreal objects, such as real seashells and those cut out of paper.

**OBJECTIVES**

Students will distinguish between fact and nonfact.

### Skills Finder

**Fact and Nonfact**

| Introduce | 167A-B |
|-----------|--------|
| Review | 199E-F, 221G-H, 433A-B, 463E-F, 493A-B |
| Test | Unit 2, Unit 4 |
| Maintain | 627 |

### TEACHING TIP

**OPINIONS AND INFERENCES** Explain to students that opinions (expressions of someone's feelings or ideas about something) are different from facts and nonfacts. Opinions may be based on facts, but they cannot be proven true. Explain that sometimes a reader uses facts to make an inference that is not directly stated in the text. Encourage them to identify supporting facts for any inferences they make.

# Review Fact and Nonfact

### PREPARE

**Discuss Fact and Nonfact**

Review with students that a statement that can be proven true is a fact, and a statement that cannot be proven true is a nonfact. Discuss ways of proving something true. Ask: Where would you expect to find facts or nonfacts? In an encyclopedia? A novel? A newspaper article? A science book? A fantasy? Which resources might have both?

### TEACH

**Read the Passage and Model the Skill**

Display **Teaching Chart 103.** Have the students look for facts and nonfacts as the story is read.

**What Happened?**

"Hey, look what I found?" Leah called out. Christina saw that Leah was pointing to the ground.

"What is it?" Christina asked.

"Well, it's a turtle's house and he doesn't seem to be home," Leah replied as she tapped the shell with a stick. It sounded hollow. "This turtle has gone for a walk without his shell. Let's look for him."

"Leah, you're teasing. A turtle can't crawl out of its shell," Christina said.

"Are you sure?" Leah asked.

Teaching Chart 103

**MODEL** I know it is a fact that the girls found a turtle shell and that it was empty. However, I wonder if a turtle sheds its shell like a snake sheds its skin. I'll have to look that up in an encyclopedia or science book to determine whether it's a fact or nonfact.

**Identify Fact and Nonfact**

Discuss with students why they think the turtle's shell is empty. Have students circle the facts and underline the nonfacts in the story.

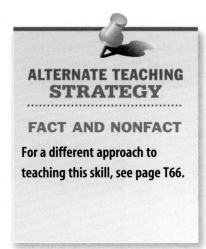

## PRACTICE

**Create a Fact and Nonfact Chart**

GROUP

Using a Fact and Nonfact chart, have students record the facts and nonfacts from the story. If there is something that they need to investigate further before determining whether it is fact or nonfact, have them check the Not Sure column. ▶ **Interpersonal/Spatial**

| STATEMENT | FACT | NON-FACT | NOT SURE |
|---|---|---|---|
| The shell sounded hollow. | √ | | |
| The shell was empty. | √ | | |
| The turtle had gone for a walk without his shell. | | | √ |

## ASSESS/CLOSE

**Distinguish Between Fact and Nonfact**

PARTNERS

Have students write several paragraphs on a familiar topic. Have them include at least two statements that are nonfacts. The rest of the information should be factual. Have partners exchange papers and use a chart to list the facts and nonfacts.

### ALTERNATE TEACHING STRATEGY

**FACT AND NONFACT**

For a different approach to teaching this skill, see page T66.

**Intervention** ▶ **Skills Intervention Guide,** for direct instruction and extra practice with fact and nonfact

# Meeting Individual Needs for Comprehension

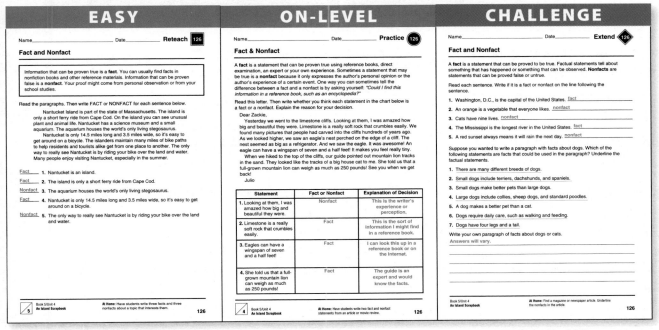

Reteach, 126     Practice, 126     Extend, 126

**OBJECTIVES**

Students will understand how to distinguish between fact and nonfact.

# Apply Fact and Nonfact

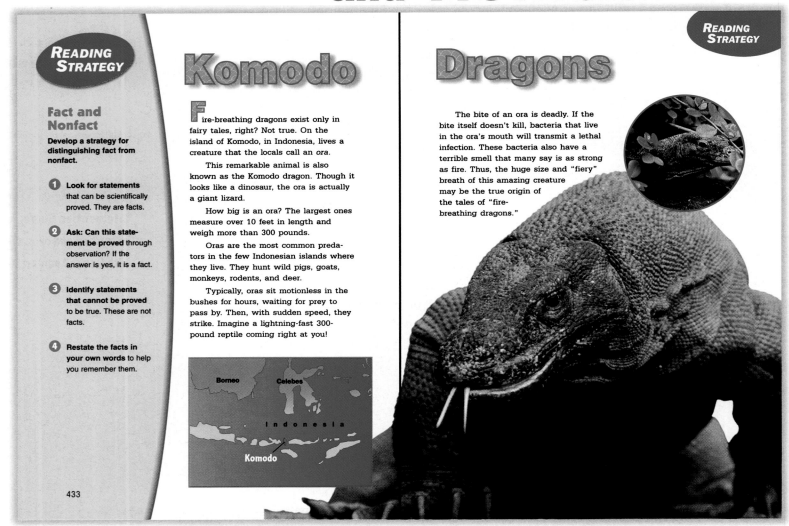

**READING STRATEGY**

**READING STRATEGY**

## Komodo Dragons

### Fact and Nonfact

Develop a strategy for distinguishing fact from nonfact.

**1** **Look for statements** that can be scientifically proved. They are facts.

**2** **Ask: Can this statement be proved** through observation? If the answer is yes, it is a fact.

**3** **Identify statements that cannot be proved** to be true. These are not facts.

**4** **Restate the facts in your own words** to help you remember them.

Fire-breathing dragons exist only in fairy tales, right? Not true. On the island of Komodo, in Indonesia, lives a creature that the locals call an *ora*.

This remarkable animal is also known as the Komodo dragon. Though it looks like a dinosaur, the ora is actually a giant lizard.

How big is an ora? The largest ones measure over 10 feet in length and weigh more than 300 pounds.

Oras are the most common predators in the few Indonesian islands where they live. They hunt wild pigs, goats, monkeys, rodents, and deer.

Typically, oras sit motionless in the bushes for hours, waiting for prey to pass by. Then, with sudden speed, they strike. Imagine a lightning-fast 300-pound reptile coming right at you!

The bite of an ora is deadly. If the bite itself doesn't kill, bacteria that live in the ora's mouth will transmit a lethal infection. These bacteria also have a terrible smell that many say is as strong as fire. Thus, the huge size and "fiery" breath of this amazing creature may be the true origin of the tales of "fire-breathing dragons."

Borneo  Celebes

Indonesia

Komodo

433

**PREVIEW** Have students preview "Komodo Dragons" by reading the title and studying the map. Ask:

- What does the title tell you about the passage? (The passage will be about a kind of dragon.)
- Where does this creature live? (on an island in Indonesia)

**SET PURPOSES** Explain that students will apply what they have learned about distinguishing fact and nonfact as they read "Komodo Dragons."

**APPLY THE STRATEGY** Discuss this strategy for distinguishing fact and nonfact.

- Can you prove scientifically that the ora's bite is deadly?
- Can you prove that oras hunt pigs and goats? How?
- Can you prove that the Komodo dragon may be the original fire-breathing dragon? If not, it is a nonfact, or an opinion.
- Restate the facts you have learned about Komodo dragons in your own words.

**Activity** Have students reread the passage and side notes. Then have them create a Fact and Nonfact chart for the passage.

# Build Background

**ocial Studies**

## Concept: Living on an Island

## Evaluate Prior Knowledge

**CONCEPT: LIVING ON AN ISLAND** In this selection, students will read about a mother and daughter who explore a barrier island and keep a record of their discoveries. Students should know an island is a body of land surrounded by water. Have them locate islands on a world map.

**COMPARE LANDFORMS** Introduce the terms barrier island and salt marsh to students. Challenge students to research these two kinds of landforms in an encyclopedia. Use a Venn diagram to record how they are alike and different. ▶ **Logical/Visual**

**BARRIER ISLAND**      **SALT MARSH**
**Different**    **Alike**    **Different**

*Graphic Organizer 14*

**KEEP A JOURNAL** Ask students to define the word *journal*. Tell them that naturalists, or scientists who study nature, keep journals of their explorations. Challenge students to observe nature carefully for a week and record their observations. Have them include drawings with labels or captions.

**PARTNERS** **WRITING**

## Develop Oral Language

**DISCUSS ISLAND SIGHTS** Ask students **ESL** to brainstorm a list of sights they might see on an island. (fishing nets, boats, beaches) If possible, bring in clippings of island settings from magazines and have students describe them.

Record the list of sights on the chalkboard. Discuss the meaning of each word and have students use the word in a sentence.

Ask students to imagine living on an island. Then pair non-native speakers with native speakers. Have one student be a reporter and interview the other about life on an island. Ask the pairs to add the new words they use in their conversations to the list on the board. Discuss the added words with all the students.

### TEACHING TIP

**MANAGEMENT** After you begin the Venn diagram comparison of settings with students, explain the journal-keeping activity. Have partners continue working on those activities.

As partners work, present the Develop Oral Language activity to students who need help with oral language facility.

### LANGUAGE SUPPORT

See Language Support Book, pages 137–140, for teaching suggestions for Build Background.

**434A**

**BJECTIVES**

Students will use context clues to determine the meanings of vocabulary words.

naturalist
barrier
parallel
teeming
emerge
fireball

# Vocabulary

## Teach Vocabulary in Context

**Identify Vocabulary Words**  Display **Teaching Chart 104** and read the passage with students. Have volunteers circle each vocabulary word and underline other words that are clues to its meaning.

**naturalist** (p. 453)  a person who specializes in the study of nature

**barrier** (p. 447)  something that blocks the way

**parallel** (p. 447)  being the same distance apart at all points

**teeming** (p. 441)  to be full; swarming

**emerge** (p. 445)  to come out

**fireball** (p. 438)  a sphere of glowing light

**Learning About Bats**

1. Joan, a naturalist, studies animals and plants living on trop-ical islands. 2. She enjoys island life and says the surrounding water provides a natural barrier, protecting her from the hus-tle and bustle of city life. 3. Today, Joan drove along the shoreline on a road running parallel to the beach. 4. The sky was teeming with bats, more than she had ever seen at one time. 5. The bats emerge from their cave each evening at dusk, coming out to look for food. 6. That's the time the sun, a giant fireball, descends into the horizon and cools the island.

Teaching Chart 104

### Story Words

These words from the selection may be unfamil-iar. Before students read, have them check the meanings and pronuncia-tions of the words in the Glossry beginning on page 760 or in a dictionary.

- pelicans, p. 445
- windswept, p. 445
- erosion, p. 454

**Discuss Meanings**  Ask questions like these to help clarify word meanings:

- What might a naturalist study?
- When might you erect a barrier?
- Name an object running parallel to the floor.
- Where might you see an anthill teeming with ants?
- Who is likely to emerge from a firehouse?
- Which celestial body could be called a fireball?

## Practice

**Island Talk**

PARTNERS

Have pairs of students pick a vocabulary word from the pile. The chooser must use the word in a sentence about islands.

▶ **Kinesthetic/Linguistic**

fireball   parallel   barrier

> Word Building Manipulative Cards

**Write a Poem**

WRITING

Have students use vocabulary words to write poems. Tell them to use as many vocabulary words as they can in their rhymes. Have students refer to the Glossary as needed. ▶ **Linguistic**

## Assess Vocabulary

**Use Words in Context**

GROUP

Divide students into small groups. Challenge each group to write and solve riddles about each of the vocabulary words. The riddles may use clues like what content area the word comes from, the word's definition, and a synonym or antonym of the word.

SPELLING/VOCABULARY CONNECTIONS
See Spelling Challenge Words, pages 4630–463P.

**LANGUAGE SUPPORT**

See the Language Support Book, pages 137–140, for teaching suggestions for Vocabulary.

**Vocabulary PuzzleMaker**

Provides vocabulary activities

# Meeting Individual Needs for Vocabulary

| EASY | ON-LEVEL | ON-LEVEL | CHALLENGE |
|---|---|---|---|

**Reteach, 127**

**Practice, 127**

**Practice, 127a**
**Take-Home Story**

**Extend, 127**

# Comprehension

## Prereading Strategies

**PREVIEW AND PREDICT** Have students read the title of the story and look at the illustrations. Explain that the selection tells a story through the main text, the illustrations, and the captions accompanying the illustrations. Ask:

- Which do you think you'll read first—the story or the captions? Why?
- What will the story most likely be about?
- Do you think this is a fiction or nonfiction story? Why? (Nonfiction. A scrapbook usually has information about events that really happened.) *Genre*

Have students prepare a Predictions chart telling what they think they will learn in reading the story.

| PREDICTIONS | WHAT HAPPENED |
|---|---|
| I will learn about sea animals and plants. | |
| I will learn what it is like to live on a barrier island. | |

**SET PURPOSES** What questions do students want answered?

- What is a barrier island?
- Why does the author include drawings in the story?

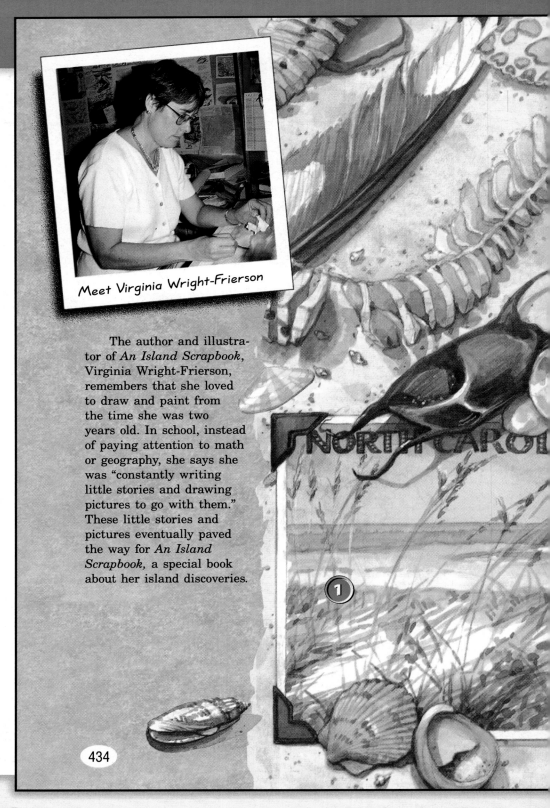

Meet Virginia Wright-Frierson

The author and illustrator of *An Island Scrapbook*, Virginia Wright-Frierson, remembers that she loved to draw and paint from the time she was two years old. In school, instead of paying attention to math or geography, she says she was "constantly writing little stories and drawing pictures to go with them." These little stories and pictures eventually paved the way for *An Island Scrapbook*, a special book about her island discoveries.

①

434

# Meeting Individual Needs • Grouping Suggestions for Strategic Reading

| EASY | ON-LEVEL | CHALLENGE |
|---|---|---|
| **Read Together** Read the story together or invite students to use the **Listening Library.** Have students use the Fact and Nonfact scorecard from page 435 to record information as they read. Comprehension and Intervention prompts offer additional help with vocabulary and comprehension. | **Guided Instruction** Choose from the Comprehension questions after the students have read the selection with a partner or listened to the **Listening Library.** Have students use the Fact and Nonfact scorecard to record information. | **Read Independently** Set up a chart with students, as on page 435, and have them fill it in as they read. After reading, students can use their charts to summarize the story and discuss what they learned about plant and animal life on a barrier island. |

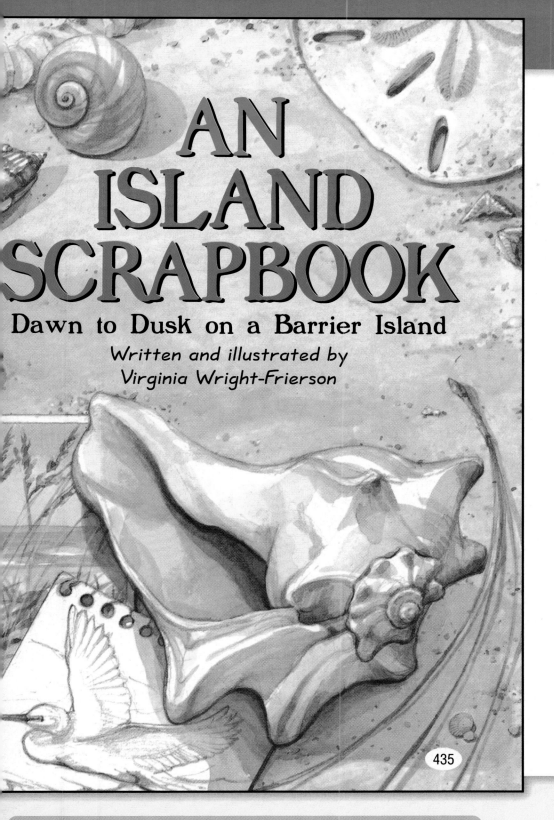

# AN ISLAND SCRAPBOOK

## Dawn to Dusk on a Barrier Island

Written and illustrated by
Virginia Wright-Frierson

435

A blackline master of the Fact and
Nonfact scorecard is available in the
**Language Support Book.**

LANGUAGE SUPPORT, 141

# Comprehension

☑ **Apply Fact and Nonfact**

☑ **Apply Draw Conclusions**

**STRATEGIC READING** Being able to distinguish facts from nonfacts will help you better
understand what you read.

Before we begin, let's prepare a Fact and
Nonfact scorecard. We'll use it to record
information about interesting and unusual
statements in the story.

| STATEMENT | FACT | NON-FACT | NOT SURE |
|---|---|---|---|
| | | | |

**①** **DRAW CONCLUSIONS** Look at
pages 434 and 435. What clues about
the setting of the story can you find? Where
does the story take place? (on a barrier island
off the coast of North Carolina) Explain the
evidence that supports your conclusion.

## Genre

### Narrative Nonfiction

Explain that narrative nonfiction:

• presents information in the context of a
real-life story.

• presents interesting facts about a topic,
usually in time order.

• may include photographs, illustrations,
charts, and other visuals.

**Activity** After students read *An Island
Scrapbook*, have them identify examples of
interesting facts about turtles that are presented in this narrative.

**435**

# Comprehension

**②** The illustrations show the interior of a summer cabin. Who lives in the cabin? Who is Amy? Who is planning to leave the island? Why? (Amy and the author live in the cabin. They are shown walking down steps. Amy is the author's daughter. It is September—almost time for the school year to begin. Amy must go home to attend school.) *Make Inferences*

**②**

Amy and I are awake before dawn on this September morning. It is the last week at our island house until next summer, and we don't want to waste a minute of it. We dress quietly, grab our packs, and slip outside into the cool darkness of the salt marsh.

436

## LANGUAGE SUPPORT

**ESL** Point out the two maps on page 437 and ask students to say what they think each one shows. Ask them to read some of the notes on the pages and say in their own words what they think the notes mean.

437

# Comprehension

**3** Look at the maps on page 437. What is their relation to each other? (The smaller is a locator map of the Southeastern part of the United States. The arrow on the locator map points to the barrier island. The larger map shows the features of the island.) **Where on the island is the cabin?** (in the southwest section) *Use Graphic Features*

### TEACHING TIP

**ILLUSTRATIONS AND CAPTIONS** Allow students time to look at each illustration carefully as you read. They should use the illustrations to monitor and reinforce their comprehension of the story. They should also look for information that is only in the illustrations and captions, not in the main text.

# Comprehension

**4** How long did the sun take to rise? How do you know? Why does the author call the sun a *fireball?* (According to the notations in the lower left corners of the sketches, it took the sun about 20 minutes to rise. It was bright orange like the color of a flaming fire.) *Make Inferences*

**p/i** **MULTIPLE-MEANING WORDS** Reread the second sentence of page 438. The word *fingernail* is used in an unusual way. Do you know what it means in this case? *Syntactic Cues*

"The sun!" calls Amy. It is a fingernail sliver, glowing above the distant trees. We unpack our watercolors, brushes, and sketch pads as fast as we can. I paint a tiny study of the sunrise every few minutes until the soft orange light becomes a fireball.

438

## Writer's Craft

### METAPHOR

Explain: A metaphor compares two different things without using a comparison word such as *like* or *as*. A metaphor often connects the two unrelated things with words like *am, is,* or *was*.

Example: Read aloud the two sentences that begin page 438. Ask: What two things is the writer comparing in these sentences? (The rising sun is compared to a fingernail sliver.) Discuss how this metaphor creates a vivid image in the reader's mind.

Have students write a metaphor that involves the sun, moon, a planet, or some other celestial object such as a meteor or comet. Encourage students to make a striking comparison that creates a vivid image in the reader's mind.

**p/i** **PREVENTION/INTERVENTION**

**MULTIPLE-MEANING WORDS** The word *fingernail* can have more than one meaning. Ask students if they know what it means in this case. Is it used as a noun or an adjective? The word *fingernail* is used as an adjective to describe the sun, referring to the shape of the tip of a fingernail. Have students demonstrate their understanding by pantomiming their fingernails "rising" above the edge of a book. *Syntactic Cues*

clapper rail - often heard but rarely seen

Amy

Amy paints one sunrise study with more detail of the fiery sky and choppy water. As we work, we listen to the whisper of the rustling cordgrass, the lapping of the tide, the call of a clapper rail, and the skittering and claw-clicking of fiddler crabs. The warming breezes bring us the rich muddy smell of the salt marsh.

**5**

439

# Comprehension

**5** **FACT AND NONFACT** Let's use the Fact and Nonfact scorecard to keep track of some of the most interesting and unusual information about plant and animal life on the barrier island. For details we can verify in a science book, an encyclopedia, or other source, we'll put a check in the "fact" column. Details that cannot be verified get a check in the "nonfact" column. Details we're not sure of get a check in the "not sure" column. We'll figure out how to verify those after we finish reading.

***MODEL*** I know that often animals are given a name that reflects how they look or move. I wonder if this is why the fiddler crab has an unusual name. I'm going to put this information on my scorecard. I'm going to say that I'm not sure if this is a fact. I can find out by reading about fiddler crabs in an encyclopedia.

| STATEMENT | FACT | NON-FACT | NOT SURE |
|---|---|---|---|
| Fiddler crabs get their name from how they look. | | | √ |

# Comprehension

**6** Read the journal entry on page 440. Why do you think the author wrote it? (The entry describes a salt marsh. Since the story takes place on a salt marsh, it is important for the reader to know something about one.) *Author's Purpose*

---

### TEACHING TIP

**ILLUSTRATIONS** You may wish to show students color photographs of some of the plant and animal life mentioned in the story from an encyclopedia or other reference source. Point out to students that the art contains important text on pages 440–441 and throughout the rest of the story.

*sand fence and shadows*

440

---

## Cross Curricular: Science

**EROSION** Erosion is a natural wearing away of a surface over time. Sometimes people take measures to protect land against erosion.

• Ask students how a sand fence might help keep a beach from eroding.

**RESEARCH AND INQUIRY** Have students research measures to control wind erosion, such as those adopted during the Dust Bowl.

Have students illustrate their findings.
▶ **Linguistic/Spatial**

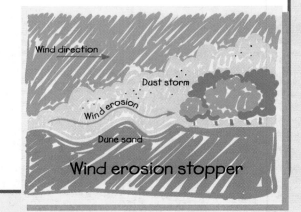

Wind direction

Dust storm

Wind erosion

Dune sand

**Wind erosion stopper**

female

ale fiddler loses his big
e other will grow large.
grow a new small claw
e of the lost one!
ale fights with the large
nd also waves it to attract
ale. He eats by scooping up
ith the small claw, sucking
ne nutrients, then discarding
st in piles of tiny mudballs.
e female can shovel in food
n both of her claws.

When our paintings are finished, we walk under the old dock to look at the mudflats teeming with fiddler crabs and patterned with the tracks of night-prowling raccoons.

One fiddler threatens us with his huge violin-shaped claw while the others vanish into their burrows. In a few hours, the water will reach the high tide mark on the dock piling. The fiddlers will plug up their tunnels with a mud-ball and wait for low tide to return.

**(7)**

**441**

# Comprehension

**(7) DRAW CONCLUSIONS** Fiddler crabs burrow tunnels into the sand. Why do they use mud balls to plug up their tunnels during high tide? What information does the story provide to support your conclusion? (Mud balls keep water from seeping into the tunnel where the crabs wait for low tide. Water entering the tunnels could collapse them and wash the crabs out to sea.)

**(p/i) MULTIPLE-MEANING WORDS** Reread the second sentence in the second paragraph. Do you know what the word *piling* means as it is used in this sentence? *Syntactic Cues*

## Minilesson

### REVIEW/MAINTAIN

### /îr/ and /ûr/

Remind students that the sound /ûr/ can have several spellings including *ur* and *er*.

- Ask students to find a word on page 441 with the /ûr/ sound spelled *ur*. (burrows)
- Ask students to find a word in the journal on page 441 with the /ûr/ sound spelled *er*. (her)
- Point out the /ûr/ sound is close to the unaccented vowel sound /ər/ in *fiddler*. Also contrast /ûr/ with the sound /îr/, as in the word *deer* on page 444. *Graphophonic Cues*

**Activity** Ask students to keep a list of /ûr/ words as they read the story. Have them keep a list of /îr/ words, too.

 **Phonics Intervention Guide**

## (p/i) PREVENTION/INTERVENTION

**MULTIPLE-MEANING WORDS** Ask students if the word *piling* is used here as a verb or a noun. (noun) Explain that *piling* has a familiar meaning as a verb but a very different and unrelated meaning when it is used as a noun. Tell students that a *pile* is a large, heavy piece of wood driven into the earth as a foundation to support a building or a deck. Several piles are referred to as *pilings*. Have students point to the pilings in the illustration and explain their purpose in order to verify their understanding. *Syntactic Cues*

# Comprehension

## SELF-MONITORING STRATEGY

**ASK FOR HELP** Students should ask for help with parts of the story they find confusing. Explain that discussing confusing passages with a partner or with the teacher will help a reader gain clarity. Encourage them to begin their discussions by saying "What does the paragraph on page 443 mean to you?"

Wax myrtle

*A pine tree knocked over during the storm*

442

Insects in the maritime forest

mosquito

no-see-ums

deer fly

ticks

horse fly

chigger (red bug)

ladybird beetle

carpenter ant

cricket

honey bee

cicada

laurel oak

dogwood

Yaupon

smilax vine

dwarf palmetto

red cedar

Our island is the northernmost range of this Sabal or cabbage

muscadine vine

We decide to walk through the maritime forest to the ocean. The springy, sandy floor is covered with acorns, palm fronds, pine cones and needles, grasses, and poison ivy. This ground cover provides food and shelter for deer, birds, and other forest animals.

**8**

443

# Comprehension

**8** Why do acorns, palm fronds, pine cones, and needles cover the ground on the barrier reef? Look in the illustration for clues. (Acorns fall from oak trees, palm fronds from palms or palmettos, and pine cones and needles from pine trees. These trees grow on the salt marsh.) *Cause and Effect*

## Minilesson

### REVIEW/MAINTAIN

### Root Words

Remind students that they might be able to determine the meaning of an unfamiliar word by looking at the root of the word.

• Explain that the root word in *maritime* is *mare*, which is Latin for the sea.

**Activity** Ask students to write a definition for *maritime forest*, keeping in mind both the root word and context clues. Have them check their definitions in the dictionary. Ask students to list other words based on the root word *mare*. (marina, marine)

# Comprehension

**9** **FACT AND NONFACT**  What interesting or unusual statements has the author made on the last few pages? Are any of the details clearly nonfact? Are there some you weren't sure of? Let's add to our Fact and Nonfact scorecard.

| STATEMENT | FACT | NON-FACT | NOT SURE |
|---|---|---|---|
| Fiddler crabs get their name from how they look. | | | √ |
| A raccoon's footprints look like tiny handprints. | √ | | |
| A blue heron is as tall as Amy. | | √ | |

Live oaks, pines, and magnolias form the canopy of the maritime forest. Their branches can withstand strong winds and salt spray. They are anchored firmly in the sandy soil by their vast root systems.

The dominant tree is the live oak, often draped with Spanish moss.

The tall trees in the canopy protect the more fragile and salt-sensitive plants in the understory: palmettos, young cedars, dogwoods, bays, hollies, and the toothache tree (Hercules' Club). Chewing its leaves or bark numbs the mouth.

**9**  Amy climbs up into her lookout tree for a bird's-eye view of the rainwater pond where the egrets roost at night.

She counts eight yellow-bellied turtles before they slip underwater. There are deer tracks and more raccoon prints (they look like tiny human handprints). Amy spots a great blue heron, almost as tall as she is, standing as still as a tree on the far bank, waiting to dart after a fish or frog.

444

# CULTURAL PERSPECTIVES

**NATURAL REMEDIES**  Herbs have been used as medicine since ancient times. Digitalis, for example, used in treating heart disease, comes from the foxglove plant. Ask students to discuss natural remedies and how they might have been discovered.

**RESEARCH AND INQUIRY**  Have students research medicinal plants.

▶ **Interpersonal/Linguistic**

*inter*NET **CONNECTION**  Students can find more information on medicinal plants by visiting **www.mhschool.com/reading**

REMEDIES
sage – the healing plant
mint balm – fever reducer
verbena – cold remedy
gentian – prevention of seasickness

We emerge from the forest shade to a beautiful view of the windswept grasses on the dunes, and the sparkling ocean stretching on forever. Pelicans fly low over the waves in a dotted line. We make our way carefully around the patches of sandspurs and prickly pear cactus to the clean, hard-packed sand of the ocean beach. Only shrimpers, fishermen, and shorebirds are out this early.

445

# Comprehension

 **WORD STRUCTURE/CONTEXT CLUES** Look at the last sentence. What do you think the word *shrimpers* means?

## PREVENTION/INTERVENTION

**WORD STRUCTURE/CONTEXT CLUES** Ask a volunteer to write *shrimpers* on the chalkboard. Ask:

- What smaller word do you see in this word? (shrimp)

- What does that word usually mean? (a small sea animal) Can it have other meanings? (yes)

- What does the suffix *-er* usually mean? (one who does)

- What do you think *shrimpers* means?

If students have trouble recognizing that *shrimpers* means "people who fish for shrimp," help them identify context clues, such as the word *fishermen*, which follows it.

# Comprehension

**10** Look at the journal on page 446. It features drawings of the fins of manta rays, sharks, and bottlenose dolphins. How are the shark fins like the manta ray fins? How are they different? (They are very similar. However, the shark fins have a squarer shape.) If you were standing on the shore and saw a fin above the water a short distance from shore, could you identify it? Explain your answer. *Compare and Contrast*

Amy being held up by the wind

We walk along, filling our hats with shells, a sand dollar, interesting pieces of driftwood, sea glass, and smoothed, round rocks. There are rows of small fish visible in the cresting waves. We munch on peanut butter crackers and stop often to watch the birds.

I make some quick pencil sketches of a snowy egret that has flown up right in front of us. Amy watches two bottlenose dolphins arching in and out of the clear water as they swim past.

446

Amy pulling her sweatshirt over her face to shield it from the blowing sand.

lls trying to fly in _____ gale.

...canes are nothing new here, and we are very ...ul and ready to leave in ...ry!

...is a [barrier] island, one ...chain of almost 300 ...e Atlantic coast from ...e to Texas.

...arrier islands protect the ...inland coast from the worst ...ds during hurricane season ...om June 1st to November 30th. ...ey are long, thin islands ...hat lie [parallel] to the coast ...and have ocean beaches, dunes, ...maritime forests with freshwater ...ponds, salt marshes, and tidal ...flats.

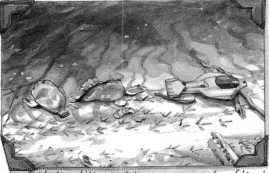

Debris still washing up a week after the hurricane. The ocean around our island is still dark brown from all the flooding of the rivers that feed into it.

A few weeks ago a small hurricane passed over the island. It was not expected to be very strong, so we were not asked to evacuate.

Amy and I were alone in our house. Luckily we live on the marsh side of the island, which is protected by the forest. **⑪** But we still spent a nearly sleepless night as the winds roared, the house leaked, and the windows were slammed open. Trees cracked and crashed around us and lightning lit up the marsh. The next morning we went outside to explore and take these photos.

447

# Comprehension

**⑪** How did the forest protect the author's house during the hurricane? (The forest protected the house against the full force of the hurricane winds.) *Make Inferences*

## Minilesson

### REVIEW/MAINTAIN
### Main Idea

Remind students that finding the main idea involves determining what a passage is about and which information supports that idea.

- Ask students to determine the main idea of the third paragraph of the scrapbook on page 447. (The paragraph describes barrier islands.)

- Discuss the details that support the students' responses. (These include the details *long, thin, parallel to coast, ocean beaches, dunes, maritime forests, ponds, marshes, tidal flats.*)

**Activity** Have students determine the main idea and supporting details for the first and last paragraphs in the scrapbook on page 444. (The first paragraph is a description of a maritime forest. The last paragraph explains the role of the island's tall trees.)

## LANGUAGE SUPPORT

**ESL** Students may not understand the term *evacuate.* Ask them to reread both sentences in the first paragraph looking for clues to its meaning. Ask students to brainstorm synonyms for *evacuate.* Then direct them to retell the paragraph using their own words. Students may use *leave, depart,* or *vacate* in place of *evacuate.*

# Comprehension

**12** Look at Amy's shell collection. How did many of the shells get their names?
(Many shells are named for their shapes: wing, silver dollar, slipper, ear, heart, razor.)
*Make Inferences*

Some beautiful shells were washed up from the ocean floor during the hurricane. Amy made a collection in an old crate she found.

448

## Activity

### Cross Curricular: Math

**GEOMETRY** Ask students to list the items in Amy's collection that have geometric shapes. The shapes needn't be exact, only representations.

- Challenge students to look at the illustrations on pages 450–451 and find spherical shapes.

Ask students to describe in writing several items on pages 448, 450, or 451 in geometrical terms. Ask partners to exchange papers and draw each item from its description.

▶ **Mathematical/Spatial**

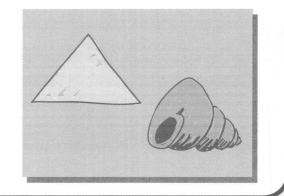

Oyster drills and moon snails can drill holes into shells to eat the creatures inside.
Shipworms burrow into driftwood (and boats. piers. and pilings).

Now we head back to our house to sort out our treasures on the front porch. Amy has gathered a pile of shiny jingle shells, and also a hat full of ark shells with holes in them for a wind chime.

She has been busy all summer making picture frames and flower pots with glued-on shells, sea glass windows, and a grapevine wreath for our door. **13**

449

# Comprehension

**13** **FACT AND NONFACT** Have you found information you would like to add to the Fact and Nonfact scorecard?

| STATEMENT | FACT | NON-FACT | NOT SURE |
|-----------|------|----------|----------|
| Fiddler crabs get their name from how they look. | | | √ |
| A raccoon's footprints look like tiny handprints. | √ | | |
| A blue heron is as tall as Amy. | | √ | |
| The wind can blow hard enough to hold a person up. | | | √ |
| Every shell once had a living thing in it. | √ | | |

# Comprehension

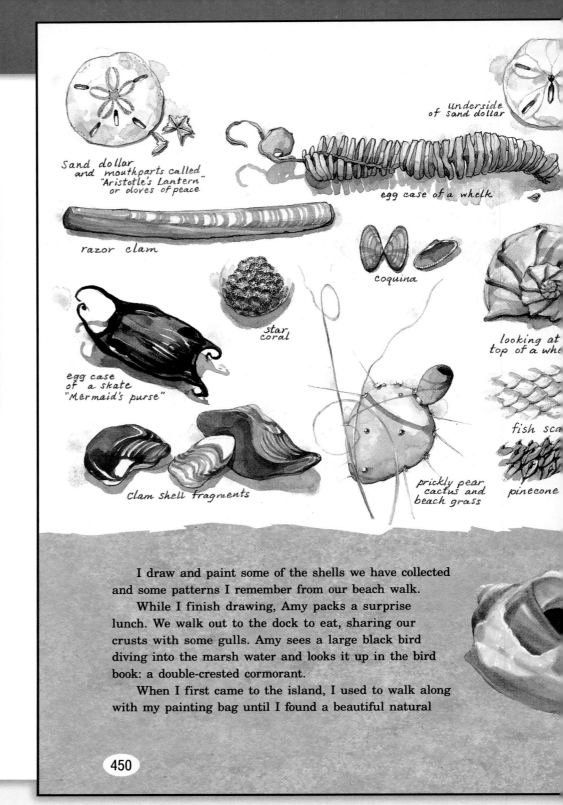

sand dollar and mouthparts called "Aristotle's Lantern" or doves of peace

underside of sand dollar

egg case of a whelk

razor clam

coquina

star coral

looking at top of a whe

egg case of a skate "Mermaid's purse"

prickly pear cactus and beach grass

fish sca

pinecone

Clam shell fragments

I draw and paint some of the shells we have collected and some patterns I remember from our beach walk.

While I finish drawing, Amy packs a surprise lunch. We walk out to the dock to eat, sharing our crusts with some gulls. Amy sees a large black bird diving into the marsh water and looks it up in the bird book: a double-crested cormorant.

When I first came to the island, I used to walk along with my painting bag until I found a beautiful natural

450

## Activity

### Cross Curricular: Art

**STILL LIFES** A still life is a visual representation of inanimate objects. The composition of a still life often begins with carefully selecting and arranging objects.

• Ask students how Wright-Frierson's "found still lifes" differ from composed still lifes.

Have students paint or draw their own "found still lifes" from the playground, their backyard, or a park. Direct them to focus on groupings of two or three items.

▶ **Kinesthetic/Visual**

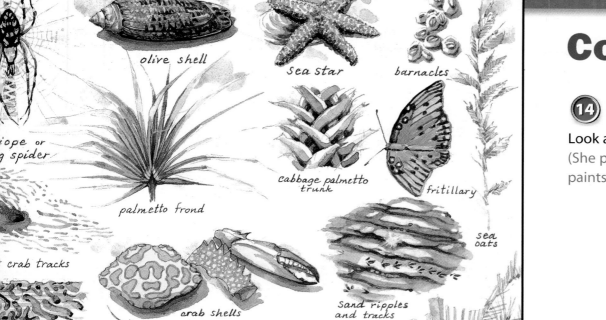

olive shell

sea star

barnacles

cabbage palmetto trunk

fritillary

palmetto frond

sea oats

crab tracks

crab shells

sand ripples and tracks

rm tunnels in wood

sand circles from sea grass

moon jellyfish

sand fence and shadows

urchin test

ope or g spider

arrangement of shells and shadows, maybe a feather or a sand dollar. I would plop down and paint it, my only rule being I couldn't touch a thing. I called these paintings "found still lifes" and sometimes I painted large oils on canvas from them, back in my studio.

Amy stays on the dock to read and I walk along the marsh to the river. I always feel like I will find something just ahead, and often I do.

451

# Comprehension

**14** What does the author mean when she writes "I painted large oils on canvas"? Look at the illustration on page 436 for clues. (She painted on stretched canvas using oil paints.) *Make Inferences*

# Comprehension

**(15) DRAW CONCLUSIONS** The author says that she hurried past the black skimmer's nest. Why? What does this tell you about the author?

*MODEL* I think the author hurried past the nest because she didn't want to disturb or frighten the bird any more than she had already. She knew the bird was faking an injury to distract her. This tells me that she knows a lot about nature. I think she also enjoys and appreciates nature.

---

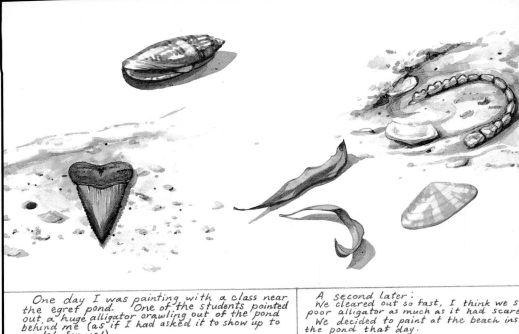

One day I was painting with a class near the egret pond. One of the students pointed out a huge alligator crawling out of the pond behind me (as if I had asked it to show up to model for us!)

A second later: We cleared out so fast, I think we sc[ared] poor alligator as much as it had scared[...] We decided to paint at the beach inste[ad of] the pond that day.

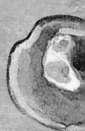

Once I found a fossil shark's tooth on the ocean beach. Once I found some false teeth sticking up out of the sand! I have heard of people losing them overboard when they get seasick.

**(15)** I see a black skimmer burst from her nest, faking a broken wing to distract me from her three small, speckled eggs. She flops and falls and limps, leading me away, then flies back, just fine, to sit on her nest again after I hurry past.

452

# Comprehension

**(16) DRAW CONCLUSIONS** Explain why the whale died. (It had eaten litter that it couldn't digest. The trash took up so much room in his stomach, there wasn't room for food. So, he starved to death.) **What can be done to protect other whales from a similar fate?** (Clean up litter from beaches and seashores. Stop littering from boats and ships.)

A month ago I came upon a dead baby whale washed up on the beach. When I called my naturalist friend to report it, she told me it was a baby sperm whale. Scientists had already studied it to learn why it had died. Its stomach had contained a marine oil bottle, nylon rope, a black plastic trash bag, a plastic buoy, and some rubber and Styrofoam. The whale had starved because there was no room for food.

453

## Minilesson

### REVIEW/MAINTAIN

### Make Inferences

Remind students that to make an inference they must read between the lines and notice what an author implies but does not state.

• Ask students to make inferences about Wright-Frierson's role in the class in the comic strip on page 452. (She was teaching the class.)

**Activity** Ask students to write two or three sentences using information from the text and the illustrations, supporting their inferences.

**453**

# Comprehension

**⑰ DRAW CONCLUSIONS** Who made the mysterious footprints? (Amy) Why did she use the jingle shells for toenails? (The illustration on page 448 says that another name for jingle shells is sailor's toenails.) **What does this tell you about Amy?** (She enjoys nature and playing tricks on her mother.)

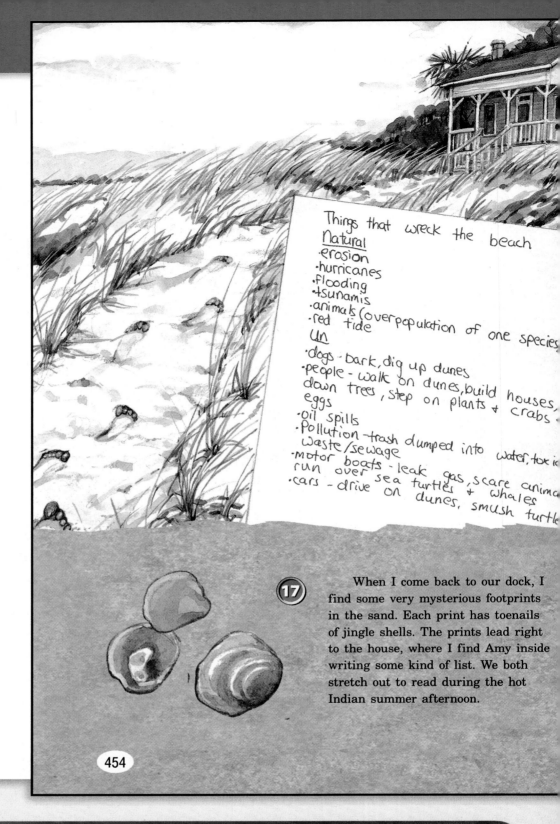

Things that wreck the beach
Natural
• erosion
• hurricanes
• flooding
• tsunamis
• animals (overpopulation of one species)
• red tide
Un
• dogs - bark, dig up dunes
• people - walk on dunes, build houses, chop down trees, step on plants & crabs eggs
• oil spills
• pollution - trash dumped into water, toxic waste/sewage
• motor boats - leak gas, scare animals, run over sea turtles & whales
• cars - drive on dunes, smush turtles

⑰ When I come back to our dock, I find some very mysterious footprints in the sand. Each print has toenails of jingle shells. The prints lead right to the house, where I find Amy inside writing some kind of list. We both stretch out to read during the hot Indian summer afternoon.

454

## Activity

### Cross Curricular: Social Studies

**TSUNAMI** *Tsunami* is the Japanese word for a very large ocean wave, caused by an underwater earthquake or volcanic eruption.

• Ask students how a tsunami could "wreck the beach."

**RESEARCH AND INQUIRY** Ask students to research tsunamis and hurricanes, listing similarities and differences on a Venn diagram. ▶ **Linguistic/Spatial**

| TSUNAMI Different | Alike | HURRICANE Different |
|---|---|---|
| • caused by earthquake • travels at 600 miles per hour | • destructive | • develops over warm ocean water • has a center called an eye |

At sunset, we walk back through the forest to the pond. Egrets are flying soundlessly down to roost in the live oaks, squawking only if one lands too close to another's sleeping spot. Soon there are so many it looks like snow has fallen on the trees. Amy counts 150 egrets, and one alligator in the middle of the pond leaving an S-shaped trail behind its powerful tail as it slowly circles in the dark water. **18**

455

# Comprehension

**18** **FACT AND NONFACT** Look over pages 450–455. What interesting or unusual information can you add to your scorecard?

| STATEMENT | FACT | NON-FACT | NOT SURE |
|---|---|---|---|
| Fiddler crabs get their name from how they look. | | | √ |
| A raccoon's footprints look like tiny handprints. | √ | | |
| A blue heron is as tall as Amy. | | √ | |
| The wind can blow hard enough to hold a person up. | | | √ |
| Every shell once had a living thing in it. | √ | | |
| A whale can starve if its stomach is full of litter. | √ | | |

## Minilesson

### REVIEW/MAINTAIN

### Figurative Language

Remind students that similes are one type of figurative language. A simile is a comparison of two unlike things using the words *like* or *as*. Authors use similes to help you form pictures in your mind about what you are reading.

- Ask students to find the simile on page 455. Ask what picture it helps them paint in their minds.

**Activity** Have students use similes to rewrite the descriptions of the sun on page 438, the fiddler crab on page 441, and the raccoon tracks on page 444.

# Comprehension

**19** **DRAW CONCLUSIONS** What guides the loggerhead turtle hatchlings toward water? (light) Support your conclusion with information from the story. (They sometimes go the wrong way when there are bright lights in the direction away from the water.)

**20** Reread the journal entry on page 456. How did the naturalists know to look for a turtle nest? How did they know where to look? (Sample answers: They keep a careful watch of the beach during nesting season. The mother's tracks led to and from the turtle nest.) *Make Inferences*

Two months ago:
We saw the tracks of the huge mother loggerhead the morning after she came ashore to lay eggs. Naturalists then fenced off the nest and covered it with wire mesh to protect the eggs from raccoons, foxes, crabs, and people. Sea turtles are now a threatened species.

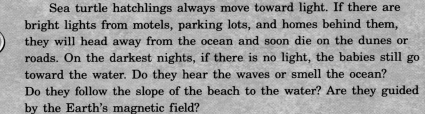

We race each other down the forest path to the beach. Reaching the dunes, we see a small group of people working to clear a path to the water...the baby loggerhead sea turtles are hatching!

Sea turtle hatchlings always move toward light. If there are bright lights from motels, parking lots, and homes behind them, they will head away from the ocean and soon die on the dunes or roads. On the darkest nights, if there is no light, the babies still go toward the water. Do they hear the waves or smell the ocean? Do they follow the slope of the beach to the water? Are they guided by the Earth's magnetic field?

456

# Comprehension

**21** **What does the photograph on this page show?** (A loggerhead sea turtle hatching from an egg.) **Why are they called hatchlings?** (because they have just hatched from eggs) ***Make Inferences***

Three days after a hatching, naturalists come back to excavate the nest. They count the empty egg shells and rescue any weak hatchlings that may not have made it to the surface. Only a licensed naturalist is allowed to touch a sea turtle or an egg or a nesting site.

Amy and I watch as the last of these little loggerheads push their way to the ocean, are tumbled back to shore by the waves, then finally swim out to deeper waters.

457

# Comprehension

**22** **FACT AND NONFACT** Let's revisit our Fact and Nonfact scorecards.

| STATEMENT | FACT | NON-FACT | NOT SURE |
|---|---|---|---|
| Fiddler crabs get their name from how they look. | | | √ |
| A raccoon's footprints look like tiny handprints. | √ | | |
| A blue heron is as tall as Amy. | | √ | |
| The wind can blow hard enough to hold a person up. | | | √ |
| Every shell once had a living thing in it. | √ | | |
| A whale can starve if its stomach is full of litter. | √ | | |
| Sea turtle hatchlings always move toward light. | √ | | |

Look at the "not sure" items. Do you think you can find evidence proving these items are facts or nonfacts? How? Where?

**RETELL THE STORY** Have students add more facts about barrier island plants and animals to their scorecards. Ask volunteers to retell the story. *Summarize*

458

## STUDENT SELF-ASSESSMENT

- How did the Fact and Nonfact strategy help me understand the story?

### TRANSFERRING THE STRATEGY

- When might I try using this strategy again? In what other reading could a Fact and Nonfact scorecard help me?

## REREADING FOR *Fluency*

 **ONE** Have students reread a section they found interesting.

**READING RATE** When you evaluate rate, have the student read aloud from the story for one minute. Place a stick-on note after the last word read. Count words read. To evaluate students' performance, see the Running

Record in the **Fluency Assessment** book.

 **Intervention** For leveled fluency lessons, passages, and norms charts, see **Skills Intervention Guide**, Part 4, Fluency.

We head quietly back to our cottage.

Tomorrow when we walk out to the ocean, the tide will have swept clean the shells and tracks from today. We will look at the ocean surface, broken by a fin from below or a boat or diving bird from above. Only traces of the hidden undersea world will wash up on the beach again: shells, bones and teeth, a jellyfish, a skate egg case.... We want to look deeper below the shining surface, to walk farther along the shoreline, to stay longer at our island home.

**22**

459

# Comprehension

## Return to Predictions and Purposes

Review with students their purposes for reading the selection. Were their predictions accurate?

| PREDICTIONS | WHAT HAPPENED |
|---|---|
| I will learn about sea animals and plants. | The selection told about and pictured plants and animals. |
| I will learn what it is like to live on a barrier island. | The author kept a scrapbook describing how she felt about living on a barrier island. |

### INFORMAL ASSESSMENT

#### FACT AND NONFACT

**HOW TO ASSESS**

- Have students review the facts in the story.
- Ask them if they think reading a selection such as *An Island Scrapbook* is a good way to learn science facts. Why?

Students should recognize that facts are statements that can be verified using reference sources or through direct observation.

**FOLLOW UP** If students are having difficulty with facts, model sorting out facts in an advertisement for a breakfast cereal.

## LITERARY RESPONSE

**QUICK-WRITE** Invite students to record their thoughts about the selection. These questions may help them:

- What are some interesting things you learned about plant and animal life on a barrier reef?

- How might this information increase your enjoyment and appreciation of nature?

**ORAL RESPONSE** Have students share their journal entries or discuss the information they found most unusual.

# Story Questions

Have the students discuss or write answers to the questions on page 460.

**Answers:**

1. Virginia Wright-Frierson, Amy's mother
   *Literal/Details*

2. Drawing and writing helps them remember what they see, increases their skill at observation, and gives them a factual record to show others. *Inferential/Draw Conclusions*

3. The scrapbook provides facts, in words, photos, and drawings, about a barrier island. *Inferential/Draw Conclusions*

4. The main idea of the selection is to describe a day on a barrier island. *Critical/Summarize*

5. The subject matter in the drawings is similar. However, Amy's and her mother's drawings are rough sketches with labels, made to record data. The picture on pages 432–433 is a composed still life meant as a work of art. *Critical/Reading Across Texts*

**Write an Observation Report** For a writing process lesson related to this suggestion, see pages 463K–463L.

# Story Questions & Activities

1. Who is telling the story?

2. Why is it important for Amy and her mother to draw exactly what they see?

3. How does the scrapbook support the facts in the rest of the selection?

4. What is the main idea of this selection?

5. Amy and her mother draw as they learn about the island. How do their drawings compare with the picture on page 432? What is one major difference?

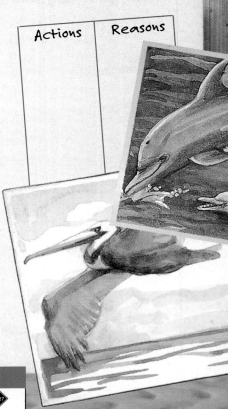

Actions    Reasons

## Write an Observation Report

"An Island Scrapbook" carefully observes and records the actions of some island creatures. Write your own observation report describing an animal you enjoy watching. Make a chart with two columns, labeled *Actions* and *Reasons*. List the animal's actions and the reasons it responds in this way. Use this chart to write an observation report of your animal.

## Meeting Individual Needs

| EASY | ON-LEVEL | CHALLENGE |
|---|---|---|

**EASY**

Name_____ Date_____ Reteach 127

**Vocabulary**

Use the words from the box to finish the sentences.

| emerge | parallel | barrier | naturalist | fireball | teeming |

1. The sand dune created an enormous _barrier_ between our house and the stormy ocean.
2. When the storm ended, we saw our cat _emerge_ from hiding.
3. Before noon, our town's _naturalist_ will be studying the storm's effect on the beach.
4. She can reach the beach on one of three _parallel_ paths that run next to each other.
5. When the sun comes out, our beach will be _teeming_ with life.
6. What does it mean when the rising sun looks like a _fireball_?

**Story Comprehension** Reteach 128

Write an answer to each question about "An Island Scrapbook."

1. Where does "An Island Scrapbook" take place? _on a barrier island_
2. What happens in "An Island Scrapbook"? _Amy and her mother spend the day observing the natural setting of their island home._
3. What kinds of observations are included in the scrapbook? _drawings of natural objects, photographs, maps, lists of observations_
4. How do you think Amy and her mother feel about the island and its natural places and creatures? _They value them and want to protect them._

At Home: Have students make one entry for an observation scrapbook about a place they really like.
127–128    An Island Scrapbook   Book 5/Unit 4   4

**Reteach, 128**

**ON-LEVEL**

Name_____ Date_____ Practice 128

**Story Comprehension**

Think about what happens in "An Island Scrapbook." Then answer the questions below. For help you may look back at the story.

1. Who is writing this story? Who are the main characters? _The author is Virginia Wright-Frierson. The main characters seem to be the author and her daughter Amy._
2. Where does the story take place? _on a barrier island_
3. How do the author and her daughter spend their days together? _They spend most of their time outside drawing, painting, and making observations._
4. Consider the title of this story. How are the handwritten notes pictured in the illustrations different from the writing throughout the rest of the story? _The handwritten notes are often like lists of facts and exact observations you'd find in a scrapbook, while the rest of the book tends to tell the overall story of what happened during their last week on the island._
5. At one point in the story the author recalls a storm that happened on the island a few weeks before, when she and Amy were alone in the summer house. What type of storm was it? _It was a hurricane that passed over the island._
6. What did they do after the storm happened? _They went out to explore, to see what damage the hurricane caused, and to take photographs_
7. What types of crafts did Amy use for her crafts? What materials did she use for her crafts? _She made picture frames and flower pots using glued-on seashells, windows made of sea glass, a grapevine wreath, a windchime using jingle shells and ark shells._
8. What was the author's one rule about painting the things she found in nature? _She could not touch anything she found in nature._

128    At Home: Have students create a craft or describe a gift they'd like to create.    An Island Scrapbook   Book 5/Unit 4   8

**Practice, 128**

**CHALLENGE**

Name_____ Date_____ Extend 127

**Vocabulary**

| barrier | emerge | fireball |
| naturalist | parallel | teeming |

In the story, "An Island Scrapbook," the author writes and draws a vivid description of wildlife on an island. Think of a place in nature that you have visited or read about. Write a paragraph describing the setting and wildlife you remember. Use as many of the vocabulary words as you can in your description. _Answers will vary but should include at least four of the vocabulary words in the appropriate context and part of speech._

Extend 128

**Story Comprehension**

Work with a partner. Find an example in "An Island Scrapbook" when the author makes a conclusion about something. Write the conclusion in the box below.

**Conclusion**

Sample answer: The sperm whale probably died of starvation.

Now make a list of the facts used by the author that led to this conclusion. Remember that a fact is a statement that can be proved true.

**Facts that Support the Conclusion**

Sample answer: The naturalist found many objects in the whale's stomach: a bottle, rope, trash bag, buoy, rubber, and Styrofoam. There was not enough room in the whale's stomach for food.

At Home: Find five facts about the wildlife on the barrier island in the story.
127–128    An Island Scrapbook   Book 5/Unit 4

**Extend, 128**

# Draw an Island Mural

Amy has been busy all summer drawing and making picture frames and flower pots with seashells. Now it's your turn. Use "An Island Scrapbook" for inspiration to draw an island mural. Work with a group of classmates to paint an ocean, trees, rocks, coastline, marshes, and beach on a long sheet of paper. Include some of the animals and plants from the selection. Give your mural a title and have your group sign it.

# Keep a Record of Facts

What's the difference between a fact and an observation? Choose three situations or actions, such as a dog rolling over, a friend laughing, and a tree rustling in the wind. After observing each action, write three facts about it in your journal.

# Find Out More

Amy and her mother create a scrapbook of the island. Pick one of the shells, fish, plants, or island creatures from the selection. Learn more about it by looking in an encyclopedia or on the Internet. Create your own scrapbook page of words and illustrations that describe your "island treasure."

461

## ART: ENVIRONMENT MOBILES

Ask students to use clothes hangers and index cards to create three different mobiles. The first mobile should show examples of insect life on Barrier Island, the second should show examples of plant life, and the third should show examples of ocean life. Students can make their own sketches or attach copies of photographs or drawings for each mobile.

**What To Look For** Three mobiles that illustrate examples of insect, plant, and ocean life on Barrier Island and that are correctly labeled.

# Story Activities

## Draw an Island Mural

**Materials:** a long sheet of paper, coloring pens or crayons

GROUP Encourage students to draw their murals to scale. Ask them to determine a way for each artist to use a similar scale. For example, make a list of items that might appear in the mural and assign each one a size. Another group may want to work on a mural in the style of Amy's collection box.

## Keep a Record of Facts

PARTNERS Discuss the differences between facts and observations. (Facts are true or real and can be verified. Observations are what a person has noticed and cannot be verified directly.) Have partners observe something of their choice and write three facts about it. Then have them compare the facts each chose to list.

## Find Out More

**RESEARCH AND INQUIRY** Direct students to the scrapbook on pages 440–441, 443, 448, and 450–451. Encourage students to choose an item with a scientific name (fritillary) rather than a common name (jingle shells). Encourage students to include as many details as possible in both their illustrations and written descriptions.

*inter*NET CONNECTION For more information about barrier islands, students can visit **www.mhschool.com/reading**

## FORMAL ASSESSMENT

After page 461, see the Selection Assessment.

# Study Skills

## GRAPHIC AIDS

**OBJECTIVES** Students will learn how to read an observation chart.

**PREPARE** Preview the animal behavior shown in the chart. Display **Teaching Chart 105.**

**TEACH** Point out that making a chart helps you keep track of and remember details. Have a student explain how the giraffe's height helps it survive.

**PRACTICE** Have students answer questions 1–5. Review the answers with them. **1.** giraffe, turtle **2.** a turtle hides in its shell; a giraffe runs **3.** hummingbirds hover and fly; giraffes stand and run. **4.** long bills on hummingbirds and long necks on giraffes help them get food; a hard shell protects a turtle **5.** It provides a factual, visual record.

**ASSESS/CLOSE** Have students make an observation chart listing details of the hurricane described in the selection.

# Study Skills

## Read an Observation Chart

As Amy and her mother discover, you can find out a great deal about an animal by observing how it eats, sleeps, reacts to danger, and interacts with other animals. An animal's behavior depends on its physical body, training, and skills. Its habitat—the place in which it lives—also influences its behavior.

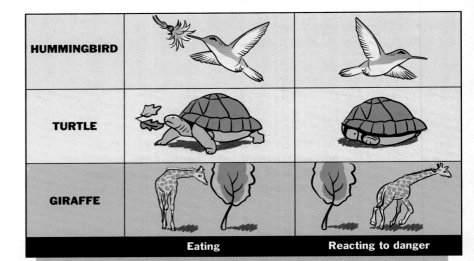

| | Eating | Reacting to danger |
| HUMMINGBIRD | | |
| TURTLE | | |
| GIRAFFE | | |

**Use the observation chart to answer these questions.**

**1** Which animals eat standing up?

**2** Compare and contrast how turtles and giraffes respond to threatening animals.

**3** Which two animals do you think use the most energy? Give two examples for each animal you choose.

**4** For each animal on the chart, choose one characteristic and explain how it helps that animal survive or adapt to its habitat.

**5** How does an observation chart help you gather facts and information?

# Meeting Individual Needs

## EASY

Name_____ Date_____ Reteach 129

**Read an Observation Chart**

An **observation chart** shows what someone has seen or noticed. The chart's title usually tells you what has been observed. Headings on the rows and columns help you find each piece of information on the chart.

Use the observation chart below to answer the questions below.

**Dogs at the Weissbergs' House**

| | Responds to Commands | Barks at Visitors | Chases other animals | Dog's age at house |
|---|---|---|---|---|
| Minnie | always | Only at Strangers | Only when she's told to | 2 months |
| Gray | about half the time | Sometimes, especially when it's dark | Only the neighbor's cat | 1 year |
| Swifty | always | Only at Strangers | often; loves to chase birds, cats, chipmunks | 3 months |

1. What is the title of the chart? Dogs at the Weissbergs' House
2. What do the column headings tell? the different ways the dogs behave
3. What do the boxes on the left tell? the names of the dogs
4. Which two dogs always respond to commands the first time? Minnie and Swifty
5. How does Minnie react when strangers visit the Weissbergs? She barks at them
6. Which dog only chases the neighbor's cat? Gray
7. How old was Gray when the Weissbergs got him? 1 year
8. Which dog do you think is the most well-trained? Why? Minnie, because she follows commands the first time; she barks only at strangers, and she chases animals only on command.

Book 5/Unit 4 An Island Scrapbook | At Home: Have students write a paragraph describing one of the dogs in the chart. They may add imaginary details that seem consistent with the chart information. | 129

**Reteach, 129**

## ON-LEVEL

Name_____ Date_____ Practice 129

**Use an Observation Chart**

Scientists and naturalists use **observation charts** to collect and organize information. Observation charts help them to monitor and track what they are studying.

Use the observation chart to answer the questions below.

1. Which baboon is pregnant? Lu-Lu
2. Which baboon is looking after Lu-Lu? Sunny
3. Which baboon took the grapefruits? Sunny
4. Which baboon is picking fights and taking food from the other baboons? Alpha
5. Which baboon is napping a great deal? Silver

Book 5/Unit 4 An Island Scrapbook | At Home: Have students make an observation chart to collect information about what happens at dinner time. | 129

**Practice, 129**

## CHALLENGE

Name_____ Date_____ Extend 129

**Read an Observation Chart**

"An Island Scrapbook" is filled with drawings and observations about the wildlife on a barrier island. You can organize information like this into an **observation chart.** An observation chart will help you see facts at a glance.

Create your own observation chart about the kinds of things that Amy and her mother take note of during their walks on the barrier island. Then fill in the chart below.

**Wildlife on the Barrier Island**

| Plants | Possible answers: red cedar, dwarf palmetto, muscadin vine, prickly pear cactus, dune grass |
|---|---|
| Insects | Possible answers: mosquito, tick, chigger, cricket, cicada, honey bee |
| Sea Animals | Possible answers: fiddler crab, yellow-bellied turtle, logger-head turtle, bottlenose dolphin, moon snail |
| Land Animals | Possible answers: raccoon, deer |
| Shell Animals | Possible answers: coquina, scallop, great heart cockle, oyster, angel wing |
| Birds | Possible answers: blue heron, pelican, black skimmer, egret |

Choose one category of animals, and use the information on the chart to write a descriptive paragraph about your category. Be sure to include facts from the story in your paragraph.

Answers will vary but should include information from chart.

Book 5/Unit 4 An Island Scrapbook | At Home: Make an observation chart about the kinds of objects you see in your kitchen. Create topic categories such as dishes, pots, and cooking utensils. | 129

**Extend, 129**

**Test Tip**

Work slowly. Be careful.

**DIRECTIONS**

**Read the sample story. Then read each question about the story.**

**SAMPLE**

## The Talent Show

During the activities club meeting on March 15, Mr. Gomez, the club advisor, announced that the Washington Elementary School would hold its first annual talent show. It would be held on May 15 in the school auditorium.

**TALENT SHOW RULES**

• Each group may enter only one act in the talent show.

• Each act must have at least two people but no more than 4 people.

• Performances longer than 10 minutes will be disqualified.

• Groups must provide their own stage props.

• All groups will be judged on the following: originality, preparation, and teamwork.

• No entry form will be accepted after April 15.

1 Which is a FACT stated in the Talent Show rules?

  A  Groups may enter as many acts as they want.

  B  Entry forms will be accepted on the night of the performance.

  C  Groups must perform a song.

  (D)  Entrants must provide their own stage props.

2 About how much time do students have to prepare for their acts?

  F  Two weeks

  (G)  Two months

  H  Six weeks

  J  Three months

463

# Test Power

THE PRINCETON REVIEW

## Read the Page

Have students read the entire page carefully.

## Discuss the Questions

**Question 1:** This question refers specifically to the talent show rules. Have students reread the rules under the boldfaced title. Then have students read each answer choice before choosing the best answer. Be sure students eliminate answer choices that do not match the information on the rules sheet.

**Question 2:** This question asks students to recall information from the portion of the passage that precedes the rules. Direct students' attention to that part of the passage. Students should note that Mr. Gomez announced the talent show on March 15th and that the talent show would be held on May 15th.

# Leveled Books

## EASY

### Tourist Trap Island

/îr/ and /ûr/

☑ **Fact and Nonfact**

☑ **Instructional Vocabulary:** *barrier, emerge, fireball, naturalist, parallel, teeming*

## Guided Reading

**PREVIEW AND PREDICT** Have students read the title and look at the illustrations through page 13. Ask them to predict what the story will be about.

**SET PURPOSES** Have students write questions they would like answered by the book.

**READ THE BOOK** Use the questions below to guide the students' reading and help them apply the strategies.

**Page 2:** List three facts from page 2. Are there any nonfacts? (Lisa is ten and a half years old. She liked living on Dungan Island and she enjoyed nature. There are no nonfacts on this page. Everything that is said can be proved.) *Fact and Nonfact*

**Pages 4–8:** What problem did the people of Dungan Island have? (They needed to raise eleven million dollars to pay for a new sewer system.) What solution did they choose? (They decided to turn Dungan Island into a tourist attraction because tourists spend money.) *Problem and Solution*

**Page 9:** When Lisa stepped into the General Store, why did she think she was in the wrong building? (The groceries were

gone and souvenirs were in their place. Lisa was confused by this.) *Draw Conclusions*

**Page 13:** Find the word **barrier** on this page. What are some other words that could have been used instead? (railing, fence, barricade) *Instructional Vocabulary*

**Pages 15–16:** Look on pages 15 and 16 for words with the /ûr/ sound as in *burn*. (person, turned, birds) Compare the spellings of the words to determine three spellings for the /ûr/ sound. (er, ur, ir) *Phonics*

**RETURN TO PREDICTIONS AND PURPOSES** Have students review their predictions. Which were accurate? Did they find answers to their questions?

**LITERARY RESPONSE** Discuss these questions:

- Do you think this is a true story? Did the people behave in realistic ways?

- What would it be like to live on a small island where everyone knew each other?

Also see the story questions and activity in *Tourist Trap Island.*

### Answers to Story Questions

1. She loved all the natural things about the island: the animals, plants, and natural beauty.
2. He did not know if the island could raise the money necessary to put in the sewer system and did not want to get in trouble with the state.
3. Accept all reasonable responses.
4. It's about an island girl who helps her neighbors realize that their beautiful island is fine just the way it is.
5. Answers will vary.

The *Story Questions* and *Activity* below appear in the *Easy Book.*

#### Story Questions and Activity

1. What did Lisa like so much about Dungan Island?
2. Why was Lisa's father, Mayor Bob, so worried when the letter came from the State?
3. What do you think would have happened to Dungan Island if many tourists had shown up?
4. What is the story mostly about?
5. How do you think the mother and daughter from *An Island Scrapbook* would have reacted to *Tourist Trap Island?* Explain your answer.

#### Attract Tourists

Suppose that your town or neighborhood was turned into a "tourist attraction." Make a sign or advertisement about something that tourists would come to see.

from *Tourist Trap Island*

# Leveled Books

## INDEPENDENT

### The Galapagos Islands

☑ **Fact and Nonfact**

☑ **Instructional Vocabulary:**
*barrier, emerge, fireball, naturalist, parallel, teeming*

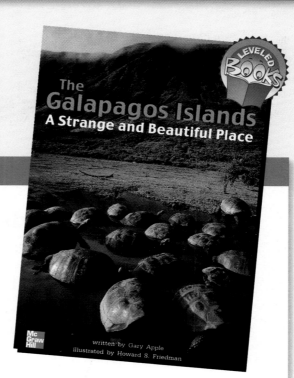

# Guided Reading

**PREVIEW AND PREDICT** Have students look at the illustrations through page 7 and predict what the book will be about.

**SET PURPOSES** Students should decide what they want to know before they read. Ask them to write a few questions they would like to have answered by the story.

**READING THE BOOK** Have the students read the book independently and then use the questions below to emphasize reading strategies.

**Page 3:** List three facts on page 3. Are there any nonfacts? (The information about the Galapagos Islands is true. All the information can be proved, so there aren't any nonfacts.) *Fact and Nonfact*

**Pages 6–7:** What led Charles Darwin to the conclusion that the Galapagos Islands were a strange and beautiful place? (Darwin found unique plant and animal life that he had never seen before, so it seemed strange. The text says the islands were "unspoiled," so they were probably quite naturally beautiful.) *Draw Conclusions*

**Page 15:** Do you agree with the story's conclusion that "The Galapagos Islands are some of the most isolated and unspoiled places on the planet"? Support your answer with information from the story. (Answers will vary.) *Draw Conclusions*

**RETURN TO PREDICTIONS AND PURPOSES** Review students' predictions and reasons for reading. Which predictions were accurate? Did the students find answers to their questions?

**LITERARY RESPONSE** Discuss these questions with students:

- What did you learn about animal life on the Galapagos Islands?

- How do you think the author gathered the information to write this story?

Also see the story questions and activity in *The Galapagos Islands*.

## Answers to Story Questions

1. They were formed by volcanoes on the ocean floor.
2. Because people had not visited there or lived there.
3. An opinion is a nonfact.
4. The Galapagos Islands are home to many rare plants and animals that should be preserved and protected.
5. Answers will vary.

The *Story Questions* and *Activity* below appear in the *Independent Book*.

### Story Questions and Activity

1. How were the Galapagos Islands formed?
2. Why did the Galapagos Islands remain so natural and unspoiled for so long?
3. One of the first visitors to the Galapagos Islands described them as "worthless." Do you think this was a fact? Explain your answer.
4. What is the main idea of the book?
5. Compare and contrast the Galapagos Islands with the barrier island described in *An Island Scrapbook*. Be sure to include plant and animal life as well as details about the islands themselves.

### Galapagos Journal

What if you were the first person to discover the Galapagos Islands? How would you write about all the different plants and animals you saw there? Write a journal entry as though you were a 16th century explorer visiting the islands for the first time. Describe all that you see and explain what you think these creatures might be.

*from The Galapagos Islands*

# Leveled Books

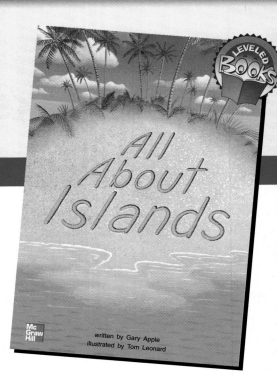

## CHALLENGE

### All About Islands

☑ **Fact and Nonfact**

☑ **Instructional Vocabulary:**
*barrier, emerge, fireball, naturalist, parallel, teeming*

written by Gary Apple
illustrated by Tom Leonard

## Guided Reading

**PREVIEW AND PREDICT** Have students read the title and the Table of Contents. Then ask them to preview the illustrations. Ask them to predict what the book will be about.

**SET PURPOSES** Students should note what they want to learn before they read the story. Have them think of a few questions they would like to have answered.

**READ THE BOOK** After students have read the book independently, return to the story to apply the following strategies.

**Page 2:** Are there any nonfacts on page 2? (All the information on page 2 can be proved. There are no nonfacts.) *Fact and Nonfact*

**Page 9:** How did Singapore become the most crowded country on Earth? (Most of its swamps and jungles were destroyed to make room for homes, farms, and factories.) *Draw Conclusions*

**Page 11:** The text says "Greenland is really not a suitable name for the island." How do you think the author drew this

conclusion? (An island named Greenland sounds like it would be covered with grass, plants, and trees. Since the story says an icecap covers most of Greenland, there's probably very little vegetation there.) *Draw Conclusions*

**Page 14:** What does the word naturalist mean? (someone who studies and appreciates nature) What are some context clues to help you? (lush plant life, scenic canyons, streams and waterfalls) *Instructional Vocabulary*

**RETURN TO PREDICTIONS AND PURPOSES** Review students' predictions and reasons for reading. Which predictions were accurate? Which were not?

**LITERARY RESPONSE** Discuss the questions with students:

• What do you find most fascinating about islands?

• What do you think Donne meant when he said, "No man is an island"?

Also see the story questions and activity in *All About Islands*.

---

## Answers to Story Questions

1. By volcanoes, by coral growth, or by rising sea level.
2. Because the private owners of the island do not welcome many visitors. You have to be invited, since no strangers are allowed on the island.
3. There are no televisions or movie theaters on the island. They have to create their own entertainment.
4. The world is filled with many different, fascinating types of islands.
5. Answers will vary.

The *Story Questions and Activity* below appear in the *Challenge Book.*

### Story Questions and Activity

1. Name two ways that islands can be formed.
2. Why is Hawaii's Niihau Island also known as Aloof Island?
3. Why do the people of Tristan da Cunha have dances every Saturday?
4. What is the main idea of the book?
5. Which of the islands mentioned in this story would the mother and daughter from *An Island Scrapbook* be the most interested in? Explain.

### Make a Choice

Reread page 9, which tells about the world's most crowded island (Singapore) and least crowded island (Baffin Island). Suppose that you had to live on one of those islands for the rest of your life. Write a short essay stating the island on which you would choose to live and why you made that choice.

*from All About Islands*

# Bringing Groups Together

## Anthology and Leveled Books

## Connecting Texts

**FACT AND NONFACT** Write the story titles on a chart. Ask students to list two facts from each story on the chart and then identify the best source to use in proving the facts true. (Discuss the difference between nonfiction and realistic fiction.) Challenge students to consider a wide variety of sources.

| An Island Scrapbook | Tourist Trap Island | The Galapagos Islands | All About Islands |
|---|---|---|---|
| • **A raccoon's footprints look like human handprints.** an encyclopedia<br><br>• **A whale can starve from eating too much litter.** a science book | • **Lisa is ten and a half.** the story<br><br>• **Lisa lives on Dungan Island.** the story | • **Giant tortoises live on the Galapagos.** an encyclopedia<br><br>• **Charles Darwin visited the Galapagos.** Darwin's biography | • **Great Britain is an island.** an atlas<br><br>• **The Inuits live on Baffin Island.** a social studies textbook |

## Viewing/Representing

**GROUP PRESENTATIONS** Divide the class into groups, one for each of the four books read in the lesson. (For *An Island Scrapbook* combine students of different reading levels.) Have each group identify an environmental issue addressed or mentioned in the story, for example, litter in our oceans or the threatened extinction of certain species. Have each group write a persuasive paragraph aimed at enlisting help for that environmental cause. Encourage students to make illustrations as well. Ask them to present their plea to the class.

**AUDIENCE RESPONSE** Ask students to listen carefully to the presentations. Ask them to assess whether the information they hear is fact or nonfact. Allow time for responses following each presentation.

## Research and Inquiry

**MORE ABOUT ISLANDS** These four stories have been about islands. Have students look at a globe and choose an island or chain of islands and find out

- how the island was formed

- what and/or who inhabits the islands

- what vegetation is native to the island

- what weather is like on the island.

Have students make a Fact Wall about island facts.

**inter NET CONNECTION** Have students log on to **www.mhschool.com/reading** to find out more about islands.

## OBJECTIVES
Students will distinguish between fact and nonfact.

### Skills Finder
**Fact and Nonfact**

| | |
|---|---|
| Introduce | 167A-B |
| Review | 199E-F, 221G-H, 433A-B, 463E-F, 493A-B |
| Test | Unit 2, Unit 4 |
| Maintain | 627 |

### TEACHING TIP

**OPINIONS** Tell students that sometimes a statement of opinion can contain both fact and nonfact.

"I believe that fire-breathing dragons really exist."

It is a *fact* that the speaker believes this. But the statement "fire-breathing dragons exist" is a *nonfact*.

### SELF-SELECTED
## Reading

*Students may choose from the following titles.*

**ANTHOLOGY**
- An Island Scrapbook

**LEVELED BOOKS**
- Tourist Trap Island
- The Galapagos Islands
- All About Islands

Bibliography, pages T78–T79

# Review Fact and Nonfact

**PREPARE**

**Discuss Fact and Nonfact**

Review: It is important to distinguish between statements or ideas that can be proven true (facts) and those that cannot be proven true (nonfacts).

**TEACH**

**Read "Old Blue" and Model the Skill**

Read "Old Blue" with the students. Ask them to think about what statements in the selection can be proven true.

---

### Old Blue

As our canoe rounds the bend, Old Blue gets up again. The great blue heron's six-foot-wide wings sweep slowly as he flies down river, his long legs trailing beneath him. Old Blue has lived on the river for years. He thinks this is the most beautiful place in the world.

Beneath the blue sky, the water flows slowly in the deeper parts and rushes noisily over rocks in the rapids. Old Blue winters in Mexico, but he returns here every summer. He likes the fishing here. He doesn't like the smelly run-off that flows into the river from the turkey farm on the hill.

Teaching Chart 106

---

Discuss clues in the story that help readers recognize fact and nonfact. Ask volunteers to underline two facts and circle a nonfact in the first paragraph.

**MODEL** Let's see...the heron's wings could be measured, so six-foot-wide wings is a fact. Long legs—that's a fact, too. But what the heron thinks? No, that is a definite nonfact!

Create a Fact and Nonfact Chart

GROUP

Using a Fact and Nonfact chart, have students record the facts and nonfacts from "Old Blue." If there is something that they need to investigate further before determining whether it is fact or nonfact, have them check the Not Sure column.

| STATEMENT | FACT | NONFACT | NOT SURE |
|---|---|---|---|
| The heron has six-foot-wide wings and long legs. | √ | | |
| The run-off comes from the turkey farm on the hill. | √ | | |
| Old Blue winters in Mexico. | | | √ |
| Old Blue doesn't like the run-off. | | √ | |

▶ Logical/Visual

ASSESS/CLOSE

Distinguish Between Fact and Nonfact

ONE

Have students list facts and nonfacts from *An Island Scrapbook*. Then have them organize these in a chart.

ALTERNATE TEACHING
STRATEGY

FACT AND NONFACT

For a different approach to teaching this skill, see page T66.

Intervention ▶ Skills
Intervention Guide, for direct instruction and extra practice with fact and nonfact

# Meeting Individual Needs for Comprehension

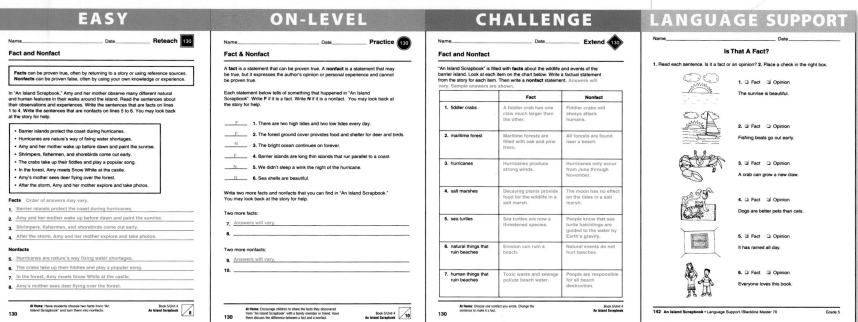

**EASY** — Reteach, 130

**ON-LEVEL** — Practice, 130

**CHALLENGE** — Extend, 130

**LANGUAGE SUPPORT** — Language Support, 142

**TESTED**

### OBJECTIVES

Students will identify important and unimportant information.

| Skills Finder | |
|---|---|
| **Important and Unimportant Information** | |
| Introduce | 409A–B |
| Review | 431E–F, 463G–H, 501E–F |
| Test | Unit 4 |

---

### TEACHING TIP

**MEDIA INFORMATION**

Have students use a two-column chart to organize important and unimportant information from a familiar story, movie, or TV show. Ask them to compare the way different media present important information.

---

## Review Important and Unimportant Information

**PREPARE**

**Discuss Important and Unimportant Information**

Review: Important information contributes to the writer's main theme or purpose. Unimportant information does not support the main idea.

**TEACH**

**Read "The Thank You Note" and Model the Skill**

Read "The Thank You Note" with students. Have students think about what information is important.

### The Thank You Note

Dear Grandma,

Thank you for the great sweater. I wore it to school on Thursday. We had a math test. And we had to stay in at recess because it was raining hard.

Everyone liked my sweater. My best friend said the colors are the coolest! When I told her that you made it, she didn't even believe me! She is really a good skater. She has been taking ice skating lessons for years.

We are ready for spring vacation. Just two more days! Marta's birthday party is in four days. I am going to wear my sweater to the party, too. Thanks again!

Love, Sandra

Teaching Chart 107

Ask students to identify the main idea of the selection.

**MODEL** I think the writer wants to thank her grandmother for a gift and let her know how much she likes it. I don't see what the math test or the weather report has to do with the sweater.

Have students draw a line under the unimportant information.

**Distinguish Between Important and Unimportant Information**

ONE

Have students chart the important and unimportant details in "The Thank You Note." ▶ **Logical/Visual**

| IMPORTANT DETAILS | UNIMPORTANT DETAILS |
|---|---|
| The friend said the sweater's colors are the coolest. | The friend is a good skater. |
| Sandra will wear the sweater to a party. | Spring vacation is in two days. |

**ASSESS/CLOSE**

**Tell Why Details Are Important or Unimportant**

Create a chart on the chalkboard, incorporating all student charts. Go through the chart with the whole class, discussing why each detail is important or unimportant. Student assessments of whether a detail is important or not may differ, but it is important that students can tell that a detail is important because it supports or develops a main idea.

---

**ALTERNATE TEACHING STRATEGY**

**IMPORTANT AND UNIMPORTANT INFORMATION**

For a different approach to teaching this skill, see page T64.

---

**Intervention** ▶ **Skills Intervention Guide,** for direct instruction and extra practice with important and unimportant information

---

# Meeting Individual Needs for Comprehension

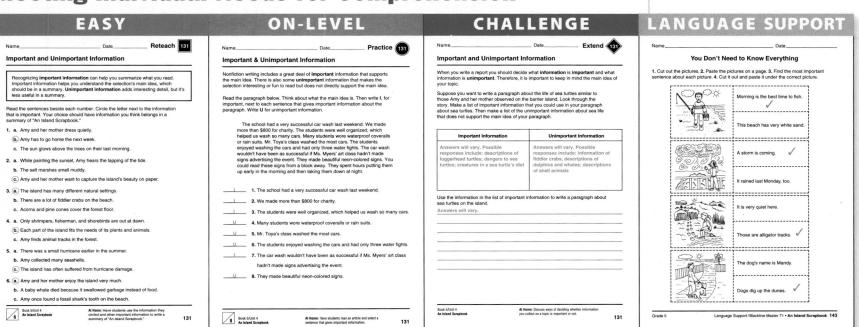

| EASY | ON-LEVEL | CHALLENGE | LANGUAGE SUPPORT |
|---|---|---|---|
| Reteach, 131 | Practice, 131 | Extend, 131 | Language Support, 143 |

## OBJECTIVES

Students will recognize suffixes *-less* and *-ment* and how they change word meaning.

### Skills Finder

**Suffixes**

| | |
|---|---|
| Introduce | 407I–J |
| Review | 463I–J, 501I–J |
| Test | Unit 4 |
| Maintain | 547, 573, 587, 635 |

---

### TEACHING TIP

**CHANGING PARTS OF SPEECH** Encourage students to use a dictionary to check the meaning of words they have figured out.

- When *-less* is added to a noun, the word changes to an adjective. Example: *pain, painless*.

- When *-ment* is added to a verb, the word changes to a noun. Example: *govern, government*.

---

# Review Suffixes

### PREPARE

**Discuss Meaning of Suffixes *-less* and *-ment***

Explain: A suffix is a word part added to the end of a base word. Suffixes have their own meanings, and they also change the meanings of words to which they are added. The suffix *-less* means "without, lacking." The suffix *-ment* means "act of," "result of," or "state of being." Knowing the meaning of a suffix can help a reader determine a word's meaning.

### TEACH

**Read the Passage and Model the Skill**

Have students read **Teaching Chart 108** with you.

**Island Incidents**

Two girls explore a barrier island, appreciating its almost untouched beauty. Each girl finds enjoyment in something different. One enjoys finding a natural arrangement of shells on the beach. With great contentment, the other watches the soundless sunset. Both spend a sleepless night listening to the winds of a small hurricane howling over the island.

Teaching Chart 108

Discuss the way the suffixes *-less* and *-ment* change a word's meaning when they are used.

**MODEL** The word *arrangement* in the third sentence ends in the suffix *-ment*. The base word is *arrange*. If *-ment* means "result of," then *arrangement* means "result of arranging." Let me read that sentence again and see if that meaning makes sense.

## PRACTICE

**Identify Suffixes and Their Meanings**

Have volunteers underline the words in the passage with the suffix *-less* or *-ment,* and then circle the suffix. Discuss how the meaning of each word changes when the suffix is added.

▶ **Visual/Linguistic**

## ASSESS/CLOSE

**Use Words with Suffixes *-less* and *-ment* in Sentences**

Have a volunteer read the three words below. Ask students to place each word where it best fits in the sentences below.

| statement | meaningless | careless |
|---|---|---|

His _____ behavior got him into trouble. (careless)

Some people think that watching television is a _____ activity. (meaningless)

I liked your _____ about saving the trees. (statement)

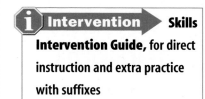

**ALTERNATE TEACHING STRATEGY**

**SUFFIXES**

For a different approach to teaching this skill, see page T63.

**i** **Intervention** ▶ **Skills Intervention Guide,** for direct instruction and extra practice with suffixes

# Meeting Individual Needs for Vocabulary

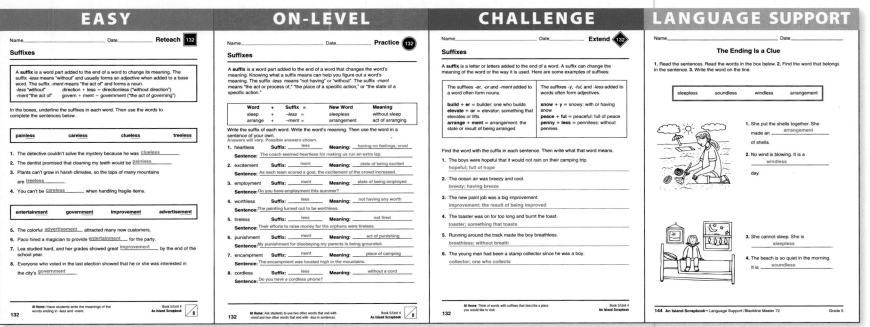

Reteach, 132          Practice, 132          Extend, 132          Language Support, 144

# Expository Writing

## GRAMMAR/SPELLING
### CONNECTIONS

See the 5-Day Grammar and Usage Plan on articles, pages 463M–463N.

See the 5-Day Spelling Plan on words with /är/ and /âr/ pages 463O–463P.

## TEACHING TIP

**Technology**
Point out to students that a spell-checker won't catch a word that has been used incorrectly, such as a *homophone*. Direct students to use a spell-checker *and* read over their work.

**Handwriting**
Remind students to use their neatest handwriting when publishing. Write on one side of the paper only and leave wide margins on all sides. For specific instruction on hand-writing, see pages T68–T73.

**Handwriting CD-ROM**

## Prewrite

**WRITE AN OBSERVATION REPORT**
Present the following assignment: *An Island Scrapbook* carefully observes and records the actions of some island creatures. Report your own observations of an animal. Make a chart with two columns, labeled *Action* and *Reason*. Use this chart to note observations of your animal.

**GATHER INFORMATION** Have students study an animal. Remind them to get both their parents' and the owner's permission if they are observing someone else's pet. Have students gather information about the animal's repeated behaviors and the cause(s) for them. Explain that on the two-column chart, they should record their observations under *Action* and why they think the animal is acting in a particular way under *Reason*.

**Strategy: Work with a Partner** Tell partners to share and discuss what they saw. Ask them to exchange ideas about what the animals' actions mean. Urge partners to rehearse what they might say in their reports and to get feedback from one another.

| ACTION | REASON |
|--------|--------|
|        |        |
|        |        |

**Graphic Organizer 31**

## Draft

**USE THE CHART** Ask students to review their charts before starting to write. Remind them that their purpose is to inform.

## Revise

**SELF-QUESTIONING** Ask students to assess their drafts for improvement.

- Is the topic of my report stated?
- Are there details missing that would tell more about the animal's behavior?
- Does the report state logical reasons the animal is behaving a particular way?

Have partners trade reports to get more feedback about clarity and the appropriateness of details and conclusions. Then ask students to create a second draft.

## Edit/Proofread

**CHECK FOR ERRORS AND DETAILS** Students should reread their reports for spelling, grammar, details, and punctuation. Have them revise once more to make the report as informative as possible.

## Publish

**SHARE THE REPORTS** In small groups, have volunteers read their reports aloud.

### An Observation Report on Squirrels

Four squirrels dash up and down the trunk of a large oak tree in my neighborhood park. I think they are a family because three of the four have slightly grayer tails than other squirrels. They scamper to other trees, but always return to the oak. When they pick up nuts, they carry them to this tree. It appears to be their home. Since it is fall, they seem to be preparing for winter. The smallest squirrel mostly stays close to this oak tree. Perhaps it feels safer here.

# Presentation Ideas

**ILLUSTRATE THE ANIMALS** Ask students to draw the animals they observed. The illustrations should show the animals demonstrating the described actions.

▶ **Viewing/Representing**

**RESPOND TO SPEAKERS** Have classmates ask the speakers about their reports.

▶ **Speaking/Listening**

Consider students' creative efforts, possibly adding a plus (+) for originality, wit, and imagination.

## Viewing and Listening

**VIEWING STRATEGIES**
After viewing the drawings, encourage students to:

• explain how details in the illustrations support the report.

**LISTENING STRATEGIES**
As students listen to reports, have them:

• make eye contact with the speaker.

• jot down questions they would like to ask.

## Scoring Rubric

| Excellent | Good | Fair | Unsatisfactory |
|---|---|---|---|
| **4:** The writer | **3:** The writer | **2:** The writer | **1:** The writer |
| • presents an exceptionally informative report | • presents a solid informative report | • attempts to present a factual report | • does not inform on the topic |
| • includes numerous vivid details about the observed animal | • includes clear details about what was observed | • states a few details about what was observed | • may state unclear or fragmented facts and details |
| • explains why the animal responds as it does | • describes why the animal behaves as it does | • is vague about why the animal acts as it does | • offers no information about why the animal acts as it does |
| • describes a logical connection between action and behavior. | • makes a logical connection between action and behavior. | • may or may not describe a logical connection between action and behavior. | • does not describe a logical connection between action and behavior. |

**Incomplete 0:** The writer leaves the page blank or fails to respond to the writing task. The student does not address the topic or simply paraphrases the prompt. The response is illegible or incoherent.

For a 6-point or an 8-point scale, see pages T107–T108.

# Meeting Individual Needs for Writing

## EASY

**A Favorite Animal** Have students choose their favorite animal from among those described in the selection. Next tell them to look up the animal in a reference book and sketch it. Then have students write a short caption, telling something interesting about the animal.

## ON-LEVEL

**Another Home** In the selection, the author tells why she and her daughter live on a barrier island for part of the year. Have students choose a place they would like to live part-time. Have them explain what time of year they would like to be there and give three reasons why they selected that particular place.

## CHALLENGE

**Report** In the selection, the author and her daughter enjoy observing animals that live in the marsh and ocean. Ask students to select animals they would like to observe and explain their choices in writing. Next, have students research their animals and find at least three interesting facts about them to include in their explanations.

**LANGUAGE SUPPORT**

**ESL** When ESL students have chosen the animal they are going to write about, ask them to draw a picture of it. Then have them work with English-fluent partners to describe how the animal moves. Have ESL students take notes to use as they write their reports.

 Invite students to include their observation reports in their portfolios.

PORTFOLIO

# 5 Day Grammar and Usage Plan

Demonstrate comparisons such as *small, smaller,* and *smallest* by showing real objects.

## DAILY LANGUAGE ACTIVITIES

Have students correct the sentences orally.

### Day 1

1. This summer was warmest than last summer.
2. We found the smoother sea glass of all.
3. That dock is oldest than our house.

### Day 2

1. One crab is bravest than the others.
2. This crab has one claw biggest than the other.
3. Crabs prefer the murkyer water.

### Day 3

1. Raccoons are the larger animals on the beach.
2. The beach is rockyest than I remember.
3. We took a longest walk today than yesterday.

### Day 4

1. We saw the prettyer view of all from the dunes.
2. I found the rounder sand dollar today.
3. Amy's paintings are largest than mine.

### Day 5

1. Those are the thinner fish I have ever seen.
2. The sand on the beach is cleanest than on the road.
3. These shells are shinyest than those.

Daily Language Transparency 18

**Suggested Answers on Transparency**

---

## DAY 1 — Introduce the Concept

**Oral Warm-Up**  Point to or hold up two similar items in the room, and say, "This (book) is smaller than this (book)." Ask students which word compares two things. Then ask them what form of the word to use if it compares more than two things.

**Introduce Adjectives That Compare**  Adjectives can be used to compare two or more things. Present the following:

### Adjectives That Compare

- Add *-er* to most adjectives to compare two people, places, or things.
- Add *-est* to most adjectives to compare more than two.

Present the Daily Language Activity and have students correct orally. Then have students write the comparative and superlative forms of the adjectives *short* and *narrow*.

 Assign the daily Writing Prompt on page 432C.

**Adjectives That Compare**

- Add *-er* to most adjectives to compare two people, places, or things.
- Add *-est* to most adjectives to compare more than two.

Think about the comparisons in each sentence. Then rewrite the sentence with the correct form for each underlined adjective.

1. The morning feels <u>warm</u> today than yesterday.
   The morning feels warmer today than yesterday.
2. The sun today is the <u>bright</u> I can remember.
   The sun today is the brightest I can remember.
3. This morning I noticed the <u>small</u> crabs I've ever seen.
   This morning I noticed the smallest crabs I've ever seen.
4. They move <u>fast</u> than the sand worms.
   They move faster than the sand worms.
5. One claw on the fiddler crab is <u>large</u> than the other.
   One claw on the fiddler crab is larger than the other.
6. Amy is slightly <u>tall</u> than the great blue heron.
   Amy is slightly taller than the great blue heron.
7. About 50 years ago, the <u>large</u> hurricane ever to hit this island blew in.
   About 50 years ago, the largest hurricane ever to hit this island blew in.
8. A much <u>small</u> hurricane passed through last week.
   A much smaller hurricane passed through last week.
9. After the storm, everything seemed much <u>calm</u> than the night before.
   After the storm, everything seemed much calmer than the night before.
10. That day, I found the <u>blue</u> shell in the world.
    That day, I found the bluest shell in the world.
11. The turtle is much <u>slow</u> than the alligator.
    The turtle is much slower than the alligator.
12. This shell is much <u>big</u> than that one.
    This shell is much bigger than that one.

Extension: Have students write a paragraph describing an outdoor walk, bike ride, or camping trip. Ask them to include in their description four adjectives that compare.

12 — Grade 5/Unit 4 An Island Scrapbook — 109

**GRAMMAR PRACTICE BOOK, PAGE 109**

---

## DAY 2 — Teach the Concept

**Review Adjectives That Compare**  Ask students to compare two or more places or things in a sentence.

**Introduce New Spellings**  Some adjectives change their spellings when adding *-er* or *-est*. Present:

### Adjectives That Compare

- For adjectives ending in *e*, drop the *e* before adding *-er* or *-est*.
- For adjectives ending in a consonant and *y*, change the *y* to *i* before adding *-er* or *-est*. (*happy → happiest*)
- For one-syllable adjectives that have a single vowel before a final consonant, double the final consonant before adding *-er* or *-est*.

Present the Daily Language Activity. Have students correct the sentences orally. Then ask students to write the comparative and superlative forms of the adjective *easy*.

Assign the daily Writing Prompt on page 432C.

**More Adjectives That Compare**

- For adjectives ending in *e*, drop the *e* before adding *-er* or *-est*.
- For adjectives ending in a consonant and *y*, change the *y* to *i* before adding *-er* or *-est*.
- For one-syllable adjectives that have a single vowel before the final consonant, double the final consonant before adding *-er* or *-est*.

Read each sentence. Rewrite it with the correct adjective forms.

1. This is the smellyest shell on the beach.
   This is the smelliest shell on the beach.
2. Still, it has the fineest markings of any I've seen.
   Still, it has the finest markings of any I've seen.
3. I don't think I could feel happyer than I am right now.
   I don't think I could feel happier than I am right now.
4. The sadest day for me is the day we leave the beach.
   The saddest day for me is the day we leave the beach.
5. You know, this shell is smallest than the pink one over there.
   You know, this shell is smaller than the pink one over there.
6. The prettyest shell is in the blue box.
   The prettiest shell is in the blue box.
7. I think the big sand dollar is prettyer than that.
   I think the big sand dollar is prettier than that.
8. Actually, I can't decide which is the lovelyest shell.
   Actually, I can't decide which is the loveliest shell.
9. Let's try to find the larger heron we've seen.
   Let's try to find the largest heron we've seen.
10. We should start looking near the higher point on the island.
    We should start looking near the highest point on the island.

Extension: Ask pairs of students to write and present a dialogue about a visit to a store or other type of market. Have them use at least six adjectives that compare the items that they see.

110 — Grade 5/Unit 4 An Island Scrapbook — 10

**GRAMMAR PRACTICE BOOK, PAGE 110**

# Adjectives That Compare

**Learn from the Literature** Review comparative and superlative adjectives.

Have students look at the drawing of Amy's shell collection on page 448 of *An Island Scrapbook*. Help students compare the shells. Offer examples such as, "The angel wing is bigger than the razor clam. The coquinas are the smallest shells."

**Compare Things** Present the Daily Language Activity and have students correct the sentences orally.

Have students look at the drawings of insects on page 443 of *An Island Scrapbook* and write sentences comparing them.

Assign the daily Writing Prompt on page 432D.

---

**Review Adjectives That Compare** Write the adjectives with spelling changes from the Daily Language Activities for Days 1–3 on the chalkboard. Identify the rule that applies to each. Present the Daily Language Activity for Day 4.

**Mechanics and Usage** Before students begin the daily Writing Prompt on page 432D, review how to punctuate a letter. Discuss:

### Letter Punctuation

- Begin the greeting and closing of a letter with a capital letter.
- Use a colon after the greeting in a business letter.
- Use a comma after the closing in a letter.
- Use a comma between the names of a city and a state.
- Use a comma between the day and year.

Assign the daily Writing Prompt on page 432D.

---

**Assess** Use the Daily Language Activity and page 113 of the **Grammar Practice Book** for assessment.

**Reteach** Write the adjectives from the Daily Language Activities for Days 1 through 4 on separate index cards. Put all the cards in a pile. Ask each student to pull a card and to use the adjective in a sentence comparing two or more objects. When every student has written a sentence, point out the differences in constructing comparative sentences, such as using the article *the* before adjectives with -est and the word *than* with adjectives with -er.

Use page 114 of the **Grammar Practice Book** for additional reteaching.

Assign the daily Writing Prompt on page 432D.

---

### Writing with Adjectives That Compare

- Add *-er* to most adjectives to compare two people, places, or things.
- Add *-est* to most adjectives to compare more than two.
- For adjectives ending in e, drop the e before adding -er or -est.
- For adjectives ending in a consonant and y, change the y to i before adding -er or -est.
- For one-syllable adjectives that have a single vowel before the final consonant, double the final consonant before adding -er or -est.

Write both forms of each adjective below.

1. sleepy   sleepier   sleepiest
2. red   redder   reddest
3. fine   finer   finest
4. salty   saltier   saltiest
5. cool   cooler   coolest
6. fast   faster   fastest
7. skinny   skinnier   skinniest
8. high   higher   highest
9. mad   madder   maddest
10. pretty   prettier   prettiest

Find the incorrect adjectives in these sentences. Rewrite the sentences so that the adjectives are correct.

11. These are the smaller birds on the island.
These are the smallest birds on the island.

12. The heron is the larger bird we ever see here.
The heron is the largest bird we ever see here.

13. I love to read during the hotest part of the day.
I love to read during the hottest part of the day.

14. The funnyest moment was meeting that alligator!
The funniest moment was meeting that alligator!

Extension: Ask students to write a letter to a friend from a very special place, a place the student loves to be. Encourage students to explain in their letters why they like this particular place. As they write their letters, students should use adjectives that compare.

14   Grade 5/Unit 4   An Island Scrapbook    111

---

### Letter Punctuation

- Begin the greeting and the closing of a letter with a capital letter.
- Use a colon after the greeting in a business letter.
- Use a comma after the closing in a letter.
- Use a comma between the names of a city and a state.
- Use a comma between the day and year in a date.

Read the short letters below. Correct all items that are incorrect.

August 10 1999   August 10, 1999

dear Jamie   Dear Jamie,

I'm having a fantastic time in North Carolina. The days have been warm and sunny, and there is so much to do in the bays and ocean. Hope you are well.

always   Always,

Jake

Sept. 9 1999   Sept. 9, 1999

Mr. Peter Johnson
112 Slate Road
Dover DE 19904   Dover, DE 19904

dear Sir   Dear Sir:

I am writing to urge you to do something to stop beach erosion here on the eastern islands. Please take the time to deal with this serious problem soon. Thank you very much.

Sincerely,

Megan Homer

Extension: Have groups of students write a business letter about a community problem. You might have them write to a government representative or local business. Ask groups to exchange and proofread letters for correct punctuation.

112    Grade 5/Unit 4   An Island Scrapbook   6

---

### Adjectives That Compare

Read the sentence. Look at the adjective in parentheses. Fill in the correct form of the adjective on the line to complete the sentence.

1. We think that today's sunrise is the _____ reddest _____ we have ever seen. (red)
2. This has been the _____ sunniest _____ month of the summer. (sunny)
3. July was much _____ foggier _____. (foggy)
4. Yesterday we saw the _____ larger _____ of our two favorite pond turtles. (large)
5. The oaks are the _____ tallest _____ of all the trees in the forest. (tall)
6. During the hurricane, the wind was _____ louder _____ than during the storm in May. (loud)
7. Afterward, the air seemed clearer, and the sky was much _____ bluer _____. (blue)
8. The days already are growing _____ shorter _____, aren't they? (short)
9. Each day I feel _____ sadder _____ than the day before. (sad)
10. We call this the _____ finest _____ island in the Atlantic Ocean. (fine)

10   Grade 5/Unit 4   An Island Scrapbook    113

# 5 Day Spelling Plan

To help students distinguish between /îr/ and /ûr/, say the two sounds several times. Then present contrasting pairs of words: steer/stir, fear/fir, peer/purse.

## DICTATION SENTENCES

### Spelling Words

1. Drivers must steer their cars.
2. What is your return address?
3. Let's watch the stars appear.
4. A nerve can help carry a message.
5. They traveled to the frontier.
6. We have a tall fir in the yard.
7. Who is that mysterious person?
8. She has a career in science.
9. The surface of the desk is flat.
10. A fearsome storm rages outside.
11. Her term of office is four years.
12. The cashier gave him a dollar back.
13. I saw the fish squirm on the fishhook.
14. You must have experience for this job.
15. The dark night was eerie.
16. She put her money in her purse.
17. It was a dark and dreary night.
18. Be alert to what is around you.
19. She will squirt them with a hose.
20. She made a dress from the material.

### Challenge Words

21. He made a barrier to keep us out.
22. The divers will emerge from the water.
23. The naturalist walked in the woods.
24. Cars were parked parallel.
25. The pond was teeming with fish.

## DAY 1 Pretest

**Assess Prior Knowledge** Use the Dictation Sentences at the left and **Spelling Practice Book** page 109 for the pretest. Allow students to correct their own papers. Students who require a modified list may be tested on the first ten words.

| Spelling Words | | Challenge Words |
|---|---|---|
| 1. steer | 11. term | 21. **barrier** |
| 2. **return** | 12. cashier | 22. **emerge** |
| 3. appear | 13. squirm | 23. **naturalist** |
| 4. nerve | 14. experience | 24. **parallel** |
| 5. frontier | 15. eerie | 25. **teeming** |
| 6. fir | 16. purse | |
| 7. **mysterious** | 17. dreary | |
| 8. career | 18. alert | |
| 9. **surface** | 19. squirt | |
| 10. fearsome | 20. material | |

*Note: Words in **dark type** are from the story.*

**Word Study** On page 110 of the **Spelling Practice Book** are word study steps and an at-home activity.

## DAY 2 Explore the Pattern

**Sort and Spell Words** Say *steer* and *term*. Ask what vowel sound is heard in each word. (/îr/, /ûr/) Have students read Spelling Words and sort them as below.

### Words with /îr/ spelled

| eer | ear |
|---|---|
| steer | appear |
| career | fearsome |
| eerie | dreary |

| ier | er |
|---|---|
| frontier | mysterious |
| cashier | experience |
| | material |

### /ûr/ spelled

| er | ur | ir |
|---|---|---|
| nerve | return | fir |
| term | surface | squirm |
| alert | purse | squirt |

**Word Wall** Have students create a word wall based on the word sort and add more words from their reading.

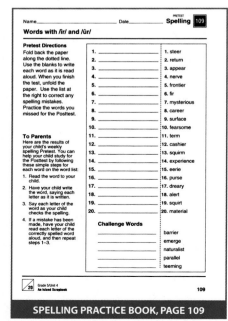

SPELLING PRACTICE BOOK, PAGE 109

**WORD STUDY STEPS AND ACTIVITY, PAGE 110**

SPELLING PRACTICE BOOK, PAGE 111

# Words with /îr/ and /ûr/

**Word Meaning: Definitions** Review that a definition is an explanation of what a word means. Have students write a definition for each Spelling Word. Then have volunteers take turns reading their definitions for classmates to match with Spelling Words.

If students need extra practice, have partners give each other a midweek test.

**Glossary** Review syllable division in the Glossary. Have students:

- write each Challenge Word.

- look up each Challenge Word in the Glossary.

- divide each Challenge Word into syllables.

**Proofread Sentences** Write these sentences on the chalkboard, including the misspelled words. Ask students to proofread, circling incorrect spellings and writing the correct spellings. There are two spelling errors in each sentence.

> I took money from my perse to pay the cashear. (purse, cashier)
>
> We were on the alurt for the feresome lion. (alert, fearsome)

Have students create additional sentences with errors for partners to correct.

**WRITING** Have students use as many Spelling Words as possible in the daily Writing Prompt on page 432D. Remind students to proofread their writing for errors in spelling, grammar, and punctuation.

**Assess Students' Knowledge** Use page 114 of the **Spelling Practice Book** or the Dictation Sentences on page 463O for the posttest.

**Personal Word List** If students have trouble with any words in the lesson, have them add to their personal list of troublesome words in their journals. Have students underline the spelling patterns of /îr/ and /ûr/ in each word.

Students should refer to their word lists during later writing activities.

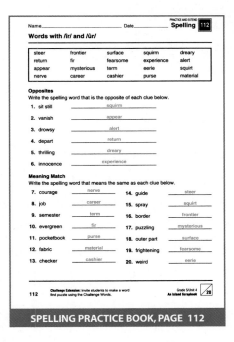

**SPELLING PRACTICE BOOK, PAGE 112**

**SPELLING PRACTICE BOOK, PAGE 113**

**SPELLING PRACTICE BOOK, PAGE 114**

**Concept**
- Storms

**Comprehension**
- Judgments and Decisions

**Vocabulary**
- atmosphere
- collision
- cycle
- data
- injured
- uneven

## Anthology

# The Big Storm

**Selection Summary** On a beautiful spring morning in late March of 1982, a mass of clouds rolled in off the Pacific Ocean. That was the beginning of a major storm that affected most of the United States.

**Stories in Art** focuses on the **comprehension** skill

**Reading Strategy** applies the **comprehension** skill

THE BIG STORM

written and illustrated by
BRUCE HISCOCK

Listening Library

**INSTRUCTIONAL** pages 466–487

**About the Author and Illustrator** Bruce Hiscock likes to stay in touch with nature. He spends some part of each day in the woods of the Adirondack Mountains in New York. It is no wonder that this nature lover would become the author of a story about a major weather event. Hiscock is also the author and illustrator of another book that explores a billion-year-old boulder located near his home.

## Leveled Books

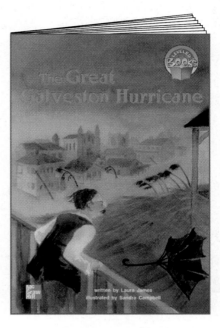

**EASY**
Lesson on pages 491A and 491D

**INDEPENDENT**
Lesson on pages 491B and 491D

**CHALLENGE**
Lesson on pages 491C and 491D

## Leveled Practice

**EASY**

**Reteach,** 133–139 Blackline masters with reteaching opportunities for each assessed skill

**INDEPENDENT/ON-LEVEL**

**Practice,** 133–139 Workbook with Take-Home stories and practice opportunities for each assessed skill and story comprehension

**CHALLENGE**

**Extend,** 133–139 Blackline masters that offer challenge activities for each assessed skill

**Quizzes Prepared by**  Accelerated Reader®

### WORKSTATION Activities

Social Studies . . . Track the Storm, *470*

Science . . . . . . . . . . . Satellites, *476*
Hurricanes, *489*

Math . . . . . . . . . . . . . . Time and Distance, *480*

Music . . . . . . . . . . . . . Storms, *472*

Language Arts . . Read Aloud, *464E*

Cultural Perspectives . . . . . Predicting the Weather, *482*

Writing . . . . . . . . . . . Report, *488*

Research and Inquiry . . . . . . Find Out More, *489*

 Internet Activities . . . . . . . . www.mhschool.com/reading

# Suggested
# Lesson Planner

| READING AND LANGUAGE ARTS |  **DAY 1** *Focus on Reading and Skills* |  **DAY 2** *Read the Literature* |
|---|---|---|

### READING AND LANGUAGE ARTS

- **Comprehension**
- **Vocabulary**
- **Phonics/Decoding**
- **Study Skills**
- **Listening, Speaking, Viewing, Representing**

---

**DAY 1** — *Focus on Reading and Skills*

 **Read Aloud: Folk Tale,** 464E
"Snowmaker Torments the People"

**Develop Visual Literacy,** 464

☑ **Review Judgments and Decisions,** 465A–465B
 **Teaching Chart 109**
 **Reteach, Practice, Extend,** 133

 **Reading Strategy:** Judgments and Decisions, 465
"A Perfect Storm"

ⓘ **Intervention Program**

---

**DAY 2** — *Read the Literature*

**Build Background,** 466A
Develop Oral Language

**Vocabulary,** 466B–466C

| atmosphere | cycle | injured |
|---|---|---|
| collision | data | uneven |

**Teaching Chart 110**
Word Building Manipulative Cards
**Reteach, Practice, Extend,** 134

 **Read the Selection,** 466–487
☑ **Judgments and Decisions**
☑ **Important and Unimportant Information**

**Genre: Narrative Nonfiction,** 467

**Cultural Perspectives,** 482

ⓘ **Intervention Program**

---

### Curriculum Connections

 **Works of Art,** 464

 **Science,** 466A

---

### Writing

 **Writing Prompt:** Write a paragraph about the most intense storm that you have ever seen. Include facts about the type of storm and the damage it may have caused.

**Writing Prompt:** The story describes spring storms because they are the most violent and active. Write a newspaper story telling about one day of the storm.

**Journal Writing,** 487
Quick-Write

---

### Grammar

**Introduce the Concept: Comparing with** *More* **and** *Most,* 491M
Daily Language Activity
1. It's the more beautiful day of the year. most
2. The air feels most frigid than usual. more
3. Was there ever a most severe storm than this? more

**Grammar Practice Book,** 115

**Teach the Concept: Comparing with** *More* **and** *Most,* 491M
Daily Language Activity
1. Which is the more powerful storm of the season? correct or most powerful
2. Winds are more strong than ever. stronger
3. The storm has become violenter. more violent

**Grammar Practice Book,** 116

---

### Spelling

**Pretest: Compound Words,** 491O
**Spelling Practice Book,** 115–116

**Explore the Pattern: Compound Words,** 491O
**Spelling Practice Book,** 117

---

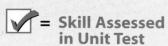 

## DAY 3 — Read the Literature

**Rereading for Fluency,** 486

**Story Questions and Activities,** 488–489
Reteach, Practice, Extend, 135

**Study Skill,** 490
✓ Read a Weather Map
**Teaching Chart 111**
Reteach, Practice, Extend, 136

**Test Power,** 491

**Read the Leveled Books,** 491A–491D
Guided Reading
/îr/ and /ûr/
✓ Judgments and Decisions
✓ Instructional Vocabulary

 **Intervention Program**

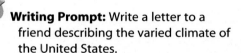 **Social Studies,** 470

**Writing Prompt:** Write a letter to a friend describing the varied climate of the United States.

**Writing Process: Expository Writing,** 491K
Prewrite, Draft

**Review and Practice: Comparing with** *More* **and** *Most,* 491N
Daily Language Activity
1. Isn't today most humid than usual? more
2. The coming storm might be the dangerousest of all. most dangerous
3. We looked for a most detailed forecast than this morning's. more detailed

**Grammar Practice Book,** 117

**Practice and Extend: Compound Words,** 491P
Spelling Practice Book, 118

## DAY 4 — Build Skills

**Read the Leveled Books and Self-Selected Books**

✓ **Review Judgments and Decisions,** 491E–491F
**Teaching Chart 112**
Reteach, Practice, Extend, 137
Language Support, 150

✓ **Review Draw Conclusions,** 491G–491H
**Teaching Chart 113**
Reteach, Practice, Extend, 138
Language Support, 151

**Minilessons,** 473, 475, 477, 479, 481, 483

**Writer's Craft,** 474

 **Intervention Program**

  **Music,** 472

**Writing Prompt:** Compare two of the most serious events that you have read about, heard about, observed, or seen on television. Write a paragraph.

**Writing Process: Expository Writing,** 491K
Revise

**Meeting Individual Needs for Writing,** 491L

**Review and Practice: Comparing with** *More* **and** *Most,* 491N
Daily Language Activity
1. The storm grew more intenser as it crossed the country. more intense
2. The clouds are more darker than usual. darker
3. Tornadoes can cause the horrendest damage. most horrendous

**Grammar Practice Book,** 118

**Proofread and Write: Compound Words,** 491P
Spelling Practice Book, 119

## DAY 5 — Build Skills

**Read Self-Selected Books**

✓ **Review Root Words,** 491I–491J
**Teaching Chart 114**
Reteach, Practice, Extend, 139
Language Support, 152

**Listening, Speaking, Viewing, Representing,** 491L

**Minilessons,** 473, 475, 477, 479, 481, 483

**Phonics Review,**
/îr/ and /ûr/, 479

**Phonics/Phonemic Awareness Practice Book,** 47–50

**Intervention Program**

**Science,** 476; **Math,** 480

**Writing Prompt:** The author found observing weather exciting. Think about one of the most exciting things that you have ever done. Write a paragraph about it.

**Writing Process: Expository Writing,** 491K
Edit/Proofread, Publish

**Assess and Reteach: Comparing with** *More* **and** *Most,* 491N
Daily Language Activity
1. I think tornadoes are most destructive than blizzards. more
2. Hail makes the more loud sound of all. loudest
3. Are people most reliable than computers? more

**Grammar Practice Book,** 119–120

**Assess and Reteach: Compound Words,** 491P
Spelling Practice Book, 120

Language Arts

# Read Aloud

## Snowmaker Torments the People
### a folk tale by Gretchen Mayo

One terrible winter Snowmaker made the icy winds howl so that even the wolves ran away to a warmer place. The people heaped their fires with wood and chips, but Snowmaker hurled the blizzards against their lodges. Soon all the fuel was gone.

When the people of the tribe went out to gather sticks and branches, cruel Snowmaker stung the noses of the children and then their ears. He breathed on the women's hands until they were raw and stiff. He piled drifts so high that some men who dared to search deep in the forest for wood never returned.

One man of the tribe, Blue Feather, stumbled home on feet like chunks of ice. "Snowmaker has grown too big! He tosses the people around and laughs!" he complained to his wife.

"Don't say those things about Snowmaker," cried his wife. "Haven't we suffered enough? Snowmaker will only heap more snow on our path and make the winds blow longer."

**Continued on pages T4–T5**

## Oral Comprehension

**LISTENING AND SPEAKING** Read the folk tale aloud. Ask students to listen for the decisions Blue Feather makes. Afterward, ask:

- What judgments did Blue Feather make about Snowmaker?

- What decisions did he make?

Help students see the connections between judgments and the decisions to which they lead. Have students think about judgments and decisions as they read other stories.

**GENRE STUDY: FOLK TALE** Discuss some of the literary devices and techniques used in "Snowmaker Torments the People."

- Point out that the characters in folk tales usually represent human qualities, either extremely good or bad. Ask: What human qualities does Blue Feather represent?

- Remind students that, in folk tales, the main character often has to defeat an enemy. Ask: How does Blue Feather defeat Snowmaker? What is the theme of this tale?

**Activity** Have students make a drawing of Blue Feather in his lodge. Ask students to include all the things Blue Feather gathered for his battle with Snowmaker. Suggest that students write a quotation or comment that summarizes the theme of the story below their drawings. Display students' finished work.
▶ **Visual/Spatial/Linguistic**

**Stories in Art**

Everything you see or imagine can give you ideas for artwork.

Look at this satellite photograph of Hurricane Andrew. How do meteorologists use satellite images to judge the path of storms? Notice the "eye" of the storm? Why do you think it is that color and shape?

Close your eyes. If you knew a hurricane was headed your way, what would you do? What could you draw to show that a hurricane was coming?

*Satellite image of Hurricane Andrew, 1992*

464

## Objective: Make Judgments and Decisions

**VIEWING** The color and the shape of a satellite image helps meteorologists make judgments about weather and the severity of storms. Invite students to describe the colors and shapes that they see in the photograph. Ask: "Where is the center of the storm? Why is it important for a meteorologist to have this information?"

Read the page with students, encouraging individual interpretations of the satellite photograph.

Have students make judgments and decisions about the image, such as:

- Which way is the hurricane spinning? (counterclockwise) What might that mean?

- The hurricane is strongest in the tunnel of whirling air. Where else might it be strong? (in the red area along the bottom of the picture)

**REPRESENTING** Have students write and report on the weather based on the satellite image. Help them judge the severity of the storm based on the picture.

**464**

**OBJECTIVES**

Students will understand how judgments and decisions are made.

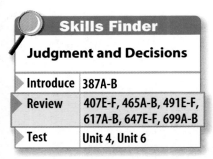

**Skills Finder**

**Judgment and Decisions**

| Introduce | 387A-B |
|-----------|--------|
| Review | 407E-F, 465A-B, 491E-F, 617A-B, 647E-F, 699A-B |
| Test | Unit 4, Unit 6 |

---

**TEACHING TIP**

**MAKE JUDGMENTS** Tell students that asking the following questions may help when they need to make a judgment. What are my options? What is the right thing to do? What is the best thing to do?

---

# Review Judgments and Decisions

**PREPARE**

**Use a Familiar Situation** Have students discuss judgments and decisions they make in their daily lives. For example, ask: How do you choose what to wear to school? Discuss the information students use to make their decisions.

**TEACH**

**Define Judgments and Decisions** Review with students that making a judgment involves applying values to determine what is right or wrong and that making a decision involves choosing a course of action.

**Safety First**

It was five o'clock in the morning and time for Mr. Harris to make a decision. He had been monitoring the weather reports since three o'clock, and he had checked in with the local division of the highway patrol as well as the local police station. The road crews had been out all night sanding the roads and overpasses. However, snow continued to fall and the predictions were for over 18 inches of snow by noon. Traffic was still moving, but very slowly. Cars and buses were slipping and sliding on the slick streets and highways. His first concern was the safety of teachers and students. So, he decided to cancel school for the day even though it meant they would have to go an additional day in the spring. "Safety first" was his motto.

Teaching Chart 109

**Read the Passage and Model the Skill** Display **Teaching Chart 109.** Have the students pay attention to judgments and decisions as the story is read.

*MODEL* To make his decision, Mr. Harris gathered information and then evaluated the situation. In his judgment, it wasn't safe to travel. Since he wanted to protect his teachers and students, he decided to cancel school.

Discuss with students how Mr. Harris made his decision. Have a volunteer underline the value judgment that influenced his decision.

**Create a Judgments and Decisions Chart**

GROUP

Using a Judgments and Decisions chart, have students work in small groups to record the judgments that Mr. Harris made in the story. Have them conclude the chart with his decision. ▶ **Logical/Spatial**

> **Judgment:** The snow was going to continue all morning.

⬇

> **Judgment:** The streets were too slick to drive on.

⬇

> **Judgment:** The safety of teachers and students was more important than adding a day to the term.

⬇

> **Decision:** Cancel school for the day.

**ASSESS/CLOSE**

**Use Judgments and Decisions**

ONE

Ask students whether or not they think Mr. Harris made the right decision. Ask them to support their answer with information from the story, making inferences as needed.

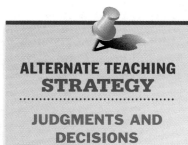

**ALTERNATE TEACHING STRATEGY**

**JUDGMENTS AND DECISIONS**

For a different approach to teaching this skill, see page T60.

 **Intervention** ▶ **Skills Intervention Guide,** for direct instruction and extra practice with judgments and decisions

# Meeting Individual Needs for Comprehension

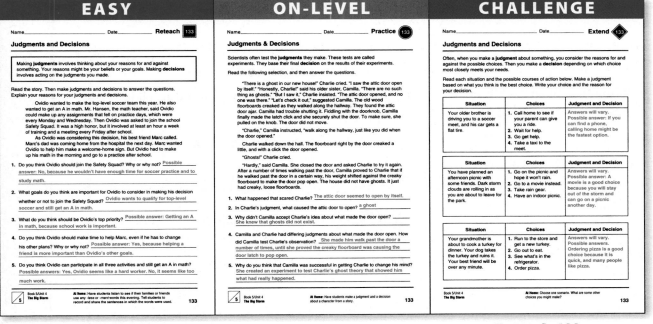

| EASY | ON-LEVEL | CHALLENGE |
|---|---|---|
| Reteach, 133 | Practice, 133 | Extend, 133 |

OBJECTIVES

Students will understand how judgments and decisions are made.

# Apply Judgments and Decisions

**READING STRATEGY**

**Judgments and Decisions**

Develop a strategy for making judgments and decisions.

1. **Think about a person's actions** in a particular situation.

2. **Examine the reasons** for those actions. Why did the captain decide to head east?

3. **Think what you would have done** in the same situation.

4. **Consider the results** of the person's actions. What happened to the men on the *Andrea Gail*?

5. **Make a judgment** about the person's actions based on facts and your own beliefs. Did it matter that the captain didn't know about the storm?

465

## A Perfect STORM

**READING STRATEGY**

In the last few days of October, 1991, the crew of the fishing boat *Andrea Gail* had a decision to make. Should they head for home or make one last run to the east in the hopes of finding plentiful swordfish? The captain chose to head east, unaware that he and his crew were heading toward one of the most powerful storms of the century.

The "October Nor'easter of 1991" developed rapidly and unexpectedly off the coast of Massachusetts. A harmless low-pressure air mass moved east into the Atlantic. There, it collided with a cold high-pressure air mass heading south. Such a combination often means bad weather. When a third storm system charged onto the scene, however, the results were extraordinary—what many have called "the perfect storm."

The third storm system was actually a worn-down hurricane named Grace. Between October 26 and 31, Grace wandered north and picked up more energy from the other two systems. The reborn hurricane produced 100-mph winds and waves up to 100 feet tall.

Nine people died in the fierce weather, including all of the men on board the *Andrea Gail*. The storm took everyone by surprise, including local weathermen. Since then, scientists have tried to be more careful predicting the weather. But they also know that, as always, you have to expect the unexpected.

**PREVIEW** Have students preview "A Perfect Storm" by reading the title and the first paragraph. Ask:

• What do you think the title means? (Answers will vary. Possible answer: The storm was perfect because it was so powerful.)

**SET PURPOSES** Explain that students will apply what they have learned about making judgments and decisions as they read "A Perfect Storm."

**APPLY THE STRATEGY** Discuss this strategy for making judgments and decisions.

• What decision did the captain make?

• Why did he make that decision?

• Would you have done the same thing if you were the captain?

• What was the result of the captain's decision?

• In your judgment, would the captain have made a different decision if he had known about the storm?

**Activity** Have students reread the passage and side notes. Then have them create a Judgments and Decisions chart for the passage.

# Build Background

**Science**

## Concept: Storms

## Evaluate Prior Knowledge

**CONCEPT: STORMS** In this selection, students will learn about a major storm that struck the eastern region of the United States in March 1982. Invite volunteers to describe their experiences dealing with major weather occurrences, such as blizzards, hurricanes, or tornadoes.

**DESCRIBE IT!** Ask students to choose a kind of storm on which to focus. Then have them use a Sense Star graphic organizer to describe the storm. ▶ **Logical/Visual**

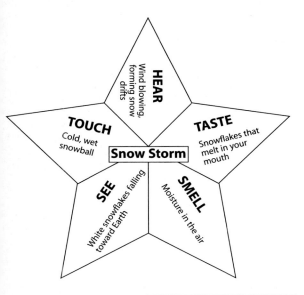

**HEAR**
Wind blowing, forming snow drifts

**TOUCH**
Cold, wet snowball

**Snow Storm**

**TASTE**
Snowflakes that melt in your mouth

**SEE**
White snowflakes falling toward Earth

**SMELL**
Moisture in the air

Graphic Organizer 35

**WRITE A NEWS BULLETIN** Have partners work together to create a news bulletin that warns listeners of a coming storm. Encourage the pairs to include suggestions on how to prepare for the storm.

**PARTNERS** **WRITING**

## Develop Oral Language

**DISCUSS WEATHER** Discuss and list
**ESL** various kinds of weather phenomena. Then have students describe the kinds of weather conditions each phenomenon produces. If students have difficulty with this task have them research weather phenomena in the encyclopedia. For example, black clouds often accompany a rain storm.

Next ask students to research and identify the geographic area most often hit by each weather phenomenon. For example, hurricanes and blizzards most often strike in the Northeast.

Have students use the information they gather to write poems or songs about the weather.

Students will use context clues to determine the meanings of vocabulary words.

atmosphere
cycle
uneven
collision
injured
data

**Definitions**

**atmosphere** (p. 473)  a layer of gases that surround Earth

**cycle** (p. 487)  a series of events that happens over and over again

**uneven** (p. 474)  not straight or regular

**collision** (p. 478)  the act of crashing against each other

**injured** (p. 480)  harmed or damaged

**data** (p. 476)  individual facts, figures, and other items of information

**Story Words**

These words from the selection may be unfamiliar. Before students read, have them check the meanings and pronunciations of the words in the Glossary beginning on page 760 or in a dictionary.

• satellite, p. 468
• tropics, p. 474
• typical, p. 477
• intense, p. 486

# Vocabulary

## Teach Vocabulary in Context

**Identify Vocabulary Words**  Display **Teaching Chart 110** and read the passage with students. Have volunteers circle each vocabulary word and underline other words that are clues to its meaning.

**A Snowy Winter**

**1.** I wonder if the clouds in the (atmosphere) around Earth will ever stop producing snow. **2.** Every day I repeat an endless (cycle) of trudging through snowdrifts and avoiding slushy puddles. **3.** I dedicate an hour each morning to removing a layer of (uneven), jagged icicles from the eaves of my house. **4.** I was almost in a (collision) last night, but avoided a crash by swerving onto the sidewalk. **5.** I wasn't (injured), not even a bruise or a scratch, but I'm one of the lucky ones. **6.** (Data) from the U.S. Weather Bureau and information from the Police Department show the number of traffic accidents this year at a record high.

Teaching Chart 110

**Discuss Meanings**  Ask questions like these to help clarify word meanings:

• What is beyond Earth's atmosphere?
• How do we measure a life cycle?
• How might a week of uneven temperatures affect you?
• What are some things that a driver can do to avoid a highway collision?
• How does a helmet protect a bicyclist from being injured?
• Why do scientists gather weather data?

## Practice

**Act It Out**

GROUP

Have students write a set of directions for acting out each vocabulary word. Then have them take turns using the directions to elicit the term from onlookers. ► **Kinesthetic/Linguistic**

collision    atmosphere    cycle

**Word Building Manipulative Cards**

**Write Context Sentences**

WRITING

Have students write sentences that must be completed with a vocabulary word and read each sentence to a partner. The partner should identify the missing term by holding up the appropriate vocabulary cards. ► **Linguistic**

## Assess Vocabulary

**Use Words in Context**

GROUP

Have students work in small groups to create the script for a TV news report about the devastation caused by a major storm. Ask students to include all of the vocabulary words in the script. Then ask each group to select one student to be the newscaster and read the report to the class.

**SPELLING/VOCABULARY CONNECTIONS**

See Spelling Challenge Words, pages 491O–491P.

**LANGUAGE SUPPORT**

See the Language Support Book, pages 145-148, for teaching suggestions for Vocabulary.

**Vocabulary PuzzleMaker**

Provides vocabulary activities

# Meeting Individual Needs for Vocabulary

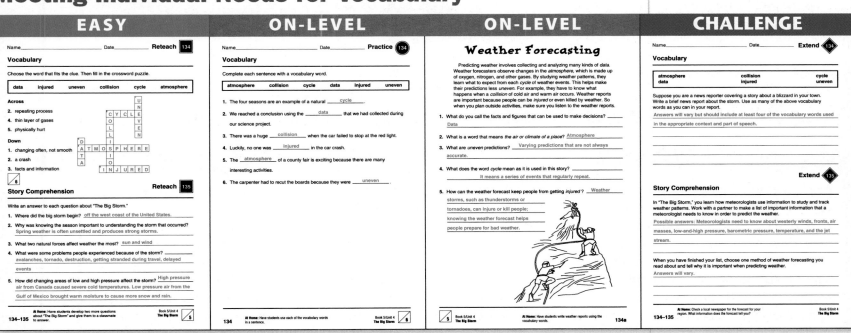

| EASY | ON-LEVEL | ON-LEVEL | CHALLENGE |
|---|---|---|---|
| Reteach, 134 | Practice, 134 | Practice, 134a<br>Take-Home Story | Extend, 134 |

# Comprehension

## Prereading Strategies

**PREVIEW AND PREDICT** Have the students preview the selection. Direct them to read the title and look at the pictures and captions, noting clues to what the selection will be about.

- What kind of information might the selection present?
- What will the story most likely be about?
- Do you think it will be a fiction or nonfiction story? Why? (Since the story will be about weather, I think it will be a nonfiction story.) *Genre*

Have students prepare a Predictions chart to record what they will learn in reading the story.

| PREDICTIONS | WHAT HAPPENED |
|---|---|
| I will learn about storms. | |
| I will learn about how people predict the weather. | |

**SET PURPOSES** What questions do students want answered?

- How do storms happen?
- What is a storm front?

## MEET BRUCE HISCOCK

Bruce Hiscock began work on *The Big Storm* by calling up weather reporters from the radio. "I had them suggest storms to write about. I wanted a spring storm because they are the most violent and active." Hiscock then studied weather for six months. He felt he had to learn all he could about weather to understand this storm fully. For details, Hiscock read newspaper accounts from towns hit by the storm. He also visited places pictured in his book.

From his cabin in the Adirondack Mountains, Hiscock stays in touch with nature. "I spend time every day in the woods with the birds and the animals. At night I watch the stars with a telescope. . . ." A billion-year-old boulder near his home is the subject of another Hiscock book, *The Big Rock*.

THE BIG ROCK
written and illustrated by
BRUCE HISCOCK

466

# Meeting Individual Needs · Grouping Suggestions for Strategic Reading

## EASY

**Read Together** Read the story together or invite students to use the **Listening Library.** Have students use the Judgment and Decision chart from page 467 to record information as they read. Comprehension and Intervention prompts offer additional help with vocabulary and comprehension.

## ON-LEVEL

**Guided Instruction** Choose from the Comprehension questions after the students have read the selection with a partner or after they have listened to the **Listening Library**. Have students use the Judgment and Decision chart to record information about the decisions people make.

## CHALLENGE

**Read Independently** Set up a chart with students, as on page 467, and have them fill it in as they read. After reading, they can use their charts to summarize the story and to discuss what they learned about the judgments and decisions people make with regard to the weather.

April 3   April 4   April 5   April

Mississippi River

Tornadoes

Rain

Appalachian Mountains

Hail Blizzards

Atlantic Ocean

# THE BIG STORM

written and illustrated by Bruce Hiscock

467

# Comprehension

☑ **Apply Judgments and Decisions**

☑ **Apply Important and Unimportant Information**

**STRATEGIC READING** Paying attention to the information on which people base judgments helps you understand their decisions. Before we begin reading, let's create a Judgment and Decision chart to record information.

| JUDGMENT | DECISION |
|----------|----------|
|          |          |

**① JUDGMENTS AND DECISIONS**
How did Bruce Hiscock prepare to write *The Big Storm*?

*MODEL* Hiscock wanted to write about a memorable storm. He interviewed forecasters and learned about a significant spring storm, which became the subject of his book. Then he learned as much as possible about the storm.

## Genre

### Narrative Nonfiction

Remind students that narrative nonfiction:

* gives facts about a topic in chronological order.
* presents information in the form of a story.
* may include maps, drawings, and diagrams.

**Activity** After students read *The Big Storm*, have them discuss how the maps and diagrams helped them learn more about the storm.

# Comprehension

**2** **IMPORTANT AND UNIMPORTANT INFORMATION** What is the most important piece of information on page 468?

**MODEL** I notice that the author gives details to establish when the storm started. He talks about the trees, the birds, and the baseball season. I guess he thinks it is important to establish the season of the storm. I think the most important piece of information is the date, March 1982.

It was a beautiful spring morning across most of the United States on the last day of March in 1982. The weather satellite, far out in space, showed clear skies stretching from the Rocky Mountains to the East Coast, where a few clouds lingered.

On the ground, signs of the changing season were everywhere. Flocks of geese and robins moved north as the days lengthened. Fresh new leaves covered the trees in the South, while up by the Great Lakes, spring peepers chirped from the ponds. With baseball season only a few days away, it looked like winter was finally over.

But spring is a time of rapidly changing weather. In the West a mass of clouds and cold, damp air rolled in off the ocean. It was the start of the big storm.

**2**

## Fluency

**READ WITH EXPRESSION** Compare the mood of the first two paragraphs on this page with the mood of the third.

**MODEL** Read the first two paragraphs in a calm voice, emphasizing words expressing beauty and excitement. Read the third paragraph in a hushed voice, indicating suspense. Place special emphasis on the words *big storm*.

Instruct students to practice reading this page with a partner until they can read the passages with expression.

# Comprehension

## LANGUAGE SUPPORT

**ESL** Relate the selection to students' native countries by having them talk about violent storms they experienced there.

• *Describe the storm. Where were you when the storm hit? What did you do? How did you feel?*

Then ask students to identify masses of clouds along the East Coast on the weather map. Have them point out where there are clouds elsewhere on the map.

# Comprehension

**3** Why did the rain turn into snow? Use the diagram at the bottom of page 470 to explain your answer. (Wind pushed the rain clouds up the mountain into colder air.) *Cause and Effect*

The clouds brought heavy rain to the Pacific Coast as the gathering storm moved inland. Like most weather systems in North America, it was carried along by the westerlies, the winds that nearly always blow from west to east across the continent.

When the storm ran up against the mountains of the Sierra Nevada range in California, the wind pushed the clouds up the steep slopes. In the cold mountain air the rain changed to snow.

470

## Cross Curricular: Social Studies

**TRACK THE STORM** Weather forecasters use maps to show weather activity.

Encourage students to map the sequence of events of the storm. Have them trace the map of the United States on pages 468–469. As they read, they can circle where the storm hit and note when it hit and what form it took.

▶ **Interpersonal/Spatial**

March 31 Heavy Snow in Sierra Nevada Mountains

It snowed hard all day in the Sierras. The flakes clung to the tall pines, coating them in heavy layers of white. But near the mountaintops, where no trees grow, the wind piled the snow into great drifts. Soon the drifts became so deep that the slopes would hold no more.

The snow began to slide from the high places, gently at first, then faster and faster, until the slides became huge avalanches. The avalanches roared down the mountains and slammed into buildings. Several people were killed.

Any storm can be dangerous as well as beautiful, but this one was a real powerhouse. And it was just getting started.

471

# Comprehension

**4** Identify a generalization on page 470. Look for clue words to help you. (The westerlies are winds that nearly always blow from west to east.) *Form Generalizations*

---

## LANGUAGE SUPPORT

**ESL** Ask students to use the illustrations on pages 470 and 471 to point out key vocabulary items from the story. For example, they can show what *moved inland* means by tracing the movement from left to right on the diagram at the bottom of page 470. *Westerlies* means "westerly winds" which are shown on the same diagram. *Steep slopes* are shown both on the diagram and in the pictures. *Heavy layers of white* and *avalanches* are both shown on page 471.

# Comprehension

**⑤** **IMPORTANT AND UNIMPORTANT INFORMATION** This page contains lots of details. Can someone summarize the page in one sentence, stating the important information? (The strong cold front moved across the Rocky Mountains to the Great Plains, bringing with it high winds and cold, violent weather.)

The storm moved swiftly over the Rocky Mountains, spreading blizzards from Montana to Arizona. In Colorado fierce winds gusted to 141 miles per hour, overturning vans and campers. In Nebraska the wind blew hard enough to move cow chips around.

The strongest winds came right at the leading edge of the storm. There a cold front marked the boundary between the warm springlike air covering most of the country and the cold, stormy air rushing in. Big masses of warm and cold air do not mix when they meet but instead push each other around. The line where the air masses bump is called a front.

**⑤** This front was a cold front because the cold air was pushing the warm air away. Strong cold fronts usually bring high winds and sometimes violent weather.

472

---

**TEACHING TIP**

**WEATHER WORDS** Clarify for students the meanings of such "weather" terms as "front," "high," and "low." If possible, have a volunteer videotape a television weather forecast and play it for the class. Have students sum up what they learn.

---

## Activity

## Cross Curricular: Music

**STORMS** Have students listen to the musical representation of a storm in an orchestral piece, such as Grofe's *Grand Canyon Suite*. Ask them to identify the stages of the storm as they listen to the piece a second time.

Have small groups orchestrate their own storm using instruments such as castanets, spoons, tambourines, recorders, and lids from pots.

The tremendous power of weather comes from the sun. Our planet is surrounded by a thin layer of air called the atmosphere, which is a mixture of gases, clouds, and dust. Heat from the sun causes the atmosphere to flow and swirl around the earth.

For instance, imagine that your city or county is covered by a blanket of cool, cloudy air. No wind stirs the leaves, and temperatures are the same everywhere.

Now let the clouds open slightly so that sunlight falls on a plowed field or a parking lot at the mall. The sun warms the earth or the pavement, which in turn heats the air right above it. Hot air rises, and soon a huge bubble of warm air is going up like an invisible balloon.

As the warm air rises, cool air flows in along the ground to take its place, causing a breeze. Temperatures begin to change. The sun has made the atmosphere move.

473

# Comprehension

**6** **IMPORTANT AND UNIMPORTANT INFORMATION** What is the most important piece of information on this page? (Heat from the sun causes Earth's atmosphere to move.) What information would you leave out in summarizing the main idea of this page? (Sunlight falls on a plowed field or a parking lot at the mall.)

## Minilesson

### REVIEW/MAINTAIN

## Cause and Effect

Remind students that an effect can be created by multiple causes working together. Ask students to reread the third paragraph on page 473 and identify the causes of a warm bubble of air.

- Ask students to create an equation that shows a cause-and-effect relationship. (sunshine + pavement = bubble of warm air)

**Activity** Have students find the cause-and-effect relationship in the last paragraph and express it as an equation.

**473**

# Comprehension

**7** **What generalization about storms does the author make on this page? What details does he provide?** (It is not easy to predict what a storm will do because so many variables affect the weather, including the sun, the ocean currents, the spinning of Earth, and the time of year.) *Form Generalizations*

## SELF-MONITORING STRATEGY

**REREAD** Rereading a part of the selection can help clarify a passage that the reader does not understand.

*MODEL* On page 474, I didn't understand how wind is created by warm air rising from the tropics meeting cold air flowing down from the North Pole. I looked back in the selection and found an explanation on page 473. Rereading previous pages helps me understand the current page.

## Writer's Craft

### EXPOSITORY TRANSITIONS

Explain: A writer uses transitions to keep a narrative moving from one event to another. Transitions also connect ideas in nonfiction writing.

Example: Read the first paragraph on page 474. Point out how the writer repeats the idea of warming air to connect the sentences. Ask: What does "this heating pattern" refer to in the third sentence? (the movement of warm and cold air) **What phrase in the next sentence does the writer use to connect "this heating pattern" with worldwide seasonal changes?** (Of course)

 Have students find examples of transitional phrases in other parts of the text.

**474** *The Big Storm*

The same sort of uneven heating keeps the atmosphere moving worldwide. Warm air rises from the tropics while cold air flows down from the poles. This heating pattern and others create the vast wind and weather systems of the planet. Of course, these weather systems change with the seasons. The long summer days provide much more sunlight to warm and lift the air than the short, cold days of winter.

The sun moves the weather, but the land and sea affect it too. Ocean currents cool or warm the air. Hills and mountains block the wind. Even the spinning of the earth changes the wind's direction.

**7** In fact, so many things affect the weather that when a storm comes up, it is not easy to predict exactly what it will do.

474

The big storm grew worse as it swept out over the Great Plains. Flocks of robins huddled on the ground, unable to fly in the blowing snow. Across the Dakotas and Minnesota, weather forecasters watched their barometers as the readings fell to record low levels. A deep low-pressure center was forming.

475

# Comprehension

 **MULTIPLE-MEANING WORDS**
Reread the first sentence. The word *swept* can have more than one meaning. What do you think it means in this case? *Semantic Cues*

## Minilesson

**REVIEW/MAINTAIN**

### Draw Conclusions

Remind students that to draw a conclusion readers use information from the story and their own body of knowledge.

- Ask students to draw a conclusion about the profession of the man in the illustration on page 475 and give three reasons to support it.

**Activity** Ask students to identify the setting of the illustration on page 470 and give three reasons that support their conclusion.

## PREVENTION/INTERVENTION

**MULTIPLE-MEANING WORDS**
Explain that the way the word *swept* is used here may be unfamiliar.

Have students suggest meanings for *swept* used in this context. Lead them to see that *swept* means to move across with speed or intensity. Ask them how this *sweeping* is similar to the motion of a broom *sweeping* a floor. *Semantic Cues*

# Comprehension

**8 JUDGMENTS AND DECISIONS**
How do weather forecasters make judgments about the weather? (They gather scientific evidence from instruments and weather stations. They compare this evidence with what they know about weather and make judgments, or forecasts.) **What decisions do forecasters make about the weather?** (They must decide what information to put in the forecasts and when to issue special bulletins, or warnings, about the weather.)

Let's put this information on our Judgment and Decision chart.

| JUDGMENT | DECISION |
|---|---|
| Make forecasts, or predictions, about the weather based on evidence. | Decide whether to issue special bulletins, or warnings, about the weather. |

Barometers measure the pressure of the air directly overhead. Air, like water, has weight, and tons of air press down on the earth. This force, called barometric or atmospheric pressure, changes constantly as the air moves.

**8** Forecasters pay close attention to these changes, for they help predict the weather to come. High pressure usually brings fair skies. Low pressure means storms, and the lower the pressure, the stronger the storm.

As the blizzard raged on, the weather stations in the storm reported the low pressure, the freezing temperatures, and the gusty wind and snow conditions to the National Meteorological Center near Washington, D.C. The data went directly into their huge computers along with data from hundreds of other weather stations, satellites, and instrument-carrying balloons.

The computer gave an overall picture of the weather to the forecasters at the National Center. Then, using more computers, they predicted what the storm would do next. These predictions were sent back to each weather station. There, a detailed forecast was made for the local area.

This work goes on every day, but with a killer storm on the loose, the forecasts were especially important.

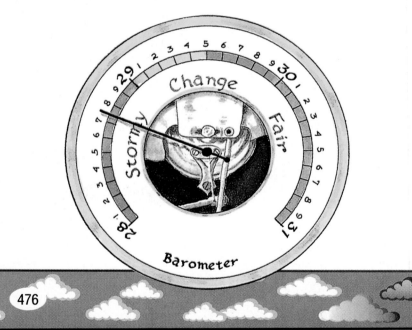

476

## Cross Curricular: Science

**SATELLITES** The first weather satellite, TIROS I, was launched in 1960. Since 1966, the Earth has been photographed at least once every day.

- Ask students what information could satellites provide that can't be gathered on land.

**RESEARCH AND INQUIRY** Have students investigate satellites and develop a time line. ▶ **Intrapersonal/Spatial**

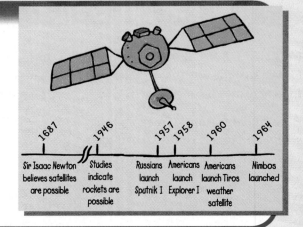

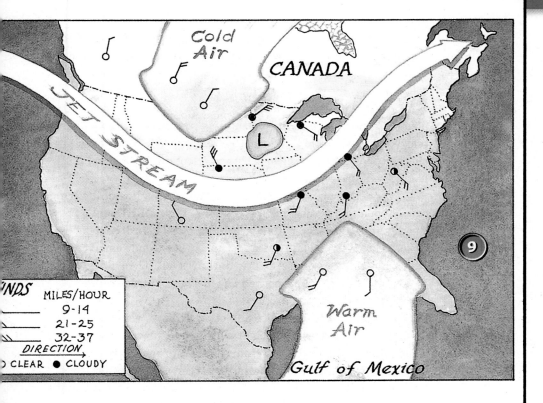

On the morning of Friday, April 2, the weather map showed strong surface winds blowing in toward the low-pressure center. Areas of low pressure push enormous amounts of air upward, causing air near the ground to rush in from all sides, like air rushing into a vacuum cleaner. Far above the surface, the jet stream, a narrow band of high-speed wind that snakes across the continent, formed a giant curve around the low.

All this was creating a huge counterclockwise swirl in the atmosphere typical of big storms. On one side of the swirl warm, moist air from the Gulf of Mexico was being drawn north. On the backside, frigid air was coming down out of Canada.

477

# Comprehension

**9** **Look at the weather map on this page. Using information from the map and its legend, generalize about the weather in Missouri on the morning of April 2.** (The weather in Missouri was warm and cloudy and the wind was blowing 21–25 miles per hour. It was a typical spring day.) **Generalize about the weather in our state on April 2.** *Form Generalizations*

**WORD STRUCTURE/CONTEXT CLUES** Reread the first sentence in the second paragraph. Do you know what *counterclockwise* means?

## Minilesson

### REVIEW/MAINTAIN

## Compound Words

A compound word is formed by combining two or more words.

Ask students to locate and define a compound word on page 476. (overhead)

Explain that sometimes words formed using a prefix, such as the word barometer, look like compound words. However, when broken down, it becomes obvious that only one part of the word can stand alone. (baro/meter)

**Activity** Have partners find and define six compound words on page 478. (thunderstorms, everyone, afternoon, airports, whirlwinds, pinpoint) Ask partners to check their definitions against the dictionary. Discuss hyphenated compounds as needed.

## PREVENTION/INTERVENTION

**WORD STRUCTURE/CONTEXT CLUES** Write *counterclockwise* on the chalkboard. Mask *counter* and ask what type of movement the work *clockwise* refers to. Demonstrate a clockwise movement with your arm and ask students to imitate it. Explain that *counter* means opposite. Ask students to demonstrate a *counterclockwise* movement.

# Comprehension

⑩ **JUDGMENTS AND DECISIONS**
Here we learn that the storm hit the Texas plains. Area airports were closed. List this decision on your Judgment and Decision chart and then fill in the judgment.

*MODEL* I know that airport managers rely on weather reports and forecasts. They know when a severe storm is coming. As airport managers, they know weather requirements for safe take-offs and landings. Do they maintain safe flying standards and inconvenience passengers as a result? This was the judgment they had to make, and their decision was to close the airports.

| JUDGMENT | DECISION |
|---|---|
| Make forecasts, or predictions, about the weather based on evidence. | Decide whether to issue special bulletins, or warnings, about the weather. |
| A dangerous situation exists, based on storm warnings. | The airports should be closed. |

## Visual Literacy

### VIEWING AND REPRESENTING

Usually the writer of a story is not also the illustrator. However, *The Big Storm* was written and illustrated by Bruce Hiscock. Ask: How might an illustrator choose what to include in drawings used to illustrate the text? (An illustrator might choose to draw familiar surroundings and people, for example.)

Ask students to read the titles on the spines of the books in the bookcase shown on page 478. Why did Hiscock choose these titles? (*The Big Rock* and *The Big Tree* are books by Hiscock; perhaps he admires Rembrandt and Homer.)

The National Severe Storm Forecast Center in Kansas City, Missouri, began plotting where these two air masses would meet. Chances were good that the collision would result in a powerful cold front, producing violent thunderstorms and tornadoes.

Local weather stations from Texas to Iowa and east were alerted. A Severe Weather Watch was announced on radio and television to warn that bad weather was possible. Forecasters checked their radar screens constantly, looking for signs of the front. Everyone waited.

⑩ The afternoon was warm and humid when a line of towering clouds appeared across the Texas plains. Lightning flashed in the distance. Soon the rumble of thunder was heard. Airports closed. Dogs whined and hid under beds. The clouds came on, churning and billowing. An eerie darkness fell. Then slashing winds hit. Rain and hail poured down. The cold front raced through. Temperatures dropped sharply.

All along the front, police and other spotters watched for tornadoes. Tornadoes are violent whirlwinds, funnel-shaped clouds that may spiral down from thunderstorms. They are extremely dangerous. The spotters watched anxiously, for they knew that weather radar can pinpoint thunderstorms but usually cannot "see" tornadoes. Eyes are better for that.

478

479

# Comprehension

## Minilesson

### REVIEW/MAINTAIN

### /îr/ and /ûr/

Remind students the /îr/ sound has several spellings, including *eer, ear, ier,* and *er*.

Ask students to find a word on page 478 with the /îr/ sound spelled the same as in *here*. (severe)

Ask students to find a word on page 478 with the /îr/ sound spelled the same as in *deer*. (eerie) Also contrast /îr/ with the sound /ûr/, as in the word *alerted* on page 478. *Graphophonic Cues*

**Activity** Challenge students to make lists of at least seven words with the /îr/ sound. The lists should cover all four spelling patterns. (examples: hear, dear, cheer, sheer, mere, pier, fierce)

 Phonics Intervention Guide

# Comprehension

**① JUDGMENTS AND DECISIONS**
What judgments did the residents of
Paris, Texas have to make? (The residents had
to make judgments about whether the severe
weather threatened their safety.) **What information did they have to consider?** (They knew
a Severe Weather Watch was in effect in their
area. They knew that temperatures had
dropped, winds were blowing, and rain and
hail were pouring down. Then, there was a
Tornado Warning.) **What decision did they
make?** (They hurried to shelter.)

Let's add this information to our Judgment
and Decision chart.

| JUDGMENT | DECISION |
|---|---|
| Make forecasts, or predictions about the weather based on evidence. | Decide whether to issue special bulletins or warnings about the weather. |
| A dangerous situation exists based on storm warnings. | The airports should be closed. |
| The weather conditions threatened their safety. | Townspeople should find shelter from the storm. |

Suddenly a tornado was sighted heading for Paris, Texas.
Sirens blew. A Tornado Warning was broadcast. Families rushed
for the nearest bathroom, closet, or basement shelter.

The tornado hit with the roar of a freight train. Houses and
churches were torn apart. Trees shattered. Cars were tossed
around.

The funnel cloud stayed down for twenty minutes, ripping a
path through the city two blocks wide and five miles long. Most of
⑪ the people in the path survived, though many were injured. Ten
people were killed.

480

## Cross Curricular: Math

**TIME AND DISTANCE** Although winds
in a tornado can swirl at 200 miles per
hour, the tornado itself moves slower on
the ground.

- Ask students how long the tornado was
  on the ground in Paris, Texas and how
  far it traveled. (20 minutes, 5 miles)

Have students determine the ground
speed of the tornado. Have them draw a
diagram expressing their findings.

▶ **Mathematical/Visual**

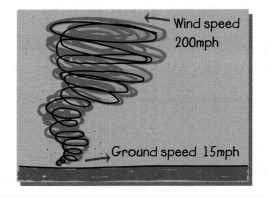

Wind speed
200mph

Ground speed 15mph

# Comprehension

**12** Look at the details in the illustration. What might happen to the neighborhood should the tornado remain on its path? *Make Predictions*

**MULTIPLE-MEANING WORDS** In the first sentence of the last paragraph on page 480, the tornado is referred to as a "funnel cloud." *Funnel* can have more than one meaning. Do you know what it means here?

## Minilesson
### REVIEW/MAINTAIN
### Sequence of Events

Remind students that the term sequence of events refers to the order in which events take place in a story.

• Ask students to make a time line showing the events on pages 478 to 482. Suggest they use a morning, afternoon, and night format.

**Activity** Have students make a time line for the storm from beginning to end.

## PREVENTION/INTERVENTION

**MULTIPLE-MEANING WORDS**
Explain that the word *funnel* is used here in an unfamiliar way. It is used as an adjective to describe the shape of the cloud. Ask students to make a funnel by rolling up a sheet of paper, and compare it with the shape of the funnel cloud in the illustration on page 481.

**481**

# Comprehension

 Compare the illustration on this page with the one on the previous page. What do they tell you about a tornado? (Tornadoes destroy anything in their path, including buildings.) *Cause and Effect*

 **IMPORTANT AND UNIMPORTANT INFORMATION** How would you summarize page 482? What is the most important information? What could be left out of a summary or considered unimportant information? (The worst series of tornadoes in the United States since 1974 killed more than thirty people and caused severe damage. The names of the individual states and the particulars of the damage wouldn't be in a summary.)

Tornado Areas April 2-3

**13**

More than eighty tornadoes touched down that afternoon and night in Texas, Oklahoma, Arkansas, Missouri, and other states as far east as Ohio. Even with the warning broadcasts, over thirty people died, and the damage was horrendous. The United States has more tornadoes than anyplace else in the world, but this was the worst outbreak since 1974.

**14**

482

---

# CULTURAL PERSPECTIVES

**PREDICTING THE WEATHER**
Advances in technology have allowed weather forecasters worldwide to predict severe weather.

- Ask students to contrast the tornado episode in *Grandma Essie's Covered Wagon* with the one in *The Big Storm*.

**RESEARCH AND INQUIRY** Ask students to research how countries of the world predict severe weather.
▶ **Interpersonal/Linguistic**

*inter***NET CONNECTION** Students can learn more about weather forecasting by visiting **www.mhschool.com/reading**

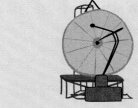

Doppler Radar allows storms to be tracked around the world.

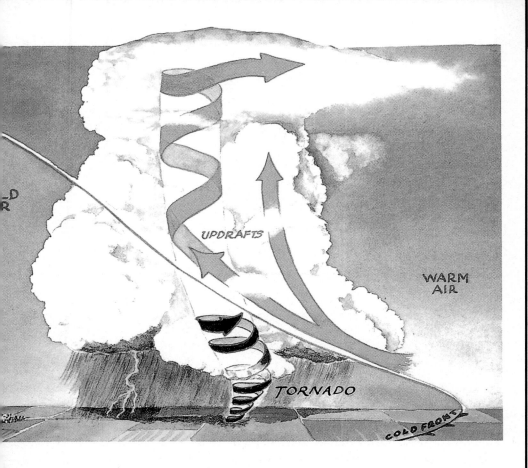

Tornadoes usually form just behind a cold front as the wedge of cold, dense air pushes in, forcing the warm, moist air to rise very quickly. This produces strong updraft winds and huge thunderclouds.

If an updraft begins to spin, it may set off a tornado. Exactly what causes the spinning is not completely understood, but once the twister is formed, it sucks in air, dirt, and anything else it touches with winds of over two hundred miles an hour. Boards, bricks, and glass become deadly flying missiles. Huge funnel clouds can even lift railroad cars.

483

# Comprehension

## Minilesson

### REVIEW/MAINTAIN

## Summarize

Remind students that it is usually not possible to remember every fact presented on a page or in a passage. Summarizing can help readers select key facts to remember.

- Ask students to identify the key fact on page 483.

**Activity** Have students write a one-sentence summary for page 483. (Tornadoes usually form just behind a cold front, with winds that can reach speeds of more than 200 miles an hour.)

# Comprehension

⑮ **IMPORTANT AND UNIMPORTANT INFORMATION** Reread page 484. As you read, make notes about how raindrops are formed. Then, use your notes to write a one-sentence explanation. (Ice crystals high in the clouds become snowflakes and then melt to become raindrops.)

ICE CRYSTAL

SNOWFLAKE

WATER VAPOR

COLD CLOUD DROPLET

RAINDROP

When the front passed, the tornadoes stopped, but thunderstorms continued throughout the South. Heavy rain drenched Alabama and Georgia. Hail the size of golf balls dented cars and broke windows in Kentucky.

Rain and hail are formed from the moisture in clouds, but they are not simply falling bits of mist and ice. The water droplets and tiny ice crystals that make up clouds are far too small to fall by themselves, and so they remain suspended in air like fog.

Surprisingly, most raindrops start out as snowflakes. High in the cloud where the air is very cold, ice crystals gradually grow into snowflakes that are heavy enough to fall. The snowflakes then melt, if it is warm near the ground, and become raindrops. A raindrop is about a million times larger than a cloud droplet. ⑮

**484**

## LANGUAGE SUPPORT

**ESL** Students who come from warm-weather countries may not be familiar with snowflakes and hailstones. Have them study the illustrations on pages 484–485 and ask them to draw their own versions of snowflakes and hailstones.

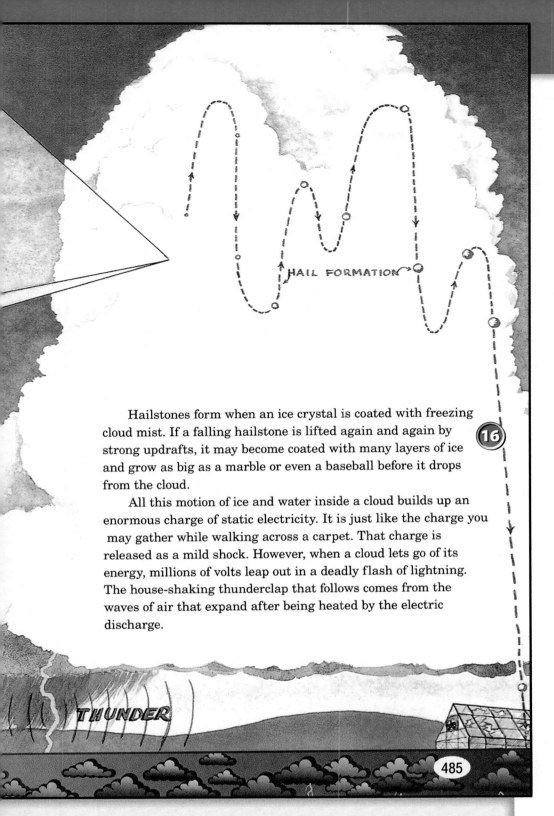

HAIL FORMATION

Hailstones form when an ice crystal is coated with freezing cloud mist. If a falling hailstone is lifted again and again by strong updrafts, it may become coated with many layers of ice and grow as big as a marble or even a baseball before it drops from the cloud.

All this motion of ice and water inside a cloud builds up an enormous charge of static electricity. It is just like the charge you may gather while walking across a carpet. That charge is released as a mild shock. However, when a cloud lets go of its energy, millions of volts leap out in a deadly flash of lightning. The house-shaking thunderclap that follows comes from the waves of air that expand after being heated by the electric discharge.

THUNDER

# Comprehension

**16** **What causes hailstones?** (They form in storm clouds from layers of ice coating ice crystals.) **What causes lightning?** (When a cloud releases built-up static electricity, millions of volts are discharged and flash as lightning.) *Cause and Effect*

**WORD STRUCTURE** Look for the words *deadly* and *discharge* on page 485. Can you identify the base words? How does the suffix or prefix change the meaning of each base word?

## PREVENTION/INTERVENTION

**WORD STRUCTURE** Explain that there are different ways to change the meaning of a word. One way is to add other word parts to the base word. Elicit from students that a prefix is added to the beginning of a base word and a suffix is added to the end.

Have students look for the meaning of the word *charge* in the dictionary. How does the prefix *dis-* change the meaning of the word? (It means the opposite.) Then discuss how the suffix *-ly* changes the meaning of *dead* to mean "in a manner that causes one to be dead."

**485**

# Comprehension

 **JUDGMENTS AND DECISIONS**
Imagine that you are the person who has to decide whether or not the New York Yankees play their game on April 6. What judgment and decision would you make?

Let's complete our Judgment and Decision chart.

| JUDGMENT | DECISION |
|---|---|
| Make forecasts, or predictions about the weather based on evidence. | Decide whether to issue special bulletins or warnings about the weather. |
| A dangerous situation exists based on storm warnings. | The airports should be closed. |
| The weather conditions threatened their safety. | Townspeople should find shelter from the storm. |
| Traveling is dangerous and the field is covered in snow. | The game should be postponed. |

**RETELL THE STORY** Ask volunteers to retell the story focusing on the important information they learned regarding the way people make judgments and decisions about the weather. They may need to refer to their Judgment and Decision charts. *Summarize*

## STUDENT SELF-ASSESSMENT

- How did the judgment and decision strategy help me understand the story?

**TRANSFERRING THE STRATEGY**

- When might I try using this strategy again? In what other reading could the chart help me?

For the next three days the huge mass of Arctic air behind the cold front brought more snow and high winds to the Midwest. Driving became very dangerous. Five hundred travelers were stranded in Michigan and had to spend the night in school gyms. Rush-hour traffic in Chicago was a tangle of accidents.

The great swirl of clouds around the low was clearly visible from space, and as the swirl drifted east, clear skies and intense cold followed it. With no blanket of clouds at night, the earth rapidly lost heat to outer space. Low temperature records were set from Idaho to the Appalachians. And still the storm was not through!

Tuesday, April 6, was opening day for the baseball season, and the New York Yankees were scheduled to play at home. The main storm center was now out at sea, but still the forecast was not good. Cold air continued to pour in, forming new lows over Pennsylvania and the New Jersey coast.

Around three in the morning, snow began to fall softly on New York City. In the Northeast the great snowstorms often begin very quietly. Soon the wind picked up. By noon it was a howling blizzard. Traffic snarled. Trains were delayed. The pace of the great city slowed to a sloppy walk.

 Over a foot of snow fell in New York before the storm moved on to Boston. It was the first blizzard ever to hit New York City in April. The Yankee game was delayed for four days. Many adults said bad things about the weather, but few kids complained. They all had a day off from school.

## REREADING FOR *Fluency*

 Have students choose a section to reread aloud. Encourage them to read a part that they found interesting during the first reading.

**READING RATE** When you evaluate rate, have the student read aloud from the story for one minute. Place a stick-on note after the last word read. Count words read. To evaluate

students' performance, see the Running Record in the **Fluency Assessment** book.

**ⓘ Intervention** For leveled fluency lessons, passages, and norms charts, see **Skills Intervention Guide**, Part 4, Fluency.

The big storm finally ended. Snow turned to slush and melted away. People cleaned up their towns. Spring returned. Birds began traveling north again, and the evenings lost their chill.

The storm is just a memory now, but every spring the  cycle repeats itself. Warm air from the south meets with cold Arctic air, triggering storms of all sizes and giving the United States one of the most varied and exciting climates on earth.

487

## LITERARY RESPONSE

**QUICK-WRITE** Invite students to record their thoughts about the selection. These questions may help them:

- What did you learn about by reading the story?

- How can you use this information to make decisions regarding your safety in severe weather?

**ORAL RESPONSE** Have students share their journal entries or discuss the information they found most interesting.

# Comprehension

## Return to Predictions and Purposes

Review with students their purposes for reading the selection. Were their predictions accurate?

| PREDICTIONS | WHAT HAPPENED |
|---|---|
| I will learn about storms. | The selection tracked the course of a severe spring storm. |
| I will learn about how people predict the weather. | Weather forecasters use information they gather from sources, such as satellites and weather balloons, to predict the weather. |

**INFORMAL ASSESSMENT**

### JUDGMENTS AND DECISIONS

**HOW TO ASSESS**

- Have students review the judgments and decisions in the story.

- Ask them if they think people in the United States use the judgments of weather forecasters to make decisions.

Students should recognize that weather forecasters make judgments that, in turn, allow people to make decisions about how to dress and what to do.

**FOLLOW UP** If students are having difficulty with judgments and decisions, model deciding what clothing to wear on a snowy day.

# Story Questions

Have the students discuss or write answers to the questions on page 488.

**Answers:**

1. It was a day of quiet, mild, typical early spring weather. *Literal/Details*

2. Many factors influence the weather. *Inferential/Draw Conclusions*

3. In spring, there is more warm air moving up from the tropics, meeting cold air from the north. *Inferential/Form Generalizations*

4. The story tells about a range of weather conditions during a turbulent, wide-ranging, long-lived spring storm. *Critical/Summarize*

5. Sample answer: similarities: destructive winds and heavy rain; differences: duration and location (water vs. land) *Critical/Reading Across Texts*

**Write a Report** For a full writing process lesson related to this suggestion, see pages 491K–491L.

# Story Questions & Activities

1. What was the weather like in most of the United States on the morning of the storm?

2. What makes it so difficult to predict what a storm will do?

3. Why do you think that "spring is a time of rapidly changing weather"? Explain.

4. How would you summarize Bruce Hiscock's findings in this selection?

5. In what way is the tornado in "The Big Storm" like the hurricane in "An Island Scrapbook"? What are the differences between the two storms?

## Write a Report

Choose a type of precipitation—rain, snow, sleet, or hail—and write a report that explains it. Start your report with a main-idea statement. Find out *how, why, when,* and *where* the precipitation might start. Write the answers as details or facts in the body of your report. End with a conclusion that summarizes your information.

# Meeting Individual Needs

| EASY | ON-LEVEL | CHALLENGE |
|---|---|---|
| Reteach, 135 | Practice, 135 | Extend, 135 |

# Create a Diorama

In an empty shoebox, create a model of a town in the middle of a bad storm. Use construction paper, cotton, sticks, stones, soil, sand, paints, and other art supplies. Build houses, streets, cars, people, and trees in the midst of a storm, such as a blizzard or a tornado. In your diorama, show the power of weather to destroy property, crops, and trees.

# Explain the Tools of the Trade

Meteorologists use instruments, computers, radar, and satellite cameras to predict the weather. Explain how these tools work together to produce a weather forecast. For example, what can the computer tell the meteorologist if changing ground temperatures, changing barometer readings, and moving clouds are studied?

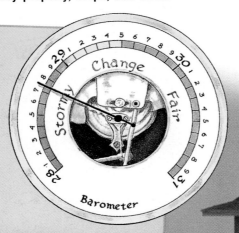

# Find Out More

Choose a place you have never been to but would like to visit. What kind of weather would you find there? Start by checking in an encyclopedia, a travel brochure, or a book about the area. Write a few sentences that describe the weather. Include the average temperature, the amount of rain- or snowfall, and the kinds of storms the area has. Show your findings on a chart or a graph.

489

# Story Activities

## Create a Diorama

**Materials:** shoebox, construction paper, cotton, cardboard, sticks, stones, soil, sand, paints

**GROUP** Have students work in small groups. Encourage them to discuss and then agree on how to take responsibility for a portion of the project.

## Explain the Tools of the Trade

**Materials:** science reference books, encyclopedias

**PARTNERS** Assign partners to investigate a specific meteorology tool. Ask them to write a short report with pictures or drawings and present it to the class.

## Find Out More

**RESEARCH AND INQUIRY** Encourage students to choose exotic locations. Ask them what special items they would need to take on their trip.

 For more information about weather in different places, students can visit **www.mhschool.com/reading**

## Activity

**SCIENCE: HURRICANES** Ask students to research five of the most destructive hurricanes in the last hundred years. Have them present the data they find in a chart that includes the name and date of the hurricane, where it touched land, and how much damage it did in lives lost and property destroyed.

**What To Look For** A 4- or 5- column chart that lists five destructive hurricanes, including their names, dates, where they touched land, damage in number of lives lost, and cost of property destroyed.

**CHALLENGE**

# Study Skills

## GRAPHIC AIDS

**OBJECTIVES** Students will

- read and interpret a weather map
- identify fronts on a weather map.

**PREPARE** Preview the map and point out which areas have rain and which have sun. Display **Teaching Chart 111.**

**TEACH** Review the information presented on the map, including the symbols. Have a student determine the prevailing wind direction.

**PRACTICE** Have students answer questions 1–5. Review the answers with them.
**1.** Southeast; Florida **2.** the Pacific Northwest; the far West **3.** yes, because there is snow in the West **4.** No, a change in the jet stream, air pressure, or humidity can change the forecast. **5.** to find out what the weather will be; to save lives

**ASSESS/CLOSE** Have students compare the large weather map in *The Big Storm* with this one and note any differences.

## Meeting Individual Needs

# Study Skills

## Read a Weather Map

The weather maps that you see on television during the weather report show many facts about weather patterns. Some weather maps show the different temperature readings for the day in several different areas. Other weather maps show wind and cloud movements, and possible rain- or snowfall.

H = High Pressure System    L = Low Pressure S

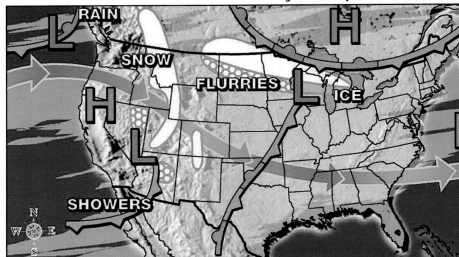

**Use the weather map to answer these questions.**

**1** In what region is there a state where it looks as if there is not a cloud in the sky? Do you know what state it is?

**2** Which parts of the country look as if they have rain showers?

**3** If the wind is moving from west to east, do you think the Middle West is going to have snow tomorrow? Explain.

**4** Can meteorologists guarantee their weather forecasts a day in advance? Why or why not?

**5** Why do you think it is important to know how to read a weather map?

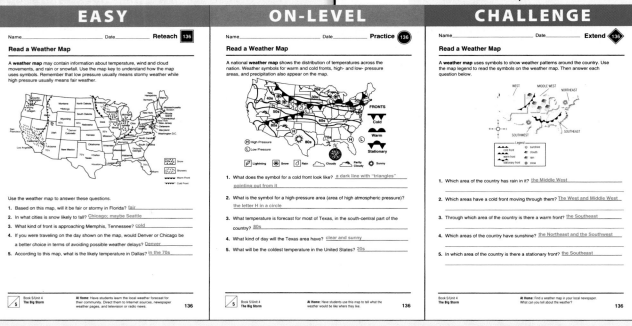

Reteach, 136            Practice, 136            Extend, 136

# TEST POWER

## Test Tip

The summary tells what the passage is mostly about.

**DIRECTIONS**

**Read the sample story. Then read each question about the story.**

SAMPLE

## Hilary Wants to Play the Drum

Hilary went down to the park every day after school to hear the drummers perform. Hilary enjoyed listening to the marches that the drum corps were practicing for the upcoming parade.

When she tried to play the same music on her drum, however, it didn't sound like the music she had heard. She couldn't get the rhythm even and smooth. Every time that she tried to repeat what she had heard at the park, she was disappointed.

One day, as the drummers were leaving, she noticed that one of them had forgotten the velvet drum cover that protected the drum when it wasn't being used.

Hilary grabbed the cover and ran after the drummers. When she caught up to one of the drummers, she gave her the cover. In return, the drummer offered Hilary a seat in the bandstand at the next parade.

1 Which of these is the best summary of the passage?

   **A** No one plays the drum better than Hilary does.

   **B** The drummers in the park liked the marches for the parade.

   **C** Hilary listened to the drummers and wanted to be like them.

   **D** Hilary spent every day in the park after her drum lesson.

2 This story mostly takes place —

   **F** in the park

   **G** at Hilary's house

   **H** at school

   **J** in a music store

491

## Read the Page

Remind students to summarize the passage in their own words.

## Discuss the Questions

**Question 1:** This question requires students to determine which is the best summary of the passage. Read each answer choice as a group. As you discuss each incorrect answer choice, have students point out *why* the answer is incorrect. The best answer will summarize the *whole* passage.

**Question 2:** This question requires students to determine where the story *mostly* takes place. Be sure to point out that the question does not ask where the *whole* story takes place, but where it *mostly* takes place. The passage refers to Hilary's visits to the *park* after school each day and to the day that she found the drum cover in the park.

# Leveled Books

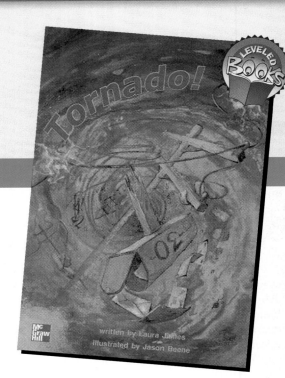

**i Intervention** ▶ **Skills**
**Intervention Guide,** for direct instruction and extra practice in vocabulary and comprehension

## EASY

### Tornado!

/îr/ and /ûr/

☑ **Judgments and Decisions**

☑ **Instructional Vocabulary:** *atmosphere, collision, cycle, data, injured, uneven*

written by Laura James
illustrated by Jason Beene

## Guided Reading

**PREVIEW AND PREDICT** Have students preview the illustrations through page 9. Ask them to predict what will happen in the story.

**SET PURPOSES** Have students write questions they would like to have answered by the story.

**READ THE BOOK** Use the questions below as students read the story to help them apply reading strategies.

**Page 2:** Look on page 2 for words with the /îr/ sound as in *pierce.* (nearby, cheerleading) Compare the spellings of *pierce, nearby,* and *cheerleading* to determine three spellings of the /îr/ sound. (ier, ear, eer) *Phonics*

**Page 3:** Why do you think some people in Jefferson County were listening to weather reports? (Many people would have observed that a thunderstorm was close. They may have been concerned that it would develop into something worse so they listened for other updates.) *Judgments and Decisions*

**Pages 4 and 5:** What causes a tornado? (A tornado is a rapidly rotating column of air caused by high fast-moving winds moving over low slower-moving winds.) *Cause and Effect*

**Page 15:** What does the word *injured* mean? (hurt) What are some context clues that helped you? (war zone, rubble, stretchers) *Instructional Vocabulary*

**Page 16:** Summarize what happened in Jefferson County, Alabama on April 8, 1998. (A tornado struck Jefferson County on April 8, 1998. It destroyed over 1,000 homes, injured 221 people, and killed 32 people.) *Summarize*

**RETURN TO PREDICTIONS AND PURPOSES** Have students review their predictions. Which ones were accurate? Did they find answers to their questions?

**LITERARY RESPONSE** Discuss these questions with students:

- What measures can be taken to help ensure your survival during a storm?

- Why do you think many people went on with their lives as usual even though there was a thunderstorm?

Also see the story questions and activity in *Tornado!*

---

**Answers to Story Questions**

1. From southwest to northeast.
2. They mostly hit the flat middle section of the country known as "tornado alley."
3. Because so many trees and poles had been splintered open by the tornado.
4. It is about the 1998 tornado in Birmingham, Alabama, what destruction it caused, and how people kept themselves safe during the disaster.
5. Answers will vary.

The *Story Questions* and *Activity* below appear in the *Easy Book*.

**Story Questions and Activity**

1. In which direction do most tornadoes travel?
2. Which part of the United States do the greatest number of tornadoes hit?
3. Why do you think the smell of fresh-cut pine is in the air the morning after the twister had passed Jefferson County?
4. What is this story mostly about?
5. Do you think this tornado was as severe a storm as the one in the story *The Big Storm*? Explain your answer.

**Try This Experiment**

You can make a miniature vortex of air. Find two table fans. Place them at right angles so that the air that one blows will intersect with the air of the other. Make sure one fan is about a foot or more higher than the other. Turn the higher-up fan on to HIGH, and the lower-down fan to LOW. At the point where the air from each intersects, there should be a vortex. Toss very small pieces of paper into the vortex to see how it's spinning.

*from Tornado!*

# Leveled Books

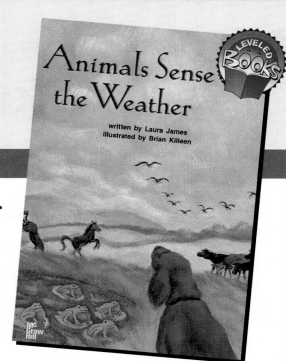

Animals Sense the Weather

written by Laura James
illustrated by Brian Killeen

## INDEPENDENT

### Animals Sense the Weather

- ☑ **Judgments and Decisions**
- ☑ **Instructional Vocabulary:**
  *atmosphere, collision, cycle, data, injured, uneven*

## Guided Reading

**PREVIEW AND PREDICT** Have students read the title and the table of contents. Ask students to preview the illustrations through page 9. Ask the students to predict what the story will be about.

**SET PURPOSES** Students should decide what they want to learn before they read and then write down a few questions they would like to have answered by the story.

**READ THE BOOK** Have students read the story independently. Then use the questions below to emphasize reading strategies.

**Page 2:** Which definition of *collision* does the author intend on this page? (crash) *Instructional Vocabulary*

**Page 5:** Why does the girl decide to have her birthday party at the park? (The girl thinks the pond is a nice spot, probably because it's pretty and green around it.) *Judgments and Decisions*

**Page 8:** List the important and unimportant information in the last paragraph on page 8. (That geese prefer to fly in calm air as it makes flying smoother is important.

The old saying in the paragraph is interesting but unimportant.) *Important and Unimportant Information*

**Page 15:** Why does the girl change the location of her party? (Her senses warn her that a storm is coming and bad weather would spoil an outdoor party. She also notices the reactions of the animals and those confirm what she has already sensed.) *Judgments and Decisions*

**RETURN TO PREDICTIONS AND PURPOSES** Review students' predictions and reasons for reading. Which predictions were accurate? Did they find answers to their questions?

**LITERARY RESPONSE** Discuss these questions with students:

- Have you ever thought an animal was trying to tell you something? Explain.

- How do you think scientists determined that animals can sense the weather? Remember the scientific process.

Also see the questions and activity in *Animals Sense the Weather.*

### Answers to Story Questions

1. Lower, because the winds up high are more turbulent.
2. It may mean that the air is dry and the frogs are swimming in the pond; the weather is good with no impending storms.
3. Accept all reasonable responses.
4. Animals can sense a change in the weather or an upcoming natural disaster, such as an earthquake. People can learn to observe changes in nature and animal behaviors to predict the weather too.
5. Answers will vary.

The *Story Questions* and *Activity* below appear in the *Independent Book.*

### Story Questions and Activity

1. Do geese fly lower or higher when a storm is coming?
2. What does it mean when frogs in a pond are not croaking very loudly?
3. After reading this book, do you think you could predict the weather without listening to a weather report?
4. What is the main idea of this book?
5. Do you think you would have been able to use your senses to detect a storm like the one that took place in *The Big Storm*?

### Observe and Predict the Weather

Keep a notebook in which you record your observations of animal behavior. For the first two weeks, watch the weather page in your newspaper to see when a storm is predicted. Then note any changes in the way animals around you are acting as the storm approaches. For the next two weeks, avoid reading the weather page or listening to weather reports. See if you can predict the weather by how the animals act.

*from Animals Sense the Weather*

# Leveled Books

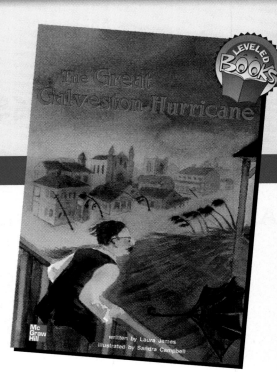

## CHALLENGE

### The Great Galveston Hurricane

☑ **Judgments and Decisions**

☑ **Instructional Vocabulary:** *atmosphere, collision, cycle, data, injured, uneven*

## Guided Reading

**PREVIEW AND PREDICT** Have students read the title and preview the illustrations through page 9. Ask them to predict what will happen in the story.

**SET PURPOSES** Students should note what they want to learn before reading the story. Have them think of a few questions they would like to have answered.

**READ THE BOOK** After students have read the book independently, return to the story to apply the following strategies.

**Page 2:** List the important information in the first paragraph on page 2. (The most deadly hurricane in United States history took place in August of 1900. It started off the west coast of Africa and traveled a great distance before it destroyed Galveston, Texas.) *Important and Unimportant Information*

**Page 5:** What does the word *data* mean here? (information) What context clues help you? (telegraph machine) *Instructional Vocabulary*

**Page 6:** When Dr. Cline received a wire saying the hurricane was headed toward Galveston, what course of action did he

take? Why? (He raised a hurricane warning flag because Galveston was in danger.) *Judgments and Decisions*

**Pages 7–8:** What did Dr. Cline do to prepare for the hurricane? Why? (Because he knew the storm was definitely going to hit Galveston, he continued to warn people. And, he decided to gather his own family at his home.) *Judgments and Decisions*

**Page 14:** Dr. Cline wrote that he believed Galveston's people would rebuild the city. How did he draw this conclusion? (They had already rebuilt the bridge. They were helping each other.) *Draw Conclusions*

**RETURN TO PREDICTIONS AND PURPOSES** Review students' predictions and reasons for reading. Which predictions were accurate? Which were not? Did they find answers to their questions?

**LITERARY RESPONSE** Discuss this with students:

- Why do you think most of the people ignored Dr. Cline's warnings?

Also see the story questions and activity in *The Great Galveston Hurricane*.

---

**Answers to Story Questions**

1. In the late summer, when ocean waters are at their warmest.
2. Sea waters were at peak temperature and winds were blowing both at the surface and at high altitude.
3. They had never experienced one as destructive as the hurricane of 1900. They also saw themselves as strong and sturdy, and did not believe it could happen to their town.
4. Using the Galveston hurricane as an example, it explains how dangerous a hurricane can be if warnings and safety rules are not followed.
5. Answers will vary.

The *Story Questions and Activity* below appear in the *Challenge Book*.

**Story Questions and Activity**

1. In what season is a hurricane most likely to form?
2. Why were the conditions off the west coast of Africa perfect for the start of a hurricane?
3. Why do you think the people of Galveston were not prepared for the hurricane?
4. What is the main idea of the book?
5. What about *The Great Galveston Hurricane* reminds you of the storm in *The Big Storm*?

**Track a Storm**

Look at the weather page in your local newspaper. Find the national weather map. Look and read for signs of a storm (a cold front or warm front) coming in at the edge of the map. Trace an outline of the country and mark where the storm is. Use dotted lines to show the track you think the storm will take across the country. Then watch the weather pages over the next several days, and mark the actual path of the front. Compare your prediction with the storm's path.

*from The Great Galveston Hurricane*

# Bringing Groups Together

## Anthology and Leveled Books

### Connecting Texts

**JUDGMENTS AND DECISIONS**
Write the story titles on a chart. Discuss with students the judgments and decisions in each story. Note the judgments for each story in the upper half of the chart and their corresponding decisions in the lower half of the chart.

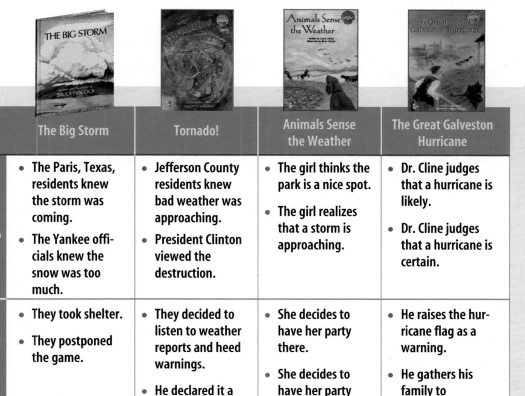

| | The Big Storm | Tornado! | Animals Sense the Weather | The Great Galveston Hurricane |
|---|---|---|---|---|
| **Judgments** | • The Paris, Texas, residents knew the storm was coming.<br>• The Yankee officials knew the snow was too much. | • Jefferson County residents knew bad weather was approaching.<br>• President Clinton viewed the destruction. | • The girl thinks the park is a nice spot.<br>• The girl realizes that a storm is approaching. | • Dr. Cline judges that a hurricane is likely.<br>• Dr. Cline judges that a hurricane is certain. |
| **Decisions** | • They took shelter.<br>• They postponed the game. | • They decided to listen to weather reports and heed warnings.<br>• He declared it a disaster area. | • She decides to have her party there.<br>• She decides to have her party indoors instead. | • He raises the hurricane flag as a warning.<br>• He gathers his family to safety. |

### Viewing/Representing

**GROUP PRESENTATIONS** Divide the class into four groups, one for each of the four books read in the lesson. (For *The Big Storm* combine students of different reading levels.) Have each group list the important, weather-related information they learned from the story. Ask them to prioritize the information and make a presentation to the class on either How Storms Form or What to Do when Bad Weather Threatens.

**AUDIENCE RESPONSE** Ask students to pay attention to the presentations. Allow time for questions after each presentation.

### Research and Inquiry

**MORE ABOUT METEOROLOGY** These four stories have all told about ways that the weather can be predicted. Ask small groups of students to

- research the types of severe weather most common in your area

- determine what tools local meteorologists use most often to predict severe weather and how they issue reports and warnings

- compare their findings and develop a weather safety chart for the classroom.

**inter NET CONNECTION** Have students log on to **www.mhschool.com/reading** to find out more about weather safety.

**LANGUAGE SUPPORT**

**ESL** Write the words *wind chill* on the chalkboard. Have volunteers pantomine the meaning of each word. Explain that wind chills the body by carrying away heat. The National Weather Service uses a wind chill index to measure the rate of heat loss from exposed skin.

## SELF-SELECTED Reading

*Students may choose from the following titles.*

**ANTHOLOGY**
- The Big Storm

**LEVELED BOOKS**
- Tornado!
- Animals Sense the Weather
- The Great Galveston Hurricane

Bibliography, pages T78–T79

# Review Judgments and Decisions

### PREPARE

**Discuss Judgments and Decisions**

Review: Making a judgment involves applying values to determine what you should do. Making a decision involves choosing a course of action.

### TEACH

**Read the Passage and Model the Skill**

Read "Snow Day?" with students. Ask them to pay attention to the reasons that a snow day might be a bad idea, as well as the reasons for calling a snow day.

### Snow Day?

By midnight the snow storm had stopped, but high winds swirled snow into drifts across highways. The temperature fell below zero, and the wind chill fell to 40 below.

Superintendent Casey listened to every weather report. The forecast for the next day was sunshine with continued cold temperatures and high winds. He had to decide whether to close the district's 23 schools. Parents would have to scramble for daycare. Some children would be left at home, unsupervised.

Superintendent Casey thought of children standing at bus stops in the morning, and of buses running late because of snowy roads. He reached for the phone. "No school tomorrow," he said.

Teaching Chart 112

Why did Superintendent Casey choose to close the schools?

***MODEL*** I think he was concerned about children waiting for the bus. Wind chills of 40 below zero are dangerous.

Have students underline reasons for closing the schools and circle reasons for keeping the schools open.

**Evaluate Choices**

GROUP

Divide students into small groups. Assign half the groups the task of defending the superintendent's decision. Tell the other half that they must find reasons to criticize the superintendent's decision.

▶ **Logical/Interpersonal**

**ASSESS/CLOSE**

**Make Judgments and Decisions**

PARTNERS

Have partners write a summary of a situation that requires people to make judgments and decisions. Suggest they use situations from stories they've read or from newspaper articles or TV news reports. Have students present their summaries to the class and discuss the judgments and decisions that should be made.

**ALTERNATE TEACHING STRATEGY**

**JUDGMENTS AND DECISIONS**

For a different approach to teaching this skill, see page T60.

**Intervention ▶ Skills**

**Intervention Guide**, for direct instruction and extra practice with judgments and decisions

# Meeting Individual Needs for Comprehension

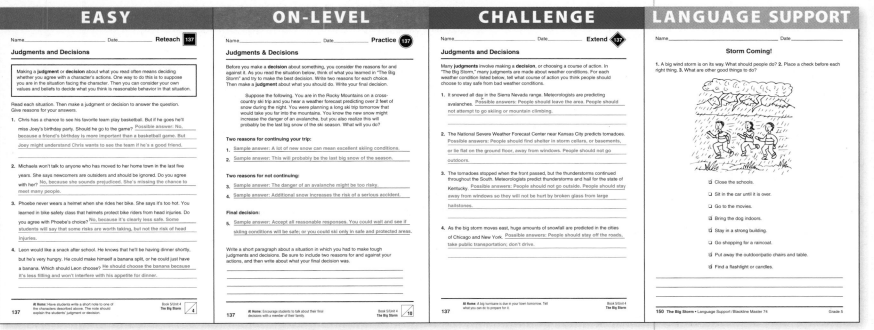

**EASY** — Reteach, 137

**ON-LEVEL** — Practice, 137

**CHALLENGE** — Extend, 137

**LANGUAGE SUPPORT** — Language Support, 150

## OBJECTIVES

**Students will**

- identify relevant information.
- draw conclusions.

### Skills Finder

**Draw Conclusions**

| Introduce | 407G–H |
|---|---|
| Review | 431G–H, 491G–H, 647G–H, 673G–H, 717G–H |
| Test | Unit 4, Unit 6 |
| Maintain | 687 |

### TEACHING TIP

**WEATHER FORECASTS**
Bring in several weather forecasts from newspapers. Point out pieces of information contained in each forecast and the conclusions that the meteorologist draws.

## Review Draw Conclusions

### PREPARE

**Discuss Drawing Conclusions**

Review: Drawing conclusions requires logical reasoning—putting together two or more ideas or pieces of information to reach a conclusion. Example: If your mother is driving you to school and you are stuck in a traffic jam and you hear lots of sirens, what conclusion do you draw?

### TEACH

**Read the Story and Model the Skill**

Read "Shep's Warning" with the students. Ask them to look for pieces of information that they can put together to draw a conclusion.

#### Shep's Warning

Susie awoke from her nap, feeling refreshed. She could have slept longer, but Shep was pawing at her arm and whining. The old <u>dog looked worried and seemed restless</u>, ready to return home.

Thick, blue-gray clouds had rolled in as Susie slept. Although it was just a little past noon, <u>the sky looked dark</u>. Overhead, clouds formed and reformed new patterns as <u>a strong east wind blew</u> them about. The <u>air felt thick and muggy</u>, almost like the air in the bathroom after a long shower.

"<u>Shower</u>," thought Susie. "No, this is not going to be a summer shower. We are in for a thunderstorm now."

**Teaching Chart 113**

Ask: What is a piece of information that helped Susie to conclude that there was going to be a thunderstorm?

**MODEL** I see that the old dog was whining and seemed worried and restless. Often animals can feel a storm coming. Susie probably based her conclusion on that.

Have students underline all of the pieces of information that Susie used to draw her conclusion. Have them circle her conclusion.

## PRACTICE

**Identify Relevant Information**

GROUP

Have students work together in small groups to list weather facts that help them to draw conclusions about the weather. Students may refer back to "The Big Storm" and to the newspaper weather forecasts. (Lists may include current temperatures, barometric pressure, direction of barometric pressure, weather to the west of your location, humidity, cloud cover.) ▶ **Logical/Interpersonal**

## ASSESS/CLOSE

**Draw Conclusions**

PARTNERS

Have partners write several paragraphs that contain information from which conclusions can be drawn. Suggest they choose a familiar topic, such as the weather. Ask sets of partners to exchange paragraphs, draw conclusions from what they read, and identify the relevant information that helped them to draw their conclusions.

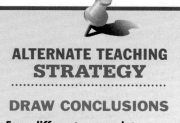

## ALTERNATE TEACHING STRATEGY

### DRAW CONCLUSIONS

For a different approach to teaching this skill, see page T62.

 **Skills Intervention Guide,** for direct instruction and extra practice with drawing conclusions

# Meeting Individual Needs for Comprehension

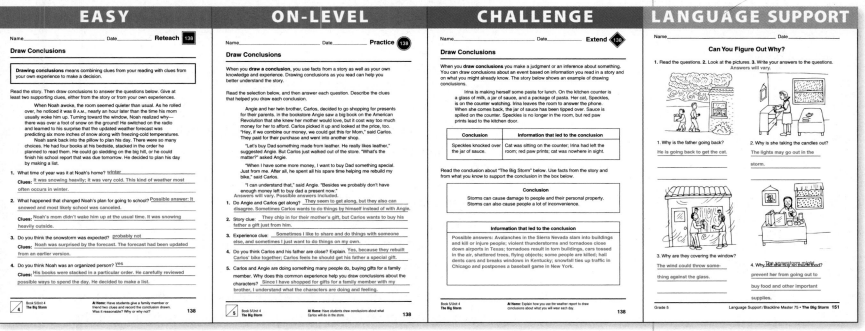

Reteach, 138          Practice, 138          Extend, 138          Language Support, 151

Students will

- **learn how a root word can help one understand a word's meaning.**

- **use root words to figure out the meaning of words.**

## Skills Finder

### Root Words

| | |
|---|---|
| Introduce | 431I–J |
| Review | 491I–J, 501G–H |
| Test | Unit 4 |

## TEACHING TIP

**ROOT WORDS** Knowing a variety of root words helps a reader figure out the meaning of many unfamiliar words.

- Share examples of root words: *log, logy* (word, study), *grat* (pleasing, thanks), *geo* (earth), *scope* (see, watch).

- Encourage partners to brainstorm one word with each root you name.

# Review Root Words

**PREPARE**

**Discuss Meaning of Root Words**

Review: A root word is a word part that carries the meaning and history of the word. In English, most root words come from Greek or Latin. Roots combine with prefixes or suffixes to form new words. Knowing the root of a word can help readers figure out the meaning of the whole word.

**TEACH**

**Read the Passage and Model the Skill**

Have students read the passage on **Teaching Chart 114.** Encourage students to look for words containing roots that may come from Greek or Latin.

### Forecasting Weather Storms

Barometers are weather instruments that measure air pressure. When a barometer shows that the air pressure in the atmosphere is falling, weather experts know that a storm is coming. They use other instruments as well to predict the weather. For example, a computer can give a picture of the weather across the nation. Satellites also provide helpful data for forecasters.

Teaching Chart 114

Model identifying roots within words and use their meanings to determine what the whole words mean.

***MODEL*** I can see the root *meter* in the word *barometer* in the first sentence. I know that *meter* means "measure," and *baro* means "weight" or "pressure," so a *barometer* must be something that measures weight or pressure. Let me read the sentence again and see if that meaning makes sense.

Have students think of other words with the root *meter*. (thermometer) Have them explain how knowing the root helps to figure out the word's meaning.

## PRACTICE

**Identify Roots to Find Meanings**

ONE

Have volunteers underline these words on the teaching chart and then circle their roots: *atmosphere, predict, computer.* Explain the roots: *Sphere* means "globe, ball"; *dicere* means "say"; *putare* means "think, reckon." Have students discuss how knowing the meaning of these roots helps them to understand each word's meaning.

▶ **Linguistic/Visual**

## ASSESS/CLOSE

**Use Roots to Find Additional Words**

GROUP

Have students work in groups to think of other words with the root words *dicere, sphere,* or *putare.* Students may want to consult a dictionary for this exercise. Have groups share and compare their lists.

▶ **Linguistic/Interpersonal**

**ALTERNATE TEACHING STRATEGY**

**ROOT WORDS**

For a different approach to teaching this skill, see page T65.

 **Intervention** ▶ **Skills Intervention Guide,** for direct instruction and extra practice with root words

# Meeting Individual Needs for Vocabulary

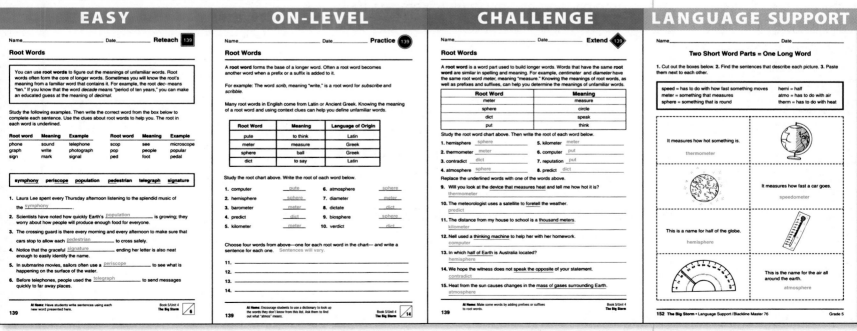

Reteach, 139          Practice, 139          Extend, 139          Language Support, 152

# Expository Writing

## GRAMMAR/SPELLING
### CONNECTIONS

See the 5-Day Grammar and Usage Plan on comparing with *more* and *most,* pages 491M–491N.

See the 5-Day Spelling Plan on compound words, pages 491O–491P.

## TEACHING TIP

**Technology**
Point out to students that it is often easier to catch mistakes on paper than on screen. For proofreading, encourage students to print out their work, mark the corrections on paper, and then enter the corrections on the file.

**Adding Details**
Have students check their work to see if any paragraphs need more details or examples. Encourage them to add further details if needed to support the main idea of each paragraph.

### Handwriting CD-ROM

## Prewrite

**WRITE A REPORT** Present the following assignment: Choose a type of precipitation— rain, snow, sleet, or hail— and write a report that explains it. Start your report with a main-idea sentence. Find out *how, why, when,* and *where* the precipitation might start. Write the answers as details or facts in the body of your report. End with a conclusion that summarizes your information.

**USE A CLUSTER MAP** Have students choose a type of precipitation and research it. Tell them to write the type of precipitation in the circle in the center. Ask students to label the surrounding circles *How?, Why?, When?,* and *Where?.* Explain that on each line, or spoke, attached to a circle they should write details that answer the question word and relate to the type of precipitation.

**Strategy: Compare Clusters** Divide students who chose the same kind of precipitation into partners and tell them to compare their cluster maps. Have partners record any additional details they discover.

## Draft

**PIECING IT TOGETHER** Tell students to write a main-idea sentence about the weather topic named in the central circle. Next, ask students to use the details on the spokes to write the body of the report. The final sentence should summarize what students learned.

## Revise

**SELF-QUESTIONING** Ask students to assess their drafts for improvement.

- Does the report start with a sentence that tells what it is about?
- Are details for each question word included in the report?
- Are there any details that do not belong?
- Are the details placed in a logical order?
- Does the last sentence tell what I learned?

PARTNERS

Have partners trade reports to get another point of view and then create a second draft. Conference with students on ways they can check the order of the details in their writing.

## Edit/Proofread

**CHECK FOR ERRORS AND DETAILS** Students should reread their reports for spelling, grammar, order of information, and punctuation. Have them revise once more to improve the introductory and summarizing sentences.

## Publish

**SHARE REPORTS** Ask volunteers to read their reports aloud in small groups.

*Rain*

Rain is part of the water cycle. Water is constantly being pulled up into the air by the sun's heat. This process is called evaporation. When the air cools, the water in it changes into clouds. After the air gets even cooler, the water changes to rain and falls back to the ground. Evaporation and rainfall are part of the cycle of moving water.

# Presentation Ideas

**DIAGRAM** Invite students to make diagrams about how, why, when, and where the selected kinds of precipitation occur.

▶ Viewing/Representing

**GIVE A TALK** Invite students to use their reports and diagrams to give talks about the types of precipitation.

▶ Speaking/Listening

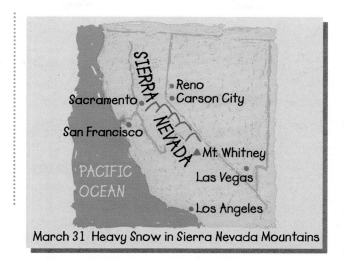

March 31 Heavy Snow in Sierra Nevada Mountains

Consider students' creative efforts, possibly adding a plus (+) for originality, wit, and imagination.

## Scoring Rubric

| Excellent | Good | Fair | Unsatisfactory |
|---|---|---|---|
| **4:** The writer | **3:** The writer | **2:** The writer | **1:** The writer |
| • presents a strong main-idea sentence that introduces the report | • has a main-idea sentence that introduces the report | • begins the report without a main-idea sentence | • begins without a main-idea sentence |
| • gives complete details and information about one type of precipitation | • gives detailed information about the type of precipitation | • provides few details about the type of precipitation | • provides few or no details about the type of precipitation |
| • concludes with a sophisticated summary. | • summarizes what was learned. | • has a weak or incomplete summary. | • may not grasp the writing assignment. |

**Incomplete 0:** The writer leaves the page blank or fails to respond to the writing task. The student does not address the topic or simply paraphrases the prompt. The response is illegible or incoherent.

For a 6-point or an 8-point scale, see pages T107–T108.

# Meeting Individual Needs for Writing

| EASY | ON-LEVEL | CHALLENGE |
|---|---|---|
| **Summary** Have students label a map of the United States. Next, help students name and list the types of weather in the article. Then have students draw the various kinds of weather on the map in the areas of the United States where they occurred. Last, tell students to label what they drew. Explain that they made a visual summary. | **Warnings** Group students in pairs, and have them imagine that they are working at the National Severe Storm Forecast Center. Ask partners to write the weather warnings for March 31–April 7. Explain that a warning names a geographic area and tells what the weather will be. Point out that on some of the days, partners will have to warn more than one area. | **Weather Report** Divide students among the various regions of the United States to report on a storm from March 31–April 7. Explain that each day students will write a short weather report for their region. Example: Day 1—bad weather forecast, Day 2—the storm, Day 3—report on the results of the storm. |

## Listening and Speaking

**LISTENING STRATEGIES**

As reports are read, have students:

• face the speaker and listen attentively.

• listen for details that tell how, why, when, and where.

**SPEAKING STRATEGIES**

Encourage students to:

• vary volume and tone of voice for emphasis.

• look up as they read to make eye contact with listeners.

• use posture appropriate for the communication setting.

---

**LANGUAGE SUPPORT**

**ESL** When English-speaking classmates are presenting their reports, encourage them to point to relevant areas of their diagrams as they talk. These actions help non-English-speaking students associate words with meaning.

Invite students to include their reports in their portfolios.

## LANGUAGE SUPPORT

**ESL** Simplify the Daily Language Activities for English learners by rewriting them with blanks to be filled in with *more* and *most*.

## DAILY LANGUAGE ACTIVITIES

Have students correct the sentences orally.

### Day 1
1. It's the more beautiful day of the year.
2. The air feels most frigid than usual.
3. Was there ever a most severe storm than this?

### Day 2
1. Which is the more powerful storm of the season?
2. Winds are more strong than ever.
3. The storm has become violenter.

### Day 3
1. Isn't today most humid than usual?
2. The coming storm might be the dangerousest of all.
3. We looked for a most detailed forecast than this morning's.

### Day 4
1. The storm grew more intenser as it crossed the country.
2. The clouds are more darker than usual.
3. Tornadoes can cause the horrendest damage.

### Day 5
1. I think tornadoes are most destructive than blizzards.
2. Hail makes the more loud sound of all.
3. Are people most reliable than computers?

**Daily Language Transparency 19**

**Suggested Answers on Transparency**

---

## DAY 1 — Introduce the Concept

**Oral Warm-Up** Ask students these questions to elicit comparative and superlative sentences: *Which is more difficult: Math or English? What is your most difficult subject?*

**Introduce *More* and *Most*** Another way to compare is to use the words *more* and *most* before an adjective. Present the following:

> **Comparing with *More* and *Most***
>
> • For long adjectives, use *more* and *most* to compare people, places, or things.
>
> • Use *more* to compare two people, places, or things.
>
> • Use *most* to compare more than two.

Present the Daily Language Activity and have students correct orally. Then, have students write sentences using *more* and *most* to compare weather conditions in your area.

 Assign the daily Writing Prompt on page 464C.

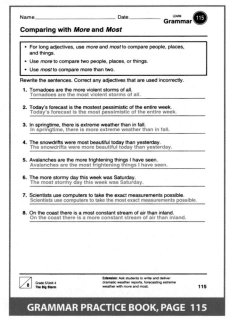

**GRAMMAR PRACTICE BOOK, PAGE 115**

---

## DAY 2 — Teach the Concept

**Review Using *More* and *Most*** Give examples such as *the most delicious cake* and *more gorgeous flowers*. Ask students to form sentences using these comparative and superlative phrases.

**Introduce Another Rule** Present and discuss:

> **Comparing with *More* and *Most***
>
> • When you use *more* and *most*, do not use the ending -*er* or -*est*.

Present the Daily Language Activity. Have students correct the sentences orally. Then have students write the corrected sentences.

 Assign the daily Writing Prompt on page 464C.

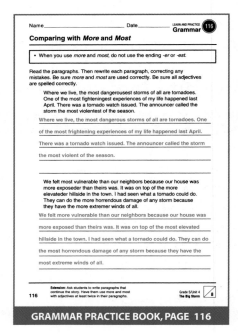

**GRAMMAR PRACTICE BOOK, PAGE 116**

# ...Comparing with *More* and *Most*

**Learn from the Literature** Review comparing with *more* and *most*. Read aloud the last sentence of *The Big Storm*.

> **Warm air from the south meets with cold Arctic air, triggering storms of all sizes and giving the United States one of <u>the most varied and exciting climates</u> on earth.**

Help students identify the comparison. Write the phrase "the most varied and exciting climates" on the chalkboard.

**Write Sentences that Compare** Present the Daily Language Activity and have students correct the sentences orally.

Have students read page 486 of *The Big Storm*. Write on the chalkboard: *Traffic snarled. Trains were delayed.* Ask students to use *more* and *most* to turn the sentences into comparatives.

 Assign the daily Writing Prompt on page 464D.

**Review Comparing with *More* and *Most*** Write the adjectives with *more* and *most* from the Daily Language Activities for Days 1 through 3 on the chalkboard. Ask students to add nouns to the adjectives to form sentences that compare. Have them identify the rule that applies to each adjective. Then present the Daily Language Activity for Day 4. Have students correct these sentences orally.

**Mechanics and Usage** Review the rules of *more* and *most*. Display and discuss:

> **Using *More* and *Most***
> - Never add *-er* and *more* to the same adjective.
> - Never add *-est* and *most* to the same adjective.

 Assign the daily Writing Prompt on page 464D.

**Assess** Use the Daily Language Activity and page 119 of the **Grammar Practice Book** for assessment.

**Reteach** Have students write the adjectives from the Daily Language Activities for Days 1 through 4. Then play a comparing game using the adjectives. Have one student say a sentence comparing two things with *more* and then call on another student to use the adjective with *most*. Repeat until all students have made up a sentence.

Have students create a classroom word wall that displays adjectives with *more* and *most* with the rule for forming each example.

Use page 120 of the **Grammar Practice Book** for additional reteaching.

 Assign the daily Writing Prompt on page 464D.

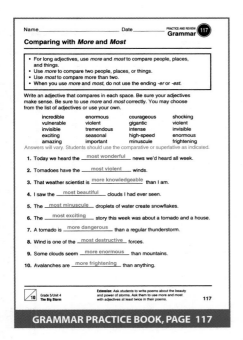

**GRAMMAR PRACTICE BOOK, PAGE 117**

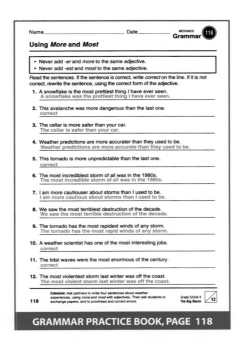

**GRAMMAR PRACTICE BOOK, PAGE 118**

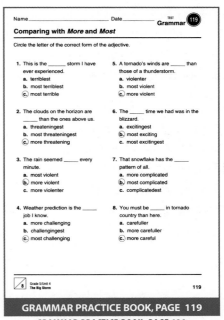

**GRAMMAR PRACTICE BOOK, PAGE 119**
**GRAMMAR PRACTICE BOOK, PAGE 120**

# 5 Day Spelling Plan

**DAY 1** Pretest

**DAY 2** Explore the Pattern

## LANGUAGE SUPPORT

Remind students to write the compound word in the correct form: as one word, as two words, or as hyphenated words. Suggest that students think of something visual to associate with a compound word and its spelling.

## DICTATION SENTENCES

### Spelling Words

1. She put the letter in the mailbox.
2. Everything will be all right.
3. The goldfish swims in the aquarium.
4. No one saw what happened.
5. They went ice-skating on the lake.
6. She became homesick at camp.
7. The post office sells stamps.
8. The ring costs twenty-five dollars.
9. Did somebody want fruit?
10. I like to eat peanut butter.
11. A raindrop landed on my hand.
12. The cold front brought dry weather.
13. Let's ride the merry-go-round.
14. She stirred in a teaspoon of sugar.
15. They left the car in a parking lot.
16. It is my thirty-third birthday.
17. Snowstorms left two feet of snow.
18. The mountaintops look green.
19. My sister-in-law is thirty years old.
20. They live northeast of the city.

### Challenge Words

21. The pollution filled the atmosphere.
22. The two cars had a collision.
23. The water cycle tells why there is rain.
24. I injured my foot in the race.
25. The sidewalk is uneven.

## DAY 1 — Pretest

**Assess Prior Knowledge** Use the Dictation Sentences at the left and **Spelling Practice Book** page 115 for the pretest. Allow students to correct their own papers. Students who require a modified list may be tested on the first ten words.

| Spelling Words | | Challenge Words |
|---|---|---|
| 1. mailbox | 11. **raindrop** | 21. **atmosphere** |
| 2. all right | 12. **cold front** | 22. **collision** |
| 3. goldfish | 13. merry-go-round | 23. **cycle** |
| 4. no one | 14. teaspoon | 24. **injured** |
| 5. ice-skating | 15. **parking lot** | 25. **uneven** |
| 6. homesick | 16. thirty-third | |
| 7. post office | 17. **snowstorms** | |
| 8. twenty-five | 18. **mountaintops** | |
| 9. somebody | 19. sister-in-law | |
| 10. peanut butter | 20. **northeast** | |

*Note: Words in **dark type** are from the story.*

**Word Study** On page 116 of the **Spelling Practice Book** are word study steps and an at-home activity.

## DAY 2 — Explore the Pattern

**Sort and Spell Words** List *mailbox, all right,* and *ice-skating* on the chalkboard. Ask how the compound words are different from each other. Have students read the Spelling Words aloud and sort them as below.

| Compound Words | |
|---|---|
| **One Word** | |
| mailbox | teaspoon |
| goldfish | snowstorms |
| homesick | mountaintops |
| somebody | northeast |
| raindrop | |
| **Two Words** | **Hyphenated** |
| all right | ice-skating |
| no one | twenty-five |
| post office | merry-go-round |
| cold front | thirty-third |
| parking lot | sister-in-law |
| peanut butter | |

**Word Wall** Have students create a word wall based on the word sort and add more words from their reading.

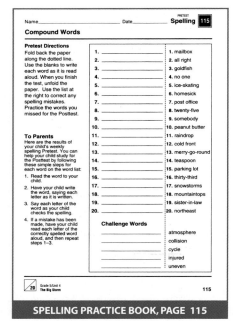

SPELLING PRACTICE BOOK, PAGE 115

WORD STUDY STEPS AND ACTIVITY, PAGE 116

SPELLING PRACTICE BOOK, PAGE 117

# Compound Words

## DAY 3 — Practice and Extend

**Word Meaning: Fill-ins** Have students fill in the blanks with Spelling Words.

- We left our car in the _____. (parking lot)
- I rode the white horse on the _____. (merry-go-round)
- I bought stamps at the _____. (post office)

If students need extra practice, have partners give each other a midweek test.

**Glossary** Review the pronunciation key. Remind students that it includes symbols and the sounds they represent. Have partners:

- find each Challenge Word in the Glossary.
- copy each Challenge Word, write its re-spelling.
- pronounce each word to each other.

## DAY 4 — Proofread and Write

**Proofread Sentences** Write these sentences on the chalkboard, including the misspelled words. Ask students to proofread, circling incorrect spellings and writing the correct spellings. There are two spelling errors in each sentence.

> I saw some-body twirl while iceskating. (somebody, ice-skating)
>
> I spread a tea-spoon of peanutbutter on my toast. (teaspoon, peanut butter)

Have students create additional sentences with errors for partners to correct.

 **WRITING** Have students use as many Spelling Words as possible in the daily Writing Prompt on page 464D. Remind students to proofread their writing for errors in spelling, grammar, and punctuation.

## DAY 5 — Assess and Reteach

**Assess Students' Knowledge** Use page 120 of the **Spelling Practice Book** or the Dictation Sentences on page 491O for the posttest.

**Personal Word List**  **JOURNAL** If students have trouble with any words in the lesson, have them add to their personal list of troublesome words in their journals. Have students list the words as one word, two words, or hyphenated words.

Students should refer to their word lists during later writing activities.

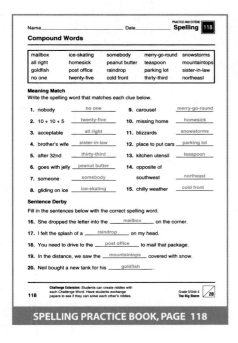

**SPELLING PRACTICE BOOK, PAGE 118**

**SPELLING PRACTICE BOOK, PAGE 119**

**SPELLING PRACTICE BOOK, PAGE 120**

**Cumulative Review** with **Expository Text**

## Time to Review

### Anthology

# Catching Up with Lewis and Clark

**Selection Summary** Historians and scientists are learning more about the explorers Lewis and Clark and their 1804 journey from St. Louis, Missouri, to the Pacific Ocean.

**Stories in Art** focuses on the **comprehension** skill

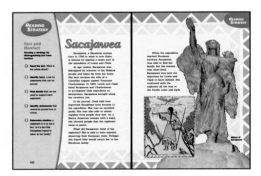

**Reading Strategy** applies the **comprehension** skill

Artist N.C. Wyeth used his imagination to paint this picture of Sacajawea, Lewis, and Clark.

**Catching Up with Lewis and Clark**

**Listening Library**

**INSTRUCTIONAL** pages 494–497

# Time to Reread

## Reread Leveled Books

**EASY**
Lesson on pages 501A and 501D

**INDEPENDENT**
Lesson on pages 501B and 501D

📖 *Take-Home version available*

**CHALLENGE**
Lesson on pages 501C and 501D

## Leveled Practice

### EASY
**Reteach, 140–146** Blackline masters with reteaching opportunities for each assessed skill

### INDEPENDENT/ON-LEVEL
**Practice, 140–146** Workbook with Take-Home stories and practice opportunities for each assessed skill and story comprehension

### CHALLENGE
**Extend, 140–146** Blackline masters that offer challenge activities for each assessed skill

**Quizzes Prepared by**  Accelerated Reader®

## WORKSTATION Activities

**Social Studies** . . . **Create a Research Journal,** *499*

**Math** . . . . . . . . . . . . . . **How Long Would It Take?,** *499*

**Art** . . . . . . . . . . . . . . . . **Draw a Cartoon,** *499*

**Language Arts** . . **Read Aloud,** *492E*

**Writing** . . . . . . . . . . . **Magazine Article,** *498*

**Research and Inquiry** . . . . . . **Find Out More,** *499*

💻 **Internet Activities** . . . . . . . . **www.mhschool.com/reading**

# Suggested Lesson Planner

| READING AND LANGUAGE ARTS | **DAY 1** *Focus on Reading and Skills* | **DAY 2** *Read the Literature* |
|---|---|---|

| | | |
|---|---|---|
| ● **Comprehension** |  **Read Aloud: Poetry,** 492E <br> "Western Wagons" | **Build Background,** 494A <br> Develop Oral Language |
| ● **Vocabulary** | **Develop Visual Literacy,** 492 | **Vocabulary,** 494B–494C |
| ● **Phonics/Decoding** | ☑ Review Fact and Nonfact, 493A–493B <br> **Teaching Chart 115** <br> Reteach, Practice, Extend, 140 | *bison*   *former*   *journal* <br> *diaries*   *glistening*   *superb* <br><br> **Teaching Chart 116** <br> Word Building Manipulative Cards <br> Reteach, Practice, Extend, 141 |
| ● **Study Skills** | **Reading Strategy:** Fact and Nonfact, 493 <br> "Sacajawea" | |
| ● **Listening, Speaking, Viewing, Representing** | | **Read the Selection,** 494–497 <br> ☑ Fact and Nonfact <br> ☑ Draw Conclusions <br><br> **Genre: Social Studies Article,** 495 |
| | ⓘ Intervention Program | ⓘ Intervention Program |

| | | |
|---|---|---|
| ● **Curriculum Connections** | **Link** Works of Art, 492 | **Link** Social Studies, 494A |

| | | |
|---|---|---|
| ● **Writing** |  **Writing Prompt:** Lewis and Clark's expedition opened the West to settlers. Write a paragraph about the best things you think it accomplished. |  **Writing Prompt:** Pretend you are with Lewis and Clark. Write a diary entry about your bad experiences with bear attacks and bitter cold. <br><br>  **Journal Writing,** 497 <br> Quick-Write |

| | | |
|---|---|---|
| ● **Grammar** | **Introduce the Concept: Comparing with** *Good* **and** *Bad,* 501M <br> Daily Language Activity <br> 1. Lewis and Clark were the goodest explorers of their time. best <br> 2. Lewis was Clark's most better friend. best <br> 3. The expedition had best than average campers. better <br><br> **Grammar Practice Book,** 121 | **Teach the Concept: Comparing with** *Good* **and** *Bad,* 501M <br> Daily Language Activity <br> 1. Was Lewis a best speller than Clark? better <br> 2. Bear attacks were the worse dangers that they faced. worst <br> 3. Cold days were worst than warm days. worse <br><br> **Grammar Practice Book,** 122 |

| | | |
|---|---|---|
| ● **Spelling** | **Pretest: Words from Social Studies,** 501O <br> **Spelling Practice Book,** 121–122 | **Explore the Pattern: Words from Social Studies,** 501O <br> **Spelling Practice Book,** 123 |

**Meeting Individual Needs**

 = **Skill Assessed in Unit Test**

 **Intervention Program Available**

---

## DAY 3 — Read the Literature

**Rereading for Fluency,** 496

**Story Questions and Activities,** 498–499
Reteach, Practice, Extend, 142

**Study Skill,** 500
☑ Use a Map
**Teaching Chart 117**
Reteach, Practice, Extend, 143

**Test Power,** 501

 **Read the Leveled Books,** 501A–501D
Guided Reading
Phonics Review
☑ Comprehension Review

 **Intervention Program**

---

## DAY 4 — Build and Review Skills

 **Read the Leveled Books and Self-Selected Books**

☑ **Review Important and Unimportant Information,** 501E–501F
**Teaching Chart 118**
Reteach, Practice, Extend, 144
Language Support, 158

☑ **Review Root Words,** 501G–501H
**Teaching Chart 119**
Reteach, Practice, Extend, 145
Language Support, 159

 **Intervention Program**

---

## DAY 5 — Build and Review Skills

 **Read Self-Selected Books**

☑ **Review Suffixes,** 501I–501J
**Teaching Chart 120**
Reteach, Practice, Extend, 146
Language Support, 160

**Listening, Speaking, Viewing, Representing,** 501L

 **Intervention Program**

---

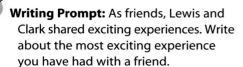 **Science,** 499

---

**Writing Prompt:** As friends, Lewis and Clark shared exciting experiences. Write about the most exciting experience you have had with a friend.

**Writing Process: Expository Writing,** 501K
Prewrite, Draft

---

**Writing Prompt:** Write a brochure for the Lewis and Clark Interpretive Center. Explain to visitors the best and worst adventures of the explorers.

**Writing Process: Expository Writing,** 501K
Revise
**Meeting Individual Needs for Writing,** 501L

---

**Writing Prompt:** Write a paragraph explaining why Sacajawea was important to the Lewis and Clark expedition.

**Writing Process: Expository Writing,** 501K
Edit/Proofread, Publish

---

**Review and Practice: Comparing with *Good* and *Bad*,** 501N
Daily Language Activity
1. The explorers kept the better maps. best
2. Some days were worst than others. worse
3. Scientists hope to find best clues to the events of their journey. better

**Grammar Practice Book,** 123

---

**Review and Practice: Comparing with *Good* and *Bad*,** 501N
Daily Language Activity
1. Clark was a worser speller than Lewis. worse
2. The better moment was reaching the Pacific. best
3. Sifting through dirt is the worse job. worst

**Grammar Practice Book,** 124

---

**Assess and Reteach: Comparing with *Good* and *Bad*,** 501N
Daily Language Activity
1. Sacajawea was the betterest guide. best
2. She spoke best English than her brother. better
3. Food and horses were their worsest problem. worst

**Grammar Practice Book,** 125–126

---

**Practice and Extend: Words from Social Studies,** 501P
Spelling Practice Book, 124

---

**Proofread and Write: Words from Social Studies,** 501P
Spelling Practice Book, 125

---

**Assess and Reteach: Words from Social Studies,** 501P
Spelling Practice Book, 126

# Read Aloud

### Western Wagons
**a poem by Rosemary and Stephen Vincent Benét**

They went with axe and rifle,
   when the trail was still
   to blaze,
They went with wife and
   children, in the prairie-
   schooner days,
With banjo and with frying
   pan—Susanna, don't you cry!
For I'm off to California to get
   rich out there or die!

We've broken land and cleared it,
but we're tired of where we are.
They say that wild Nebraska is a
   better place by far.

There's gold in far Wyoming,
   there's black earth in Ioway,
So pack up the kids and blankets,
   for we're moving out today!

The cowards never started and
   the weak died on the road,
And all across the continent the
   endless campfires glowed.
*We'd taken land and settled—*
   *but a traveler passed by—*
*And we're going West tomorrow—*
   *Lordy, never ask us why!*

**Continued on page T5**

## Oral Comprehension

**LISTENING AND SPEAKING** Read the poem aloud. Ask students to listen for factual information and for information that is not factual. Afterward, ask:

- What facts motivated people to go West?

- What nonfacts were people told about California?

- What facts and nonfacts move people today to take chances and to change their lives?

Then reread the poem. Ask: Did you enjoy listening to the poem? What kinds of poems do you enjoy most?

**GENRE STUDY: POETRY** Discuss some of the literary devices and techniques used in "Western Wagons."

- Have students write down the last word of each line

and then trace the rhyme scheme of the poem. (aabb)

- Explain that the poem was written in the exact meter of a well-known song. Ask: What song forms the basis for this poem? (Stephen Collins Foster's song, "O! Susanna")

- Point out that the poem ends with the line "But we're going West tomorrow with our future in our hands." Ask: What do you think the words "in our hands" refers to?

**Activity** Invite students to create posters about the Old West. Provide drawing paper and markers or painting materials. Students might include factual images of life on the trail and information that might motivate people to leave their homes and go West. ▶ **Visual/Spatial**

# Develop Visual Literacy

Stories in Art

Space exploration is turning fantasy into fact. Today, the make-believe world of the science-fiction writer now seems very real.

Look at this painting of space stations and spacecraft. What parts of it are already fact? What parts are not yet fact? Do you think they will become real? When? Why? How? What will life be like aboard one of these space stations? What makes you think so?

Look at the painting again. What do you think it would be like to explore new worlds? Would you like to go on such a journey? Explain.

*Ships of the Long Range Pioneer Fleet*
by Julian Balm

492

## Objective: Distinguish Between Fact and Nonfact

**VIEWING** In *Ships of the Long Range Pioneer Fleet*, Julian Balm has used geometric shapes to create a city in space. Invite students to describe the shapes they see in the painting. Ask: "Does the painting depict reality, fantasy, or something in between?"

Read the page with students, encouraging individual interpretations of the painting.

Ask students to consider scientific and technological facts when they discuss the painting. For example:

- Satellites and other spacecraft exist.
- Spacecraft can move from one place to another in space.
- Rudimentary space stations have been launched.

**REPRESENTING** Invite students to create their own drawings of how a space station might look. Encourage them to be imaginative, but to base their pictures on fact.

**OBJECTIVES**

Students will distinguish between fact and nonfact.

| Skills Finder | |
|---|---|
| **Fact and Nonfact** | |
| Introduce | 167A-B |
| Review | 199E-F, 221G-H, 433A-B, 463E-F, 493A-B |
| Test | Unit 2, Unit 4 |
| Maintain | 627 |

---

**TEACHING TIP**

**SUPPORTED INFER-ENCES** Remind students to read expository texts carefully to distinguish between inferences that are supported by facts or by opinions.

---

# Review Fact and Nonfact

**PREPARE**

**Discuss Fact and Nonfact**

Tell students that to identify a fact they should ask themselves: Can this piece of information be checked or proven true? If they determine that a piece of information cannot be proven true, then they have discovered a nonfact.

**TEACH**

**Read the Passage and Model the Skill**

Display **Teaching Chart 115.** Have students look for facts and nonfacts as the paragraph is read.

### Sacajawea

Sacajawea was a Shoshone Indian who traveled with the Lewis-and-Clark Expedition in 1805 and 1806. She was also known as Bird Woman. She was accompanied by her husband, Toussaint Charbonneau. Sacajawea could speak English and was able to interpret several Indian languages for the explorers. She was reported to have died of a fever in 1812 in what is now South Dakota. According to another account, she lived at the Shoshone Agency in Wyoming and survived until 1884.

**Teaching Chart 115**

*MODEL* I know that Sacajawea is a historical figure, so I think we could prove she was a Shoshone Indian and her husband's name was Charbonneau. However, since there are conflicting reports about the date of her death, both of the reports would have to be considered nonfacts until one is proven true. I'm not sure she was called "Bird Woman." I'll have to look that up.

**Identify Fact and Nonfact**

Have the students underline the facts and circle the nonfacts in the paragraph.

## PRACTICE

**Create a Fact and Nonfact Scorecard**

GROUP

Using a Fact and Nonfact scorecard, have students record the facts and nonfacts from "Sacajawea." If there is something that they need to investigate further before determining whether it is fact or nonfact, have them check the Not Sure column. ▶ **Interpersonal/Spatial**

| STATEMENT | FACT | NON-FACT | NOT SURE |
|---|---|---|---|
| Sacajawea traveled with the Lewis-and-Clark Expedition. | √ | | |
| She was known as Bird Woman. | | | √ |
| Sacajawea's husband was also on the expedition. | √ | | |
| Sacajawea died in 1812. | | √ | |

## ASSESS/CLOSE

**Distinguish Between Fact and Nonfact**

PARTNERS

Have partners select and read a passage from a familiar story or a newspaper or magazine article. Have them work together to list the facts and nonfacts in the piece on a chart like the one above.

# Meeting Individual Needs for Comprehension

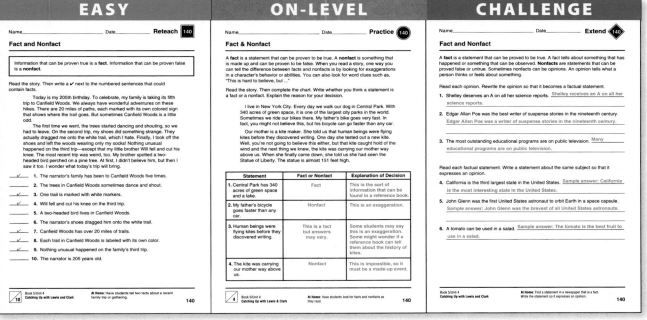

Reteach, 140          Practice, 140          Extend, 140

**493B**

**OBJECTIVES**

Students will distinguish fact from nonfact.

## Apply Fact and Nonfact

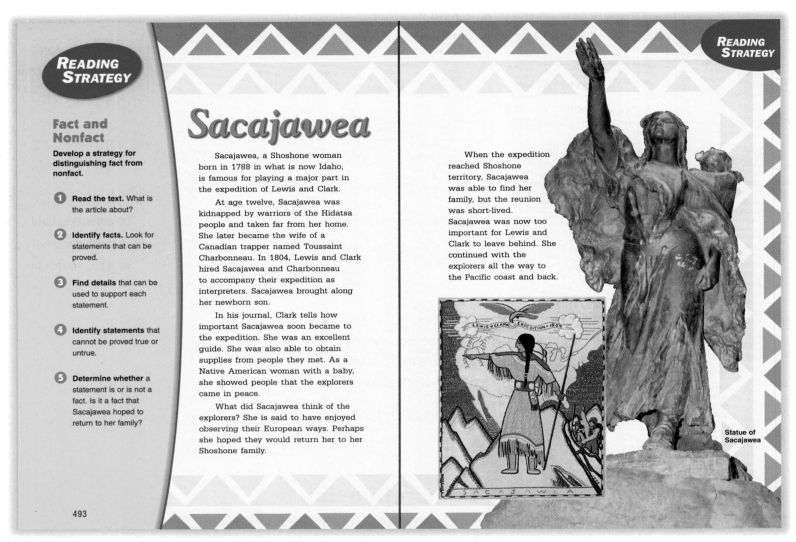

**READING STRATEGY**

### Fact and Nonfact

Develop a strategy for distinguishing fact from nonfact.

1. **Read the text.** What is the article about?

2. **Identify facts.** Look for statements that can be proved.

3. **Find details** that can be used to support each statement.

4. **Identify statements** that cannot be proved true or untrue.

5. **Determine whether** a statement is or is not a fact. Is it a fact that Sacajawea hoped to return to her family?

### Sacajawea

Sacajawea, a Shoshone woman born in 1788 in what is now Idaho, is famous for playing a major part in the expedition of Lewis and Clark.

At age twelve, Sacajawea was kidnapped by warriors of the Hidatsa people and taken far from her home. She later became the wife of a Canadian trapper named Toussaint Charbonneau. In 1804, Lewis and Clark hired Sacajawea and Charbonneau to accompany their expedition as interpreters. Sacajawea brought along her newborn son.

In his journal, Clark tells how important Sacajawea soon became to the expedition. She was an excellent guide. She was also able to obtain supplies from people they met. As a Native American woman with a baby, she showed people that the explorers came in peace.

What did Sacajawea think of the explorers? She is said to have enjoyed observing their European ways. Perhaps she hoped they would return her to her Shoshone family.

When the expedition reached Shoshone territory, Sacajawea was able to find her family, but the reunion was short-lived. Sacajawea was now too important for Lewis and Clark to leave behind. She continued with the explorers all the way to the Pacific coast and back.

**READING STRATEGY**

Statue of Sacajawea

493

---

**PREVIEW** Have students preview "Sacajawea" by reading the title and the first paragraph. Ask:

- Based on the first paragraph, what do you think the passage is about? (the part Sacajawea played in the Lewis and Clark expedition)

**SET PURPOSES** Explain that students will apply what they have learned about distinguishing between fact and nonfact as they read "Sacajawea."

**APPLY THE STRATEGY** Discuss this strategy for distinguishing between fact and nonfact.

- List some statements in the text that may be facts or nonfacts.

- What evidence can you find to support the statements you listed?

- Which statements on your list cannot be proven? They are nonfacts.

- Which statements can be proven true? They are facts.

- Mark each statement as a fact or nonfact.

**Activity** Have students reread the passage and side notes. Then have them create a Fact and Nonfact scorecard for the passage.

# Build Background

**Link**
**ocial Studies**

## Concept: Explore the West

## Evaluate Prior Knowledge

**CONCEPT: EXPLORE THE WEST** In this selection, students will read about the 1804 West Coast explorations of Lewis and Clark. Invite students to share any experiences they've had as explorers.

**COMPARE TOOLS** Guide students in recognizing that the tools available to Lewis and Clark in 1804 were quite different from those available to explorers today. Use a graphic organizer to help students compare tools then and now. ▶ **Logical/Visual**

| Tools of 1804 | Modern Tools |
|---|---|
| lantern | flashlight |
| notebook and pencil | computer |
| pick and shovel | power drill |

**Graphic Organizer 12**

**RECORD YOUR OBSERVATION** Have

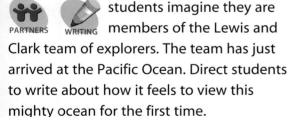

students imagine they are members of the Lewis and Clark team of explorers. The team has just arrived at the Pacific Ocean. Direct students to write about how it feels to view this mighty ocean for the first time.

### DISCUSS TRAITS OF AN EXPLORER

**ESL** Ask students what kind of personality traits they think explorers should have. Write their responses on the board. (Answers may include: *curious, brave, leadership, independent*.) Then ask them to work in pairs to role-play interviews with a reporter asking questions and an explorer answering. Remind the interviewers to find out what the explorers did, when they did it, and how they felt about their work. If time permits, change roles and repeat.

---

**TEACHING TIP**

**MANAGEMENT** As students work on their skits, visit each group, making sure everyone is working and acknowledging one another's ideas.

---

**LANGUAGE SUPPORT**

See **Language Support Book**, pages 153–156, for teaching suggestions for Build Background.

diaries
former
journal
bison
superb
glistening

Students will use context clues to determine the meanings of vocabulary words.

**Definitions**

**diaries** (p. 496) written records of one's thoughts and actions

**former** (p. 497) happening in the past

**journal** (p. 496) a regular record or account

**bison** (p. 497) a large animal with a big, shaggy head, short horns and a bump on its back

**superb** (p. 496) very fine; excellent

**glistening** (p. 496) shining with reflected light

# Vocabulary

## Teach Vocabulary in Context

**Identify Vocabulary Words**

Display **Teaching Chart 116** and read the passage with students. Have volunteers circle each vocabulary word and underline other words that are clues to its meaning.

**The Secret Diaries**

**1.** In exploring the attic, Rick came upon a pile of dusty diaries, written by a man named Lukas. **2.** He was a former occupant of the house, who had lived there in the 1800s. **3.** The diaries were written in the form of a journal. **4.** They described a location out west, where bison large, buffalo-like animals, roamed the range freely. **5.** The writing style was superb, so good that Rick felt the diaries should be published. **6.** The idea of publishing the diaries glistened in his mind like a shiny star. "Maybe, one day," Rick thought.

Teaching Chart 116

**Story Words**

These words from the selection may be unfamiliar. Before students read, have them check the meanings and pronunciations of the words in the Glossary beginning on page 760 or in a dictionary.

- historians, p. 495
- pioneers, p. 495
- waterfalls, p. 496

**Discuss Meanings**

Ask questions like these to help clarify word meaning:

- What kind of information is recorded in diaries?
- Name three of your former teachers?
- Why might an explorer keep a journal?
- Describe a bison.
- Can you think of a time when you had a superb meal?
- Have you ever seen the reflection of a full moon glistening on the surface of a lake?

# Activities

## Practice

**Demonstrating Word Meaning**

Have students discuss the meaning of each vocabulary word. Then have them choose one or two vocabulary words to use in writing a journal entry. ▶ **Linguistic**

> **Word Building Manipulative Cards**

**Write Tongue Twisters**

WRITING

Have students write tongue twisters for two vocabulary words of choice. Have them try out each other's tongue twisters to determine the most difficult. ▶ **Oral/Linguistic**

## Assess Vocabulary

**Use Words in Context**

PARTNERS

Challenge students to write a paragraph about a real or imaginary event using all of the vocabulary words, if possible. Students should then exchange papers with a partner and check that the words are used correctly.

**SPELLING/VOCABULARY CONNECTIONS**

See Spelling Challenge Words, pages 501O–501P.

**LANGUAGE SUPPORT**

See the **Language Support Book**, pages 153–156, for teaching suggestions for Vocabulary.

**Vocabulary PuzzleMaker**

Provides vocabulary activities

# Meeting Individual Needs for Vocabulary

| EASY | ON-LEVEL | ON-LEVEL | CHALLENGE |
|---|---|---|---|

### EASY

Name_____ Date_____ **Reteach 141**

**Vocabulary**

Circle the vocabulary word that correctly completes each sentence.

1. There were hundreds of (superb/**bison**) charging across the prairie.
2. After the storm passed, the leaves were (**glistening**/journal) with raindrops.
3. Each day, we recorded our experiences in our (glistening/**diaries**).
4. We had a (journal/**superb**) view of the valley from the mountaintop.
5. Luckily, I had the writings of a (**former**/journal) nature guide to help me.
6. She left a (**journal**/bison) filled with both facts and personal responses.

**Reteach 142**

**Story Comprehension**

Answer these questions about "Catching Up with Lewis and Clark."

1. What part of the current United States did Lewis and Clark explore? the west, the northwest, and the midwest
2. What was one goal of their journey? to expand United States trade by finding a water route from the Mississippi River to the Pacific Ocean
3. Who helped Lewis and Clark communicate with the Native Americans they met along the trail? Sacajawea, an English-speaking Shoshone
4. Which President asked Lewis to explore the Louisiana Purchase? President Thomas Jefferson
5. Why is it difficult for researchers today to find the actual trail Lewis and Clark followed? They left very little physical evidence of their journey.

**At Home:** Have students draw a picture of a bison. They may need to check a reference source first.
141–142 **Catching Up with Lewis and Clark** Book 5/Unit 4 **4**

### ON-LEVEL

Name_____ Date_____ **Practice 141**

**Vocabulary**

Complete each sentence with a vocabulary word.

| bison | diaries | former | glistening | journal | superb |
|---|---|---|---|---|---|

1. The coach keeps _____ diaries _____ every year to record his team's progress.
2. The movie was better than good— it was _____ superb _____!
3. I keep a _____ journal _____ to help me keep track of each day's events.
4. You can find herds of _____ bison _____ out west in Yellowstone National Park.
5. Our _____ former _____ school principal came back to see our science fair.
6. Have you ever seen winter frost _____ glistening _____ in early morning light?

**At Home:** Have students use each of the vocabulary words in a sentence.
141 **Catching Up with Lewis and Clark** Book 5/Unit 4 **6**

### ON-LEVEL

## The Ranch

This just might be the best vacation we've ever had. It has been *superb* so far! This week we went to visit my mother's *former* professor, Ms. Berry. She lives on a ranch in the western state of Wyoming. We had to drive for miles up a dirt road to get to her place. On the way, we saw these huge shaggy creatures with horns.

"BUFFALO!" my brother cried. My mother turned politely and said, "Actually, Ms. Berry runs a *bison* ranch."

My brother immediately recorded this information in his travel *journal*. Every day he makes notes of new facts and the miles we've traveled. I'm keeping two *diaries*. I write in one at the end of each day, and I write in the other only when I have something important to say about what we've seen.

After lunch, Ms. Berry took us out to explore the ranch. This place looked very dry, so I was surprised to find a small pond. The water was a deep emerald green and was *glistening* in the sun. Staying at Ms. Berry's ranch was the perfect place to end our vacation.

1. What is a word that means "excellent"? superb
2. What does it mean that Ms. Berry was the mother's *former* professor? _____ It means that in the past, Ms. Berry was her professor.
3. What is another word for the word "buffalo"? bison
4. How is a diary different from a *journal*? Consider how both words are used in this story. In this story, the journal is a daily written account of factual information; the diary, while kept on a regular basis, is not a daily record and the writing is more personal.
5. Why did it surprise the narrator to find a pond of *glistening* water in Wyoming? _____ The state of Wyoming can be very dry, so the narrator didn't expect to find a pond there.

Book 5/Unit 4 **5** **Catching Up with Lewis and Clark** **At Home:** Have students write about a vacation they would like to take using vocabulary words. 141a

### CHALLENGE

Name_____ Date_____ **Extend 141**

**Vocabulary**

| bison | diaries | former |
|---|---|---|
| glistening | journal | superb |

Imagine you are witnessing a scene in which Sacajawea is guiding Lewis and Clark through the Rocky Mountains. Write the conversation they might have had with one another. Use as many vocabulary words as you can.

Answers will vary but should include at least four vocabulary words used in the correct context or part of speech.

_____

_____

**Extend 142**

**Story Comprehension**

Scientists have found what they believe to be remains of the Lewis and Clark expedition. They have uncovered a tall wooden wall from a campsite and some beads and ammunition. What do you think scientists could conclude from these findings? Write a paragraph to explain your conclusion.

Possible answer: It takes a long time to build a wooden wall, so Lewis and Clark may have stayed at the campsite for a period of time, maybe in the winter when snow made traveling impossible. The beads may have come from meeting and trading with Native Americans. Ammunition may have been used to hunt for food or for defense.

_____

**At Home:** Have students write a journal entry for today using vocabulary words.
141–142 **Catching Up with Lewis and Clark** Book 5/Unit 4

**Reteach, 141** **Practice, 141** **Practice, 141a** **Take-Home Story** **Extend, 141**

# Comprehension

## Prereading Strategies

**PREVIEW AND PREDICT** Have students read the title and look at the photos and illustrations. Direct them to the captions for clues about the article.

- Who are the people featured in this article?
- What will the article most likely be about?
- How do you know the article is nonfiction? (The photographs are of actual people, and Lewis and Clark are historical figures.) *Genre*

Have students record their predictions about the article in their journals.

**SET PURPOSES** What do students hope to find out by reading the article? For example:

- What did Lewis and Clark do?
- Who was Sacajawea?
- Why are researchers following the footsteps of Lewis and Clark?

Artist N.C. Wyeth used his imagination to paint this picture of Sacajawea, Lewis, and Clark.

## Catching Up with Lewis and Clark

494

# Meeting Individual Needs · Grouping Suggestions for Strategic Reading

| EASY | ON-LEVEL | CHALLENGE |
|---|---|---|
| **Read Together** Read the article together with students or have them use the **Listening Library.** Have students use the Fact and Nonfact scorecard on page 496 to record information as they read. Comprehension questions offer additional help with comprehension. | **Guided Instruction** Choose from the Comprehension questions as you read the article with students or after they have played the **Listening Library.** Have students use the Fact and Nonfact scorecard as they read to record information from the article. | **Read Independently** Set up a Fact and Nonfact scorecard with students, as on page 496, and ask them to fill it in as they read. After reading, they can use their charts to verify any statements they were unsure of and to summarize the article. |

# Hot on Lewis and Clark's Trail

## Historians and scientists follow in the footsteps of two of America's brave explorers

Nobody likes a litterbug, but historians wish that Meriwether Lewis and William Clark had left more behind as they bravely traveled across the North American continent nearly 200 years ago. They cleaned up so well after themselves that it's hard to tell exactly where they stopped on their journey from St. Louis, Missouri, to the Pacific Ocean.

But researchers hope to answer age-old questions about these great trailblazers of the West, whose work made it possible for the U.S. government to claim the Oregon territory. This led to pioneers settling the West in the mid-1800s.

In 1803, President Thomas Jefferson asked Lewis to explore the Louisiana Purchase, a huge area of land that the United States was about to buy from France. He hoped to learn of a water route between the Mississippi River and the Pacific Ocean that would help U.S. trade.

**Ken Karsmizki has been busy digging up the facts about Lewis and Clark.**

**The red dashes show the explorers' route. They wintered at Fort Mandan and Fort Clatsop and split up on the way back.**

495

# Comprehension

☑ **Apply Fact and Nonfact**
☑ **Apply Draw Conclusions**

**STRATEGIC READING** Being aware of facts and nonfacts as you read will help you evaluate information.

**1** **FACT AND NONFACT** Look at the painting and read the caption on page 494. Does the picture show us exactly how the characters looked? (No. Although based on fact, it was painted from Wyeth's imagination.) Let's put this information on a Fact and Nonfact scorecard and add other information to it as we read.

**2** **DRAW CONCLUSIONS** Why did Lewis and Clark follow the rivers instead of taking a more direct route over land? (They hoped to find a water route to the Pacific.)

## Genre

### Social Studies Article

Remind students that a social studies article:

• reflects the most recent research available when it is written.

• includes special text features, such as headings, sidebars, captions, charts, and diagrams.

• presents facts in logical order.

**Activity** After students read *Catching Up with Lewis and Clark*, have them describe some of the special text features that this article contains.

## LANGUAGE SUPPORT

This chart is available as a blackline master in the **Language Support Book**.

**LANGUAGE SUPPORT, 157**

**495**

# Comprehension

**3** **DRAW CONCLUSIONS** Do you think the scientists will be able to fully document the Lewis and Clark expedition? List information from the article that supports your conclusion.

**4** Reread the information about Sacajawea in the inset on page 497. Who can summarize in one or two sentences who Sacajawea was and the role she played in the Lewis and Clark Expedition? (Sacajawea was an English-speaking Shoshone Indian who traveled with Lewis and Clark and helped them communicate with and get help from the Indians they met along the way.) *Summarize*

**5** **FACT AND NONFACT** Review the article. Are there more statements you would like to add to your Fact and Nonfact scorecard? How can you verify information that you were not sure of?

| STATEMENT | FACT | NON-FACT | NOT SURE |
|---|---|---|---|
| The painting is an actual portrait of Lewis and Clark. | | √ | |
| Lewis and Clark followed the Missouri River and the Yellowstone River. | √ | | |
| Lewis and Clark kept detailed diaries. | √ | | |
| Scientists have found items that were once used by Lewis and Clark. | | | √ |

**ORGANIZE INFORMATION** Ask volunteers to organize the information they gathered while reading the article. Students may refer to their scorecards. Then have students write a one- or two-sentence summary of the article. Have them focus on the facts and nonfacts. *Summarization*

RIGHT AND FAR RIGHT: BRUCE SELYEM/MUSEUM OF THE ROCKIES

**Sifting dirt through a giant strainer can reveal important finds at Great Falls, Montana.**

Lewis and his best friend, Clark, left St. Louis in May 1804 with a party of 42 men. They never found the water route, but they became the first U.S. citizens to see many of America's wonders—the endless Great Plains, the jagged Rocky Mountains, and the glistening Pacific. They faced many hardships and dangers, including bear attacks and bitter cold. In Great Falls, Montana, they carried heavy canoes for weeks around waterfalls under the hot sun. At times they had little food to eat and almost starved.

More than 500 days and 4,000 miles after they had set out, Lewis and Clark reached the Pacific. "Ocian in view! O! the joy!" wrote Clark in his journal. (Clark was smart and brave, but not a very good speller.)

The explorers kept superb maps and diaries. They were the first to describe 122 kinds of animals and 178 plants, and to meet many native tribes. But they left barely a trace behind at their campsites. That makes it hard for historians to say "Lewis and Clark were here!" **3**

**PINNING DOWN LEWIS AND CLARK**

Montana scientist Ken Karsmizki and others have been trying to pin down such facts. They have been digging in the soil at Great Falls and at Fort Clatsop, Oregon, where the pair rested before making their way home. Recently, a campsite was found

**FIND OUT MORE**
Visit our website:
***www.mhschool.com/reading***

***inter*NET**
**CONNECTION**

## REREADING FOR *Fluency*

**PARTNERS** Have students choose a favorite section of the article to read to a partner. Encourage students to read with feeling and expression.

**READING RATE** When you evaluate rate, have the student read aloud from the story for one minute. Place a stick-on note after the last word read. Count words read. To evaluate stu-

dents' performance, see the Running Record in the **Fluency Assessment** book.

**i Intervention** For leveled fluency lessons, passages, and norms charts, see **Skills Intervention Guide,** Part 4, Fluency.

near Great Falls. Scientists think it may be one of Lewis and Clark's camps, but they are not sure. Beads and ammunition were found at Fort Clatsop. Scientists think the remains belonged to the explorers.

In fact, scientists will be digging around Fort Clatsop for years to come. "Lewis and Clark wintered here for 106 days," explains Cindy Orlando, head of the Fort Clatsop National Memorial. Scientists have found the remains of what may have been a wooden wall from the original campsite. "What we're finding could prove to be from Lewis and Clark's trip," says Orlando.

### JOIN THE CELEBRATION!

As the 200th anniversary of their journey approaches, Americans are getting plenty of chances to learn about the brave pioneers. Visitors to Great Falls can visit the Lewis and Clark Interpretive Center. And special events to mark the anniversary. will take place along the route from 2003 to 2006.

"When Lewis and Clark left, we were a seaboard collection of former colonies," says Ken Burns, who made a movie about the two explorers. "What they saw transformed us from a small country into a great one."

Scientists say the bison bone (top) and the iron pushpin are both from the time of Lewis and Clark.

### Sacajawea

When Lewis and Clark needed a guide to help them talk with Indians they met on their trip, they turned to Sacajawea. (Her name means Bird Woman.) Sacajawea was an English-speaking Shoshone Indian who traveled with the explorers in 1805 and 1806. During her travels, she visited what are now the states of Montana, Idaho, Washington, and Oregon.

When the group arrived in the Rocky Mountains, the explorers met a band of Shoshone Indians whose chief was Sacajawea's brother. She helped the explorers communicate with him and with his band. Sacajawea also helped Lewis and Clark get horses and food from the Shoshone. Her work made it possible for the group to continue on to the Pacific. A number of monuments have been built in Western states to honor her.

**4**

**5**

Based on an article in *TIME FOR KIDS*.

497

# Comprehension

## Return to Predictions and Purposes

Review with students their predictions and purposes for reading. Were their predictions correct? Did they find out what they wanted to know?

### INFORMAL ASSESSMENT

#### FACT AND NONFACT

**HOW TO ASSESS**

- Have students review the facts and nonfacts presented in the article.
- Then ask them why the scientists want to know more about Lewis and Clark.

Students should recognize that although we have diaries and maps from Lewis and Clark, it is difficult after the passage of 200 years to verify the physical details of their expedition.

**FOLLOW UP** If students have difficulty with fact and nonfact, model comparing the photo of Ken Karsmizki on page 495 with the painting of Sacajawea on page 494.

---

## LITERARY RESPONSE

**QUICK WRITE** Invite students to record their thoughts about the article. This question might help them start:

- Why are Lewis and Clark important figures in American history?

**ORAL RESPONSE** Have students share their journal writings and discuss what part of the article they found most interesting.

**RESEARCH AND INQUIRY** Have students find out more about:

- the maps and diaries kept by Lewis and Clark
- the remains found at Fort Clatsop and Great Falls
- the Louisiana Purchase

**inter**NET **CONNECTION** To learn more about Lewis and Clark, have students visit **www.mhschool.com/reading**

# Story Questions

Have the students discuss or write answers to the questions on page 498.

**Answers:**

1. Lewis and Clark led an expedition in 1803 to explore the Louisiana Purchase. *Literal/Main Idea*

2. Researchers have discovered campsite remains, such as beads and ammunition. These facts are physical proof of the explorers' trip. *Inferential/Fact and Nonfact*

3. The information from their expedition told pioneers how to get to the Pacific and what they might encounter along the way. *Inferential/Draw Conclusions*

4. Researchers are trying to pinpoint the trail Lewis and Clark took. *Critical/Summarize*

5. Jamestown was one site with many artifacts. Lewis and Clark traveled over 4,000 miles and left few remains. *Critical/Reading Across Texts*

**Write a magazine article** For a full writing process lesson, see pages 501K–501L.

# Story Questions & Activities

1. Who were Lewis and Clark?

2. What facts have researchers discovered about the journey of Lewis and Clark? Why are they important?

3. How did the work of Lewis and Clark make it possible for pioneers to settle the West?

4. What is the main idea of this selection?

5. In "Digging Up the Past" archaeologists and historians have created an accurate picture of how early colonists lived. Why are such people having a difficult time piecing together a picture of the Lewis and Clark expedition?

## Write a Magazine Article

Write a short magazine article about the Lewis and Clark expedition. Focus on a question such as "What route did they take?" or "What did they find?" Start by looking in your social studies textbook or in a book about Lewis and Clark. Check your facts in two sources to make sure they are correct. Then include your facts in the middle of your article. Summarize your findings at the end.

## Meeting Individual Needs

| EASY | ON-LEVEL | CHALLENGE |
|------|----------|-----------|
| Reteach, 142 | Practice, 142 | Extend, 142 |

# Draw a Cartoon

Imagine that you are either Lewis or Clark. The time is 1804. You have been traveling west for months. Draw a cartoon describing your journey. Remember that Lewis and Clark are human beings just like you. Perhaps Lewis is tired of hearing Clark complain about his sore feet or tired back. Label your cartoon with a thought balloon or a clever caption.

# Create a Research Journal

Recently, a Montana scientist has found a campsite that may be one of Lewis and Clark's. Create an archaeologist's journal of drawings of objects found along the Lewis and Clark trail. These could include beads, ammunition, a carved bison bone, a pushpin, or a wooden wall from the original campsite. Write a sentence or two under each object. Identify it, and explain why it was important to the explorers.

# Find Out More

Sacajawea joined Lewis and Clark on their journey. Who was she? Why did the explorers ask her to join them? How did she learn English? Why were they lucky to have her along? Find out more about Sacajawea in an encyclopedia or a book about her life. List five facts about her and share them with your classmates.

# Story Activities

## Draw a Cartoon

**Materials:** paper, coloring pens

GROUP

Encourage students to brainstorm ideas for the cartoons. Remind them to consider the weather that the Lewis and Clark party encountered.

## Create a Research Journal

**Materials:** pencil, paper

PARTNERS

Encourage students to model their drawings after the photos on page 497. Brainstorm why these items would have been left behind.

## Find Out More

**RESEARCH AND INQUIRY** Encourage

GROUP

at least two groups to investigate the same questions using different resources. Have them compare their findings and speculate about differences they found.

*inter***NET** **CONNECTION** For more information about the Lewis-and-Clark expedition, students can visit ***www.mhschool.com/reading***

### FORMAL ASSESSMENT

After page 501, see Selection and Unit Assessment.

**MATH: HOW LONG WOULD IT TAKE?** Challenge students to figure out how long it would take Lewis and Clark to get from St. Louis to Seattle if they were living today. They should figure out the length of the trip by car or bus, by train, and by jet.

**What To Look For** Students should do three math problems, based on their research into the distance by road, rail, and air between St. Louis and Seattle multiplied by how many miles per hour an average car, train, and jet can go. Some students may look into rail connections between the two cities for a more accurate answer.

**CHALLENGE**

# Study Skills

## GRAPHIC AIDS

**OBJECTIVES** Students will

- interpret information from a map
- use a map key.

**PREPARE** Read the passage with students. Display **Teaching Chart 117.**

**TEACH** Review how to read a historical map. Have a student trace the route of Lewis and Clark.

**PRACTICE** Have students answer questions 1–5. Review the answers with them. **1.** 1804–1806 **2.** Missouri, Columbia **3.** Spain, Great Britain, and Russia **4.** to learn the geography of this huge piece of land; to open the West to settlement **5.** The map reveals the journey's path and scope.

**ASSESS/CLOSE** Have students use information from the map to evaluate the vast importance of this journey to the nation.

# Study SKILLS

## Use a Map

From 1804 to 1806, Lewis and Clark mapped more than 3,000 miles. The maps that Lewis and Clark drew on their trip and the detailed diaries they kept made it easier for the pioneers to follow the way west.

Look at this map of the Louisiana Purchase and of the route of Lewis and Clark.

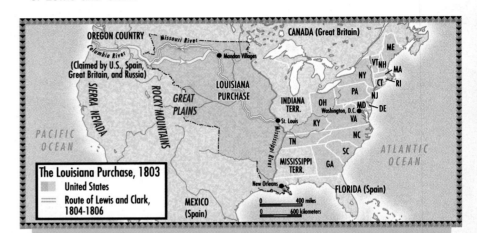

**Use the map to answer these questions.**

1. What were the years of the Lewis and Clark expedition?

2. What rivers did Lewis and Clark travel?

3. Which countries in Europe claimed areas that later became the United States?

4. The United States bought the land in the Louisiana Purchase from France in 1803. Why do you think Jefferson wanted Lewis and Clark to explore the Louisiana Purchase and all the land to the Pacific Ocean?

5. How can this map help you understand the journey of Lewis and Clark?

## Meeting Individual Needs

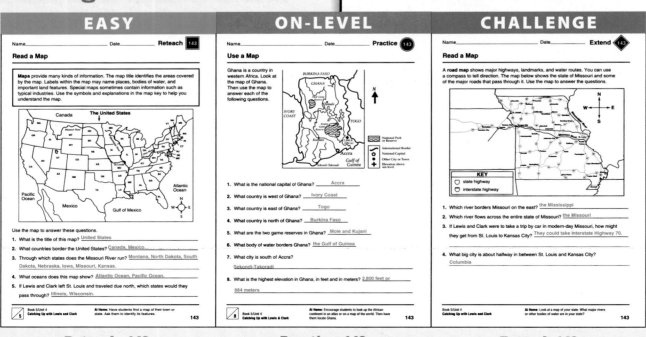

**EASY**    Reteach, 143

**ON-LEVEL**    Practice, 143

**CHALLENGE**    Extend, 143

# TEST POWER

**Test Tip**

Take your time as you do your work.

**DIRECTIONS**

**Read the sample story. Then read each question about the story.**

**SAMPLE**

## Darlene's Adventure

Darlene and her mother had planned the canoe trip for weeks. The trip was now only days away.

Darlene looked again through the pictures and at the <u>brochures</u> they had gotten about their trip. This is one of the pamphlets she studied:

### PALMER LAKE CANOE VENTURES

- You can rent a canoe on Palmer Lake anytime between May 1st and October 31st.
- No experience is required to rent a canoe. Trained instructors are always available to help you understand the basics of proper canoeing.
- Canoe rentals are $20 for the day. Paddles are included.
- A canoe can hold three adults and some light supplies.
- During the summer months, you may reserve a canoe up to three days in advance.

**1** In this passage, <u>brochures</u> means—

  **A** postage stamps

  **B** experiences

  **C** calendar

  **(D)** booklets

**2** Which is the best summary of this passage?

  **F** Darlene and her mother plan their vacation.

  **(G)** Darlene reviews information about a place she will visit.

  **H** Darlene and her mother decide between biking and canoeing.

  **J** Palmer Lake rents canoes during the summer.

## Test Power

**THE PRINCETON REVIEW**

### Read the Page

Have students read *all* the information on the pamphlet. Explain the importance of reading the description above the pamphlet as well.

### Discuss the Questions

**Question 1:** This question asks students to define a word in context. Ask students to find the clue or clues that help them answer this question even when they are unsure what <u>brochures</u> means. Review the sentence that follows the underlined word. It says, "This is one of the pamphlets she studied." Ask students how this information helps them answer the question.

**Question 2:** This question asks students to find the best summary of the passage. Wrong answer choices often give details that *are stated* in the passage but will not be what the passage is *mostly* about.

**ⓘ Intervention ➤ Skills**
**Intervention Guide,** for direct instruction and extra practice in vocabulary and comprehension

## Phonics

- /ô/ and /ôr/
- /âr/ and /är/
- /îr/ and /ûr/

## ☑ Comprehension

- **Judgments and Decisions**
- **Important and Unimportant Information**
- **Draw Conclusions**
- **Fact and Nonfact**

### Answers to Story Questions

Answers will vary and should include details and examples from stories students have read.

---

### EASY

#### Story Questions for Selected Reading

1. What is the main idea of the book?
2. What is the setting?
3. Describe the main character.
4. Summarize the book.
5. What did you learn from reading the book?

#### Information Sources

In each of these stories, a problem is solved when the right information is found. Choose a character from one of the books. How did the character find information? Think of another way in which it could be found.

---

## EASY

### UNIT SKILLS REVIEW

Phonics
☑ **Comprehension**

Help students self-select an Easy Book to read and apply phonics and comprehension skills.

# Guided Reading

**PREVIEW AND PREDICT** Ask students to read the titles and preview the illustrations. Ask them to predict what the book will be about.

**SET PURPOSES** Have students write down two questions they would like answered by the story.

**READ THE BOOK** Use items like the following to guide students' reading.

- Write the sounds listed in the "Phonics" side column on the chalkboard. Look at the pronunciation key in the glossary of your text and make a list of the possible spellings of each of these sounds. Look for words with these sounds as you read. *Phonics*

- Identify a judgment in the story. List the information the author or a character used to make a decision. *Judgments and Decisions*

- Choose a paragraph or a page and list all the important information. Explain how each piece of information is important to the plot of the book. *Important and Unimportant Information*

- Identify a conclusion in the story drawn by the author or one of the characters and the information used to draw the conclusion. *Draw Conclusions*

- Choose a page and identify the facts and nonfacts it contains. Explain how you know which is which. *Fact and Nonfact*

**RETURN TO PREDICTIONS AND PURPOSES** Discuss the students' predictions. Which were close to what really happened in the story and which were not? Were their questions answered?

**LITERARY RESPONSE** Have children discuss questions such as the following:

- What part of the book was most interesting?

- What would be another good title for the book? Why?

**EVALUATE** As students demonstrate success, encourage them to attempt more challenging books. Once a week set aside a longer period of time for them to read independently while you work with students needing support.

# Self-Selected Reading
# Leveled Books

## INDEPENDENT

### UNIT SKILLS REVIEW

☑ **Comprehension**

Help students self-select an Independent Book to read and apply comprehension skills.

## Guided Reading

**PREVIEW AND PREDICT** Ask students to read the titles and preview the illustrations. Ask them to predict what the book will be about.

**SET PURPOSES** Have students write down two questions they would like answered by the story.

**READ THE BOOK** Use items such as the following to guide students' reading.

- Identify a judgment in the story. List the information the author or a character used to make a decision. *Judgments and Decisions*

- Choose a paragraph or a page and list all the important information it contains. How is this information necessary to the story? *Important and Unimportant Information*

- Identify a conclusion in the story drawn by the author or one of the characters. Identify the information the author or the character used to draw the conclusion. *Draw Conclusions*

- Choose a paragraph or a page and identify the facts and nonfacts it contains. Explain how you know which is which. *Fact and Nonfact*

**RETURN TO PREDICTIONS AND PURPOSES** Discuss the students' predictions. Which were close to what really happened in the story and which were not? Have students review their purposes for reading. Were their questions answered?

**LITERARY RESPONSE** Have children discuss questions like the following:

- Who was your favorite character? Why?

- Would you recommend this book to a friend? Why or why not?

**EVALUATE** Use these guidelines to assign books for instructional-level (guided) and independent-level reading:

- Instructional-level texts should contain no more than about 1 in 10 words that is difficult for the reader.

- Independent-level texts should contain no more than about 1 in 20 words that is difficult for the reader.

☑ **Comprehension**

- **Judgments and Decisions**

- **Important and Unimportant Information**

- **Draw Conclusions**

- **Fact and Nonfact**

**Answers to Story Questions**

Answers will vary and should include details and examples from stories children have read.

### INDEPENDENT

**Story Questions for Selected Reading**

1. What is the main idea of the book?
2. What is the setting?
3. Who is the main character? How does he or she solve the problem?
4. Briefly summarize the book.
5. What did you learn by reading the book?

**Information Sources**

In each one of these stories, a solution to a problem is discovered when the right information is found. Could this problem be solved without that information? How?

# Self-Selected Reading
# Leveled Books

## CHALLENGE

☑ **Comprehension**

- Judgments and Decisions

- Important and Unimportant Information

- Draw Conclusions

- Fact and Nonfact

**Answers to Story Questions**

Answers will vary and should include details and examples from stories children have read.

### CHALLENGE

**Story Questions for Selected Reading**

1. What is the main idea of the book?

2. What is the setting?

3. Name and describe the main character and tell why the character acts as he or she does.

4. Briefly summarize the book.

5. What did you learn by reading the book?

**Information Sources**

Think of a time when you had to solve a problem. Write a paragraph describing how you found the information you needed.

---

**UNIT SKILLS REVIEW**

☑ **Comprehension**

Help students self-select a Challenge Book to read and apply comprehension skills.

## Guided Reading

**PREVIEW AND PREDICT** Ask students to predict what the book will be about based on the title, illustrations, and chapter headings.

**SET PURPOSES** Have students write down two questions they would like answered by the story.

**READ THE BOOK** Use items like the following to guide students' reading.

- Identify a judgment in the story. List the information the author or a character used to make a decision. Do you agree with the decision? Why or why not? *Judgments and Decisions*

- Choose a paragraph or a page and list all the important information it contains. Explain why that information is important to the story. *Important and Unimportant Information*

- Identify a conclusion in the story drawn by the author or one of the characters. Identify the information the author or the character used to draw the conclusion. Was the conclusion correct? *Draw Conclusions*

- Choose a paragraph or a page and identify the facts and nonfacts it contains. Explain how you know which is which. *Fact and Nonfact*

**RETURN TO PREDICTIONS AND PURPOSES** Discuss the students' predictions. Which were close to what really happened in the story and which were not? Were their questions answered?

**LITERARY RESPONSE** Have children discuss questions like the following:

- What would be another good title for the book? Why?

- What questions would you ask the author?

**EVALUATE** Monitor students' reading rate during sustained silent reading to make sure they are reading with ease for increasing periods of time. A typical fifth grader reads about 100 words per minute.

# Bringing Groups Together

## Anthology and Leveled Books

## Connecting Texts

**FRAYER MODEL** Select four of the leveled books and write the story titles on a Frayer Model graphic organizer. Write the name of the unit theme in the center of the model and ask students to tell where the search for answers led characters in the story.

**On Track**
- to each crime scene to sketch tracks
- to observe all tracks

**The Galapagos Islands**
- to islands off of South America

**INVESTIGATE!**

**The Great Galveston Hurricane**
- to his telegraph machine
- to the Gulf shore
- to his horse-and-buggy
- home

**The Ladder of Truth**
- to many lumber yards
- to an attic

## Viewing/Representing

**GROUP PRESENTATIONS** Divide the class into groups. Ask students to choose their favorite title and summarize the story in comic strip form. Suggest they begin by listing story events as they happened. Then they can decide which events to include in their comic strip. Have them write captions and use speech balloons to accompany their scene sketches. Their captions should clarify how conclusions were drawn in the story.

**AUDIENCE RESPONSE** Ask students to listen quietly to the presentation and to save their questions. Allow time for questions after each group presents.

## Research and Inquiry

**MORE ON MYSTERIES** Have students choose a well-known mystery to research. How was it solved? Ask them to:

- list a few questions about their topic

- think about ways to find information (nonfiction books, magazines, organizations)

- make notes as they gather information

- create a class book of famous mysteries with their findings.

**interNET CONNECTION** Have students log on to **www.mhschool.com/reading** for links to web pages about scientific investigations.

## OBJECTIVES

Students will distinguish between important and unimportant information.

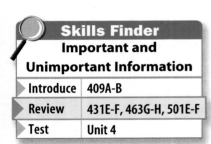

| Skills Finder | |
|---|---|
| **Important and Unimportant Information** | |
| Introduce | 409A–B |
| Review | 431E–F, 463G–H, 501E–F |
| Test | Unit 4 |

---

**TEACHING TIP**

**IMPORTANT INFORMA- TION** Point out that different types of information are important for different purposes. For example, if you are planning a picnic, then information about the weather is important. If you are going to a movie, then weather information is less important.

---

## SELF-SELECTED Reading

*Students may choose from the following titles.*

**ANTHOLOGY**

• Catching Up with Lewis and Clark

**LEVELED BOOKS**

• All titles for the unit

Bibliography, pages T78–T79

Instruct students to choose books at an appropriate level of difficulty—books in which they can read at least nine words out of ten and can use context and language-structure clues and letter-sound correspondences to decode the rest.

# Review Important and Unimportant Information

**PREPARE**

**Discuss Important and Unimportant Information**

Review: Important information contributes to the writer's main theme or purpose. Unimportant information does not support the main idea.

**TEACH**

**Read "Sacajawea" and Model the Skill**

Display **Teaching Chart 118** and read "Sacajawea" with students. Have students think about what information is important.

---

**Sacajawea**

Two eleven-year-old Shoshone girls (played near the Missouri River) in about 1800. (Their fathers were away hunting.) A raiding party from the Minnetaree people captured eight Shoshone children, but (six of them escaped.)

Though they were captives of the Minnetaree, the girls were treated more like family. The Minnetaree named one of the girls Sacajawea, because she had bright eyes and quick movements like a bird. Later, Sacajawea left the Minnetaree and became the wife of a white man, Touissaint Charbonneau.

*Teaching Chart 118*

---

Ask students what information is important to the main idea of the passage.

**MODEL** I think the author wants to give information about Sacajawea's life. I think her age when she was captured and how she got her name are important. I don't think the name of the river is important.

Have students circle words that give unimportant information.

## PRACTICE

**Chart Important and Unimportant Facts**

GROUP

Have students chart the important and unimportant facts in the teaching chart passage. ▶ **Visual/Logical**

| IMPORTANT FACTS | UNIMPORTANT FACTS |
|---|---|
| Sacajawea was eleven when she was captured. | The girls were captured near the Missouri River. |
| Sacajawea had bright eyes and quick movements like a bird. | Six children escaped. |

## ASSESS/CLOSE

**Distinguish Between Important and Unimportant Information**

PARTNERS

Have students choose a familiar historical person or a character from a familiar story, movie, or show. Ask them to write two or three paragraphs that include both important and unimportant information about the person. Have partners exchange paragraphs and identify the important and unimportant information. Suggest they list the information on a chart.

### ALTERNATE TEACHING STRATEGY

#### IMPORTANT AND UNIMPORTANT INFORMATION

For a different approach to teaching this skill, see page T64.

**ⓘ Intervention ▶ Skills Intervention Guide,** for direct instruction and extra practice with important and unimportant information

---

# Meeting Individual Needs for Comprehension

| EASY | ON-LEVEL | CHALLENGE | LANGUAGE SUPPORT |
|---|---|---|---|

**EASY**

Name_____ Date_____ **Reteach 144**

**Important and Unimportant Information**

One way to recognize **important and unimportant information** is to ask yourself what would happen if the information were left out of the selection. Important information cannot be removed without affecting a main idea of the selection. Unimportant information can be left out without changing the main idea.

Read the stories. Then circle YES or NO to tell whether the underlined information is important or unimportant. Test your choice by rereading the story without the underlined information.

1. Jon's ride was late again. It was the third time this month. This time, she came 12 minutes after 8 o'clock. She always called to say she would be late, but that didn't help Jon get to school on time.
   Yes  (No)

2. Aunt Hattie makes fantastic lunches. Her black-eyed peas are the best I've ever had. She also makes great corn bread. I look forward all week to Sunday lunch at her house.
   (Yes)  No

3. Joellyn works late at night. Her shift starts at midnight. When she gets tired, she drinks a glass of cold water to wake up.
   (Yes)  No

4. Wait until you hear this! Jim's Dad was backing out of his garage, and he tore off the garage door right off. He had lifted the door up but I guess not far enough. Anyway, the door is totally smashed.
   Yes  (No)

5. Quentin comes from a big family. They need four long tables when everyone eats together on special holidays. He always has someone to talk to.
   (Yes)  No

At Home: Expand one of the stories by adding an important or an unimportant piece of information. Tell which kind of information you have added.
144    Book 5/Unit 4  Catching Up with Lewis & Clark  5

**ON-LEVEL**

Name_____ Date_____ **Practice 144**

**Important & Unimportant Information**

In "Catching Up with Lewis & Clark" the **important information** supports the main idea—trying to find the remains of an old Lewis and Clark campsite. There is also **unimportant information** that might be interesting for the reader, but does not support the main idea.

Place a ✓next to each sentence that states important information for "Catching Up with Lewis & Clark."

____  1. Scientists have been digging for remains of the Lewis and Clark journey in Great Falls, Montana, and Fort Clatsop, Oregon.

✓  2. Lewis and Clark made it possible for people from the East to settle the West.

____  3. The Lewis and Clark expedition had to fight off bears and carry heavy canoes for weeks overland.

✓  4. Lewis and Clark kept maps and diaries, so scientists have a good idea where they might have camped.

____  5. It took more than 500 days for Lewis and Clark to reach the Pacific Ocean.

✓  6. It is hard for scientists to say, "Lewis and Clark camped here," because the explorers left barely anything behind.

✓  7. Scientists have to sift dirt through a giant strainer to find things that might have belonged to Lewis and Clark on their journey.

____  8. A number of monuments have been built to honor Sacajawea.

____  9. The bison bone and pushpin are from the time of Lewis and Clark.

✓  10. Scientists think the ammunition and beads found at Fort Clatsop in Oregon might have belonged to the explorers.

At Home: Encourage children to talk about the most important information they learned from reading "Catching Up with Lewis & Clark."
144    Book 5/Unit 4  Catching Up with Lewis & Clark  10

**CHALLENGE**

Name_____ Date_____ **Extend 144**

**Important and Unimportant Information**

When you write a report about a topic, you need to identify the purpose, or main idea, of your report. Then you determine which information you want to include to support your main idea. This is **important information**. **Unimportant information** can add interest but is not needed to support a main idea.

"Catching Up with Lewis and Clark" discusses the journey of these explorers. Suppose you wanted to write an article about where they traveled and what they saw on their journey. First find the important information that you will include in your article to support your main idea. Then write a brief article titled, "The Journey of Lewis and Clark."

Articles and lists should include states through which Lewis and Clark traveled, rivers and mountains they journeyed across, the dates of their expedition, and what they saw along the way.

_____

_____

_____

At Home: Use reference materials to find out more about the journey of Lewis and Clark. Add important information to your article.
144    Book 5/Unit 4  Catching Up with Lewis & Clark

**LANGUAGE SUPPORT**

Name_____ Date_____

**How Much Does It Matter?**

1. Read the sentences. Study the pictures. 2. Which sentence is more important?
3. Place a check before that sentence.

▣ There is a waterfall ahead.
❑ They have come five miles today.

❑ Her name means "Bird Woman."
▣ She can speak English and Shoshone.

▣ It is not safe to cross the mountains in winter.
❑ This mountain range is about 3,200 miles long.

▣ Eating this plant will make you sick.
❑ This plant has pretty leaves.

158 Catching Up With Lewis and Clark • Language Support/Blackline Master 78    Grade 5

**Reteach, 144**   **Practice, 144**   **Extend, 144**   **Language Support, 158**

**501F**

 **OBJECTIVES**

Students will:

- recognize the roots of words.
- use root words to determine the meaning of unfamiliar words.

### Skills Finder

**Root Words**

| Introduce | 431I-J |
|-----------|--------|
| Review | 491I-J, 501G-H |
| Test | Unit 4 |

### TEACHING TIP

**ROOT WORDS** The more root words a reader knows, the better able he or she is to figure out the meanings of unfamiliar words.

- Share examples of root words: *ped* (foot), *scrib* (write).

# Review Root Words

**PREPARE**

**Discuss Meaning of Root Words**

Review: A root word is a word from which other words are derived. Often a root word cannot stand alone. Knowing the root of a word can help readers figure out the meaning of the whole word.

**TEACH**

**Read the Passage and Model the Skill**

Have students read the passage on **Teaching Chart 119.**

---

#### When the Trail Is 200 Years Old

Although Lewis and Clark kept a journal describing their expedition, historians still have questions about exactly where they camped. We do know that they stayed for some time at Fort Clatsop, where a national <u>memorial</u> is now established. There, scientists have found a wooden wall of what may have been Lewis and Clark's <u>original</u> campsite. To know for certain where else they stayed, though, historians require more evidence.

Teaching Chart 119

---

Model using knowledge of root words to clarify word meaning.

*MODEL* In the first sentence I can see that the word *questions* has the root word *quest.* This root comes from the Latin word *quaerere*, meaning "to seek, ask." So a question is something that is asked.

Have students discuss other words with the same root. (quest, query, inquire, require, request) Have them notice how knowing the root word is a key to understanding word meaning.

## PRACTICE

**Use Root Words to Determine Meaning**

ONE

Have volunteers underline the words *memorial* and *original* in the teaching chart passage. Tell students that the root of *memorial* is *memor*, "mindful" and the root of *original* is *origin*, "rise." Have students explain how the root words are keys to the underlined words' meanings. ▶ **Linguistic**

## ASSESS/CLOSE

**Use Root Words to Create Word Trees**

GROUP

Provide groups of students with large sheets of paper. Have students create "groves" of word trees, using root words that they know as the roots of the trees. Groups can combine their groves to make a forest.

▶ **Visual/Interpersonal**

---

---

# Meeting Individual Needs for Vocabulary

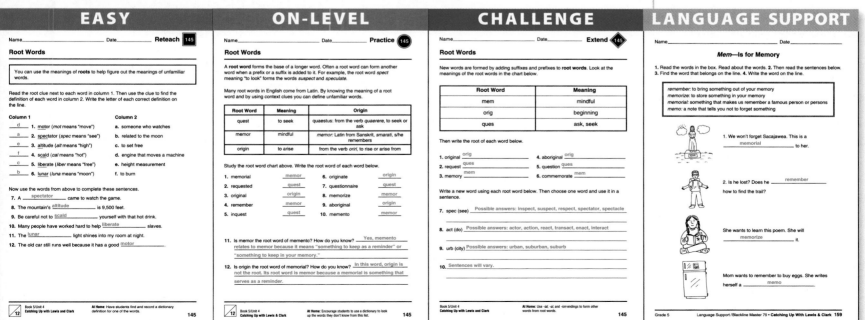

| EASY | ON-LEVEL | CHALLENGE | LANGUAGE SUPPORT |
|---|---|---|---|
| Reteach, 145 | Practice, 145 | Extend, 145 | Language Support, 159 |

## OBJECTIVES

**Students will**

- understand the meaning of suffixes *-less* and *-ment*.
- figure out the meaning of words ending with suffixes *-less* and *-ment*.

### Skills Finder

**Suffixes**

| | |
|---|---|
| Introduce | 407I–J |
| Review | 463I–J, 501I–J |
| Test | Unit 4 |
| Maintain | 547, 573, 587, 635 |

### TEACHING TIP

**SUFFIXES** Sometimes the *y* at the end of a word changes to *i* before the suffix is added. Example: *penny, penniless.*

- Not all words ending with *-less* or *-ment* have suffixes. Examples: *bless, cement.*
- Have volunteers look up other meanings of the suffix *-ment* in different dictionaries and share them with the class.

# Review Suffixes

### PREPARE

**Discuss Meaning of Suffixes *-less* and *-ment***

Review: A suffix is a word part that is added to the end of a word. The suffix *-less* means "without, lacking." The suffix *-ment* means "act of," "result of," or "state of being." The more suffixes a reader knows, the more unfamiliar words he or she will be able to figure out.

### TEACH

**Read the Passage and Model the Skill**

Have students read the passage on **Teaching Chart 120.**

**Expedition Extraordinaire**

The United States made a payment of $15 million to France for the Louisiana Purchase. The Lewis-and-Clark Expedition helped the United States government by exploring this land and laying claim to much land west of the Mississippi River. To get to the Pacific Ocean, the expedition had to cross the endless Great Plains. The tireless efforts of the Expedition crew lasted over two years and won them President Jefferson's praise for their magnificent accomplishment.

Teaching Chart 120

Discuss how suffixes change the meaning of words, and how knowing what suffixes mean helps to figure out the meaning of words.

**MODEL** I see in the first sentence that *payment* ends with the suffix *-ment.* The base word is *pay.* If *-ment* means "act or result of" or "state of being," then *payment* means "act or result of paying" or "state of being paid."

## PRACTICE

**Identify Words with Suffixes -less and -ment**

ONE

Have students underline the words in the teaching chart passage with the suffixes *-less* and *-ment*, and then circle the suffix. Have them discuss how understanding the meaning of the suffix helped them to understand the words. ▶ **Linguistic**

## ASSESS/CLOSE

**Create Words with Suffixes -less and -ment**

GROUP

Have students brainstorm lists of words with the suffixes *-less* and *-ment*. Have groups of students write the base words and suffixes from the list on separate word cards, with one root or one suffix on each card. Distribute cards to each group, one card per student. Have students physically "match" themselves up to form the whole words.

▶ **Kinesthetic/Interpersonal**

**ALTERNATE TEACHING STRATEGY**
...................................

**SUFFIXES**

For a different approach to teaching this skill, see page T63.

**i  Intervention ▶ Skills Intervention Guide,** for direct instruction and extra practice with suffixes

# Meeting Individual Needs for Vocabulary

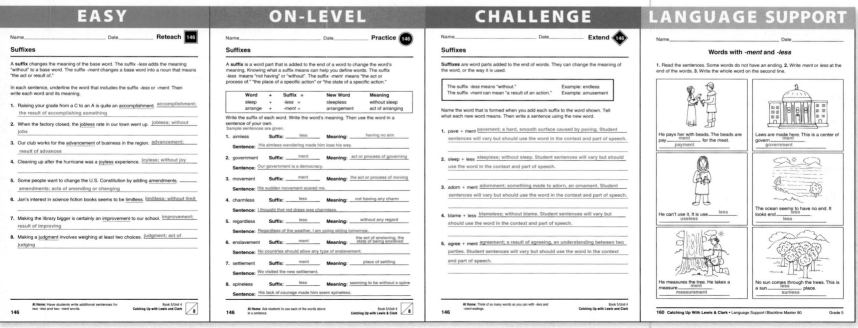

**EASY**   Reteach, 146

**ON-LEVEL**   Practice, 146

**CHALLENGE**   Extend, 146

**LANGUAGE SUPPORT**   Language Support, 160

# Expository Writing

**GRAMMAR/SPELLING**
**CONNECTIONS**

See the 5-Day Grammar and Usage Plan on comparing with *good* and *bad*, pages 501M–501N.

See the 5-Day Spelling Plan on words from Social Studies, pages 501O–501P.

## TEACHING TIP

**Technology**
Point out that many magazine articles are written in column format. Mention that some word-processing programs allow you to set up your page layout to accommodate column format. Have a volunteer show how to use the column format feature.

**Supporting Facts**
Remind students that the facts used to support an idea must clearly relate to the focus of the article. Facts that do not relate clearly to the focus should not be included.

**Handwriting CD-ROM**

## Prewrite

**WRITE A MAGAZINE ARTICLE** Present this writing assignment: Write a short magazine article about the Lewis and Clark expedition. Focus on a question. Examples: What route did they take? What did they find? Start by checking in your social studies textbook, an encyclopedia, or a book about Lewis and Clark. Check your facts in two sources to make sure they are correct. Present your main idea in the introduction. Support it with facts in the middle of your article. Summarize your findings at the end.

**TAKE NOTES** Urge students to write notes on index cards as they gather information.

**Strategy: Organize Information** Suggest that students keep their note cards in three groups that correspond with the beginning, middle, and end of the article.

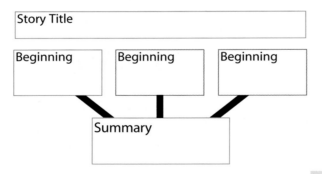

Story Title

Beginning | Beginning | Beginning

Summary

## Draft

**SUMMARIZING THE GRAPHIC ORGANIZER** Begin by asking students to write the title of their magazine article in the Story Title box. Next ask them to review their notes and then write a draft summary on the graphic organizer—the main idea in the Beginning box, supporting facts and details in the Middle box, and ideas to be summa-

rized in the Summary box. Students are now ready to write their first draft.

## Revise

**SELF-QUESTIONING** Ask students to assess the organization of their drafts.

- Is the main idea introduced in the first paragraph?
- Does the body of the article support the main idea with facts?
- Does the final paragraph summarize the article?

**PARTNERS**
Have students reread their own magazine article and create a second draft.

## Edit/Proofread

**CHECK FOR ERRORS AND DETAILS** Students should reread their articles for spelling, grammar, and clarity. Have them revise once to strengthen their summaries.

## Publish

**SHARE MAGAZINE ARTICLES** Have students add headings or other graphic features to their articles and create a Table of Contents. Bind the articles into a magazine, and have volunteers read their articles aloud.

*An Amazing Journey*

The Lewis and Clark Expedition (1804–1806) explored and mapped land that Americans knew very little about. This group struggled up the Missouri River from St. Louis almost to its source. It took nearly a month to carry the boats around the Great Falls.

At the Continental Divide, the explorers expected to see the Pacific. Instead they saw more mountains. After climbing over them, they followed the Clearwater River, the Snake River, and the Columbia River to the Pacific. Finally, the explorers returned to St. Louis. Along the way, Lewis and Clark made maps and drew pictures of the animals and plants they discovered.

What were results of the Lewis and Clark trip? Americans knew how wide the United States was. The drawings in Lewis' journal showed many unknown animals and plants. Due to their maps, much more was known about the land along the Missouri River.

# Presentation Ideas

**ILLUSTRATE THE ARTICLE** Encourage students to submit illustrations with their magazine articles. ▶ **Viewing/Representing**

**DRAMATIZE THE EXPEDITION** Encourage students to act out key parts of the Lewis and Clark expedition.

▶ **Speaking/Listening**

Consider students' creative efforts, possibly adding a plus (+) for originality, wit, and imagination.

## Scoring Rubric

| Excellent | Good | Fair | Unsatisfactory |
|---|---|---|---|
| **4:** The writer | **3:** The writer | **2:** The writer | **1:** The writer |
| • clearly states the main idea in the introduction. | • states the main idea in the introduction. | • may provide a description of the main idea. | • offers some explanation of the main idea. |
| • describes the trip with exceptionally interesting details. | • supports the main idea with accurate facts. | • provides a few facts related to the topic. | • provides a few related and some unrelated facts. |
| • concludes with an accurate, detailed summary of the findings. | • clearly summarizes the findings in the conclusion. | • offers a vague or incomplete summary. | • does not summarize findings. |

**Incomplete 0:** The writer leaves the page blank or fails to respond to the writing task. The student does not address the topic or simply paraphrases the prompt. The response is illegible or incoherent.

For a 6-point or an 8-point scale, see pages T107–T108.

# Meeting Individual Needs for Writing

## EASY

**Book Jacket** Have students make a book jacket. On the front, there should be a title, a picture showing Lewis and Clark or a scene from the trip, and the name of the author (the student). The back cover should include a brief summary of the trip.

## ON-LEVEL

**Travel Brochure** Have students trace Lewis and Clark's path on a map and label three to five important places. Next fold the map in half horizontally to make the outside of a brochure. Tell students to write the tour company's name on the front and list the places of interest on the back.

## CHALLENGE

**A Press Release** Invite students to research the Lewis and Clark expedition. Next, have them write a press release for radio or television about the adventure. Have students describe how the expected and actual outcomes differed in their explanations.

## Listening and Speaking

**LISTENING STRATEGIES**
As students watch the dramatization, encourage them to:

• reflect on what they are learning about Lewis and Clark.

• make notes about parts that could be clearer.

**SPEAKING STRATEGIES**
Encourage students to:

• use appropriate gestures to engage the audience.

• project their words so that they are clear to all.

**LANGUAGE SUPPORT**

**ESL** Gather materials: pictures of Lewis and Clark, map of their route, illustrated history book or a video (*Lewis and Clark* by Ken Burns). Use the visuals to demonstrate what the selection describes. Ask students to take notes and use this information as they write their introductions.

 **PORTFOLIO** Invite students to include their magazine articles in their portfolios.

# 5 Day Grammar and Usage Plan

**ESL** Show students a diagram showing the weather over a five-day period. Help them describe each day's weather using *good, better, best, bad, worse,* and *worst.*

## DAILY LANGUAGE ACTIVITIES

Have students correct the sentences orally.

### Day 1
1. Lewis and Clark were the goodest explorers of their time.
2. Lewis was Clark's most better friend.
3. The expedition had best than average campers.

### Day 2
1. Was Lewis a best speller than Clark?
2. Bear attacks were the worse dangers that they faced.
3. Cold days were worst than warm days.

### Day 3
1. The explorers kept the better maps.
2. Some days were worst than others.
3. Scientists hope to find best clues to the events of their journey.

### Day 4
1. Clark was a worser speller than Lewis.
2. The better moment was reaching the Pacific.
3. Sifting through dirt is the worse job.

### Day 5
1. Sacajawea was the betterest guide.
2. She spoke best English than her brother.
3. Food and horses were their worst problem.

**Daily Language Transparency 20**

**Suggested Answers on Transparency**

## DAY 1 — Introduce the Concept

**Oral Warm-Up** Discuss a comparative situation with students such as: *I think vanilla ice cream is good, but strawberry is better, and chocolate is best. What do you think?*

**Introduce Comparing with *Good*** Some adjectives have special forms for comparing. Present the following:

### Comparing with *Good*
- Use *better* to compare two people, places, or things.
- Use *best* to compare more than two.

Present the Daily Language Activity and have students correct orally. Then, ask students to write sentences using *better* and *best.*

 **WRITING** Assign the daily Writing Prompt on page 492C.

## DAY 2 — Teach the Concept

**Review Comparing with *Good* and *Bad*** Continue discussion of personal preferences with students using *good, better,* and *best.*

**Introduce Comparing with *Bad*** The adjective *bad* also has special forms for comparing. Present:

### Comparing with *Bad*
- Use *worse* to compare two people, places, or things.
- Use *worst* to compare more than two.

Present the Daily Language Activity. Have students correct the sentences orally. Then have students write sentences using *worse* and *worst.*

 **WRITING** Assign the daily Writing Prompt on page 492C.

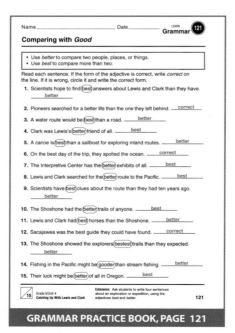

**GRAMMAR PRACTICE BOOK, PAGE 121**

**GRAMMAR PRACTICE BOOK, PAGE 122**

# .... Comparing with *Good* and *Bad*

## DAY 3 — Review and Practice

**Learn from the Literature** Review comparing with *good* and *bad*. Read aloud from page 496 *Catching Up with Lewis and Clark.*

> **Lewis and his best friend, Clark, left St. Louis in May 1804 with a party of 42 men.**

Ask students what they think "a best friend" means. How many friends does this compare?

**Write Comparative Sentences**
Present the Daily Language Activity and have students correct the sentences orally.

Have students read the rest of page 496 of *Catching Up with Lewis and Clark.* Ask them to write comparative sentences about the exploration using *better, best, worse,* and *worst.*

 Assign the daily Writing Prompt on page 492D.

## DAY 4 — Review and Practice

**Review Comparing with *Good* and *Bad*** Have students write the corrected sentences from the Daily Language Activities for Days 1 through 3 under columns labeled Comparing Two and Comparing More Than Two. Then present the Daily Language Activity for Day 4. Have students correct the sentences orally.

**Mechanics and Usage** Before students begin the Daily Writing Prompt on page 492D, review the rules of proper adjectives. Display and discuss:

### Proper Adjectives

- A proper adjective is formed from a proper noun.
- A proper adjective begins with a capital letter.

 Assign the daily Writing Prompt on page 492D.

## DAY 5 — Assess and Reteach

**Assess** Use the Daily Language Activity and page 125 of the **Grammar Practice Book** for assessment.

**Reteach** Have a student volunteer a statement about something they think is *good* or *bad.* Ask volunteers to state what they think is *better* or *worse* and *best* or *worst.*

Write the students' sentences on a chalkboard or white board. Then have students create a classroom word wall by grouping the sentences under the headings Comparing Two and Comparing More Than Two.

Use page 126 of the **Grammar Practice Book** for additional reteaching.

 Assign the daily Writing Prompt on page 492D.

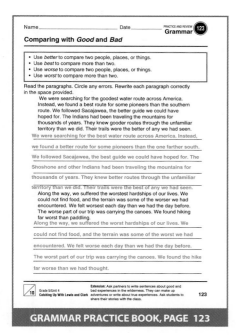

**GRAMMAR PRACTICE BOOK, PAGE 123**

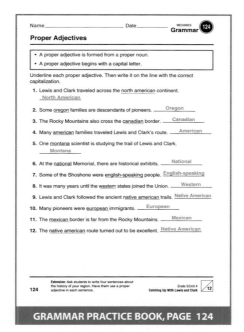

**GRAMMAR PRACTICE BOOK, PAGE 124**

**GRAMMAR PRACTICE BOOK, PAGE 125**

**GRAMMAR PRACTICE BOOK, PAGE 126**

**501N**

# 5 Day Spelling Plan

## LANGUAGE SUPPORT

Remind students that a syllable contains a vowel sound. Have students identify the syllables by tapping out the vowel sounds in each Spelling Word.

## DICTATION SENTENCES

### Spelling Words

1. We saw many places on our journey.
2. We went across the lake in canoes.
3. They traveled to many states.
4. Take the route around the lake.
5. The travel service helps tourists.
6. Their hardships included snowstorms.
7. The trail goes through the valley.
8. The explorer found new places.
9. We communicate with words.
10. A travel agency plans our trips.
11. Boats float down the canal.
12. A fort protects the farmers.
13. I am a native of this town.
14. There were ten cars in the caravan.
15. This agreement ends the war.
16. The expedition will study plants.
17. What is the elevation of the hill?
18. The canyon is deep.
19. They dwell in homes near a lake.
20. Our campsite had many tents.

### Challenge Words

21. Bison are often called buffalo.
22. I have kept several diaries.
23. He went back to his former home.
24. She wrote stories in her journal.
25. Her superb soup tastes great.

## DAY 1 Pretest

**Assess Prior Knowledge** Use the Dictation Sentences at the left and **Spelling Practice Book** page 121 for the pretest. Allow students to correct their own papers. Students who require a modified list may be tested on the first ten words.

| Spelling Words | | Challenge Words |
|---|---|---|
| 1. **journey** | 11. canal | 21. **bison** |
| 2. **canoes** | 12. **fort** | 22. **diaries** |
| 3. **traveled** | 13. **native** | 23. **former** |
| 4. **route** | 14. caravan | 24. **journal** |
| 5. service | 15. agreement | 25. **superb** |
| 6. **hardships** | 16. **expedition** | |
| 7. **trail** | 17. elevation | |
| 8. **explorer** | 18. canyon | |
| 9. **communicate** | 19. dwell | |
| 10. agency | 20. **campsite** | |

*Note: Words in **dark type** are from the story.*

**Word Study** On page 122 of the **Spelling Practice Book** are word study steps and an at-home activity.

## DAY 2 Explore the Pattern

**Sort and Spell Words** Say *communicate*. Ask students how many syllables they heard in *communicate*. (4) Have students read the Spelling Words aloud and sort them as below.

### Words with

| One Syllable | Two Syllables | |
|---|---|---|
| route | journey | canal |
| trail | canoes | native |
| fort | traveled | canyon |
| dwell | service | campsite |
| | hardships | |

| Three Syllables | Four Syllables |
|---|---|
| explorer | communicate |
| agency | expedition |
| caravan | elevation |
| agreement | |

**Word Wall** Have students create a word wall based on the word sort and add more words from their reading.

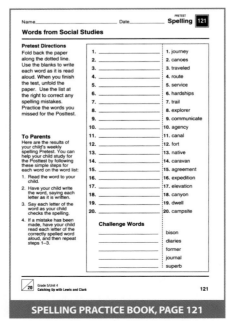

SPELLING PRACTICE BOOK, PAGE 121

WORD STUDY STEPS AND ACTIVITY, PAGE 122

SPELLING PRACTICE BOOK, PAGE 123

# Words from Social Studies

## DAY 3 — Practice and Extend

**Word Meaning: Synonyms** Review that a *synonym* has almost the same meaning as another word. Have students think of synonyms for the Spelling Words. (Examples: trail/path, journey/trip)

If students need extra practice, have partners give each other a midweek test.

**Glossary** Ask students to read the word history for *diaries* in the Glossary. Ask:

- From what language did the word *diary* come? (Latin)

- From what Latin word did *diary* come? (diarium)

- How are the words *diary* and *daily* related? (People often write daily in their diaries.)

## DAY 4 — Proofread and Write

**Proofread Sentences** Write these sentences on the chalkboard, including the misspelled words. Ask students to proofread, circling incorrect spellings and writing the correct spellings. There are two spelling errors in each sentence.

> Let's take a journy in a canew. (journey, canoe)
>
> What rout will the carrivan take? (route, caravan)

Have students create additional sentences with errors for partners to correct.

Have students use as many Spelling Words as possible in the daily Writing Prompt on page 492D. Remind students to proofread their writing for errors in spelling, grammar, and punctuation.

## DAY 5 — Assess and Reteach

**Assess Students' Knowledge** Use page 126 of the **Spelling Practice Book** or the Dictation Sentences on page 501O for the posttest.

**Personal Word List** If students have trouble with any words in the lesson, have them add to their personal list of troublesome words in their journals. Have students write a context sentence for each word.

Students should refer to their word lists during later writing activities.

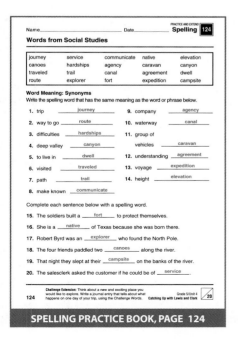

**SPELLING PRACTICE BOOK, PAGE 124**

**SPELLING PRACTICE BOOK, PAGE 125**

**SPELLING PRACTICE BOOK, PAGE 126**

# Wrap Up the Theme

## Investigate!

*We never know where the search for answers might lead us.*

**REVIEW THE THEME** Remind students that all of the selections in this unit relate to the theme Investigate! Were students surprised at any of the ways the characters investigated the world around them? Ask students to name other stories or movies they know that also fit the theme Investigate!

**READ THE POEM** Read "Early Spring" by Shonto Begay aloud to students. As they listen, ask students to think about how the poet feels. After reading, discuss how the poem connects to the theme Investigate! What is the poet investigating on the mesa?

Reread the poem, asking the class to join in reading the last line aloud.

🔘 📼 **Listening Library** The poem is available on **audiocassette** or on **compact disc.**

**MAKE CONNECTIONS** Have students work in small groups to brainstorm a list of ways that the stories, poems, and the *Time for Kids* magazine article relate to the theme Investigate! Groups can then compare their lists as they share them with the class.

If students listened to any selections or poetry on audiocassette or compact disc, have them explain what they liked or disliked about experiencing the literature in that way.

# Early Spring

In the early spring, the snowfall is light
upon the mesa.
It does not stick to the ground very long.
I walk through this patchwork of snow and earth,
watching the ground for early signs.
Signs of growth. Signs of rebirth.

Larkspur and wild onions are still
within the warmth of the earth.
I hear cries of crows off in the distance.
A rabbit bounds off into the sagebrush flat.
A shadow of a hawk disturbs the landscape momentarily.
It sees food and life abundant below that I cannot see.
The cycle of life continues.

Even as I stand here shivering in the afternoon chill,
just below me, young seedlings start
their upward journey.
Insects begin to stir.
Rodents and snakes are comfortable in their burrows.
Maybe to them we also disappear with the cold.
Not to be seen until spring.

For this generation, and many more to come,
this land is beautiful and filled with mysteries.
They reveal themselves and their stories—
if you look very carefully, and listen....

by *Shonto Begay*

502

## LOOKING AT GENRE

Have students review *Carlos and the Skunk* and *The Big Storm*. What makes one realistic fiction? What makes the other nonfiction?

Help students list the characteristics of each genre. Can they name other stories that have these same characteristics?

| REALISTIC FICTION: *CARLOS AND THE SKUNK* | NONFICTION: *THE BIG STORM* |
|---|---|
| • Fictional story takes place in a setting that could be real. | • Story is about real people, places, and events. |
| • Realistic fiction is written mainly to entertain. | • Nonfiction is written to inform or to entertain. |
| • Sometimes uses humor to poke fun at characters who are like real people. | • Information is organized around main ideas. |

503

# Research and Inquiry

 **Complete the Theme Project** Have students work in teams to complete their group project. Remind students that the information they have gathered can be presented in any creative way. Encourage them to share the tasks involved in developing their presentation. Each member of the team should contribute to the project.

**Make a Classroom Presentation** Have teams take turns presenting their projects. Suggest that students pay attention to each oral presentation, listening not only for literal information, but also making inferences and evaluating what is said. Be sure to include time for questions from the audience.

**Draw Conclusions** Have students draw conclusions about what they learned from researching and preparing their projects. Was the resource chart they made helpful? What other resources did they use? What conclusions have students made about their topic? Was their presentation effective? Finally, ask students if doing the research has changed their opinion in any way about the issue they chose. What can they conclude from this?

**Ask More Questions/Revise Questions** What additional questions do students now have about the issue they chose to investigate? What else would students like to find out? Do students have questions about other issues that might be offshoots of the one they explored? You might encourage the teams to continue their research and prepare another presentation.

## LEARNING ABOUT POETRY

**Literary Devices: Imagery** Read the poem aloud, asking students to close their eyes and imagine the mesa as the poet describes it. Explain that the poet uses imagery to give the reader a mental picture of the mesa. Ask students to list all the things the poet found "in this patchwork of snow and earth." Each image is a building block, making up the total vision in the poem.

**Response Activity** Ask students to choreograph a dance based on the discoveries the poet makes on the mesa. One student might be the poet, others might portray the additional living things described in the poem. Students can present their dance as one student reads the poem, or they may dance to music representative of spring.

**503**

# Reading for Information

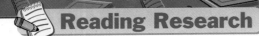

## Reading Research

When you write a report, you must first do research on your topic. It is important that you read various sources to get enough information. Taking notes from multiple sources will help you gather different facts about your topic. As you research, select the best sources for your information, and check the accuracy of the facts you use.

**Research Report**

### Use Research Methods

1. **Locate sources of information.** Use the library to find books and other sources. Cross-checking is also important—checking questionable or conflicting facts in a second or third source.

2. **Take notes on useful information.** Also record information about the source. You may need to list your sources in a bibliography.

3. **Organize your information.** Put your notes in categories based on the main ideas of your topic. Then use these categories to make a logical outline for your report.

4. **Write your report in your own words.** Be sure to write clear sentences that your readers will understand.

748   *Reading for Information*

---

**Locate several sources of information for your topic.** This seems like a good source for my topic, Georgia O'Keeffe.

**Take notes.** This is an important fact for my report.

**Organize.** The early years of O'Keeffe will be a main part of my outline.

**Write.** I'll use my notes and outline to write my report.

*Here is part of an article from a source that you will find listed on page 750.*

### Georgia O'Keeffe, American Artist

Georgia O'Keeffe was born in Wisconsin in 1887. By the age of ten, she knew she wanted to be a painter.

Her work was finally recognized when she was nearly thirty. She sent some drawings to a friend in New York. The friend gave them to the photographer Alfred Stieglitz, who ran an art gallery in New York. Stieglitz loved O'Keeffe's drawings and exhibited them immediately. From then on, people were eager to see her work.

Georgia O'Keeffe continued to develop her own unique style. Her paintings show natural forms such as flowers, shells, skulls, clouds, and hills. They also show skyscrapers and city streets. O'Keeffe's forms are drawn simply, and the colors are vivid.

*See also* Stieglitz, Alfred.

*Reading Research*   749

**Anthology pages 748–749**

---

# Reading Research

**OBJECTIVES** Students will:

- learn to use a variety of sources to research information for a report
- understand techniques for organizing and documenting information in a report

**INTRODUCE**   Ask students to read the opening paragraph on page 748. Invite volunteers to say in their own words what they will need to do to write an effective report. Then have students read the four points listed under **Use Research Methods** and discuss the importance of these guidelines.

*MODEL*   Finding the right sources is a key first step for researching a report. I try to find up-to-date books and magazines. That way, I can be more confident that my facts are correct. I also look for sources that are written by experts who can be trusted to present information fairly.

**PRACTICE/APPLY**   Ask students to read "Georgia O'Keeffe, American Artist" on page 749. Have students discuss why each numbered suggestion would be helpful when researching and writing a report. Ask:

- Why is it important to use more than one source?
- What might happen if you wrote without an outline?
- How does retelling information in your own words help you learn?

As students **preview** pages 750–751, ask: how might the writer of the report on Georgia O'Keeffe have used these guidelines? *(Set Purposes)*

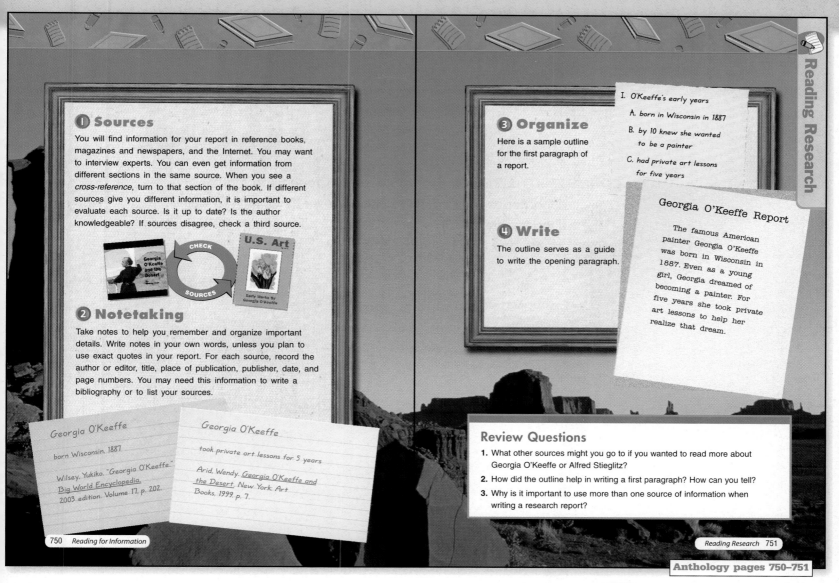

**Anthology pages 750–751**

## ANSWERS TO REVIEW QUESTIONS

**1.** Answers will vary. A biography of O'Keeffe or Stieglitz would be helpful; encyclopedia and magazine articles would be other useful sources.

**2.** The author developed the main and supporting details in the outline into paragraphs; the first paragraph closely follows Part I of the outline.

**3.** Using more than one source (cross-referencing) lets a writer check questionable or conflicting facts; different sources also present different information and points of view.

## TRANSFER THE STRATEGY

**Ask:** How does "Georgia O'Keeffe, American Artist" follow the guidelines for writing reports?

**Explain:** What did you learn in this lesson that will help you write reports in social studies or science?

**Discuss:** List five careers that would require good research skills. Explain.

## Activity

### Look It Up!

**What to Do:**

**1.** Using research sources, write five statements about well-known people or events. Some of the statements you write should be true, and a few should be false. Write each statement on a separate 3 x 5 note card.

**2.** Exchange cards with a partner.

**3.** Now use research sources to find out whether the statements on your partner's cards are true or false.

**4.** On each note card, write *true* or *false,* and give exact details about the source where you checked the fact.

**5.** The first partner to research all five statements correctly wins.

# Expository Writing

**CONNECT TO LITERATURE** In *An Island Scrapbook,* a mother and daughter explore an island and discover its beauty, as well as the dangers that threaten them. Have the class review the different animals, plants, and habitats in the story.

**GROUP**

### A Treasured Waterway

Chesapeake Bay is the biggest American bay on the Atlantic coast. Maryland, Virginia, and Delaware all touch Chesapeake Bay. The weather can be rough. Sometimes the waves get so high that you seem to be on the ocean.

The Chesapeake is famous for its fishing industry. Long before sun-rise, oyster and crab boats are out hauling in their catch. These fishermen are very proud of their profession. Many of them help to preserve and protect the natural wildlife.

People go to this place for its natural beauty, good seafood, and history. It is an American treasure.

# Prewrite

**PURPOSE AND AUDIENCE** Students will write informative reports about a natural place they know. Have them focus on specific examples of the plant and animal life, or things unique to this environment. Remind them that since their main purpose is to inform, they should try to present information clearly.

**STRATEGY: RESEARCH THE TOPIC** Have students choose a natural environment to write about. Then have them gather facts from various sources. Suggest they organize their facts in an outline.

Use **Writing Process Transparency 4A** to model an outline.

## FEATURES OF EXPOSITORY WRITING

- **presents factual information on a specific topic**
- **expands the main idea with factual elaboration and detailed description**
- **may draw a thoughtful conclusion based on facts**

### PREWRITE TRANSPARENCY

**My Topic:** The Duck Pond

**I. Introduction**
   **A.** What the place is
   **B.** Where it is

**II. What visitors can see there**
   **A.** Kinds of wildlife
      1. mallard ducks
      2. trumpeter swans
      3. catfish
      4. field mice, rabbits
   **B.** Kinds of plants
      1. wildflowers, such as daisies
      2. berry bushes
   **C.** Other things of interest
      1. a stone wall
      2. a walking trail

**III. Conclusion**
   **A.** Why people like It
      1 It's clean and quiet.
      2. It's peaceful, beautiful.
      3. The ducks and swans are not afraid of people.

# Expository Writing

# Draft

**STRATEGY: EXPAND THE MAIN IDEA** Remind students to begin with a strong opening statement that introduces the main idea. In this phase of the writing process, they should focus on expanding their outlines with facts and descriptive details. Encourage them to include pertinent observations or anecdotes that will help bring their subject to life.

**WORD CHOICE** Point out that in expository writing, it is important to show how ideas are connected to one another. Good writers learn to use transition words and phrases that connect ideas logically between sentences and between paragraphs. Such transition words and phrases include *and, also, therefore, as a result, when, but, thus, for example, after a while, however, because,* and *consequently*.

Use **Writing Process Transparency 4B** as a model for discussion.

**LANGUAGE SUPPORT**

Some students may need help organizing their ideas. Guide them to reflect on their own experiences in the natural place. Have them focus on detailing two or three of the most interesting features. Encourage them to start small and add more features.

*DRAFT* TRANSPARENCY

**The Duck Pond**

The Silver lining Duck Pond are in the state park. You can see mallard ducks and graceful trumpeter swans. They are not at all afraid of people and will swim very near if you stay stille. People come from far away to enjoy the natural wonders of those beautiful place.

It's very peaceful to set on an stone wall under the soft spanish moss that hangs from the trees. You can read, draw or watch catfish swam by with their long whiskers.

Because it is in the state park their is the walking trail. You'll see many kinds of wild flours. There are also bushs of berrys which the birds love to eat. Sometimes you can spot little animals.

# Revise

Have students work in small teams to review each other's drafts. Ask them to write comments for each classmate on a separate page. Circulate and work with each team to guide their revision process.

Use **Writing Process Transparency 4C** for classroom discussion on the revision process. Ask students to comment on how revisions may have improved this writing example.

**STRATEGY: ELABORATION** Ask students to consider how an audience might react to their writing in a magazine or almanac. Invite them to think about audience while asking themselves the following questions:

- Do I keep my focus on the main idea?

- Are my facts presented in logical order?

- Do I expand on each fact with more information and realistic details?

- Does my writing give a real feeling of the place?

## TEACHING TIP

**TEACHER CONFERENCE**
Discuss with students various ways to improve their informative reports. Use the following questions as a foundation for your discussion. Make a chalkboard list of their responses.

- Does your writing clearly describe the physical features of the place?
- What kind of personal comments might make the report more interesting?
- What's the most important thing you can say to conclude your report?

*REVISE* TRANSPARENCY

Our own Silver Lining
~~The Duck Pond~~

The Silver lining Duck Pond are in the state park. You can see colorful mallard ducks and graceful trumpeter swans. They are not at all afraid of people and will swim very near if you stay stille. People come from far away to enjoy the natural wonders of those beautiful place.

It's very peaceful to set on an stone wall under the soft spanish moss that hangs from the trees. You can read, draw or watch catfish swam by with their long whiskers.

Because it is in the state park their is the walking trail. You'll see many kinds of wild flours, such as daisies. There are also bushs of berrys, dark red which the birds love to eat. Sometimes you can spot little animals. brown field mice and long-eared rabbits.

# Expository Writing

# Edit/Proofread

After students finish revising their reports, have them proofread for final corrections and additions.

## GRAMMAR/SPELLING CONNECTIONS

See the 5-Day Grammar and Usage Plans, pages 407M–407N, 431M–431N, 463M–463N, 491M–491N, and 501M–501N.

See the 5-Day Spelling Plans, pages 407O–407P, 431O–431P, 463O–463P, 491O–491P, 501O–501P.

### GRAMMAR, MECHANICS, USAGE

- Use helping verbs and linking verbs correctly.
- Use demonstrative adjectives correctly.
- Use the correct article (*a, an,* or *the*) with singular and plural nouns.

# Publish

**MAKE A GUIDEBOOK** Bind students' reports into a class guide to "Beautiful Places We Know" and share it with other classes.

Use **Writing Process Transparency 4D** as a proofreading model and **Writing Process Transparency 4E** to discuss presentation ideas.

---

### PROOFREAD TRANSPARENCY

Our own Silver Lining

**The Duck Pond**

The Silver lining Duck Pond are in the state park. You can see colorful mallard ducks and graceful trumpeter swans. They are not at all afraid of people and will swim very near if you stay still. People come from far away to enjoy the natural wonders of those beautiful place.

It's very peaceful to set on an stone wall under the soft spanish moss that hangs from the trees. You can read, draw, or watch catfish swam by with their long whiskers.

Because it is in the state park their is the walking trail. You'll see many kinds of wild flours, such as daisies. There are also bushs of berrys which the birds love to eat. Sometimes you can spot little animals. brown field mice and long-eared rabbits.

---

### PUBLISH TRANSPARENCY

**Our Own Silver Lining**

The Silver Lining Duck Pond is in the state park. You can see colorful mallard ducks and graceful trumpeter swans. They are not at all afraid of people and will swim very near if you stay still.

It's very peaceful to sit on a stone wall under the soft Spanish moss that hangs from the trees. You can read, draw, or watch catfish swim by with their long whiskers.

Because it is in the state park, there is a walking trail. You'll see many kinds of wildflowers, such as daisies. There are also bushes of dark red berries, which the birds love to eat. Sometimes you can spot little brown field mice and long-eared rabbits.

People come from far away to enjoy the natural wonders of this beautiful place.

# Presentation Ideas

**MAKE A DISPLAY** Have students arrange a classroom display of samples or pictures of the areas described in their reports. Have volunteers present their reports and discuss the display with the class.
▶ Representing/Speaking

**DRAW A MAP** Have students draw a map of their place. Ask them to include an image of themselves in the map. Have volunteers display their maps on a classroom or hall bulletin board. ▶ Spatial/Viewing

# Assessment

- Ask students to self-assess their writing. Present the writing features, page 503B, in question form on a chart.

- For a 6-point or an 8-point scale, see the writing rubrics on T107–T108.

## Scoring Rubric: 6-Trait Writing

| **4** Excellent | **3** Good | **2** Fair | **1** Unsatisfactory |
|---|---|---|---|
| **Ideas & Content** devises a focused, thoroughly detailed report on a familiar natural environment; makes fresh, accurate connections between key facts and observations. | **Ideas & Content** presents a clear, carefully researched report; details show knowledge of the place described; shares accurate information and observations. | **Ideas & Content** has some control of the topic, but details and ideas are vague, undeveloped, or do not fit; makes obvious or predictable observations about the environment. | **Ideas & Content** does not successfully report on an environment; writer may not grasp the purpose, or may offer very limited facts and ideas. |
| **Organization** careful, effective structure moves the reader logically through the text; information and paragraphs are smoothly tied together; inviting beginning and satisfying conclusion. | **Organization** shows a conscious, capable structure; logic is easy to follow from beginning to end; details fit, and reinforce facts; ideas, paragraphs, and sentences are connected. | **Organization** tries to shape a report, but may have trouble ordering facts and comments; reader may be confused by vague or disconnected details. | **Organization** shows extreme lack of organization; logic is hard to follow; ideas and details are disconnected; no sense of a clear beginning or ending. |
| **Voice** shows deep involvement with the topic; distinct style enlivens the factual content; personal message is skillfully linked to the purpose and audience. | **Voice** sounds like a real person behind the words; is involved with the topic; devises a real personal style that relates to the topic and audience. | **Voice** may not connect a distinct personal message or style to the facts; is not very involved with the topic, or an audience. | **Voice** is not involved in the topic; does not try to convey a personal style; does not consciously address ideas to an audience. |
| **Word Choice** effective use of precise, colorful language makes the message clear and interesting; vocabulary is vivid and diverse. | **Word Choice** uses a variety of words to create an accurate picture for the reader; experiments with some challenging words, or uses everyday words in a fresh way. | **Word Choice** gets the message across, in an average way; experiments with few new words; some words may not fit the topic. | **Word Choice** chooses words that don't fit, or that confuse reader; no new words are attempted; familiar words are overused. |
| **Sentence Fluency** effective use of simple and complex sentences; varied beginnings, lengths, and patterns add interest to the topic. | **Sentence Fluency** crafts simple and complex sentences that are easy to read aloud; has stronger control of simple sentences; lengths and patterns vary, and fit together well. | **Sentence Fluency** most sentences are understandable, but may be choppy, monotonous, or run-on; writer may have trouble with more complex sentences; may not vary beginnings, lengths, or patterns. | **Sentence Fluency** constructs incomplete or confusing sentences; does not grasp how words and sentences fit together; writing doesn't follow natural sentence patterns, and is hard to read aloud. |
| **Conventions** is skilled in most writing conventions; proper use of the rules of English enhances clarity, style, and cohesion of ideas; editing is largely unnecessary. | **Conventions** uses a variety of conventions correctly; some editing may be needed; errors are few and don't make the paper hard to understand. | **Conventions** makes noticeable mistakes that prevent a smooth reading of the text; extensive need for editing and revision. | **Conventions** makes repeated errors in word choice, punctuation and usage; reader has a hard time getting through the text; spelling errors make it hard to guess what words are meant. |

**Incomplete** This piece is blank or fails to respond to the writing task. The topic is not addressed, or the student simply paraphrases the prompt. The response may be illegible or incoherent.

# Unit Assessment

## VOCABULARY

To review vocabulary, have each student create a joke or riddle that incorporates and defines the vocabulary words for one of the selections.

### Unit Review

**Carlos and the Skunk**

| | | |
|---|---|---|
| nestled | stunned | unbearable |
| peculiar | tortillas | unpleasant |

**How to Think Like a Scientist**

| | | |
|---|---|---|
| assignments | carelessly | observations |
| automatically | normally | swerved |

**An Island Scrapbook**

| | | |
|---|---|---|
| barrier | fireball | parallel |
| emerge | naturalist | teeming |

**The Big Storm**

| | | |
|---|---|---|
| atmosphere | cycle | injured |
| collision | data | uneven |

**Catching Up with Lewis and Clark**

| | | |
|---|---|---|
| bison | former | journal |
| diaries | glistening | superb |

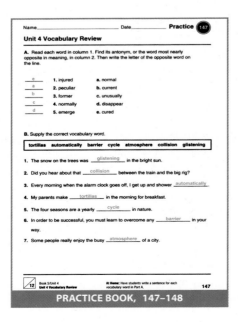

## GRAMMAR

To review the skills covered in the grammar lessons, assign one lesson to each of five groups. Have the groups create a skit that illustrates the key points of their lesson. Then have groups perform their skits for the class.

### Unit Review

**Carlos and the Skunk**
Adjectives

**How to Think Like a Scientist**
Articles

**An Island Scrapbook**
Adjectives That Compare

**The Big Storm**
Comparing with *More* and *Most*

**Catching Up with Lewis and Clark**
Comparing with *Good* and *Bad*

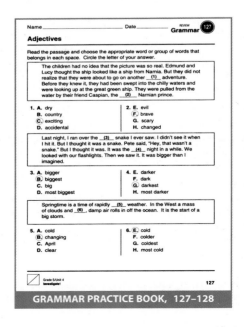

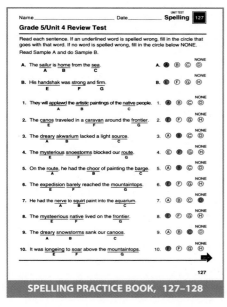

Have partners write the review words on slips of paper. One student picks up a slip of paper and states clues about the word to the other student. The other student must then identify the mystery word by spelling it and using it in a sentence. Partners switch roles and continue play until all slips have been drawn.

## Unit Review

### /ô/, /ôr/
applaud
longing
source
soar
chore

### /är/, /âr/
barge
artistic
barely
stairway
aquarium

### /îr/, /ûr/
dreary     nerve
mysterious  squirt
frontier

### Compound Words
snowstorms
mountaintops
peanut butter
thirty-third
sister-in-law

### Social Studies Words
route
canoes
native
caravan

---

Name_____ Date_____ **Spelling** `127`

**Grade 5/Unit 4 Review Test**

Read each sentence. If an underlined word is spelled wrong, fill in the circle that goes with that word. If no word is spelled wrong, fill in the circle below NONE.
Read Sample A and do Sample B.

A. The <u>sailur</u> is <u>home</u> from the <u>sea</u>.          A. ● Ⓑ Ⓒ Ⓓ
   A        B         C

B. His <u>handshak</u> was <u>strong</u> and <u>firm</u>.        B. ● Ⓕ Ⓖ Ⓗ
   E         F         G

1. They will <u>applawd</u> the <u>artistic</u> paintings of the <u>native</u> people.   1. Ⓐ Ⓑ Ⓒ Ⓓ
             A            B                       C

2. The <u>canos</u> traveled in a <u>caravan</u> around the <u>frontier</u>.   2. Ⓔ Ⓕ Ⓖ Ⓗ
       E                F                    G

3. The <u>dreary</u> <u>akwarium</u> lacked a light <u>source</u>.   3. Ⓐ ● Ⓒ Ⓓ
       A        B                    C

4. The <u>mysterious</u> <u>snoestorms</u> blocked our <u>route</u>.   4. Ⓔ Ⓕ Ⓖ Ⓗ
       E            F                  G

5. On the <u>route</u>, he had the <u>choor</u> of painting the <u>barge</u>.   5. Ⓐ ● Ⓒ Ⓓ
          A               B                    C

6. The <u>expedision</u> <u>barely</u> reached the <u>mountaintops</u>.   6. Ⓔ Ⓕ Ⓖ Ⓗ
       E            F                 G

7. He had the <u>nerve</u> to <u>squirt</u> paint into the <u>aquarium</u>.   7. Ⓐ Ⓑ Ⓒ ●
             A        B                    C

8. The <u>mysterious</u> <u>native</u> lived on the <u>frontier</u>.   8. Ⓔ Ⓕ Ⓖ Ⓗ
       E           F                G

9. The <u>dreary</u> <u>snowstorms</u> sank our <u>canoos</u>.   9. Ⓐ Ⓑ ● Ⓓ
       A          B                C

10. It was <u>longeing</u> to <u>soar</u> above the <u>mountaintops</u>.   10. ● Ⓕ Ⓖ Ⓗ
           E           F                G

127

**SPELLING PRACTICE BOOK, 127–128**

## Comprehension

☑ Judgments and Decisions
☑ Draw Conclusions
☑ Important and Unimportant Information
☑ Fact and Nonfact

## Vocabulary Strategies

☑ Suffixes
☑ Root Words

## Study Skills

☑ Graphic Aids

## Writing

☑ Expository Writing

MCGRAW-HILL READING

**Unit Test**

Student Name:_____

Date:_____

Grade 5 • Unit 4

# Assessment
# Follow-Up

Use the results of the informal and formal assessment opportunities in the unit to help you make decisions about future instruction.

| SKILLS AND STRATEGIES | Reteaching Blackline Masters | Alternate Teaching Strategies | Skills Intervention Guide |
|---|---|---|---|
| **Comprehension** | | | |
| Judgments and Decisions | 112, 116, 133, 137 | T60 | ✓ |
| Draw Conclusions | 117, 124, 138 | T62 | ✓ |
| Important and Unimportant Information | 119, 123, 131, 144 | T64 | ✓ |
| Fact and Nonfact | 126, 130, 140 | T66 | ✓ |
| **Vocabulary Strategy** | | | |
| Suffixes | 118, 132, 146 | T63 | ✓ |
| Root Words | 125, 139, 145 | T65 | ✓ |
| **Study Skills** | | | |
| Graphic Aids | 115, 122, 129, 136, 143 | T61 | ✓ |

| Writing | Alternate Writing Project—Easy | Unit Writing Process Lesson |
|---|---|---|
| Expository Writing | 407L, 431L, 463L, 491L, 501L | 503C–H |

McGraw-Hill School
**TECHNOLOGY**

*inter***NET** Research and Inquiry Ideas.
**CONNECTION** Visit **www.mhschool.com/reading**

# Glossary

Introduce students to the Glossary by reading through the introduction and looking over the pages with them. Encourage the class to talk about what they see.

Words in a glossary, like words in a dictionary, are listed in **alphabetical order.** Point out the **guide words** at the top of each page that tell the first and last words appearing on that page.

Point out examples of **entries** and **main entries.** Read through a simple entry with the class, identifying each part. Have students note the order in which information is given: entry word(s), definition(s), example sentence, syllable division, pronunciation respelling, part of speech, plural/verb/adjective forms.

Note that if more than one definition is given for a word, the definitions are numbered. Note also the format used for a word that is more than one part of speech.

Review the parts of speech by identifying each in a sentence:

| *inter.* | *adj.* | *n.* | *conj.* | *adj.* | *n.* |
|----------|--------|------|---------|--------|------|
| Wow! | A | dictionary | and | a | glossary |

| *v.* | *adv.* | *pron.* | *prep.* | *n.* |
|------|--------|---------|---------|------|
| tell | almost | everything | about | words! |

Explain the use of the **pronunciation key** (either the **short key,** at the bottom of every other page, or the **long key,** at the beginning of the glossary). Demonstrate the difference between **primary** stress and **secondary** stress by pronouncing a word with both.

Point out an example of the small triangle signaling a homophone. **Homophones** are words with different spellings and meanings but with the same pronunciation. Explain that a pair of words with the superscripts **1** and **2** are **homographs**—words that have the same spelling, but different origins and meanings, and in some cases, different pronunciations.

The **Word History** feature tells what language a word comes from and what changes have occurred in its spelling and/or meaning. Many everyday words have interesting and surprising stories behind them. Note that word histories can help us remember the meanings of difficult words.

Allow time for students to further explore the Glossary and make their own discoveries.

# Glossary

This Glossary can help you find the **meanings** of words in this book that you may not know. It will also help you pronounce these words. The words in the Glossary are listed in **alphabetical order. Guide words** at the top of each page tell you the first and last words on the page.

Each word is divided into syllables. The way to pronounce the word is given next. You can understand the pronunciation respelling by using the **Pronunciation Key** at the right. A shorter key appears at the bottom of every other page. When a word has more than one syllable, a dark accent mark (´) shows which syllable is stressed. In some words, a light accent mark (´) shows which syllable has a less heavy stress.

Glossary entries are based on entries in *The Macmillan/McGraw-Hill School Dictionary 1.*

## Sample Entry

Main entry — **adobe** A sandy kind of clay used to make bricks. Bits of straw are sometimes mixed with the clay, and the bricks are dried in the sun. Many buildings in Mexico and the southwestern United States are made of *adobe*. — Definition

Example sentence

Syllable division — **a•do•be** (ə dō´ bē) *noun, plural* **adobes.** — Part of speech

Plural form / Pronunciation

| | | | |
|---|---|---|---|
| a | at, bad | d | dear, soda, bad |
| ā | ape, pain, day, break | f | five, defend, leaf, off, cough, elephant. |
| ä | father, car, heart | | |
| âr | care, pair, bear, their, where | g | game, ago, fog, egg |
| e | end, pet, said, heaven, friend | h | hat, ahead |
| ē | equal, me, feet, team, piece, key | hw | white, whether, which |
| i | it, big, English, hymn | j | joke, enjoy, gem, page, edge |
| ī | ice, fine, lie, my | k | kite, bakery, seek, tack, cat |
| îr | ear, deer, here, pierce | l | lid, sailor, feel, ball, allow |
| o | odd, hot, watch | m | man, family, dream |
| ō | old, oat, toe, low | n | not, final, pan, knife |
| ô | coffee, all, taught, law, fought | ng | long, singer, pink |
| ôr | order, fork, horse, story, pour | p | pail, repair, soap, happy |
| oi | oil, toy | r | ride, parent, wear, more, marry |
| ou | out, now | s | sit, aside, pets, cent, pass |
| u | up, mud, love, double | sh | shoe, washer, fish, mission, nation |
| ū | use, mule, cue, feud, few | t | tag, pretend, fat, button, dressed |
| ü | rule, true, food | th | thin, panther, both, |
| ů | put, wood, should | th | this, mother, smooth |
| ûr | burn, hurry, term, bird, word, courage | v | very, favor, wave |
| ə | about, taken, pencil, lemon, circus | w | wet, weather, reward |
| | | y | yes, onion |
| b | bat, above, job | z | zoo, lazy, jazz, rose, dogs, houses |
| ch | chin, such, match | zh | vision, treasure, seizure |

760 · 761

---

## Aa

**abalone** A large sea snail that has a flat, pearly shell; its meat is used for food. For dinner we ordered *abalone* at the restaurant.
**ab•a•lo•ne** (ab´ə lō´nē) *noun, plural* **abalones.**

**abolitionist** A person who was in favor of ending slavery in the United States before the Civil War. The *abolitionists* wanted to set the slaves free.
**a•bo•li•tion•ist** (ab´ə lish´ə nist) *noun, plural* **abolitionists.**

**accurate** Correct, exact, or precise. The newspaper stories about the accident were not *accurate*.
▲ **Synonym:** precise
**ac•cu•rate** (ak´yər it) *adjective.*

### Language Note

A **synonym** is a word that has the same meaning as another word. A synonym for *accurate* is *precise*.

**acre** A measure of land equal to 43,560 square feet. An acre is slightly smaller in size than a football field. The farmer planted one *acre* of corn.
**a•cre** (ā´kər) *noun, plural* **acres.**

**adobe** 1. A brick made of clay, sometimes mixed with straw, and dried in the sun. They built the house entirely of *adobe* bricks. 2. A building made with adobe bricks, popular in Mexico and the southwestern United States. On our drive through New Mexico, many of the houses we saw were *adobes*.
**a•do•be** (ə dō´bē) *noun, plural* **adobes.**

**afford** 1. To have enough money to pay for. Can you *afford* a new car? 2. To be able to give or do. They couldn't *afford* the time to help us.
**af•ford** (ə fôrd´) *verb,* **afforded, affording.**

**amplify** 1. To make louder or stronger. The microphone will *amplify* the speaker's voice so that everyone can hear. 2. To give more details about; explain more. The teacher asked me to *amplify* my report by giving more details.
**am•pli•fy** (am´plə fī´) *verb,* **amplified, amplifying.**

---

**anchor** A heavy metal device that is attached to a ship by a chain or cable. When an *anchor* is dropped overboard, it digs into the ground below the water and keeps the ship from drifting. *Noun.*—To hold something in place with an anchor. We will *anchor* the boat while we fish. *Verb.*
**an•chor** (ang´kər) *noun, plural* **anchors;** *verb,* **anchored, anchoring.**

### Word History

*Anchor* comes from the Greek word *ankyra*. It was first used in the English language in the 12th century.

**apologize** To say one is sorry or embarrassed; make an apology. I *apologized* to my parents for being rude.
**a•pol•o•gize** (ə pol´ə jīz´) *verb,* **apologized, apologizing.**

**approve** 1. To have or give a favorable opinion. My parents don't *approve* of my staying up very late. 2. To consent or agree to officially; authorize. The town *approved* the construction of a public swimming pool.
**ap•prove** (ə prüv´) *verb,* **approved, approving.**

**arrowhead** The pointed tip or head of an arrow. The scientists found *arrowheads* on the site of ancient hunting grounds.
**ar•row•head** (ar´ō hed´) *noun, plural* **arrowheads.**

arrowhead

**arroyo** A ditch with steep sides that has been cut in the ground by the force of running water; gully. Arroyos are dry most of the year. During the rainy season, the rains cut *arroyos* into the ground.
**ar•roy•o** (ə roi´ō) *noun, plural* **arroyos.**

**assignment** 1. Something that is assigned. My arithmetic *assignment* is to do ten multiplication problems. 2. The act of assigning. The company's president is responsible for the *assignment* of tasks to employees.
**as•sign•ment** (ə sīn´mənt) *noun, plural* **assignments.**

**astound** To surprise very much; amaze; astonish. The first flight into outer space *astounded* the whole world.
▲ **Synonym:** surprise
**as•tound** (ə stound´) *verb,* **astounded, astounding.**

at; āpe; fär; câre; end; mē; it; īce; pîerce; hot; ōld; sông; fôrk; oil; out; up; ūse; rüle; půll; tûrn; chin; sing; shop; thin; this; hw in white; zh in treasure. The symbol ə stands for the unstressed vowel sound in about, taken, pencil, lemon, and circus.

762 · 763

**athletic 1.** Of or having to do with an athlete or athletics. Our school has just bought new *athletic* equipment. **2.** Active and strong. My grandparents are very *athletic;* they love to swim and ice-skate.
**ath•let•ic** (ath let'ik) *adjective.*

**atmosphere 1.** The layer of gases that surrounds the Earth. The atmosphere is made up of oxygen, nitrogen, carbon dioxide, and other gases. Outer space lies beyond the Earth's *atmosphere.* **2.** The layer of gases that surrounds any heavenly body. Scientists do not think people could live in the *atmosphere* of Mars.
**at•mos•phere** (at'məs fir') *noun,* plural **atmospheres.**

**auction** A public sale at which things are sold to the person who offers the most money. My cousin bid five dollars for a rocking chair at the village *auction. Noun.*—To sell at an auction. We *auctioned* off our old furniture. *Verb.*
**auc•tion** (ôk'shən) *noun, plural* **auctions;** *verb,* **auctioned, auctioning.**

**automatically** Done in a manner without a person's control. I breathe *automatically.*
**au•to•mat•i•cal•ly** (ô'tə mat'i kəl lē) *adverb.*

**avalanche** The swift, sudden fall of a mass of snow, ice, earth, or rocks down a mountain slope. The *avalanche* completely covered the village with mud.
**av•a•lanche** (av'ə lanch') *noun, plural* **avalanches.**

**awesome** Causing wonder or fear. The huge whale was an *awesome* sight.
**awe•some** (ô'səm) *adjective.*

**banner** A piece of cloth that has a design and sometimes writing on it. *Noun.* —Important; outstanding. With the hedges and roadsides full of raspberries, it was a *banner* season for raspberry pickers. *Adjective.*
**ban•ner** (ban'ər) *noun, plural* **banners;** *adjective.*

**Word History**

The word ***banner*** appeared in the English language during the 13th century and is thought to have come from the language of the Goths. Their word *bandwo* meant "sign."

---

**barrier** Something that blocks the way. The fallen tree was a *barrier* to traffic on the road.
**bar•ri•er** (bar'ē ər) *noun, plural* **barriers.**

**bashful** Shy around people. The *bashful* child hid behind the chair.
**bash•ful** (bash'fəl) *adjective.*

**billow** To rise or swell in billows. The sail of the boat *billowed* in the wind. *Verb.*—A great swelling wave of something. *Billows* of smoke poured from the smokestack. *Noun.*
**bil•low** (bil'ō) *verb,* **billowed, billowing;** *noun, plural* **billows.**

**bison** A large animal that has a big, shaggy head, short horns, and a hump on its back; buffalo. Bison are found in North America. Herds of *bison* once roamed the American prairies.
**bi•son** (bī'sən) *noun, plural* **bison.**

**board** To provide lodging and meals for pay. I *boarded* with a family from France last summer. *Verb.*—A long, flat piece of sawed wood, used in building houses and other things. The carpenters hammered nails into the *boards* on the floor. *Noun.*
**board** (bôrd) *verb,* **boarded, boarding;** *noun, plural* **boards.**

**boon** A help; benefit. The rain was a *boon* to my vegetable garden after the dry weather.
▲ **Synonym:** favor
**boon** (bün) *noun, plural* **boons.**

**border** To lie along the edge of. California *borders* Oregon. *Verb.*—A line where one country or other area ends and another begins; boundary. The tourists crossed the *border* into Mexico. *Noun.*
**bor•der** (bôr'dər) *verb,* **bordered, bordering;** *noun, plural* **borders.**

**boulder** A large, usually rounded rock. We saw many huge *boulders* at the foot of the mountain.
**boul•der** (bōl'dər) *noun, plural* **boulders.**

at; āpe; fär; câre; end; mē; it; īce; pîerce; hot; ōld; sông; fôrk; oil; out; up; ūse; rūle; pûll; tûrn; chin; sing; shop; thin; this; hw in white; zh in treasure. The symbol ə stands for the unstressed vowel sound in about, taken, pencil, lemon, and circus.

---

**bruise** To cause a bruise on the skin of. The hard fall *bruised* my knee. *Verb.* —An injury that does not break the skin but discolors it. A *bruise* can be caused by a fall, blow, or bump. *Noun.*
**bruise** (brüz) *verb,* **bruised, bruising;** *noun, plural* **bruises.**

**bullet** A small piece of rounded or pointed metal, made to be shot from a small firearm, such as a gun or rifle. Never play with a gun, even if it is not loaded with *bullets.*
**bul•let** (bùl'it) *noun, plural* **bullets.**

**burglar** A person who breaks into a house, store, or other place to steal something. The *burglar* crawled in the open window and stole the silverware.
▲ **Synonym:** thief
**bur•glar** (bûr'glər) *noun, plural* **burglars.**

**bushel** A measure for grain, fruit, vegetables, and other dry things. A *bushel* is equal to 4 pecks, or 32 quarts.
**bush•el** (bùsh'əl) *noun, plural* **bushels.**

**canvas** A strong, heavy cloth. My sneakers are made of *canvas.*
**can•vas** (kan'vəs) *noun, plural* **canvases.**

**capture** To succeed in expressing something. The story *captures* what it is like to be an only child. *Verb.* —The act of catching and holding a person, animal, or thing. The *capture* of the bank robber took place the day after the robbery. *Noun.*
**cap•ture** (kap'chər) *verb,* **captured, capturing;** *noun, plural* **captures.**

**carelessly 1.** In a manner showing a lack of attention. I *carelessly* ran down the stairs, and I tripped and fell. **2.** Done without close attention or care. You will not get a good grade on your report if you *carelessly* make spelling mistakes.
**care•less•ly** (kâr'lis lē) *adverb.*

**cemetery** A place where the dead are buried. While at the *cemetery,* I put flowers on my grandmother's grave.
▲ **Synonym:** graveyard
**cem•e•ter•y** (sem'ə ter' ē) *noun, plural* **cemeteries.**

**Word History**

*Cemetery* comes from the Greek word *koimeterion,* meaning "sleeping chamber."

---

**characteristic** A quality that belongs to and helps to identify a person or thing. Kindness and honesty are two good *characteristics* of my neighbor. *Noun.* —Belonging to and helping to identify a person or thing; typical. The *characteristic* taste of a lemon is sour. *Adjective.*
**char•ac•ter•is•tic** (kar'ik tə ris'tik) *noun, plural* **characteristics;** *adjective.*

**charcoal** A soft, black form of carbon, made by partially burning wood, used as a fuel and in pencils for drawing. The burning wood turned into *charcoal.*
**char•coal** (chär'kōl) *noun.*

**chase** The act of running and trying to catch. The *chase* ended when the police caught the criminal. *Noun.* —To run after and try to catch. The dog *chased* the bouncing ball. *Verb.*
**chase** (chās) *noun, plural* **chases;** *verb,* **chased, chasing.**

**chemical** A substance made by or used in chemistry. Ammonia is a *chemical* used in household cleaners. *Noun.* —Having to do with or made by chemistry. Rusting is a *chemical* process in which metal combines with oxygen. *Adjective.*
**chem•i•cal** (kem'i kəl) *noun, plural* **chemicals;** *adjective.*

**chile** A hot pepper. Mama puts *chiles* in the salsa to make it spicy.
**chil•e** (chil' ē) *noun, plural* **chiles.**

**cleft** A space or opening made by splitting; crack. You can climb the cliff by holding on to the *clefts* in the rocks. *Noun.*—Divided by a crack or split. Two of my cousins have *cleft* chins. *Adjective.*
**cleft** (kleft) *noun, plural* **clefts;** *adjective.*

**coax** To persuade or influence by mild urging. I *coaxed* my parents into letting me go to camp next summer.
**coax** (kōks) *verb,* **coaxed, coaxing.**

**cockpit** The space in an airplane or a small boat where the pilot sits. The pilot showed us the airplane's control panel in the *cockpit.*
**cock•pit** (kok'pit') *noun, plural* **cockpits.**

at; āpe; fär; câre; end; mē; it; īce; pîerce; hot; ōld; sông; fôrk; oil; out; up; ūse; rūle; pûll; tûrn; chin; sing; shop; thin; this; hw in white; zh in treasure. The symbol ə stands for the unstressed vowel sound in about, taken, pencil, lemon, and circus.

**Glossary**

**G3**

**collision** The act of colliding; a crash. The *collision* of the two cars made a great noise.
col•li•sion (kə lizh'ən) *noun, plural* **collisions.**

**commotion** A noisy confusion; disorder. There was a *commotion* at the stadium as the crowd booed the referee's decision.
com•mo•tion (kə mō'shən) *noun, plural* **commotions.**

**concentrate** 1. To focus one's mind on something. *Concentrate* on your homework. 2. To bring together into one place. The population of our country is *concentrated* in the cities.
con•cen•trate (kon'sən trāt') *verb,* **concentrated, concentrating.**

**confirm** 1. To show to be true or correct. The newspaper *confirmed* the reports of a flood. 2. To consent to; approve. The Senate *confirmed* the trade agreement.
con•firm (kən fûrm') *verb,* **confirmed, confirming.**

**confront** To meet or face. A difficult problem *confronted* us.
▲ **Synonym:** face
con•front (kən frunt') *verb,* **confronted, confronting.**

**congratulate** To give good wishes or praise for someone's success or for something nice that has happened. We *congratulated* them on doing such a good job.
con•grat•u•late (kən grach'ə lāt') *verb,* **congratulated, congratulating.**

**conquer** To overcome; defeat. We *conquered* our fears.
con•quer (kong'kər) *verb,* **conquered, conquering.**

**consent** To give permission; agree. My parents *consented* to my going camping. *Verb.*—Permission. My parents gave me their *consent* to go camping. *Noun.*
con•sent (kən sent') *verb,* **consented, consenting;** *noun, plural* **consents.**

**convenience** 1. Ease; comfort. I like the *convenience* of canned foods. 2. Something that gives ease or comfort. A washing machine is a modern *convenience.*
con•ven•ience (kən vēn'yəns) *noun, plural* **conveniences.**

768

**cove** A small, sheltered bay or inlet. The pirates hid their ship in the *cove.*
cove (kōv) *noun, plural* **coves.**

**credentials** Letters or documents that give the right to exercise authority. Without the proper *credentials* you cannot become president.
cre•den•tials (kri den' shəlz) *plural noun.*

**cripple** 1.To injure badly. A car accident *crippled* him. 2. To disable or incapacitate; keep from working properly. The power failure *crippled* the entire city.
crip•ple (krip'əl) *verb,* **crippled, crippling.**

> **Word History**
>
> *Cripple* appeared in the English language before the 12th century. It comes from the Old English word *creopan,* meaning "to creep."

**cycle** 1. A series of events that happen one after another in the same order, over and over again: the *cycle* of the four seasons of the year. *Noun.*—To ride a bicycle, tricycle, or motorcycle. I dream of *cycling* across America. *Verb.*
cy•cle (sī'kəl) *noun, plural* **cycles;** *verb,* **cycled, cycling.**

**dangle** 1. To hang or swing loosely. An old kite *dangled* from a tree. 2. To tease by offering something as a treat. I *dangled* a bone in front of the dog.
dan•gle (dang'gəl) *verb,* **dangled, dangling.**

**data** 1. Individual facts, figures, and other items of information. These *data* from the computer don't seem to be accurate. 2. Information as a whole. Adequate *data* on that subject is sometimes difficult to find.
▲ Used with either a singular or plural verb.
da•ta (dā'tə *or* dat'ə) *plural noun.*

769

**debt** 1. Something that is owed to another. I paid my *debts* when I got my allowance. 2. The condition of owing. My parents are in *debt* because they borrowed money to buy our house.
debt (det) *noun, plural* **debts.**

**dedicate** To set apart for a special purpose or use. Their parents *dedicated* their weekends to playing with their children.
ded•i•cate (ded'i kāt') *verb,* **dedicated, dedicating.**

**defiantly** Boldly refusing to obey or respect authority. The child *defiantly* slammed the door because he didn't want to go to bed.
de•fi•ant•ly (di fī'ənt lē) *adverb.*

**delivery** 1. The act of taking something to the proper place or person. We get a mail *delivery* every day except Sundays and holidays. 2. A way of doing something. The pitcher's *delivery* was low and outside.
de•liv•er•y (di liv'ə rē) *noun, plural* **deliveries.**

**delta** An area of land at the mouth of a river. A delta is formed by deposits of mud, sand, and pebbles. It is often shaped like a triangle. The Mississippi *Delta* is the area of land at the mouth of the Mississippi River.
del•ta (del'tə) *noun, plural* **deltas.**

delta

**depict** To show in pictures or words; describe. The artist tried to *depict* the movement of the ocean's waves. The story *depicted* a day in the life of a typical Chinese family.
de•pict (di pikt') *verb,* **depicted, depicting.**

**despair** A complete loss of hope. The family was filled with *despair* when the fire destroyed their house. *Noun.*—To give up or lose hope; be without hope. I *despaired* of ever finding my lost watch in the pond. *Verb.*
de•spair (di spâr') *noun; verb,* **despaired, despairing.**

**desperation** A willingness to try anything to change a hopeless situation. They gripped the log in *desperation* as they floated toward the waterfall.
des•per•a•tion (des'pə rā'shən) *noun.*

770

**destruction** 1. The act of destroying. The *destruction* of the old building became a media event. 2. Great damage or ruin. The earthquake caused widespread *destruction.*
de•struc•tion (di struk'shən) *noun.*

**detect** To find out or notice; discover. I called the fire department after I *detected* smoke coming from the garage.
de•tect (di tekt') *verb,* **detected, detecting.**

**devastation** The act of destruction; ruin. The hurricane left *devastation* in its wake in the small towns along the coast.
dev•as•ta•tion (dev'ə stā' shən) *noun.*

**devour** 1. To eat greedily; consume. The hungry child *devoured* the sandwich. 2. To consume destructively. The flames *devoured* the house.
de•vour (di vour') *verb,* **devoured, devouring.**

**diary** A written record of the things that one has done or thought each day. I keep my *diary* hidden.
di•a•ry (dī' ə rē) *noun, plural* **diaries.**

> **Word History**
>
> The word *diary* appeared in its English form in the late 1500s. It comes from the Latin word *diarium,* derived from *dies,* meaning "day."

**dimension** 1. A measurement of length, width, or height. A cube has three *dimensions.* 2. Size or importance.
di•men•sion (di men'shən) *noun, plural* **dimensions.**

**discount** An amount subtracted from the regular price. I bought a suit on sale at a 25 percent *discount.*
▲ **Synonym:** reduction
dis•count (dis' kount') *noun, plural* **discounts.**

**disgrace** To bring shame to. Poor losers *disgrace* their teams. *Verb.*—The loss of honor or respect; shame. The president resigned in *disgrace* when the police learned about the stolen money. *Noun.*
dis•grace (dis grās') *verb,* **disgraced, disgracing;** *noun, plural* **disgraces.**

771

**dismay** A feeling of fear or alarm. The family was filled with *dismay* when they saw the fire approaching their house. *Noun.*—To trouble or discourage. The rising flood *dismayed* the people of the town. *Verb.*
**dis•may** (dis mā′) *noun; verb,* **dismayed, dismaying.**

**disobey** To refuse or fail to obey. The driver *disobeyed* the traffic laws by not stopping at the red light.
**dis•o•bey** (dis′ə bā′) *verb,* **disobeyed, disobeying.**

**distinguish 1.** To know or show that there is a difference between certain things. The jeweler *distinguished* the real diamond from the fake one. **2.** To make something special or different; set apart. The male cardinal's bright red feathers *distinguish* it from the female.
**dis•tin•guish** (di sting′gwish) *verb,* **distinguished, distinguishing.**

**distress** Great pain or sorrow; misery. My grandfather's illness was a great *distress* to me. *Noun.*—To cause pain, sorrow, or misery. The bad news *distressed* us. *Verb.*
**dis•tress** (di stres′) *noun; verb,* **distressed, distressing.**

**division 1.** One of the parts into which something is divided. Asian history is one of the *divisions* of our social studies course. **2.** The act of dividing or the condition of being divided. The *division* of the house into apartments provided homes for five families.
**di•vi•sion** (di vizh′ən) *noun, plural* **divisions.**

**divorce** To legally end a marriage. Our parents have been *divorced* for one year. *Verb.*—The legal ending of a marriage. The marriage ended with a *divorce. Noun.*
**di•vorce** (di vôrs′) *verb,* **divorced, divorcing;** *noun, plural* **divorces.**

**donate** To give; contribute. The family *donated* their old clothes to people who needed them.
▲ **Synonyms:** present, bestow
**do•nate** (dō′nāt) *verb,* **donated, donating.**

**driftwood** Wood that floats on water or is brought to the shore by water. We walked up the beach and collected the *driftwood* the waves washed in.
**drift•wood** (drift′ wu̇d′) *noun.*

772

---

**drought** A long period of time when there is little or no rainfall at all. Our garden suffered in the *drought.*
**drought** (drout) *noun, plural* **droughts.**

**dynamite** A substance that explodes with great force. Dynamite is used to blow up old buildings and blast openings in rocks. Using *dynamite* is very dangerous. *Noun.*—To blow something up with dynamite. The builders *dynamited* the mountain so that they could put a road through. *Verb.*
**dy•na•mite** (dī′nə mīt′) *noun; verb,* **dynamited, dynamiting.**

## Ee

**elementary** Dealing with the simple basic parts or beginnings of something. We learned about addition and subtraction when we studied *elementary* arithmetic.
**el•e•men•ta•ry** (el′ə men′tə rē *or* el′ə men′trē) *adjective.*

**emerge 1.** To come into view. The sun *emerged* from behind a cloud. **2.** To come out; become known. New facts about the case *emerged* during the trial.
**e•merge** (i mûrj′) *verb,* **emerged, emerging.**

emerge

**enlist 1.** To join or persuade to join the armed forces. Many *enlisted* in the Navy as soon as the war broke out. **2.** To get the help or support of. The mayor *enlisted* the entire town in the drive to clean up the streets.
**en•list** (en list′) *verb,* **enlisted, enlisting.**

**erosion** A wearing, washing, or eating away. *Erosion* usually happens gradually, over a long period of time.
**e•ro•sion** (i rō′zhən) *noun.*

**escort** One or more ships or airplanes that travel with or protect another ship or airplane. The battleship's *escort* included three destroyers. *Noun.* —To act as an escort. The police *escorted* the mayor in the parade. *Verb.*
**es•cort** (es′kôrt *for noun;* e skôrt′ *or* es′kôrt *for verb) noun, plural* **escorts;** *verb,* **escorted, escorting.**

at; āpe; fär; câre; end; mē; it; īce; pîerce; hot; ōld; sông; fôrk; oil; out; up; ūse; rūle; pu̇ll; tûrn; chin; sing; shop; thin; this; hw in white; zh in treasure. The symbol ə stands for the unstressed vowel sound in about, taken, pencil, lemon, and circus.

773

---

**eventually** At the end; finally. We waited and waited for our friends, but *eventually* we went to the movies without them.
**e•ven•tu•al•ly** (i ven′chü ə lē) *adverb.*

**explosive** Something that can explode or cause an explosion. The bomb squad searched the building for *explosives. Noun.*—Likely to explode or cause an explosion. A bomb is an *explosive* device. *Adjective.*
**ex•plo•sive** (ek splō′siv) *noun, plural* **explosives;** *adjective.*

## Ff

**fertile 1.** Able to produce crops and plants easily and plentifully. *Fertile* soil is the best soil for growing vegetables. **2.** Able to produce eggs, seeds, pollen, or young. An animal is *fertile* when it can give birth to young.
**fer•tile** (fûr′təl) *adjective.*

**fireball** A ball of fire. The sun was a magnificent *fireball* in the evening sky.
**fire•ball** (fīr′bôl′) *noun, plural* **fireballs.**

**flabbergast** To overcome with shock or surprise. I was *flabbergasted* when I saw my low grade on the test, because I had really studied for it.
**flab•ber•gast** (fla′ bər gast′) *verb,* **flabbergasted, flabbergasting.**

**flail** To wave or move about wildly. The turtle *flailed* its legs when it was turned on its back.
▲ **Synonym:** thrash
**flail** (flāl) *verb,* **flailed, flailing.**

**former 1.** Belonging to or happening in the past; earlier. In *former* times, people used fireplaces to heat their houses. **2.** The first of two. Greenland and Madagascar are both islands; the *former* island is in the North Atlantic Ocean, and the latter island is in the Indian Ocean.
**for•mer** (fôr′mər) *adjective.*

**fraction 1.** A part of a whole. Only a small *fraction* of the people watching the football game left before it was over. **2.** A number that stands for one or more equal parts of a whole. A fraction shows the division of one number by a second number. 2/3, 3/4, and 1/16 are *fractions.*
**frac•tion** (frak′shən) *noun, plural* **fractions.**

774

---

**fume** To be very angry or irritated. The driver *fumed* while stuck in traffic. *Verb.*—A smoke or gas that is harmful or has a bad smell. The *fumes* from the traffic made us sick. *Noun.*
**fume** (fūm) *verb,* **fumed, fuming;** *noun, plural* **fumes.**

## Gg

**glisten** To shine with reflected light. The spiderweb *glistened* in the sun.
**glis•ten** (glis′ən) *verb,* **glistened, glistening.**

**glory 1.** Great praise; honor; fame. They both did the work, but only one got the *glory.* **2.** Great beauty; splendor. The sun shone in all its *glory.*
**glo•ry** (glôr′ē) *noun, plural* **glories.**

**gorge** A deep, narrow valley with steep, rocky walls. Over millions of years the river cut a *gorge* in the land. *Noun.*—To eat in a greedy way. Don't *gorge* your food. *Verb.*
**gorge** (gôrj) *noun, plural* **gorges;** *verb,* **gorged, gorging.**

**granite** A hard kind of rock used to build monuments and buildings. The builders lifted the *granite* block to its place at the top of the monument.
**gran•ite** (gran′it) *noun.*

**gratitude** A feeling of gratefulness. We are full of *gratitude* for your help.
▲ **Synonym:** thankfulness
**grat•i•tude** (grat′i tüd′ *or* grat′i tūd′) *noun.*

**grit** Very small bits of sand or stone. The strong winds carried *grit* through the air. *Noun.* —To press together hard; grind. I *gritted* my teeth. *Verb.*
**grit** (grit) *noun; verb,* **gritted, gritting.**

## Hh

**hail** A motion or call used as a greeting or to attract attention. *Hails* from the crowd greeted the politician as he walked into the auditorium. *Noun.* —To greet or to attract the attention of by calling or shouting. We *hailed* a taxi by waving our arms. *Verb.*
**hail** (hāl) *noun, plural* **hails;** *verb,* **hailed, hailing.**

at; āpe; fär; câre; end; mē; it; īce; pîerce; hot; ōld; sông; fôrk; oil; out; up; ūse; rūle; pu̇ll; tûrn; chin; sing; shop; thin; this; hw in white; zh in treasure. The symbol ə stands for the unstressed vowel sound in about, taken, pencil, lemon, and circus.

775

**Glossary**

**G5**

**hasty 1.** Quick; hurried. We barely had time for a *hasty* breakfast. **2.** Too quick; careless or reckless. Don't make a *hasty* decision that you'll be sorry for later.
    **hast•y** (hās′ tē) *adjective*, **hastier, hastiest;** *adverb*, **hastily;** *noun* **hastiness.**

**herb 1.** Any plant or plant part that is used for flavor in cooking, or in making medicines or perfumes and cosmetics. She used *herbs* in her cooking. **2.** Any flowering plant that does not form a woody stem, but instead dies down to the ground at the end of each growing season. Her garden of *herbs* supplies the whole neighborhood.
    **herb** (ûrb *or* hûrb) *noun, plural* **herbs.**

**heritage** Something handed down from earlier generations or from the past; tradition. The right to free speech is an important part of our American *heritage.*
    **her•i•tage** (her′i tij) *noun, plural* **heritages.**

**heroic 1.** Very brave; courageous. The firefighter's *heroic* rescue of the child from the burning house made all the newspapers. **2.** Describing the deeds of heroes. I wrote a *heroic* poem about Chief Crazy Horse.
    **he•ro•ic** (hi rō′ik) *adjective.*

**hoist** To lift or pull up. We *hoisted* the bags onto the table. *Verb.*—A device used to lift or pull up something heavy. The sailors used a *hoist* to raise the cargo. *Noun.*
    **hoist** (hoist) *verb,* **hoisted, hoisting;** *noun, plural* **hoists.**

**host** To serve as host for. I *hosted* a party for our friends. *Verb.*—A person who invites people to visit as guests. We thanked our *host* for a wonderful party. *Noun.*
    **host** (hōst) *verb,* **hosted, hosting;** *noun, plural* **hosts.**

**hull** The sides and bottom of a boat or ship. The waves crashed against the *hull* of the ship. *Noun.*—To remove the outer covering from a seed or fruit. Birds *hull* seeds before they eat them. *Verb.*
    **hull** (hul) *noun, plural* **hulls;** *verb,* **hulled, hulling.**

776

---

**husk** To take off the husk from. We cracked and *husked* the coconuts. *Verb.*—The dry outside covering of some vegetables and fruits. We took the green *husks* off the corn. *Noun.*
    **husk** (husk) *verb,* **husked, husking;** *noun, plural* **husks.**

## Ii

**immortal** One who lives or is remembered forever. The ancient Greek gods were considered *immortals.*
    **im•mor•tal** (i môr′təl) *noun, plural* **immortals.**

**incorrectly** In a manner that is not right or correct. You must redo this problem because you answered it *incorrectly.*
    **in•cor•rect•ly** (in′kə rekt′ lē) *adverb.*

**influence** To have an effect on, especially by giving suggestions or by serving as an example. The older members of my family *influence* me in many ways. *Verb.*—The power of a person or thing to produce an effect on others without using force or a command. Use your *influence* to persuade your friend to study harder. *Noun.*
    **in•flu•ence** (in′flü əns) *verb,* **influenced, influencing;** *noun, plural* **influences.**

**injure** To cause harm to; damage or hurt. I *injured* myself when I fell off my bicycle.
    **in•jure** (in′jər) *verb,* **injured, injuring.**

**inquire** To ask for information. We stopped at a gas station to *inquire* about the way to the park.
    **in•quire** (in kwīr′) *verb,* **inquired, inquiring.**

**insistent 1.** Firm or persistent. Although we were having a good time, my cousin was *insistent* on going home. **2.** Demanding attention. The *insistent* ringing of the doorbell woke us.
    **in•sis•tent** (in sis′ tənt) *adjective.*

at; āpe; fär; câre; end; mē; it; īce; pîerce; hot; ōld; sông; fôrk; oil; out; up; ūse; rūle; pu̇ll; tûrn; chin; sing; shop; thin; this; hw in white; zh in treasure. The symbol ə stands for the unstressed vowel sound in about, taken, pencil, lemon, and circus.

777

---

**intense 1.** Very great or strong; extreme. The heat from the iron was so *intense* that it burned a hole in the cloth. **2.** Having or showing strong feeling, purpose, or effort; concentrated. The worried parent had an *intense* look.
    **in•tense** (in tens′) *adjective.*

**interpret 1.** To explain the meaning of. The teacher *interpreted* what the author meant in the poem. **2.** To change from one language to another; translate. Since my friends couldn't speak Spanish, I *interpreted* what my cousin from Mexico was saying.
    **in•ter•pret** (in tûr′prit) *verb,* **interpreted, interpreting.**

**isolate** To place or set apart; separate from others. I was *isolated* from my sister and brother when I had the mumps so that they wouldn't get it.
    **i•so•late** (ī′sə lāt′) *verb,* **isolated, isolating.**

## Jj

**journal 1.** A regular record or account; diary. Each student was told to keep a *journal* during the summer. The scientist entered the results of the experiments in a *journal.* **2.** A magazine or newspaper. The medical *journal* published a report on the doctor's most recent discoveries.
    **jour•nal** (jûr′nəl) *noun, plural* **journals.**

## Kk

**keg** A small metal or wooden barrel. Beer is often put in *kegs.*
    **keg** (keg) *noun, plural* **kegs.**

## Ll

**lament** To express sorrow, regret, or grief. The people sang a sad song to *lament* the loss of their leader.
    ▲ **Synonym:** mourn
    **la•ment** (lə ment′) *verb,* **lamented, lamenting.**

**landlord** A person or organization that owns houses, apartments, or rooms to be rented to other people. At the end of the month I have to send my *landlord* the rent for my apartment.
    **land•lord** (land′lôrd′) *noun, plural* **landlords.**

778

---

**landscape** A stretch of land that can be seen from a place; view. The train passengers watched the passing *landscape. Noun.*—To make an area of land more beautiful by planting trees, shrubs, and other plants, and by designing gardens. A gardener *landscaped* the grounds around these offices. *Verb.*
    **land•scape** (land′skāp′) *noun, plural* **landscapes;** *verb,* **landscaped, landscaping.**

**lecture** To give a talk to an audience. The scientist *lectures* on the history of aviation at the college. *Verb.*—A scolding. I got a *lecture* from my parents for breaking the window. *Noun.*
    **lec•ture** (lek′chər) *verb,* **lectured, lecturing;** *noun, plural* **lectures.**

**legislator** One who makes laws, especially for a political organization. The Senator knew all of the *legislators* in the state.
    **leg•is•la•tor** (lej′is lā′tər) *noun, plural* **legislators.**

**livestock** Animals raised on a farm or ranch for profit. Cows, horses, sheep, and pigs are livestock. We enjoy seeing the *livestock* when we go to the county fair.
    **live•stock** (līv′stok′) *noun.*

**logger** A person who cuts down trees for a living; lumberjack. The *loggers* cut down the trees.
    **log•ger** (lô′gər) *noun, plural* **loggers.**

**lush** Thick, rich, and abundant. That land is covered with *lush* forests.
    ▲ **Synonym:** luxuriant
    **lush** (lush) *adjective,* **lusher, lushest.**

**luxury 1.** Something that gives much comfort and pleasure but is not necessary. Eating dinner at the fancy restaurant was a *luxury* for our family. **2.** A way of life that gives comfort and pleasure. The opera star is used to *luxury.*
    **lux•u•ry** (luk′shə rē *or* lug′zhə rē) *noun, plural* **luxuries.**

at; āpe; fär; câre; end; mē; it; īce; pîerce; hot; ōld; sông; fôrk; oil; out; up; ūse; rūle; pu̇ll; tûrn; chin; sing; shop; thin; this; hw in white; zh in treasure. The symbol ə stands for the unstressed vowel sound in about, taken, pencil, lemon, and circus.

779

Glossary

# Mm

**maiden** A girl or young unmarried woman. The boy hoped one day to meet the *maiden* of his dreams. *Noun.*—First or earliest. The ship's *maiden* voyage was from England to New York. *Adjective.*
**maid•en** (mā′dən) *noun, plural* **maidens;** *adjective.*

**masthead** The top of a mast. From the shore we could see the ship's *masthead* in the distance.
**mast•head** (mast′hed′) *noun, plural* **mastheads.**

**meagre** Also **meager.** Very little; hardly enough. The sick child ate a *meagre* meal of tea and toast.
▲ **Synonyms:** small, scanty
**mea•gre** (mē′gər) *adjective.*

**mildew** A kind of fungus that looks like white powder or fuzz. It grows on plants and materials such as cloth, leather, and paper when they are left damp. *Mildew* grows in the shower if the bathroom is always damp.
**mil•dew** (mil′dü) *noun.*

**mongoose** A slender animal with a pointed face, a long tail, and rough, shaggy fur. Mongooses live in Africa and Asia, are very quick, and eat rats and mice. On television we saw the quick *mongoose* fight a snake.
**mon•goose** (mong′güs′) *noun, plural* **mongooses.**

**monument 1.** A building, statue, or other object made to honor a person or event. The Lincoln Memorial is a *monument* to Abraham Lincoln. **2.** An achievement of lasting importance. The discovery of a polio vaccine was a *monument* in medicine.
**mon•u•ment** (mon′yə mənt) *noun, plural* **monuments.**

**murky** Dark and gloomy; cloudy. We couldn't see beneath the surface of the *murky* water in the pond.
**mur•ky** (mûr′kē) *adjective,* **murkier, murkiest.**

**musket** A gun with a long barrel, used before modern rifles were invented. The soldiers loaded their *muskets* for battle.
**mus•ket** (mus′kit) *noun, plural* **muskets.**

**mutiny** An open rebellion against authority. The sailors who led the *mutiny* were punished. *Noun.*—To take part in an open rebellion. The crew *mutinied* against their captain. *Verb.*
**mu•ti•ny** (mū′tə nē) *noun, plural* **mutinies;** *verb,* **mutinied, mutinying.**

780

# Nn

**naturalist** A person who specializes in the study of things in nature, especially animals and plants. The *naturalists* walked through the forest to study the plants and animals unique to the region.
**nat•u•ral•ist** (nach′ər ə list) *noun, plural* **naturalists.**

**navigate 1.** To sail, steer, or direct the course of. They *navigated* the ship through the storm. **2.** To sail on or across. Ships can *navigate* the Atlantic in under a week.
**nav•i•gate** (nav′i gāt) *verb,* **navigated, navigating.**

> **Word History**
> The word *navigate* comes from two Latin words: *navis,* meaning "ship," and *agere,* meaning "to drive." Sailors *navigate* ships.

**nestle** To get very close to; snuggle; cuddle. The kittens *nestled* against their mother.
▲ **Synonym:** cuddle
**nes•tle** (nes′əl) *verb,* **nestled, nestling.**

**nightfall** The beginning of night; the end of the day. My parents told me to be sure to be home before *nightfall.*
**night•fall** (nīt′fôl′) *noun.*

**normally 1.** Under ordinary circumstances; regularly; usually. Heavy rain *normally* falls at this time of year. **2.** In an accepted or normal manner. In a traffic jam, cars move slower than they *normally* do.
**nor•mal•ly** (nôr′mə lē) *adverb.*

**nostril** One of the two outer openings of the nose. In the cold air, smoke seemed to billow from the mountain climber's *nostrils.*
**nos•tril** (nos′trəl) *noun, plural* **nostrils.**

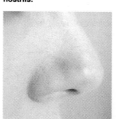

at; āpe; fär; câre; end; mē; it; īce; pîerce; hot; ōld; sông; fôrk; oil; out; up; ūse; rūle; pull; tûrn; chin; sing; shop; thin; **this; hw** in white; **zh** in treasure. The symbol ə stands for the unstressed vowel sound in about, taken, pencil, lemon, and circus.

781

# Oo

**oblige 1.** To make thankful for a service or favor. We are *obliged* to you for your help. **2.** To make a person do something by law, promise, or sense of duty. My parents were *obliged* to pay for the window I broke.
**o•blige** (ə blīj′) *verb,* **obliged, obliging.**

**observation 1.** The act or power of noticing. The detective's careful *observation* helped solve the crime. **2.** The condition of being seen; notice. The thief escaped *observation.*
**ob•ser•va•tion** (ob′zər vā′shən) *noun, plural* **observations.**

**offend** To cause resentment, anger, or displeasure. Your rude remark *offended* me.
▲ **Synonym:** insult
**of•fend** (ə fend′) *verb,* **offended, offending.**

**ominous** Foretelling trouble or bad luck to come; threatening. There were *ominous* black storm clouds coming in from the sea.
**om•i•nous** (om′ə nəs) *adjective.*

**onlooker** A spectator. The *onlookers* stood on the sidewalk, watching the parade go by.
**on•look•er** (on′ lùk′ ər) *noun, plural* **onlookers.**

**onlookers**

**orphanage** A place that takes in and cares for children without parents. The *orphanage* finds good homes for children.
**or•phan•age** (ôr′fə nij) *noun, plural* **orphanages.**

**ozone** A form of oxygen. It is formed by lightning or other electricity in the air. Ozone is used to kill germs and freshen the air. A layer of *ozone* in the atmosphere protects the Earth from some of the sun's harmful rays.
**o•zone** (ō′zōn′) *noun.*

# Pp

**parallel** Always the same distance apart. The road runs *parallel* to the river. *Adverb.*—Being the same distance apart at all points. If lines are parallel, they never meet or cross each other. The rails of a railroad track are *parallel. Adjective.*
**par•al•lel** (par′ə lel′) *adverb, adjective.*

782

**paralyze 1.** To take away the power to move or feel in a part of the body. After the accident, my right arm was *paralyzed.* **2.** To make helpless, powerless, or inactive. The bus strike *paralyzed* the city.
**par•a•lyze** (par′ə līz′) *verb,* **paralyzed, paralyzing.**

**parapet** A wall or railing built for protection. The rebels retreated to the *parapet* for safety.
**par•a•pet** (par′ ə pet′) *noun, plural* **parapets.**

**peculiar 1.** Not usual; strange; queer. It's *peculiar* that the sky is so dark at noon. **2.** Belonging to a certain person, group, place, or thing. The kangaroo is *peculiar* to Australia and New Guinea.
**pe•cul•iar** (pi kūl′yər) *adjective; adverb,* **peculiarly.**

**pelican** A large bird that lives near the water and has a pouch under its long bill. The *pelican* flew overhead, carrying a fish in its pouch.
**pel•i•can** (pel′i kən) *noun, plural* **pelicans.**

**pelt** To strike over and over with small hard things. Hail *pelted* the roof. *Verb.*—The skin of an animal with its fur or hair still on it. Pelts are used to make clothing and rugs. The trappers traded the animal *pelts* for supplies for their camp. *Noun.*
**pelt** (pelt) *verb,* **pelted, pelting;** *noun,* **pelts.**

**perish** To be destroyed; die. Many people *perished* when the ship sank.
▲ **Synonym:** expire
**per•ish** (per′ish) *verb,* **perished, perishing.**

**permission** A consent from someone in authority. You should ask your parents for *permission* to stay overnight at my house.
**per•mis•sion** (pər mish′ən) *noun.*

**persuade** To cause to do or believe something by pleading or giving reasons; convince. They *persuaded* me to go with them.
**per•suade** (pər swād′) *verb,* **persuaded, persuading;** *noun,* **persuasion.**

at; āpe; fär; câre; end; mē; it; īce; pîerce; hot; ōld; sông; fôrk; oil; out; up; ūse; rūle; pull; tûrn; chin; sing; shop; thin; **this; hw** in white; **zh** in treasure. The symbol ə stands for the unstressed vowel sound in about, taken, pencil, lemon, and circus.

783

**petition** A formal request that is made to a person in authority. All the people on our street signed a *petition* asking the city to put a stop sign on the corner. *Noun.*—To make a formal request to. The students in our school *petitioned* the principal to keep the library open after school. *Verb.*
**pe•ti•tion** (pə tish'ən) *noun, plural* **petitions;** *verb,* **petitioned, petitioning.**

**pier 1.** A structure built out over the water, used as a landing place for boats or ships. We walked to the end of the *pier* and watched the boats. **2.** A pillar or other support used to hold up a bridge. Modern bridges have steel piers to support them. Engineers design *piers* that can hold up bridges during an earthquake.
▲ Another word that sounds like this is **peer.**
**pier** (pîr) *noun, plural* **piers.**

**pioneer** A person who is among the first to explore and settle a region. *Pioneers* settled the American West. *Noun.*—To be among the first to explore or develop. American scientists *pioneered* in sending human beings to the moon. *Verb.*
**pi•o•neer** (pī'ə nîr') *noun, plural* **pioneers;** *verb,* **pioneered, pioneering.**

---

**Word History**

*Pioneer* was first used in the English language in 1523. It is based on the Old French word *peonier,* which means "foot soldier."

---

**pneumonia** A disease in which the lungs become inflamed and fill with fluid. Pneumonia is caused by a virus. A person with pneumonia might cough or have a hard time breathing. I was relieved when the doctor said I didn't have *pneumonia.*
**pneu•mo•nia** (nŭ mōn'yə *or* nŭ mōn'yə) *noun.*

**polio** A short form of the word **poliomyelitis.** Polio is a contagious disease that can cause paralysis by attacking the central nervous system. It is caused by a virus. President Franklin Delano Roosevelt was stricken with *polio* and lost the use of his legs.
**po•li•o** (pō'lē ō) *noun.*

784

---

**prediction 1.** The act of predicting something. The weather forecaster's job is the *prediction* of the weather. **2.** Something predicted. My *prediction* that our team would win has come true.
**pre•dic•tion** (pri dik'shən) *noun, plural* **predictions.**

**presence 1.** The fact of being in a place at a certain time. The *presence* of the growling dog at the door made me nervous. **2.** The area around or near a person. The document was signed in the *presence* of a witness.
**pres•ence** (prez'əns) *noun.*

**prosper** To be successful; do very well. The town *prospered* when several companies moved their offices there.
▲ Synonym: succeed
**pros•per** (pros'pər) *verb,* **prospered, prospering.**

**protective** Keeping from harm; protecting. We put a *protective* coating of wax on the floors.
**pro•tec•tive** (prə tek'tiv) *adjective.*

**provision 1.** A supply of food. Their ship has *provisions* for one month. **2.** The act of planning ahead for a future need. Has any *provision* been made for the party if it rains?
**pro•vi•sion** (prə vizh'ən) *noun, plural* **provisions.**

**provoke 1.** To make angry. Their rudeness *provoked* me. **2.** To stir; excite. Unfair laws *provoked* the people to riot.
**pro•voke** (prə vōk') *verb,* **provoked, provoking.**

**prow** The front part of a boat or ship; bow. The *prow* of the ship cut through the waves.
**prow** (prou) *noun, plural* **prows.**

**publicity 1.** Information given out to bring a person or thing to the attention of the public. The *publicity* about the band brought a large crowd to hear it perform. **2.** The attention of the public. Most politicians like *publicity.*
**pub•lic•i•ty** (pu blis'i tē) *noun.*

**pulverize** To reduce to very small pieces; demolish; grind; crush. We *pulverized* the corn before cooking it.
▲ Synonym: crush
**pul•ver•ize** (pul'və rīz') *verb,* **pulverized, pulverizing.**

---

at; āpe; fär; câre; end; mē; it; īce; pîerce; hot; ōld; sŏng; fôrk; oil; out; up; ūse; rūle; pull; tûrn; chin; sing; shop; thin; this; hw in white; zh in treasure. The symbol ə stands for the unstressed vowel sound in about, taken, pencil, lemon, and circus.

---

785

---

**quarry** A place where stone is cut or blasted out. The crane lifted the blocks of limestone out of the *quarry.*
**quar•ry** (kwôr'ē) *noun, plural* **quarries.**

**quench 1.** To put an end to by satisfying. I *quenched* my thirst with iced tea. **2.** To make something stop burning; put out; extinguish. I *quenched* the fire.
**quench** (kwench) *verb,* **quenched, quenching.**

**radar** A device used to find and track objects such as aircraft and automobiles. It uses reflected radio waves. The Navy detected the planes with *radar* before they flew over the city.
**ra•dar** (rā'där) *noun.*

---

**Word History**

The word *radar* is short for *ra*dio *d*etecting *a*nd *r*anging.

---

**rascal 1.** A mischievous character. That pup is a real *rascal.* **2.** A dishonest person; rogue. That *rascal* took off with my pocket watch.
**ras•cal** (ras'kəl) *noun, plural* **rascals.**

**rebuild** To build again. After the earthquake in California, the people *rebuilt* what had been destroyed.
**re•build** (rē bild') *verb,* **rebuilt, rebuilding.**

**refreshment 1.** Food or drink. What *refreshments* will you serve at the party? **2.** A refreshing or being refreshed. I needed *refreshment* after working all day.
**re•fresh•ment** (ri fresh'mənt) *noun, plural* **refreshments.**

786

---

**register** To have one's name placed on a list or record. Voters must *register* before they can vote. *Verb.*—An official list or record, or a book used for this. I signed my name in the guest *register. Noun.*
**reg•is•ter** (rej'ə stər) *verb,* **registered, registering;** *noun, plural* **registers.**

**regulation 1.** A law, rule, or order. Smoking is against school *regulations.* **2.** The act of regulating or the state of being regulated. A thermostat controls the *regulation* of heat in the building.
**reg•u•la•tion** (reg'yə lā'shən) *noun, plural* **regulations.**

**reject** To refuse to accept, allow, or approve. The voters *rejected* the tax plan.
**re•ject** (ri jekt') *verb,* **rejected, rejecting;** *noun,* **rejection.**

**reliable** Able to be depended on and trusted. We know she will do a good job because she is a *reliable* worker.
▲ Synonyms: dependable, responsible, trustworthy
**re•li•a•ble** (ri lī'ə bəl) *adjective; adverb,* **reliably;** *noun,* **reliability.**

**reluctant** Unwilling. I am *reluctant* to lend you the book because you seldom return what you borrow.
**re•luc•tant** (ri luk'tənt) *adjective; adverb,* **reluctantly.**

**reserved 1.** Set apart for a person or purpose. The only available seats in the theater are *reserved.* **2.** Keeping one's thoughts and feelings to oneself. He is a quiet and *reserved* man.
**re•served** (ri zûrvd') *adjective.*

**reverence** A feeling of deep love and respect. Everyone in the town had *reverence* for the old doctor.
**rev•er•ence** (rev'ər əns) *noun.*

**revolt** To rebel against a government or other authority. The ill-treated prisoners *revolted. Verb.*—An uprising or rebellion against a government or other authority. The citizens staged a *revolt* against the tyrant. *Noun.*
**re•volt** (ri vōlt') *verb,* **revolted, revolting;** *noun, plural* **revolts;** *adjective,* **revolting.**

**ruddy** Having a healthy redness. She has a *ruddy* complexion.
**rud•dy** (rud'ē) *adjective,* **ruddier, ruddiest.**

---

at; āpe; fär; câre; end; mē; it; īce; pîerce; hot; ōld; sŏng; fôrk; oil; out; up; ūse; rūle; pull; tûrn; chin; sing; shop; thin; this; hw in white; zh in treasure. The symbol ə stands for the unstressed vowel sound in about, taken, pencil, lemon, and circus.

---

787

Glossary

# Ss

**sacred 1.** Belonging to God or a god; having to do with religion. Our choir sings *sacred* music. **2.** Regarded as deserving respect. The memory of the dead hero was *sacred* to the town. **sa•cred** (sā′krid) *adjective.*

**salsa** A spicy sauce or relish made mostly with tomatoes and chiles. Many cooks spoon *salsa* on eggs. **sal•sa** (säl′sə) *noun.*

**satellite 1.** A spacecraft that moves in an orbit around the Earth, the moon, or other bodies in space. *Satellites* are used to forecast the weather, to connect radio, telephone, and television communications, and to provide information about conditions in space. **2.** A heavenly body that moves in an orbit around another body larger than itself. The moon is the earth's only natural satellite. All the planets in our solar system are *satellites* that orbit the sun. **sat•el•lite** (sat′ə lit′) *noun, plural* **satellites.**

**scheme** A plan or plot for doing something. The crooks had a *scheme* for robbing the bank. *Noun.*—To plan or plot. The rebels *schemed* to capture the king and queen. *Verb.* **scheme** (skēm) *noun, plural* **schemes;** *verb,* **schemed, scheming.**

**scholarship 1.** Money given to a student to help pay for his or her studies. The university awarded her a *scholarship* for her good grades. **2.** Knowledge or learning. The professor is respected for her *scholarship.* **schol•ar•ship** (skol′ər ship′) *noun, plural* **scholarships.**

**scorch** To burn slightly on the surface. I *scorched* my shirt with the iron. *Verb.*—A slight burn. A necktie will cover that *scorch. Noun.* **scorch** (skôrch) *verb,* **scorched, scorching;** *noun, plural* **scorches.**

---

### Word History

The word *scorch* is thought to be of Scandinavian origin, based on the Old Norse word *skorpna,* meaning "to shrivel up."

---

**scratch** To scrape or cut with nails, claws, or anything sharp and pointed. The cat *scratched* my arm. **scratch** (skrach) *verb,* **scratched, scratching.**
▲ **from scratch** From the beginning; with no resources. When their business failed, they had to start again *from scratch. Adverb.*

**scroll** A roll of paper, parchment, or other material with writing on it, often wound around a rod or rods. The official unrolled the *scroll* and read the message from the king. *Noun.*—To move the text on a computer up or down in order to read it. I *scrolled* through the document to look for words I misspelled. *Verb.* **scroll** (skrōl) *noun, plural* **scrolls;** *verb,* **scrolled, scrolling.**

**sculpture** A figure or design that is usually done by carving stone, wood, or marble, modeling in clay, or casting in bronze or another metal. That statue is a beautiful piece of *sculpture. Noun.*—To carve, model, or cast figures or designs in such a way. The artist *sculptured* a lion. *Verb.* **sculp•ture** (skulp′chər) *noun, plural* **sculptures;** *verb,* **sculptured, sculpturing.**

**settler** A person who settles in a new land or country. The first European *settlers* of Florida were from Spain. **set•tler** (set′lər) *noun, plural* **settlers.**

**severe 1.** Very strict; harsh. The dictator established many *severe* laws. **2.** Dangerous; serious. The soldier had a *severe* wound. **3.** Causing great difficulty or suffering. A *severe* storm is expected. **se•vere** (sə vîr′) *adjective.*

**shabby 1.** Worn-out and faded. The beggar wore a *shabby* coat. **2.** Mean or unfair. It's cruel and *shabby* to make fun of other people. **shab•by** (shab′ē) *adjective,* **shabbier, shabbiest.**

**shoreline** The line where a body of water meets the land. We took a helicopter ride up the *shoreline* and saw people swimming in the ocean. **shore•line** (shôr′lin′) *noun, plural* **shorelines.**

**shrivel** To shrink, wrinkle, or wither. The plant *shriveled* because it was too hot in the room. **shriv•el** (shriv′əl) *verb,* **shriveled, shriveling;** *adjective,* **shriveled.**

**sizzle** To make a hissing or sputtering sound. The bacon *sizzled* as it cooked in the frying pan. **siz•zle** (siz′əl) *verb,* **sizzled, sizzling.**

---

at; āpe; fär; câre; end; mē; it; īce; pîerce; hot; ōld; sông; fôrk; oil; out; up; ūse; rūle; pùll; tûrn; chin; sing; shop; thin; this; hw in white; zh in treasure. The symbol ə stands for the unstressed vowel sound in about, taken, pencil, lemon, and circus.

---

**skeleton 1.** A framework that supports and protects the body of an animal. Birds, fish, and humans have skeletons made up of bones or cartilage. Many different types of bones make up the human *skeleton.* **2.** Any framework or structure used as a support. The workers built the steel *skeleton* of the building first. **skel•e•ton** (skel′i tən) *noun, plural* **skeletons.**

**skeptical** Having or showing doubt or disbelief. My classmates were *skeptical* of my plan to get the governor to visit our class. **skep•ti•cal** (skep′ti kəl) *adjective.*

**sledgehammer** A heavy hammer with a long handle that is held with both hands. The workers broke the rocks with their *sledgehammers.* **sledge•ham•mer** (slej′ham′ər) *noun, plural* **sledgehammers.**

**snoop** One who looks or pries, especially in a sneaky manner. I caught the *snoop* looking through my personal things. *Noun.*—To look or pry in a sneaky manner. *Verb.* The detective *snooped* around the office. **snoop** (snüp) *noun; verb,* **snooped, snooping.**

**soot** A black, greasy powder that forms when such fuels as wood, coal, and oil are burned. The chimney sweep was covered with *soot.* **soot** (sút *or* süt) *noun.*

**soothe** To quiet, calm, or ease. The nurse *soothed* the crying child with a lullaby. **soothe** (süth) *verb,* **soothed, soothing.**

**speechless 1.** Temporarily unable to speak. Her news left me *speechless;* I didn't know what to say. **2.** Not having the power of speech; mute. **speech•less** (spēch′lis) *adjective; adverb,* **speechlessly;** *noun,* **speechlessness.**

**spire** A tall, narrow structure that tapers to a point, built on the top of a tower. The church *spire* towered above all the other buildings in the town. **spire** (spir) *noun, plural* **spires.**

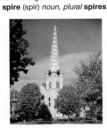

**spiritual** A religious folk song, especially one originated by blacks in the southern United States. The group sang beautiful *spirituals. Noun.*—Of or having to do with religion. Priests, ministers, and rabbis are *spiritual* leaders. *Adjective.* **spir•i•tu•al** (spir′i chü əl) *noun, plural* **spirituals;** *adjective.*

**sprawl 1.** To lie or sit with the body stretched out in an awkward or careless manner. I *sprawled* in the chair with one leg hooked over the arm. **2.** To spread out in a way that is not regular or organized. New houses *sprawl* across the countryside. **sprawl** (sprôl) *verb,* **sprawled, sprawling.**

**spurt** To pour out suddenly in a stream. Water *spurted* from the broken pipe. *Verb.*—A sudden pouring out or bursting forth. A *spurt* of water came out of the hose. *Noun.* **spurt** (spûrt) *verb,* **spurted, spurting;** *noun, plural* **spurts.**

**squirm** To turn or twist the body. The child *squirmed* in her seat. **squirm** (skwûrm) *verb,* **squirmed, squirming.**

**stadium** A structure made up of rows of seats built around an open field. The crowd filled the *stadium* to watch the soccer match.
▲ **Synonym:** arena
**sta•di•um** (stā′dē əm) *noun, plural* **stadiums.**

**standard** Anything used to set an example or serve as a model. New cars must meet strict safety *standards. Noun.*—Widely used or usual. It's our *standard* practice to send bills on the first day of the month. *Adjective.* **stand•ard** (stan′dərd) *noun, plural* **standards;** *adjective.*

**starvation** The state of suffering from lack of nourishment. Too many people are dying of *starvation.* **star•va•tion** (stär vā′shən) *noun.*

**statue** A likeness of a person or animal, made out of stone, bronze, or clay. The *statue* of the turtle looked so real that you couldn't tell it was made of stone. **stat•ue** (stach′ü) *noun, plural* **statues.**

**stern** The rear part of a boat or ship. The sailor stood at the *stern* of the ship and waved good-bye. *Noun.* —Harsh or strict. Our parents were *stern* when it came to our homework. *Adjective.* **stern** (stûrn) *noun, plural* **sterns;** *adjective,* **sterner, sternest;** *adverb,* **sternly.**

---

at; āpe; fär; câre; end; mē; it; īce; pîerce; hot; ōld; sông; fôrk; oil; out; up; ūse; rūle; pùll; tûrn; chin; sing; shop; thin; this; hw in white; zh in treasure. The symbol ə stands for the unstressed vowel sound in about, taken, pencil, lemon, and circus.

---

**G9**

**stifle** To smother; suffocate. The smoke was so thick I thought it would *stifle* us.
sti•fle (stī′ fəl) *verb*, **stifled, stifling.**

**strict 1.** Following or enforcing a rule in a careful, exact way. The teacher is *strict* about spelling. **2.** To be followed in a careful, exact way; carefully enforced. That school has *strict* rules.
strict (strikt) *adjective*, **stricter, strictest;** *adverb*, **strictly;** *noun*, **strictness.**

**stun 1.** To shock. We were *stunned* by the news. **2.** To make unconscious. The robin was *stunned* when it flew into the window.
stun (stun) *verb*, **stunned, stunning.**

**submit 1.** To present. *Submit* your book reports on Monday. **2.** To yield to power or authority. The children *submitted* to their parents' wishes
sub•mit (səb mit′) *verb*, **submitted, submitting.**

**summon 1.** To ask to come. We *summoned* the police to the scene of the accident. **2.** To stir up; arouse. I *summoned* my courage and dived off the high diving board.
sum•mon (sum′ən) *verb*, **summoned, summoning.**

**superb** Very fine; excellent. The actor gave a *superb* performance.
▲ **Synonym:** outstanding
su•perb (sü pûrb′) *adjective*; *adverb*, **superbly.**

**survey** To look at or study in detail. The mayor *surveyed* the damage to the city after the storm. *Verb.*—A detailed study. The company conducted a *survey* to find out who bought its products. *Noun.*
sur•vey (sər vā′ *for verb;* sûr′vā *or* sər vā′ *for noun*) *verb*, **surveyed, surveying;** *noun, plural* **surveys;** *noun*, **surveyor.**

**survival 1.** The act of surviving. The *survival* of all the bus passengers in the accident seemed a miracle. **2.** A thing that survives. The custom of throwing rice at a bride and groom is a *survival* from the past.
sur•viv•al (sər vī′ vəl) *noun*.

**swerve** To turn aside suddenly. The driver *swerved* to avoid hitting a dog. *Verb.*—The act of swerving. The *swerve* of the car upset the driver's cup of coffee. *Noun.*
swerve (swûrv) *verb*, **swerved, swerving;** *noun, plural* **swerves.**

**swollen** Made larger by swelling. I can't get the ring off my *swollen* finger.
swol•len (swō′lən) *adjective.*

## Tt

**tavern** A place where travelers stay overnight; inn. The weary travelers stopped to rent a room at the *tavern* for the night.
tav•ern (tav′ərn) *noun, plural* **taverns.**

**teem** To be full of; swarm. The creek near our house *teems* with fish.
▲ **Synonym:** swarm
teem (tēm) *verb*, **teemed, teeming.**

**tempestuous** Stormy; turbulent. The *tempestuous* seas tossed the boat around like a toy.
tem•pes•tu•ous (tem pes′chü əs) *adjective.*

tempestuous

**thickness 1.** The quality of having space between one side or surface and the other. The *thickness* of the walls makes the house quiet. **2.** The distance between two sides or surfaces of something; the measurement other than the length or width. The *thickness* of this board is 1 inch.
thick•ness (thik′nis) *noun, plural* **thicknesses.**

**thief** A person who steals. The *thief* broke into the house and stole the television.
▲ **Synonym:** robber
thief (thēf) *noun, plural* **thieves.**

**thrive** To be successful; do well. This plant *thrives* in the sun.
thrive (thrīv) *verb*, **thrived** *or* **throve, thrived** *or* **thriven, thriving.**

at; āpe; fär; câre; end; mē; it; īce; pîerce; hot; ōld; sông; fôrk; oil; out; up; ūse; rūle; pùll; tûrn; chin; sing; shop; thin; this; hw in white; zh in treasure. The symbol ə stands for the unstressed vowel sound in about, taken, pencil, lemon, and circus.

**tiller** A bar or handle used to turn the rudder of a boat. The pilot steadied the boat by holding the *tiller.*
till•er (til′ər) *noun, plural* **tillers.**

**timber 1.** A large, heavy piece of wood; beam. The strength of its *timbers* kept the building standing. **2.** Wood that is used in building things; lumber. The stack of *timber* was our only clue that they were planning to build something.
tim•ber (tim′bər) *noun, plural* **timbers.**

**tiresome** Exhausting; tedious. It was *tiresome* writing my paper.
tire•some (tīr′səm) *adjective.*

**tombstone** A stone that marks a grave. Tombstones often show the dead person's name and the dates of birth and death. The *tombstones* marked the spot where the old graveyard was.
tomb•stone (tüm′stōn′) *noun, plural* **tombstones.**

**tornado** A powerful storm with winds that whirl in a dark cloud shaped like a funnel. It can cause great destruction. Luckily, the *tornado* touched down in a field and didn't cause much damage to the houses.
tor•na•do (tôr nā′dō) *noun, plural* **tornadoes** *or* **tornados.**

### Word History

*Tornado* first appeared in the English language around 1556. It is a modification of the Spanish word *tronada*, which means "thunderstorm."

**tortilla** A thin, round, flat bread made from water and cornmeal. For lunch I ate rice and beans wrapped in a *tortilla.*
tor•til•la (tôr tē′yə) *noun, plural* **tortillas.**

**track** To follow the marks, path, or course of. The dogs *tracked* the fox. The scientists *tracked* the flight of the missile on their radar. *Verb.*—A mark left by a person, animal, or object as it moves over a surface. We followed the deer *tracks* in the snow. *Noun.*
track (trak) *verb*, **tracked, tracking;** *noun, plural* **tracks.**

**treacherous 1.** Full of danger; hazardous. The waters near the cape were *treacherous*. **2.** Betraying one's country or friends; disloyal. The *treacherous* soldier gave secrets to the enemy.
treach•er•ous (trech′ər əs) *adjective.*

**tribute** Something done or given to show thanks or respect. The statue was a *tribute* to the soldiers who had died in the war.
trib•ute (trib′ūt) *noun, plural* **tributes.**

**trifle** To treat something in a careless way. Don't *trifle* with the camera. *Verb.*—Something that is small in amount or importance. One twin is just a *trifle* taller than the other. *Noun.*
tri•fle (trī′fəl) *verb*, **trifled, trifling;** *noun, plural* **trifles.**

**tropical** Relating to or found in the tropics. In the cold of winter I often wish our weather were more *tropical.*
trop•i•cal (trop′i kəl) *adjective.*

## Uu

**unbearable** Unable to be endured or put up with. Some of us found the singer's voice *unbearable.*
▲ **Synonym:** intolerable
un•bear•able (un bâr′ ə bəl) *adjective.*

**uneven 1.** Not straight, smooth, or regular. The car bounced along the *uneven* road. **2.** Being an odd number. 1, 3, and 5 are *uneven* numbers.
un•ev•en (un ē′vən) *adjective.*

**unique** Not having an equal; being the only one of its kind. Landing on the moon was a *unique* achievement.
u•nique (ū nēk′) *adjective.*

**unpleasant** Not pleasing; disagreeable. An *unpleasant* odor came from the sewer.
un•pleas•ant (un plez′ənt) *adjective.*

**uproot 1.** To tear or pull up by the roots. The bulldozers *uprooted* bushes and trees. **2.** To cause to leave; displace. The flood *uprooted* many families from their homes.
up•root (up rüt′ *or* up rùt′) *verb*, **uprooted, uprooting.**

at; āpe; fär; câre; end; mē; it; īce; pîerce; hot; ōld; sông; fôrk; oil; out; up; ūse; rūle; pùll; tûrn; chin; sing; shop; thin; this; hw in white; zh in treasure. The symbol ə stands for the unstressed vowel sound in about, taken, pencil, lemon, and circus.

**usher** To act as an usher; lead. The waiter *ushered* us to a table by the window. *Verb.*—One who leads people to their seats in a church, theater, or other place. We showed the *usher* our ticket stubs. *Noun.*
    **ush•er** (ush′ər) *verb,* **ushered, ushering;** *noun, plural* **ushers.**

**vague 1.** Not clearly expressed or understood. The directions to the party were *vague,* so I was unsure where to go. **2.** Not having a precise meaning. To me the meaning of the poem was *vague.*
    **vague** (vāg) *adjective.*
    **vague•ly** (vāg′ le) *adverb.*

**variety 1.** A number of different things. We bought a *variety* of foods. **2.** Change or difference; lack of sameness. A job that has no *variety* can become boring.
    **va•ri•e•ty** (və rī′i tē) *noun, plural* **varieties.**

**violent 1.** Acting with or resulting from strong physical force. The falling branch gave the gardener a *violent* blow on the head. **2.** Caused by or showing strong feeling or emotion. My friend has a *violent* temper.
    **vi•o•lent** (vī′ ə lənt) *adjective.*

**waterfall** A natural stream of water falling from a high place. The crash of water over the *waterfall* made a thunderous noise.
    **wa•ter•fall** (wô′tər fôl′) *noun, plural* **waterfalls.**

**width** The distance from one side of something to the other side. The *width* of a football field is 52 1/3 yards.
    **width** (width) *noun, plural* **widths.**

**wildlife** Wild animals that live naturally in an area. In the forest we saw much of the local *wildlife.*
    **wild•life** (wīld′līf′) *noun.*

**woe** Great sadness or suffering. The story told of the hunger, sickness, and other *woes* of the settlers of the frontier.
    ▲ **Synonym:** sorrow
    **woe** (wō) *noun, plural* **woes.**

**wonderland** A place of delicate beauty or magical charm. After the snowstorm the neighborhood looked like a winter *wonderland.*
    **won•der•land** (wun′ dər land′) *noun.*

**writhe** To twist or contort. The fish *writhed* about when we took it out of the water.
    **writhe** (rith) *verb,* **writhed, writhing.**

**Cover Illustration:** Greg Newbold

***The publisher gratefully acknowledges permission to reprint the following copyrighted material:***

"Archimedes and the King's Gold Crown" from CRICKET, May 1989 by Linda Walvoord Girard. Reprinted by permission of the author.

THE BEST TOWN IN THE WORLD. Reprinted with the permission of Atheneum Books for Young Readers, an imprint of Simon & Schuster Children's Division from THE BEST TOWN IN THE WORLD by Byrd Baylor. Copyright © 1982 by the author.

"The Boy Who Caught the Wind" from THE RESCUE OF THE SUN AND OTHER TALES FROM THE FAR NORTH by Edythe W. Newell. Copyright © 1970 by Edythe W. Newell. Used by permission.

"Break, Break, Break" from THE OXFORD AUTHORS ALFRED TENNYSON edited by Adam Roberts. Copyright © 2000 Oxford University Press. Used by permission.

"For old times' sake: a tree speaks" by James Kirkup and the University of Salzburg Press for extract from COLLECTED SHORTER POEMS vols. I & II.

"Fox Fools Eagle" from IN A CIRCLE LONG AGO by Nancy Van Laan. Text copyright © 1995 by Nancy Van Laan. Reprinted by permission of Alfred A. Knopf, Inc.

"The Golden Touch" from CHILDREN'S ANTHOLOGY. Copyright © 1988, Macmillan Publishing Co. Used by permission.

"Harriet Tubman" Text copyright © 1978 by Eloise Greenfield. Used by permission of Harper Collins Publishers.

"How the World Got Wisdom" from THE ADVENTURES OF SPIDER by Joyce Cooper Arkhurst. Copyright © 1964 by Joyce Cooper Arkhurst (text); Illustrations © by Barker/Blade Studios Inc. By permission of Little, Brown and Company.

"In Geometry Land" by Sandra Liatsos. Copyright © 1993 by Sandra Liatsos. Used by permission of Marian Reiner for the author.

From "Jamestown, New World Adventure" by James E. Knight. Copyright © 1982 Troll Communications, LLC., published by Troll Communications, LLC. Reprinted by permission of Troll Communications, LLC.

"Kids On Strike" by Susan Campbell Bartoletti. Copyright © 1999 Houghton Mifflin Company. Used by permission.

"The Lobster and the Crab" from FABLES by Arnold Lobel. Copyright © 1980 by Arnold Lobel. Used by permission of HarperCollins Publishers.

## ACKNOWLEDGMENTS

*The publisher gratefully acknowledges permission to reprint the following copyrighted material.*

AMISTAD RISING by Veronica Chambers, illustrated by Paul Lee. Text copyright © 1998 by Veronica Chambers. Illustrations copyright © 1998 by Paul Lee. Used by permission of Harcourt, Brace & Company.

Poem "Lemon Tree" by Jennifer Clement. Copyright © 1995. Used by permission of the author.

"The Big Storm" by Bruce Hiscock. Copyright © 1993 by Bruce Hiscock. Reprinted with permission of Atheneum Books for Young Readers, Simon & Schuster Children's Publishing Division.

"Breaker's Bridge" from THE RAINBOW PEOPLE by Laurence Yep. Text copyright © 1989 by Laurence Yep. Reprinted by permission of HarperCollins Publishers.

CARLOS AND THE SKUNK by Jan Romero Stevens, illustrated by Jeanne Arnold. Text copyright © 1997 by Jan Romero Stevens. Illustrations copyright © 1997 by Jeanne Arnold. Reprinted by permission of Northland Publishing, Flagstaff, Arizona.

"Dear Mr. Henshaw" from DEAR MR. HENSHAW by Beverly Cleary. Copyright © 1983 by Beverly Cleary. Used by permission of Morrow Junior Books, a division of William Morrow & Company, Inc. Used by permission of HarperCollins Publishers.

"Early Spring" from NAVAJO: VISIONS AND VOICES ACROSS THE MESA by Shonto Begay. Copyright © 1995 by Shonto Begay. Published by Scholastic, Inc. Used by permission.

"First Flight" by Frank Richards from THE PENGUIN BOOK OF LIMERICKS, compiled and edited by E.O. Parrott. Copyright © 1983 by E.O. Parrott.

"Frederick Douglass 1817–1895" from COLLECTED POEMS by Langston Hughes. Copyright © 1994 by the Estate of Langston Hughes. Reprinted by permission of Alfred A. Knopf, Inc.

GOING BACK HOME: AN ARTIST RETURNS TO THE SOUTH interpreted and written by Toyomi Igus, illustrated by Michele Wood. Pictures copyright © 1996 by Michele Wood, story copyright © 1996 by Toyomi Igus. Reprinted with permission of the publisher, Children's Book Press, San Francisco, CA.

"The Gold Coin" from THE GOLD COIN by Alma Flor Ada. Copyright © 1991 by Alma Flor Ada. Illustrations copyright © 1991 by Neil Waldman. Reprinted with permission from Atheneum Books for Young Readers, an imprint of Simon & Schuster Children's Publishing Division.

"Grandma Essie's Covered Wagon" by David Williams, illustrated by Wiktor Sadowski. Text copyright © 1993 by David Williams. Illustrations copyright © 1993 by Wiktor Sadowski. Reprinted by permission.

"How to Think Like a Scientist" by Stephen P. Kramer. Text copyright © 1987 by Stephen P. Kramer. Used by permission of HarperCollins Publishers.

AN ISLAND SCRAPBOOK written and illustrated by Virginia Wright-Frierson. Copyright © 1998 by Virginia Wright-Frierson. Reprinted with permission of Simon & Schuster Books for Young Readers, Simon & Schuster Children's Publishing Division. All rights reserved.

"It's Our World, Too!" from IT'S OUR WORLD TOO! by Phillip Hoose. Copyright © 1993 by Phillip Hoose. Used by permission of Little, Brown and Company.

From JOHN HENRY by Julius Lester. Copyright © 1994 by Julius Lester. Used by permission of Dial Books for Young Readers, a division of Penguin Putnam Inc.

Text of "Knoxville, Tennessee" from BLACK TALK, BLACK FEELING, BLACK JUDGMENT by Nikki Giovanni. Text Copyright © 1968, 1970 by Nikki Giovanni. By permission of William Morrow and Company, Inc. Used by permission of HarperCollins Publishers.

"Life in Flatland" from FLATLAND: A Romance of Many Dimensions written and illustrated by Edwin Abbott. Copyright © 1998 by World Book Publishing. Used by permission.

"The Marble Champ" from BASEBALL IN APRIL AND OTHER STORIES, copyright © 1990 by Gary Soto. Reprinted by permission of Harcourt, Inc.

THE PAPER DRAGON by Marguerite W. Davol, illustrated by Robert Sabuda. Text copyright © 1997 by Marguerite W. Davol. Illustrations copyright © 1997 by Robert Sabuda. Used by permission of Atheneum Books for Young Readers, an imprint of Simon & Schuster Children's Publishing Division.

"Paper I" by Carl Sandburg from THE COMPLETE POEMS OF CARL SANDBURG. Copyright © 1970, 1969 by Lilian Steichen Sandburg, Trustee, reprinted by permission of Harcourt, Inc.

"Philbert Phlurk" from THE SHERIFF OF ROTTENSHOT by Jack Prelutsky. Text copyright © 1982 by the author. Illustration: By permission of Greenwillow Books, a division of William Morrow & Company, Inc. Used by permission of HarperCollins Publishers.

From THE RIDDLE by Adele Vernon. Copyright © 1987 by Adele Vernon. Used by permission of Grasset & Dunlap, Inc., a division of Penguin Putnam Inc.

"Rip Van Winkle" by Washington Irving, adapted by Adele Thane, is reprinted by permission from Plays, Inc., the Drama Magazine for Young People. Copyright © 1966, 1977, 1983 by Plays, Inc. This play may be used for reading purposes only. For permission to produce, write to Plays, Inc., 1 Boylston St., Boston, MA 02116.

THE SEA MAIDENS OF JAPAN by Lili Bell. Used by permission of Ideals Children's Books, an imprint of Hambleton-Hill Publishing, Inc. Text copyright © 1996 by Lili Bell. Illustrations copyright © 1996 by Hambleton-Hill Publishing, Inc.

"The Sidewalk Racer or On the Skateboard" from THE SIDEWALK RACER AND OTHER POEMS OF SPORTS AND MOTION by Lillian Morrison. Copyright © 1977 by Lillian Morrison. Reprinted by permission of the author.

"The Silent Lobby" by Mildred Pitts Walter. Copyright © 1990 by Mildred Pitts Walter. Reprinted by permission of McIntosh & Otis, Inc.

"To Dark Eyes Dreaming" by Zilpha Keatley Snyder. Copyright © 1969. —TODAY IS SATURDAY—Atheneum.

"To Make a Prairie" by Emily Dickinson from CELEBRATE AMERICA IN POETRY AND ART. Collection copyright © 1994. Published by Hyperion Books for Children, in association with the National Museum of American Art, Smithsonian Institution. Used by permission.

"Tonweya and the Eagles" from TONWEYA AND THE EAGLES by Rosebud Yellow Robe, illustrated by Jerry Pinkney. Text copyright © 1979 by Rosebud Yellow Rose Frantz. Illustrations copyright © 1979 by Jerry Pinkney. Used by permission of Viking Penguin, a division of Penguin Putnam, Inc.

THE VOYAGE OF THE DAWN TREADER by C. S. Lewis copyright © C.S. Lewis Pte. Ltd. 1952. Extract reprinted by permission.

WILMA UNLIMITED by Kathleen Krull, illustrated by David Diaz. Text copyright © 1996 by Kathleen Krull. Illustrations copyright © 1996 by David Diaz. Used by permission of Harcourt, Brace & Company.

THE WISE OLD WOMAN retold by Yoshiko Uchida, illustrated by Martin Springett. Text copyright © 1994 by The Estate of Yoshiko Uchida. Illustrations copyright © 1994 by Martin Springett. Used by permission of Margaret K. Elderry Books, a division of Simon & Schuster, Inc.

"The Wreck of the Zephyr" from THE WRECK OF THE ZEPHYR by Chris Van Allsburg. Copyright © 1983 by Chris Van Allsburg. Reprinted by permission of Houghton Mifflin Company. All rights reserved.

**Cover Illustration**
Greg Newbold

**Illustration**
Lori Lohstoeter, 16; Rose Zgodzinski, 42; Stanford Kay, 64; Stanford Kay, 92; Stanford Kay, 122; Tuko Fujisaki, 123; Cliff Faust, 134–135;

"Ma Lien and the Magic Brush" copyright © 1966 by Kaisei-sha Publishing Co., Ltd. Originally published in 1966 in Japanese under the title "Maiyan To Maho No Fude" by Kaisei-sha Publishing Co., Ltd.

"Martin Luther King" from YEAR-ROUND PROGRAMS FOR YOUNG PLAYERS by Aileen Fisher. Copyright © 1985, 1986 by Aileen Fisher. Used by permission of Plays, Inc.

"Prairie" from COMPLETE POEMS by Carl Sandburg. Copyright © 1950. Used by permission.

"The Princess on the Pea" from TWELVE TALES by Hans Christian Andersen. Translation copyright © 1994 by Erik Blegvad. Reprinted with the permission of Margaret K. McElderry Books, an imprint of Simon & Schuster Children's Publishing Division.

Sally Vitsky, 136; Rose Zgodzinski, 164; Annie Bissett, 198; Adam Gordon, 199; Rose Zgodzinski, 220; Tuko Fujisaki, 221; Rose Zgodzinski, 240; Joe LeMonnier, 250; Rose Zgodzinski, 251; Nancy Stahl, 252–253; Selina Alko, 254; Stanford Kay, 272; Stanford Kay, 306; Stanford Kay, 338; Chuck Gonzales, 339; Annie Bissett, 370; Chris Lensch, 380; Danuta Jarecka, 382–383; Tim Jessell, 384; Rose Zgodzinski, 406; Annie Bissett, 430; Stanford Kay, 462; Rose Zgodzinski, 463; Daniel DelValle, 489; Dave Merrill, 490; Joe LeMonnier, 500; Annie Bissett, 501; Shonto Begay, 502–503; Michael Maydak, 504; Patrick Gnan, 509; Rose Zgodzinski, 530; Wallace Keller, 532–545; Annie Bissett, 552; Stanford Kay, 578; Adam Gordon, 579; Rose Zgodzinski, 600; Chuck Gonzales, 601; Rose Zgodzinski, 610; Bryan Leister, 612–613; Joan Hall, 614; Joe LeMonnier, 646; Annie Bissett, 647; Stanford Kay, 672; Annie Bissett, 696; Annie Bissett 716; Adam Gordon, 717; Annie Bissett, 726; Chuck Gonzales, 727; John Carrozza, 765; Chuck Gonzales, 768, 771, 793; Katie Lee, 777, 783

**Photography**

5: Don Lloyd/Weatherstock. 7: Association for the Preservation of Virginia Antiquities. 9: Robb Dewall. 13: Matthew McVay/SABA. 15: Paul Edmondson/Tony Stone Images. 18: The British Library, London/The Bridgeman Art Library, London/Superstock. 20: The Bancroft Library, University of California, Berkley, photo by Gordon Honda. 44: National Museum of American Art, Washington, DC/Art Resource, NY. 66: Corbis Images. 68: b. Courtesy, Harcourt Brace and Company/t. Paul Brewer/Courtesy, Harcourt Brace and Company. 70–71 bkgd. PhotoDisc. 72–73 bkgd. PhotoDisc. 74–75: bkgd. PhotoDisc. 76–77: bkgd. PhotoDisc. 78–79: bkgd. PhotoDisc. 80–81: bkgd. PhotoDisc. 84: bkgd. PhotoDisc. 85: bkgd. PhotoDisc. 89: i. AP/Wide World Photos. 91: Express Newspapers/Archive Photos. 94: Collection of Mr and Mrs Paul Mellon, Upperville, VA. 124: Explorer, Paris/Superstock. 130: c. Timothy Marshall/Liasion International. 131: c. Howard Blustein/Photo Researchers. 138: The Granger Collection. 140: Courtesy, Alma Flor Ada. 163: c.r. The Smithsonian Institute. 166: Courtesy of the Westtown School/The Brandywine River Museum. 168: t. Penguin Putnam Books for Young Readers/b. Penguin Putnam, Inc., photo by Myles C Pinkney. 200: n/a Dorothy Zeiman/AXA Financial Inc. 217: Photo courtesy Little Brown & Co. 219: b. David M. Grossman/Photo Researchers Inc. 222–223: © David Hockney/The J. Paul Getty Museum, Los Angeles. 242: Wolfgang Kaehler. 248: b. Sidney E. King/MHSD. 249: t. Association for the Preservation of Virginia Antiquities/b. Association for the Preservation of Virginia Antiquities. 256: Superstock. 271: b. Louis Glanzman/NGS Image Collection. 274: Barnes Foundation, Merion, PA/Superstock. 276: t. Courtesy, Marquerite W. Davol/b. Simon & Schuster Children's Division. 305: c.l. Arne Hodalic/Corbis. 308: Lady Lever Gallery, Port Sunlight, England/Bridgeman Art Library, London/Superstock. 340: National Museum of American Art, Washington, DC/Art Resource, NY. 369: b.r. Corbis. 372: Culver Pictures. 378: Robb Dewall. 379: b.r. Library of Congress/Corbis. 386: Private Collection/Superstock. 388: t. Courtesy, Northland Publishing, Flagstaff, AZ./b. Courtesy, Northland Publishing, Flagstaff, AZ. 405: b.r. Werner Forman Archive/Maxwell Museum of Anthropology/Art Resource, NY. 408: Motion Picture and Television Photo Archive. 429: b.l. The Granger Collection. 432: Hermitage, St Petersburg, Russia/The Bridgeman Art Library International. 464: NOAA/Science Photo Library/Photo Researchers, Inc. 488–89: c. Warren Faidley/International Stock. 492: Julian Baum/Science Photo Library/Photo Researchers, Inc. 499: b.r. The Granger Collection/m.l. Bruce Selyem/Museum of the Rockies/t.l. Bruce Selyem/Museum of the Rockies. 506: The Grand Design, Leeds, England/Superstock. 508: r. Bill Smith Studio. 529: b. Paul Sisul/Tony Stone Images. 532: © 2003 Estate of Pablo Picasso/Artists Rights Society (ARS), New York/Milwaukee Art Museum, Gift of Mrs Harry Lynde Bradley. 554: Musees des Beaux-Arts de Belgique, Brussels/The Bridgeman Art Library International. 580: Werner Forman Archive/Art Resource, NY. 596: b.r. courtesy, Lawrence Yep. 602: Courtesy, Gilbert Elementary School, Gilbert, AZ. 609: i. Phillip Gould/Corbis. 616: Ashley Bryan/Islesford Artists. 644: b. Jacques Jangoux/Photo Researchers. 645: c.l. The Granger Collection/b.r. The Granger Collection. 648: Royal Ontario Museum, Toronto/The Bridgeman Art Library International. 671: t.l. North Wind Pictures. 674: David David Gallery, Philadelphia/Superstock. 695: t.r. Felicia Martinez/Photo Edit. 698: The Smithsonian Institute. 713: Courtesy, Mildred Pitts Walter. 715: t. Matt Heron/Take Star/Black Star. 718: Kathleen Norris Cook. 728: Daniel J. Cox/Natural Exposures. 728: b.r. The Granger Collection. 728–9: Daniel J. Cox/Natural Exposures.

**Reading for Information**
**Table of Contents, pp. 730–731**

Chess pieces, tl, Wides + Hall/FPG; Earth, mcl, M. Burns/Picture Perfect; CD's, mcl, Michael Simpson/FPG; Newspapers, bl, Craig Orsini/Index Stock/PictureQuest; Clock, tc, Steve McAlister/The Image Bank; Kids circle, bc, Daniel Pangbourne Media/FPG; Pencils, tr, W. Cody/Corbis; Starfish, tc, Darryl Torckler/Stone; Keys, cr, Randy Faris/Corbis; Cells, br, Spike Walker/Stone; Stamps, tr, Michael W. Thomas/Focus Group/PictureQuest; Books, cr, Siede Preis/PhotoDisc; Sunflower, cr, Jeff LePore/Natural Selection; Mouse, br, Andrew Hall/Stone; Apples, tr, Siede Preis/PhotoDisc; Watermelons, br, Neil Beer/PhotoDisc; Butterfly, br, Stockbyte

***All photographs are by Macmillan/McGraw-Hill (MMH); Sidney E. King for MMH; and Richard Hutchings for MMH, except as noted below:***

733: b. Ralph A. Clevenger/Corbis. 734: Jack Stein Grove/ProFiles West. 739: b. G Buttner/Naturbild/OKAPIA/Photo Researchers Inc./b. G Buttner/Naturbild/OKAPIA/Photo Researchers Inc; 737: t.l. Andre Jenny/Unicorn Stock Photos/t.r. John Elk/Stock Boston; 740–741: NASA. 748: t.r. Stone/b.r. Corbis/l. Tony Vaccaro/Archive Photos/l. Tony Vaccaro/Archive Photos/t.c. Corbis; 749: b.r. PhotoDisc/bl. Georgia O'Keefe, 1987–1986, White Shell With Red, 1938, pastel on wood pulp laminate board, 54.6x69.8 cm, Alfred Stieglitz Collection, bequest of Georgia O'Keefe, 1987.250.5. Copyright 2000, The Art Institute of Chicago. All rights reserved. 750: l. Tony Vaccaro/Archive Photos/r. Corbis; 750–751: background: Stone; 754: Brown Brothers; 755: National Museum of American History/Smithsonian; 756–7: b PhotoLink/PhotoDisc. 758: bl Tony Freeman/PhotoEdit; 758–9: bkgd S. Solum/PhotoLink/PhotoDisc. 762: L. Newman and A. Flowers. 763: t.r. Francois Gohier/Photo Researchers. 766: bl. Tom Croke/Liaison Agency, Inc. 769: t.l. Francois Gohier/Photo Researchers, Inc. 770: t.r. Thomas Schmitt/Image Bank. 772: William Johnson/Stock Boston. 774: Superstock. 775: Anselm Sring/Image Bank. 776: Chris Close/Image Bank. 779: Jonathan Nourok/Photo Edit. 781: Frederic Jorez/Image Bank. 782: G.M. Cassidy/The Picture Cube/Index Stock Photography. 784: Index Stock Photography. 785: Magnus Rietz/Image Bank. 786: t. Michael Melford/Image Bank/b. Ian O'Leary/Stone. 788: David Ducros/Photo Researchers, Inc. 790: Rafael Macia/Photo Researchers, Inc. 791: Bob Abraham/Corbis-Stock Market. 794: Derik Murray/Image Bank. 795: Pete Seaward/Stone.

**Reading Strategy Credits**

Craig Spearing, 19–19A; Kevin Beilfuss, 257–257A; Liz Callen, 275–275A; Mike DiGiorgio, 433, 603A, 719A; Luigi Galante, 507–507A; Alexi Natchev, 555–555A; Arvis Stewart, 581–581A; Tom Barrett, 649–649A; The Granger Collection. Pages 45–45a, Grant V. Faint/The Image Bank; pages 67–67a, Jean Lorre/Photo Researchers; page 67a (inset), AP/Wide World Photos; pages 95–95a, Lawson Wood/Corbis; page 95a (inset), PhotoDisc; pages 125–125a, Burton McNeely/The Image Bank; pages 125–125a (inset), Wesley Bocxe/Photo Researchers; page 139, Christopher Cormack/Corbis; pages 139–139a, Randy Duchaine/The Stock Market; pages 167–167a, Corbis/Bettmann; page 201, Courtesy Kids Helping Kids in Crisis; pages 201–201a, AFP/Corbis; pages 223–223a, Copyright Janusz Kawa; page 243, Tim Wright/Corbis; page 243a, David Muench/Corbis; page 309a, Corbis/Bettmann; page 341, AP/Wide World Photos; page 341a, Photograph (c) 2001 The Museum of Modern Art, New York; pages 373–373a, Rafael Macia/Photo Researchers; pages 387–387a, Ed Eckstein/Corbis; page 387a (right), PhotoDisc; pages 409–409a, Reuters NewMedia/Corbis; page 409a (top), Stephen J. Krasemann/Photo Researchers; page 433a (top), Gavriel Jecan/The Stock Market; page 433a (bottom), Superstock; pages 465–465a, The Kobal Collection; page 465a (inset), NOAA; page 493a (left), Georgiana Harbeson/Wood River Gallery/PictureQuest; page 493a (right), Corbis/Bettmann; pages 533–533a, Joseph Sohm/Corbis; page 533a (inset), PhotoDisc; page 603, Craig Hammell/The Stock Market; page 603a, Jon Feingersh/The Stock Market; page 617 (top), Kelly-Mooney/Corbis; pages 617–617a, James P. Blair/Corbis; page 617a (inset), Corbis/Bettmann; page 675, Farrell Grehan/Corbis; page 675 (inset), GK & Vikki Hart/The Image Bank; page 675a, Jeffrey L. Rotman/Corbis; page 675a (inset), Steve Woit/Stock Boston/PictureQuest; page 699a, Corbis/Bettmann; pages 719–719a, Phil Schermeister/Corbis.

"Sioux" Reprinted with the permission of Margaret K. McElderry Books, an imprint of Simon & Schuster Children's Publishing Division from FIRST CAME THE INDIANS by M.J. Wheeler. Text copyright © 1983 M.J. Wheeler.

"Snowmaker Torments the People" from EARTHMAKER'S TALES by Gretchen Will Mayo. Copyright © 1989 by Gretchen Will Mayo. Reprinted with permission of Walker and Company.

"Souvenir" from THE SINGING GREEN by Eve Merriam. Text copyright © 1992 by the Estate of Eve Merriam. Used by permission of Marian Reiner.

"The Steam Shovel" from STORY-TELLER POEMS by Rowena Bennett. Copyright © 1948 by Rowena Bennett.

"The Sticks of Truth" from STORIES TO SOLVE by George Shannon. Text copyright © 1985 by George W. B. Shannon. Used by permission of Greenwillow Books, a division of William Morrow & Company, Inc.

"Stormalong" from AMERICAN TALL TALES by Mary Pope Osborne. Text copyright 1991 by Mary Pope Osborne. Illustrations copyright 1991 by Michael McCurdy. Used by permission of Alfred A. Knopf.

"That's What Friends Are For" by Carole Bayer Sager and Burt Bacharach. Copyright © 1985 WB Music Corp. (ASCAP), New Hidden Valley Music (ASCAP), Carole Bayer Sager Music (BMI). All Rights jointly administered by WB Music Corp. (ASCAP) & Warner-Tamerlane Publishing Corp. (BMI). All Rights Reserved. Used by permission of Warner Bros. Publications U.S. Inc.,

"There's Just So Much To Go Around" by Neil Fishman and Harvey Edelman. Copyright © 1995 Macmillan/McGraw-Hill School Publishing Company. Used by permission.

"Touch the Moon," from FANTASTIC STORIES by Terry Jones. Copyright © 1992 Terry Jones, text. Used by permission of Viking Penguin, a division of Penguin Putnam Inc.

"A Tug of War" from IN A CIRCLE LONG AGO by Nancy Van Laan. Text copyright © 1995 by Nancy Van Laan. Illustrations copyright © 1995 by Lisa Desimini. Used by permission of Apple Soup Books, an imprint of Alfred A. Knopf.

Reprinted with permission from "Turtle's Race with Beaver" in HEROES & HEROINES, MONSTERS & MAGIC: Native American Legends & Folktales told by Joseph Bruchac © 1985. Published by The Crossing Press, P. O. Box 1048, Freedom, CA 95019.

"Western Wagons" by Stephen Vincent Benét. From *A Book of Americans* by Rosemary and Stephen Vincent Benét. Holt, Rinehart & Winston, Inc. Copyright © 1933 by Rosemary and Stephen Vincent Benét. Copyright renewed © 1961 by Rosemary Carr Benét. Reprinted by permission of Brandt & Brandt Literary Agents, Inc.

"You" from SPORTS PAGES by Arnold Adoff. Text copyright © 1986 by Arnold Adoff. Used by permission of HarperCollins Publishers.

ZB Font Method Copyright © 1996 Zaner-Bloser. Handwriting Models, Manuscript and Cursive. Used by permission.

**Photography**

All photographs by Macmillan/McGraw-Hill except as noted below.
135A left: Daniel Pangbourne Media/FPG. 135A right: M. Burns/Picture Perfect. 253A left: Jeff LePore/Natural Selection. 253A right: Stockbyte.

# Backmatter Contents

## The Lobster and the Crab
**by Arnold Lobel**

On a stormy day, the Crab went strolling along the beach. He was surprised to see the Lobster preparing to set sail in his boat.

"Lobster," said the Crab, "it is foolhardy to venture out on a day like this."

"Perhaps so," said the Lobster, "but I love a squall at sea!"

"I will come with you," said the Crab. "I will not let you face such danger alone."

The Lobster and the Crab began their voyage. Soon they found themselves far from shore. Their boat was tossed and buffeted by the turbulent waters.

"Crab!" shouted the Lobster above the roar of the wind. "For me, the splashing of the salt spray is thrilling! The crashing of every wave takes my breath away!"

"Lobster, I think we are sinking!" cried the Crab.

▶ "Yes, of course, we are sinking," said the Lobster. "This old boat is full of holes. Have courage, my friend. Remember, we are both creatures of the sea."

The little boat capsized and sank.

"Horrors!" cried the Crab.

"Down we go!" shouted the Lobster.

The Crab was shaken and upset. The Lobster took him for a relaxing walk along the ocean floor.

"How brave we are," said the Lobster. "What a wonderful adventure we have had!"

The Crab began to feel somewhat better. Although he usually enjoyed a quieter existence, he had to admit that the day had been pleasantly out of the ordinary.

*Even the taking of small risks will add excitement to life.*

---

## Archimedes and the King's Gold Crown
**a story from Sicily**
**by Linda Walvoord Girard**

King Hiero, who lived in Syracuse on the island of Sicily, had a new crown of solid gold. The king had given his goldsmith pure gold and ordered him to hammer and mold it into just the crown the king wanted.

At last the crown was finished, and the king wore it all day. It was rather large, but the king was happy, for kings love to wear golden crowns that sway a bit as they walk.

Not until King Hiero was ready to go to sleep did he reach up to remove the crown. Hmm, he said to himself. This solid gold crown isn't as heavy as I thought it would be. It looks like solid gold. It shines. It's the right size. But it seems a bit light. He bounced it in his hands.

A black thought crept into the king's mind. Maybe his royal goldsmith had cheated him by melting the gold and mixing it with silver. Silver is much lighter than gold, and it's also cheaper than gold. Every king knows that. Had the ▶goldsmith kept some of that gold for himself, and had he stretched out the gold for the king's crown with silver?

All night the king lay awake worrying about his crown. By morning he knew what to do. "Wrap up my crown and get a horse ready," King Hiero said to his courier. "You must take my crown to Archimedes. I have a great problem and I need a smart man like him to solve it."

When Archimedes received the king's courier, he was astonished. There lay the crown, sparkling in the sunlight, and with it the king's secret message about his suspicions.

Archimedes was flattered by the king's trust. But he was worried, too, for he had no idea how he could answer the king. How could he *prove* beyond all doubt that the crown was or was not pure gold? He couldn't just lift the crown himself and say to the king, "Yes, it's the right weight, I think." Or, "No, it's too light, I think." He needed a scientific way to test that crown.

In his fine laboratory Archimedes put the king's crown on one side of a scale, and pieces of pure, shining gold on the other until they balanced. He had the crown's weight in gold. But now what? Now, whenever Archimedes was puzzled by a problem, he did two things to make his great brain work even harder. First, he talked to himself, repeating the facts. What did he know? Well, he knew the crown had been made to the exact size the king had ordered. He knew its weight in gold. And he knew that gold is more dense than silver. Or that, for the same volume (the amount of space), gold is heavier than silver.

The second thing Archimedes always did—his secret trick in solving problems—was to form a lot of "If, then—" sentences.

*Read Aloud*     ▶ Continue reading here.

He started imagining crowns in his mind. If two crowns, one gold and one silver, were the same size, he thought, then the gold crown would be heavier. And if two crowns, one gold and one silver, were the same weight, then the silver crown would be larger. If two crowns were both solid gold and were exactly the same size, then they must also weigh the same. And, he thought, putting his hand on his forehead and closing his eyes, if two crowns were both pure gold, and both weighed the same, then…then they would also be the same size.

But now what?

Something was missing—a way to compare the size. He wished he could squash the crown somehow, like a mass of clay, into one hunk, without all the turrets and curves, so he could see its real size. Or else, he wished he could take those gold hunks himself and fashion them into a copy of the crown, the exact size of the king's.

But I can't do that, Archimedes thought. I am not a goldsmith. I am a philosopher, a thinker, a mathematician. I have to think my way out of this.

But he was stumped.

At last, hours later, Archimedes was ready to give up and go home for dinner. He was hot. So he decided he would stop at the baths.

At the bath chamber a servant filled the tub to the rim. Archimedes was tired. He sighed as he stepped in. *Whoosh. Splash.* As he sank into the tub with an *aah*, water flowed over the rim. And that's when something clicked in his mind. The water that spilled out was making room for whatever went into the tub. When he sank into that tub, his body was taking up space. The amount of water that had spilled was exactly the same amount of space that he had occupied.

Well, that was it. The spilled water was a way to measure size!

Archimedes was so happy that he leaped out of the tub and ran naked out of the bathhouse into the streets, laughing, shouting, and crying, "*Eureka!*" which is Greek for "I have found it!"

The passers-by all stared. "Oh well, it's only Archimedes the philosopher," one man said. "He's a little crazy. Somebody get him a towel."

It wasn't long before Archimedes stood in the king's royal court, watching the goldsmith swagger in and sit down.

"What's this all about? I'm busy," the goldsmith said.

"Archimedes, please proceed," said the king.

Archimedes now brought forth his scale and his gold weights, his water, his bowls, and the king's crown.

"What are you doing, preparing lunch?" asked the goldsmith.

Archimedes put the crown on one side of his scale. Then he put gold weights on the other side of the scale, just as he had done in his laboratory. "I have here," said Archimedes, pointing to the perfectly balanced scale, "the exact weight of this lovely crown in pure gold."

Archimedes then asked a servant to fill two bowls exactly to the rim with water and to be ready to catch the water that overflowed.

Archimedes took the pure gold weights from the scale and lowered them into a large bowl of water. The servant caught all the water that spilled out as the gold sank.

Next, Archimedes lowered the crown into the second water-filled bowl. Again, the servant caught all the water that spilled out as the crown sank.

"I now have two amounts of water," Archimedes announced.

"Congratulations," said the goldsmith with a brave sneer. "So what?"

But the king knew so what. Archimedes held up the two glass containers of water that had spilled.

The king stood up. "So they are not the same," he said, glaring at the goldsmith. "If my crown were gold through and through, then it would spill exactly the same amount of water as its weight in gold. But it didn't; it spilled more. So you cheated me. You used something else!"

Within five minutes the king had clapped the greedy goldsmith into prison. And that very day he ordered the crown melted down and made over of pure gold. And the king gave many honors and gifts to Archimedes for solving his problem.

Today the name of that king is hardly remembered. His kingdom is gone. And the crown is lost.

But because Archimedes saw something in a new way and used it to solve a problem, his name has never been forgotten. Today we'd call him a true scientist. You might remember him, too, whenever you lean back in your bath, and—*whoosh, slosh*—the water moves to make room for you.

## Souvenir

**by Eve Merriam**

I bring back a shell so I can always hear
the music of the ocean when I hold it to my ear:

then I feel again the grains of sand
trickle sun-warm through my hand

the sea gulls dip and swoop and cry
as they dive for fish then climb the sky

the sailboats race with wings spread wide
as the wind spins them round and they glide ride glide

my lips taste a crust of salty foam
and sandpipers skitter and crabs scuttle home

where I build a castle of Yesterday
that the high tide washes away away

while I keep the shell so I can always hear
the music of the ocean when I hold it to my ear.

## Snowmaker Torments the People

**by Gretchen Mayo**

One terrible winter Snowmaker made the icy winds howl so that even the wolves ran away to a warmer place. The people heaped their fires with wood and chips, but Snowmaker hurled the blizzards against their lodges. Soon all the fuel was gone.

When the people of the tribe went out to gather sticks and branches, cruel Snowmaker stung the noses of the children and then their ears. He breathed on the women's hands until they were raw and stiff. He piled drifts so high that some men who dared to search deep in the forest for wood never returned.

One man of the tribe, Blue Feather, stumbled home on feet like chunks of ice. "Snowmaker has grown too big! He tosses the people around and laughs!" he complained to his wife.

"Don't say those things about Snowmaker," cried his wife. "Haven't we suffered enough? Snowmaker will only heap more snow on our path and make the winds blow longer."

So Blue Feather kept his silence. But he thought, "Snow-maker needs to be taught a lesson." Then, while the icy gales roared outside, Blue Feather chiseled and carved from his largest log a wooden bowl.

In time the sun grew warmer and Snowmaker grew quiet. Little by little he shrank away from the village. Soon nothing was left of Snowmaker but a patch of icy snow hidden in the cool, shadowy forest. This was when Blue Feather took out his wooden bowl. Before Snowmaker could vanish completely, Blue Feather scooped the last of the snow into his bowl, then he carried it to a rock and let the hot sun beat down, melting the snow.

"Ha! Cruel Snowmaker!" he shouted. "You only torment the people when Father Sun is gone. Now you are not so big. Now I laugh at you and I am not afraid!"

But a chill little wind came out of the north at just that moment, winding itself around Blue Feather and overturning the bowl. "Just wait!" it whispered. "Just wait!"

When autumn came again, Blue Feather worked harder than anyone else in the village. His firewood heaped as high as his lodge. He had many furs. But he did more. He saved the fat of the animals he killed and instead of using it for food he made oil, which he kept in his wooden bowl. Then, when the cold winds tore the last leaf from the forest branches, Blue Feather knew Snowmaker would come back to settle their fight, so he built a lodge for himself away from his wife and children.

The days grew shorter and Blue Feather saw signs that Snowmaker was preparing to attack. The ground turned cold and hard. The grasses withered. But when Snowmaker froze his meat and berries, Blue Feather used his fire to warm them.

Then one day, Father Sun was gone and Snowmaker came into the village, swirling snow and wailing his cruel laughter. Blue Feather pulled on his warm moccasins and gathered his fur robes around him.

Snowmaker heaped snow on the village all day, but he waited until night when the people were asleep to sweep boldly into Blue Feather's lodge.

Snowmaker spread a white rug for himself and sat down. He blew his icy breath, laughing, and made Blue Feather shiver. He shook his great snowy head, killing the flames of Blue Feather's fire.

"I have never been so frozen," thought Blue Feather as he felt the cold squeeze the life from him. "Maybe if I go to sleep, Snowmaker will leave." But Blue Feather called upon his last bit of strength and reached out instead for the oil he had saved, flinging it on the dying fire. The flames roared alive, leaping to the smoke hole, lighting up the lodge.

While new life came to Blue Feather, Snowmaker shrank away from the flames, sweating and gasping. When Blue Feather let his fur robes drop from his shoulders and threw more oil on his fire, Snowmaker crouched against the wall of the lodge, sweat pouring from him in a stream.

"You have beaten me," hissed Snowmaker in a small weak voice. Then the shrunken bully stumbled out of Blue Feather's lodge, leaving only a wet trail behind him.

Snowmaker still comes again and again to torment the people, but because of Blue Feather he has lost some of his power, and the people are strong. When the hills turn golden, the children gather wood. The women store away the dried meat and the berries. And the men bring home warm furs, saving the oil to make their winter fires burn brightly.

## Western Wagons
**by Rosemary and Stephen Vincent Benét**

They went with axe and rifle, when the trail was still to blaze,
They went with wife and children, in the prairie-schooner
   days,
With banjo and with frying pan—Susanna, don't you cry!
For I'm off to California to get rich out there or die!

We've broken land and cleared it, but we're tired of where
   we are.
They say that wild Nebraska is a better place by far.
There's gold in far Wyoming, there's black earth in Ioway,
So pack up the kids and blankets, for we're moving out today!

The cowards never started and the weak died on the road,
And all across the continent the endless campfires glowed.
*We'd taken land and settled—but a traveler passed by—*
*And we're going West tomorrow—Lordy, never ask us why!*

We're going West tomorrow, where the promises can't fail,
O'er the hills in legions, boys, and crowd the dusty trail!
We shall strive and freeze and suffer. We shall die, and tame
   the lands.
But we're going West tomorrow, with our fortune in our
   hands.

▶ Continue reading here.

## Practice 112

Name_____ Date_____ **Practice** 112

### Judgments & Decisions

Before you make a **decision** about something, you consider the reasons for and against the decision. Read each situation below. List two reasons for each choice, and then make a **judgment** about what you should do. Write your final decision.

Suppose the following: After three weekends in a row of cold rain, this weekend is sunny and warm. You are having friends over for two hours. One of them is bringing a new video that you want to see. How would you decide to spend the day? Should you stay indoors, or should you go outside?

1. Two reasons for staying indoors: Answers will vary. Sample answer: You should stay indoors to watch the video you want to see. You have a friend over who wants to watch it with you.

2. Two reasons for going outdoors: Answers will vary. Sample answer: You should go outside because it is the first sunny and warm weekend you've had for a long time. It's healthy to go outside.

3. Final decision: Answers will vary.
_____

Suppose the following: Two of your friends have had a misunderstanding that has led to bad feelings between them. Should you try to get them to be friends again, or should you let them figure things out on their own?

1. Two reasons for trying to get them to be friends again: Answers will vary. Sample answers: You may help them understand each other's viewpoints. Explain they have been friends and that friendship is important.

2. Two reasons for letting them figure things out on their own: Answers will vary. Sample answers: People sometimes need to work out their differences on their own; by trying to help them you may make it worse.

3. Final decision: Sample answer: You could try talking to each friend separately at first to see if they would like you to help them work out their differences.

6 Book 5/Unit 4
Carlos and the Skunk

**At Home:** Have students list the reasons why they should and should not buy something. Then ask them to make a judgment about what they should do and write their final decision.

112

## Practice 113

Name_____ Date_____ **Practice** 113

### Vocabulary

Write a vocabulary word from the list that means almost the same thing as the underlined words in the sentences.

| nestled | peculiar | stunned | tortillas | unbearable | unpleasant |
|---|---|---|---|---|---|

1. The cold water was _____ unbearable _____. The temperature was intolerable.

2. The star of the film was very _____ unpleasant _____. She had a disagreeable personality.

3. We were all shocked to hear she had won the prize. It _____ stunned _____ us.

4. I like _____ tortillas _____. They remind me of thin pancakes.

5. After a long day of hiking, we lay comfortably _____ nestled _____ in our tent. That night we snuggled in our sleeping bags to stay warm.

6. The story is a little odd. Some people think what happened is _____ peculiar _____.

## Very Good Cooking

"I could go for some good food," Maria thought to herself. "I could go for some *tortillas*. I could make them myself. How hard could it be?"

Usually, Maria thought cooking was *unpleasant*, but this time she was actually enjoying herself. Maria poured corn flour and water into a bowl just like she had seen her grandmother do. "That's *peculiar*," said Maria. "There must be more ingredients in the recipe." But Maria didn't have the recipe. So she decided to create her own. She found a box of raisins *nestled* in a drawer. She added those. Then she added some molasses and a little sugar.

Maria was finishing cooking her tortillas when her grandmother came into the kitchen. Maria proudly told her the recipe she had invented. Her grandmother was *stunned*. "Well, normally, you need only flour and water, but yours does sound interesting. I'm sure it won't be *unbearable*," said her grandmother. "I'm sure we'll enjoy eating them." They did enjoy eating them. They were very good!

1. What did Maria decide to cook? tortillas

2. What did Maria think was *peculiar*? There were only two ingredients she could remember.

3. What was *nestled* in the drawer? a box of raisins

4. How did Maria's grandmother react to her recipe? She was stunned.

5. Why do you think Maria's grandmother said the tortillas would not be *unbearable*? She didn't want to hurt Maria's feelings; also the tortillas had sweet ingredients so they probably would taste fine.

5 Book 5/Unit 4
Carlos and the Skunk

**At Home:** Have students write a story about a time they cooked.

113a

## Practice 114

Name_____ Date_____ **Practice** 114

### Story Comprehension

Answer the questions about "Carlos and the Skunk."

1. Who is Gloria? Is she a main character? Why is she important to the story? Gloria is Carlos's best friend. She is a main character and is important to the story because she is the one Carlos wants to impress.

2. What happens to Carlos's feelings for Gloria as they grow older? His feelings about Gloria change. He likes her more as a girlfriend and not just as a childhood friend. He wants to impress her so that she likes him.

3. Who is Dos Dedos (Two Toes)? Why is Dos Dedos important to the story? Dos Dedos is the skunk that Carlos tries to catch. Dos Dedos sets up the plot by spraying Carlos and ruining his shoes.

4. What does Carlos think will happen if he picks up the skunk by its tail? He thinks he will not be sprayed if he catches the skunk by its tail.

5. How does Carlos try to get rid of the skunk smell? He first runs to the river to wash the skunk's stinky odor off his body and his clothes. Then he takes a bath, using the juice of fresh tomatoes, to get rid of the smell.

6. How does the fact that Carlos forgets to clean his shoes affect the plot? He has to wear them to church, and they still smell.

7. What happens at church that embarrasses Carlos? The odor from his shoes fills the church with such a bad smell that people have to leave.

8. How do you know Carlos's father knows about the skunk and Carlos's smelly shoes? Explain. Carlos's father offers to buy him new shoes. Then he makes a remark about catching a skunk by the tail.

# Carlos and the Skunk • PRACTICE

## Read a Diagram

A **diagram** is a simple drawing of an object. In a diagram, the important parts of an object are labeled. Below is the diagram of a suspension bridge.

Use the diagram to answer these questions.

1. What part of the bridge supports the towers from below? _the pier_

2. How is the bridge supported from above? _By cables that run over the top of the two towers._

3. What is the name of the part of the bridge where the cables run over the top of the tower? _the saddle_

4. How are the cables anchored to the ground at each end of the bridge? _____ They are anchored to an anchorage._

5. Cables are heavy ropes of twisted steel. What do you think would happen if the ends of the cables were not anchored into the ground? _Answers will vary._ The cables could not be held tight, so they would not support the bridge. The bridge could sag or collapse.

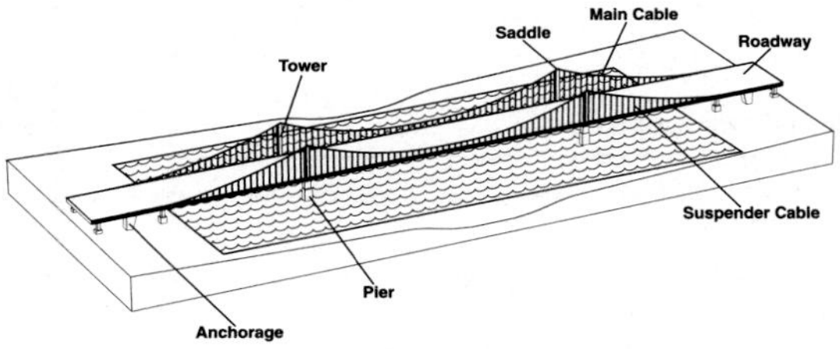

Labels: Tower, Saddle, Main Cable, Roadway, Suspender Cable, Pier, Anchorage

**At Home:** Have students look up other types of bridges and make a diagram for one of them.

---

## Judgments & Decisions

When reading a story, you make **judgments** about the characters and the things they say or do. Think about the **decisions** made by the main characters in "Carlos and the Skunk." Answer each question below. Then explain your answers.
Answers will vary. Students may cite their own knowledge as well as story clues.

1. "Carlos, you'd better be careful," whispered Gloria as Carlos inched along on his stomach near the skunk. In your opinion, do you think this was wise advice? Why or why not? _____

2. Beginning to think he (Carlos) smelled better, he crawled into bed and fell asleep quickly after his very unpleasant day. Why do you think Carlos went straight to bed? Was what happened to Carlos unpleasant? _____

3. The women began vigorously fanning their faces with their church programs. The children started squirming and pinched their noses. Little by little the strange behavior began working its way toward the back of the church. Do you think this is the way people should act when they are in a large group? Do you think Carlos' dad knew what was going on? _____

4. Embarrassed, Carlos pushed his way out of the church. He heard Gloria calling to him, but he bolted through the door and ran all the way home. Would you do the same thing Carlos did or would you have handled the situation differently? _____

**At Home:** Encourage students to talk about one thing that a main character in "Carlos and the Skunk" said or did that, in their opinion, was either right or wrong. Ask them to explain their opinions.

---

## Draw Conclusions

Since authors don't always tell readers exactly how the characters in a story feel, it is necessary to **draw** your own **conclusions**. To draw a conclusion, you rely on what you know from your own life experience and story clues.

Read the situations below and answer each question. Then describe the clues that helped you draw each conclusion. Use one clue from the story, and one from your own life experience.

In the long afternoon sun, Sula and Kwame swung gently back and forth on the porch swing. They were talking quietly, sharing their thoughts with each other, when three of their pals from school came by. They asked Sula and Kwame if they wanted to walk to the store with them. "No, thanks," said Kwame.
"We're sort of busy right now," explained Sula.

1. How do Sula and Kwame feel about each other? _Sample answer: They are good friends who enjoy spending time together._

2. Story clue: _They would rather talk alone together than join their pals._

3. Life Experience clue: _Sample answer: My best friend and I enjoy sharing our thoughts with each other, and we need to take time to do that._

Julia stomped down the hallway to her room. Then Arnie and Mrs. Kosasky heard the loud slam of a door. Arnie didn't know what to do or say. After a few awkward seconds that seemed to last forever, he turned to Mrs. Kosasky and said, "Well, I guess I'd better be going now, or I'll be late for the game. Thanks for lunch."

4. How does Julia feel? _She's probably really angry and upset._

5. Story clue: _She stomped off, and slammed the door._

6. Life Experience clue: _Sample answer: I have been angry and have had to leave places immediately. I have also been with friends who have gotten angry, and I have had to leave them alone._

**At Home:** Ask students to draw conclusions about the characters in their favorite book.

---

## Suffixes

A **suffix** is a word part that can be added to the end of a word to change the word's meaning. Knowing what a suffix means can help you define the word. The suffix -less means "not having" or "without." The suffix -able means "able to be" or "cause to be."

| Word | + | Suffix = | New Word | Meaning |
|------|---|----------|----------|---------|
| hope | + | less = | hopeless | without hope |
| bear | + | able = | bearable | tolerable |

Write the suffix of each word. Write the word's meaning. Then use the word in a sentence of your own.

1. breathless  Suffix: _less_  Meaning: _without breath_
   Sentence: _Sample answer: The race left me breathless._

2. likable  Suffix: _able_  Meaning: _pleasing_
   Sentence: _Sample answer: Sonya was a likable person._

3. powerful  Suffix: _ful_  Meaning: _full of power, very strong_
   Sentence: _Sample answer: Paul Bunyan was a very powerful character._

4. laughable  Suffix: _able_  Meaning: _causing laughter or scorn_
   Sentence: _Sample answer: His attempt to paint the door was laughable._

5. homeless  Suffix: _less_  Meaning: _not having a home_
   Sentence: _Sample answer: How do you help the homeless?_

6. thoughtful  Suffix: _ful_  Meaning: _full of thought, considerate_
   Sentence: _Sample answer: Jorge is very thoughtful towards his grandfather._

7. youthful  Suffix: _ful_  Meaning: _having the qualities of youth_
   Sentence: _Sample answer: That eighty-year-old woman looks very youthful._

8. agreeable  Suffix: _able_  Meaning: _pleasant_
   Sentence: _Sample answer: His answer seemed agreeable._

**At Home:** Ask students to name two other words that end with -ful and two other words that end with -less. Have them write each word's meaning, and then use each word in a sentence.

# Carlos and the Skunk • RETEACH

## Judgments and Decisions

> Making a **judgment** means deciding whether something or someone is right or wrong. It can also mean determining if you would behave as story characters do and if their **decisions** make story situations better or worse.

Read the story. Then make judgments and decisions about the characters' actions. Answer the questions below.

It was a chilly September day, but Jill planned to go swimming. She grabbed her swimsuit and towel and rushed down the stairs. When she reached the back door, she heard her mom shouting, "Jill, what about some breakfast? Isn't it a little cold to go swimming?"

"No thanks, Mom. I can't stop to eat. I'll never win that swim meet if I don't practice every day," replied Jill as she hopped on her bike.

Jill pedaled furiously to the pool. At the pool, the gusty wind created little waves. Jill liked the waves because they made her swim harder.

1. Do you think Jill's choice to go swimming is wise? Explain. _Practice improves_ _performance, but it was not wise to go because she might get chilled from_ _being wet in cold weather._

2. Do you agree with Jill's decision not to have breakfast? Why or why not? _____ _Possible answer: No, because you need energy for physical activity._ _____

3. If you were Jill's mother, would you let her go swimming on such a day? _____ _Answers will vary. Some will say yes, because Jill is clearly committed to her_ _sport; others will say no, because the cold weather may make Jill catch a_ _cold._

4. Would you welcome a gusty wind if you were going swimming? Explain. _No, if you_ _were swimming for pleasure; yes, if you were swimming to get stronger and_ _wanted extra resistance to push against._

Book 5/Unit 4
**Carlos and the Skunk** 4

**At Home:** Have students record at least three decisions they made during the day.

112

---

## Vocabulary

Complete each sentence using the correct vocabulary word.

| unbearable | peculiar | unpleasant | stunned | tortillas | nestled |
|---|---|---|---|---|---|

1. When she dines in a Mexican restaurant, Kate usually orders _tortillas_ wrapped around cheese with sour cream.

2. The house was _nestled_ between a stone ledge and a hill covered with apple trees.

3. After cleaning the barn and working in the fields, Lucas thought his clothing smelled _unbearable_.

4. When Dawn was accidentally hit hard by the ball, she was so _stunned_ that it took her some time to realize what had happened.

5. Samir felt sick. His homework had mistakes, and he forgot his lunch. All in all, it was turning out to be a very _unpleasant_ day.

6. Jaime never went anywhere without his guitar. He played constantly. So everyone thought it was _peculiar_ when he stopped playing.

6

## Story Comprehension

Read each sentence about "Carlos and the Skunk." Write T if the sentence is true and F it is false.

1. Carlos didn't want to touch the skunk. _F_
2. Carlos avoided Gloria for a while. _T_
3. The church service ended earlier than usual. _T_
4. Carlos didn't know where the terrible smell was coming from. _F_
5. Carlos asked his father for a new pair of shoes. _F_

**At Home:** Have students tell what clues helped them realize why Carlos was avoiding Gloria.

113–114

Book 5/Unit 4
**Carlos and the Skunk** 5

---

## Read a Diagram

A **diagram** is an illustration that can show how something is put together or how something works. The parts are often labeled with their names. Look at this diagram of an airplane. Then answer the questions.

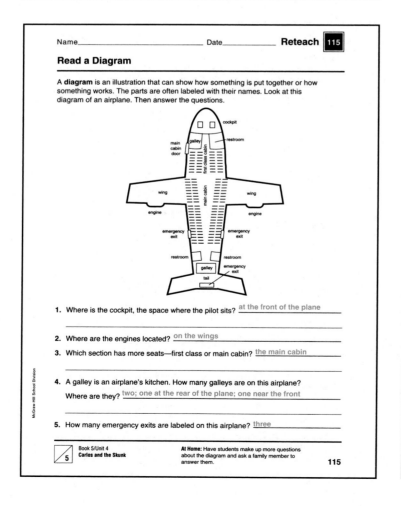

1. Where is the cockpit, the space where the pilot sits? _at the front of the plane_

2. Where are the engines located? _on the wings_

3. Which section has more seats—first class or main cabin? _the main cabin_

4. A galley is an airplane's kitchen. How many galleys are on this airplane? Where are they? _two; one at the rear of the plane; one near the front_

5. How many emergency exits are labeled on this airplane? _three_

Book 5/Unit 4
**Carlos and the Skunk** 5

**At Home:** Have students make up more questions about the diagram and ask a family member to answer them.

115

---

## Judgments and Decisions

> You make **judgments** about how characters act in a story. Using these judgements can help you make **decisions** about the story and its characters. You should be able to give reasons for the judgments and decisions you make.

Here are some decisions Carlos and Gloria made in "Carlos and the Skunk." For each decision, write YES or NO to tell whether or not you agree with it.
_Answers will vary._

1. Gloria warns Carlos not to believe everything that he hears. _Yes_
2. Carlos decides that he will impress Gloria if he can catch the skunk. _Yes_
3. Carlos washes out his clothing in the river to try and get rid of the odor. _Yes_
4. When he gets home, Carlos leaves his shoes outside of the house. _Yes_
5. Carlos forgets to clean his shoes and wears them to church. _Yes_
6. Gloria calls to him as he leaves the church. _Yes_

Share your judgments about each story character by answering the questions. Give reasons for your answers.

7. Would you like to have Carlos as a friend? _Possible answer: Yes. He is a nice_ _person. Even though he is trying to impress Gloria, he is trying to do the right_ _thing._

8. Would you ask Gloria for advice or Carlos? Why? _Possible answer: Gloria._ _She seems to be a much more logical and practical thinker._

9. Would you ask Carlos for help if you wanted to catch a skunk? _Possible answer:_ _No. Since Carlos had such a bad experience, he probably would not be a_ _good person to ask._

116

**At Home:** Have students make a judgment about an action they observe at home. Ask them to give reasons for their judgment.

Book 5/Unit 4
**Carlos and the Skunk** 9

# Carlos and the Skunk • RETEACH

## Draw Conclusions

> Sometimes stories don't tell you all information directly. You have to **draw conclusions** about characters or situations from clues given in the story. You can also use experiences from your own life to help you draw conclusions.

Read each of the stories. Then circle the letter next to the conclusion you can draw from the information provided. Remember to think about your own experience as you read the stories.

1. Susanna has read six books written about time travel. She's also written a story for a magazine called "Imaginary Journeys."

   (a.) Susanna enjoys fantasy stories.

   b. Susanna is ten years old.

2. Cameron wants to go to swimming camp next summer. He signed up for an extra day of newspaper delivery to make more money to pay for camp. Also, he's working for the neighbors doing odd jobs.

   a. Cameron is a good swimmer.

   (b.) Cameron wants to go to swimming camp very badly.

3. In Meghan's classroom, the walls are covered with green stripes. The paintings are framed with green paper. The teacher gave each student a green pencil at the beginning of the year.

   a. There are a lot of paintings in Meghan's classroom.

   (b.) Meghan's teacher likes the color green.

4. Zach described the giant mouse. He said it could talk and was dressed in fancy velvet clothes. Zach explained that the mouse could play the violin.

   (a.) Zach has probably made up the giant mouse.

   b. Zach knows something about mice that the rest of us don't.

Book 5/Unit 4
**Carlos and the Skunk**
4

**At Home:** Have students draw a conclusion about the kind of day someone else has had. Ask them to tell what information they used to draw their conclusion.

117

---

## Suffixes

> **Suffixes** are word parts added to the ends of base words to change their meanings or their parts of speech. The suffix *-less* means "without." The suffix *-able* means "able to be" or "to cause to be."

Circle the suffix *-less* or *-able* in each word. Think about the meanings of the base word and the suffix. Then write a meaning for the whole word.

1. end(less)      without end; going on forever
2. care(less)      without care; not careful
3. meaning(less)      without meaning
4. comfort(able)      able to be with comfort
5. worth(less)      without worth; not important
6. reach(able)      able to be reached

Now write a word from above to complete each sentence.

7. The sparkling stones were really glass, so the necklace that looked so valuable was actually __worthless__ .

8. She went camping and was not __reachable__ by phone.

9. The ship had very __comfortable__ cabins.

10. In June, summer vacation seemed like an __endless__ adventure, but the children soon became bored and missed going to school.

11. Malik apologized for teasing his sister, but the apology was not sincere so it felt __meaningless__ .

12. Leaving her new bike out in the rain was a __careless__ act.

118

**At Home:** Ask students to add *-less* to weight, joy and harm and to use the new words in sentences.

Book 5/Unit 4
**Carlos and the Skunk**
12

## Extend 112

Name_____ Date_____

### Judgments and Decisions

When you make a **decision** about something, you choose a course of action. For example, you might make a decision about whether or not to go to a certain movie. When you make a **judgment**, you apply a value to something. For example, you might describe the movie as the best or worst you ever saw.

For each sentence below, tell whether the person is making a decision or a judgment.

1. Ronda chose to wear the blue pants instead of the brown skirt. _decision_

2. The Cooper family decided to go to the New Jersey Shore for their family vacation. _decision_

3. Jeremy likes watching baseball on television more than watching basketball. _judgment_

4. Both Lee and Roy thought the game was the most exciting one they had ever seen. _judgment_

5. After careful consideration, Miles decided to join the choir on Wednesday night instead of taking flute lessons. _decision_

6. Keisha thought that her classmates were being unfair about choosing parts for the play. _judgment_

Think of a character from a story you've read who faced a problem that required him or her to make certain judgments. What decisions did the character come to based on his or her judgments? Write your answers on the lines below. If you need to, you can use a separate sheet of paper.

_____
_____
_____

Book 5/Unit 4
**Carlos and the Skunk**

**At Home:** Take a group vote of your favorite television programs for the evening. Then decide which ones you will watch.

112

---

## Extend 113

Name_____ Date_____

### Vocabulary

| nestled | peculiar | stunned |
| tortillas | unbearable | unpleasant |

Suppose that Carlos writes about the things that happen to him each day in a journal. Write a journal entry for the day that Carlos encountered the skunk. Use as many of the vocabulary words in the box as you can.

_Answers will vary but should be written in correct context and with correct parts of speech._

_____
_____
_____

## Extend 114

### Story Comprehension

The main character of "Carlos and the Skunk" is a boy named Carlos. His best friend is a girl named Gloria, but the story doesn't give many details about her. What inferences can you make about what Gloria is like? Reread the parts of the story where Gloria is mentioned. Write a description of Gloria.

_Answers will vary. Students may say that Gloria is wiser about the ways of skunks than Carlos. She laughs when she tells him not to believe everything he has heard, so she probably also laughs when the skunk sprays Carlos. But she must also be sympathetic to Carlos, since they are still good friends at the end of the story._

_____
_____

**At Home:** Talk about animals you see around your home or the home of a friend or relative. What do they do when they meet up with a person? Has anyone in your family ever encountered a skunk?

113–114

Book 5/Unit 4
**Carlos and the Skunk**

---

## Extend 115

Name_____ Date_____

### Read a Diagram

A **diagram** is a drawing that shows how something is put together, or how something works. Diagrams usually have labels that name the parts.

The diagram below shows the floor plan of a castle. Study the diagram, then answer the questions.

1. If you could not leave the castle through the main gate, how else could you get out? _by the secret passage that leaves from the Queen's Tower_

2. In what direction does the main gate face? How do you know? _It faces north. You can tell the direction from the West and East towers._

3. To what other parts of the castle does the king's chamber lead? _the Great Hall, the Guards' Quarters, and the Stable._

4. Write a paragraph describing an afternoon visit to this castle. Use the diagram to describe what happens during your visit. _Answers will vary. For instance, a student might first enter through the big walls of the Main Gate; view the countryside from the West Tower; see the Queen's beautiful horses in the Stables; eat lunch at a banquet table in the Great Hall._

Book 5/Unit 4
**Carlos and The Skunk**

**At Home:** Make a diagram of the floor plan of your home. Label the parts.

115

---

## Extend 116

Name_____ Date_____

### Judgments and Decisions

People make **judgments** and **decisions** about the events that happen in their lives. Read each passage from "Carlos and the Skunk" below. Then answer each question. Use examples in the stories to back up your reasons.

1. Carlos wants to impress Gloria so he tries to get as close as he can to the skunk. Do you think this a good idea? Do you think Gloria will be impressed?
   _Answers will vary._

2. Several families began heading for the door. The priest dismissed the service early. Why do you think the priest decided to end the service early?
   _Answers will vary._

3. Carlos's father tells Carlos at dinner that it is time for a new pair of shoes. Do you think this was a good way for Carlos's father to handle the situation? Why or why not?
   _Answers will vary._

4. At the end of the story, do you think Carlos made the right decision when he told his father that he did not want to try and catch the skunk? Why or why not?
   _Answers will vary._

**At Home:** What are some animals you should be careful around? Tell what to do if you see one.

116

Book 5/Unit 4
**Carlos and the Skunk**

---

# Carlos and the Skunk • EXTEND

## Draw Conclusions

When you read fiction, you can use clues and facts from the story to **draw conclusions** about characters' feelings and what the characters are like. In the story "Carlos and the Skunk," Carlos and Gloria have been good friends since they were very young. You could draw the conclusion that they will continue to be friends for a long time.

The chart below lists some events from the story. Write a sentence that shows a conclusion you might make about the personality or feeling of the character described.

| Story Events | Conclusion About the Character |
|---|---|
| **1.** Gloria feared that the skunk would spray her if she got to close to it. | Gloria _Possible answer: is careful and doesn't like to upset things._ |
| **2.** Carlos hesitated, then winked at Gloria before he reached out and grabbed the tail. | Carlos _Possible answer: likes to play and wants to show off a bit._ |
| **3.** "Carlos, you look very nice for church this morning," said his mother. | Carlos's mother _Possible answer: is a kind, thoughtful person._ |
| **4.** "Carlos, I've noticed your shoes are looking a little small," said Papa with a glance toward Mama. | Papa _Possible answer: is tactful. He knows how Carlos is feeling and wants him to feel better._ |

**At Home:** Choose one character from the story. Create a list of words that describe the personality of that character.

---

## Suffixes

A **suffix** is a word part added to the end of a word. A suffix can change the meaning of a word. For example, *adapt* means "to adjust." When the suffix *–able* is added, the new word, *adaptable*, means "capable to adjust." The suffix *–less* means "without." *Shoeless* means "without shoes."

Use the suffix *-able* or *-less* to change the meaning of each word below. Then write sentences using the words you created.

**1.** like _able_____ Sentences will vary.

**2.** move _able_____ Sentences will vary.

**3.** fear _less_____ Sentences will vary.

**4.** tire _less_____ Sentences will vary.

**5.** bear _able_____ Sentences will vary.

**6.** care _less_____ Sentences will vary.

**At Home:** The suffix *-ton* is added to the names of many towns. Look on a map to find towns that end in *-ton* in your state.

**T11**

# Carlos and the Skunk • GRAMMAR

## Adjectives

- An **adjective** is a word that describes a noun and tells *what kind* or *how many*.
- An adjective can come after the noun it describes. The noun and the adjective are connected by a linking verb.

Complete each of the following sentences with one of the adjectives from the box.

| doubting | strange | unbearable | shiny | foolish |
|----------|---------|------------|-------|---------|
| uneasy | one | best | adobe | striped |

1. Carlos and Gloria played in the garden where _____ shiny _____ chiles grew.

2. The children lived in thick-walled _____ adobe _____ homes.

3. In just _____ one _____ year, Carlos had grown several inches.

4. Dos Dedos had a _____ striped _____ tail.

5. Gloria thought that Carlos was _____ foolish _____ .

6. The _____ doubting _____ girl told him not to believe everything he heard.

7. The smell of Carlos's clothes was _____ unbearable _____ .

8. Carlos wore his _____ best _____ shirt and pants to church.

9. He felt _____ uneasy _____ when Mama asked him where his shoes were.

10. People in the church made _____ strange _____ faces and held their noses.

**Extension:** Have students write eight sentences about an embarrassing incident they have experienced. Ask them to include at least six adjectives and to circle each one.

---

## Demonstrative Adjectives

- A **demonstrative adjective** tells *which one*.
- Use *this* and *that* with singular nouns. Use *these* and *those* with plural nouns.
- *This* and *these* refer to nouns that are nearby; *that* and *those* refer to nouns that are farther away.

Read each sentence. Rewrite it using the correct form of the demonstrative adjective.

1. Carlos thought, "I wonder if this tomatoes are ripe."
   Carlos thought, "I wonder if these tomatoes are ripe."

2. "What is those?" Gloria yelled suddenly and pointed to a skunk.
   "What is that?" Gloria yelled suddenly and pointed to a skunk.

3. Carlos said, "These is the biggest skunk I ever saw."
   Carlos said, "This is the biggest skunk I ever saw."

4. He said, "I will catch these animal."
   He said, "I will catch this animal."

5. "Those is a bad idea," said Gloria.
   "That is a bad idea," said Gloria.

6. She watched the skunk spray Carlos and said, "These is a boy in trouble."
   She watched the skunk spray Carlos and said, "This is a boy in trouble."

7. Carlos said, "This shoes smell really bad."
   Carlos said, "These shoes smell really bad."

8. His friend said, "That pants are ruined, too."
   His friend said, "Those pants are ruined, too."

9. Mama ordered, "Get rid of these striped creature!"
   Mama ordered, "Get rid of that striped creature!"

10. Carlos nodded, "These is a smelly pest."
    Carlos nodded, "This is a smelly pest."

---

## Adjectives

- An **adjective** is a word that describes a noun and tells *what kind* or *how many*.
- An adjective can come after the noun it describes. The noun and the adjective are connected by a linking verb.
- A **demonstrative adjective** tells *which* one.
- Use *this* and *that* with singular nouns. Use *these* and *those* with plural nouns.
- *This* and *these* refer to nouns that are nearby. *That* and *those* refer to nouns that are farther away.

Underline each adjective that is connected to a noun by a linking verb. Circle each linking verb. Then write the noun it describes on the line.

1. Jan Romero Stevens's books about Carlos (are) wonderful. _____ books _____

2. *Carlos and the Squash Plant* (was) first.
   _____ Carlos and the Squash Plant _____

3. The Carlos series (has been) popular. _____ series _____

4. The books (are) amusing. _____ books _____

5. Their southwest setting (is) interesting. _____ setting _____

Read each sentence. Write the correct demonstrative adjective—*this, that, these,* or *those*—in each blank space.

6. _____ This _____ book here is my favorite.

7. _____ Those _____ books by the window are Pap's.

8. I wish there were more books to read like _____ these _____ Carlos books here.

9. I like _____ that _____ one over there.

10. Would you please bring me _____ that _____ one from the shelf?

**Extension:** Have students write a description of a favorite animal book. Ask them to include in their writing six examples of adjectives and at least two demonstrative adjectives.

---

## Proper Adjectives

- A proper adjective is formed from a proper noun.
- A proper adjective begins with a capital letter.

Rewrite each sentence. Add the correct proper adjective for each underlined proper noun. Use the dictionary for help with spelling.

1. The Carlos series was written by an <u>America</u> author.
   The Carlos series was written by an American author.

2. The books often tell about <u>Mexico</u> food.
   The books often tell about Mexican food.

3. Many foods mentioned in the books are used in <u>Italy</u> recipes.
   Many foods mentioned in the books are used in Italian recipes.

4. <u>Rome</u> cooks use tomatoes to make fine sauces.
   Roman cooks use tomatoes to make fine sauces.

5. Tomatoes are popular in <u>Greece</u> dishes, too.
   Tomatoes are popular in Greek dishes, too.

6. <u>Spain</u> people also enjoy tomatoes.
   Spanish people also enjoy tomatoes.

7. Spicy foods are liked by <u>China</u> diners and by diners in Mexico.
   Spicy foods are liked by Chinese diners and by diners in Mexico.

8. Many <u>Africa</u> recipes also use spices.
   Many African recipes also use spices.

9. <u>France</u> cooks use spices, too.
   French cooks use spices, too.

10. Spicy foods are even found in <u>England</u> restaurants.
    Spicy foods are even found in English restaurants.

**Extension:** Have students write an article for a travel magazine in which they describe scenic places, food, and people in other countries. Tell them to use at least five examples of proper adjectives.

# Carlos and the Skunk • GRAMMAR

## Adjectives

Add adjectives to the following sentences. Answers will vary

1. Carlos and Gloria have always been _____ friends.

2. They spend hours playing in their _____ garden.

3. One day, they discovered a _____ skunk.

4. _____ Carlos decided to catch the animal.

5. The _____ skunk sprayed Carlos from head to toe.

6. The odor was _____.

7. Carlos ran to the _____ river and jumped in.

8. He scrubbed and scrubbed himself and his _____ clothes.

9. He left his _____ shoes outside the door

10. Mama asked, "What is that _____ odor?"

11. The next day in church, something _____ happened.

12. Carlos felt _____ when he realized his shoes made the whole church smell.

13. "I think that Carlos's shoes are too _____," said Papa.

14. Papa bought Carlos a _____ pair of boots.

15. That night, Carlos ate _____ tortillas for dinner.

McGraw-Hill School Division

## Adjectives

- An **adjective** is a word that describes a noun and tells *what kind* or *how many*.
- An adjective can come after the noun it describes. The noun and the adjective are connected by a linking verb.
- A **demonstrative adjective** tells which one.
- Use *this* and *that* with singular nouns. Use *these* and *those* with plural nouns.
- *This* and *these* refer to nouns that are nearby. *That* and *those* refer to nouns that are farther away.

### Mechanics

- A proper adjective is formed from a proper noun.
- A proper adjective begins with a capital letter.

Use the following adjectives to help you write a paragraph about Carlos. Then draw a scene from your story below.

| nervous   black   spicy   smelly   troubled   tall   funny   best |

_____

_____

_____

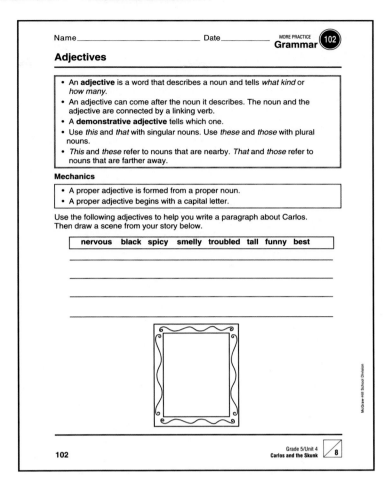

McGraw-Hill School Division

**T13**

# Carlos and the Skunk • SPELLING

## Page 97

Name_____ Date_____ **Spelling 97**

### Words with /ô/ and /ôr/

**Pretest Directions**

Fold back the paper along the dotted line. Use the blanks to write each word as it is read aloud. When you finish the test, unfold the paper. Use the list at the right to correct any spelling mistakes. Practice the words you missed for the Posttest.

**To Parents**

Here are the results of your child's weekly spelling Pretest. You can help your child study for the Posttest by following these simple steps for each word on the word list:

1. Read the word to your child.

2. Have your child write the word, saying each letter as it is written.

3. Say each letter of the word as your child checks the spelling.

4. If a mistake has been made, have your child read each letter of the correctly spelled word aloud, and then repeat steps 1–3.

1. _____ 1. forward
2. _____ 2. course
3. _____ 3. audience
4. _____ 4. aboard
5. _____ 5. bore
6. _____ 6. fawn
7. _____ 7. install
8. _____ 8. longing
9. _____ 9. performing
10. _____ 10. astronaut
11. _____ 11. soar
12. _____ 12. chore
13. _____ 13. withdraw
14. _____ 14. wallpaper
15. _____ 15. coffee
16. _____ 16. border
17. _____ 17. source
18. _____ 18. applaud
19. _____ 19. coarse
20. _____ 20. forecast

**Challenge Words**

_____ nestled
_____ peculiar
_____ stunned
_____ unbearable
_____ unpleasant

Grade 5/Unit 4
Carlos and the Skunk
20

97

## Page 98

Name_____ Date_____ **Spelling 98**

### Words with /ô/ and /ôr/

**Using the Word Study Steps**

1. LOOK at the word.
2. SAY the word aloud.
3. STUDY the letters in the word.
4. WRITE the word.
5. CHECK the word.
   Did you spell the word right?
   If not, go back to step 1.

**Spelling Tip**

Homophones are words that sound alike but are spelled differently and have different meanings. Learn the meanings of common homophones to help you choose the ones you want. For example:

**course** (route) **coarse** (rough)
**sore** (painful) **soar** (fly)

**Hidden in Plain Sight**

Circle each of the spelling words in this puzzle.

```
withdrawbrechoresoartodinstallforecastezrs
wallpapertihaudiencendforwardborderborelm
performingtymcoursenisourcefaboardfawnz
alongingpcoffeeastronautitysecoarsenthoun
applaudabcnkfghitranwilaofngroychentrsuvx
```

**To Parents or Helpers:**

Using the Word Study Steps above as your child comes across any new words will help him or her spell words effectively. Review the steps as you both go over this week's spelling words.

Go over the Spelling Tip with your child. Help your child list and define other homophones, such as **bore** and **boar**.

Help your child complete the spelling activity by finding the spelling words in the puzzle.

98

Grade 5/Unit 4
Carlos and the Skunk
20

## Page 99

Name_____ Date_____ **Spelling 99**

### Words with /ô/ and /ôr/

| | | | | |
|---|---|---|---|---|
| forward | bore | performing | withdraw | source |
| course | fawn | astronaut | wallpaper | applaud |
| audience | install | soar | coffee | coarse |
| aboard | longing | chore | border | forecast |

Sort each spelling word by finding the sound and spelling pattern to which it belongs. Write the spelling words with the /ô/ sound spelled:

**au**

1. audience
2. astronaut
3. applaud

**aw**

4. fawn
5. withdraw

**a**

6. install
7. wallpaper

**o**

8. longing
9. coffee

Write the spelling words with the /ôr/ sound spelled:

**or**

10. forward
11. performing
12. border

**our**

13. course
14. source

**oar**

15. aboard
16. soar
17. coarse

**ore**

18. bore
19. chore
20. forecast

Grade 5/Unit 4
Carlos and the Skunk
20

99

## Page 100

Name_____ Date_____ **Spelling 100**

### Words with /ô/ and /ôr/

| | | | | |
|---|---|---|---|---|
| forward | bore | performing | withdraw | source |
| course | fawn | astronaut | wallpaper | applaud |
| audience | install | soar | coffee | coarse |
| aboard | longing | chore | border | forecast |

**We Go Together**

Write the spelling word that matches each clue below.

1. clap — applaud
2. put in — install
3. predict — forecast
4. listeners — audience
5. task — chore
6. draw back — withdraw
7. fly high — soar

8. rough — coarse
9. edge or rim — border
10. make a hole — bore
11. deer — fawn
12. acting — performing
13. craving — longing
14. onward — forward

Write a sentence using each of the spelling words below.

15. aboard _____
16. course _____
17. astronaut _____
18. wallpaper _____
19. coffee _____
20. source _____

100

**Challenge Extension:** Have students write fill-in sentences for each Challenge Word. Then have each student exchange his/her sentences with a partner and try to fill them in correctly.

Grade 5/Unit 4
Carlos and the Skunk
20

# Carlos and the Skunk • SPELLING

## Words with /ô/ and /ôr/

### Proofreading Activity

Find the six spelling errors in the diary entry below. Circle each incorrectly spelled word. Write the words correctly on the lines below.

Gloria and I had a great time at the pet show. We saw a preforming dog named Pepe. Pepe walked foreward on his hind legs. Then he climbed abored a toy rocket. You should have seen that rocket sore! The audiense loved Pepe. His dancing made everyone aplaud.

1. performing
2. forward
3. aboard
4. soar
5. audience
6. applaud

### Writing Activity

Imagine having Pepe for a pet. Write a paragraph about what you and Pepe might do together. Use four words from the spelling list.

_____

_____

_____

_____

_____

## Words with /ô/ and /ôr/

Look at the words in each set below. One word in each set is spelled correctly. Use a pencil to fill in the circle next to the correct word. Before you begin, look at the sample sets of words. Sample A has been done for you. Do Sample B by yourself. When you are sure you know what to do, you may go on with the rest of the page.

**Sample A:**
- (A) exploar
- (B) exploir
- (C) explor
- (D) explore ●

**Sample B:**
- (A) craul
- (B) crual
- (C) crawl ●
- (D) crall

1.
- (A) fourcast
- (B) foarecast
- (C) forcast
- (D) forecast ●

2.
- (E) applawd
- (F) applad
- (G) applaud ●
- (H) applod

3.
- (A) coarse ●
- (B) corse
- (C) corrse
- (D) corese

4.
- (E) caffee
- (F) coffee ●
- (G) cauffee
- (H) cawffee

5.
- (A) source ●
- (B) sorce
- (C) soarce
- (D) sorece

6.
- (E) bourder
- (F) bauder
- (G) border ●
- (H) boreder

7.
- (A) waullpaper
- (B) wallpaper ●
- (C) wawllpaper
- (D) wollpaper

8.
- (E) withdrauw
- (F) withdrow
- (G) withdra
- (H) withdraw ●

9.
- (A) choare
- (B) chore ●
- (C) choure
- (D) chor

10.
- (E) sor
- (F) sawr
- (G) soar ●
- (H) saor

11.
- (A) astronawt
- (B) astronat
- (C) astronaut ●
- (D) astronot

12.
- (E) longing ●
- (F) lawnging
- (G) launging
- (H) langing

13.
- (A) faun
- (B) fawn ●
- (C) fon
- (D) fawne

14.
- (E) instaull
- (F) instawll
- (G) install ●
- (H) instoll

15.
- (A) perfurmance
- (B) perfoarmance
- (C) perforemance
- (D) performance ●

16.
- (E) bore ●
- (F) bor
- (G) boure
- (H) boare

17.
- (A) abord
- (B) aboard ●
- (C) abourd
- (D) abored

18.
- (E) awdience
- (F) adience
- (G) audience ●
- (H) oudience

19.
- (A) course ●
- (B) corse
- (C) corrse
- (D) corese

20.
- (E) fourward
- (F) foarward
- (G) foreward
- (H) forward ●

**T15**

# How to Think Like a Scientist • PRACTICE

**Important & Unimportant Information**

Nonfiction writing includes **important** information that supports the main idea. There is also **unimportant** information that makes the selection interesting or fun to read, but may not directly support the main idea.

Read the paragraph below. Decide what information is important and what information is unimportant. Write **I** next to the sentence if the information is important, and **U** next to the sentence if the information is unimportant.

Watching too much television can be dangerous for your health. There are good programs on television, but watching too much television is not good for anyone. The average fifth grader in North America watches 25 hours of television a week. That's at least three and a half hours a day spent sitting in front of a television instead of doing something productive. Children could spend more time actively doing things to develop their minds and bodies. Besides watching television, they can do things such as playing baseball or another sport, playing an instrument, walking, dancing, working on a science project, or reading. Being physically active helps keep weight down and muscles strong. Taking part in team sports teaches the important skill of interacting with others.

__I__ 1. Watching too much television can be dangerous for your health.

__U__ 2. There are good programs on television.

__I__ 3. Children need to spend more time actively doing things to develop their minds and their bodies.

__I__ 4. Being active in body and mind is healthier than sitting and watching television.

__U__ 5. Children can do many things besides watching television, such as playing baseball or another sport, playing an instrument, walking, dancing, working on a science project, or reading.

5 Book 5/Unit 4
How to Think Like a Scientist
**At Home:** Have students create a list of activities that they can do instead of watching television.
**119**

---

**Vocabulary**

Label each sentence **True** or **False**. If a sentence is false, write the correct definition of the word in italics.

1. If you think carefully before answering a question, you are answering *automatically*.
   __False__ ___Automatically means you answer without thought.___

2. Things you see and take note of are *observations*. __True__

3. If you get many *assignments* in different subjects you have a lot of homework to do.
   __True__

4. Crossing a busy street *carelessly* is not dangerous. __False__
   ___If you carelessly cross a busy street, you could get hit by a car.___

5. If you ride your bike to school every day, then you don't *normally* take the school bus or walk there. __True__

6. If you drove carefully and slowly up a winding mountain road, you would have *swerved* often. __False__ ___Swerve means to turn aside suddenly, so if you___ ___are driving slowly and carefully, you should not have to swerve.___

**120** **At Home:** Have students use each of the vocabulary words in a sentence.
Book 5/Unit 4
How to Think Like a Scientist
6

---

# Stay Alert!

Every Wednesday at two o'clock, Ms. Yee *automatically* hands out homework. She gives us *assignments* for four subjects: math, English, social studies, and earth sciences. *Normally* I am the first student to get any handouts because I sit right next to her desk.

This time, however, Ms. Yee *swerved* around my desk and went directly to the back of the room. When she was finished, she asked us if we had noticed anything different about the way she had handed out the homework today. A few of us remarked that she had begun at the back of the room, which was unusual.

"Good." said Ms. Yee. "I want you all to get into the habit of making *observations* about things. Lately, some of you have been working *carelessly*—you need to pay closer attention to your work."

1. What does it mean to do something *automatically*? _____
   It means to do it without having to think about it.

2. What is a word that means "tasks or jobs that have been given out"? assignments

3. What is another word for "usually"? normally

4. What does it mean to make *observations*? It means to see or notice things.

5. Ms. Yee *swerved* around the student's desk at the front and went directly to the back of the room. Why did she do this? She wanted to do something that she didn't usually do to see if the students noticed. She did this to help the students learn to make observations about what is happening around them.

5 Book 5/Unit 4
How to Think Like a Scientist
**At Home:** Have students write about some observations they have made at school.
**120a**

---

**Story Comprehension**

The author of "How to Think Like a Scientist" asks questions for which there are correct answers and then offers reasons for why people give incorrect answers. Use what you learned in "How to Think Like a Scientist" to complete the chart below. Begin by stating the question asked in the beginning of the three sections listed below.

| Question | Correct Answer | Reason for Incorrect Answer |
|---|---|---|
| Watching the Murphys: 1. Is someone stealing something from the Murphys? | 2. yes | 3. incorrectly using information from an observation |
| The Zoo Comes to the Classroom: 4. What kind of fish is in the bowl? | 5. guppies | 6. relying too much on an another person's knowledge |
| The Math Assignment: 7. Is Ms. Wilson going to collect the math assignment on Monday morning? | 8. yes | 9. basing answer on wishful thinking |

10. What was the author's purpose for writing "How to Think Like a Scientist"? _____
    to show some common mistakes that people make when answering questions

**121** **At Home:** Have students retell the story and explain why people sometimes give incorrect answers.
Book 5/Unit 4
How to Think Like a Scientist
10

# How to Think Like a Scientist • PRACTICE

## Use an Outline

Using an **outline** can help you to group facts and organize information. In an outline, a Roman numeral is placed before each main idea. Beneath that, capital letters organize the important facts that support the main idea. Study this section of an outline. Then answer the questions below. Answers may vary.

III. Women Pilots in the Thirties
  A. Beryl Markham survives crash on Cape Breton.
  B. Jean Batten sets record for South Atlantic flight.
  C. Louise Thaden wins Bendix Trophy in 1936.
  D. Amelia Earhart makes last flight, 1937.

1. Which section of the outline is presented here? the third section

2. What is the main idea of this section? How do you know what it is about? The main idea is about women pilots in the 1930s; I can tell because it is written next to a Roman numeral.

3. What sort of information follows the capital letters? facts that support the main idea

4. If you found out about another woman pilot in the 1930s, how would you include her in the outline? Explain. I would add another capital letter (E) to this section and put the information about her there or if she was in the early 1930s, put her in the correct place chronologically and reorder the entries.

5. How could you use an outline to help you study a textbook to prepare for a test? I could make an outline of each chapter in the textbook to find the main ideas and supporting facts.

Book 5/Unit 4
5 How to Think Like a Scientist

**At Home:** Encourage students to explain how they would use an outline for their next research report.

122

---

## Important & Unimportant Information

In "How to Think Like A Scientist," the **important information** supports the main idea of the article, which is how to answer questions correctly.

Place a ✓ next to each sentence that states important information from "How to Think Like A Scientist." You may look back at the story for help.

✓ 1. You must use information carefully to answer a question correctly.

_____ 2. Ralphie really did see men taking things out of the Murphy's house.

_____ 3. The gastromorph is a dangerous fish that will bite you if you put your hand in the fish bowl.

✓ 4. Don't base your answer on what someone else says.

_____ 5. One girl knew the fish were really guppies because her sister had some at home.

✓ 6. You will probably make mistakes if you depend too much on other people's answers to questions.

✓ 7. Sometimes we choose an answer to a question because it is the answer we like, and that can lead to making the wrong choice.

_____ 8. If a great movie is playing and you have a math assignment due the next morning, it's best to spend the evening at home working on your math.

_____ 9. At class on Monday morning, Pat asked Ms. Wilson how her weekend was, hoping that she'd then forget to ask for the math assignments.

✓ 10. Finding an answer that is correct is more difficult than finding an answer you like.

123

**At Home:** Encourage students to talk about the most important information they learned from reading "How to Think Like a Scientist."

Book 5/Unit 4
How to Think Like a Scientist 10

---

## Draw Conclusions

Since authors don't always tell readers exactly how the characters in a story feel, you must sometimes draw your own conclusions. To **draw a conclusion**, you rely on what you know from personal life experience and story clues.

Read the situation below, and answer each question. Then describe the clues that helped you draw each conclusion.

Andrea and Mario had been working in their grandfather's garden all afternoon. Mario squinted into the sun. It was time for a rest. He slumped down in the shade and wiped his sweaty brow. Then he reached for the water bottle for a cool, refreshing drink. Andrea stopped weeding and joined him under the pear tree. He passed her the cold water bottle from their picnic basket. Andrea quickly gulped down what was left of it. As usual, Mario hadn't left much for her. Andrea went to back to work, while Mario rested.

1. From what you just read, how do you think Andrea and Mario are related? They are either brother and sister or cousins.

2. Story clue: They are working in their grandfather's garden; they know each other's habits.

3. What is the weather like? It is hot and sunny.

4. Story clue: Mario squinted into the sun; he slumped down in the shade to rest; his brow was sweaty.

5. What kind of worker is Andrea? She is a hard worker; she rests for only a short time.

6. Story clue: Andrea goes right back to work; she doesn't rest very long.

Book 5/Unit 4
6 How to Think Like a Scientist

**At Home:** Encourage students to draw conclusions about some stories that they have read.

124

---

## Root Words

You can make a **root word** into another word by adding a prefix or a suffix. For example, the word fresh is the root word for the words refresh and freshness. Knowing the meaning of the root word can help you define unknown words. For example, the word aquarium has a root word aqua that means water. Often root words originally come from the ancient Latin and Greek languages.

| Root Word | Meaning | Language of Origin |
|-----------|---------|--------------------|
| aqua | water | Latin |
| tele | far off | Greek |
| phone | voice, sound | Greek |
| form | shape, form | Latin |

Use the root word chart above to write the root of each word below.

1. aquatic — aqua
2. telescope — tele
3. phonics — phone
4. information — form
5. headphone — phone
6. aquamarine — aqua
7. telephone — tele/phone
8. aquaplane — aqua
9. formula — form
10. microphone — phone
11. aqueduct — aqua
12. misinform — form

Choose four words from above, and write a sentence using each word.

13. Sample answer: I saw the surface of the moon with my new telescope.
14. _____
15. _____
16. _____

125

**At Home:** Have students use a dictionary to look up more root words.

Book 5/Unit 4
How to Think Like a Scientist 16

T17

# How to Think Like a Scientist • RETEACH

## Important and Unimportant Information

Not all the **information** in your reading is equally **important**. Information that helps you understand the main idea is most important. Facts and information that just add detail to the main idea can be **unimportant**.

Read this story. Then write a ✔ next to each sentence below the story that gives important information about the story.

Ernesto was making a model of a school locker with a roll-up door similar to the kind you see on a garage. He planned to paint it red like his real school locker. But Ernesto had a problem. His invention was due in school Wednesday morning at exactly 8:00 A.M. The material he needed to make the sliding door had arrived this morning and today was already Monday! If that wasn't bad enough, the sliding door company hadn't sent enough plastic parts for the sliding door, so now it closed only halfway. What could he do? Suddenly Ernesto had a flash of brilliance. He cut a piece of wood to cover the lower part of the locker's opening. Now the sliding door had to come only partway down the opening, and people could still see how the idea worked. Ernesto just might win the Fifth Annual Invention Contest after all!

1. _____ The invention was due at school at exactly 8:00 A.M.
2. ___✔___ Ernesto had just two days to finish his invention.
3. ___✔___ Ernesto was missing key material to build his invention.
4. ___✔___ The invention was a locker with a roll-up sliding door.
5. _____ Ernesto planned to paint his model locker red.
6. ___✔___ By covering part of the opening, Ernesto completed the locker.
7. ___✔___ Ernesto was able to compete in the Invention Contest after all.
8. _____ This is the fifth year of the Invention Contest.

Book 5/Unit 4
How to Think Like a Scientist
8

At Home: Have students add three unimportant facts to Ernesto's story without changing the important information.

119

## Vocabulary

Read each clue. Then circle the vocabulary word in the row of letters.

| automatically normally | carelessly observations | assignments swerved |
|---|---|---|

1. turned quickly — u b o (s w e r v e d) i p e r d v c
2. tasks — t a y i n w (a s s i g n m e n t s)
3. not carefully — m i l g g y (c a r e l e s s l y) o
4. as usual — a (n o r m a l l y) s s g n l l m t
5. things noticed — c a u o u (o b s e r v a t i o n s)
6. without thinking — s (a u t o m a t i c a l l y) p w z

6

## Story Comprehension

Read each of the two answers below the questions about "How to Think Like a Scientist." Then underline the answer to each question.

1. What reason did Jim's grandfather give for people throwing dead snakes over tree branches in the past?
   They wanted to make it rain.     They wanted to scare away other snakes.

2. What did Ralphie's sister do that led to her mistake about the events at the Murphys' house?
   She believed an expert.     <u>She used the information from her observation incorrectly.</u>

3. What key information did Ralphie provide that should have helped his sister see the situation more clearly?
   The men drove a van.     <u>The men didn't take a television set with them.</u>

4. What mistake did the zookeeper make before his school visit?
   <u>He took the wrong fish.</u>     He tried to trick the students.

5. Why did the girl decide she was wrong about the kind of fish the zookeeper brought?
   She didn't trust her own eyes.     <u>She didn't want to question an expert.</u>

At Home: Have students make their own hidden-word grids for the vocabulary and give them to classmates to solve.

120–121

Book 5/Unit 4
How to Think Like a Scientist
5

## Use an Outline

Suppose you want to write a report about weather. You can use an outline to organize your information before you start writing. An **outline** is one way to show the main ideas in your report.

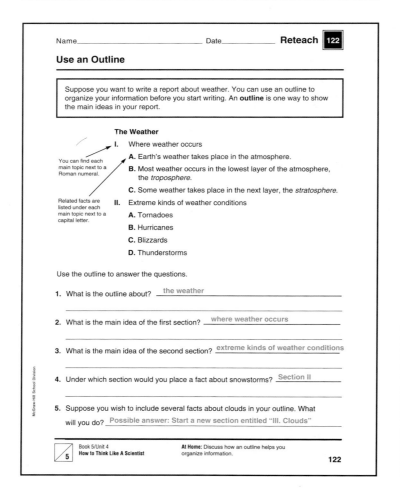

**The Weather**

You can find each main topic next to a Roman numeral.

I. Where weather occurs
   A. Earth's weather takes place in the atmosphere.
   B. Most weather occurs in the lowest layer of the atmosphere, the *troposphere*.
   C. Some weather takes place in the next layer, the *stratosphere*.

Related facts are listed under each main topic next to a capital letter.

II. Extreme kinds of weather conditions
   A. Tornadoes
   B. Hurricanes
   C. Blizzards
   D. Thunderstorms

Use the outline to answer the questions.

1. What is the outline about? ___the weather___

2. What is the main idea of the first section? ___where weather occurs___

3. What is the main idea of the second section? ___extreme kinds of weather conditions___

4. Under which section would you place a fact about snowstorms? ___Section II___

5. Suppose you wish to include several facts about clouds in your outline. What will you do? ___Possible answer: Start a new section entitled "III. Clouds"___

Book 5/Unit 4
How to Think Like A Scientist
5

At Home: Discuss how an outline helps you organize information.

122

## Important and Unimportant Information

**Important information** helps you understand a selection's main idea. **Unimportant information** usually just adds detail to the main idea.

Read the selection. Find the main idea for each paragraph. Then decide if each underlined phrase contains important information or unimportant information. Write important information on lines 1 to 4. Write unimportant information on lines 5 to 8.

There is incredible variety among fish. Some are tiny while others are enormous. Some are brightly colored, and some are very plain. Some live in salt water; some need fresh water.

In spite of these differences, fish share many common features. For example, all fish breathe through gills. These flaps on the side of the fish's head absorb oxygen from the water. Most fish have scales covering their bodies. The scales help fish slide through the water. A few fish have no scales. Catfish are examples of fish without scales. Most fish lay eggs from which baby fish are hatched. Some sharks give birth to fully formed young fish instead.

**Important Information** that supports that main idea.

1. There is incredible variety among fish.
2. Fish share many common features.
3. All fish breathe through gills.
4. Most fish lay eggs.

**Unimportant Information** that only adds detail to the main idea.

5. Some are very plain.
6. Flaps on the side of the head absorb oxygen.
7. The scales help fish slide through the water.
8. Catfish are examples of fish without scales

123

At Home: Have students give three important facts that describe a prized possession to someone who's never seen it.

Book 5/Unit 4
How to Think Like a Scientist
8

# How to Think Like a Scientist • RETEACH

## Draw Conclusions

> **Drawing conclusions** means making decisions based on information. The information can come from clues in your reading or from your own experience.

Read each story. Then circle YES or NO after each sentence to tell whether or not it contains a conclusion that can be drawn from the story. Give at least one clue for each *Yes* answer. Remember to use clues from your own experience.

> Tomás couldn't reach the light switch. He began to cry. Stomping his feet, he tugged furiously on his mother's pant leg until she noticed him. Smiling, his mother scooped Tomás up in her arms. She saw him point at the light switch, so she quickly turned it on.

1. Tomás is a very young child. **(Yes)  No**

   Clues: Possible answers: He can't reach light; he cries in frustration; he
   reaches only to his mother's pant leg; she can carry him.

2. Tomás's mother is impatient with him. **Yes  (No)**

   Clues: (None.)
   _____

> Sweat poured down Shasta's back as she ran across the pavement rippling with heat. It was only 6:00 A.M. Shasta paused briefly. She always took a short break during her workout to help herself regain her strength. Still, she had to get going. She had another 10 miles to run that morning.

3. The story is set in a very cold place. **Yes  (No)**

   Clues: (None.)
   _____

4. Shasta is a serious long-distance runner. **(Yes)  No**

   Clues: Possible answers: She was out jogging at 6:00 A.M; she had a workout
   plan based on experience; she had 10 more miles to run.

---

## Root Words

> A **root word** is a word or word part that forms the core of a longer word. The root word, which often comes from an older language, carries important information about the meaning of the whole word. You can use this information to figure out what a word you don't know means.

The roots *cycl* and *cycle* come from a Greek word that means "wheel, circle, ring." Underline the root in each word on the tree. Then write the word that goes with each definition below. You can use the clues next to the definition to help you figure out the word's meaning.

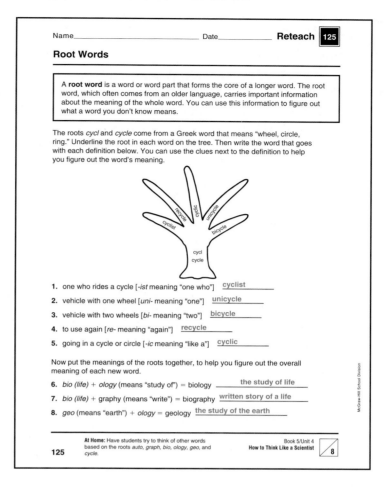

1. one who rides a cycle [-*ist* meaning "one who"]  cyclist

2. vehicle with one wheel [*uni-* meaning "one"]  unicycle

3. vehicle with two wheels [*bi-* meaning "two"]  bicycle

4. to use again [*re-* meaning "again"]  recycle

5. going in a cycle or circle [-*ic* meaning "like a"]  cyclic

Now put the meanings of the roots together, to help you figure out the overall meaning of each new word.

6. *bio (life)* + *ology* (means "study of") = biology  the study of life

7. *bio (life)* + *graphy* (means "write") = biography  written story of a life

8. *geo* (means "earth") + *ology* = geology  the study of the earth

**At Home:** Have students try to think of other words based on the roots *auto, graph, bio, ology, geo,* and *cycle.*
125   Book 5/Unit 4
How to Think Like a Scientist   8

# How to Think Like a Scientist • EXTEND

## Important and Unimportant Information

When you read a selection, you need to recognize the difference between **important and unimportant information**. To do this, you should focus on your purpose for reading the selection.

As you read the selection below, look for information about a snake's "body structure." Write the information about this topic in the column on the left. Write information that is unimportant to the topic in the column on the right.

> Snakes are reptiles. They do not have any limbs, and their bodies are covered with scales. These reptiles come in many different sizes. The South American anaconda, for instance, can grow as long as 27 feet. The thread snake is as small as 5 inches long. Snakes are carnivores, or meat-eating animals. Their jaws are constructed so that they can open very wide. The lower jaw stretches sideways. This helps the snake swallow very large animals. The teeth of the snake curve toward the back of the mouth. This prevents the animal being swallowed from escaping. Other reptiles include lizards, turtles, alligators, and crocodiles.

**Body Structure of Snakes**

| Important Information | Unimportant Information |
|---|---|
| Snakes do not have limbs. Snakes are covered with scales. Snakes' jaws are constructed so that they can open very wide. The lower jaw stretches sideways. A snake's teeth curve toward the back of the mouth. | Snakes are reptiles. They come in many sizes. The South American anaconda can grow to 27 feet. The thread snake is as small as 5 inches long. Snakes are carnivores. Other reptiles include lizards, turtles, alligators, and crocodiles. |

**At Home:** Find a magazine or newspaper article. Decide what the main idea of the article is. List the important information.

---

## Vocabulary

| assignments normally | automatically observations | carelessly swerved |
|---|---|---|

Think about a scientific investigation you have done or read about. Write a paragraph describing the investigation. Use as many of the vocabulary words as you can in your paragraph.

Answers will vary but should include at least four vocabulary words used in the correct context and parts of speech.

## Story Comprehension

A **conclusion** is an opinion or judgment that you make based upon information. Scientists often draw conclusions when they use the scientific method. In "How to Think Like a Scientist," Jim's grandfather said that a person could make it rain by throwing a dead snake over a tree branch.

Suppose you were to try an experiment. Lacking a dead snake, you decide to throw a rubber snake over a tree branch every night for one week. It rains on two days. What conclusion could you draw? On what information is your conclusion based?

Answers will vary. Students may respond that you cannot draw a conclusion because there are other factors involved in the occurrence of rain and because the experiment has no scientific basis.

**At Home:** Look up the word conclusion in a Thesaurus. List other words that have the same meaning.

---

## Use an Outline

If you were asked to write a report about galaxies, how would you organize your information? An **outline** such as the one below would help you get started.

**Galaxies**
I. Definition of a galaxy
   A. a group of stars, gas, and dust that usually rotates around a central core
   B. Most stars are found in galaxies.
   C. The universe contains hundreds of billions of galaxies.
II. The Milky Way
   A. galaxy that contains our Solar System
   B. holds more than 100 billion stars, including our sun
   C. one of the larger galaxies in the universe
III. Types of galaxies
   A. spiral shape
   B. barred-spiral shape
   C. elliptical shape
   D. irregular shape

1. What are the main topics of this outline? How do you know?
   The main topics are a definition of a galaxy, description of the Milky Way, and types of galaxies. These three topics are listed next to the Roman numerals.

2. Where would you place this fact on the outline? **The Milky Way is more than 100 thousand light-years across.**
   in Section II., "the Milky Way"

3. Where would you place facts about spiral galaxies?
   in Section III. A., "types of galaxies—spiral shape"

4. How are outlines organized?
   The main topics are listed next to Roman numerals. The facts for each main topic are listed beneath that topic next to capital letters.

**At Home:** Ask students to find and outline an interesting article in a newspaper or magazine.

---

## Important and Unimportant Information

One way to answer a question is to determine which information is **important** and which is unimportant **information**.

1. The first story in "How to Think Like a Scientist" asks the question, "Is someone stealing from the neighbor's house?" What information does Ralphie use to answer the question? He sees someone in the Murphys' backyard. The person is leaving the house carrying something that is covered. The man goes back into the house. Ralphie thinks that someone is stealing from the house.

2. What information does Ralphie's sister use to answer the question? She sees a TV repair truck and decides that it is a TV repair person going into the Murphys' house.

3. What information is important in determining that the person going into the Murphys' house was a burglar and not a TV repair person? The Johnsons were watching a repairman fix their TV all afternoon, so the person going into the Murphys' house could not have been a repair person.

4. Why is it important to use information carefully? You must be sure that your information is correct and that you have all of the important information that will help you answer a question.

**At Home:** Think of your favorite mystery story. What information in the story is important in solving the mystery?

---

# How to Think Like a Scientist • EXTEND

## Draw Conclusions

The characters in all three stories answer questions by **drawing conclusions**. Choose one story in "How to Think Like a Scientist." Use the drawing conclusions chart to show how the character arrived at his or her conclusion. Make sure you fill in the important information.

**What is the Question?**

Possible Answers: Is someone stealing from the Murphys? What kind of fish is in the bowl? Is Ms. Wilson going to collect the math assignment on Monday?

**Examples of Important Information**    Answers will vary.

| | | |
|---|---|---|
| Someone goes into the Murphys' house and carries out a covered item. | You know what guppies look like. | Ms. Wilson has collected papers late before. |

**Conclusion**

Answers will vary.
The Murphys are being robbed.
The fish in the bowl are guppies.
Ms. Wilson won't collect papers on Monday.

Was the conclusion correct? Explain. Answers will vary.

Yes._____

Yes._____

No._____

**At Home:** The newspaper is missing from your front porch. The neighbor's dog was seen chewing on something. Does the neighbor's dog have your paper? What conclusions do you make?

---

## Root Words

A **root word** is a word part that can be used to build other words. Many modern English words have roots from Greek and Latin. Knowing root words can help you determine the meaning of unknown words. For example, the word *autograph* includes the root word *graph* meaning "write" and the prefix *auto* meaning "self."

| Root Word | Meaning |
|---|---|
| aqua | water |
| graph | write |
| phon | sound, voice |
| act | do |

Study the root chart above, then write the root of each word below.

1. graphic  graph

2. action  act

3. aquarium  aqua

4. photograph  graph

5. telephone  phon

6. react  act

Use the clues below to find a new word. Then write a sentence using the new word.

7. act + or (one who) = actor      That actor has a leading role.
_____

8. sym (together) + phon + y = symphony      We listened to the symphony again.
_____

9. tele (distant) + graph = telegraph      She sent me a telegraph.
_____

10. therm (heat) + o + meter (measure) = thermometer   The thermometer tells how

hot it is outside._____

**At Home:** Look in a newspaper or magazine for words with prefixes and suffixes. Find the root word.

**T21**

# How to Think Like a Scientist • GRAMMAR

## The Articles *A*, *An*, and *The*

- The words *a*, *an*, and *the* are special adjectives called **articles**.
- Use *a* and *an* with singular nouns.
- Use *a* if the next word starts with a consonant sound.
- Use *an* if the next word starts with a vowel sound.

Rewrite each sentence, adding the correct article *a* or *an*.

1. "Someone's stealing television from the Murphys' house."
   "Someone's stealing a television from the Murphys' house."

2. She saw TV repair truck through the front window.
   She saw a TV repair truck through the front window.

3. Ralph saw man go back inside the Murphys' house
   Ralphie saw a man go back inside the Murphys' house.

4. Later we learned that the thieves had stolen violin belonging to Mr. Murphy.
   Later we learned that the thieves had stolen a violin belonging to Mr. Murphy.

5. Repairman was fixing the Johnsons' TV.
   A repairman was fixing the Johnsons' TV.

6. The Murphys' house does not have burglar alarm.
   The Murphys' house does not have a burglar alarm.

7. Ralphie made observation from his sister's room.
   Ralphie made an observation from his sister's room.

8. Your observation was not incorrect one.
   Your observation was not an incorrect one.

9. Having information does not always mean you will answer question correctly.
   Having information does not always mean you will answer a question correctly.

10. Bad information can lead to wrong answer.
    Bad information can lead to a wrong answer.

---

## The Article *The*

- Use *the* with singular nouns that name a particular person, place, or thing.
- Use *the* before all plural nouns.

Read each sentence. Rewrite it, adding the correct article.

1. "Someone's stealing stuff from house across the street."
   "Someone's stealing stuff from the house across the street."

2. "No way! TV repair truck is out front."
   "No way! A TV repair truck is out front."

3. "The men are taking something besides TV."
   "The men are taking something besides the TV."

4. We heard different story from each person.
   We heard a different story from each person.

5. The Johnsons didn't notice what was going on because repairman was fixing their TV.
   The Johnsons didn't notice what was going on because the repairman was fixing their TV.

6. Almost all of neighbors were gone during the day.
   Almost all of the neighbors were gone during the day.

7. Why did two people have different answers to same observations?
   Why did two people have different answers to the same observations?

8. One person assumed TV truck was there for the Murphys' house.
   One person assumed the TV truck was there for the Murphys' house.

9. Other person saw things that were being stolen and knew better.
   The other person saw the things that were being stolen and knew better.

10. When you know information, it does not mean you will get right answer.
    When you know information, it does not mean you will get the right answer.

**Extension:** Ask students to write a story about a person who stops a burglary. When they have finished writing, have them circle all the articles in the story. | 104 | Grade 5/Unit 4
How to Think Like A Scientist: Answering
Questions by the Scientific Method | 10

---

## Articles

- The words *a*, *an*, and *the* are special adjectives called **articles**.
- Use *a* and *an* with singular nouns.
- Use *a* if the next word starts with a consonant sound.
- Use *an* if the next word starts with a vowel sound.
- Use *the* with singular nouns that name a particular person, place, or thing.
- Use *the* before all plural nouns.

Write *a*, *an*, or *the* on the line before each noun. Answers may vary.

1. the students
2. an answer
3. a city
4. a telephone
5. an observation
6. the stories
7. the guppies
8. a screen
9. an iguana
10. an aquarium

Fix each incorrect article in the following sentences. Answers may vary.

11. Are a guppies in that bowl?
    Are the guppies in that bowl?

12. Don't always agree with a opinion of another person.
    Don't always agree with the opinion of another person.

13. We will have an math assignment over the weekend.
    We will have a math assignment over the weekend.

14. There are many things to do instead of a assignment.
    There are many things to do instead of the assignment.

15. Whenever you get a assignment, it's important to get it done on time.
    Whenever you get an assignment, it's important to get it done on time.

---

## Quotations

- Use quotation marks to set off a direct quotation from the rest of the sentence.
- Use a comma before the quotation when the speaker's name comes first.
- Use a comma, a question mark, or an exclamation point to end the quotation when the speaker's name comes last.

Rewrite each sentence. Add quotation marks and commas where needed.

1. Who can name these animals asked the teacher.
   "Who can name these animals?" asked the teacher.

2. I can said Freida.
   "I can," said Freida.

3. What is the name of the lizard asked Ron.
   "What is the name of the lizard?" asked Ron.

4. Freida said That's an iguana.
   Freida said, "That's an iguana."

5. Watch out for the fierce fish said the zookeeper.
   "Watch out for the fierce fish!" said the zookeeper.

6. They will bite anything that moves he continued.
   "They will bite anything that moves," he continued.

7. Angelo asked What is that animal called.
   Angelo asked, "What is that animal called?"

8. That's a mongoose said Libby.
   "That's a mongoose," said Libby.

9. That's right agreed the zookeeper.
   "That's right," agreed the zookeeper.

10. We hope you come back and show us other animals said Jason.
    "We hope you come back and show us other animals," said Jason.

# How to Think Like a Scientist • GRAMMAR

## Articles and Quotation Marks

Add articles to the following sentences. Use quotation marks when needed. Answers may vary.

1. We have assignment due on Monday.
   We have an assignment due on Monday.

2. It's math assignment.
   It's a math assignment.

3. Did you do math assignment, Sam? asked Ralph.
   "Did you do the math assignment, Sam?" asked Ralph.

4. Yes, I also have science experiment due on Monday said Sam.
   "Yes, I also have a science experiment due on Monday," said Sam.

5. Almost everyone turned in assignment.
   Almost everyone turned in the assignment.

6. One boy went to movies instead.
   One boy went to the movies instead.

7. He assumed teacher would forget to collect it.
   He assumed the teacher would forget to collect it.

8. Sometimes people want only particular answer to a question.
   Sometimes people want only a particular answer to a question.

9. One good way to answer questions is to use scientific method.
   One good way to answer questions is to use the scientific method.

10. Good scientists often use experiment to find out answers.
    Good scientists often use an experiment to find out answers.

## Adjectives

- The words *a*, *an*, and *the* are special adjectives called articles.
- Use *a* and *an* with singular nouns.
- Use *a* if the next word starts with a consonant sound.
- Use *an* if the next word starts with a vowel sound.
- Use *the* with singular nouns that name a particular person, place, or thing.
- Use *the* before all plural nouns.

### Mechanics

- Use quotation marks to set off a direct quotation from the rest of the sentence.
- Use a comma before the quotation when the speaker's name comes first.
- Use a comma, a question mark, or an exclamation point to end the quotation when the speaker's name comes last.

Read each sentence aloud to a partner. Have your partner add the correct articles in the appropriate place. Then write the sentences and put commas and quotation marks wherever needed. Answers may vary.

1. Pete ran over snake with his bicycle.
   Pete ran over a snake with his bicycle.

2. Jim said It's probably inner tube.
   Jim said, "It's probably an inner tube."

3. The boys looked in dark for the snake.
   The boys looked in the dark for the snake.

4. Fortunately, they each had flashlight.
   Fortunately, they each had a flashlight.

5. Soon they saw enormous gopher snake.
   Soon they saw an enormous gopher snake.

6. They watched while snake crawled into the bushes.
   They watched while the snake crawled into the bushes.

7. That's rain snake for sure said Jim.
   "That's a rain snake for sure," said Jim.

8. Do you really believe snake could cause rain asked Pete.
   "Do you really believe a snake could cause rain?" asked Pete.

9. If you put it in tree replied Jim.
   "If you put it in a tree," replied Jim.

10. Anyway, my grandpa said big snake would bring rain.
    "Anyway, my grandpa said a big snake would bring rain."

# How to Think Like a Scientist • SPELLING

## Page 103

Name_____ Date_____ **Spelling** `103`

PRETEST

### Words with /är/ and /âr/

**Pretest Directions**

Fold back the paper along the dotted line. Use the blanks to write each word as it is read aloud. When you finish the test, unfold the paper. Use the list at the right to correct any spelling mistakes. Practice the words you missed for the Posttest.

**To Parents**

Here are the results of your child's weekly spelling Pretest. You can help your child study for the Posttest by following these simple steps for each word on the word list:

1. Read the word to your child.
2. Have your child write the word, saying each letter as it is written.
3. Say each letter of the word as your child checks the spelling.
4. If a mistake has been made, have your child read each letter of the correctly spelled word aloud, and then repeat steps 1–3.

1. _____
2. _____
3. _____
4. _____
5. _____
6. _____
7. _____
8. _____
9. _____
10. _____
11. _____
12. _____
13. _____
14. _____
15. _____
16. _____
17. _____
18. _____
19. _____
20. _____

1. cards
2. carve
3. barely
4. stairway
5. remark
6. vary
7. rare
8. airline
9. scar
10. scarce
11. chart
12. square
13. repairman
14. target
15. aquarium
16. barge
17. beware
18. lair
19. artistic
20. regard

**Challenge Words**

_____ assignments
_____ automatically
_____ normally
_____ observations
_____ swerved

Grade 5/Unit 4
How to Think Like a Scientist

`20`     **103**

## Page 104

Name_____ Date_____ **Spelling** `104`

AT-HOME WORD STUDY

### Words with /är/ and /âr/

**Using the Word Study Steps**

1. LOOK at the word.
2. SAY the word aloud.
3. STUDY the letters in the word.
4. WRITE the word.
5. CHECK the word.
   Did you spell the word right? If not, go back to step 1.

**Spelling Tip**

Make up clues to help you remember how a word is spelled. For example, there's a **scar** in **scarce**.

**What Does It Mean?**

Match each clue below with a word from the spelling list.

1. ferry boat ____barge____
2. fix-it man ____repairman____
3. graph ____chart____
4. plane company ____airline____
5. look at ____regard____
6. four-sided figure ____square____
7. good at art ____artistic____
8. home for fish ____aquarium____
9. comment ____remark____
10. game ____cards____

11. scarcely ____barely____
12. warning ____beware____
13. extraordinary ____rare____
14. limited amount ____scarce____
15. change ____vary____
16. den ____lair____
17. bull's-eye ____target____
18. cut ____carve____
19. healed injury ____scar____
20. passageway ____stairway____

**To Parents or Helpers:**

Using the Word Study Steps above as your child comes across any new words will help him or her spell words effectively. Review the steps as you both go over this week's spelling words.

Go over the Spelling Tip with your child. Help your child create clues for the spelling words, based on each word's sound or letters.

Help your child complete the spelling activity by matching the clues with a word from the spelling list.

**104**     Grade 5/Unit 4
How to Think Like a Scientist     `20`

## Page 105

Name_____ Date_____ **Spelling** `105`

EXPLORE THE PATTERN

### Words with /är/ and /âr/

| cards | remark | scar | repairman | beware |
|-------|--------|------|-----------|--------|
| carve | vary | scarce | target | lair |
| barely | rare | chart | aquarium | artistic |
| stairway | airline | square | barge | regard |

This week's spelling words contain /är/ and /âr/. Write each spelling word under the matching spelling. Write the spelling words with the sound /är/ spelled:

**ar**

1. ____cards____
2. ____carve____
3. ____remark____
4. ____scar____
5. ____chart____
6. ____target____
7. ____barge____
8. ____artistic____
9. ____regard____

Write the spelling words with the /âr/ sound spelled:

**are**

10. ____barely____
11. ____rare____
12. ____square____
13. ____beware____

**air**

14. ____stairway____
15. ____airline____
16. ____repairman____
17. ____lair____

**ar**

18. ____vary____
19. ____scarce____
20. ____aquarium____

Grade 5/Unit 4
How to Think Like a Scientist

`20`     **105**

## Page 106

Name_____ Date_____ **Spelling** `106`

PRACTICE AND EXTEND

### Words with /är/ and /âr/

| cards | remark | scar | repairman | beware |
|-------|--------|------|-----------|--------|
| carve | vary | scarce | target | lair |
| barely | rare | chart | aquarium | artistic |
| stairway | airline | square | barge | regard |

**Complete the Sentences**

Complete each sentence with a spelling word.

1. Can you fit a ____square____ peg in a round hole?
2. We called the ____repairman____ to fix the broken oven.
3. I send birthday ____cards____ to my friends.
4. There are many fish swimming in the ____aquarium____.
5. The sign said, "____Beware____ of the tiger."
6. Thank you for the kind ____remark____.
7. The ____airline____ flies around the world.
8. My sister is very ____artistic____; she can paint and draw well.

**Similar Meanings**

Write the spelling word which has the same, or a similar, meaning as the following word or words.

9. cut ____carve____
10. hardly ____barely____
11. staircase ____stairway____
12. change ____vary____
13. unusual ____rare____
14. graph ____chart____

15. goal ____target____
16. boat ____barge____
17. den ____lair____
18. consider ____regard____
19. mark ____scar____
20. hard to find ____scarce____

**Challenge Extension:** Have students scramble the letters in each Challenge Word. Then have students exchange papers with a partner to solve.

**106**     Grade 5/Unit 4
How to Think Like a Scientist     `20`

# How to Think Like a Scientist • SPELLING

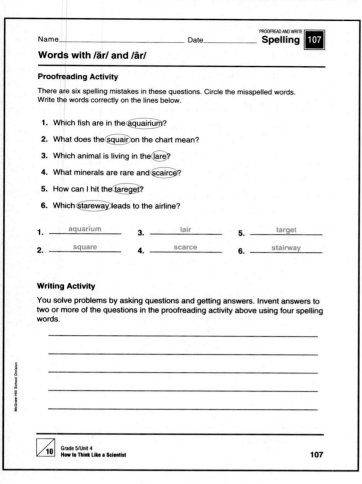

## Words with /är/ and /âr/

### Proofreading Activity

There are six spelling mistakes in these questions. Circle the misspelled words. Write the words correctly on the lines below.

1. Which fish are in the aquairium?
2. What does the squair on the chart mean?
3. Which animal is living in the lare?
4. What minerals are rare and scairce?
5. How can I hit the tareget?
6. Which stareway leads to the airline?

1. _____aquarium_____   3. _____lair_____   5. _____target_____
2. _____square_____   4. _____scarce_____   6. _____stairway_____

### Writing Activity

You solve problems by asking questions and getting answers. Invent answers to two or more of the questions in the proofreading activity above using four spelling words.

_____
_____
_____
_____
_____

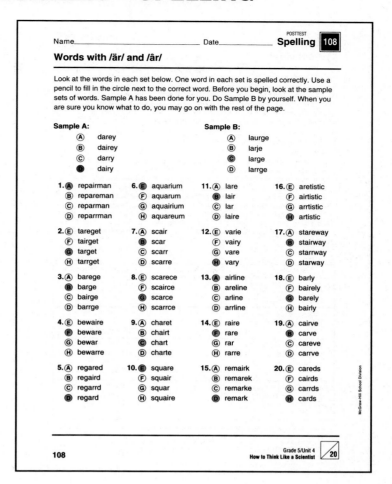

## Words with /är/ and /âr/

Look at the words in each set below. One word in each set is spelled correctly. Use a pencil to fill in the circle next to the correct word. Before you begin, look at the sample sets of words. Sample A has been done for you. Do Sample B by yourself. When you are sure you know what to do, you may go on with the rest of the page.

**Sample A:**
- Ⓐ darey
- Ⓑ dairey
- Ⓒ darry
- ⬤ dairy

**Sample B:**
- Ⓐ laurge
- Ⓑ larje
- ⬤ large
- Ⓓ larrge

1. Ⓐ repairman
   Ⓑ repareman
   Ⓒ reparman
   Ⓓ reparrman

2. Ⓔ tareget
   Ⓕ tairget
   Ⓖ target
   Ⓗ tarrget

3. Ⓐ barege
   Ⓑ barge
   Ⓒ bairge
   Ⓓ barrge

4. Ⓔ bewaire
   Ⓕ beware
   Ⓖ bewar
   Ⓗ bewarre

5. Ⓐ regared
   Ⓑ regaird
   Ⓒ regarrd
   Ⓓ regard

6. Ⓔ aquarium
   Ⓕ aquarum
   Ⓖ aquairium
   Ⓗ aquareum

7. Ⓐ scair
   Ⓑ scar
   Ⓒ scarr
   Ⓓ scarre

8. Ⓔ scarece
   Ⓕ scairce
   Ⓖ scarce
   Ⓗ scarrce

9. Ⓐ charet
   Ⓑ chairt
   Ⓒ chart
   Ⓓ charte

10. Ⓔ square
    Ⓕ squair
    Ⓖ squar
    Ⓗ squaire

11. Ⓐ lare
    Ⓑ lair
    Ⓒ lar
    Ⓓ laire

12. Ⓔ varie
    Ⓕ vairy
    Ⓖ vare
    Ⓗ vary

13. Ⓐ airline
    Ⓑ areline
    Ⓒ arline
    Ⓓ arrline

14. Ⓔ raire
    Ⓕ rare
    Ⓖ rar
    Ⓗ rarre

15. Ⓐ remairk
    Ⓑ remarek
    Ⓒ remarke
    Ⓓ remark

16. Ⓔ aretistic
    Ⓕ airtistic
    Ⓖ arrtistic
    Ⓗ artistic

17. Ⓐ stareway
    Ⓑ stairway
    Ⓒ starrway
    Ⓓ starway

18. Ⓔ barly
    Ⓕ bairely
    Ⓖ barely
    Ⓗ bairly

19. Ⓐ cairve
    Ⓑ carve
    Ⓒ careve
    Ⓓ carrve

20. Ⓔ careds
    Ⓕ cairds
    Ⓖ carrds
    Ⓗ cards

**Annotated Workbooks**

---

Name_____ Date_____ Practice 126

## Fact & Nonfact

A **fact** is a statement that can be proven true using reference books, direct examination, an expert or your own experience. Sometimes a statement that may be true is a **nonfact** because it only expresses the author's personal opinion or the author's experience of a certain event. One way you can sometimes tell the difference between a fact and a nonfact is by asking yourself: *"Could I find this information in a reference book, such as an encyclopedia?"*

Read this letter. Then write whether you think each statement in the chart below is a fact or a nonfact. Explain the reason for your decision.

Dear Zackie,

Yesterday we went to the limestone cliffs. Looking at them, I was amazed how big and beautiful they were. Limestone is a really soft rock that crumbles easily. We found many pictures that people had carved into the cliffs hundreds of years ago. As we looked higher, we saw an eagle's nest perched on the edge of a cliff. The nest seemed as big as a refrigerator. And we saw the eagle. It was awesome! An eagle can have a wingspan of seven and a half feet! It makes you feel really tiny.

When we hiked to the top of the cliffs, our guide pointed out mountain lion tracks in the sand. They looked like the tracks of a big house cat to me. She told us that a full-grown mountain lion can weigh as much as 250 pounds! See you when we get back!

Julio

| Statement | Fact or Nonfact | Explanation of Decision |
|---|---|---|
| 1. Looking at them, I was amazed how big and beautiful they were. | Nonfact | This is the writer's experience or perception. |
| 2. Limestone is a really soft rock that crumbles easily. | Fact | This is the sort of information I might find in a reference book. |
| 3. Eagles can have a wingspan of seven and a half feet! | Fact | I can look this up in a reference book or on the Internet. |
| 4. She told us that a full-grown mountain lion can weigh as much as 250 pounds! | Fact | The guide is an expert and would know the facts. |

4 / Book 5/Unit 4
An Island Scrapbook

**At Home:** Have students write two fact and nonfact statements from an article or movie review.

126

---

Name_____ Date_____ Practice 127

## Vocabulary

Complete each sentence by writing a vocabulary word from the box on each line.

| barrier | emerge | fireball | naturalist | parallel | teeming |
|---|---|---|---|---|---|

1. The railroad tracks run ___parallel___ to each other.

2. The flower garden was ___teeming___ with butterflies of different colors and sizes.

3. Have you ever seen a butterfly ___emerge___ from its cocoon in the warm springtime?

4. The herd of sheep on the road acted as a ___barrier___ to the traffic and the honking cars made a terrible noise.

5. A great ___fireball___ erupted from the volcano and lit up the sky for a great distance.

6. We had a ___naturalist___ as our guide on a field trip to the marshland that was to the north of our town.

127

**At Home:** Have students use each of the vocabulary words in a sentence.

Book 5/Unit 4
An Island Scrapbook / 6

---

## School's Out!

Every Friday afternoon all the students *emerge* from the school doors. Suddenly the whole area is *teeming* with people laughing, running, and talking loudly. The safety monitors form a *barrier* along the sidewalk to keep younger students from wandering onto the driveway. The monitors line up within an arm's length of each other *parallel* to the road. They wear orange safety vests that are as bright as a *fireball*.

A *naturalist* watching this scene might be able to compare the activities to what goes on in a bee hive or ant colony.

1. What is a word that means "to come into view or appear"? ___emerge___

2. What does it mean to be *teeming with people*? ___It means to be full of or abounding with people.___

3. What is a vocabulary word for *obstacle*? ___barrier___

4. How is the word *fireball* used in this story? ___It is used as figurative language; it's a simile showing how bright the orange safety vests are.___

5. Why would a *naturalist* compare the activity at the end of school on Friday to an insect colony? ___Answers will vary. Sample response: A naturalist is interested in studying animal activity and behavior. A naturalist can draw parallels to the teeming of students and the way the monitors organize for safety to the way insects swarm and organize themselves for important tasks.___

5 / Book 5/Unit 4
An Island Scrapbook

**At Home:** Have students use the vocabulary words to write about something a naturalist might see.

127a

---

Name_____ Date_____ Practice 128

## Story Comprehension

Think about what happens in "An Island Scrapbook." Then answer the questions below. For help you may look back at the story.

1. Who is writing this story? Who are the main characters? ___The author is Virginia Wright-Frierson. The main characters seem to be the author and her daughter Amy.___

2. Where does the story take place? ___on a barrier island___

3. How do the author and her daughter spend their days together? ___They spend most of their time outside drawing, painting, and making observations.___

4. Consider the title of this story. How are the handwritten notes pictured in the illustrations different from the writing throughout the rest of the story? ___The handwritten notes are often like lists of facts and exact observations you'd find in a scrapbook, while the rest of the book tends to tell the overall story of what happened during their last week on the island.___

5. At one point in the story the author recalls a storm that happened on the island a few weeks before, when she and Amy were alone in the summer house. What type of storm was it? ___It was a hurricane that passed over the island.___

6. What did they do after the storm happened? ___They went out to explore, to see what damage the hurricane caused, and to take photographs___

7. What types of crafts did Amy make that summer? What materials did she use for her crafts? ___She made picture frames and flower pots using glued-on seashells, windows made of sea glass, a grapevine wreath, a windchime using jingle shells and ark shells.___

8. What was the author's one rule about painting the things she found in nature? ___She could not touch anything she found in nature.___

128

**At Home:** Have students create a craft or describe a gift they'd like to create.

Book 5/Unit 4
An Island Scrapbook / 8

---

**T26** *Annotated Workbooks*

# An Island Scrapbook • PRACTICE

## Use an Observation Chart

Scientists and naturalists use **observation charts** to collect and organize information. Observation charts help them to monitor and track what they are studying.

Use the observation chart to answer the questions below.

1. Which baboon is pregnant? __Lu-Lu__

2. Which baboon is looking after Lu-Lu? __Sunny__

3. Which baboon took the grapefruits? __Sunny__

4. Which baboon is picking fights and taking food from the other baboons? __Alpha__

5. Which baboon is napping a great deal? __Silver__

5 Book 5/Unit 4
An Island Scrapbook

**At Home:** Have students make an observation chart to collect information about what happens at dinner time.

129

---

## Fact & Nonfact

A **fact** is a statement that can be proven true. A **nonfact** is a statement that may be true, but it expresses the author's opinion or personal experience and cannot be proven true.

Each statement below tells of something that happened in "An Island Scrapbook". Write **F** if it is a fact. Write **N** if it is a nonfact. You may look back at the story for help.

__F__ 1. There are two high tides and two low tides every day.

__F__ 2. The forest ground cover provides food and shelter for deer and birds.

__N__ 3. The bright ocean continues on forever.

__F__ 4. Barrier islands are long thin islands that run parallel to a coast.

__N__ 5. We didn't sleep a wink the night of the hurricane.

__N__ 6. Sea shells are beautiful.

Write two more facts and nonfacts that you can find in "An Island Scrapbook." You may look back at the story for help.

Two more facts:

7. __Answers will vary.__

8. _____

Two more nonfacts:

9. __Answers will vary.__

10. _____

130 **At Home:** Encourage children to share the facts they discovered from "An Island Scrapbook" with a family member or friend. Have them discuss the difference between a fact and a nonfact.

Book 5/Unit 4
An Island Scrapbook 10

---

## Important & Unimportant Information

Nonfiction writing includes a great deal of **important** information that supports the main idea. There is also some **unimportant** information that makes the selection interesting or fun to read but does not directly support the main idea.

Read the paragraph below. Think about what the main idea is. Then write **I**, for important, next to each sentence that gives important information about the paragraph. Write **U** for unimportant information.

The school had a very successful car wash last weekend. We made more than $800 for charity. The students were well organized, which helped us wash so many cars. Many students wore waterproof coveralls or rain suits. Mr. Toya's class washed the most cars. The students enjoyed washing the cars and had only three water fights. The car wash wouldn't have been as successful if Ms. Myers' art class hadn't made signs advertising the event. They made beautiful neon-colored signs. You could read these signs from a block away. They spent hours putting them up early in the morning and then taking them down at night.

__I__ 1. The school had a very successful car wash last weekend.

__I__ 2. We made more than $800 for charity.

__I__ 3. The students were well organized, which helped us wash so many cars.

__U__ 4. Many students wore waterproof coveralls or rain suits.

__U__ 5. Mr. Toya's class washed the most cars.

__U__ 6. The students enjoyed washing the cars and had only three water fights.

__I__ 7. The car wash wouldn't have been as successful if Ms. Myers' art class hadn't made signs advertising the event.

__U__ 8. They made beautiful neon-colored signs.

8 Book 5/Unit 4
An Island Scrapbook

**At Home:** Have students read an article and select a sentence that gives important information.

131

---

## Suffixes

A **suffix** is a word part added to the end of a word that changes the word's meaning. Knowing what a suffix means can help you figure out a word's meaning. The suffix -less means "not having" or "without". The suffix -ment means "the act or process of," "the place of a specific action," or "the state of a specific action."

| Word | + | Suffix | = | New Word | Meaning |
|------|---|--------|---|----------|---------|
| sleep | + | –less = | | sleepless | without sleep |
| arrange | + | –ment = | | arrangement | act of arranging |

Write the suffix of each word. Write the word's meaning. Then use the word in a sentence of your own.
Answers will vary. Possible answers shown.

1. heartless **Suffix:** __less__ **Meaning:** __having no feelings; cruel__
   **Sentence:** The coach seemed heartless for making us run an extra lap.

2. excitement **Suffix:** __ment__ **Meaning:** __state of being excited__
   **Sentence:** As each team scored a goal, the excitement of the crowd increased.

3. employment **Suffix:** __ment__ **Meaning:** __state of being employed__
   **Sentence:** Do you have employment this summer?

4. worthless **Suffix:** __less__ **Meaning:** __not having any worth__
   **Sentence:** The painting turned out to be worthless.

5. tireless **Suffix:** __less__ **Meaning:** __not tired__
   **Sentence:** Their efforts to raise money for the orphans were tireless.

6. punishment **Suffix:** __ment__ **Meaning:** __act of punishing__
   **Sentence:** My punishment for disobeying my parents is being grounded.

7. encampment **Suffix:** __ment__ **Meaning:** __place of camping__
   **Sentence:** The encampment was located high in the mountains.

8. cordless **Suffix:** __less__ **Meaning:** __without a cord__
   **Sentence:** Do you have a cordless phone?

132 **At Home:** Ask students to use two other words that end with -ment and two other words that end with -less in sentences.

Book 5/Unit 4
An Island Scrapbook 8

**T27**

## Reteach 126

Name_____ Date_____

### Fact and Nonfact

Information that can be proven true is a **fact**. You can usually find facts in nonfiction books and other reference materials. Information that can be proven false is a **nonfact**. Your proof might come from personal observation or from your school studies.

Read the paragraphs. Then write FACT or NONFACT for each sentence below.

Nantucket Island is part of the state of Massachusetts. The island is only a short ferry ride from Cape Cod. On the island you can see unusual plant and animal life. Nantucket has a science museum and a small aquarium. The aquarium houses the world's only living stegosaurus.

Nantucket is only 14.5 miles long and 3.5 miles wide, so it's easy to get around on a bicycle. The islanders maintain many miles of bike paths to help residents and tourists alike get from one place to another. The only way to really see Nantucket is by riding your bike over the land and water. Many people enjoy visiting Nantucket, especially in the summer.

<u>Fact</u>   1. Nantucket is an island.

<u>Fact</u>   2. The island is only a short ferry ride from Cape Cod.

<u>Nonfact</u>   3. The aquarium houses the world's only living stegosaurus.

<u>Fact</u>   4. Nantucket is only 14.5 miles long and 3.5 miles wide, so it's easy to get around on a bicycle.

<u>Nonfact</u>   5. The only way to really see Nantucket is by riding your bike over the land and water.

5 / Book 5/Unit 4
An Island Scrapbook

**At Home:** Have students write three facts and three nonfacts about a topic that interests them.

126

---

## Reteach 127

Name_____ Date_____

### Vocabulary

Use the words from the box to finish the sentences.

| emerge | parallel | barrier | naturalist | fireball | teeming |
|---|---|---|---|---|---|

1. The sand dune created an enormous <u>barrier</u> between our house and the stormy ocean.

2. When the storm ended, we saw our cat <u>emerge</u> from hiding.

3. Before noon, our town's <u>naturalist</u> will be studying the storm's effect on the beach.

4. She can reach the beach on one of three <u>parallel</u> paths that run next to each other.

5. When the sun comes out, our beach will be <u>teeming</u> with life.

6. What does it mean when the rising sun looks like a <u>fireball</u>?

☐ 6

---

## Reteach 128

### Story Comprehension

Write an answer to each question about "An Island Scrapbook."

1. Where does "An Island Scrapbook" take place? <u>on a barrier island</u>

2. What happens in "An Island Scrapbook"? <u>Amy and her mother spend the day observing the natural setting of their island home.</u>

3. What kinds of observations are included in the scrapbook? <u>drawings of natural objects, photographs, maps, lists of observations</u>

4. How do you think Amy and her mother feel about the island and its natural places and creatures? <u>They value them and want to protect them.</u>

**At Home:** Have students make one entry for an observation scrapbook about a place they really like.

127–128

Book 5/Unit 4
An Island Scrapbook / 4

---

## Reteach 129

Name_____ Date_____

### Read an Observation Chart

An **observation chart** shows what someone has seen or noticed. The chart's title usually tells you what has been observed. Headings on the rows and columns help you find each piece of information on the chart.

Use the observation chart below to answer the questions below.

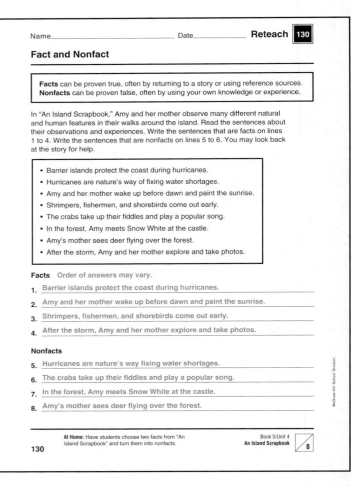

**Dogs at the Weissbergs' House**

| | Responds to commands | Barks at visitors | Chases other animals | Dog's age at arrival at house |
|---|---|---|---|---|
| Minnie | always | Only at strangers | Only when she's told to | 2 months |
| Gray | about half the time | Sometimes, especially when it's dark | Only the neighbor's cat | 1 year |
| Swifty | always | Only at strangers | often; loves to chase birds, cats, chipmunks | 3 months |

1. What is the title of the chart? <u>Dogs at the Weissbergs' House</u>

2. What do the column headings tell? <u>the different ways the dogs behave</u>

3. What do the boxes on the left tell? <u>the names of the dogs</u>

4. Which two dogs always respond to commands the first time? <u>Minnie and Swifty</u>

5. How does Minnie react when strangers visit the Weissbergs? <u>She barks at them</u>

6. Which dog only chases the neighbor's cat? <u>Gray</u>

7. How old was Gray when the Weissbergs got him? <u>1 year</u>

8. Which dog do you think is the most well-trained? Why? <u>Minnie, because she follows commands the first time; she barks only at strangers, and she chases animals only on command.</u>

8 / Book 5/Unit 4
An Island Scrapbook

**At Home:** Have students write a paragraph describing one of the dogs in the chart. They may add imaginary details that seem consistent with the chart information.

129

---

## Reteach 130

Name_____ Date_____

### Fact and Nonfact

**Facts** can be proven true, often by returning to a story or using reference sources. **Nonfacts** can be proven false, often by using your own knowledge or experience.

In "An Island Scrapbook," Amy and her mother observe many different natural and human features in their walks around the island. Read the sentences about their observations and experiences. Write the sentences that are facts on lines 1 to 4. Write the sentences that are nonfacts on lines 5 to 6. You may look back at the story for help.

- Barrier islands protect the coast during hurricanes.
- Hurricanes are nature's way of fixing water shortages.
- Amy and her mother wake up before dawn and paint the sunrise.
- Shrimpers, fishermen, and shorebirds come out early.
- The crabs take up their fiddles and play a popular song.
- In the forest, Amy meets Snow White at the castle.
- Amy's mother sees deer flying over the forest.
- After the storm, Amy and her mother explore and take photos.

**Facts**   Order of answers may vary.

1. <u>Barrier islands protect the coast during hurricanes.</u>

2. <u>Amy and her mother wake up before dawn and paint the sunrise.</u>

3. <u>Shrimpers, fishermen, and shorebirds come out early.</u>

4. <u>After the storm, Amy and her mother explore and take photos.</u>

**Nonfacts**

5. <u>Hurricanes are nature's way fixing water shortages.</u>

6. <u>The crabs take up their fiddles and play a popular song.</u>

7. <u>In the forest, Amy meets Snow White at the castle.</u>

8. <u>Amy's mother sees deer flying over the forest.</u>

**At Home:** Have students choose two facts from "An Island Scrapbook" and turn them into nonfacts.

130

Book 5/Unit 4
An Island Scrapbook / 8

# An Island Scrapbook • RETEACH

**Important and Unimportant Information**

> Recognizing **important information** can help you summarize what you read. Important information helps you understand the selection's main idea, which should be in a summary. **Unimportant information** adds interesting detail, but it's less useful in a summary.

Read the sentences beside each number. Circle the letter next to the information that is important. Your choice should have information you think belongs in a summary of "An Island Scrapbook."

1. **a.** Amy and her mother dress quietly.
   **b.** Amy has to go home the next week. *(circled)*
   **c.** The sun glows above the trees on their last morning.

2. **a.** While painting the sunset, Amy hears the lapping of the tide.
   **b.** The salt marshes smell muddy.
   **c.** Amy and her mother want to capture the island's beauty on paper. *(circled)*

3. **a.** The island has many different natural settings. *(circled)*
   **b.** There are a lot of fiddler crabs on the beach.
   **c.** Acorns and pine cones cover the forest floor.

4. **a.** Only shrimpers, fisherman, and shorebirds are out at dawn.
   **b.** Each part of the island fits the needs of its plants and animals. *(circled)*
   **c.** Amy finds animal tracks in the forest.

5. **a.** There was a small hurricane earlier in the summer.
   **b.** Amy collected many seashells.
   **c.** The island has often suffered from hurricane damage. *(circled)*

6. **a.** Amy and her mother enjoy the island very much. *(circled)*
   **b.** A baby whale died because it swallowed garbage instead of food.
   **c.** Amy once found a fossil shark's tooth on the beach.

6 | Book 5/Unit 4
An Island Scrapbook

**At Home:** Have students use the information they circled and other important information to write a summary of "An Island Scrapbook."

131

---

**Suffixes**

> A **suffix** is a word part added to the end of a word to change its meaning. The suffix -*less* means "without" and usually forms an adjective when added to a base word. The suffix -*ment* means "the act of" and forms a noun.
> -*less* "without"     direction + less = directionless ("without direction")
> -*ment* "the act of"     govern + ment = government ("the act of governing")

In the boxes, underline the suffixes in each word. Then use the words to complete the sentences below.

| pain**less** | care**less** | clue**less** | tree**less** |
|---|---|---|---|

1. The detective couldn't solve the mystery because he was clueless_____.
2. The dentist promised that cleaning my teeth would be painless_____.
3. Plants can't grow in harsh climates, so the tops of many mountains are treeless_____.
4. You can't be careless_____ when handling fragile items.

| entertain**ment** | govern**ment** | improve**ment** | advertise**ment** |
|---|---|---|---|

5. The colorful advertisement___ attracted many new customers.
6. Paco hired a magician to provide entertainment___ for the party.
7. Lea studied hard, and her grades showed great improvement___ by the end of the school year.
8. Everyone who voted in the last election showed that he or she was interested in the city's government___.

132

**At Home:** Have students write the meanings of the words ending in -*less* and -*ment*.

Book 5/Unit 4
An Island Scrapbook | 8

# An Island Scrapbook • EXTEND

## Fact and Nonfact

A **fact** is a statement that can be proved to be true. Factual statements tell about something that has happened or something that can be observed. **Nonfacts** are statements that can be proved false or untrue.

Read each sentence. Write if it is a fact or nonfact on the line following the sentence.

1. Washington, D.C., is the capital of the United States. _fact_
2. An orange is a vegetable that everyone likes. _nonfact_
3. Cats have nine lives. _nonfact_
4. The Mississippi is the longest river in the United States. _fact_
5. A red sunset always means it will rain the next day. _nonfact_

Suppose you wanted to write a paragraph with facts about dogs. Which of the following statements are facts that could be used in the paragraph? Underline the factual statements.

1. There are many different breeds of dogs.
2. Small dogs include terriers, dachshunds, and spaniels.
3. Small dogs make better pets than large dogs.
4. Large dogs include collies, sheep dogs, and standard poodles.
5. A dog makes a better pet than a cat.
6. Dogs require daily care, such as walking and feeding.
7. Dogs have four legs and a tail.

Write your own paragraph of facts about dogs or cats.
Answers will vary.
_____
_____
_____
_____
_____

Book 5/Unit 4
**An Island Scrapbook**

**At Home:** Find a magazine or newspaper article. Underline the nonfacts in the article.

126

## Vocabulary

| barrier | emerge | fireball |
|---------|--------|----------|
| naturalist | parallel | teeming |

In the story, "An Island Scrapbook," the author writes and draws a vivid description of wildlife on an island. Think of a place in nature that you have visited or read about. Write a paragraph describing the setting and wildlife you remember. Use as many of the vocabulary words as you can in your description.
Answers will vary but should include at least four of the vocabulary words in the
appropriate context and part of speech.
_____
_____
_____
_____
_____

## Story Comprehension

Work with a partner. Find an example in "An Island Scrapbook" when the author makes a conclusion about something. Write the conclusion in the box below.

**Conclusion**

Sample answer: The sperm whale probably died of starvation.

Now make a list of the facts used by the author that led to this conclusion. Remember that a fact is a statement that can be proved true.

**Facts that Support the Conclusion**

Sample answer: The naturalist found many objects in the whale's stomach: a bottle, rope, trash bag, buoy, rubber, and Styrofoam. There was not enough room in the whale's stomach for food.

**At Home:** Find five facts about the wildlife on the barrier island in the story.

127–128

Book 5/Unit 4
**An Island Scrapbook**

## Read an Observation Chart

"An Island Scrapbook" is filled with drawings and observations about the wildlife on a barrier island. You can organize information like this into an **observation chart**. An observation chart will help you see facts at a glance.

Create your own observation chart about the kinds of things that Amy and her mother take note of during their walks on the barrier island. Then fill in the chart below.

**Wildlife on the Barrier Island**

| Plants | Possible answers: red cedar, dwarf palmetto, muscadin vine, prickly pear cactus, dune grass |
|--------|----------------------------------------------------------------------------------------------|
| Insects | Possible answers: mosquito, tick, chigger, cricket, cicada, honey bee |
| Sea Animals | Possible answers: fiddler crab, yellow-bellied turtle, logger-head turtle, bottlenose dolphin, moon snail |
| Land Animals | Possible answers: raccoon, deer |
| Shell Animals | Possible answers: coquina, scallop, great heart cockle, oyster, angel wing |
| Birds | Possible answers; blue heron, pelican, black skimmer, egret |

Choose one category of animals, and use the information on the chart to write a descriptive paragraph about your category. Be sure to include facts from the story in your paragraph.
Answers will vary but should include information from chart.
_____
_____
_____
_____
_____

Book 5/Unit 4
**An Island Scrapbook**

**At Home:** Make an observation chart about the kinds of objects you see in your kitchen. Create topic categories such as dishes, pots, and cooking utensils.

129

## Fact and Nonfact

"An Island Scrapbook" is filled with **facts** about the wildlife and events of the barrier island. Look at each item on the chart below. Write a factual statement from the story for each item. Then write a **nonfact** statement. Answers will vary. Sample answers are shown.

| | Fact | Nonfact |
|---|------|---------|
| 1. fiddler crabs | A fiddler crab has one claw much larger than the other. | Fiddler crabs will always attack humans. |
| 2. maritime forest | Maritime forests are filled with oak and pine trees. | All forests are found near a beach. |
| 3. hurricanes | Hurricanes produce strong winds. | Hurricanes only occur from June through November. |
| 4. salt marshes | Decaying plants provide food for the wildlife in a salt marsh. | The moon has no effect on the tides in a salt marsh. |
| 5. sea turtles | Sea turtles are now a threatened species. | People know that sea turtle hatchlings are guided to the water by Earth's gravity. |
| 6. natural things that ruin beaches | Erosion can ruin a beach. | Natural events do not hurt beaches. |
| 7. human things that ruin beaches | Toxic waste and sewage pollute beach water. | People are responsible for all beach destruction. |

**At Home:** Choose one nonfact you wrote. Change the sentence to make it a fact.

130

Book 5/Unit 4
**An Island Scrapbook**

# An Island Scrapbook • EXTEND

## Important and Unimportant Information

When you write a report you should decide what **information** is **important** and what information is **unimportant**. Therefore, it is important to keep in mind the main idea of your topic.

Suppose you want to write a paragraph about the life of sea turtles similar to those Amy and her mother observed on the barrier island. Look through the story. Make a list of important information that you could use in your paragraph about sea turtles. Then make a list of the unimportant information about sea life that does not support the main idea of your paragraph.

| Important Information | Unimportant Information |
|---|---|
| Answers will vary. Possible responses include: descriptions of loggerhead turtles; dangers to sea turtles; creatures in a sea turtle's diet | Answers will vary. Possible responses include: information of fiddler crabs, descriptions of dolphins and whales; descriptions of shell animals |

Use the information in the list of important information to write a paragraph about sea turtles on the island.

Answers will vary.

_____
_____
_____
_____
_____
_____
_____

Book 5/Unit 4
An Island Scrapbook

**At Home:** Discuss ways of deciding whether information you collect on a topic is important or not.

131

## Suffixes

A **suffix** is a letter or letters added to the end of a word. A suffix can change the meaning of the word or the way it is used. Here are some examples of suffixes:

| | |
|---|---|
| The suffixes -er, -or and -ment added to a word often form nouns.<br><br>**build** + **er** = builder: one who builds<br>**elevate** + **or** = elevator: something that elevates or lifts<br>**arrange** + **ment** = arrangement: the state or result of being arranged | The suffixes -y, -ful, and -less added to words often form adjectives.<br><br>**snow** + **y** = snowy: with or having snow<br>**peace** + **ful** = peaceful: full of peace<br>**penny** + **less** = penniless: without pennies |

Find the word with the suffix in each sentence. Then write what that word means.

1. The boys were hopeful that it would not rain on their camping trip.
   hopeful; full of hope

2. The ocean air was breezy and cool.
   breezy; having breeze

3. The new paint job was a big improvement.
   improvement; the result of being improved

4. The toaster was on for too long and burnt the toast.
   toaster; something that toasts

5. Running around the track made the boy breathless.
   breathless; without breath

6. The young man had been a stamp collector since he was a boy.
   collector; one who collects

**At Home:** Think of words with suffixes that describe a place you would like to visit.

132

Book 5/Unit 4
An Island Scrapbook

**T31**

## Page 109

### Adjectives That Compare

- Add *-er* to most adjectives to compare two people, places, or things.
- Add *-est* to most adjectives to compare more than two.

Think about the comparisons in each sentence. Then rewrite the sentence with the correct form for each underlined adjective.

1. The morning feels <u>warm</u> today than yesterday.
   The morning feels warmer today than yesterday.

2. The sun today is the <u>bright</u> I can remember.
   The sun today is the brightest I can remember.

3. This morning I noticed the <u>small</u> crabs I've ever seen.
   This morning I noticed the smallest crabs I've ever seen.

4. They move <u>fast</u> than the sand worms.
   They move faster than the sand worms.

5. One claw on the fiddler crab is <u>large</u> than the other.
   One claw on the fiddler crab is larger than the other.

6. Amy is slightly <u>tall</u> than the great blue heron.
   Amy is slightly taller than the great blue heron.

7. About 50 years ago, the <u>large</u> hurricane ever to hit this island blew in.
   About 50 years ago, the largest hurricane ever to hit this island blew in.

8. A much <u>small</u> hurricane passed through last week.
   A much smaller hurricane passed through last week.

9. After the storm, everything seemed much <u>calm</u> than the night before.
   After the storm, everything seemed much calmer than the night before.

10. That day, I found the <u>blue</u> shell in the world.
    That day, I found the bluest shell in the world.

11. The turtle is much <u>slow</u> than the alligator.
    The turtle is much slower than the alligator.

12. This shell is much <u>big</u> than that one.
    This shell is much bigger than that one.

12 | Grade 5/Unit 4
**An Island Scrapbook**

**Extension:** Have students write a paragraph describing an outdoor walk, bike ride, or camping trip. Ask them to include in their description four adjectives that compare.

109

## Page 110

### More Adjectives That Compare

- For adjectives ending in *e*, drop the *e* before adding *-er* or *-est*.
- For adjectives ending in a consonant and *y*, change the *y* to *i* before adding *-er* or *-est*.
- For one-syllable adjectives that have a single vowel before the final consonant, double the final consonant before adding *-er* or *-est*.

Read each sentence. Rewrite it with the correct adjective forms.

1. This is the smellyest shell on the beach.
   This is the smelliest shell on the beach.

2. Still, it has the fineest markings of any I've seen.
   Still, it has the finest markings of any I've seen.

3. I don't think I could feel happyer than I am right now.
   I don't think I could feel happier than I am right now.

4. The sadest day for me is the day we leave the beach.
   The saddest day for me is the day we leave the beach.

5. You know, this shell is smallest than the pink one over there.
   You know, this shell is smaller than the pink one over there.

6. The prettyest shell is in the blue box.
   The prettiest shell is in the blue box.

7. I think the big sand dollar is prettyer than that.
   I think the big sand dollar is prettier than that.

8. Actually, I can't decide which is the lovelyest shell.
   Actually, I can't decide which is the loveliest shell.

9. Let's try to find the larger heron we've seen.
   Let's try to find the largest heron we've seen.

10. We should start looking near the higher point on the island.
    We should start looking near the highest point on the island.

**Extension:** Ask pairs of students to write and present a dialogue about a visit to a store or other type of market. Have them use at least six adjectives that compare the items that they see.

110 | Grade 5/Unit 4
**An Island Scrapbook** | 10

## Page 111

### Writing with Adjectives That Compare

- Add *-er* to most adjectives to compare two people, places, or things.
- Add *-est* to most adjectives to compare more than two.
- For adjectives ending in *e*, drop the *e* before adding *-er* or *-est*.
- For adjectives ending in a consonant and *y*, change the *y* to *i* before adding *-er* or *-est*.
- For one-syllable adjectives that have a single vowel before the final consonant, double the final consonant before adding *-er* or *-est*.

Write both forms of each adjective below.

| | | | | | | |
|---|---|---|---|---|---|---|
| 1. sleepy | sleepier | sleepiest | 6. fast | faster | fastest |
| 2. red | redder | reddest | 7. skinny | skinnier | skinniest |
| 3. fine | finer | finest | 8. high | higher | highest |
| 4. salty | saltier | saltiest | 9. mad | madder | maddest |
| 5. cool | cooler | coolest | 10. pretty | prettier | prettiest |

Find the incorrect adjectives in these sentences. Rewrite the sentences so that the adjectives are correct.

11. These are the smaller birds on the island.
    These are the smallest birds on the island.

12. The heron is the larger bird we ever see here.
    The heron is the largest bird we ever see here.

13. I love to read during the hotest part of the day.
    I love to read during the hottest part of the day.

14. The funnyest moment was meeting that alligator!
    The funniest moment was meeting that alligator!

14 | Grade 5/Unit 4
**An Island Scrapbook**

**Extension:** Ask students to write a letter to a friend from a very special place, a place the student loves to be. Encourage students to explain in their letters why they like this particular place. As they write their letters, students should use adjectives that compare.

111

## Page 112

### Letter Punctuation

- Begin the greeting and the closing of a letter with a capital letter.
- Use a colon after the greeting in a business letter.
- Use a comma after the closing in a letter.
- Use a comma between the names of a city and a state.
- Use a comma between the day and year in a date.

Read the short letters below. Correct all items that are incorrect.

August 10 1999   August 10, 1999

dear Jamie   Dear Jamie,

I'm having a fantastic time in North Carolina. The days have been warm and sunny, and there is so much to do in the bays and ocean. Hope you are well.

always   Always,

Jake

Sept. 9 1999   Sept. 9, 1999

Mr. Peter Johnson
112 Slate Road
Dover DE  19904   Dover, DE  19904

dear Sir   Dear Sir:

I am writing to urge you to do something to stop beach erosion here on the eastern islands. Please take the time to deal with this serious problem soon. Thank you very much.

Sincerely,

Megan Homer

**Extension:** Have groups of students write a business letter about a community problem. You might have them write to a government representative or local business. Ask groups to exchange and proofread letters for correct punctuation.

112 | Grade 5/Unit 4
**An Island Scrapbook** | 6

# An Island Scrapbook • GRAMMAR

## Adjectives That Compare

Read the sentence. Look at the adjective in parentheses. Fill in the correct form of the adjective on the line to complete the sentence.

1. We think that today's sunrise is the ___reddest___ we have ever seen. *(red)*

2. This has been the ___sunniest___ month of the summer. *(sunny)*

3. July was much ___foggier___. *(foggy)*

4. Yesterday we saw the ___larger___ of our two favorite pond turtles. *(large)*

5. The oaks are the ___tallest___ of all the trees in the forest. *(tall)*

6. During the hurricane, the wind was ___louder___ than during the storm in May. *(loud)*

7. Afterward, the air seemed clearer, and the sky was much ___bluer___ . *(blue)*

8. The days already are growing ___shorter___, aren't they? *(short)*

9. Each day I feel ___sadder___ than the day before. *(sad)*

10. We call this the ___finest___ island in the Atlantic Ocean. *(fine)*

## Adjectives That Compare

- Add *-er* to most adjectives to compare two people, places, or things. Add *-est* to most adjectives to compare more than two.

- For adjectives ending in *e*, drop the *e* before adding *-er* or *-est*. For adjectives ending in a consonant and *y*, change the *y* to *i* before adding *-er* or *-est*. For one-syllable adjectives that have a single vowel before the final consonant, double the final consonant before adding *-er* or *-est*.

**Mechanics:**

- Begin the greeting and the closing of a letter with a capital letter. Use a comma after the closing in a letter.

- Use a comma between the names of a city and a state and between the day and year in a date.

Read the postcard carefully. Look for errors in adjectives, commas, and capital letters. Then rewrite the postcard correctly.

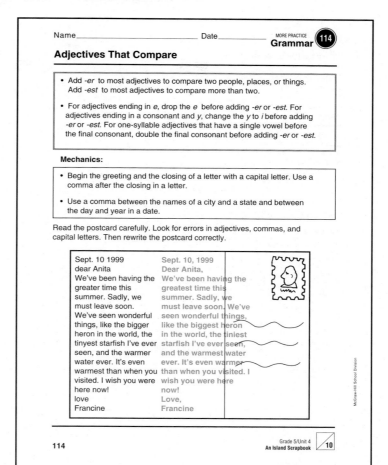

| | |
|---|---|
| Sept. 10 1999<br>dear Anita<br>We've been having the<br>greater time this<br>summer. Sadly, we<br>must leave soon.<br>We've seen wonderful<br>things, like the bigger<br>heron in the world, the<br>tinyest starfish I've ever<br>seen, and the warmer<br>water ever. It's even<br>warmest than when you<br>visited. I wish you were<br>here now!<br>love<br>Francine | Sept. 10, 1999<br>Dear Anita,<br>We've been having the<br>greatest time this<br>summer. Sadly, we<br>must leave soon. We've<br>seen wonderful things,<br>like the biggest heron<br>in the world, the tiniest<br>starfish I've ever seen,<br>and the warmest water<br>ever. It's even warmer<br>than when you visited. I<br>wish you were here<br>now!<br>Love,<br>Francine |

**T33**

# An Island Scrapbook • SPELLING

---

## Page 109

### Words with /îr/ and /ûr/

**Pretest Directions**

Fold back the paper along the dotted line. Use the blanks to write each word as it is read aloud. When you finish the test, unfold the paper. Use the list at the right to correct any spelling mistakes. Practice the words you missed for the Posttest.

**To Parents**

Here are the results of your child's weekly spelling Pretest. You can help your child study for the Posttest by following these simple steps for each word on the word list:

1. Read the word to your child.
2. Have your child write the word, saying each letter as it is written.
3. Say each letter of the word as your child checks the spelling.
4. If a mistake has been made, have your child read each letter of the correctly spelled word aloud, and then repeat steps 1–3.

| | |
|---|---|
| 1. _____ | 1. steer |
| 2. _____ | 2. return |
| 3. _____ | 3. appear |
| 4. _____ | 4. nerve |
| 5. _____ | 5. frontier |
| 6. _____ | 6. fir |
| 7. _____ | 7. mysterious |
| 8. _____ | 8. career |
| 9. _____ | 9. surface |
| 10. _____ | 10. fearsome |
| 11. _____ | 11. term |
| 12. _____ | 12. cashier |
| 13. _____ | 13. squirm |
| 14. _____ | 14. experience |
| 15. _____ | 15. eerie |
| 16. _____ | 16. purse |
| 17. _____ | 17. dreary |
| 18. _____ | 18. alert |
| 19. _____ | 19. squirt |
| 20. _____ | 20. material |

**Challenge Words**

_____ barrier
_____ emerge
_____ naturalist
_____ parallel
_____ teeming

Grade 5/Unit 4
An Island Scrapbook
20
109

---

## Page 110

### Words with /îr/ and /ûr/

**Using the Word Study Steps**

1. LOOK at the word.
2. SAY the word aloud.
3. STUDY the letters in the word.
4. WRITE the word.
5. CHECK the word.
   Did you spell the word right? If not, go back to step 1.

**Spelling Tip**

If you're not sure how to spell a word, try to remember how it looks. Have you seen the word in signs, ads, or other things you've read? Write the word in different ways to see which one looks correct.

~~career~~   ~~carreer~~
career

**All Mixed Up**

Unscramble each set of letters to make a spelling word.

1. userp — purse
2. stqrui — squirt
3. arapep — appear
4. ertal — alert
5. eceerienxp — experience
6. eesomarf — fearsome
7. rurnet — return
8. rnvee — nerve
9. eaydrr — dreary
10. eerst — steer
11. eiousrstmy — mysterious
12. sirmqu — squirm
13. etrm — term
14. fierntro — frontier
15. eearrc — career
16. sacefur — surface
17. eialrtma — material
18. irf — fir
19. rieee — eerie
20. aerhisc — cashier

**To Parents or Helpers:**

Using the Word Study Steps above as your child comes across any new words will help him or her spell words effectively. Review the steps as you both go over this week's spelling words.

Go over the Spelling Tip with your child. Encourage your child to write some of the spelling words in different ways and see which one looks correct.

Help your child complete the spelling activity by unscrambling the words.

110
Grade 5/Unit 4
An Island Scrapbook
20

---

## Page 111

### Words with /îr/ and /ûr/

| steer | frontier | surface | squirm | dreary |
|---|---|---|---|---|
| return | fir | fearsome | experience | alert |
| appear | mysterious | term | eerie | squirt |
| nerve | career | cashier | purse | material |

This week's spelling words contain /îr/ and /ûr/. Sort each spelling word by finding the sound and spelling pattern to which it belongs.

Write the spelling words with the sound /îr/ spelled:

**eer**
1. steer
2. career
3. eerie

**ear**
6. appear
7. fearsome
8. dreary

**ier**
4. frontier
5. cashier

**er**
9. mysterious
10. experience
11. material

Write the spelling words with the sound /ûr/ spelled:

**er**
12. nerve
13. term
14. alert

**ur**
18. return
19. surface
20. purse

**ir**
15. fir
16. squirm
17. squirt

Grade 5/Unit 4
An Island Scrapbook
20
111

---

## Page 112

### Words with /îr/ and /ûr/

| steer | frontier | surface | squirm | dreary |
|---|---|---|---|---|
| return | fir | fearsome | experience | alert |
| appear | mysterious | term | eerie | squirt |
| nerve | career | cashier | purse | material |

**Opposites**

Write the spelling word that is the opposite of each clue below.

1. sit still — squirm
2. vanish — appear
3. drowsy — alert
4. depart — return
5. thrilling — dreary
6. innocence — experience

**Meaning Match**

Write the spelling word that means the same as each clue below.

7. courage — nerve
8. job — career
9. semester — term
10. evergreen — fir
11. pocketbook — purse
12. fabric — material
13. checker — cashier
14. guide — steer
15. spray — squirt
16. border — frontier
17. puzzling — mysterious
18. outer part — surface
19. frightening — fearsome
20. weird — eerie

**Challenge Extension:** Invite students to make a word find puzzle using the Challenge Words.

112
Grade 5/Unit 4
An Island Scrapbook
20

---

# An Island Scrapbook • SPELLING

## Words with /ir/ and /ûr/

### Proofreading Activity

There are six spelling mistakes in this journal entry. Circle the misspelled words. Write the words correctly on the lines below.

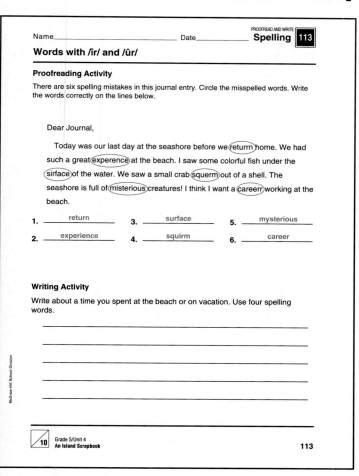

Dear Journal,

Today was our last day at the seashore before we (returrn) home. We had such a great (experence) at the beach. I saw some colorful fish under the (sirface) of the water. We saw a small crab (squerm) out of a shell. The seashore is full of (misterious) creatures! I think I want a (careerr) working at the beach.

1. ___return___    3. ___surface___    5. ___mysterious___
2. ___experience___    4. ___squirm___    6. ___career___

### Writing Activity

Write about a time you spent at the beach or on vacation. Use four spelling words.

_____
_____
_____
_____
_____

---

## Words with /ir/ and /ûr/

Look at the words in each set below. One word in each set is spelled correctly. Use a pencil to fill in the circle next to the correct word. Before you begin, look at the sample sets of words. Sample A has been done for you. Do Sample B by yourself. When you are sure you know what to do, you may go on with the rest of the page.

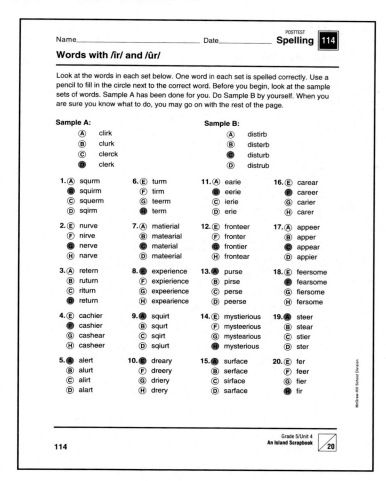

**Sample A:**
- Ⓐ clirk
- Ⓑ clurk
- Ⓒ clerck
- ⬤ clerk

**Sample B:**
- Ⓐ distirb
- Ⓑ disterb
- ⬤ disturb
- Ⓓ distrub

1. Ⓐ squrm
   ⬤ squirm
   Ⓒ squerm
   Ⓓ sqirm

2. Ⓔ nurve
   Ⓕ nirve
   ⬤ nerve
   Ⓗ narve

3. Ⓐ retern
   Ⓑ ruturn
   Ⓒ riturn
   ⬤ return

4. Ⓔ cachier
   ⬤ cashier
   Ⓖ cashear
   Ⓗ casheer

5. ⬤ alert
   Ⓑ alurt
   Ⓒ alirt
   Ⓓ alart

6. Ⓔ turm
   Ⓕ tirm
   Ⓖ teerm
   ⬤ term

7. Ⓐ matierial
   Ⓑ mataerial
   ⬤ material
   Ⓓ mateerial

8. Ⓔ experience
   Ⓕ expierience
   Ⓖ expeerience
   Ⓗ expearience

9. ⬤ squirt
   Ⓑ squrt
   Ⓒ sqirt
   Ⓓ sqiurt

10. Ⓔ dreary
    Ⓕ dreery
    Ⓖ driery
    Ⓗ drery

11. Ⓐ earie
    ⬤ eerie
    Ⓒ ierie
    Ⓓ erie

12. Ⓔ fronteer
    Ⓕ fronter
    ⬤ frontier
    Ⓗ frontear

13. Ⓐ purse
    Ⓑ pirse
    Ⓒ perse
    Ⓓ peerse

14. Ⓔ mystierious
    Ⓕ mysteerious
    Ⓖ mystearious
    ⬤ mysterious

15. Ⓐ surface
    Ⓑ serface
    Ⓒ sirface
    Ⓓ sarface

16. Ⓔ carear
    ⬤ career
    Ⓖ carier
    Ⓗ carer

17. Ⓐ appeer
    Ⓑ apper
    ⬤ appear
    Ⓓ appier

18. Ⓔ feersome
    ⬤ fearsome
    Ⓖ fiersome
    Ⓗ fersome

19. ⬤ steer
    Ⓑ stear
    Ⓒ stier
    Ⓓ ster

20. Ⓔ fer
    Ⓕ feer
    Ⓖ fier
    ⬤ fir

**T35**

## Practice 133

Name_____ Date_____

### Judgments & Decisions

Scientists often test the **judgments** they make. These tests are called experiments. They base their final **decision** on the results of their experiments.

Read the following selection, and then answer the questions.

"There is a ghost in our new house!" Charlie cried. "I saw the attic door open by itself." "Honestly, Charlie!" said his older sister, Camilla. "There are no such thing as ghosts." "But I saw it," Charlie insisted. "The attic door opened, and no one was there." "Let's check it out," suggested Camilla. The old wood floorboards creaked as they walked along the hallway. They found the attic door ajar. Camilla had trouble shutting it. Fiddling with the doorknob, Camilla finally made the latch click and she securely shut the door. To make sure, she pulled on the knob. The door did not move.

"Charlie," Camilla instructed, "walk along the hallway, just like you did when the door opened."

Charlie walked down the hall. The floorboard right by the door creaked a little, and with a click the door opened.

"Ghosts!" Charlie cried.

"Hardly," said Camilla. She closed the door and asked Charlie to try it again. After a number of times walking past the door, Camilla proved to Charlie that if he walked past the door in a certain way, his weight shifted against the creaky floorboard to make the door pop open. The house did not have ghosts. It just had creaky, loose floorboards.

1. What happened that scared Charlie? The attic door seemed to open by itself.

2. In Charlie's judgment, what caused the attic door to open? a ghost

3. Why didn't Camilla accept Charlie's idea about what made the door open? _____
She knew that ghosts did not exist.

4. Camilla and Charlie had differing judgments about what made the door open. How did Camilla test Charlie's observation? She made him walk past the door a number of times, until she proved the creaky floorboard was causing the door latch to pop open.

5. Why do you think that Camilla was successful in getting Charlie to change his mind? She created an experiment to test Charlie's ghost theory that showed him what had really happened.

---

## Practice 134

Name_____ Date_____

### Vocabulary

Complete each sentence with a vocabulary word.

| atmosphere | collision | cycle | data | injured | uneven |
|---|---|---|---|---|---|

1. The four seasons are an example of a natural _____ cycle _____.

2. We reached a conclusion using the _____ data _____ that we had collected during our science project.

3. There was a huge _____ collision _____ when the car failed to stop at the red light.

4. Luckily, no one was _____ injured _____ in the car crash.

5. The _____ atmosphere _____ of a county fair is exciting because there are many interesting activities.

6. The carpenter had to recut the boards because they were _____ uneven _____.

---

# Weather Forecasting

Predicting weather involves collecting and analyzing many kinds of *data*. Weather forecasters observe changes in the *atmosphere*, which is made up of oxygen, nitrogen, and other gases. By studying weather patterns, they learn what to expect from each *cycle* of weather events. This helps make their predictions less *uneven*. For example, they have to know what happens when a *collision* of cold air and warm air occurs. Weather reports are important because people can be *injured* or even killed by weather. So when you plan outside activities, make sure you listen to the weather reports.

1. What do you call the facts and figures that can be used to make decisions? _____
Data

2. What is a word that means *the air or climate of a place*? Atmosphere

3. What are *uneven* predictions? Varying predictions that are not always accurate.

4. What does the word *cycle* mean as it is used in this story? _____
It means a series of events that regularly repeat.

5. How can the weather forecast keep people from getting *injured*? Weather storms, such as thunderstorms or tornadoes, can injure or kill people; knowing the weather forecast helps people prepare for bad weather.

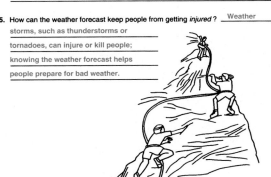

---

## Practice 135

Name_____ Date_____

### Story Comprehension

Complete each sentence with information from "The Big Storm." You may look back at the story for help.

1. The westerlies are winds that blow in what direction across the United States?
They blow from west to east.

2. What does a barometer measure? It measures barometric pressure, the pressure of the air directly overhead.

3. What does a low-pressure reading usually mean? _____
It usually means there is a storm coming.

4. What different instruments do weather forecasters use to make their predictions?
computers, weather stations, satellites, and weather balloons

5. What atmospheric conditions can cause a tornado to occur? A wedge of cold dense air forces warm air rapidly upward creating strong updraft winds.

6. According to the map on page 477, where does the frigid air blowing into the United States often come from? What type of weather conditions does it often bring?
Canada; cold air, snow and high winds

7. What do raindrops start out as inside of clouds? snowflakes

8. What causes thunder to occur? A lightning bolt that heats the air causing the air waves to rapidly expand.

# The Big Storm • PRACTICE

## Read a Weather Map

A national **weather map** shows the distribution of temperatures across the nation. Weather symbols for warm and cold fronts, high- and low- pressure areas, and precipitation also appear on the map.

FRONTS

▼▼ Cold

◖◖ Warm

◖▼◖▼ Stationary

Ⓗ High Pressure
Ⓛ Low Pressure

⚡ Lightning   ❄ Snow   ◖ Rain   ☁ Cloudy   ⛅ Partly Cloudy   ☀ Sunny

1. What does the symbol for a cold front look like? __a dark line with "triangles"__ __pointing out from it__

2. What is the symbol for a high-pressure area (area of high atmospheric pressure)? __the letter H in a circle__

3. What temperature is forecast for most of Texas, in the south-central part of the country? __80s__

4. What kind of day will the Texas area have? __clear and sunny__

5. What will be the coldest temperature in the United States? __20s__

Book 5/Unit 4
The Big Storm

At Home: Have students use this map to tell what the weather would be like where they live.

136

---

## Judgments & Decisions

Before you make a **decision** about something, you consider the reasons for and against it. As you read the situation below, think of what you learned in "The Big Storm" and try to make the best decision. Write two reasons for each choice. Then make a **judgment** about what you should do. Write your final decision.

Suppose the following. You are in the Rocky Mountains on a cross-country ski trip and you hear a weather forecast predicting over 2 feet of snow during the night. You were planning a long ski trip tomorrow that would take you far into the mountains. You know the new snow might increase the danger of an avalanche, but you also realize this will probably be the last big snow of the ski season. What will you do?

**Two reasons for continuing your trip:**

1. __Sample answer: A lot of new snow can mean excellent skiing conditions.__

2. __Sample answer: This will probably be the last big snow of the season.__

**Two reasons for not continuing:**

3. __Sample answer: The danger of an avalanche might be too risky.__

4. __Sample answer: Additional snow increases the risk of a serious accident.__

**Final decision:**

5. __Sample answer: Accept all reasonable responses. You could wait and see if__ __skiing conditions will be safe; or you could ski only in safe and protected areas.__

Write a short paragraph about a situation in which you had to make tough judgments and decisions. Be sure to include two reasons for and against your actions, and then write about what your final decision was.

_____
_____
_____
_____

137

At Home: Encourage students to talk about their final decisions with a member of their family.

Book 5/Unit 4
The Big Storm  10

---

## Draw Conclusions

When you **draw a conclusion**, you use facts from a story as well as your own knowledge and experience. Drawing conclusions as you read can help you better understand the story.

Read the selection below, and then answer each question. Describe the clues that helped you draw each conclusion.

Angie and her twin brother, Carlos, decided to go shopping for presents for their parents. In the bookstore Angie saw a big book on the American Revolution that she knew her mother would love, but it cost way too much money for her to afford. Carlos picked it up and looked at the price, too. "Hey, if we combine our money, we could get this for Mom," said Carlos. They paid for their purchase and went into another shop.

"Let's buy Dad something made from leather. He really likes leather," suggested Angie. But Carlos just walked out of the store. "What's the matter?" asked Angie.

"When I have some more money, I want to buy Dad something special. Just from me. After all, he spent all his spare time helping me rebuild my bike," said Carlos.

"I can understand that," said Angie. "Besides we probably don't have enough money left to buy dad a present now."

Answers will vary. Possible answers included.

1. Do Angie and Carlos get along? __They seem to get along, but they also can__ __disagree. Sometimes Carlos wants to do things by himself instead of with Angie.__

2. Story clue: __They chip in for their mother's gift, but Carlos wants to buy his__ __father a gift just from him.__

3. Experience clue: __Sometimes I like to share and do things with someone__ __else, and sometimes I just want to do things on my own.__

4. Do you think Carlos and his father are close? Explain. __Yes, because they rebuilt__ __Carlos' bike together; Carlos feels he should get his father a special gift.__

5. Carlos and Angie are doing something many people do, buying gifts for a family member. Why does this common experience help you draw conclusions about the characters? __Since I have shopped for gifts for a family member with my__ __brother, I understand what the characters are doing and feeling.__

Book 5/Unit 4
The Big Storm

At Home: Have students draw conclusions about what Carlos will do in the store.

138

---

## Root Words

A **root word** forms the base of a longer word. Often a root word becomes another word when a prefix or a suffix is added to it.

For example: The word _scrib_, meaning "write," is a root word for _subscribe_ and _scribble_.

Many root words in English come from Latin or Ancient Greek. Knowing the meaning of a root word and using context clues can help you define unfamiliar words.

| Root Word | Meaning | Language of Origin |
|-----------|---------|--------------------|
| pute | to think | Latin |
| meter | measure | Greek |
| sphere | ball | Greek |
| dict | to say | Latin |

Study the root chart above. Write the root of each word below.

1. computer _____ __pute__      6. atmosphere _____ __sphere__

2. hemisphere _____ __sphere__   7. diameter _____ __meter__

3. barometer _____ __meter__     8. dictate _____ __dict__

4. predict _____ __dict__        9. biosphere _____ __sphere__

5. kilometer _____ __meter__     10. verdict _____ __dict__

Choose four words from above—one for each root word in the chart— and write a sentence for each one.   Sentences will vary.

11. _____
12. _____
13. _____
14. _____

139

At Home: Encourage students to use a dictionary to look up the words they don't know from this list. Ask them to find out what "atmos" means.

Book 5/Unit 4
The Big Storm  14

# The Big Storm • RETEACH

## Reteach 133

Name_____ Date_____

### Judgments and Decisions

> Making **judgments** involves thinking about your reasons for and against something. Your reasons might be your beliefs or your goals. Making **decisions** involves acting on the judgments you made.

Read the story. Then make judgments and decisions to answer the questions. Explain your reasons for your judgments and decisions.

Ovidio wanted to make the top-level soccer team this year. He also wanted to get an A in math. Mr. Hansen, the math teacher, said Ovidio could make up any assignments that fell on practice days, which were every Monday and Wednesday. Then Ovidio was asked to join the school Safety Squad. It was a high honor, but it involved at least an hour a week of training and a meeting every Friday after school.

As Ovidio was considering this decision, his best friend Marc called. Marc's dad was coming home from the hospital the next day. Marc wanted Ovidio to help him make a welcome-home sign. But Ovidio had to make up his math in the morning and go to a practice after school.

1. Do you think Ovidio should join the Safety Squad? Why or why not? <u>Possible answer: No, because he wouldn't have enough time for soccer practice and to study math.</u>

2. What goals do you think are important for Ovidio to consider in making his decision whether or not to join the Safety Squad? <u>Ovidio wants to qualify for top-level soccer and still get an A in math.</u>

3. What do you think should be Ovidio's top priority? <u>Possible answer: Getting an A in math, because school work is important.</u>

4. Do you think Ovidio should make time to help Marc, even if he has to change his other plans? Why or why not? <u>Possible answer: Yes, because helping a friend is more important than Ovidio's other goals.</u>

5. Do you think Ovidio can participate in all three activities and still get an A in math? <u>Possible answers: Yes, Ovidio seems like a hard worker. No, it seems like too much work.</u>

Book 5/Unit 4
**The Big Storm**
5

At Home: Have students listen to see if their families or friends use any -less or -ment words this evening. Tell students to record and share the sentences in which the words were used.

133

## Reteach 134

Name_____ Date_____

### Vocabulary

Choose the word that fits the clue. Then fill in the crossword puzzle.

| data | injured | uneven | collision | cycle | atmosphere |

**Across**

2. repeating process
4. thin layer of gases
5. physically hurt

**Down**

1. changing often, not smooth
2. a crash
3. facts and information

Crossword answers: CYCLE, ATMOSPHERE, INJURED, UNEVEN, COLLISION, DATA

6

## Reteach 135

### Story Comprehension

Write an answer to each question about "The Big Storm."

1. Where did the big storm begin? <u>off the west coast of the United States.</u>

2. Why was knowing the season important to understanding the storm that occurred? <u>Spring weather is often unsettled and produces strong storms.</u>

3. What two natural forces affect weather the most? <u>sun and wind</u>

4. What were some problems people experienced because of the storm? <u>avalanches, tornado, destruction, getting stranded during travel, delayed events</u>

5. How did changing areas of low and high pressure affect the storm? <u>High pressure air from Canada caused severe cold temperatures. Low pressure air from the Gulf of Mexico brought warm moisture to cause more snow and rain.</u>

134–135

At Home: Have students develop two more questions about "The Big Storm" and give them to a classmate to answer.

Book 5/Unit 4
**The Big Storm**
5

## Reteach 136

Name_____ Date_____

### Read a Weather Map

A **weather map** may contain information about temperature, wind and cloud movements, and rain or snowfall. Use the map key to understand how the map uses symbols. Remember that low pressure usually means stormy weather while high pressure usually means fair weather.

Use the weather map to answer these questions.

1. Based on this map, will it be fair or stormy in Florida? <u>fair</u>

2. In what cities is snow likely to fall? <u>Chicago; maybe Seattle</u>

3. What kind of front is approaching Memphis, Tennessee? <u>cold</u>

4. If you were traveling on the day shown on the map, would Denver or Chicago be a better choice in terms of avoiding possible weather delays? <u>Denver</u>

5. According to this map, what is the likely temperature in Dallas? <u>in the 70s</u>

Book 5/Unit 4
**The Big Storm**
5

At Home: Have students learn the local weather forecast for their community. Direct them to Internet sources, newspaper weather pages, and television or radio news.

136

## Reteach 137

Name_____ Date_____

### Judgments and Decisions

> Making a **judgment** or **decision** about what you read often means deciding whether you agree with a character's actions. One way to do this is to suppose you are in the situation facing the character. Then you can consider your own values and beliefs to decide what you think is reasonable behavior in that situation.

Read each situation. Then make a judgment or decision to answer the question. Give reasons for your answers.

1. Chris has a chance to see his favorite team play basketball. But if he goes he'll miss Joey's birthday party. Should he go to the game? <u>Possible answer: No, because a friend's birthday is more important than a basketball game. But Joey might understand Chris wants to see the team if he's a good friend.</u>

2. Michaela won't talk to anyone who has moved to her home town in the last five years. She says newcomers are outsiders and should be ignored. Do you agree with her? <u>No, because she sounds prejudiced. She's missing the chance to meet many people.</u>

3. Phoebe never wears a helmet when she rides her bike. She says it's too hot. You learned in bike safety class that helmets protect bike riders from head injuries. Do you agree with Phoebe's choice? <u>No, because it's clearly less safe. Some students will say that some risks are worth taking, but not the risk of head injuries.</u>

4. Leon would like a snack after school. He knows that he'll be having dinner shortly, but he's very hungry. He could make himself a banana split, or he could just have a banana. Which should Leon choose? <u>He should choose the banana because it's less filling and won't interfere with his appetite for dinner.</u>

137

At Home: Have students write a short note to one of the characters described above. The note should explain the students' judgment or decision.

Book 5/Unit 4
**The Big Storm**
4

# The Big Storm • RETEACH

Name Date **Reteach** 138

## Draw Conclusions

> **Drawing conclusions** means combining clues from your reading with clues from your own experience to make a decision.

Read the story. Then draw conclusions to answer the questions below. Give at least two supporting clues, either from the story or from your own experiences.

> When Noah awoke, the room seemed quieter than usual. As he rolled over, he noticed it was 8 A.M., nearly an hour later than the time his mom usually woke him up. Turning toward the window, Noah realized why—there was over a foot of snow on the ground! He switched on the radio and learned to his surprise that the updated weather forecast was predicting six more inches of snow along with freezing-cold temperatures.
>
> Noah sank back into the pillow to plan his day. There were so many choices. He had four books at his bedside, stacked in the order he planned to read them. He could go sledding on the big hill, or he could finish his school report that was due tomorrow. He decided to plan his day by making a list.

1. What time of year was it at Noah's home? winter

   **Clues:** It was snowing heavily; it was very cold. This kind of weather most often occurs in winter.

2. What happened that changed Noah's plan for going to school? Possible answer: It snowed and most likely school was canceled.

   **Clues:** Noah's mom didn't wake him up at the usual time. It was snowing heavily outside.

3. Do you think the snowstorm was expected? probably not

   **Clues:** Noah was surprised by the forecast. The forecast had been updated from an earlier version.

4. Do you think Noah was an organized person? yes

   **Clues:** His books were stacked in a particular order. He carefully reviewed possible ways to spend the day. He decided to make a list.

Book 5/Unit 4
**The Big Storm**  4

**At Home:** Have students give a family member or friend two clues and record the conclusion drawn. Was it reasonable? Why or why not?

**138**

---

Name Date **Reteach** 139

## Root Words

> You can use **root words** to figure out the meanings of unfamiliar words. Root words often form the core of longer words. Sometimes you will know the root's meaning from a familiar word that contains it. For example, the root *dec-* means "ten." If you know that the word *decade* means "period of ten years," you can make an educated guess at the meaning of *decimal*.

Study the following examples. Then write the correct word from the box below to complete each sentence. Use the clues about root words to help you. The root in each word is underlined.

| Root word | Meaning | Example | Root word | Meaning | Example |
|-----------|---------|---------|-----------|---------|---------|
| phone | sound | telephone | scop | see | microscope |
| graph | write | photograph | pop | people | popular |
| sign | mark | signal | ped | foot | pedal |

> symphony    periscope    population    pedestrian    telegraph    signature

1. Laura Lee spent every Thursday afternoon listening to the splendid music of the symphony .

2. Scientists have noted how quickly Earth's population is growing; they worry about how people will produce enough food for everyone.

3. The crossing guard is there every morning and every afternoon to make sure that cars stop to allow each pedestrian to cross safely.

4. Notice that the graceful signature ending her letter is also neat enough to easily identify the name.

5. In submarine movies, sailors often use a periscope to see what is happening on the surface of the water.

6. Before telephones, people used the telegraph to send messages quickly to far away places.

**At Home:** Have students write sentences using each new word presented here.

**139**

Book 5/Unit 4
**The Big Storm**  6

**T39**

# The Big Storm • EXTEND

## Judgments and Decisions

Often, when you make a **judgment** about something, you consider the reasons for and against the possible choices. Then you make a **decision** depending on which choice most closely meets your needs.

Read each situation and the possible courses of action below. Make a judgment based on what you think is the best choice. Write your choice and the reason for your decision.

| Situation | Choices | Judgment and Decision |
|---|---|---|
| Your older brother is driving you to a soccer meet, and his car gets a flat tire. | 1. Call home to see if your parent can give you a ride. 2. Wait for help. 3. Go get help. 4. Take a taxi to the meet. | Answers will vary. Possible answer: If you can find a phone, calling home might be the fastest option. |

| Situation | Choices | Judgment and Decision |
|---|---|---|
| You have planned an afternoon picnic with some friends. Dark storm clouds are rolling in as you are about to leave for the park. | 1. Go on the picnic and hope it won't rain. 2. Go to a movie instead. 3. Take rain gear. 4. Have an indoor picnic. | Answers will vary. Possible answer: A movie is a good choice because you will stay out of the storm and can go on a picnic another day. |

| Situation | Choices | Judgment and Decision |
|---|---|---|
| Your grandmother is about to cook a turkey for dinner. Your dog takes the turkey and ruins it. Your best friend will be over any minute. | 1. Run to the store and get a new turkey. 2. Go out to eat. 3. See what's in the refrigerator. 4. Order pizza. | Answers will vary. Possible answers. Ordering pizza is a good choice because it is quick, and many people like pizza. |

Book 5/Unit 4
The Big Storm

**At Home:** Choose one scenario. What are some other choices you might make?

133

## Vocabulary

| atmosphere | collision | cycle |
|---|---|---|
| data | injured | uneven |

Suppose you are a news reporter covering a story about a blizzard in your town. Write a brief news report about the storm. Use as many of the above vocabulary words as you can in your report.

Answers will vary but should include at least four of the vocabulary words used in the appropriate context and part of speech.

## Story Comprehension

In "The Big Storm," you learn how meteorologists use information to study and track weather patterns. Work with a partner to make a list of important information that a meteorologist needs to know in order to predict the weather.

Possible answers: Meteorologists need to know about westerly winds, fronts, air masses, low-and-high pressure, barometric pressure, temperature, and the jet stream.

When you have finished your list, choose one method of weather forecasting you read about and tell why it is important when predicting weather.

Answers will vary.

**At Home:** Check a local newspaper for the forecast for your region. What information does the forecast tell you?

134–135

Book 5/Unit 4
The Big Storm

## Read a Weather Map

A **weather map** uses symbols to show weather patterns around the country. Use the map legend to read the symbols on the weather map. Then answer each question below.

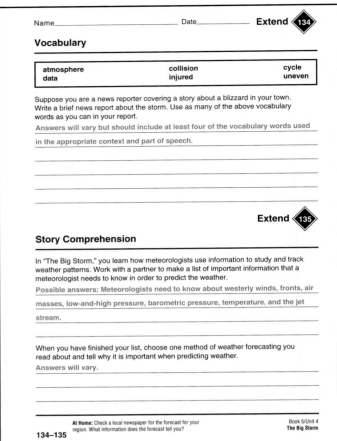

1. Which area of the country has rain in it? the Middle West

2. Which areas have a cold front moving through them? The West and Middle West

3. Through which area of the country is there a warm front? the Southeast

4. Which areas of the country have sunshine? the Northeast and the Southwest

5. In which area of the country is there a stationary front? the Southeast

Book 5/Unit 4
The Big Storm

**At Home:** Find a weather map in your local newspaper. What can you tell about the weather?

136

## Judgments and Decisions

Many **judgments** involve making a **decision**, or choosing a course of action. In "The Big Storm," many judgments are made about weather conditions. For each weather condition listed below, tell what course of action you think people should choose to stay safe from bad weather conditions.

1. It snowed all day in the Sierra Nevada range. Meteorologists are predicting avalanches. Possible answers: People should leave the area. People should not attempt to go skiing or mountain climbing.

2. The National Severe Weather Forecast Center near Kansas City predicts tornadoes. Possible answers: People should find shelter in storm cellars, or basements, or lie flat on the ground floor, away from windows. People should not go outdoors.

3. The tornadoes stopped when the front passed, but the thunderstorms continued throughout the South. Meteorologists predict thunderstorms and hail for the state of Kentucky. Possible answers: People should not go outside. People should stay away from windows so they will not be hurt by broken glass from large hailstones.

4. As the big storm moves east, huge amounts of snowfall are predicted in the cities of Chicago and New York. Possible answers: People should stay off the roads, take public transportation; don't drive.

**At Home:** A big hurricane is due in your town tomorrow. Tell what you can do to prepare for it.

137

Book 5/Unit 4
The Big Storm

# The Big Storm • EXTEND

## Draw Conclusions

When you **draw conclusions** you make a judgment or an inference about something. You can draw conclusions about an event based on information you read in a story and on what you might already know. The story below shows an example of drawing conclusions.

Irina is making herself some pasta for lunch. On the kitchen counter is a glass of milk, a jar of sauce, and a package of pasta. Her cat, Speckles, is on the counter watching. Irina leaves the room to answer the phone. When she comes back, the jar of sauce has been tipped over. Sauce is spilled on the counter. Speckles is no longer in the room, but red paw prints lead to the kitchen door.

| Conclusion | Information that led to the conclusion |
|---|---|
| Speckles knocked over the jar of sauce. | Cat was sitting on the counter; Irina had left the room; red paw prints; cat was nowhere in sight. |

Read the conclusion about "The Big Storm" below. Use facts from the story and from what you know to support the conclusion in the box below.

| Conclusion |
|---|
| Storms can cause damage to people and their personal property. Storms can also cause people a lot of inconvenience. |

| Information that led to the conclusion |
|---|
| Possible answers: Avalanches in the Sierra Nevada slam into buildings and kill or injure people; violent thunderstorms and tornadoes close down airports in Texas; tornadoes result in torn buildings, cars tossed in the air, shattered trees, flying objects; some people are killed; hail dents cars and breaks windows in Kentucky; snowfall ties up traffic in Chicago and postpones a baseball game in New York. |

## Root Words

A **root word** is a word part used to build longer words. Words that have the same **root word** are similar in spelling and meaning. For example, *centimeter* and *diameter* have the same root word *meter*, meaning "measure." Knowing the meanings of root words, as well as prefixes and suffixes, can help you determine the meanings of unfamiliar words.

| Root Word | Meaning |
|---|---|
| meter | measure |
| sphere | circle |
| dict | speak |
| put | think |

Study the root word chart above. Then write the root of each word below.

1. hemisphere  sphere
2. thermometer  meter
3. contradict  dict
4. atmosphere  sphere
5. kilometer  meter
6. computer  put
7. reputation  put
8. predict  dict

Replace the underlined words with one of the words above.

9. Will you look at the device that measures heat and tell me how hot it is?
   thermometer

10. The meteorologist uses a satellite to foretell the weather.
    predict

11. The distance from my house to school is a thousand meters.
    kilometer

12. Nell used a thinking machine to help her with her homework.
    computer

13. In which half of Earth is Australia located?
    hemisphere

14. We hope the witness does not speak the opposite of your statement.
    contradict

15. Heat from the sun causes changes in the mass of gases surrounding Earth.
    atmosphere

**T41**

# The Big Storm • GRAMMAR

---

Name_____ Date_____

## Comparing with *More* and *Most*

- For long adjectives, use *more* and *most* to compare people, places, and things.
- Use *more* to compare two people, places, or things.
- Use *most* to compare more than two.

Rewrite the sentences. Correct any adjectives that are used incorrectly.

1. Tornadoes are the more violent storms of all.
   Tornadoes are the most violent storms of all.

2. Today's forecast is the mostest pessimistic of the entire week.
   Today's forecast is the most pessimistic of the entire week.

3. In springtime, there is extreme weather than in fall.
   In springtime, there is more extreme weather than in fall.

4. The snowdrifts were most beautiful today than yesterday.
   The snowdrifts were more beautiful today than yesterday.

5. Avalanches are the more frightening things I have seen.
   Avalanches are the most frightening things I have seen.

6. The more stormy day this week was Saturday.
   The most stormy day this week was Saturday.

7. Scientists use computers to take the exact measurements possible.
   Scientists use computers to take the most exact measurements possible.

8. On the coast there is a most constant stream of air than inland.
   On the coast there is a more constant stream of air than inland.

8 | Grade 5/Unit 4
The Big Storm

Extension: Ask students to write and deliver dramatic weather reports, forecasting extreme weather with more and most.

115

---

Name_____ Date_____

## Comparing with *More* and *Most*

- When you use *more* and *most*, do not use the ending *-er* or *-est*.

Read the paragraphs. Then rewrite each paragraph, correcting any mistakes. Be sure *more* and *most* are used correctly. Be sure all adjectives are spelled correctly.

Where we live, the most dangerousest storms of all are tornadoes. One of the most fighteningest experiences of my life happened last April. There was a tornado watch issued. The announcer called the storm the most violentest of the season.

Where we live, the most dangerous storms of all are tornadoes. One

of the most frightening experiences of my life happened last April.

There was a tornado watch issued. The announcer called the storm

the most violent of the season.

_____

We felt most vulnerable than our neighbors because our house was more exposeder than theirs was. It was on top of the more elevateder hillside in the town. I had seen what a tornado could do. They can do the more horrendous damage of any storm because they have the more extremer winds of all.

We felt more vulnerable than our neighbors because our house was

more exposed than theirs was. It was on top of the most elevated

hillside in the town. I had seen what a tornado could do. They can do

the most horrendous damage of any storm because they have the

most extreme winds of all.

116 | Grade 5/Unit 4
The Big Storm

Extension: Ask students to write paragraphs that continue the story. Have them use more and most with adjectives at least twice in their paragraphs.

8

---

Name_____ Date_____

## Comparing with *More* and *Most*

- For long adjectives, use *more* and *most* to compare people, places, and things.
- Use *more* to compare two people, places, or things.
- Use *most* to compare more than two.
- When you use *more* and *most*, do not use the ending *-er* or *-est*.

Write an adjective that compares in each space. Be sure your adjectives make sense. Be sure to use *more* and *most* correctly. You may choose from the list of adjectives or use your own.

| | | | |
|---|---|---|---|
| incredible | enormous | courageous | shocking |
| vulnerable | violent | gigantic | violent |
| invisible | tremendous | intense | invisible |
| exciting | seasonal | high-speed | enormous |
| amazing | important | minuscule | frightening |

Answers will vary. Students should use the comparative or superlative as indicated.

1. Today we heard the ___most wonderful___ news we'd heard all week.

2. Tornadoes have the ___most violent___ winds.

3. That weather scientist is ___more knowledgeable___ than I am.

4. I saw the ___most beautiful___ clouds I had ever seen.

5. The ___most minuscule___ droplets of water create snowflakes.

6. The ___most exciting___ story this week was about a tornado and a house.

7. A tornado is ___more dangerous___ than a regular thunderstorm.

8. Wind is one of the ___most destructive___ forces.

9. Some clouds seem ___more enormous___ than mountains.

10. Avalanches are ___more frightening___ than anything.

10 | Grade 5/Unit 4
The Big Storm

Extension: Ask students to write poems about the beauty and power of storms. Ask them to use more and most with adjectives at least twice in their poems.

117

---

Name_____ Date_____

## Using *More* and *Most*

- Never add *-er* and *more* to the same adjective.
- Never add *-est* and *most* to the same adjective.

Read the sentences. If the sentence is correct, write *correct* on the line. If it is not correct, rewrite the sentence, using the correct form of the adjective.

1. A snowflake is the most prettiest thing I have ever seen.
   A snowflake was the prettiest thing I have ever seen.

2. This avalanche was more dangerous than the last one.
   correct

3. The cellar is more safer than your car.
   The cellar is safer than your car.

4. Weather predictions are more accurater than they used to be.
   Weather predictions are more accurate than they used to be.

5. This tornado is more unpredictable than the last one.
   correct

6. The most incrediblest storm of all was in the 1980s.
   The most incredible storm of all was in the 1980s.

7. I am more cautiouser about storms than I used to be.
   I am more cautious about storms than I used to be.

8. We saw the most terriblest destruction of the decade.
   We saw the most terrible destruction of the decade.

9. The tornado has the most rapidest winds of any storm.
   The tornado has the most rapid winds of any storm.

10. A weather scientist has one of the most interesting jobs.
    correct

11. The tidal waves were the most enormous of the century.
    correct

12. The most violentest storm last winter was off the coast.
    The most violent storm last winter was off the coast.

118 | Grade 5/Unit 4
The Big Storm

Extension: Ask partners to write four sentences about weather experiences, using more and most with adjectives. Then ask students to exchange papers, and to proofread and correct errors.

12

---

# The Big Storm • GRAMMAR

## Page 119

Name_____ Date_____

**TEST Grammar 119**

### Comparing with *More* and *Most*

Circle the letter of the correct form of the adjective.

1. This is the _____ storm I have ever experienced.
   a. terriblest
   b. most terriblest
   c. most terrible

2. The clouds on the horizon are _____ than the ones above us.
   a. threateningest
   b. most threateningest
   c. more threatening

3. The rain seemed _____ every minute.
   a. most violent
   b. more violent
   c. more violenter

4. Weather prediction is the _____ job I know.
   a. more challenging
   b. challengingest
   c. most challenging

5. A tornado's winds are _____ than those of a thunderstorm.
   a. violenter
   b. most violent
   c. more violent

6. The _____ time we had was in the blizzard.
   a. excitingest
   b. most exciting
   c. most excitingest

7. That snowflake has the _____ pattern of all.
   a. more complicated
   b. most complicated
   c. complicatedest

8. You must be _____ in tornado country than here.
   a. carefuller
   b. more carefuller
   c. more careful

8 Grade 5/Unit 4
The Big Storm

**119**

## Page 120

Name_____ Date_____

**MORE PRACTICE Grammar 120**

### Comparing with *More* and *Most*

- For long adjectives, use *more* and *most* to compare people, places, and things.
- Use *more* to compare two people, places, or things.
- Use *most* to compare more than two.

**Mechanics**

- Never add *-er* and *more* to the same adjective.
- Never add *-est* and *most* to the same adjective.

Work with a partner. One of you reads the sentences aloud. The other proofreads. Look for the proper forms of *more* and *most* with adjectives. Take out *more* and *most* where they are not needed. Rewrite the sentences correctly.

1. Those clouds are enormouser than these are.
   Those clouds are more enormous than these are.

2. The tornado was the most frighteningest one ever.
   The tornado was the most frightening one ever.

3. Yesterday's sirens were the more piercing of all.
   Yesterday's sirens were the most piercing of all.

4. The air near the North Pole is more frigider than anywhere.
   The air near the North Pole is more frigid than anywhere.

5. I think tornadoes are more better than tidal waves.
   I think tornadoes are better than tidal waves.

6. Hailstones are more harder than snowflakes.
   Hailstones are harder than snowflakes.

7. Snow is more beautifuler than rain.
   Snow is more beautiful than rain.

8. I think floods are the most scariest of all disasters.
   I think floods are the scariest of all disasters.

**120**

Grade 5/Unit 4
The Big Storm 8

**T43**

# The Big Storm • SPELLING

## Spelling 115 — Compound Words

Name_____ Date_____ **Spelling** 115

**Compound Words**

**Pretest Directions**
Fold back the paper along the dotted line. Use the blanks to write each word as it is read aloud. When you finish the test, unfold the paper. Use the list at the right to correct any spelling mistakes. Practice the words you missed for the Posttest.

**To Parents**
Here are the results of your child's weekly spelling Pretest. You can help your child study for the Posttest by following these simple steps for each word on the word list:

1. Read the word to your child.
2. Have your child write the word, saying each letter as it is written.
3. Say each letter of the word as your child checks the spelling.
4. If a mistake has been made, have your child read each letter of the correctly spelled word aloud, and then repeat steps 1–3.

1. _____
2. _____
3. _____
4. _____
5. _____
6. _____
7. _____
8. _____
9. _____
10. _____
11. _____
12. _____
13. _____
14. _____
15. _____
16. _____
17. _____
18. _____
19. _____
20. _____

1. mailbox
2. all right
3. goldfish
4. no one
5. ice-skating
6. homesick
7. post office
8. twenty-five
9. somebody
10. peanut butter
11. raindrop
12. cold front
13. merry-go-round
14. teaspoon
15. parking lot
16. thirty-third
17. snowstorms
18. mountaintops
19. sister-in-law
20. northeast

**Challenge Words**
_____ atmosphere
_____ collision
_____ cycle
_____ injured
_____ uneven

20 Grade 5/Unit 4
The Big Storm
115

---

Name_____ Date_____ **Spelling** 116

**Compound Words**

**Using the Word Study Steps**
1. LOOK at the word
2. SAY the word aloud.
3. STUDY the letters in the word.
4. WRITE the word.
5. CHECK the word.
   Did you spell the word right? If not, go back to step 1.

**Spelling Tip**
Remember not to add or take away letters when two smaller words are combined to make a compound word.
For example:
mail + box = mailbox
north + east = northeast

**Bits and Pieces**
Join the first word on the left with the second word on the right that completes each compound spelling word. Match the words in column 1–10 first, then 11–20.

1. mail __box__        butter
2. home __sick__       -five
3. peanut __butter__   one
4. some __body__       sick
5. ice __-skating__    fish
6. all __right__       -skating
7. twenty __-five__    office
8. post __office__     right
9. no __one__          box
10. gold __fish__      body

11. north __east__     lot
12. tea __spoon__      storms
13. snow __storms__    -third
14. cold __front__     spoon
15. sister __-in-law__ front
16. thirty __-third__  tops
17. merry __-go-round__ east
18. mountain __tops__  drop
19. parking __lot__    -go-round
20. rain __drop__      -in-law

**To Parents or Helpers:**
Using the Word Study Steps above as your child comes across any new words will help him or her spell the words effectively. Review the steps as you both go over this week's spelling words.
Go over the Spelling Tip with your child. Help your child find the two smaller words in each of the compound words on the list.
Help your child complete the spelling activity.

116
Grade 5/Unit 4
The Big Storm 20

---

Name_____ Date_____ **Spelling** 117

**Compound Words**

| mailbox | ice-skating | somebody | merry-go-round | snowstorms |
| all right | homesick | peanut butter | teaspoon | mountaintops |
| goldfish | post office | raindrop | parking lot | sister-in-law |
| no one | twenty-five | cold front | thirty-third | northeast |

**Open or Closed?**
Sort the spelling words according to the pattern by which they form compound words.

**One Word**
1. _mailbox_
2. _goldfish_
3. _homesick_
4. _somebody_
5. _raindrop_
6. _teaspoon_
7. _snowstorms_
8. _mountaintops_
9. _northeast_

**Two Words**
10. _all right_
11. _no one_
12. _post office_
13. _cold front_
14. _parking lot_
15. _peanut butter_

**Hyphenated**
16. _ice-skating_
17. _twenty-five_
18. _merry-go-round_
19. _thirty-third_
20. _sister-in-law_

20 Grade 5/Unit 4
The Big Storm
117

---

Name_____ Date_____ **Spelling** 118

**Compound Words**

| mailbox | ice-skating | somebody | merry-go-round | snowstorms |
| all right | homesick | peanut butter | teaspoon | mountaintops |
| goldfish | post office | raindrop | parking lot | sister-in-law |
| no one | twenty-five | cold front | thirty-third | northeast |

**Meaning Match**
Write the spelling word that matches each clue below.

1. nobody — _no one_
2. 10 + 10 + 5 — _twenty-five_
3. acceptable — _all right_
4. brother's wife — _sister-in-law_
5. after 32nd — _thirty-third_
6. goes with jelly — _peanut butter_
7. someone — _somebody_
8. gliding on ice — _ice-skating_
9. carousel — _merry-go-round_
10. missing home — _homesick_
11. blizzards — _snowstorms_
12. place to put cars — _parking lot_
13. kitchen utensil — _teaspoon_
14. opposite of southwest — _northeast_
15. chilly weather — _cold front_

**Sentence Derby**
Fill in the sentences below with the correct spelling word.

16. She dropped the letter into the _mailbox_ on the corner.
17. I felt the splash of a _raindrop_ on my head.
18. You need to drive to the _post office_ to mail that package.
19. In the distance, we saw the _mountaintops_ covered with snow.
20. Neil bought a new tank for his _goldfish_.

**Challenge Extension:** Students can create riddles with each Challenge Word. Have students exchange papers to see if they can solve each other's riddles.

118
Grade 5/Unit 4
The Big Storm 20

---

# The Big Storm • SPELLING

## Compound Words

### Proofreading Activity

There are six spelling mistakes in this weather report. Circle the misspelled words. Write the words correctly on the lines below.

The (cold-front) is moving in from the northeast tonight. Expect (snow storms) by mid-morning. Be careful of ice when you drive into any outdoor (parkinglot). (Noone) is traveling more than twenty-five miles per hour. Everything will be (allright.) If this weather continues, you'll be able to go (iceskating) soon!

1. _____cold front_____     3. _____parking lot_____     5. _____all right_____

2. _____snowstorms_____     4. _____No one_____     6. _____ice-skating_____

### Writing Activity

Think about the last big storm you saw in person, on TV, or in the movies. What happened during the storm? What did you see and hear? Write a report about the storm. Use four spelling words.

_____

_____

_____

_____

_____

## Compound Words

Look at the words in each set below. One word in each set is spelled correctly. Use a pencil to fill in the circle next to the correct word. Before you begin, look at the sample sets of words. Sample A has been done for you. Do Sample B by yourself. When you are sure you know what to do, you may go on with the rest of the page.

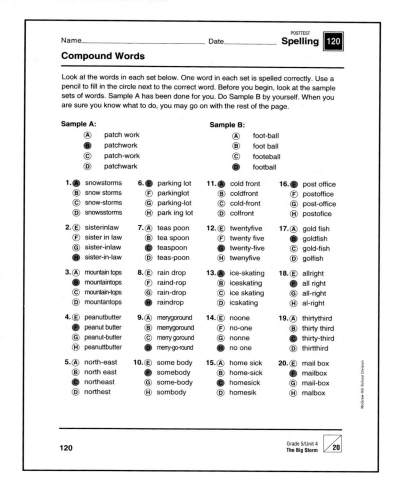

**Sample A:**
- Ⓐ patch work
- Ⓑ patchwork
- Ⓒ patch-work
- Ⓓ patchwark

**Sample B:**
- Ⓐ foot-ball
- Ⓑ foot ball
- Ⓒ footeball
- Ⓓ football

1.
- Ⓐ snowstorms
- Ⓑ snow storms
- Ⓒ snow-storms
- Ⓓ snowsstorms

2.
- Ⓔ sisterinlaw
- Ⓕ sister in law
- Ⓖ sister-inlaw
- Ⓗ sister-in-law

3.
- Ⓐ mountain tops
- Ⓑ mountaintops
- Ⓒ mountain-tops
- Ⓓ mountantops

4.
- Ⓔ peanutbutter
- Ⓕ peanut butter
- Ⓖ peanut-butter
- Ⓗ peanuttbutter

5.
- Ⓐ north-east
- Ⓑ north east
- Ⓒ northeast
- Ⓓ northest

6.
- Ⓔ parking lot
- Ⓕ parkinglot
- Ⓖ parking-lot
- Ⓗ park ing lot

7.
- Ⓐ teas poon
- Ⓑ tea spoon
- Ⓒ teaspoon
- Ⓓ teas-poon

8.
- Ⓔ rain drop
- Ⓕ raind-rop
- Ⓖ rain-drop
- Ⓗ raindrop

9.
- Ⓐ meryground
- Ⓑ merrygoround
- Ⓒ merry goround
- Ⓓ merry-go-round

10.
- Ⓔ some body
- Ⓕ somebody
- Ⓖ some-body
- Ⓗ sombody

11.
- Ⓐ cold front
- Ⓑ coldfront
- Ⓒ cold-front
- Ⓓ colfront

12.
- Ⓔ twentyfive
- Ⓕ twenty five
- Ⓖ twenty-five
- Ⓗ twenyfive

13.
- Ⓐ ice-skating
- Ⓑ iceskating
- Ⓒ ice skating
- Ⓓ icskating

14.
- Ⓔ noone
- Ⓕ no-one
- Ⓖ nonne
- Ⓗ no one

15.
- Ⓐ home sick
- Ⓑ home-sick
- Ⓒ homesick
- Ⓓ homesik

16.
- Ⓔ post office
- Ⓕ postoffice
- Ⓖ post-office
- Ⓗ postofice

17.
- Ⓐ gold fish
- Ⓑ goldfish
- Ⓒ gold-fish
- Ⓓ golfish

18.
- Ⓔ allright
- Ⓕ all right
- Ⓖ all-right
- Ⓗ al-right

19.
- Ⓐ thirtythird
- Ⓑ thirty third
- Ⓒ thirty-third
- Ⓓ thirtthird

20.
- Ⓔ mail box
- Ⓕ mailbox
- Ⓖ mail-box
- Ⓗ malbox

**T45**

## Practice 140

Name_____ Date_____ **Practice 140**

### Fact & Nonfact

A **fact** is a statement that can be proven to be true. A **nonfact** is something that is made up and can be proven to be false. When you read a story, one way you can tell the difference between facts and nonfacts is by looking for exaggerations in a character's behavior or abilities. You can also look for word clues such as, "This is hard to believe, but ..."

Read the story. Then complete the chart. Write whether you think a statement is a fact or a nonfact. Explain the reason for your decision.

I live in New York City. Every day we walk our dog in Central Park. With 340 acres of green space, it is one of the largest city parks in the world. Sometimes we ride our bikes there. My father's bike goes very fast. In fact, you might not believe this, but his bicycle can go faster than any car.

Our mother is a kite maker. She told us that human beings were flying kites before they discovered writing. One day she tested out a new kite. Well, you're not going to believe this either, but that kite caught hold of the wind and the next thing we knew, the kite was carrying our mother way above us. When she finally came down, she told us she had seen the Statue of Liberty. The statue is almost 151 feet high.

| Statement | Fact or Nonfact | Explanation of Decision |
|---|---|---|
| **1.** Central Park has 340 acres of green space and a lake. | Fact | This is the sort of information that can be found in a reference book. |
| **2.** My father's bicycle goes faster than any car. | Nonfact | This is an exaggeration. |
| **3.** Human beings were flying kites before they discovered writing. | This is a fact but answers may vary. | Some students may say this is an exaggeration. Some might wonder if a reference book can tell them about the history of kites. |
| **4.** The kite was carrying our mother way above us. | Nonfact | This is impossible, so it must be a made-up event. |

---

## Practice 141

Name_____ Date_____ **Practice 141**

### Vocabulary

Complete each sentence with a vocabulary word.

| bison | diaries | former | glistening | journal | superb |
|---|---|---|---|---|---|

1. The coach keeps ____diaries____ every year to record his team's progress.

2. The movie was better than good— it was ____superb____!

3. I keep a ____journal____ to help me keep track of each day's events.

4. You can find herds of ____bison____ out west in Yellowstone National Park.

5. Our ____former____ school principal came back to see our science fair.

6. Have you ever seen winter frost ____glistening____ in early morning light?

---

## The Ranch

This just might be the best vacation we've ever had. It has been *superb* so far! This week we went to visit my mother's *former* professor, Ms. Berry. She lives on a ranch in the western state of Wyoming. We had to drive for miles up a dirt road to get to her place. On the way, we saw these huge shaggy creatures with horns.

"BUFFALO!" my brother cried. My mother turned politely and said, "Actually, Ms. Berry runs a *bison* ranch."

My brother immediately recorded this information in his travel *journal*. Every day he makes notes of new facts and the miles we've traveled. I'm keeping two *diaries*. I write in one at the end of each day, and I write in the other only when I have something important to say about what we've seen.

After lunch, Ms. Berry took us out to explore the ranch. This place looked very dry, so I was surprised to find a small pond. The water was a deep emerald green and was *glistening* in the sun. Staying at Ms. Berry's ranch was the perfect place to end our vacation.

1. What is a word that means "excellent"? ___superb___

2. What does it mean that Ms. Berry was the mother's *former* professor? _____
   It means that in the past, Ms. Berry was her professor.

3. What is another word for the word "buffalo"? ___bison___

4. How is a diary different from a *journal*? Consider how both words are used in this story. ___In this story, the journal is a daily written account of factual information; the diary, while kept on a regular basis, is not a daily record and the writing is more personal.

5. Why did it surprise the narrator to find a pond of *glistening* water in Wyoming? ___
   The state of Wyoming can be very dry, so the narrator didn't expect to find a pond there.

---

## Practice 142

Name_____ Date_____ **Practice 142**

### Story Comprehension

Think about what happens in "Catching Up with Lewis & Clark." Then answer the questions below. You may look back at the story for help.

1. What did Meriwether Lewis and William Clark do nearly 200 years ago that no other United States citizen had done? ___They made their way across the continent to the Pacific Ocean.

2. Where did they begin their journey? ___St. Louis, Missouri

3. Why did President Thomas Jefferson want Lewis and Clark to explore the area that was part of the Louisiana Purchase? ___He wanted them to find a water route between the Mississippi River and the Pacific Ocean.

4. How long did it take the expedition to get to the ocean? How many miles did they travel? ___500 days; 4,000 miles

5. Did the explorers set out on their journey all alone? Did they travel only on foot? ___No; 42 people traveled with them when they set out. They traveled by canoe and horse, as well as on foot.

6. Who was Sacajawea? ___She was their Shoshone guide.

7. Why was Sacajawea so important? ___She was important because she spoke English, so she was able to get horses and food for Lewis and Clark from the Shoshone; without her help they probably would not have made it to the Pacific.

8. What makes it so difficult to find any trace of Lewis and Clark's journey? ___It's hard to know exactly where they stopped because they didn't leave any material behind at their campsites.

# Catching Up with Lewis and Clark • PRACTICE

## Use a Map

Ghana is a country in western Africa. Look at the map of Ghana. Then use the map to answer each of the following questions.

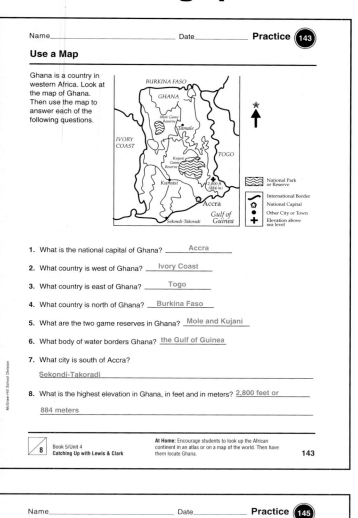

1. What is the national capital of Ghana? ___Accra___

2. What country is west of Ghana? ___Ivory Coast___

3. What country is east of Ghana? ___Togo___

4. What country is north of Ghana? ___Burkina Faso___

5. What are the two game reserves in Ghana? ___Mole and Kujani___

6. What body of water borders Ghana? ___the Gulf of Guinea___

7. What city is south of Accra?

   ___Sekondi-Takoradi___

8. What is the highest elevation in Ghana, in feet and in meters? ___2,800 feet or___

   ___884 meters___

---

## Important & Unimportant Information

In "Catching Up with Lewis & Clark" the **important information** supports the main idea—*trying to find the remains of an old Lewis and Clark campsite.* There is also **unimportant information** that might be interesting for the reader, but does not support the main idea.

Place a ✓ next to each sentence that states important information for "Catching Up with Lewis & Clark."

___✓___ 1. Scientists have been digging for remains of the Lewis and Clark journey in Great Falls, Montana, and Fort Clatsop, Oregon.

_____ 2. Lewis and Clark made it possible for people from the East to settle the West.

_____ 3. The Lewis and Clark expedition had to fight off bears and carry heavy canoes for weeks overland.

___✓___ 4. Lewis and Clark kept maps and diaries, so scientists have a good idea where they might have camped.

_____ 5. It took more than 500 days for Lewis and Clark to reach the Pacific Ocean.

___✓___ 6. It is hard for scientists to say, "Lewis and Clark camped here," because the explorers left barely anything behind.

___✓___ 7. Scientists have to sift dirt through a giant strainer to find things that might have belonged to Lewis and Clark on their journey.

_____ 8. A number of monuments have been built to honor Sacajawea.

_____ 9. The bison bone and pushpin are from the time of Lewis and Clark.

___✓___ 10. Scientists think the ammunition and beads found at Fort Clatsop in Oregon might have belonged to the explorers.

---

## Root Words

A **root word** forms the base of a longer word. Often a root word can form another word when a prefix or a suffix is added to it. For example, the root word *spect* meaning "to look" forms the words *suspect* and *speculate.*

Many root words in English come from Latin. By knowing the meaning of a root word and by using context clues you can define unfamiliar words.

| Root Word | Meaning | Origin |
|---|---|---|
| quest | to seek | *quaestus:* from the verb *quaerere,* to seek or ask |
| memor | mindful | *memor:* Latin from Sanskrit, *smarati,* s/he remembers |
| origin | to arise | from the verb *oriri,* to rise or arise from |

Study the root word chart above. Write the root word of each word below.

1. memorial ___memor___
2. requested ___quest___
3. original ___origin___
4. remember ___memor___
5. inquest ___quest___
6. originate ___origin___
7. questionnaire ___quest___
8. memorize ___memor___
9. aboriginal ___origin___
10. memento ___memor___

11. Is memor the root word of memento? How do you know? ___Yes, memento___ relates to memor because it means "something to keep as a reminder" or "something to keep in your memory."

12. Is origin the root word of memorial? How do you know? ___In this word, origin is___ not the root. Its root word is memor because a memorial is something that serves as a reminder.

---

## Suffixes

A **suffix** is a word part that is added to the end of a word to change the word's meaning. Knowing what a suffix means can help you define words. The suffix *-less* means "not having" or "without". The suffix *-ment* means "the act or process of." "the place of a specific action" or "the state of a specific action."

| Word | + | Suffix | = | New Word | Meaning |
|---|---|---|---|---|---|
| sleep | + | *-less* = | | sleepless | without sleep |
| arrange | + | *-ment* = | | arrangement | act of arranging |

Write the suffix of each word. Write the word's meaning. Then use the word in a sentence of your own.
Sample sentences are given.

1. aimless **Suffix:** ___less___ **Meaning:** ___having no aim___
   **Sentence:** His aimless wandering made him lose his way.

2. government **Suffix:** ___ment___ **Meaning:** ___act or process of governing___
   **Sentence:** Our government is a democracy.

3. movement **Suffix:** ___ment___ **Meaning:** ___the act or process of moving___
   **Sentence:** His sudden movement scared me.

4. charmless **Suffix:** ___less___ **Meaning:** ___not having any charm___
   **Sentence:** I thought that red dress was charmless.

5. regardless **Suffix:** ___less___ **Meaning:** ___without any regard___
   **Sentence:** Regardless of the weather, I am going skiing tomorrow.

6. enslavement **Suffix:** ___ment___ **Meaning:** ___the act of enslaving, the state of being enslaved___
   **Sentence:** No countries should allow any type of enslavement.

7. settlement **Suffix:** ___ment___ **Meaning:** ___place of settling___
   **Sentence:** We visited the new settlement.

8. spineless **Suffix:** ___less___ **Meaning:** ___seeming to be without a spine___
   **Sentence:** His lack of courage made him seem spineless.

**T47**

## Reteach 140

Name_____ Date_____

### Fact and Nonfact

> Information that can be proven true is a **fact**. Information that can be proven false is a **nonfact**.

Read the story. Then write a ✔ next to the numbered sentences that could contain facts.

Today is my 205th birthday. To celebrate, my family is taking its fifth trip to Canfield Woods. We always have wonderful adventures on these hikes. There are 20 miles of paths, each marked with its own colored sign that shows where the trail goes. But sometimes Canfield Woods is a little odd.

The first time we went, the trees started dancing and shouting, so we had to leave. On the second trip, my shoes did something strange. They actually dragged me onto the white trail, which I hate. Finally, I took off the shoes and left the woods wearing only my socks! Nothing unusual happened on the third trip—except that my little brother Will fell and cut his knee. The most recent trip was weird, too. My brother spotted a two-headed bird perched on a pine tree. At first, I didn't believe him, but then I saw it too. I wonder what today's trip will bring.

- ✔ **1.** The narrator's family has been to Canfield Woods five times.
- _____ **2.** The trees in Canfield Woods sometimes dance and shout.
- ✔ **3.** One trail is marked with white markers.
- ✔ **4.** Will fell and cut his knee on the third trip.
- _____ **5.** A two-headed bird lives in Canfield Woods.
- _____ **6.** The narrator's shoes dragged him onto the white trail.
- ✔ **7.** Canfield Woods has over 20 miles of trails.
- ✔ **8.** Each trail in Canfield Woods is labeled with its own color.
- ✔ **9.** Nothing unusual happened on the family's third trip.
- _____ **10.** The narrator is 205 years old.

Book 5/Unit 4
**Catching Up with Lewis and Clark** 10

At Home: Have students tell two facts about a recent family trip or gathering.

140

## Reteach 141

Name_____ Date_____

### Vocabulary

Circle the vocabulary word that correctly completes each sentence.

1. There were hundreds of (superb/**bison**) charging across the prairie.
2. After the storm passed, the leaves were (**glistening**/journal) with raindrops.
3. Each day, we recorded our experiences in our (glistening/**diaries**).
4. We had a (journal/**superb**) view of the valley from the mountaintop.
5. Luckily, I had the writings of a (**former**/journal) nature guide to help me.
6. She left a (**journal**/bison) filled with both facts and personal responses.

6

## Reteach 142

### Story Comprehension

Answer these questions about "Catching Up with Lewis and Clark."

1. What part of the current United States did Lewis and Clark explore? <u>the west, the northwest, and the midwest</u>

2. What was one goal of their journey? <u>to expand United States trade by finding a water route from the Mississippi River to the Pacific Ocean</u>

3. Who helped Lewis and Clark communicate with the Native Americans they met along the trail? <u>Sacajawea, an English-speaking Shoshone</u>

4. Which President asked Lewis to explore the Louisiana Purchase? <u>President Thomas Jefferson</u>

5. Why is it difficult for researchers today to find the actual trail Lewis and Clark followed? <u>They left very little physical evidence of their journey.</u>

At Home: Have students draw a picture of a bison. They may need to check a reference source first.

141–142

Book 5/Unit 4
**Catching Up with Lewis and Clark** 4

## Reteach 143

Name_____ Date_____

### Read a Map

> **Maps** provide many kinds of information. The map title identifies the areas covered by the map. Labels within the map may name places, bodies of water, and important land features. Special maps sometimes contain information such as typical industries. Use the symbols and explanations in the map key to help you understand the map.

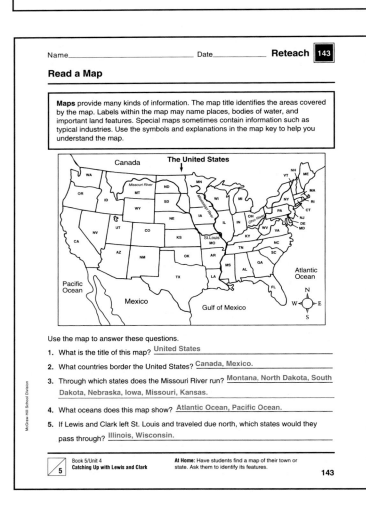

Use the map to answer these questions.

1. What is the title of this map? <u>United States</u>

2. What countries border the United States? <u>Canada, Mexico.</u>

3. Through which states does the Missouri River run? <u>Montana, North Dakota, South Dakota, Nebraska, Iowa, Missouri, Kansas.</u>

4. What oceans does this map show? <u>Atlantic Ocean, Pacific Ocean.</u>

5. If Lewis and Clark left St. Louis and traveled due north, which states would they pass through? <u>Illinois, Wisconsin.</u>

Book 5/Unit 4 5
**Catching Up with Lewis and Clark**

At Home: Have students find a map of their town or state. Ask them to identify its features.

143

## Reteach 144

Name_____ Date_____

### Important and Unimportant Information

> One way to recognize **important and unimportant information** is to ask yourself what would happen if the information were left out of the selection. Important information cannot be removed without affecting a main idea of the selection. Unimportant information can be left out without changing the main idea.

Read the stories. Then circle YES or NO to tell whether the underlined information is important or unimportant. Test your choice by rereading the story without the underlined information.

1. Jon's ride was late again. It was the third time this month. <u>This time, she came 12 minutes after 8 o'clock.</u> She always called to say she would be late, but that didn't help Jon get to school on time.

    Yes    (**No**)

2. <u>Aunt Hattie makes fantastic lunches.</u> Her black-eyed peas are the best I've ever had. She also makes great corn bread. I look forward all week to Sunday lunch at her house.

    (**Yes**)    No

3. Joellyn works late at night. Her shift starts at midnight. <u>When she gets tired, she drinks a glass of cold water to wake up.</u>

    Yes    (**No**)

4. <u>Wait until you hear this!</u> Jim's Dad was backing out of his garage, and he tore the garage door right off. He had lifted the door up but I guess not far enough. Anyway, the door is totally smashed.

    Yes    (**No**)

5. <u>Quentin comes from a big family.</u> They need four long tables when everyone eats together on special holidays. He always has someone to talk to.

    (**Yes**)    No

At Home: Expand one of the stories by adding an important or an unimportant piece of information. Tell which kind of information you have added.

144

Book 5/Unit 4
**Catching Up with Lewis and Clark** 5

# Catching Up with Lewis and Clark • RETEACH

**Root Words**

> You can use the meanings of **roots** to help figure out the meanings of unfamiliar words.

Read the root clue next to each word in column 1. Then use the clue to find the definition of each word in column 2. Write the letter of each correct definition on the line.

**Column 1**

_d_ 1. motor (*mot* means "move")

_a_ 2. spectator (*spec* means "see")

_e_ 3. altitude (*alt* means "high")

_f_ 4. scald (*cal* means "hot")

_c_ 5. liberate (*liber* means "free")

_b_ 6. lunar (*luna* means "moon")

**Column 2**

**a.** someone who watches

**b.** related to the moon

**c.** to set free

**d.** engine that moves a machine

**e.** height measurement

**f.** to burn

Now use the words from above to complete these sentences.

7. A ___spectator___ came to watch the game.

8. The mountain's ___altitude___ is 9,500 feet.

9. Be careful not to ___scald___ yourself with that hot drink.

10. Many people have worked hard to help ___liberate___ slaves.

11. The ___lunar___ light shines into my room at night.

12. The old car still runs well because it has a good ___motor___.

Book 5/Unit 4
**Catching Up with Lewis and Clark** 12

At Home: Have students find and record a dictionary definition for one of the words.

145

**Suffixes**

A **suffix** changes the meaning of the base word. The suffix *-less* adds the meaning "without" to a base word. The suffix *-ment* changes a base word into a noun that means "the act or result of."

In each sentence, underline the word that includes the suffix *-less* or *-ment*. Then write each word and its meaning.

1. Raising your grade from a C to an A is quite an <u>accomplishment</u>. ___accomplishment; the result of accomplishing something___

2. When the factory closed, the <u>jobless</u> rate in our town went up. ___jobless; without jobs___

3. Our club works for the <u>advancement</u> of business in the region. ___advancement; result of advances___

4. Cleaning up after the hurricane was a <u>joyless</u> experience. ___joyless; without joy___

5. Some people want to change the U.S. Constitution by adding <u>amendments</u>. ___amendments; acts of amending or changing___

6. Jan's interest in science fiction books seems to be <u>limitless</u>. ___limitless; without limit___

7. Making the library bigger is certainly an <u>improvement</u> to our school. ___improvement; result of improving___

8. Making a <u>judgment</u> involves weighing at least two choices. ___judgment; act of judging___

At Home: Have students write additional sentences for two *-less* and two *-ment* words.

146

Book 5/Unit 4
**Catching Up with Lewis and Clark** 8

**T49**

# Catching Up with Lewis and Clark • EXTEND

## Fact and Nonfact

A **fact** is a statement that can be proved to be true. A fact tells about something that has happened or something that can be observed. **Nonfacts** are statements that can be proved false or untrue. Sometimes nonfacts can be opinions. An opinion tells what a person thinks or feels about something.

Read each opinion. Rewrite the opinion so that it becomes a factual statement.

1. Shelley deserves an A on all her science reports. _Shelley receives an A on all her_
   _science reports._

2. Edgar Allan Poe was the best writer of suspense stories in the nineteenth century.
   _Edgar Allan Poe was a writer of suspense stories in the nineteenth century._

3. The most outstanding educational programs are on public television. _Many_
   _educational programs are on public television._

Read each factual statement. Write a statement about the same subject so that it expresses an opinion.

4. California is the third largest state in the United States. _Sample answer: California_
   _is the most interesting state in the United States._

5. John Glenn was the first United States astronaut to orbit Earth in a space capsule.
   _Sample answer: John Glenn was the bravest of all United States astronauts._

6. A tomato can be used in a salad. _Sample answer: The tomato is the best fruit to_
   _use in a salad._

Book 5/Unit 4
Catching Up with Lewis and Clark

**At Home:** Find a statement in a newspaper that is a fact.
Write the statement so it expresses an opinion.

140

## Vocabulary

| bison | diaries | former |
|-------|---------|--------|
| glistening | journal | superb |

Imagine you are witnessing a scene in which Sacajawea is guiding Lewis and Clark through the Rocky Mountains. Write the conversation they might have had with one another. Use as many vocabulary words as you can.

Answers will vary but should include at least four vocabulary words used in the

correct context or part of speech.

_____

_____

_____

## Story Comprehension

Scientists have found what they believe to be remains of the Lewis and Clark expedition. They have uncovered a tall wooden wall from a campsite and some beads and ammunition. What do you think scientists could conclude from these findings? Write a paragraph to explain your conclusion.

Possible answer: It takes a long time to build a wooden wall, so Lewis and Clark

may have stayed at the campsite for a period of time, maybe in the winter when

snow made traveling impossible. The beads may have come from meeting and

trading with Native Americans. Ammunition may have been used to hunt for food

or for defense.

**At Home:** Have students write a journal entry for today
using vocabulary words.

141–142

Book 5/Unit 4
Catching Up with Lewis and Clark

## Read a Map

A **road map** shows major highways, landmarks, and water routes. You can use a compass to tell direction. The map below shows the state of Missouri and some of the major roads that pass through it. Use the map to answer the questions.

**KEY**
◯ state highway
◯ interstate highway

1. Which river borders Missouri on the east? _the Mississippi_

2. Which river flows across the entire state of Missouri? _the Missouri_

3. If Lewis and Clark were to take a trip by car in modern-day Missouri, how might
   they get from St. Louis to Kansas City? _They could take Interstate Highway 70._

4. What big city is about halfway in between St. Louis and Kansas City?
   _Columbia_

Book 5/Unit 4
Catching Up with Lewis and Clark

**At Home:** Look at a map of your state. What major rivers
or other bodies of water are in your state?

143

## Important and Unimportant Information

When you write a report about a topic, you need to identify the purpose, or main idea, of your report. Then you determine which information you want to include to support your main idea. This is **important information**. **Unimportant information** can add interest but is not needed to support a main idea.

"Catching Up with Lewis and Clark" discusses the journey of these explorers. Suppose you wanted to write an article about where they traveled and what they saw on their journey. First find the important information that you will include in your article to support your main idea. Then write a brief article titled, "The Journey of Lewis and Clark."

Articles and lists should include states through which Lewis and Clark traveled,

rivers and mountains they journeyed across, the dates of their expedition, and

what they saw along the way.

**At Home:** Use reference materials to find out more about the
journey of Lewis and Clark. Add important information to
your article.

144

Book 5/Unit 4
Catching Up with Lewis and Clark

# Catching Up with Lewis and Clark • EXTEND

## Root Words

New words are formed by adding suffixes and prefixes to **root words**. Look at the meanings of the root words in the chart below.

| Root Word | Meaning |
|-----------|---------|
| mem | mindful |
| orig | beginning |
| ques | ask, seek |

Then write the root of each word below.

**1.** original _orig_____

**2.** request _ques_____

**3.** memory _mem_____

**4.** aboriginal _orig_____

**5.** question _ques_____

**6.** commemorate _mem_____

Write a new word using each root word below. Then choose one word and use it in a sentence.

**7.** spec (see) _Possible answers: inspect, suspect, respect, spectator, spectacle_

**8.** act (do) _Possible answers: actor, action, react, transact, enact, interact_

**9.** urb (city) _Possible answers: urban, suburban, suburb_

**10.** _Sentences will vary._

Book 5/Unit 4
**Catching Up with Lewis and Clark**

**At Home:** Use *-ial*, *-al*, and *-ion* endings to form other words from root words.

**145**

## Suffixes

**Suffixes** are word parts added to the end of words. They can change the meaning of the word, or the way it is used.

> The suffix *-less* means "without."     Example: endless
> The suffix *-ment* can mean "a result of an action."     Example: amusement

Name the word that is formed when you add each suffix to the word shown. Tell what each new word means. Then write a sentence using the new word.

**1.** pave + ment _pavement; a hard, smooth surface caused by paving. Student sentences will vary but should use the word in the context and part of speech._

**2.** sleep + less _sleepless; without sleep. Student sentences will vary but should use the word in the context and part of speech._

**3.** adorn + ment _adornment; something made to adorn, an ornament. Student sentences will vary but should use the word in the context and part of speech._

**4.** blame + less _blameless; without blame. Student sentences will vary but should use the word in the context and part of speech._

**5.** agree + ment _agreement; a result of agreeing, an understanding between two parties. Student sentences will vary but should use the word in the context and part of speech._

**146**

**At Home:** Think of as many words as you can with *-less* and *-ment* endings.

Book 5/Unit 4
**Catching Up with Lewis and Clark**

# Catching Up with Lewis and Clark • GRAMMAR

## Comparing with *Good*

- Use *better* to compare two people, places, or things.
- Use *best* to compare more than two.

Read each sentence. If the form of the adjective is correct, write *correct* on the line. If it is wrong, circle it and write the correct form.

1. Scientists hope to find (best) answers about Lewis and Clark than they have.
   better

2. Pioneers searched for a better life than the one they left behind. ____ correct

3. A water route would be (best) than a road. ____ better

4. Clark was Lewis's (better) friend of all. ____ best

5. A canoe is (best) than a sailboat for exploring inland routes. ____ better

6. On the best day of the trip, they spotted the ocean. ____ correct

7. The Interpretive Center has the (better) exhibits of all. ____ best

8. Lewis and Clark searched for the (better) route to the Pacific. ____ best

9. Scientists have (best) clues about the route than they had ten years ago.
   better

10. The Shoshone had the (better) trails of anyone. ____ best

11. Lewis and Clark had (best) horses than the Shoshone. ____ better

12. Sacajawea was the best guide they could have found. ____ correct

13. The Shoshone showed the explorers (bestest) trails than they expected.
    better

14. Fishing in the Pacific might be (gooder) than stream fishing. ____ better

15. Their luck might be (better) of all in Oregon. ____ best

15 | Grade 5/Unit 4
**Catching Up With Lewis and Clark**

**Extension:** Ask students to write four sentences about an exploration or expedition, using the adjectives *best* and *better*.

121

---

## Comparing with *Bad*

- Use *worse* to compare two people, places, or things.
- Use *worst* to compare more than two.

Rewrite the sentences, correcting forms of *good* and *bad* where necessary.

1. Lewis and Clark suffered the worse hardships in their lives.
   Lewis and Clark suffered the worst hardships in their lives.

2. Having sore feet was not the worse of their troubles.
   Having sore feet was not the worst of their troubles.

3. Ferocious bears were one of the worser surprises on the whole trip.
   Ferocious bears were one of the worst surprises on the whole trip.

4. Grizzlies seemed worst than any animal in the East.
   Grizzlies seemed worse than any animal in the East.

5. In the mountains, the weather became worser than it had been.
   In the mountains, the weather became worse than it had been.

6. Hunting was worst in the mountains than it was in the valleys.
   Hunting was worse in the mountains than it was in the valleys.

7. The worstest part of the trip was the hunger.
   The worst part of the trip was the hunger.

8. You must be prepared for the worse conditions ever.
   You must be prepared for the worst conditions ever.

9. The heat is worser today than it was yesterday.
   The heat is worse today than it was yesterday.

10. The worser hours of the whole day were spent hauling canoes.
    The worst hours of the day were spent hauling canoes.

**Extension:** Ask students to read library books about the journey of Lewis and Clark. Then ask them to write paragraphs about the explorers' worst dangers and hardships. Remind them to use worse and worst correctly.

122 | Grade 5/Unit 4
**Catching Up With Lewis and Clark** | 10

---

## Comparing with *Good* and *Bad*

- Use *better* to compare two people, places, or things.
- Use *best* to compare more than two.
- Use *worse* to compare two people, places, or things.
- Use *worst* to compare more than two.

Read the paragraphs. Circle any errors. Rewrite each paragraph correctly in the space provided.

   We were searching for the goodest water route across America. Instead, we found a best route for some pioneers than the southern route. We followed Sacajawea, the better guide we could have hoped for. The Indians had been traveling the mountains for thousands of years. They knew gooder routes through the unfamiliar territory than we did. Their trails were the better of any we had seen.

We were searching for the best water route across America. Instead,

we found a better route for some pioneers than the one farther south.

We followed Sacajawea, the best guide we could have hoped for. The

Shoshone and other Indians had been traveling the mountains for

thousands of years. They knew better routes through the unfamiliar

territory than we did. Their trails were the best of any we had seen.

   Along the way, we suffered the worstest hardships of our lives. We could not find food, and the terrain was some of the worser we had encountered. We felt worsest each day than we had the day before. The worse part of our trip was carrying the canoes. We found hiking far worst than paddling.

Along the way, we suffered the worst hardships of our lives. We

could not find food, and the terrain was some of the worst we had

encountered. We felt worse each day than we had the day before.

The worst part of our trip was carrying the canoes. We found the hike

far worse than we had thought.

10 | Grade 5/Unit 4
**Catching Up With Lewis and Clark**

**Extension:** Ask partners to write sentences about good and bad experiences in the wilderness. They can make up adventures or write about true experiences. Ask students to share their stories with the class.

123

---

## Proper Adjectives

- A proper adjective is formed from a proper noun.
- A proper adjective begins with a capital letter.

Underline each proper adjective. Then write it on the line with the correct capitalization.

1. Lewis and Clark traveled across the north american continent.
   North American

2. Some oregon families are descendants of pioneers. ____ Oregon

3. The Rocky Mountains also cross the canadian border. ____ Canadian

4. Many american families traveled Lewis and Clark's route. ____ American

5. One montana scientist is studying the trail of Lewis and Clark.
   Montana

6. At the national Memorial, there are historical exhibits. ____ National

7. Some of the Shoshone were english-speaking people. ____ English-speaking

8. It was many years until the western states joined the Union. ____ Western

9. Lewis and Clark followed the ancient native american trails. ____ Native American

10. Many pioneers were european immigrants. ____ European

11. The mexican border is far from the Rocky Mountains. ____ Mexican

12. The native american route turned out to be excellent. ____ Native American

**Extension:** Ask students to write four sentences about the history of your region. Have them use a proper adjective in each sentence.

124 | Grade 5/Unit 4
**Catching Up With Lewis and Clark** | 12

---

# Catching Up with Lewis and Clark • GRAMMAR

## Comparing with *Good* and *Bad*

**A.** Circle the letter of the adjective that completes the sentence correctly.

1. It was the _____ day of our entire journey.
   a. best
   b. goodest
   c. better

2. The _____ danger we encountered was the grizzly.
   a. worse
   b. worser
   c. worst

3. The view of the Pacific was the _____ thing they had ever seen.
   a. goodest
   b. better
   c. best

4. The freezing days were _____ than the hot ones.
   a. worst
   b. worse
   c. worser

5. The Oregon Trail is _____ than the California Trail.
   a. better
   b. gooder
   c. worst

**B.** Circle the letter of the proper adjective in each sentence.

1. Lewis and Clark crossed the Rockies near the Canadian border.
   a. Lewis
   b. Rockies
   c. Canadian

2. A Shoshone named Sacajawea led the explorers over Indian territory.
   a. Sacajawea
   b. explorers
   c. Indian

3. A Montana scientist is digging for clues.
   a. Montana
   b. scientist
   c. clues

## Comparing with *Good* and *Bad*

- Use *better* to compare two people, places, or things.
- Use *best* to compare more than two.
- Use *worse* to compare two people, places, or things.
- Use *worst* to compare more than two.

**Mechanics**

- A proper adjective is formed from a proper noun.
- A proper adjective begins with a capital letter.

Read the sentences about the picture. Rewrite the sentences correctly. Look for forms of the adjectives *good* and *bad*. Be sure all proper adjectives are capitalized.

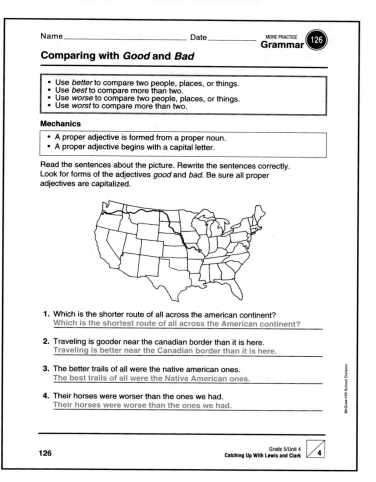

1. Which is the shorter route of all across the american continent?
   Which is the shortest route of all across the American continent?

2. Traveling is gooder near the canadian border than it is here.
   Traveling is better near the Canadian border than it is here.

3. The better trails of all were the native american ones.
   The best trails of all were the Native American ones.

4. Their horses were worser than the ones we had.
   Their horses were worse than the ones we had.

# Catching Up with Lewis and Clark • SPELLING

Name_____ Date_____

## Words from Social Studies

### Pretest Directions
Fold back the paper along the dotted line. Use the blanks to write each word as it is read aloud. When you finish the test, unfold the paper. Use the list at the right to correct any spelling mistakes. Practice the words you missed for the Posttest.

### To Parents
Here are the results of your child's weekly spelling Pretest. You can help your child study for the Posttest by following these simple steps for each word on the word list:

1. Read the word to your child.
2. Have your child write the word, saying each letter as it is written.
3. Say each letter of the word as your child checks the spelling.
4. If a mistake has been made, have your child read each letter of the correctly spelled word aloud, and then repeat steps 1–3.

1. _____
2. _____
3. _____
4. _____
5. _____
6. _____
7. _____
8. _____
9. _____
10. _____
11. _____
12. _____
13. _____
14. _____
15. _____
16. _____
17. _____
18. _____
19. _____
20. _____

1. journey
2. canoes
3. traveled
4. route
5. service
6. hardships
7. trail
8. explorer
9. communicate
10. agency
11. canal
12. fort
13. native
14. caravan
15. agreement
16. expedition
17. elevation
18. canyon
19. dwell
20. campsite

**Challenge Words**

_____ bison
_____ diaries
_____ former
_____ journal
_____ superb

---

Name_____ Date_____

## Words from Social Studies

### Using the Word Study Steps
1. LOOK at the word.
2. SAY the word aloud.
3. STUDY the letters in the word.
4. WRITE the word.
5. CHECK the word.
   Did you spell the word right? If not, go back to step 1.

**Spelling Tip**
Say the word to yourself one syllable at a time. Then write the word the same way.

For example:
jour + ney = journey
hard + ships = hardships

### X the Word
Put an X on the word in each row that has the same number of syllables as the spelling word on the left.

| | | | | |
|---|---|---|---|---|
| 1. journey | ~~hello~~ | smart | jail | |
| 2. caravan | construction | carton | crayon | |
| 3. dwell | yellow | ~~fine~~ | weather | |
| 4. canal | can't | clip | ~~cannot~~ | |
| 5. agency | ~~agreement~~ | against | always | |
| 6. service | serve | ~~notice~~ | enemy | |
| 7. communicate | compete | commune | ~~disagreement~~ | |
| 8. route | ~~tough~~ | ruin | riddle | |
| 9. campsite | clamp | ~~camper~~ | sight | |
| 10. expedition | ~~situation~~ | explore | perhaps | |

### To Parents or Helpers:
Using the Word Study Steps above as your child comes across any new words will help him or her spell well. Review the steps as you both go over this week's spelling words.
Go over the Spelling Tip with your child.
Help your child complete the spelling activity.

---

Name_____ Date_____

## Words from Social Studies

| | | | | |
|---|---|---|---|---|
| journey | service | communicate | native | elevation |
| canoes | hardships | agency | caravan | canyon |
| traveled | trail | canal | agreement | dwell |
| route | explorer | fort | expedition | campsite |

Sort each spelling word according to the number of syllables. Then write the words on the lines below.

**one syllable**

1. route
2. trail
3. fort
4. dwell

**two syllables**

5. journey
6. canoes
7. traveled
8. service
9. hardships
10. canal
11. native
12. canyon
13. campsite

**three syllables**

14. explorer
15. agency
16. caravan
17. agreement

**four syllables**

18. communicate
19. expedition
20. elevation

---

Name_____ Date_____

## Words from Social Studies

| | | | | |
|---|---|---|---|---|
| journey | service | communicate | native | elevation |
| canoes | hardships | agency | caravan | canyon |
| traveled | trail | canal | agreement | dwell |
| route | explorer | fort | expedition | campsite |

### Word Meaning: Synonyms
Write the spelling word that has the same meaning as the word or phrase below.

1. trip ___journey___
2. way to go ___route___
3. difficulties ___hardships___
4. deep valley ___canyon___
5. to live in ___dwell___
6. visited ___traveled___
7. path ___trail___
8. make known ___communicate___

9. company ___agency___
10. waterway ___canal___
11. group of vehicles ___caravan___
12. understanding ___agreement___
13. voyage ___expedition___
14. height ___elevation___

Complete each sentence below with a spelling word.

15. The soldiers built a ___fort___ to protect themselves.
16. She is a ___native___ of Texas because she was born there.
17. Robert Byrd was an ___explorer___ who found the North Pole.
18. The four friends paddled two ___canoes___ along the river.
19. That night they slept at their ___campsite___ on the banks of the river.
20. The salesclerk asked the customer if he could be of ___service___.

# Catching Up with Lewis and Clark • SPELLING

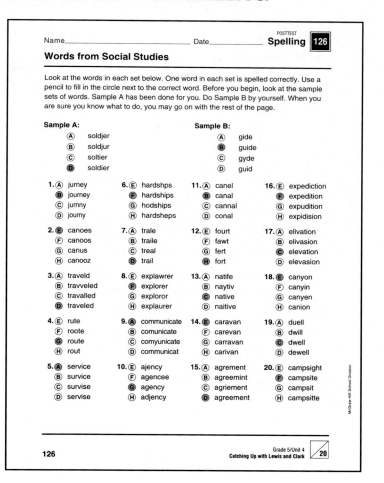

## Page 125

### Words from Social Studies

**Proofreading Activity**

There are six spelling mistakes in the paragraph below. Circle the misspelled words. Write the words correctly on the lines below.

Lewis and Clark could not find the words to comunicate the beauty of the land. But one member of their expidition was an artist. He traveld with the explorers and drew all the wonders he saw. Often, he would climb a mountain for the view. From this elvation he could draw the beauty of the land for miles around. He also drew pictures of the natife people they met along the way. The artist's work is the only picture record of Lewis and Clark's jurny.

1. communicate
2. expedition
3. traveled
4. elevation
5. native
6. journey

**Writing Activity**

Suppose that you were with Lewis and Clark as they went across the country. Write about what you would see. Use four spelling words in your writing.

_____

_____

_____

_____

_____

## Page 126

### Words from Social Studies

Look at the words in each set below. One word in each set is spelled correctly. Use a pencil to fill in the circle next to the correct word. Before you begin, look at the sample sets of words. Sample A has been done for you. Do Sample B by yourself. When you are sure you know what to do, you may go on with the rest of the page.

**Sample A:**
- (A) soldjer
- (B) soldjur
- (C) soltier
- (D) soldier ●

**Sample B:**
- (A) gide
- (B) guide ●
- (C) gyde
- (D) guid

1.
- (A) jurney
- (B) journey ●
- (C) jurnny
- (D) journy

2.
- (E) canoes ●
- (F) canoos
- (G) canus
- (H) canooz

3.
- (A) traveld
- (B) travveled
- (C) travalled
- (D) traveled ●

4.
- (E) rute
- (F) roote
- (G) route ●
- (H) rout

5.
- (A) service ●
- (B) survice
- (C) survise
- (D) servise

6.
- (E) hardshps
- (F) hardships ●
- (G) hodships
- (H) hardsheps

7.
- (A) trale
- (B) traile
- (C) treal
- (D) trail ●

8.
- (E) explawrer
- (F) explorer ●
- (G) exploror
- (H) explaurer

9.
- (A) communicate ●
- (B) comunicate
- (C) comyunicate
- (D) communicat

10.
- (E) ajency
- (F) agencee
- (G) agency ●
- (H) adjency

11.
- (A) canel
- (B) canal ●
- (C) cannal
- (D) conal

12.
- (E) fourt
- (F) fawt
- (G) fert
- (H) fort ●

13.
- (A) natife
- (B) naytiv
- (C) native ●
- (D) naitive

14.
- (E) caravan
- (F) carevan
- (G) carravan
- (H) carivan

15.
- (A) agrement
- (B) agreemint
- (C) agriement
- (D) agreement ●

16.
- (E) expediction
- (F) expedition ●
- (G) expudition
- (H) expidision

17.
- (A) elivation
- (B) elivasion
- (C) elevation ●
- (D) elevasion

18.
- (E) canyon ●
- (F) canyin
- (G) canyen
- (H) canion

19.
- (A) duell
- (B) dwill
- (C) dwell ●
- (D) dewell

20.
- (E) campsight
- (F) campsite ●
- (G) campsit
- (H) campsitte

## Practice 147

Name_____ Date_____ **Practice** 147

### Unit 4 Vocabulary Review

**A.** Read each word in column 1. Find its antonym, or the word most nearly opposite in meaning, in column 2. Then write the letter of the opposite word on the line.

| | | |
|---|---|---|
| _e_ | **1.** injured | **a.** normal |
| _a_ | **2.** peculiar | **b.** current |
| _b_ | **3.** former | **c.** unusually |
| _c_ | **4.** normally | **d.** disappear |
| _d_ | **5.** emerge | **e.** cured |

**B.** Supply the correct vocabulary word.

| tortillas | automatically | barrier | cycle | atmosphere | collision | glistening |
|---|---|---|---|---|---|---|

**1.** The snow on the trees was ___glistening___ in the bright sun.

**2.** Did you hear about that ___collision___ between the train and the big rig?

**3.** Every morning when the alarm clock goes off, I get up and shower ___automatically___.

**4.** My parents make ___tortillas___ in the morning for breakfast.

**5.** The four seasons are a yearly ___cycle___ in nature.

**6.** In order to be successful, you must learn to overcome any ___barrier___ in your way.

**7.** Some people really enjoy the busy ___atmosphere___ of a city.

12 Book 5/Unit 4
Unit 4 Vocabulary Review

At Home: Have students write a sentence for each vocabulary word in Part A.

**147**

## Practice 148

Name_____ Date_____ **Practice** 148

### Unit 4 Vocabulary Review

**A.** Answer each question.

**1.** What sort of an animal is a **bison**? ___Sample answer: It is a large, ox-like animal with dark shaggy fur and curved horns. It is also called a buffalo.___

**2.** What is **data** and what is it used for? ___Sample answer: Data is a collection of facts and figures often used to make a decision.___

**3.** What sort of things are **parallel** to each other? ___Sample answers include: the railroad tracks or the double yellow lines down a highway.___

**4.** What do you find **unpleasant**? ___Sample answer: Getting caught in the rain without an umbrella.___

**B.** Write the vocabulary word that means almost the same thing as the underlined word.

| swerved | observations | teeming | peculiar | naturalist | superb |
|---|---|---|---|---|---|

**1.** The concert was <u>excellent</u>. You should go if you can. ___superb___

**2.** The picnic basket was <u>swarming</u> with small insects. ___teeming___

**3.** Did the scientists make any <u>comments</u> about the event? ___observations___

**4.** I want to become a <u>scientist who works with nature</u>. ___naturalist___

**5.** I thought the chair looked <u>odd</u> painted pink. ___peculiar___

**6.** We quickly <u>turned</u> our bikes to avoid the deeper mud puddles. ___swerved___

148 At Home: Have students write a question for each vocabulary word in Part B. Then have them answer the questions. They can use Part A as a guide.

Book 5/Unit 4
Unit 4 Vocabulary Review

10

## Reteach 147

Name_____ Date_____ **Reteach** 147

### Unit 4 Vocabulary Review

**A.** Use words from the list to finish the crossword puzzle.

| naturalist | bison | teeming | data |
|---|---|---|---|
| superb | uneven | observations | stunned |

**Across**

**2.** things you see
**6.** nature expert
**8.** large prairie animal

**Down**

**1.** not even
**3.** crawling or covered with
**4.** fabulous
**5.** information, facts
**7.** shocked

*(Crossword answers:* OBSERVATIONS, NATURALIST, BISON, UNEVEN, STUNNED, SUPERB, DATA, TEEMING*)*

**B.** Supply the correct word from the list.

| glistening | emerge | assignments | journal | peculiar | atmosphere |
|---|---|---|---|---|---|

**1.** Lauren felt a ___peculiar___ feeling in her elbow when she fell off her bike.

**2.** The tasks of taking notes and keeping time will be Hannah's ___assignments___.

**3.** We watched the baby bird ___emerge___ from its nest and look around.

**4.** Chemicals in the air will hurt the ___atmosphere___.

**5.** Would-be writers keep a ___journal___ for jotting down ideas.

**6.** After swimming, Seth's skin was ___glistening___ with water.

14 Book 5/Unit 4
Unit 4 Vocabulary Review

At Home: Have students write a brief paragraph about one of the Unit 4 selections, using at least three vocabulary words.

**147**

## Reteach 148

Name_____ Date_____ **Reteach** 148

### Unit 4 Vocabulary Review

**A.** Read each clue. Then find the vocabulary word in the row of letters and circle it.

| swerved | parallel | injured | diaries |
|---|---|---|---|
| collision | fireball | carelessly | |

**1.** turned sharply   i n l l x y (s w e r v e d) v g e
**2.** daily writings   d i a s c x i e r (d i a r i e s)
**3.** harmed, hurt   p a r (i n j u r e d) j c v u e r
**4.** crash   (c o l l i s i o n) y c g u h e o
**5.** equally apart   x u q o x d l (p a r a l l e l) z
**6.** without care   x u e d o d (c a r e l e s s l y)
**7.** the sun   g i x n (f i r e b a l l) p i v b

**B.** Read the sentences and fill in the correct words.

| former | barrier | normally | unpleasant |
|---|---|---|---|
| observations | cycle | automatically | |

I hope the change in plans is not ___unpleasant___ news.

I realize that ___normally___ the ___cycle___ of classes begins on Mondays and ends on Fridays. However, we are lucky enough to have a visit from a ___former___ student who is quite successful. She knows a lot about the ___barrier___ islands of our region. Her ___observations___ should add a great deal of information to our discussions. The computer has ___automatically___ shifted all classes ahead by one day to make time for Ms. Liberatore's visit.

148 At Home: Look and listen for these vocabulary words in conversations, on signs, and in personal reading. Write any words you come across in a vocabulary log.

Book 5/Unit 4
Unit 4 Vocabulary Review

14

## Extend 147

Name_____ Date_____ **Extend** 147

**Vocabulary Review**

Read each clue below to complete the crossword puzzle.

**Across**
1. to settle oneself snugly
6. the gases, clouds, and dust that surround Earth
7. an equal distance apart at all points of the globe
8. to come forth
9. a mammal with a large shaggy head; buffalo
10. not straight; bumpy

**Down**
1. a person who studies natural science
2. factual information
3. something done with lack of care or attention
4. to come together; crash
5. very high quality; excellent

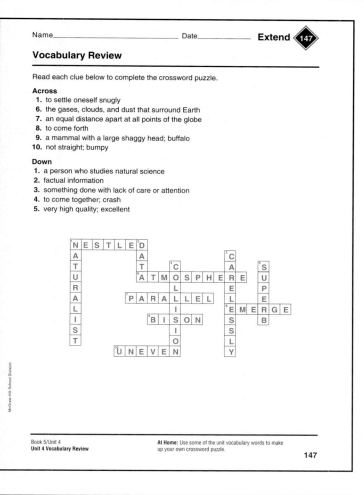

Crossword solution: NESTLED, NATURALIST, DATA, ATMOSPHERE, CARELESS, CAUSE, SUPERB, PARALLEL, EMERGE, BISON, COLLISION, UNEVEN

**Book 5/Unit 4**
**Unit 4 Vocabulary Review**

**At Home:** Use some of the unit vocabulary words to make up your own crossword puzzle.

147

---

## Extend 148

Name_____ Date_____ **Extend** 148

**Vocabulary Review**

Look at each bold face word. Use the clue word to complete a sentence that makes sense. Be creative when completing your sentences. Answers will vary.

1. One of Ivan's class **assignments** is to Answers will vary but should use the word in the correct context and part of speech.

2. The car **swerved** in order to Answers will vary but should use the word in the correct context and part of speech.

3. His leg became **injured** when he Answers will vary but should use the word in the correct context and part of speech.

4. The traveler's **journal** gave a vivid account of Answers will vary but should use the word in the correct context and part of speech.

5. After the meeting, the sports committee was **stunned** by the Answers will vary but should use the word in the correct context and part of speech.

6. The small pond was **teeming** with Answers will vary but should use the word in the correct context and part of speech.

7. After Sasha gets home from school, she **normally** Answers will vary but should use the word in the correct context and part of speech.

8. The huge **fireball** in the sky had been caused by Answers will vary but should use the word in the correct context and part of speech.

**At Home:** Write sentences using the words *convenience* and *naturalist*.

**Book 5/Unit 4**
**Unit 4 Vocabulary Review**

148

---

## Grammar 127

Name_____ Date_____ REVIEW **Grammar** 127

**Adjectives**

Read the passage and choose the appropriate word or group of words that belongs in each space. Circle the letter of your answer.

> The children had no idea that the picture was so real. Edmund and Lucy thought the ship looked like a ship from Narnia. But they did not realize that they were about to go on another __(1)__ adventure. Before they knew it, they had been swept into the chilly waters and were looking up at the great green ship. They were pulled from the water by their friend Caspian, the __(2)__ Narnian prince.

1. **A.** dry
   **B.** country
   **C.** exciting ⟵ (circled)
   **D.** accidental

2. **E.** evil
   **F.** brave ⟵ (circled)
   **G.** scary
   **H.** changed

> Last night, I ran over the __(3)__ snake I ever saw. I didn't see it when I hit it. But I thought it was a snake. Pete said, "Hey, that wasn't a snake." But I thought it was. It was the __(4)__ night in a while. We looked with our flashlights. Then we saw it. It was bigger than I imagined.

3. **A.** bigger
   **B.** biggest ⟵ (circled)
   **C.** big
   **D.** most biggest

4. **E.** darker
   **F.** dark
   **G.** darkest ⟵ (circled)
   **H.** most darker

> Springtime is a time of rapidly __(5)__ weather. In the West a mass of clouds and __(6)__, damp air rolls in off the ocean. It is the start of a big storm.

5. **A.** cold
   **B.** changing ⟵ (circled)
   **C.** April
   **D.** clear

6. **E.** cold ⟵ (circled)
   **F.** colder
   **G.** coldest
   **H.** most cold

Grade 5/Unit 4
**Investigate!**

127

---

## Grammar 128

Name_____ Date_____ REVIEW **Grammar** 128

**Adjectives**

> There are many powerful types of storms. The __(7)__ storms are tornadoes. Last year we had the most terrible storms anyone can remember. I remember one tornado that was __(8)__ than the others. It destroyed fifteen houses. Even the snow storms were the heaviest in years.

7. **A.** most powerfulest
   **B.** most powerfuler
   **C.** powefullest
   **D.** most powerful ⟵ (circled)

8. **E.** more violenter
   **F.** violenter
   **G.** violentest
   **H.** more violent ⟵ (circled)

> Lewis and Clark explored the American West. They were trying to find the __(9)__ route across the country. Some of the trails they found were better than others. The best were the Native American trails, though some were __(10)__ than others. With the help of Native Americans, Lewis and Clark finally reached the Pacific Ocean.

9. **A.** bestest
   **B.** worst
   **C.** best ⟵ (circled)
   **D.** better

10. **E.** worser
    **F.** badder
    **G.** worse ⟵ (circled)
    **H.** more bad

128

Grade 5/Unit 4
**Investigate!** 10

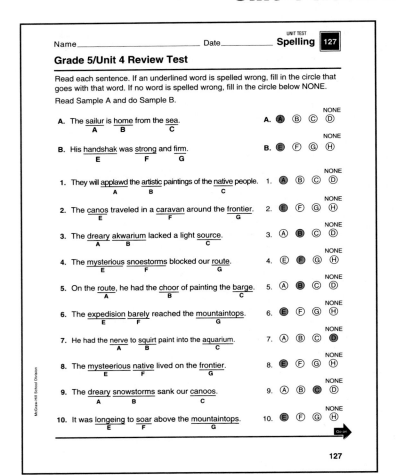

Name_____ Date_____

## Grade 5/Unit 4 Review Test

Read each sentence. If an underlined word is spelled wrong, fill in the circle that goes with that word. If no word is spelled wrong, fill in the circle below NONE.

Read Sample A and do Sample B.

A. The <u>sailur</u> is <u>home</u> from the <u>sea</u>.   A. Ⓐ Ⓑ Ⓒ Ⓓ
   A      B       C          NONE

B. His <u>handshak</u> was <u>strong</u> and <u>firm</u>.   B. Ⓔ Ⓕ Ⓖ Ⓗ
      E         F    G          NONE

1. They will <u>applawd</u> the <u>artistic</u> paintings of the <u>native</u> people.  1. Ⓐ Ⓑ Ⓒ Ⓓ
          A        B            C

2. The <u>canos</u> traveled in a <u>caravan</u> around the <u>frontier</u>.  2. Ⓔ Ⓕ Ⓖ Ⓗ
      E          F            G

3. The <u>dreary</u> <u>akwarium</u> lacked a light <u>source</u>.  3. Ⓐ Ⓑ Ⓒ Ⓓ
        A     B         C

4. The <u>mysterious</u> <u>snoestorms</u> blocked our <u>route</u>.  4. Ⓔ Ⓕ Ⓖ Ⓗ
        E        F         G

5. On the <u>route</u>, he had the <u>choor</u> of painting the <u>barge</u>.  5. Ⓐ Ⓑ Ⓒ Ⓓ
       A          B           C

6. The <u>expedision</u> <u>barely</u> reached the <u>mountaintops</u>.  6. Ⓔ Ⓕ Ⓖ Ⓗ
        E      F         G

7. He had the <u>nerve</u> to <u>squirt</u> paint into the <u>aquarium</u>.  7. Ⓐ Ⓑ Ⓒ Ⓓ
         A    B         C

8. The <u>mysteerious</u> <u>native</u> lived on the <u>frontier</u>.  8. Ⓔ Ⓕ Ⓖ Ⓗ
        E      F        G

9. The <u>dreary</u> <u>snowstorms</u> sank our <u>canoos</u>.  9. Ⓐ Ⓑ Ⓒ Ⓓ
       A       B        C

10. It was <u>longeing</u> to <u>soar</u> above the <u>mountaintops</u>.  10. Ⓔ Ⓕ Ⓖ Ⓗ
       E      F        G

Go on ➤

---

Name_____ Date_____

## Grade 5/Unit 4 Review Test

11. The <u>mysterious</u> weather on the <u>frontier</u> was <u>dreery</u>.  11. Ⓐ Ⓑ Ⓒ Ⓓ
        A            B        C

12. Cleaning an <u>aquarium</u> is not an <u>artistic</u> <u>chor</u>.  12. Ⓔ Ⓕ Ⓖ Ⓗ
        E         F    G

13. My <u>sister-in-law</u> ate <u>peanut butter</u> on the <u>expedition</u>.  13. Ⓐ Ⓑ Ⓒ Ⓓ
      A        B         C

14. The <u>aquarium</u> was the <u>saurce</u> of a <u>mysterious</u> leak.  14. Ⓔ Ⓕ Ⓖ Ⓗ
       E       F      G

15. My <u>sister-in-law</u> has a <u>rare</u> kite that can <u>soar</u>.  15. Ⓐ Ⓑ Ⓒ Ⓓ
      A       B       C

16. He was <u>longing</u> to climb the <u>stareway</u> to the <u>thirty-third</u> floor.  16. Ⓔ Ⓕ Ⓖ Ⓗ
       E       F       G

17. Our <u>roote</u> took us over the <u>frontier</u> <u>mountaintops</u>.  17. Ⓐ Ⓑ Ⓒ Ⓓ
      A        B       C

18. We will <u>applaud</u> my <u>sister-in-law</u> on her <u>thirty-third</u> birthday.  18. Ⓔ Ⓕ Ⓖ Ⓗ
       E      F      G

19. She <u>barely</u> had the <u>nirve</u> to <u>applaud</u> the singer.  19. Ⓐ Ⓑ Ⓒ Ⓓ
      A      B      C

20. The <u>expedition</u> followed a <u>route</u> over the <u>mountantops</u>.  20. Ⓔ Ⓕ Ⓖ Ⓗ
      E      F      G

21. It was a <u>chore</u> to move the <u>caravan</u> in <u>snowstorms</u>.  21. Ⓐ Ⓑ Ⓒ Ⓓ
      A      B      C

22. The <u>expedition</u> traveled to the <u>fronteer</u> by <u>barge</u>.  22. Ⓔ Ⓕ Ⓖ Ⓗ
      E      F      G

23. You have <u>nerve</u> to sit on the <u>stairway</u> and eat <u>peanut butter</u>.  23. Ⓐ Ⓑ Ⓒ Ⓓ
      A      B      C

24. He was <u>longing</u> for a <u>source</u> of <u>native</u> art.  24. Ⓔ Ⓕ Ⓖ Ⓗ
      E      F      G

25. I will <u>skwirt</u> the <u>barge</u> with water for the <u>thirty-third</u> time.  25. Ⓐ Ⓑ Ⓒ Ⓓ
      A      B      C

Grade 5/Unit 4
Unit Review Test  /25

# Notes

# Judgments and Decisions

**OBJECTIVES** Students will evaluate decisions through designing a new form of transportation, preparing for a journey, and performing a group story. Students will make and analyze judgments.

## Alternate Activities

## Visual

### WHAT'S THE BEST DESIGN?

**Materials:** drawing paper or poster board, crayons or colored pencils

Students will make decisions in designing a form of transportation to meet given criteria.

- Organize students into groups of 4 or 5. Ask each group to imagine and draw a new type of transportation they could take for a long journey. Ask them to create something that will work equally well on land, on water, and in the air.

- Have each group explain the vehicle it created and how it fits the criteria.

- Have classmates vote on the top design and brainstorm a name for the vehicle.
  ▶ **Spatial**

## Kinesthetic

### WHAT TO PACK?

**Materials:** 5 or 6 shoe boxes, magazines or catalogs showing clothing, scissors, tape or paste, index cards, crayons or colored pencils

Using pictures and shoe boxes, students will discuss and determine what to pack for a long journey.

- Give each group a shoe-box "suitcase" and magazines or catalogs and other materials.

- Have each group select clothing they would pack if they could take just one suitcase on a trip where the weather could be both hot and cold.

- Have students cut out pictures of the clothing, paste them on index cards, and "pack" them.

- Have one student in each group make a chart of the items of clothing they packed and the reasons why they chose each item.

- Have groups share their suitcases and charts.
  ▶ **Logical/Mathematical**

## Auditory

### AND SO THE STORY GOES

**Materials:** pencils, paper

Students will take turns completing a story. Then each group will act out its completed story for the class as one group member reads it aloud.

- Organize students into groups of 4 or 5. Give each group a paper with this story prompt at the top: *It all happened because the Smiths were so excited about leaving on their month-long family vacation.*

 Ask each group to complete the story based on the prompt. Each group member will add a sentence to the story until the group decides it is complete.

- Have one student in each group read the final story to the class as other members act it out. Discuss how the group writers made decisions on how to continue and conclude the story.

- Discuss the differences and similarities of the final stories.
  ▶ **Linguistic**

**See Reteach 112, 116, 133, 137**

# Graphic Aids

**OBJECTIVES** Students will make maps, create time lines, and write news reports to identify and use various graphic aids.

## Alternate Activities

### Visual

#### STATE MAPS

**Materials:** individual worksheets with outline of your state, maps of the U.S., road maps of your state, markers or colored pencils

By making and labeling a map of their state, students will use a graphic aid to assemble information.

- Have students identify the major rivers, roads, lakes, and any state or national parks; the capital city; and three other big cities in your state.

- Have students present this information on their map outlines, using different colored pencils and markers.

- Challenge students to locate your school on their maps.
  ▶ **Spatial**

### Kinesthetic

#### "BEEP-BEEP" TIME LINES

**Materials:** large sheets of drawing paper, tape or glue, markers or colored pencils

Students will create a time line to organize information in a memorable format.

- Each student will draw and label an event from history that interests him or her.

- Students will then research their events in order to label their drawing with the correct date.

- After all the drawings have been labeled, have the students line up in chronological order, displaying their drawings face out in the front of them.

  ▶ **Logical/Mathematical**

### Auditory

#### TV REPORTS

**Materials:** paper and pencils, newspapers

In this activity, students will write various types of reports and read the reports like television announcers.

- Organize students into groups of 4 or 5.

- Assign each group to locate a different type of report in the newspaper—weather report, traffic report, school report, sports report, farm report, and so on.

 Have students write up a script of the report as a TV announcer would deliver it. Also ask them to draw a graphic aid that displays the information from the report in a simple, clear way.

- Invite each group to give their report orally before the class.
  ▶ **Interpersonal**

See Reteach 115, 122, 129, 136, 143

# Draw Conclusions

 **OBJECTIVES** Students will create riddles, play a verbal location game, and play a description game as they derive conclusions by using logical reasoning.

## Alternate

## Visual

### DRAW CONCLUSION RIDDLES

 **Materials:** books of riddles, index cards, pencils

By writing and solving riddles, students will give logical answers that draw conclusions.

- Give each set of partners a riddle book to enjoy and to use as a model for writing.

On the index cards, have students create an original riddle. You might suggest that they use vocabulary or information from the unit. For example: Why did the chicken go out in the rain? *Because chickens love foul weather.*

- Have students challenge each other to solve their riddles.
  ▶ **Logical/Mathematical**

## Kinesthetic

### HIDE-AND-SEEK

**Materials:** small object, paper and pencils

Students will ask two or three questions about the location of an object hidden in the room and use logical reasoning to draw a conclusion about where the object has been hidden.

- Have students pick a number close to one you are thinking of to determine who starts.
- Send the first player out of the room. Hide the object.

- Call the player back in and let him or her ask just three questions about where the object is hidden.
- Students may call out "Hot" or "Cold" to indicate when the player is getting closer to or farther away from the object.
- If the player finds the object, he or she gets to choose the next player. If not, the teacher selects another player and repeats the routine.
  ▶ **Bodily/Kinesthetic**

## Auditory

### I'M THINKING OF SOMETHING...

Students will use verbal clues to challenge others to guess what they are describing.

- Arrange students in a circle. Ask each student to think of a particular item. You may wish to state a general theme, such as things on a farm, things in the classroom, things at the circus.
- Ask a volunteer to begin. Have the students say, "I'm thinking of something that sounds [or looks, or smells] like…" and then provide a verbal clue to the item.
- The student will continue to provide one clue at a time until the item is guessed by someone in the circle. Encourage discussion of what clues were most helpful and why. Continue until everyone has had a turn to challenge the others.
  ▶ **Logical/Mathematical**

**See Reteach 117, 124, 138**

# Suffixes

**OBJECTIVES** Students will write a poem, play word bingo, and tape record a story to identify and use suffixes.

## Alternate
## Activities

## *Visual*

### FIVE-LINE POEMS

**Materials:** individual worksheets, pencils or colored pencils

Students will use words with suffixes *-less* and *-ment* in writing a five-line poem.

Have students write five-line poems that follow these guidelines: Line 1 is one word taken from a unit story, such as "voyage" or "storm"; line 2 is two words using suffixes *-less* and *-ment* that describe line 1; line 3 is three words expressing action; line 4 is a four-word phrase; line 5 is one word ending with *-less* or *-ment* that sums up the whole poem. For example:

Poetry—
Breathless amazement.
Singing, speaking, playing
Like music of words—
Enjoyment!

* Have students read their poems aloud and post them on the bulletin board.
  ▶ **Intrapersonal**

## *Kinesthetic*

### WORD BINGO

**Materials:** bingo cards, beans or markers, large jar or bowl, small strips of paper

Using a bingo format, students will identify words with the suffixes *-less* and *-ment*.

* Have each student create a bingo card with three squares across and three squares down.

* Write a list of 20 or 25 *-less* and *-ment* words on the chalkboard. Write each word also on a small strip of paper, and put the strips in a jar or bowl. Have students choose 9 of the words on the board and write them in the 9 blank spaces on their bingo cards.

* Give each student beans or markers. As you pick and call a word, they should cover that word.

* When the first student with a completed line calls out bingo, have the student uncover the words and give their meanings.
  ▶ **Bodily/Kinesthetic**

## *Auditory*

### THE STORY OF LESS AND MENT

Students will write a story about the Suffix family of Less and Ment.

Have each group write a short story using this writing prompt: *Once upon a time the Suffix family lived in the small town of Wordville. There were two happy children in the family, twins named Less and Ment. One sunny summer day Less and Ment went for a walk in the woods and got lost.*

* Encourage students to use *-less* and *-ment* words in their stories.

* Have each group present its story orally for the class.
  ▶ **Linguistic**

**See Reteach 118, 132, 142**

# Important and Unimportant Information

OBJECTIVES Students will draw from memory, create a news program, and give game directions to choose what is most important.

## Alternate Activities

### Visual

#### WHAT AM I WEARING?

**Materials:** writing and drawing paper, pencils and colored pencils

By writing or drawing a detailed description of what another is wearing, students will choose or summarize the important information.

Seat partners back-to-back on the floor. Have one partner write from memory a description of what the other is wearing.

• When students have finished writing, let them face each other and check how accurate they were in describing from memory. Discuss if they got the most important information.

• Repeat the activity. This time have the non-writing partner draw what the other partner is wearing.

• Discuss <u>how</u> there may have been differences in reporting important or unimportant information depending upon writing or drawing.
▶ **Spatial**

### Kinesthetic

#### ACTION NEWS TEAMS

**Materials:** copies of age-appropriate magazines, newspapers, newsletters

Students will read and identify important information from assigned news articles. Teams will use this information to perform mock news programs for the class.

• Organize students into groups of four. Provide each group with a news source.

• Invite each group to select a story. As students read their stories, ask them to record all the important information onto index cards.

• Ask each group to use the information on the index cards to act out a news program for the rest of the class.
▶ **Bodily/Kinesthetic**

### Auditory

#### FOLLOW THE DIRECTIONS

**Materials:** index cards and pencils

Students will read a set of directions, identify important information, and follow directions.

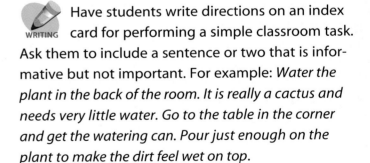Have students write directions on an index card for performing a simple classroom task. Ask them to include a sentence or two that is informative but not important. For example: *Water the plant in the back of the room. It is really a cactus and needs very little water. Go to the table in the corner and get the watering can. Pour just enough on the plant to make the dirt feel wet on top.*

• Put the index cards in a pile.

• Have players take turns selecting a card, reading the directions aloud, telling which parts are unimportant, and following the directions.
▶ **Linguistic**

**See Reteach 119, 123, 131, 144**

# Root Words

**OBJECTIVES** Students will create word maps, play a word relay, and listen to the rhythm in words to identify and use root words.

## Visual

### WORD MAPS

**Materials:** paper and pencils or colored pencils, vocabulary lists

By designing word maps, students will identify root words. Create a vocabulary list of words with root words. Put the list on the chalkboard.

- Give each set of partners drawing paper. Let them draw a word map that consists of a small circle on the left, connected with a line to a large circle in the middle, connected with a line to a small circle on the right.

- Have each set of partners choose five words from the word list to create word maps. Ask them to write the root words in the large center circle, prefixes in the left small circle, and suffixes in the right small circle.

- Discuss how knowing the meaning of the root word can help them find the meaning of an unfamiliar word with prefixes and suffixes.
  ▶ Linguistic

## Kinesthetic

### ROOT WORD RELAY

**Materials:** paper strips, three basket-type holders, colored chalk, score board, vocabulary lists

Students will identify root words.

- Organize the students into two teams.

- Write on the board two identical lists of words that have root words in them. Have students write the root words on strips of paper and put the strips of paper in a basket holder for their team.

- Follow the rules for running a relay. Give the first team member a paper strip with the root word. That student has to run up to the word list, put a tally mark by the word having the root word, deposit the used strip in the middle basket, draw another paper strip from the basket holder, and hand the new strip to a teammate.

- Repeat until all students have had a turn.
  ▶ Bodily/Kinesthetic

## Auditory

### RHYTHM ROOTS

**Materials:** poster board, colored pencils or markers, root word list

Students will clap the beat or rhythm to the syllables in words with prefixes, roots, and suffixes.

- Have students form pairs and create a chart on poster board: left column labeled *prefixes*, middle column *roots*, right column *suffixes*.

- Put a list of words with root words on the chalkboard. Have students go over each word and clap the number of syllables.

- Have partners go through the word list, clap the syllables, and write the word parts in the correct columns on the chart.
  ▶ Musical

**See Reteach 125, 139, 145**

# Fact and Nonfact

**OBJECTIVES** Students will create a travel scrapbook, play a circle game, and chart information in advertisements to identify and use facts and nonfacts.

## Alternate Activities

## Visual

### TRAVEL FACTS

**Materials:** travel brochures, large construction paper pages, scissors, paste, colored pencils or markers

Students will identify statements as true or false.

- Organize students into groups of 4 or 5. Give each group travel brochures for a different destination.

- Have students create a scrapbook page of pictures and text from the brochures. Ask them to divide the page into two categories: (1) facts, or things demonstrably true, and (2) nonfacts, or claims that can't be proved.

- Have a spokesperson for each group present their scrapbook page to the class and explain what they learned about this travel destination by categorizing information as fact or nonfact.

- Put all the pages together to make a travel scrapbook for the class to consult.

  ▶ **Interpersonal**

## Kinesthetic

### HOT POTATO FACTS

**Materials:** bean bag or soft item that can be tossed in a circle, a stopwatch or clock with a second hand

Students will play a game of "Hot Potato" in which they make true and false statements when they are tossed the bean bag.

- Have students stand in a circle. Start the game by tossing the bean bag to someone in the circle. When the student catches the bag, the thrower says either "fact" or "non-fact." The student catching the bean bag has ten seconds to respond with an appropriate statement. If the student is successful, he or she may toss the bag to another person; if not, the student must sit out the round.

- Continue until all students have had a turn, or only one student is left standing.

  ▶ **Bodily/Kinesthetic**

## Auditory

### FOOD FACTS

 **Materials:** magazines that can be cut up, construction paper, scissors, paste, colored pencils or markers

Students will read magazine ads and then chart whether the statements are facts or nonfacts.

- Have students work as partners. Give each pair a magazine with food ads. Have students read the ads aloud to each other and select several for a fact/nonfact chart.

- Create a chart with columns headed *Fact* and *Nonfact*.

- Invite students to cut out and paste statements from their magazine ads in the appropriate column.

- Ask partners to explain why the statements are facts or nonfacts.

  ▶ **Spatial**

**See Reteach 126, 130, 140**

## A Communication Tool

Although typewriters and computers are readily available, many situations continue to require handwriting. Tasks such as keeping journals, completing forms, taking notes, making shopping or organizational lists, and the ability to read hand-written manuscript or cursive writing are a few examples of practical application of this skill.

### BEFORE YOU BEGIN

Before children begin to write, certain fine motor skills need to be developed. Examples of activities that can be used as warm-up activities are:

- **Simon Says** Play a game of Simon Says using just finger positions.
- **Finger Plays and Songs** Sing songs that use Signed English, American Sign Language or finger spelling.
- **Mazes** Mazes are available in a wide range of difficulty. You can also create mazes that allow children to move their writing instruments from left to right.

## Determining Handedness

Keys to determining handedness in a child:

- Which hand does the child eat with? This is the hand that is likely to become the dominant hand.
- Does the child start coloring with one hand and then switch to the other? This may be due to fatigue rather than lack of hand preference.
- Does the child cross midline to pick things up or use the closest hand? Place items directly in front of the child to see if one hand is preferred.
- Does the child do better with one hand or the other?

## The Mechanics of Writing

### DESK AND CHAIR

- Chair height should allow for the feet to rest flat on the floor.
- Desk height should be two inches above the level of the elbows when the child is sitting.
- The chair should be pulled in allowing for an inch of space between the child's abdomen and the desk.
- Children sit erect with the elbows resting on the desk.
- Children should have models of letters on the desk or at eye level, not above their heads.

### PAPER POSITION

- **Right-handed children** should turn the paper so that  the lower left-hand corner of the paper points to the abdomen.
- **Left-handed children** should turn the paper so that 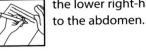 the lower right-hand corner of the paper points to the abdomen.
- The nondominant hand should anchor the paper near the top so that the paper doesn't slide.
- The paper should be moved up as the child nears the bottom of the paper. Many children won't think of this and may let their arms hang off the desk when they reach the bottom of a page.

## The Writing Instrument Grasp

For handwriting to be functional, the writing instrument must be held in a way that allows for fluid dynamic movement.

### FUNCTIONAL GRASP PATTERNS

- **Tripod Grasp** With open web space, the writing instrument  is held with the tip of the thumb and the index finger and rests against the side of the third finger. The thumb and index finger form a circle.
- **Quadrupod Grasp** With open web space, the writing  instrument is held with the tip of the thumb and index finger and rests against the fourth finger. The thumb and index finger form a circle.

### INCORRECT GRASP PATTERNS

- **Fisted Grasp** The writing instrument is held in a fisted hand.

- **Pronated Grasp** The writing instrument is held diagonally 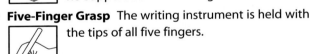 within the hand with the tips of the thumb and index finger on the writing instrument but with no support from other fingers.
- **Five-Finger Grasp** The writing instrument is held with  the tips of all five fingers.

### TO CORRECT WRITING INSTRUMENT GRASPS

- Have children play counting games with an eye dropper and water.
- Have children pick up small objects with a tweezer.
- Do counting games with children picking up small coins using just the thumb and index finger.

### FLEXED OR HOOKED WRIST

- The writing instrument can be held in a variety of grasps with the wrist flexed or bent. This is typically seen with left-handed writers but is also present in some right-handed writers. To correct wrist position, have children check their writing posture and paper placement.

# Evaluation Checklist

Functional writing is made up of two elements, legibility and functional speed.

## LEGIBILITY

### MANUSCRIPT

**Formation and Strokes**

- ☑ Does the child begin letters at the top?
- ☑ Do circles close?
- ☑ Are the horizontal lines straight?
- ☑ Do circular shapes and extender and descender lines touch?
- ☑ Are the heights of all upper-case letters equal?
- ☑ Are the heights of all lower-case letters equal?
- ☑ Are the lengths of the extenders and descenders the same for all letters?

**Directionality**

- ☑ Are letters and words formed from left to right?
- ☑ Are letters and words formed from top to bottom?

**Spacing**

- ☑ Are the spaces between letters equidistant?
- ☑ Are the spaces between words equidistant?
- ☑ Do the letters rest on the line?
- ☑ Are the top, bottom and side margins even?

### CURSIVE

**Formation and Strokes**

- ☑ Do circular shapes close?
- ☑ Are the downstrokes parallel?
- ☑ Do circular shapes and downstroke lines touch?
- ☑ Are the heights of all upper-case letters equal?
- ☑ Are the heights of all lower-case letters equal?
- ☑ Are the lengths of the extenders and descenders the same for all letters?
- ☑ Do the letters which finish at the top join the next letter? (*l, o, v, w*)
- ☑ Do the letters which finish at the bottom join the next letter? (*a, c, d, h, i, k, l, m, n, r, s, t, u, x*)
- ☑ Do letters with descenders join the next letter? (*f, g, j, p, q, y, z*)
- ☑ Do all letters touch the line?
- ☑ Is the vertical slant of all letters consistent?

**Directionality**

- ☑ Are letters and words formed from left to right?
- ☑ Are letters and words formed from top to bottom?

**Spacing**

- ☑ Are the spaces between letters equidistant?
- ☑ Are the spaces between words equidistant?
- ☑ Do the letters rest on the line?
- ☑ Are the top, bottom and side margins even?

## SPEED

The prettiest handwriting is not functional for classroom work if it takes the child three times longer than the rest of the class to complete work assignments. After the children have been introduced to writing individual letters, begin to add time limitations to the completion of copying or writing assignments. Then check the child's work for legibility.

# Handwriting Models—Manuscript

# Handwriting Models—Cursive

A B C D E F G H I

J K L M N O P Q R

S T U V W X Y Z

a b c d e f g h i j

k l m n o p q r s

t u v w x y z

# Handwriting Models—Slant

A B C D E F G H

I J K L M N O P

Q R S T U V W

X Y Z

a b c d e f g h

i j k l m n o p

q r s t u v w

x y z

# Handwriting Practice

## Selection Titles

## Honors, Prizes, and Awards

**THE WISE OLD WOMAN**
Unit 1, p. 20
by *Yoshiko Uchida*
Illustrated by *Martin Springett*

**Author: Yoshiko Uchida,** winner of Commonwealth Club of California Book Award (1972) for *Samurai of Gold Hill*; Bay Area Book Reviewers Association Award (1986) for *The Happiest Ending*; Friends of Children and Literature Award (1986) for *A Jar of Dreams*

**VOYAGE OF THE *DAWN TREADER***
Unit 1, p. 46
by *C.S. Lewis*
Illustrated by *Amy Hill*

**Author: C.S. Lewis,** winner of Lewis Carroll Shelf Award (1962) for *The Lion, the Witch, and the Wardrobe;* Carnegie Medal (1956) for *The Last Battle*

**WILMA UNLIMITED**
Unit 1, p. 68
by *Kathleen Krull*
Illustrated by *David Diaz*

**Booklist Editor's Choice, Parent's Choice Award (1996), School Library Journal Best Book of the Year, ALA Notable, Jane Addams Book Award (1997)**
**Illustrator: David Diaz,** winner of Caldecott Medal (1995) for *Smoky Nights*

**WRECK OF THE *ZEPHYR***
Unit 1, p. 96
by *Chris Van Allsburg*

**Booklist Editor's Choice, IRA Teacher's Choice, New York Times Best Illustrated Children's Books of the Year (1983), Publishers Weekly, ALA Notable (1984)**
**Author/Illustrator: Chris Van Allsburg,** winner of ALA Notable, Caldecott Medal, Boston Globe-Horn Book Honor (1982) for *Jumanji*; ALA Notable, Boston Globe-Horn Book Honor, Caldecott Medal (1986) for *The Polar Express*; NSTA Outstanding Science Trade Book for Children (1988), IRA-CBC Children's Choice (1989) for *Two Bad Ants*; ALA Notable (1994) for *The Sweetest Fig*

**KNOXVILLE, TENNESSEE**
Unit 1, p. 134
by *Nikki Giovanni*

**Poet: Nikki Giovanni,** winner of ALA Best Book for Young Adults commendation (1973) for *My House*; Children's Reading Roundtable of Chicago Award (1988) for *Vacation Time*

**ORANGES**
Unit 2, p. 136
by *Jean Little*

**Poet: Jean Little,** winner of Canadian Library Association Awards Book of the Year for Children (1985) for *Mama's Going to Buy You a Mockingbird*; Boston Globe-Horn Book Honor Book, ALA Notable (1988) for *Little by Little: A Writer's Education*

| Selection Titles | Honors, Prizes, and Awards |
|---|---|
| **THE GOLD COIN**<br>Unit 2, p. 140<br>by *Alma Flor Ada*<br>Illustrated by *Neil Waldman* | **Christopher Award (1992)** |
| **JOHN HENRY**<br>Unit 2, p. 168<br>by *Julius Lester*<br>Illustrated by *Jerry Pinkney* | **Center for Children's Books Blue Ribbon (1994), ALA Notable, Caldecott Medal Honor Book, Boston Globe-Horn Book Award (1995)**<br>**Illustrator: Jerry Pinkney,** winner of Newbery Medal, Boston Globe-Horn Book Honor (1977) for *Roll of Thunder, Hear My Cry*; ALA Notable, Cadelcott Honor, Coretta Scott King Award (1989) for *Mirandy and Brother Wind*; ALA Notable, Caldecott Honor, Coretta Scott King Honor (1990) for *Talking Eggs*; ALA Notable (1991) for *Further Tales of Uncle Remus*; ALA Notable, Christopher Award, Coretta Scott King Award (1997) for *Minty* |
| **IT'S OUR WORLD, TOO**<br>Unit 2, p. 202<br>by *Phillip Hoose*<br>Illustrated by *Robert Rober* | **Christopher Award (1994)** |
| **DEAR MR. HENSHAW**<br>Unit 2, p. 224<br>by *Beverly Cleary*<br>Illustrated by *R. J. Shay* | **Newbery Medal, Christopher Award (1984), Dorothy Canfield Fisher Children's Book Award (1985)** |
| **THE SIDEWALK RACER OR ON THE SKATEBOARD**<br>Unit 3, p. 254<br>by *Lillian Morrison* | **Poet: Lillian Morrison,** winner of ALA Notable (1965) for *Sprints and Distances: Sports in Poetry and the Poetry in Sports* |
| **THE MARBLE CHAMP**<br>Unit 3, p. 258<br>by *Gary Soto*<br>Illustrated by *Ken Spengler* | **Author: Gary Soto,** winner of Academy of American Poets Award (1975); California Library Association's John And Patricia Beatty Award, Best Books for Young Adults Awards (1991) for *Baseball in April and Other Stories*; Americás Book Award, Honorable Mention (1995) for *Chato's Kitchen*; Americás Book Award, Commended List (1995) for *Canto Familiar*; (1996) for *The Old Man and His Door*; (1997) for *Buried Onions* |

## Selection Titles | Honors, Prizes, and Awards

**THE PAPER DRAGON**
Unit 3, p. 276
by *Marguerite W. Davol*
Illustrated by *Robert Sabuda*

**Golden Kite Award (1997), ALA Notable, Notable Children's Trade Book in the Field of Social Studies (1998)**

---

**GRANDMA ESSIE'S COVERED WAGON**
Unit 3, p. 310
by *David Williams*
Illustrated by *Wiktor Sadowski*

**Notable Trade Book in the Field of Social Studies (1994)**

---

**GOING BACK HOME: AN ARTIST RETURNS TO THE SOUTH**
Unit 3, p. 342
by *Toyomi Igus*
Illustrated by **Michele Wood**

**Center for Children's Books Blue Ribbon (1996), American Book Award Winner (1997)**

---

**TO DARK EYES DREAMING**
Unit 3, p. 382
by *Zilpha Keatley Snyder*

**Poet: Zilpha Keatley Snyder,** winner of Newbery Medal Honor Book (1968) and George G. Stone Center for Children's Books Recognition of Merit Award (1973) for *The Egypt Game*; ALA Notable (1971) and Christopher Award (1974) for *The Headless Cupid*

---

**CARLOS AND THE SKUNK**
Unit 4, p. 388
by *Jan Romero Stevens*
Illustrated by *Jeanne Arnold*

**Author: Jan Romero Stevens,** winner of Consortium of Latin American Studies Programs (CLASP) Americás Award for Children's and Young Adult Literature, Commended List (1997)

---

**AN ISLAND SCRAPBOOK**
Unit 4, p. 434
by *Virginia Wright-Frierson*

**Notable Children's Book in the Language Arts, Outstanding Nature Book for Children by John Burroughs Association (1998), Outstanding Science Trade Book for Children (1999)**

---

**THE RIDDLE**
Unit 5, p. 510
by **Adele Vernon**
Illustrated by **Robert Rayevsky and Vladimir Radunsky**

**Booklist Editor's Choice**

---

| Selection Titles | Honors, Prizes, and Awards |
|---|---|
| **TONWEYA AND THE EAGLES**<br>Unit 5, p. 556<br>by *Rosebud Yellow Robe*<br>Illustrated by *Richard Red Owl* | **ALA Notable (1979)** |
| **BREAKER'S BRIDGE**<br>Unit 5, p. 582<br>by *Laurence Yep*<br>Illustrated by *David Wisniewski* | **Author: Laurence Yep,** winner of Newbery Honor Book Award (1976) for *Dragonwings;* (1994) for *Dragon's Gate;* Boston Globe-Horn Book Honor (1977) for *Child of the Owl* |
| **PHILBERT PHLURK**<br>Unit 5, p. 612<br>by *Jack Prelutsky* | **Poet: Jack Prelutsky,** winner of New York Times Notable Book (1980) for *The Headless Horseman Rides Tonight;* ALA Notable (1983) for *Random House Book of Poetry for Children;* (1985) for *New Kid on the Block;* (1991) for *Something Big Has Been Here* |
| **PAPER I**<br>Unit 6, p. 614<br>by *Carl Sandburg* | **Poet: Carl Sandburg**, winner of Pulitzer Prize in poetry (1919) for *Corn Huskers;* (1951) for *Complete Poems;* Pulitzer Prize in history (1940) for *Abraham Lincoln: The War Years;* Poetry Society of America's Frost Medal for Distinguished Achievement (1952); ALA Notable (1982) for *Rainbows are Made: Poems of Carl Sandburg* |
| **AMISTAD RISING**<br>Unit 6, p. 618<br>by *Veronica Chambers*<br>Illustrated by *Paul Lee* | **Author: Veronica Chambers,** winner of ALA Best Book for Young Adults (1996) for *Mama's Girl* |
| **THE SILENT LOBBY**<br>Unit 6, p. 700<br>by *Mildred Pitts Walter*<br>Illustrated by *Gil Ashby* | **Author: Mildred Pitts Walter,** winner of Coretta Scott King Award (1984) for *My Mama Needs Me;* (1987) for *Justin and the Best Biscuits in the World* |
| **FREDERICK DOUGLASS 1817–1895**<br>Unit 6, p. 728<br>by *Langston Hughes* | **Poet: *Langston Hughes,*** winner of Witter Bynner Prize (1926); Harmon Foundation Literature Award (1931); American Academy of Arts and Letters Grant (1946); Spingarn Medal (1960) |

## CARLOS AND THE SKUNK

## HOW TO THINK LIKE A SCIENTIST

## Trade Books

**A**dditional fiction and nonfiction trade books related to each selection can be shared with students throughout the unit.

### Bill Pickett: Rodeo-Ridin' Cowboy
Andrea D. Pinkney, illustrated by Brian Pinkney (Harcourt Brace, 1996)

The story of the cowboy whose dream it was to become the most famous black rodeo performer. *Biography*

### The Abacus Contest: Stories from Taiwan and China
Priscilla Wu (Fulcrum, 1996)

Six stories about life in modern Taiwan depict cultural differences while illustrating the common themes concerning all children around the world. *Realistic Fiction*

### The Cricket in Times Square
George Selden (Bantam Doubleday Dell, 1997)

Chester, a Connecticut cricket, finds success in New York City but longs for the peace of his country home. *Fantasy*

### The Real McCoy: The Life of an African-American Inventor
Wendy Towle, illustrated by Wil Clay (Scholastic, 1995)

A picture-book biography of Elijah McCoy, a pioneer in engineering. *Biography*

### The Librarian Who Measured the Earth
Kathryn Lasky, illustrated by Kevin Hawkes (Little, Brown, 1994)

Meet Eratosthenes, the ancient Greek librarian and geographer who measured the circumference of the Earth to within 200 feet of today's measurements. *Biography*

### Brainstorm! The Stories of Twenty American Kid Inventors
Tom Tucker, illustrated by Richard Loehle (Farrar, Straus & Giroux, 1995)

Learn about the inventions of twenty young creative thinkers throughout the last three centuries. *Social Studies Nonfiction*

## Technology

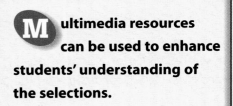

**M**ultimedia resources can be used to enhance students' understanding of the selections.

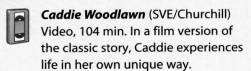 ***Caddie Woodlawn*** (SVE/Churchill) Video, 104 min. In a film version of the classic story, Caddie experiences life in her own unique way.

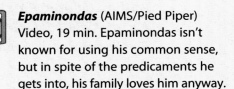 ***Epaminondas*** (AIMS/Pied Piper) Video, 19 min. Epaminondas isn't known for using his common sense, but in spite of the predicaments he gets into, his family loves him anyway.

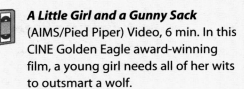 ***A Little Girl and a Gunny Sack*** (AIMS/Pied Piper) Video, 6 min. In this CINE Golden Eagle award-winning film, a young girl needs all of her wits to outsmart a wolf.

 ***Scientific Method and Measurement*** (United Learning) Video, 17 min. Scientific method is examined and demonstrated.

 ***Scientific Measurement*** (SVE) Videodisc CAV, 18 min. A demonstration of scientific techniques.

 ***Elementary Science Series—The Scientific Method*** (National Geographic Society) Video, 20 min. Video series explains how the scientific method applies to the work of some scientists.

## AN ISLAND SCRAPBOOK

**Grand Canyon: Exploring a Natural Wonder**
*Wendell Minor (Scholastic, 1998)*

The author/illustrator explores and sketches the Grand Canyon. *Social Studies Nonfiction*

**Maria de Sautuola: The Bulls in the Cave**
*Dennis Brindell Fradin, illustrated by Ed Martinez (Silver Burdett, 1997)*

A young Spanish girl discovers prehistoric cave drawings, to both the tragedy and triumph of her family. *Historical Fiction*

**The Most Beautiful Roof in the World: Exploring the Rainforest Canopy**
*Kathryn Lasky (Harcourt Brace, 1997)*

Visit the unique world of the rainforest canopy at a site in Belize with biologist Meg Lowman. *Photo Essay*

 *Deserts* (Ambrose Video) Video, 30 min. Insight into the conditions that create deserts.

 *U.S. Geography: The Southwest* (SVE/Churchill Media) CD-ROM. Students will see some of the fastest growing cities in Arizona, New Mexico, Oklahoma, and Texas.

 *One Small Square–Seashore* (ESI) CD-ROM, Macintosh, Windows. A powerful look at nature and the many forms of life that can be found in one tiny area of seashore.

## THE BIG STORM

**Trapped by the Ice! Shackleton's Amazing Antarctic Adventure**
*Michael McCurdy (Walker, 1997)*

A riveting account of Sir Ernest Shackleton's 1914 expedition to the Antarctic, where his ship, the *Endurance*, became trapped by ice and sank. *Social Studies Nonfiction*

**Tornado**
*Betsy Byars (HarperCollins, 1997)*

A family driven to the storm cellar by an approaching tornado is entertained by a farmhand's tales of his childhood pet, a dog named Tornado. *Fiction*

**El Niño: Stormy Weather for People and Wildlife**
*Caroline Arnold (Clarion Books, 1998)*

Everything you ever wanted to know about El Niño with a glossary, color photographs, diagrams, maps, and a bibliography. *Science Nonfiction*

 *Violent Storms* (Coronet/MTI) Video or videodisc, 14 min. A photographic and cinematographic record of a thunderstorm.

 *Hurricanes and Tornadoes* (Library Video Company) Video, 23 min. Shows how meteorologists use data from satellite images, Doppler radar, and other technology.

 *Wind* (AIMS Multimedia) Video, 12 min. How the wind functions and how it changes the land.

*TIME FOR KIDS*

## CATCHING UP WITH LEWIS AND CLARK

**How We Crossed the West: Adventures of Lewis and Clark**
*Rosalyn Schanzer (National Geographic Society, 1997)*

Using the actual words of the explorers, the author recreates the Lewis and Clark expedition. *Historical Fiction*

**Off the Map: The Journals of Lewis and Clark**
*Peter and Connie Roop, eds., illustrated by Tim Tanner (Walker, 1993)*

Entries and excerpts from the Lewis and Clark journals describe their adventurous expedition. *Journal*

**Sacajawea**
*Judith St. George (G. P. Putnam's Sons, 1997)*

The story of the Lewis and Clark expedition is told from the point of view of sixteen-year-old Sacajawea, the Shoshone woman who was the interpreter for the journey. *Historical Fiction*

 *Lewis and Clark* (National Geographic) CD-ROM, Macintosh, Windows. Students experience the journey of Lewis and Clark as they search for a Northwest passage.

 *The Oregon Trail* (MECC) CD-ROM, Macintosh, Windows. Students explore American frontier life in this interactive program about the Oregon Trail.

 *The Song of Sacagawea* (AIMS/Pied Piper) Video, 30 min. A profile of Sacagawea, the young Native American who served as a guide to Lewis and Clark.

**Directory of Resources** *(sidebar)*

**Aladdin Paperbacks**
(Imprint of Simon & Schuster Children's
Publishing)

**Alaska Northwest Books**
(Division of Graphic Arts Center
Publishing Co.)
3019 NW Yeon Ave.
Box 10306
Portland, OR 97296-0306
(503) 226-2402 • (800) 452-3032
Fax (503) 223-1410
www.gacpc.com

**Annick Press**
(Imprint of Firefly Books, Ltd.)

**Atheneum**
(Imprint of Simon & Schuster Children's
Publishing)

**Avon Books**
(Division of Hearst Corp.)
1350 Avenue of the Americas
New York, NY 10019
(212) 261-6800 • (800) 238-0658
Fax (800) 223-0239
www.avonbooks.com

**Bantam Doubleday Dell Books for
Young Readers**
(Imprint of Random House)

**Peter Bedrick Books**
156 Fifth Ave., Suite 817
New York, NY 10010
(800) 788-3123 • Fax (212) 206-3741

**Beech Tree Books**
(Imprint of William Morrow & Co.)

**Blackbirch Press**
260 Amity Road
Woodbridge, CT 06525
(203) 387-7525 • (800) 831-9183
www.blackbirch.com

**Blue Sky Press**
(Imprint of Scholastic)

**Bradbury Press**
(Imprint of Simon & Schuster Children's
Publishing)

**BridgeWater Books**
(Distributed by Penguin Putnam, Inc.)

**Candlewick Press**
2067 Massachusetts Avenue
Cambridge, MA 02140
(617) 661-3330 • Fax (617) 661-0565
www.candlewick.com

**Carolrhoda Books**
(Division of Lerner Publications Co.)

**Cartwheel Books**
(Imprint of Scholastic)

**Children's Book Press**
246 First St., Suite 101
San Francisco, CA 94105
(415) 995-2200 • Fax (415) 995-2222

**Children's Press** (Division of Grolier, Inc.)
P.O. Box 1795
Danbury, CT 06816-1333
(800) 621-1115 • www.grolier.com

**Chronicle Books**
85 Second Street, Sixth Floor
San Francisco, CA 94105
(415) 537-3730 • Fax (415) 537-4460
(800) 722-6657
www.chroniclebooks.com

**Clarion Books**
(Imprint of Houghton Mifflin, Inc.)
215 Park Avenue South
New York, NY 10003
(212) 420-5800 • (800) 225-3362
www.houghtonmifflinbooks.com/clarion

**Crabtree Publishing Co.**
350 Fifth Ave., Suite 3308
New York, NY 10118
(212) 496-5040 • (800) 387-7650
Fax (800) 355-7166
www.crabtree-pub.com

**Creative Education**
The Creative Co.
123 S. Broad Street
P.O. Box 227
Mankato, MN 56001
(507) 388-6273 • (800) 445-6209
Fax (507) 388-2746

**Crowell** (Imprint of HarperCollins)

**Crown Publishing Group**
(Imprint of Random House)

**Delacorte**
(Imprint of Random House)

**Dial Books**
(Imprint of Penguin Putnam, Inc.)

**Discovery Enterprises, Ltd.**
31 Laurelwood Dr.
Carlisle, MA 01741
(978) 287-5401 • (800) 729-1720
Fax (978) 287-5402

**Disney Press**
(Division of Disney Book Publishing, Inc.,
A Walt Disney Co.)
114 Fifth Ave.
New York, NY 10011
(212) 633-4400 • Fax (212) 633-4833
www.disneybooks.com

**Dorling Kindersley** (DK Publishing)
95 Madison Avenue
New York, NY 10016
(212) 213-4800 • Fax (212) 213-5240
(888) 342-5357 • www.dk.com

**Doubleday** (Imprint of Random House)

**E. P. Dutton Children's Books**
(Imprint of Penguin Putnam, Inc.)

**Farrar Straus & Giroux**
19 Union Square West
New York, NY 10003
(212) 741-6900 • Fax (212) 741-6973
(888) 330-8477

**Firefly Books, Ltd.**
PO Box 1338
Endicott Station
Buffalo, NY 14205
(416) 499-8412 • Fax (800) 565-6034
(800) 387-5085
www.firefly.com

**Four Winds Press**
(Imprint of Macmillan, see Simon &
Schuster Children's Publishing)

**Fulcrum Publishing**
350 Indiana Street, Suite 350
Golden, CO 80401
(303) 277-1623 • (800) 992-2908
Fax (303) 279-7111
www.fulcrum-books.com

**Greenwillow Books**
(Imprint of William Morrow & Co, Inc.)

**Gulliver Green Books**
(Imprint of Harcourt Brace & Co.)

**Harcourt Brace & Co.**
6277 Sea Harbor Drive
Orlando, FL 32337
(407) 345-2000 • (800) 225-5425
www.harcourtbooks.com

**Harper & Row** (Imprint of HarperCollins)

**HarperCollins Children's Books**
1350 Avenue of the Americas
New York, NY 10017
(212) 261-6500 • Fax (212) 261-6689
(800) 242-7737 www.harperchildrens.com

**Harper Trophy**
(Imprint of HarperCollins)

**Holiday House**
425 Madison Avenue
New York, NY 10017
(212) 688-0085 • Fax (212) 421-6134

**Henry Holt and Company**
115 West 18th Street
New York, NY 10011
(212) 886-9200 • (212) 633-0748
(888) 330-8477 • www.henryholt.com/byr/

**Houghton Mifflin**
222 Berkeley Street
Boston, MA 02116
(617) 351-5000 • Fax (617) 351-1125
(800) 225-3362
www.houghtonmifflinbooks.com

**Hyperion Books**
(Division of ABC, Inc.)
77 West 66th Street
New York, NY 10023
(212) 456-0100 • (800) 343-9204
www.disney.com

**Just Us Books**
356 Glenwood Avenue
E. Orange, NJ 07017
(973) 672-7701 • Fax (973) 677-7570
www.justusbooks.com

**Kane/Miller Book Publishers**
P.O. Box 310529
Brooklyn, NY 11231-0529
(718) 624-5120 • Fax (718) 858-5452
www.kanemiller.com

**Alfred A. Knopf**
(Imprint of Random House)

**Lee & Low Books**
95 Madison Avenue, Room 606
New York, NY 10016
(212) 779-4400 • Fax (212) 683-1894

**Lerner Publications Co.**
241 First Avenue North
Minneapolis, MN 55401
(612) 332-3344 • Fax (612) 332-7615
(800) 328-4929 • www.lernerbooks.com

**Little, Brown & Co.**
3 Center Plaza
Boston, MA 02108
(617) 227-0730 • Fax (617) 263-2864
(800) 759-0190 • www.littlebrown.com

**Lothrop Lee & Shepard**
(Imprint of William Morrow & Co.)

**Macmillan**
(Imprint of Simon & Schuster
Children's Publishing)

**Mikaya Press**
(Imprint of Firefly Books, Ltd.)

**Millbrook Press, Inc.**
2 Old New Milford Road
Brookfield, CT 06804
(203) 740-2220 • (800) 462-4703
Fax (203) 740-2526
www.millbrookpress.com

**William Morrow & Co.**
(Imprint of HarperCollins)

**Morrow Junior Books**
(Imprint of HarperCollins)

**National Geographic Society**
1145 17th Street, NW
Washington, DC 20036
(800) 638-4077
www.nationalgeographic.com

**Northland Publishing**
(Division of Justin Industries)
Box 1389
Flagstaff, AZ 86002
(520) 774-5251 • Fax (800) 744-0592
(800) 346-3257 • www.northlandpub.com

**Orchard Books** (A Grolier Company)
95 Madison Avenue
New York, NY 10016
(212) 951-2600 • Fax (212) 213-6435
www.grolier.com

**Oxford University Press, Inc.**
198 Madison Ave.
New York, NY 10016-4314
(212) 726-6000 • (800) 451-7556
www.oup-usa.org

**Penguin Putnam, Inc.**
375 Hudson Street
New York, NY 10014
(212) 366-2000
(800) 631-8571
www.penguinputnam.com

**Philomel Books**
(Imprint of Penguin Putnam, Inc.)

**Pippin Press**
Gracie Station, Box 1347
229 E. 85th Street
New York, NY 10028
(212) 288-4920 • Fax (732) 225-1562

**Puffin Books**
(Imprint of Penguin Putnam, Inc.)

**G.P. Putnam's Sons Publishing**
(Imprint of Penguin Putnam, Inc.)

**Random House**
1540 Broadway
New York, NY 10036
(212) 782-9000 • Fax (212) 782-9452
(800) 200-3552
www.randomhouse.com/kids

**Rising Moon**
(Imprint of Northland Publishing)

**Scholastic**
555 Broadway
New York, NY 10012
(212) 343-7500 • Fax (212) 965-7442
(800) SCHOLASTIC • www.scholastic.com

**Sierra Club Books for Children**
85 Second Street, Second Floor
San Francisco, CA 94105-3441
(415) 977-5500 • Fax (415) 977-5793
(800) 935-1056 • www.sierraclub.org

**Silver Burdett Press**
(Division of Pearson Education)
299 Jefferson Rd.
Parsippany, NJ 07054-0480
(973) 739-8000 • (800) 848-9500
www.sbgschool.com

**Simon & Schuster Children's Books**
1230 Avenue of the Americas
New York, NY 10020
(212) 698-7200 • (800) 223-2336
www.simonsays.com/kidzone

**Gareth Stevens, Inc.**
River Center Bldg.
1555 N. River Center Dr., Suite 201
Milwaukee, WI 53212
(414) 225-0333 • (800) 341-3569
Fax (414) 225-0377
www.gsinc.com

**Sunburst**
(Imprint of Farrar Straus & Giroux)

**Tricycle Press**
(Division of Ten Speed Press)
P.O. Box 7123
Berkeley, CA 94707
(510) 559-1600 • (800) 841-2665
Fax (510) 559-1637
www.tenspeed.com

**Viking Children's Books**
(Imprint of Penguin Putnam, Inc.)

**Voyager**
(Imprint of Harcourt Brace & Co.)

**Walker & Co.**
435 Hudson Street
New York, NY 10014
(212) 727-8300 • (212) 727-0984
(800) AT-WALKER

**Warwick Publishing**
162 John St.
Toronto, CAN M5V2E5
(416) 596-1555
www.warwickgp.com

**Watts Publishing**
(Imprint of Grolier Publishing;
see Children's Press)

**Yearling Books**
(Imprint of Random House)

# Multimedia Resources

**AIMS Multimedia**
9710 DeSoto Avenue
Chatsworth, CA 91311-4409
(800) 367-2467
www.AIMS-multimedia.com

**Ambrose Video and Publishing**
28 West 44th Street, Suite 2100
New York, NY 10036
(800) 526-4663 • Fax (212) 768-9282
www.AmbroseVideo.com

**BFA Educational Media**
(see The Phoenix Learning Group)

**Boston Federal Reserve Bank**
Community Affairs Dept.
P.O. Box 2076
Boston, MA 02106-2076
(617) 973-3459
www.bos.frb.org

**Britannica**
310 South Michigan Avenue
Britannica Center
Chicago, IL 60604-4293
(800) 621-3900 • Fax (800) 344-9624

**Broderbund**
(Parsons Technology;
also see The Learning Company)
500 Redwood Blvd.
Novato, CA 94997
(800) 395-0277
www.broderbund.com

**Carousel Film and Video**
260 Fifth Avenue, Suite 705
New York, NY 10001
(212) 683-1660 • e-mail:
carousel@pipeline.com

**CBS/Fox Video**
1330 Avenue of the Americas
New York, NY 10019
(800) 457-0686

**Cornell University Audio/Video Resource Ctr.**
8 Business & Technology Park
Ithaca, NY 14850
(607) 255-2091

**Coronet/MTI**
(see The Phoenix Learning Group)

**Direct Cinema, Ltd.**
P.O. Box 10003
Santa Monica, CA 90410-1003
(310) 636-8200

**Encyclopaedia Britannica Educational Corp.**
310 South Michigan Avenue
Chicago, IL 60604
(800) 522-8656 • www.eb.com

**ESI/Educational Software**
4213 S. 94th Street
Omaha, NE 68127
(800) 955-5570 • www.edsoft.com

**Films for the Humanities and Sciences**
P.O. Box 2053
Princeton, NJ 08543-2053
(800) 257-5126 • Fax (609) 275-3767
www.films.com

**GPN/Reading Rainbow**
University of Nebraska-Lincoln
P.O. Box 80669
Lincoln, NE 68501-0669
(800) 228-4630 • www.gpn.unl.edu

**Journal Films and Videos**
1560 Sherman Avenue, Suite 100
Evanston, IL 60201
(800) 323-9084

**Kaw Valley Films**
P.O. Box 3900
Shawnee, KS 66208
(800) 332-5060

**Library Video Company**
P.O. Box 580
Wynnewood, PA 19096
(800) 843-3620
www.libraryvideo.com

**Listening Library**
One Park Avenue
Greenwich, CT 06870-1727
(800) 733-3000 • www.listeninglib.com

**Macmillan/McGraw-Hill**
(see SRA/McGraw-Hill)

**Marshmedia**
P.O. Box 8082
Shawnee Mission, KS 66208
(800) 821-3303 • Fax (816) 333-7421
marshmedia.com

**MECC**
(see The Learning Company)

**National Geographic Society School Publishing**
P.O. Box 10597
Des Moines, IA 50340-0597
(888) 225-5647
www.nationalgeographic.com

**New Jersey Network**
1573 Parkside Ave.
Trenton, NJ 08625-0777
(609) 530-5180

**PBS Video**
1320 Braddock Place
Alexandria, VA 22314
(800) 344-3337 • www.pbs.org

**Phoenix Films**
(see The Phoenix Learning Group)

**The Phoenix Learning Group**
2348 Chaffee Drive
St. Louis, MO 63146
(800) 221-1274 • e-mail:
phoenixfilms@worldnet.att.net

**Pied Piper** (see AIMS Multimedia)

**Rainbow Educational Video**
170 Keyland Court
Bohemia, NY 11716
(800) 331-4047

**Social Studies School Service**
10200 Jefferson Boulevard, Room 14
P.O. Box 802
Culver City, CA 90232-0802
(800) 421-4246 • Fax (310) 839-2249
socialstudies.com

**SRA/McGraw-Hill**
220 East Danieldale Road
De Soto, TX 75115
(888) 772-4543 • www.sra4kids.com

**SVE/Churchill Media**
6677 North Northwest Highway
Chicago, IL 60631
(800) 829-1900 • www.svemedia.com

**Tom Snyder Productions** (also see ESI)
80 Coolidge Hill Rd.
Watertown, MA 02472
(800) 342-0236 • www.teachtsp.com

**Troll Associates**
100 Corporate Drive
Mahwah, NJ 07430
(888) 998-7655 • Fax (800) 979-8765
www.troll.com

**United Learning**
6633 W. Howard St.
Niles, IL 60714-3389
(800) 424-0362
www.unitedlearning.com

**Weston Woods**
12 Oakwood Avenue
Norwalk, CT 06850
(800) 243-5020 • Fax (203) 845-0498

**Zenger Media**
10200 Jefferson Blvd., Room 94
P.O. Box 802
Culver City, CA 90232-0802
(800) 421-4246 • Fax (800) 944-5432
www.Zengermedia.com

# UNIT 1

## Vocabulary

## Spelling

### THE WISE OLD WOMAN

**banner**
**conquered**
**prospered**
**reluctantly**
**scroll**
**summoned**

#### Words with Short Vowels

| | | | |
|---|---|---|---|
| **tasks** | club | **wisdom** | **threatened** |
| rent | **son** | **solve** | slippery |
| weapon | grant | pump | occupy |
| twin | dreadful | smother | **sudden** |
| fond | lend | cash | blister |

### THE VOYAGE OF THE *DAWN TREADER*

**approve**
**bruised**
**convenience**
**offend**
**presence**
**vaguely**

#### Words with long *a* and long *e*

| | | | |
|---|---|---|---|
| paste | evening | decorate | **delay** |
| aim | receive | **indeed** | heal |
| **spray** | drain | theme | concrete |
| leader | pace | indicate | greet |
| creep | flea | faith | decay |

### WILMA UNLIMITED

**astounding**
**athletic**
**bushel**
**concentrating**
**luxury**
**scholarship**

#### Words with long *i* and long *o*

| | | | |
|---|---|---|---|
| excite | loaf | fold | enclose |
| grind | obey | goal | type |
| **notice** | site | code | console |
| spy | **fight** | despite | notion |
| hose | rely | gigantic | slightly |

### THE WRECK OF THE *ZEPHYR*

**hull**
**ominous**
**shoreline**
**spire**
**timbers**
**treacherous**

#### Words with /ū/ and /ü/

| | | | |
|---|---|---|---|
| nephew | include | dispute | reunion |
| **boom** | **lose** | cruel | suitcase |
| truly | **view** | contribute | boost |
| **grew** | cucumber | assume | rumor |
| juicy | **flew** | **prove** | remove |

### TIME FOR KIDS: TORNADOES!

**destruction**
**detect**
**predictions**
**reliable**
**severe**
**stadium**

#### Words from Science

| | | | |
|---|---|---|---|
| **twister** | rainfall | **damage** | device |
| **computers** | **instruments** | horizon | energy |
| hurricane | front | **satellites** | sleet |
| **strength** | **warning** | surge | humid |
| condense | **conditions** | debris | cyclone |

**Boldfaced** words appear in the selection.

# UNIT 2

|  | Vocabulary | Spelling |
| --- | --- | --- |

## THE GOLD COIN

**Vocabulary**
- **despair**
- **distressed**
- **insistent**
- **shriveled**
- **speechless**
- **stifling**

### Syllable Patterns

| | | | |
| --- | --- | --- | --- |
| lotion | luggage | gravy | agent |
| subject | **silence** | lantern | stifle |
| ugly | victim | active | baggage |
| **simply** | **moment** | bacon | spiral |
| pony | bubble | fable | blender |

## JOHN HENRY

**Vocabulary**
- **acre**
- **commotion**
- **dynamite**
- **grit**
- **pulverized**
- **rebuild**

### Words with Consonant Clusters

| | | | |
| --- | --- | --- | --- |
| scramble | screech | scrape | scribble |
| **strange** | **straightest** | stray | strain |
| sprang | sprout | sprain | script |
| schoolyard | schedule | scholar | strawberry |
| throughout | throat | throne | strategy |

## IT'S OUR WORLD, TOO!

**Vocabulary**
- **auction**
- **dangled**
- **deliveries**
- **donate**
- **lecture**
- **publicity**

### Words with /z/, /j/, and /f/

| | | | |
| --- | --- | --- | --- |
| dizzy | gem | telegraph | trophy |
| **manage** | lizard | fudge | zipper |
| squeeze | average | represent | praise |
| lodge | budge | margin | postage |
| paragraph | **refuse** | **challenge** | physical |

## DEAR MR. HENSHAW

**Vocabulary**
- **afford**
- **permission**
- **rejected**
- **reserved**
- **snoop**
- **submitted**

### Plurals

| | | | |
| --- | --- | --- | --- |
| losses | potatoes | studios | wives |
| **stories** | atlases | heroes | rodeos |
| reefs | difficulties | crutches | **tomatoes** |
| shelves | gulfs | possibilities | **thieves** |
| pianos | wolves | beliefs | echoes |

## TIME FOR KIDS: DIGGING UP THE PAST

**Vocabulary**
- **arrowheads**
- **bullet**
- **eventually**
- **fraction**
- **starvation**
- **violent**

### Words from Social Studies

| | | | |
| --- | --- | --- | --- |
| **capital** | liberty | property | empire |
| **colonists** | senator | immigrant | civil |
| ancestor | justice | governor | **settlement** |
| territory | **settlers** | plantation | **historians** |
| congress | culture | politics | federal |

**Boldfaced** words appear in the selection.

# UNIT 3

## Vocabulary | Spelling

### THE MARBLE CHAMP

**Vocabulary**
- **accurate**
- **congratulated**
- **division**
- **elementary**
- **glory**
- **onlookers**

**Spelling — Words with /ou/ and /oi/**

| | | | |
|---|---|---|---|
| **join** | mount | couch | background |
| outfit | shower | rejoice | prowl |
| howl | employee | loyalty | sour |
| hoist | broil | doubt | turquoise |
| destroy | eyebrow | drowsy | trousers |

### THE PAPER DRAGON

**Vocabulary**
- **billowed**
- **devour**
- **heroic**
- **quench**
- **scorched**
- **uprooted**

**Spelling — Words with /u̇/ and /yu̇/**

| | | | |
|---|---|---|---|
| **looked** | understood | lure | rural |
| bureau | tourist | barefoot | fishhook |
| **surely** | mural | gourmet | tournament |
| poor | assure | bulletin | jury |
| cushion | childhood | textbook | purify |

### GRANDMA ESSIE'S COVERED WAGON

**Vocabulary**
- **bashful**
- **canvas**
- **cemetery**
- **granite**
- **orphanage**
- **tornado**

**Spelling — Words with /sh/ and /ch/**

| | | | |
|---|---|---|---|
| **sheets** | polish | vanish | publish |
| especially | ancient | commercial | gracious |
| **chopped** | cheap | **orchard** | arch |
| **kitchen** | clutch | latch | hitch |
| patient | caution | nation | function |

### GOING BACK HOME: AN ARTIST RETURNS TO THE SOUTH

**Vocabulary**
- **heritage**
- **influenced**
- **livestock**
- **survival**
- **thrive**
- **tiresome**

**Spelling — Adding -ed and -ing**

| | | | |
|---|---|---|---|
| slammed | pitied | **fascinated** | regretted |
| **exploring** | skimmed | envied | **easing** |
| **copied** | deserved | referring | qualified |
| jogging | applied | collapsed | forbidding |
| amusing | dripping | relied | complicated |

### TIME FOR KIDS: A MOUNTAIN OF A MONUMENT

**Vocabulary**
- **awesome**
- **dedicate**
- **explosives**
- **hail**
- **nostril**
- **sculpture**

**Spelling — Words from the Arts**

| | | | |
|---|---|---|---|
| **carving** | gallery | quality | texture |
| **monument** | portrait | technique | jewelry |
| **memorial** | impression | original | charcoal |
| **displays** | style | fabric | glaze |
| **process** | decoration | medium | creative |

**Boldfaced** words appear in the selection.

# UNIT 4

| | Vocabulary | Spelling |
|---|---|---|

## CARLOS AND THE SKUNK

**Vocabulary**
- **nestled**
- **peculiar**
- **stunned**
- **tortillas**
- **unbearable**
- **unpleasant**

**Words with /ô/ and /ôr/**

| | | | |
|---|---|---|---|
| forward | fawn | soar | border |
| course | install | **chore** | **source** |
| audience | longing | withdraw | applaud |
| aboard | performing | wallpaper | coarse |
| bore | astronaut | coffee | forecast |

## HOW TO THINK LIKE A SCIENTIST

**Vocabulary**
- **assignments**
- **automatically**
- **carelessly**
- **normally**
- **observations**
- **swerved**

**Words with /är/ and /âr/**

| | | | |
|---|---|---|---|
| **cards** | vary | chart | barge |
| carve | rare | square | beware |
| **barely** | airline | **repairman** | lair |
| stairway | scar | target | artistic |
| remark | scarce | **aquarium** | regard |

## AN ISLAND SCRAPBOOK

**Vocabulary**
- **barrier**
- **emerge**
- **fireball**
- **naturalist**
- **parallel**
- **teeming**

**Words with /îr/ and /ûr/**

| | | | |
|---|---|---|---|
| steer | fir | term | purse |
| **return** | **mysterious** | cashier | dreary |
| appear | career | squirm | alert |
| nerve | **surface** | experience | squirt |
| frontier | fearsome | eerie | material |

## THE BIG STORM

**Vocabulary**
- **atmosphere**
- **collision**
- **cycle**
- **data**
- **injured**
- **uneven**

**Compound Words**

| | | | |
|---|---|---|---|
| mailbox | homesick | **raindrop** | thirty-third |
| all right | post office | **cold front** | **snowstorms** |
| goldfish | twenty-five | merry-go-round | **mountaintops** |
| no one | somebody | teaspoon | sister-in-law |
| ice-skating | peanut butter | **parking lot** | **northeast** |

## TIME FOR KIDS: CATCHING UP WITH LEWIS AND CLARK

**Vocabulary**
- **bison**
- **diaries**
- **former**
- **glistening**
- **journal**
- **superb**

**Words from Social Studies**

| | | | |
|---|---|---|---|
| **journey** | **hardships** | canal | **expedition** |
| **canoes** | **trail** | **fort** | elevation |
| **traveled** | **explorer** | **native** | canyon |
| **route** | **communicate** | caravan | dwell |
| service | agency | agreement | **campsite** |

**Boldfaced** words appear in the selection.

# UNIT 5

## Vocabulary    Spelling

### THE RIDDLE

**Vocabulary**

**apologized**
**debt**
**hasty**
**inquired**
**lamented**
**refreshment**

**Spelling — Words with /ər/, /əl/, and /ən/**

| | | | |
|---|---|---|---|
| labor | **answer** | chosen | **twinkle** |
| legal | regular | **castle** | central |
| captain | single | **clever** | sweater |
| fasten | camel | apron | grammar |
| tunnel | **pardon** | terror | **riddle** |

### LIFE IN FLATLAND

**Vocabulary**

**dimensions**
**distinguished**
**landscape**
**thickness**
**trifle**
**unique**

**Spelling — Spelling Unstressed Syllables**

| | | | |
|---|---|---|---|
| **constant** | distance | torrent | ransom |
| consult | compose | focus | **method** |
| neglect | dozen | purchase | emblem |
| patrol | collage | payment | hammock |
| accuse | **compass** | possess | support |

### TONWEYA AND THE EAGLES

**Vocabulary**

**cleft**
**consented**
**defiantly**
**gratitude**
**sacred**
**tribute**

**Spelling — Words with Silent Letters**

| | | | |
|---|---|---|---|
| **sign** | autumn | column | campaign |
| wrist | knuckle | knowledge | **handwriting** |
| knit | wring | wrench | bough |
| **lightning** | naughty | brighten | solemn |
| gnaw | gnat | dough | gnarled |

### BREAKER'S BRIDGE

**Vocabulary**

**dismay**
**gorge**
**immortals**
**murky**
**piers**
**scheme**

**Spelling — Contractions**

| | | | |
|---|---|---|---|
| aren't | hasn't | they're | there'll |
| we'd | you'd | how's | must've |
| would've | haven't | needn't | who'd |
| **we'll** | where'd | she's | who'll |
| **you've** | what'll | mustn't | should've |

### TIME FOR KIDS: CLEANING UP AMERICA'S AIR

**Vocabulary**

**fumes**
**protective**
**regulations**
**standards**
**stricter**
**width**

**Spelling — Words from Health**

| | | | |
|---|---|---|---|
| **illness** | **kidneys** | **headaches** | **smog** |
| **breathing** | safety | vitamin | artery |
| oxygen | organ | hazard | **ozone** |
| **health** | **lungs** | substance | symptom |
| **heart** | **reaction** | **particle** | allergy |

**Boldfaced** words appear in the selection.

# UNIT 6

| Vocabulary | Spelling |
|---|---|

### AMISTAD RISING: A STORY OF FREEDOM

**Vocabulary**

- **coax**
- **escorted**
- **navigate**
- **nightfall**
- **perished**
- **ushered**

**Homophones and Homographs**

| | | | |
|---|---|---|---|
| **died** | **bound** | main | hall |
| stable | pane | sole | currant |
| pain | waist | haul | soul |
| wound | vault | current | mane |
| waste | **dyed** | idle | idol |

### RIP VAN WINKLE

**Vocabulary**

- **husking**
- **keg**
- **landlord**
- **oblige**
- **rascals**
- **sprawled**

**Words with Prefixes**

| | | | |
|---|---|---|---|
| preschool | preview | precook | prearrange |
| **replaced** | regain | recall | **revisit** |
| unknown | **unseen** | unable | unaware |
| disobey | discomfort | dishonest | disapprove |
| invisible | incorrect | inexpensive | incredible |

### SEA MAIDENS OF JAPAN

**Vocabulary**

- **cove**
- **disgrace**
- **driftwood**
- **flail**
- **host**
- **sizzle**

**Words with Suffixes**

| | | | |
|---|---|---|---|
| remarkable | reasonable | respectable | honorable |
| peaceful | **graceful** | harmful | **flavorful** |
| countless | painless | meaningless | defenseless |
| foolishness | weakness | softness | nervousness |
| **excitement** | amusement | treatment | announcement |

### THE SILENT LOBBY

**Vocabulary**

- **interpret**
- **pelted**
- **persuade**
- **register**
- **shabby**
- **soothing**

**Words with Suffixes**

| | | | |
|---|---|---|---|
| instruction | selection | **election** | concentration |
| suggestion | confusion | perfection | consideration |
| information | invitation | conversation | **demonstration** |
| education | attraction | location | **constitution** |
| imagination | reservation | population | correction |

### TIME FOR KIDS: AMAZON ALERT!

**Vocabulary**

- **confirmed**
- **isolated**
- **lush**
- **tropical**
- **variety**
- **wonderland**

**Words from Math**

| | | | |
|---|---|---|---|
| **ordered** | multiply | product | **estimated** |
| equal | frequency | liter | angle |
| range | mathematics | ratio | portion |
| **difference** | centimeter | bar graph | **one-eighth** |
| volume | formula | millimeter | quotient |

**Boldfaced** words appear in the selection.

# Listening, Speaking, Viewing, Representing

☑ Tested Skill

Tinted panels show skills, strategies, and other teaching opportunities

| | K | 1 | 2 | 3 | 4 | 5 | 6 |
|---|---|---|---|---|---|---|---|

## LISTENING

Learn the vocabulary of school (numbers, shapes, colors, directions, and categories)

Identify the musical elements of literary language, such as rhymes, repetition, onomatopoeia, alliteration, assonance

Determine purposes for listening (get information, solve problems, enjoy and appreciate)

Understand and follow directions

Listen critically and responsively; recognize barriers to effective listening

Ask and answer relevant questions (for clarification; to follow up on ideas)

Listen critically to interpret and evaluate

Listen responsively to stories and other texts read aloud, including selections from classic and contemporary works

Connect and compare own experiences, feelings, ideas, and traditions with those of others

Apply comprehension strategies in listening activities

Understand the major ideas and supporting evidence in spoken messages

Participate in listening activities related to reading and writing (such as discussions, group activities, conferences)

Listen to learn by taking notes, organizing, and summarizing spoken ideas

Know personal listening preferences

## SPEAKING

Uses repetition, rhyme, and rhythm in oral texts (such as in reciting songs, poems, and stories with repeating patterns)

Learn the vocabulary of school (numbers, shapes, colors, directions, and categories)

Use appropriate language, grammar, and vocabulary learned to describe ideas, feelings, and experiences

Ask and answer relevant questions (for clarification; to follow up on ideas)

Communicate effectively in everyday situations (such as discussions, group activities, conferences, conversations)

Demonstrate speaking skills (audience, purpose, occasion, clarity, volume, pitch, intonation, phrasing, rate, fluency)

Clarify and support spoken messages and ideas with objects, charts, evidence, elaboration, examples

Use verbal communication in effective ways when, for example, making announcements, giving directions, or making introductions

Use nonverbal communication in effective ways such as eye contact, facial expressions, gestures

Retell a story or a spoken message by summarizing or clarifying

Connect and compare own experiences, ideas, and traditions with those of others

Determine purposes for speaking (inform, entertain, compare, describe, give directions, persuade, express personal feelings and opinions)

Recognize differences between formal and informal language

Demonstrate skills of reporting and providing information

Demonstrate skills of interviewing, requesting and providing information

Apply composition strategies in speaking activities

Monitor own understanding of spoken message and seek clarification as needed

## VIEWING

Demonstrate viewing skills (focus attention, organize information)

Understand and use nonverbal cues

Respond to audiovisual media in a variety of ways

Participate in viewing activities related to reading and writing

Apply comprehension strategies in viewing activities, including main idea and details

Recognize artists' craft and techniques for conveying meaning

Interpret information from various formats such as maps, charts, graphics, video segments, technology

Knows various types of mass media (such as film, video, television, billboards, and newspapers)

Evaluate purposes of various media, including mass media (information, appreciation, entertainment, directions, persuasion)

Use media, including mass media, to compare ideas, information, and points of view

## REPRESENTING

Select, organize, or produce visuals to complement or extend meanings

Produce communication using appropriate media to develop a class paper, multimedia or video reports

Show how language, medium, and presentation contribute to the message

# Reading: Alphabetic Principle, Sounds/Symbols

☑ Tested Skill

Tinted panels show skills, strategies, and other teaching opportunities

| | K | 1 | 2 | 3 | 4 | 5 | 6 |
|---|---|---|---|---|---|---|---|
| **PRINT AWARENESS** | | | | | | | |
| Know the order of the alphabet | | | | | | | |
| Recognize that print represents spoken language and conveys meaning | | | | | | | |
| Understand directionality (tracking print from left to right; return sweep) | | | | | | | |
| Understand that written words and sentences are separated by spaces | | | | | | | |
| Know the difference between individual letters and printed words | | | | | | | |
| Understand that spoken words are represented in written language by specific sequence of letters | | | | | | | |
| Recognize that there are correct spellings for words | | | | | | | |
| Know the difference between capital and lowercase letters | | | | | | | |
| Recognize how readers use capitalization and punctuation to comprehend | | | | | | | |
| Recognize the distinguishing features of a letter, word, sentence, paragraph | | | | | | | |
| Understand appropriate book handling | | | | | | | |
| Recognize that parts of a book (such as cover/title page and table of contents) offer information | | | | | | | |
| **PHONOLOGICAL AWARENESS** | | | | | | | |
| Listen for environmental sounds | | | | | | | |
| Identify spoken words and sentences | | | | | | | |
| Divide spoken sentence into individual words | | | | | | | |
| Produce rhyming words and distinguish rhyming words from nonrhyming words | | | | | | | |
| Identify, segment, and combine syllables within spoken words | | | | | | | |
| Blend and segment onsets and rimes | | | | | | | |
| Identify and isolate the initial, medial, and final sound of a spoken word | | | | | | | |
| Add, delete, or substitute sounds to change words (such as *cow* to *how*, *pan* to *fan*) | | | | | | | |
| Blend sounds to make spoken words | | | | | | | |
| Segment one-syllable spoken words into individual phonemes | | | | | | | |
| **PHONICS AND DECODING** | | | | | | | |
| Alphabetic principle: Letter/sound correspondence | ☑ | ☑ | ☑ | | | | |
| Blending CVC words | ☑ | ☑ | | | | | |
| Segmenting CVC words | ☑ | | | | | | |
| Blending CVC, CVCe, CCVC, CVCC, CVVC words | ☑ | ☑ | ☑ | | | | |
| Segmenting CVC, CVCe, CCVC, CVCC, CVVC words and sounds | ☑ | ☑ | ☑ | | | | |
| Initial and final consonants: /n/n, /d/d, /s/s, /m/m, /t/t, /k/c, /f/f, /r/r, /p/p, /l/l, /k/k, /g/g, /b/b, /h/h, /w/w, /v/v, /ks/x, /kw/qu, /j/j, /y/y, /z/z | ☑ | ☑ | | | | | |
| Initial and medial short vowels: *a, i, u, o, e* | ☑ | ☑ | ☑ | | | | |
| Long vowels: *a-e, i-e, o-e, u-e* (vowel-consonant-e) | | ☑ | ☑ | | | | |
| Long vowels, including *ay, ai; e, ee, ie, ea; o, oa, oe, ow; i, y, igh* | | ☑ | ☑ | | | | |
| Consonant Digraphs: *sh, th, ch, wh* | | ☑ | | | | | |
| Consonant Blends: continuant/continuant, including *sl, sm, sn, fl, fr, ll, ss, ff* | | ☑ | | | | | |
| Consonant Blends: continuant/stop, including *st, sk, sp, ng, nt, nd, mp, ft* | | ☑ | | | | | |
| Consonant Blends: stop/continuant, including *tr, pr, pl, cr, tw* | | ☑ | | | | | |
| Variant vowels: including /ù/oo; /ô/a, aw, au; /ü/ue, ew | | ☑ | ☑ | | | | |
| Diphthongs, including /ou/ou, ow; /oi/oi, oy | | ☑ | ☑ | | | | |
| r-controlled vowels, including /âr/are; /ôr/or, ore; /îr/ear | | | ☑ | | | | |
| Soft *c* and soft *g* | | | ☑ | | | | |
| *nk* | | ☑ | ☑ | | | | |
| Consonant Digraphs: *ck* | ☑ | ☑ | | | | | |
| Consonant Digraphs: *ph, tch, ch* | | | ☑ | | | | |
| Short *e: ea* | | | ☑ | | | | |
| Long *e: y, ey* | | | ☑ | | | | |
| /ü/oo | | ☑ | ☑ | | | | |
| /är/ar; /ûr/ir, ur, er | | ☑ | ☑ | | | | |
| Silent letters: including *l, b, k, w, g, h, gh* | | | ☑ | | | | |
| Schwa: /ər/er; /ən/en; /əl/le; | | | ☑ | | | | |
| Reading/identifying multisyllabic words | | ☑ | ☑ | | | | |
| Using graphophonic cues | | | | | | | |

T89

# Reading: Vocabulary/Word Identification

| WORD STRUCTURE | K | 1 | 2 | 3 | 4 | 5 | 6 |
|---|---|---|---|---|---|---|---|
| Common spelling patterns | | | | | | | |
| Syllable patterns | | | | | | | |
| Plurals | | ☑ | | | | | |
| Possessives | | ☑ | | | | | |
| Contractions | | ☑ | | | | | |
| Root, or base, words and inflectional endings (-s, -es, -ed, -ing) | | ☑ | ☑ | ☑ | | ☑ | |
| Compound Words | | ☑ | ☑ | ☑ | ☑ | ☑ | ☑ |
| Prefixes and suffixes (such as un-, re-, dis-, non-; -ly, -y, -ful, -able, -tion) | | | ☑ | ☑ | ☑ | ☑ | ☑ |
| Root words and derivational endings | | | | ☑ | ☑ | ☑ | ☑ |

| WORD MEANING | K | 1 | 2 | 3 | 4 | 5 | 6 |
|---|---|---|---|---|---|---|---|
| Develop vocabulary through concrete experiences, word walls, other people | | | | | | | |
| Develop vocabulary through selections read aloud | | | | | | | |
| Develop vocabulary through reading | | | | | | | |
| Cueing systems: syntactic, semantic, graphophonic | | | | | | | |
| Context clues, including semantic clues (word meaning), syntactical clues (word order), and graphophonic clues | ☑ | ☑ | ☑ | ☑ | ☑ | ☑ | ☑ |
| High-frequency words (such as the, a, and, said, was, where, is) | ☑ | ☑ | | | | | |
| Identify words that name persons, places, things, and actions | | | | | | | |
| Automatic reading of regular and irregular words | | | | | | | |
| Use resources and references (dictionary, glossary, thesaurus, synonym finder, technology and software, and context) | | | | | | | |
| Classify and categorize words | | | | | | | |
| Synonyms and antonyms | | | ☑ | ☑ | ☑ | ☑ | ☑ |
| Multiple-meaning words | | | ☑ | | ☑ | ☑ | ☑ |
| Figurative language | | | ☑ | ☑ | ☑ | ☑ | ☑ |
| Decode derivatives (root words, such as like, pay, happy with affixes, such as dis-, pre-, un-) | | | | | | | |
| Systematic study of words across content areas and in current events | | | | | | | |
| Locate meanings, pronunciations, and derivations (including dictionaries, glossaries, and other sources) | | | | | | | |
| Denotation and connotation | | | | | | | ☑ |
| Word origins as aid to understanding historical influences on English word meanings | | | | | | | |
| Homophones, homographs | | | | | | | |
| Analogies | | | | | | | ☑ |
| Idioms | | | | | | | |

# Reading: Comprehension

| PREREADING STRATEGIES | K | 1 | 2 | 3 | 4 | 5 | 6 |
|---|---|---|---|---|---|---|---|
| Preview and predict | | | | | | | |
| Use prior knowledge | | | | | | | |
| Set and adjust purposes for reading | | | | | | | |
| Build background | | | | | | | |

| MONITORING STRATEGIES | K | 1 | 2 | 3 | 4 | 5 | 6 |
|---|---|---|---|---|---|---|---|
| Adjust reading rate | | | | | | | |
| Reread, search for clues, ask questions, ask for help | | | | | | | |
| Visualize | | | | | | | |
| Read a portion aloud, use reference aids | | | | | | | |
| Use decoding and vocabulary strategies | | | | | | | |
| Paraphrase | | | | | | | |
| Create story maps, diagrams, charts, story props to help comprehend, analyze, synthesize and evaluate texts | | | | | | | |

(continued on next page

*(Reading: Comprehension continued)*

| SKILLS AND STRATEGIES | K | 1 | 2 | 3 | 4 | 5 | 6 |
|---|---|---|---|---|---|---|---|
| Recall story details, including character and setting | ✓ | ✓ | | | | | |
| Use illustrations | ✓ | ✓ | | | | | |
| Distinguish reality and fantasy | ✓ | ✓ | ✓ | | | | |
| Classify and categorize | ✓ | | | | | | |
| Make predictions | ✓ | ✓ | ✓ | ✓ | ✓ | ✓ | ✓ |
| Recognize sequence of events (tell or act out) | ✓ | ✓ | ✓ | ✓ | ✓ | ✓ | ✓ |
| Recognize cause and effect | ✓ | ✓ | ✓ | ✓ | ✓ | ✓ | ✓ |
| Compare and contrast | ✓ | ✓ | ✓ | ✓ | ✓ | ✓ | ✓ |
| Summarize | ✓ | ✓ | ✓ | ✓ | ✓ | ✓ | ✓ |
| Make and explain inferences | | ✓ | ✓ | ✓ | ✓ | ✓ | ✓ |
| Draw conclusions | | ✓ | ✓ | ✓ | ✓ | ✓ | ✓ |
| Distinguish important and unimportant information | | | | | ✓ | ✓ | ✓ |
| Recognize main idea and supporting details | ✓ | ✓ | ✓ | ✓ | ✓ | ✓ | ✓ |
| Form conclusions or generalizations and support with evidence from text | | | ✓ | ✓ | ✓ | ✓ | ✓ |
| Distinguish fact and opinion (including news stories and advertisements) | | | | ✓ | ✓ | ✓ | ✓ |
| Recognize problem and solution | | | ✓ | ✓ | ✓ | ✓ | ✓ |
| Recognize steps in a process | | ✓ | ✓ | ✓ | ✓ | ✓ | ✓ |
| Make judgments and decisions | | | | ✓ | ✓ | ✓ | ✓ |
| Distinguish fact and nonfact | | | | ✓ | ✓ | ✓ | ✓ |
| Recognize techniques of persuasion and propaganda | | | | | | | ✓ |
| Evaluate evidence and sources of information, including checking other sources and asking experts | | | | | | | ✓ |
| Identify similarities and differences across texts (including topics, characters, problems, themes, cultural influences, treatment, scope, or organization) | | | | | | | |
| Practice various questions and tasks (test-like comprehension questions) | | | | | | | |
| Paraphrase and summarize to recall, inform, and organize | | | | | | | |
| Answer various types of questions (open-ended, literal, interpretative, test-like such as true-false, multiple choice, short-answer) | | | | | | | |
| Use study strategies to learn and recall (preview, question, reread, and record) | | | | | | | |

| LITERARY RESPONSE | K | 1 | 2 | 3 | 4 | 5 | 6 |
|---|---|---|---|---|---|---|---|
| Listen to stories being read aloud | | | | | | | |
| React, speculate, join in, read along when predictable and patterned selections are read aloud | | | | | | | |
| Respond to a variety of stories and poems through talk, movement, music, art, drama, and writing | | | | | | | |
| Show understanding through writing, illustrating, developing demonstrations, and using technology | | | | | | | |
| Connect ideas and themes across texts | | | | | | | |
| Support responses by referring to relevant aspects of text and own experiences | | | | | | | |
| Offer observations, make connections, speculate, interpret, and raise questions in response to texts | | | | | | | |
| Interpret text ideas through journal writing, discussion, enactment, and media | | | | | | | |

| TEXT STRUCTURE/LITERARY CONCEPTS | K | 1 | 2 | 3 | 4 | 5 | 6 |
|---|---|---|---|---|---|---|---|
| Distinguish forms and functions of texts (lists, newsletters, signs) | | | | | | | |
| Use text features to aid comprehension | | | | | | | |
| Understand story structure | | | | | | | |
| Identify narrative (for entertainment) and expository (for information) | | | | | | | |
| Distinguish fiction from nonfiction, including fact and fantasy | | | | | | | |
| Understand literary forms (stories, poems, plays, and informational books) | | | | | | | |
| Understand literary terms by distinguishing between roles of author and illustrator | | | | | | | |
| Understand title, author, and illustrator across a variety of texts | | | | | | | |
| Analyze character, character's motive, character's point of view, plot, setting, style, tone, mood | | ✓ | ✓ | ✓ | ✓ | ✓ | ✓ |
| Compare communication in different forms | | | | | | | |
| Understand terms such as *title, author, illustrator, playwright, theater, stage, act, dialogue,* and *scene* | | | | | | | |
| Recognize stories, poems, songs, myths, legends, folktales, fables, tall tales, limericks, plays, biographies, autobiographies | | | | | | | |
| Judge internal logic of story text | | | | | | | |
| Recognize that authors organize information in specific ways | | | | | | | |
| Recognize author's purpose: to inform, influence, express, or entertain | | | | | | | |
| Describe how author's point of view affects text | | | | ✓ | ✓ | ✓ | ✓ |
| Recognize biography, historical fiction, realistic fiction, modern fantasy, informational texts, and poetry | | | | | | | |
| Analyze ways authors present ideas (cause/effect, compare/contrast, inductively, deductively, chronologically) | | | | | | | |
| Recognize literary techniques such as imagery, repetition, flashback, foreshadowing, symbolism | | | | | | | |

*(continued on next page)*

*(Reading: Comprehension continued)*

| VARIETY OF TEXT | K | 1 | 2 | 3 | 4 | 5 | 6 |
|---|---|---|---|---|---|---|---|
| Read a variety of genres and understand their distinguishing features | | | | | | | |
| Use expository and other informational texts to acquire information | | | | | | | |
| Read for a variety of purposes | | | | | | | |
| Select varied sources when reading for information or pleasure | | | | | | | |
| Know preferences for reading literary and nonfiction texts | | | | | | | |
| **FLUENCY** | | | | | | | |
| Read regularly in independent-level and instructional-level materials | | | | | | | |
| Read orally with fluency from familiar texts | | | | | | | |
| Self-select independent-level reading | | | | | | | |
| Read silently for increasing periods of time | | | | | | | |
| Demonstrate characteristics of fluent and effective reading | | | | | | | |
| Adjust reading rate to purpose | | | | | | | |
| Read aloud in selected texts, showing understanding of text and engaging the listener | | | | | | | |
| **CULTURES** | | | | | | | |
| Connect own experience with culture of others | | | | | | | |
| Compare experiences of characters across cultures | | | | | | | |
| Articulate and discuss themes and connections that cross cultures | | | | | | | |
| **CRITICAL THINKING** | | | | | | | |
| Experiences (comprehend, apply, analyze, synthesize, evaluate) | | | | | | | |
| Make connections (comprehend, apply, analyze, synthesize, evaluate) | | | | | | | |
| Expression (comprehend, apply, analyze, synthesize, evaluate) | | | | | | | |
| Inquiry (comprehend, apply, analyze, synthesize, evaluate) | | | | | | | |
| Problem solving (comprehend, apply, analyze, synthesize, evaluate) | | | | | | | |
| Making decisions (comprehend, apply, analyze, synthesize, evaluate) | | | | | | | |

## Study Skills

| INQUIRY/RESEARCH AND STUDY STRATEGIES | K | 1 | 2 | 3 | 4 | 5 | 6 |
|---|---|---|---|---|---|---|---|
| Follow and give directions | | | | | | | |
| Use alphabetical order | | | | | | | |
| Use text features and formats to help understand text (such as boldface, italic, or highlighted text; captions; headings and subheadings; numbers or symbols) | | | | | | | |
| Use study strategies to help read text and to learn and recall information from text (such as preview text, set purposes, and ask questions; use SQRRR; adjust reading rate; skim and scan; use KWL) | | | | | | | |
| Identify/frame and revise questions for research | | | | | | | |
| Obtain, organize, and summarize information: classify, take notes, outline, web, diagram | | | | | | | |
| Evaluate research and raise new questions | | | | | | | |
| Use technology for research and/or to present information in various formats | | | | | | | |
| Follow accepted formats for writing research, including documenting sources | | | | | | | |
| Use test-taking strategies | | | | | | | |
| Use text organizers (book cover; title page—title, author, illustrator; contents; headings; glossary; index) | | ☑ | ☑ | ☑ | ☑ | ☑ | ☑ |
| Use graphic aids, such as maps, diagrams, charts, graphs, schedules, calendars | | ☑ | ☑ | ☑ | ☑ | ☑ | ☑ |
| Read and interpret varied texts, such as environmental print, signs, lists, encyclopedia, dictionary, glossary, newspaper, advertisement, magazine, calendar, directions, floor plans, online resources | | ☑ | ☑ | ☑ | ☑ | ☑ | ☑ |
| Use print and online reference sources, such as glossary, dictionary, encyclopedia, telephone directory, technology resources, nonfiction books | | ☑ | ☑ | ☑ | ☑ | ☑ | ☑ |
| Recognize Library/Media center resources, such as computerized references; catalog search—subject, author, title; encyclopedia index | | ☑ | ☑ | ☑ | ☑ | ☑ | ☑ |

# Writing

| MODES AND FORMS | K | 1 | 2 | 3 | 4 | 5 | 6 |
|---|---|---|---|---|---|---|---|
| Interactive writing | | | | | | | |
| Descriptive writing | | | ☑ | | | | |
| Personal narrative | | | ☑ | ☑ | ☑ | ☑ | ☑ |
| Writing that compares | | ☑ | ☑ | ☑ | ☑ | ☑ | ☑ |
| Explanatory writing | | | ☑ | ☑ | ☑ | ☑ | ☑ |
| Persuasive writing | | | | ☑ | ☑ | ☑ | ☑ |
| Writing a story | | ☑ | ☑ | ☑ | ☑ | ☑ | ☑ |
| Expository writing; research report | | ☑ | ☑ | ☑ | ☑ | ☑ | ☑ |
| Write using a variety of formats, such as advertisement, autobiography, biography, book report/report, comparison-contrast, critique/review/editorial, description, essay, how-to, interview, invitation, journal/log/notes, message/list, paragraph/multi-paragraph composition, picture book, play (scene), poem/rhyme, story, summary, note, letter | | | | | | | |

| PURPOSES/AUDIENCES | K | 1 | 2 | 3 | 4 | 5 | 6 |
|---|---|---|---|---|---|---|---|
| Dictate sentences and messages such as news and stories for others to write | | | | | | | |
| Write labels, notes, and captions for illustrations, possessions, charts, and centers | | | | | | | |
| Write to record, to discover and develop ideas, to inform, to influence, to entertain | | | | | | | |
| Exhibit an identifiable voice | | | | | | | |
| Use literary devices (suspense, dialogue, and figurative language) | | | | | | | |
| Produce written texts by organizing ideas, using effective transitions, and choosing precise wording | | | | | | | |

| PROCESSES | K | 1 | 2 | 3 | 4 | 5 | 6 |
|---|---|---|---|---|---|---|---|
| Generate ideas for self-selected and assigned topics using prewriting strategies | | | | | | | |
| Develop drafts | | | | | | | |
| Revise drafts for varied purposes, elaborate ideas | | | | | | | |
| Edit for appropriate grammar, spelling, punctuation, and features of published writings | | | | | | | |
| Proofread own writing and that of others | | | | | | | |
| Bring pieces to final form and "publish" them for audiences | | | | | | | |
| Use technology to compose, revise, and present text | | | | | | | |
| Select and use reference materials and resources for writing, revising, and editing final drafts | | | | | | | |

| SPELLING | K | 1 | 2 | 3 | 4 | 5 | 6 |
|---|---|---|---|---|---|---|---|
| Spell own name and write high-frequency words | | | | | | | |
| Words with short vowels (including CVC and one-syllable words with blends CCVC, CVCC, CCVCC) | | | | | | | |
| Words with long vowels (including CVCe) | | | | | | | |
| Words with digraphs, blends, consonant clusters, double consonants | | | | | | | |
| Words with diphthongs | | | | | | | |
| Words with variant vowels | | | | | | | |
| Words with r-controlled vowels | | | | | | | |
| Words with /ər/, /əl/, and /ən/ | | | | | | | |
| Words with silent letters | | | | | | | |
| Words with soft c and soft g | | | | | | | |
| Inflectional endings (including plurals and past tense and words that drop the final e and double a consonant when adding -ing, -ed) | | | | | | | |
| Compound words | | | | | | | |
| Contractions | | | | | | | |
| Homonyms | | | | | | | |
| Suffixes such as -able, -ly, -ful, or -less, and prefixes such as dis-, re-, pre-, or un- | | | | | | | |
| Spell words ending in -tion and -sion, such as station and procession | | | | | | | |
| Accurate spelling of root or base words | | | | | | | |
| Orthographic patterns and rules such as keep/can; sack/book; out/now; oil/toy; match/speech; ledge/cage; consonant doubling, dropping e, changing y to i | | | | | | | |
| Multisyllabic words using regularly spelled phonogram patterns | | | | | | | |
| Syllable patterns (including closed, open, syllable boundary patterns) | | | | | | | |
| Synonyms and antonyms | | | | | | | |
| Words from Social Studies, Science, Math, and Physical Education | | | | | | | |
| Words derived from other languages and cultures | | | | | | | |
| Use resources to find correct spellings, synonyms, and replacement words | | | | | | | |
| Use conventional spelling of familiar words in writing assignments | | | | | | | |
| Spell accurately in final drafts | | | | | | | |

(continued on next page)

☑ Tested Skill

☐ Tinted panels show skills, strategies, and other teaching opportunities

| | K | 1 | 2 | 3 | 4 | 5 | 6 |
|---|---|---|---|---|---|---|---|
| **GRAMMAR AND USAGE** | | | | | | | |
| Understand sentence concepts (word order, statements, questions, exclamations, commands) | | | | | | | |
| Recognize complete and incomplete sentences | | | | | | | |
| Nouns (common, proper, singular, plural, irregular plural, possessives) | | | | | | | |
| Verbs (action, helping, linking, irregular) | | | | | | | |
| Verb tense (present, past, future, perfect, and progressive) | | | | | | | |
| Pronouns (possessive, subject and object, pronoun-verb agreement) | | | | | | | |
| Use objective case pronouns accurately | | | | | | | |
| Adjectives | | | | | | | |
| Adverbs that tell how, when, where | | | | | | | |
| Subjects, predicates | | | | | | | |
| Subject-verb agreement | | | | | | | |
| Sentence combining | | | | | | | |
| Recognize sentence structure (simple, compound, complex) | | | | | | | |
| Synonyms and antonyms | | | | | | | |
| Contractions | | | | | | | |
| Conjunctions | | | | | | | |
| Prepositions and prepositional phrases | | | | | | | |
| **PENMANSHIP** | | | | | | | |
| Write each letter of alphabet (capital and lowercase) using correct formation, appropriate size and spacing | | | | | | | |
| Write own name and other important words | | | | | | | |
| Use phonological knowledge to map sounds to letters to write messages | | | | | | | |
| Write messages that move left to right, top to bottom | | | | | | | |
| Gain increasing control of penmanship, pencil grip, paper position, beginning stroke | | | | | | | |
| Use word and letter spacing and margins to make messages readable | | | | | | | |
| Write legibly by selecting cursive or manuscript as appropriate | | | | | | | |
| **MECHANICS** | | | | | | | |
| Use capitalization in sentences, proper nouns, titles, abbreviations and the pronoun *I* | | | | | | | |
| Use end marks correctly (period, question mark, exclamation point) | | | | | | | |
| Use commas (in dates, in addresses, in a series, in letters, in direct address) | | | | | | | |
| Use apostrophes in contractions and possessives | | | | | | | |
| Use quotation marks | | | | | | | |
| Use hyphens, semicolons, colons | | | | | | | |
| **EVALUATION** | | | | | | | |
| Identify the most effective features of a piece of writing using class/teacher-generated criteria | | | | | | | |
| Respond constructively to others' writing | | | | | | | |
| Determine how his/her own writing achieves its purpose | | | | | | | |
| Use published pieces as models for writing | | | | | | | |
| Review own written work to monitor growth as writer | | | | | | | |

# Scoring Chart

The Scoring Chart is provided for your convenience in grading your students' work.

- Find the column that shows the total number of items.
- Find the row that matches the number of items answered correctly.
- The intersection of the two rows provides the percentage score.

## TOTAL NUMBER OF ITEMS

| NUMBER CORRECT | 1 | 2 | 3 | 4 | 5 | 6 | 7 | 8 | 9 | 10 | 11 | 12 | 13 | 14 | 15 | 16 | 17 | 18 | 19 | 20 | 21 | 22 | 23 | 24 | 25 | 26 | 27 | 28 | 29 | 30 |
|---|---|---|---|---|---|---|---|---|---|---|---|---|---|---|---|---|---|---|---|---|---|---|---|---|---|---|---|---|---|---|
| 1 | 100 | 50 | 33 | 25 | 20 | 17 | 14 | 13 | 11 | 10 | 9 | 8 | 8 | 7 | 7 | 6 | 6 | 6 | 5 | 5 | 5 | 5 | 4 | 4 | 4 | 4 | 4 | 4 | 3 | 3 |
| 2 | | 100 | 66 | 50 | 40 | 33 | 29 | 25 | 22 | 20 | 18 | 17 | 15 | 14 | 13 | 13 | 12 | 11 | 11 | 10 | 10 | 9 | 9 | 8 | 8 | 8 | 7 | 7 | 7 | 7 |
| 3 | | | 100 | 75 | 60 | 50 | 43 | 38 | 33 | 30 | 27 | 25 | 23 | 21 | 20 | 19 | 18 | 17 | 16 | 15 | 14 | 14 | 13 | 13 | 12 | 12 | 11 | 11 | 10 | 10 |
| 4 | | | | 100 | 80 | 67 | 57 | 50 | 44 | 40 | 36 | 33 | 31 | 29 | 27 | 25 | 24 | 22 | 21 | 20 | 19 | 18 | 17 | 17 | 16 | 15 | 15 | 14 | 14 | 13 |
| 5 | | | | | 100 | 83 | 71 | 63 | 56 | 50 | 45 | 42 | 38 | 36 | 33 | 31 | 29 | 28 | 26 | 25 | 24 | 23 | 22 | 21 | 20 | 19 | 19 | 18 | 17 | 17 |
| 6 | | | | | | 100 | 86 | 75 | 67 | 60 | 55 | 50 | 46 | 43 | 40 | 38 | 35 | 33 | 32 | 30 | 29 | 27 | 26 | 25 | 24 | 23 | 22 | 21 | 21 | 20 |
| 7 | | | | | | | 100 | 88 | 78 | 70 | 64 | 58 | 54 | 50 | 47 | 44 | 41 | 39 | 37 | 35 | 33 | 32 | 30 | 29 | 28 | 27 | 26 | 25 | 24 | 23 |
| 8 | | | | | | | | 100 | 89 | 80 | 73 | 67 | 62 | 57 | 53 | 50 | 47 | 44 | 42 | 40 | 38 | 36 | 35 | 33 | 32 | 31 | 30 | 29 | 28 | 27 |
| 9 | | | | | | | | | 100 | 90 | 82 | 75 | 69 | 64 | 60 | 56 | 53 | 50 | 47 | 45 | 43 | 41 | 39 | 38 | 36 | 35 | 33 | 32 | 31 | 30 |
| 10 | | | | | | | | | | 100 | 91 | 83 | 77 | 71 | 67 | 63 | 59 | 56 | 53 | 50 | 48 | 45 | 43 | 42 | 40 | 38 | 37 | 36 | 34 | 33 |
| 11 | | | | | | | | | | | 100 | 92 | 85 | 79 | 73 | 69 | 65 | 61 | 58 | 55 | 52 | 50 | 48 | 46 | 44 | 42 | 41 | 39 | 38 | 37 |
| 12 | | | | | | | | | | | | 100 | 92 | 86 | 80 | 75 | 71 | 67 | 63 | 60 | 57 | 55 | 52 | 50 | 48 | 46 | 44 | 43 | 41 | 40 |
| 13 | | | | | | | | | | | | | 100 | 93 | 87 | 81 | 76 | 72 | 68 | 65 | 62 | 59 | 57 | 54 | 52 | 50 | 48 | 46 | 45 | 43 |
| 14 | | | | | | | | | | | | | | 100 | 93 | 88 | 82 | 78 | 74 | 70 | 67 | 64 | 61 | 58 | 56 | 54 | 52 | 50 | 48 | 47 |
| 15 | | | | | | | | | | | | | | | 100 | 94 | 88 | 83 | 79 | 75 | 71 | 68 | 65 | 63 | 60 | 58 | 56 | 54 | 52 | 50 |
| 16 | | | | | | | | | | | | | | | | 100 | 94 | 89 | 84 | 80 | 76 | 73 | 70 | 67 | 64 | 62 | 59 | 57 | 55 | 53 |
| 17 | | | | | | | | | | | | | | | | | 100 | 94 | 89 | 85 | 81 | 77 | 74 | 71 | 68 | 65 | 63 | 61 | 59 | 57 |
| 18 | | | | | | | | | | | | | | | | | | 100 | 95 | 90 | 86 | 82 | 78 | 75 | 72 | 69 | 67 | 64 | 62 | 60 |
| 19 | | | | | | | | | | | | | | | | | | | 100 | 95 | 90 | 86 | 83 | 79 | 76 | 73 | 70 | 68 | 66 | 63 |
| 20 | | | | | | | | | | | | | | | | | | | | 100 | 95 | 91 | 87 | 83 | 80 | 77 | 74 | 71 | 69 | 67 |
| 21 | | | | | | | | | | | | | | | | | | | | | 100 | 95 | 91 | 88 | 84 | 81 | 78 | 75 | 72 | 70 |
| 22 | | | | | | | | | | | | | | | | | | | | | | 100 | 96 | 92 | 88 | 85 | 81 | 79 | 76 | 73 |
| 23 | | | | | | | | | | | | | | | | | | | | | | | 100 | 96 | 92 | 88 | 85 | 82 | 79 | 77 |
| 24 | | | | | | | | | | | | | | | | | | | | | | | | 100 | 96 | 92 | 89 | 86 | 83 | 80 |
| 25 | | | | | | | | | | | | | | | | | | | | | | | | | 100 | 96 | 93 | 89 | 86 | 83 |
| 26 | | | | | | | | | | | | | | | | | | | | | | | | | | 100 | 96 | 93 | 90 | 87 |
| 27 | | | | | | | | | | | | | | | | | | | | | | | | | | | 100 | 96 | 93 | 90 |
| 28 | | | | | | | | | | | | | | | | | | | | | | | | | | | | 100 | 97 | 93 |
| 29 | | | | | | | | | | | | | | | | | | | | | | | | | | | | | 100 | 97 |
| 30 | | | | | | | | | | | | | | | | | | | | | | | | | | | | | | 100 |

# Expository Writing

## 6-Point Scoring Rubric

| 6. Exceptional | 5. Excellent | 4. Good | 3. Fair | 2. Poor | 1. Unsatisfactory |
|---|---|---|---|---|---|
| • **Ideas & Content** crafts an accurate, richly detailed report on a familiar natural environment; shares fresh observations on unique features of the place. | • **Ideas & Content** devises a focused, detailed report; makes some fresh observations about the place. | • **Ideas & Content** crafts a solid, factual report; details clarify key features of the topic place. | • **Ideas & Content** has some control of reporting on a place; some ideas or details are vague, limited, or do not fit the topic. | • **Ideas & Content** has little control of the task, or seems unsure of the topic; facts and details are few, repeated, or inaccurate. | • **Ideas & Content** does not present a report; writer is unfocused or unsure of what s/he wants to say. |
| • **Organization** thoughtful, effective strategy smoothly connects ideas, paragraphs, and sentences; strong beginning and conclusion. | • **Organization** logical sequence of facts and ideas moves a reader easily through the text; strong beginning and satisfying conclusion. | • **Organization** orders facts and ideas logically; details fit where they are placed; reader can follow the writer's logic; clear beginning and ending. | • **Organization** tries to structure a report, but the logic may be hard to follow; ideas, sentences, or paragraphs may need clearer transitions or sequencing. | • **Organization** lacks a clear structure; order is hard to follow; beginning and ending are incomplete or undeveloped; ideas/ details don't fit where they are placed. | • **Organization** extreme lack of structure makes the text hard to follow; ideas are disjointed; facts and details, if any, are incomplete, irrelevant, or vague. |
| • **Voice** inventive use of accurate language adds interest to the facts; sophisticated descriptions bring the place to life. | • **Voice** reaches the reader with a personal involvement in the topic; original style shows who is behind the words, and enlivens the facts. | • **Voice** attempts to bring an original personal tone to the report; writing style connects the reader with the place described. | • **Voice** may not seem consistently involved with the topic; attempts to connect the writing style with the purpose and audience. | • **Voice** is not involved in sharing ideas with a reader; writing may be lifeless, with no sense of who is behind the words. | • **Voice** does not attempt to deal with the topic; does not try to share a personal message or tone. |
| • **Word Choice** thoughtfully uses varied, precise words to create a clear picture of the place; explores new words, or uses everyday words in a fresh way. | • **Word Choice** conveys the main idea; uses a variety of words that fit the purpose, but that may not create memorable pictures of the environment. | • **Word Choice** describes a place in an ordinary way; may try to use a range of words, but some do not relate; shows little experimentation with new words. | • **Word Choice** does not use words that convey images of a natural place; some words are overused, or may take away from the meaning. | • **Word Choice** uses words that do not fit, or are vague or confusing; no new words are attempted; may overuse familiar words. | |
| • **Sentence Fluency** simple and complex sentences flow smoothly and naturally; text is easy to follow and read aloud; a variety of lengths, beginnings, and endings adds appeal to the information. | • **Sentence Fluency** creatively uses well-paced simple and complex sentences; a variety of lengths, beginnings, and patterns fit together, and are easy to follow. | • **Sentence Fluency** uses simple and complex structures, with stronger control of simple sentences; fluid, easy-to-read sentences vary in lengths, beginnings, and patterns. | • **Sentence Fluency** most sentences are readable, with a limited range of lengths and patterns; some rereading may be required to follow the text; some sentences may be awkward; has trouble with more complicated sentences. | • **Sentence Fluency** sentences are choppy or awkward; patterns are similar or monotonous; text is hard to understand or read aloud. | • **Sentence Fluency** incomplete, rambling, or confusing sentences make the text hard to follow and read aloud. |
| • **Conventions** is skilled in most writing conventions; proper usage enhances clarity, meaning, and style; paragraphs are placed to support the structure. | • **Conventions** is skilled in most conventions; proper usage makes the text easy to read and understand; little need for editing. | • **Conventions** may make some errors in spelling, capitalization, punctuation, or usage, which do not interfere with understanding the text; some editing is needed. | • **Conventions** has basic control of conventions; makes enough errors to prevent an easy reading of the text; significant editing is needed. | • **Conventions** makes frequent, significant errors in most conventions; paper is difficult to read, and requires heavy revision. | • **Conventions** makes severe errors in most conventions; spelling errors may make it hard to guess what words are meant; some parts of the text are impossible to follow. |

**0 Incomplete:** This piece is either blank, or fails to respond to the writing task. The topic is not addressed, or the student simply paraphrases the prompt. The response may be illegible or incoherent.

# Expository Writing

## 8–Point Scoring Rubric

| 8 | 7 | 6 | 5 | 4 | 3 | 2 | 1 |
|---|---|---|---|---|---|---|---|
| The writer<br><br>• has used a wide array of research sources to construct an outstanding report.<br><br>• makes insightful observations that express a unique understanding of the topic.<br><br>• crafts fluent sentences, and chooses sophisticated words, to reinforce explanations.<br><br>• makes strong connections between ideas, and draws an innovative conclusion based on research findings.<br><br>• consistently elaborates the report with well-articulated details that further support and enliven the facts. | The writer<br><br>• has used numerous research sources to craft an excellent report.<br><br>• makes many interesting observations that expand the main idea.<br><br>• constructs varied sentences, and uses excellent word choices, to support main points.<br><br>• makes connections between ideas, and draws an original conclusion based on research findings.<br><br>• frequently elaborates facts. | The writer<br><br>• has used several research sources to present a good factual report.<br><br>• enhances the main idea with relevant personal observations.<br><br>• exhibits a good organizational strategy, and chooses words carefully to communicate ideas.<br><br>• draws an apt conclusion based on research findings.<br><br>• usually elaborates facts. | The writer<br><br>• uses a couple of research sources to present a solid report.<br><br>• uses some valid personal observations to support the main idea.<br><br>• exhibits a good overall organizational structure, with minor digressions that do not distract from appreciation of the report's main findings.<br><br>• uses some fitting word choices to explain ideas and facts.<br><br>• elaborates on important facts. | The writer<br><br>• uses one or two research sources to write a factual report.<br><br>• uses simple personal observations to reinforce some of the main facts of the report.<br><br>• exhibits an adequate organizational structure, with digressions that occasionally distract from understanding certain points.<br><br>• uses grade-level vocabulary to draw conclusions and explain meaning.<br><br>• occasionally elaborates on major facts. | The writer<br><br>• uses one research source to present some relevant facts about the topic.<br><br>• may show an uneven or limited vocabulary for the writing task.<br><br>• may exhibit organizational problems, such as an illogically structured list of facts and ideas.<br><br>• demonstrates a lack of follow-through on the main idea.<br><br>• exhibits an inconsistent control of language conventions.<br><br>• may not have drawn a relevant conclusion based on the facts presented. | The writer<br><br>• uses few, if any, verifiable facts to explain the topic.<br><br>• employs a limited vocabulary to articulate ideas.<br><br>• exhibits organizational difficulties and problems with language serious enough to detract from the main ideas of the report.<br><br>• does not draw a relevant conclusion about the topic. | The writer<br><br>• does not use research or facts to explain the topic of the report.<br><br>• uses the most basic vocabulary to explain ideas.<br><br>• may not grasp how to connect words and sentences.<br><br>• may show repeated errors in basic conventions.<br><br>• cannot be easily understood. |

**0 Incomplete:** This piece is either blank, or fails to respond to the writing task. The topic is not addressed, or the student simply paraphrases the prompt. The response may be illegible or incoherent.